A DICTIONARY OF
RELIGIOUS ORDERS

By the same author and published by Burns & Oates

THE LITURGICAL DICTIONARY OF
EASTERN CHRISTIANITY

A DICTIONARY OF RELIGIOUS ORDERS

Peter Day

BURNS & OATES
London and New York

First published in Great Britain in 2001 by
BURNS & OATES
A Continuum imprint
The Tower Building, 11 York Road
London SE1 7NX

British Library Cataloguing-in-Publication Data
A catalogue record for this book is available from the
British Library.

ISBN 0 860 12314 6

Typeset by CentraServe Ltd, Saffron Walden, Essex
Printed and bound in Great Britain by The Bath Press, Bath

CONTENTS

PREFACE AND ACKNOWLEDGEMENTS

This book is intended to be a reference tool for those seeking information about religious Orders and Congregations, Institutes, Societies, and Public Associations, both defunct and active, male and female, in the Western Church. Some Equestrian Orders have merited an entry on account of their religious foundation, although many of those still in existence are now purely secular.

Each entry will normally have the foundation's headquarters, or mother house, indicated as 'Location', foundation details, post-nominal abbreviations and a brief description of the habit originally worn. This is followed by the main entry, below which, in some cases, I have listed, under the symbol ✚, common alternative names by which the Congregation may be known. At the end of the dictionary there are to be found a glossary, a list of abbreviations, a list of alternative names in alphabetical order and a summary (at a glance) list of the orders contained in the dictionary, which will help with identification.

To help undertake this task I had access to P. Bonanni's *Catalogi Ordinum Religiosorum* (1706), *Religiosarum* (1707) and *Catalogus Ordinum Equestrium* (1711), P. Helyot's *Dictionnaire des Ordres Religieux* (1847) and Tiron's work on religious Orders. Current information has come largely from the archivists of the various Congregations themselves. Since this is a dictionary, and not a directory, although I have tried to be as inclusive as possible, inevitably the constraints of space and time have meant that not all Orders and Congregations have been included.

I hope the dictionary will be of use to a wide-ranging group of readers who are looking for immediate access to historical and current information and that it provides a useful introduction to this field. It would have been impossible to produce without the editing and computing skills of my wife, Anne, to whom I am greatly indebted. I would also like to acknowledge the generosity and encouragement of all those superiors and archivists of the many religious Orders and Congregations who responded to my queries and pleas for help. My thanks go to Philip and Rosalind Lund of Cambridge, England, who provided me with books and many obscure details, to Fr Adrian Graffy and past colleagues at St John's Seminary, Wonersh, England, and to Fr Timothy Brien of Ruthin, Wales, a fellow Australian, for his encouragement and kindness and Dr Hans van der Hoeven of The Hague for his interest and enthusiasm.

P.D.D.
Cromer, Norfolk. England
28 August 2000
Feast of St Augustine

To my wife and co-worker, Anne

A

ABANDONED AGED, SISTERS OF THE

Location: Spain (Valencia)
RC (female) founded in Spain in 1872 by St Teresa
of Jesus (canonized 1974)

St Teresa of Jesus (1843–97) was born in Aytona, Catalonia and tried her vocation to the religious life with the Poor Clares at Briviesca, but her concern for the plight of old people who had no families to care for them led her to form the Congregation of Sisters of the Abandoned Aged. Although the growth of the Congregation was not rapid, there are now houses in Valencia (the mother house), and Saragossa in Spain and also in the USA.

ABRAHAM-MEN

Defunct

Following the dissolution of the monasteries in England in the 16th century, this was a name given to homeless, wandering monks who travelled the countryside begging for their living. The term 'Bedlam' (an abbreviation of Bethlehem) was also one used to denote a person who was licensed to beg and who may have been released from a mental asylum. Bedlam Beggars wore a small tin plate on the arm to identify them as legitimate beggars.

☩ Bedlam Beggars
Tom o'Bedlam's Men

ACOEMETAE

Defunct
RC (male and female) founded in Alexandria in
c.400 by Alexander, a Byzantine nobleman
Original habit: tradition claims that it was green
with a red cross on the breast; female religious
may have worn an additional black veil and cape.

Literally 'the ones without rest', or 'the sleepless ones', the Acoemetae were a group of Orthodox monks and nuns established at Alexandria around the beginning of the 5th century. They lived a life of great austerity, their main work being perpetual adoration of the Blessed Sacrament, which they maintained night and day. The communities established a great reputation for working with manuscripts, which enhanced the prestige of their libraries. They were also noted for their orthodoxy, especially during the christological controversies caused by Nestorius and Eutyches. Some monks succumbed to the Nestorian heresy and were excommunicated in the 6th century by Pope John II (533–35). There is no mention of the Acoemetae beyond the 12th century, at which time a monastery is known to have moved from Alexandria to Constantinople.

✠ Studites
  Watchers

ADORATION OF THE MOST PRECIOUS BLOOD, SISTERS OF THE

Location: USA (O'Fallon, Missouri)
RC (female) founded in Switzerland in 1845
Abbr: CPPS

A Congregation which had its beginnings in Switzerland when the Community of the Precious Blood was founded at Steinerberg by Fr Karl Rollfuss and Mother Theresa Weber. This community later moved to French Alsace, and some of the Sisters went to Gurtweil in Baden, at the request of the local priest, to help with the care and education of children. A school and novitiate followed. In 1870 the community was invited to send some Sisters to the USA, to conduct parish schools in Illinois. The *Kulturkampf* in Germany, which closed many religious houses, saw more of the Sisters leaving for the USA, and a foundation was made at O'Fallon, Missouri, in 1875. Members of this Congregation are now to be found in Italy, Finland and Estonia, as well as in many parts of the USA, where they teach at all levels, care for the elderly and conduct parish and pastoral ministries.

✠ Precious Blood Sisters

ADORATION REPARATRICE, SISTERS OF THE INSTITUTE OF

Location: France (Paris)
RC (female) founded in France in 1848 by Theodoline Dubouche (Mother Mary Thérèse of the Heart of Jesus)
Original habit: a dark brown woollen robe with a round white collar and a red ribbon bearing the cross of the Congregation; a scapular, a black veil and choir cloak. Auxiliary Sisters wore a black habit.

The work of the Institute is to offer reparation for sins and offences committed against the Blessed Sacrament, for which purpose there is perpetual exposition. There were originally two branches of this Order, (a) contemplative, or community Sisters who were enclosed and recited the daily office of the Blessed Sacrament in choir, and (b) auxiliary Sisters who looked after the manual work of the community. Practical work is now undertaken in running nursing homes and making altar breads and vestments. The Sisters observe a modified Carmelite Rule, adapted for the purpose of the Institute. Several lay associations are connected with the Institute, the members undertaking various devotions and observing part of the Rule.

AFRICAN MISSIONS, SOCIETY OF

Location: Italy (Rome)
RC (male) founded in France in 1856 by Mgr Melchior de Marion-Bresillac and the Abbé Planque
Abbr: SMA
Original habit: secular.

A society of priests and lay brothers established under the authority of the Sacred Congregation of Propaganda with the aim of evangelizing the negroes of Africa. The first mission, led by Bresillac and Planque in 1859, went to Freetown, Sierra Leone, where all but Fr Planque died during a yellow fever epidemic. A second mission led by Fr Planque, to Dahomey in 1861, was more successful. The membership of the Society grew, and Provinces were established throughout Europe and North America. As well as undertaking foreign missions, members of the Society work in their own countries with African immigrants and students. Also known as the Lyons Missionaries, the priests live under a common Rule of life. No vows are taken, but all must make a solemn undertaking to spend their lives in the service of the African missions.

✠ Lyons Missionaries

AGNES, SISTERS OF ST – Dordrecht

Defunct
RC (female) founded in The Netherlands in 1491 by
the Chevalier Gerard Heemskerke
Original habit: a white tunic and scapular with a
black veil; a white ruff was worn around the neck.

The Order was founded at Dordrecht, near
Rotterdam, where a previous monastic settlement, founded in 1326 by Walburga, a
Norwegian noblewoman, had existed. The
succeeding nunnery, dedicated to the virgin
St Agnes, was founded on the advice of
Duke John of Bavaria. It was a cloistered
community, which observed the Augustinian Rule; the main occupation of the Sisters
was prayer.

AGNES, SISTERS OF ST – Fond du Lac

Location: USA (Fond du Lac, Wisconsin)
RC (female) founded the USA in 1858 by Caspar
Rehrl
Abbr: CSA

A Pontifical Institute with simple vows
and an active apostolate involved with education at most levels from elementary
school through to college. The training of
nurses is also undertaken, and practical
nursing care of the aged together with the
provision of pastoral and social welfare
ministries as needed. Foreign missions in
Central America have been included in the
apostolate and are presently concentrated
in Nicaragua.

ALBATI, ORDER OF

Defunct
RC (male) founded in Italy c.1400 during the
pontificate of Pope Boniface IX (1389–1404)
Original habit: white with a red and white cross set
within a circle of black; a large hood was worn in
such a way that the face was mostly hidden.

The Albati were Italian hermits, their name
deriving from their white habits, who were
formed into loose bands which roamed
around Italy and Provence staging nine-
day-long processions, during which they
would flagellate themselves and chant
hymns. The origin of the group can possibly
be traced to the Archconfraternity of the
Gonfalone, which had been established in
Rome in 1264, when St Bonaventure set out
the Rule and habit for a group whose work
included caring for the sick and dying and
burying the dead. The hermits also undertook to provide medical care for those unable to afford it for themselves.

✠ Bianchi

ALCÁNTARA, KNIGHTS OF

Defunct
RC (male Equestrian Order) founded in Spain in the
13th century by the Knights of St Julian de Pereiro
Original habit: knights and clerics originally wore a
plain black habit without any insignia, but from
the beginning of the 14th century a green cross
fleury was added.

The Order grew from a small group, known
as the Knights of St Julian, which was active
in Spain, in Leon and Castile, and which
gained papal recognition as a religious
Order in 1183. Needing the support of a
larger body, they placed themselves, in
1187, under the jurisdiction of the more
powerful Knights of Calatreve, retaining
some autonomy. A grant of land at Alcántara was given to the Knights of Calatreve
in 1217, parts of which were ceded to the
Knights of St Julian, who were then
renamed the Order of the Knights of Alcántara. The Order continued successfully until
the end of the 15th century. At one time
there were some six hundred knights and
over two thousand foot soldiers.

ALEXIUS, BROTHERS OF ST

Location: USA (Signal Mountain, Tennessee)
RC (male) founded in The Netherlands in the 14th
century by Tobias ver Hooven
Abbr: CFA
Original habit: a black tunic, scapular and hood
with a black cloak extending below the knee.

The origin of this community is to be found in an informal gathering of men at Mechlin (Brabant) under Tobias ver Hooven in the 14th century. They concerned themselves with the care of the sick and burial of the victims of the Black Death, hence their alternative name Cellites (from *cella* – a cell, or grave). When this group later adopted St Alexius as the patron saint of their chapel at Aix-la-Chapelle, they became known as the Alexian Fathers, or Alexians. In 1472, Pope Sixtus V approved and confirmed the Alexian Brothers under the Augustinian Rule, and many foundations were made throughout Germany and the Low Countries. The French Revolution reduced their numbers. After the Concordat with Napoleon, only three Brothers remained in the community at Aachen (Aix-la-Chapelle), but the communities were rebuilt and the headquarters was moved to Aachen in the late 19th century. In 1866 the Alexian Brothers' hospital for men and boys was established in Chicago, Illinois, but was later destroyed by fire. The work in the USA expanded to St Louis, Missouri, and Elizabeth, New Jersey. There are now houses in the USA, Ireland, the United Kingdom, Africa, Belgium, Germany and South America, where the members continue in their apostolate of caring for the sick, the old, the poor and the insane as well as the maintenance of cemeteries. The Brothers also run missions in the Philippines and India. Their motto is 'The Charity of Christ Urges Us'.

✠ Alexian Brothers
    Cellites

ALEXIUS, SISTERS OF ST

Defunct
RC (female)
Original habit: a black tunic and mantle with white
cap.

The Order was founded as an associate Congregation to work with the Brothers of St Alexius (see previous entry) and was largely concerned with the care of the sick. The nuns observed the Rule of St Augustine.

✠ Alexian Nuns
    Black Sisters
    Cellitine Sisters

ALL HALLOWS, COMMUNITY OF

Location: England (Bungay, Suffolk)
Anglican (female) founded in England in 1855 by
Lavinia Crosse
Abbr: CAH

An Anglican foundation, following the Augustinian Visitation Rule, established for the purposes of education of the young and care of the infirm. The founder, Lavinia Crosse, had agreed to become superintendent of a rescue mission house for women and girls at Shipmeadow, in Suffolk. In 1855 she took the three vows of religion, those of poverty, chastity and obedience, and was joined by two young novices. A move to larger premises took the community to Ditchingham, Suffolk, where a House of Mercy was built and opened in 1864. There was provision in the Constitution of the community for Magdalens, penitent and reformed women, who might be seeking the religious life, to join and live under a religious Rule if they so wished. By the end of the 19th century other foundations had been made, including one in the

USA, at Yale, and one in Canada, on the Fraser River in British Columbia, where schooling was provided for both Canadian and native Indian girls. In England, a House of Mercy was opened at Norwich, Norfolk, and a refuge at Ipswich, Suffolk. To meet the needs of the times the Sisters are now concerned with an AIDS ministry, while their social welfare programme has an innovative provision for Family Contact days, when children and separated parents can be reconciled in safe and neutral surroundings. The Sisters also run guest houses, conduct retreats, visit prisons and work in areas of spiritual direction. They also work with disturbed adolescent girls and the provision of shelters for the needy.

ALL SAINTS SISTERS OF THE POOR

Location: USA (Catonsville, Maryland)
Episcopalian (female) founded in the USA in 1856 (1890) through affiliation
Abbr: ASSP
Original habit: a black habit, scapular, girdle and veil with a white linen collar and wimple and a small wooden cross; a black coat was worn outdoors.

An American Congregation which arose in 1890 when the American foundation in Baltimore, Maryland, was affiliated to the English Congregation of the same name, which had been founded by Fr W. Upton Richards and Harriet Brownlow Byron in London in 1851. The Sisters now work by providing altar breads and caring for convalescent women. They also run St Anna's Home, in Philadelphia, where they look after elderly women.

ALL SAINTS SISTERS OF THE POOR, SOCIETY OF

Location: England (Oxford)
Anglican (female) founded in England in 1851 by Harriet Brownlow Byron

Abbr: ASSP
Original habit: a black tunic and girdle, with a small wooden cross, and a plain, round, white collar, black veil and scapular. A black outdoor cloak was also worn.

The foundation was made in London, where Harriet Byron began her vocation by caring for three incurable invalids and two orphans in rented accommodation. Others joined her, and three more houses were taken over, which provided space for the small community and its orphans. Harriet Byron made her profession in 1856 and was installed as superior for life, the community at that time numbering no more than five members. The way of life was austere, with a Rule of Silence observed during the day and the Great Silence after Compline and until Terce the following day. The community, which observes the Rule of St Augustine, developed and moved to Colney House in Hertfordshire, and the work began to extend throughout England and Scotland and into South Africa and India, with affiliated houses in the USA at Baltimore and Philadelphia. The apostolate is to provide care for those in need, in hospitals, orphanages, schools and rest homes. The Sisters are well known for running the children's hospice, Helen House, in England, which gives valuable support to terminally sick children and their families. They also conduct retreats, care for the aged, and run drop-in centres for the homeless and a hostel for students. They help to support themselves by making altar breads and church vestments. The community includes some Outer Sisters, women who live in their own homes but are associated with the community and follow an abridged Rule.

ALOYSIUS GONZAGO, BROTHERS OF ST

Location: The Netherlands (Oudenbosch)
RC (male) founded in The Netherlands in 1840
Abbr: CSA

The Congregation, which received the Decree of Praise in 1922, has an apostolate in the education of the young and youth work.

ALUMBRADOS

Defunct
RC (male and female) existing in Spain in the 16th century

A group of recluses in Spain who spent their lives in prayer and contemplation and were regarded with favour and respect by the Reformed Franciscans and Jesuits of the time. Although many of the members are thought to have been unbalanced, others were saintly people, some of whom were later canonized. The group suffered badly under the Spanish Inquisition because of their possible doctrinal unorthodoxy and the claim of many of their number to have received visions and other spiritual experiences. Their alternative name, 'Illuminati', has also been given to other groups, such as the Rosicrucians and a masonic sect existing in 18th-century Bavaria. The Alumbrados groups were united only in their religious fervour and an unshakeable belief that they alone had received divine illumination.

✠ Illuminati

AMADISTS

Defunct
RC (male) founded in Italy in 1461 by Amadeo Menez da Silva

Amadeo da Silva began his religious life in the Hieronymite monastery of Our Lady of Guadalupe in Spain. After ten years he left to enter the Franciscan community at Assisi in Italy, where he established a reputation for saintliness and miracle-working. Anxious to explore a stricter observance of the Rule of St Francis, he left Assisi with a few companions, spent some time in other monasteries, and eventually founded the convent of Santa Maria Bressanoro, where his reforms could be observed. In all some twenty-eight houses were established throughout Italy. Pope Sixtus IV (1471–84) gave him full control over the houses and provided him with a headquarters in Rome. These reformed Franciscan houses flourished until 1568, when Pope St Pius V (1566–72) suppressed them, uniting them, along with other branches of the Franciscan Order, under the name of the Friars Minor Observants.

✠ Amadeans
   Friends of God

AMANTI, CANONS REGULAR OF THE PRIORY OF

Defunct
RC (male) – date of foundation unknown
Original habit: a white tunic and rochet with a black biretta.

Evidence of this priory comes from the writings of St Gregory of Tours (539–96). The priory church was in the diocese of Rouen, France, and dedicated to St Mary Magdalen.

✠ Canons Regular of the Priory of the Two
   Lovers

AMARANTA, KNIGHTS OF

Defunct
RC (male Equestrian Order) founded in Sweden in 1653 by Queen Christina of Sweden (1632–54)
Original habit: a distinctive purple mantle; (insignia) the mantle was decorated with a gold oval stud with the letter 'A' upright, standing on an inverted 'A', all enclosed in a laurel wreath bounded by white bands on which is inscribed 'Dolce Nella Memoria' (Sweet in the Memory). The same emblem is suspended from a gold neck chain.

Queen Christina of Sweden established this Equestrian Order at Stockholm in the penultimate year of her life for the purpose of defending the faithful and promoting virtue and justice.

AMBROSE, OBLATES OF ST

Defunct (suppressed 1844 – re-erected 1848 – now defunct)
RC (male) founded in Italy in the 16th century by St Charles Borromeo (canonized 1610)
Original habit: secular.

A Society of secular priests who took vows of obedience to the diocesan bishop, who could then use the members in order to overcome the opposition of some cathedral canons to any proposed reforms. St Charles Borromeo was very committed to reform of both religious and secular clergy and this is reflected in the Constitutions he drew up in four books for the Oblates of St Ambrose, with the recommendation that they should take a vow of poverty. Laymen were also admitted to the society and were expected to remain for life. In the mid-19th century a Congregation was established in England, in the Westminster archdiocese, but the Order is now defunct.

✤ Ambrosians
   Oblates of St Charles

AMBROSE, ORDER OF ST

Defunct
RC (male) founded in Italy, in c.1441 by Alexander Grivelli (or Crivelli) and others
Original habit: a brown habit with a scapular and a short cape; sandals were worn.

The original founders, each desiring to lead the life of a hermit, left Milan and went to live in some woodland not far from the town. Others joined them and there were soon several offshoot settlements in existence, all observing the Rule of St Augustine. In 1441 Pope Eugenius IV (1431–47) ordered them to come together in Milan to form the Congregation of St Ambrose at Nemus, and the earlier eremitical way of life was superseded. At the end of the 16th century, following a successful reform by St Charles Borromeo, the Brothers of the Apostles of the Poor Life were united with the Order of St Ambrose. Pope Paul V (1605–21) added the name of St Barnabas to the new Congregation and approved the new Constitutions in 1606. The Order was dissolved by Pope Innocent X (1644–55) in 1650.

✤ Congregation of St Ambrose and St Barnabas
   Congregation of the Apostle Brothers of the Poor Life

AMBROSE, SISTERS OF ST

Defunct
RC (female) founded in Italy in 1474 by Blessed Catarina Morigia of Pallanza (cult approved 1769, but never officially beatified)
Original habit: reputedly a white habit with a black veil was worn, but it is also suggested that the Blessed Catarina changed this for a brown habit similar in style to that worn by the Brothers of the Congregation of St Ambrose at Nemus (see previous entry).

The Blessed Catarina was a solitary who went to live an eremitical way of life on top of Mount Varese, near Lake Maggiore, and was joined there by others. They dedicated their community to Our Lady of the Mount and adopted the Rule of St Augustine. The community was approved in 1474.

✤ Ambrosian Sisters

AMEDIANS

Defunct
RC (male) founded in Italy c.1400
Original habit: a grey habit with a cord girdle; wooden shoes were worn.

An Italian Congregation which at one time had twenty-eight convents. The Order was united with the Cistercians by Pope Pius V (1504–72).

✠ Friends of God

ANAWIM

Location: USA (Corning, New York)
RC (male)

A Public Association. This is a community of priests and laity, both single and married, who want to dedicate their lives to Christ in the service of the Church and in so doing encourage others to a life of holiness. The members, who take no vows, live in community and are characterized by fidelity both to the pope and to the diocesan bishop.

ANDREW, COMMUNITY OF ST

Location: England (London)
Anglican (female) founded in England in 1861 by Elizabeth Ferard
Abbr: CSA

Following her ordination as a deaconess, Elizabeth Ferard and six other women formed the London Diocesan Deaconess Institution, whose purpose was to provide training for other deaconesses and to promote the cause of women's work in the London diocese; the Institution included within it the smaller St Andrew's Community. The members observed a common Rule of life which, since 1887, includes the daily recitation of the day hours. Traditional vows were not taken at first, but all members made a promise of celibacy and recognized the authority of a head Sister. Vows were incorporated into the Rule in 1917. The community soon developed into a Sisterhood, with its members all ordained as deaconesses and closely subject to the authority of the diocesan bishop, whose

approval of the election and appointment of office-bearers in the community had to be sought. The present-day Rule allows for full individual development. The programme of training provides for a three-month postulancy followed by a two-year novitiate. Temporary profession is taken annually for two years, after which the candidate is presented to the bishop for ordination to the diaconate, and on the same day she takes her final vows. At present the community, which is involved in parish work, hospitality, chaplaincy, conference and retreat work, includes several women priests.

✠ Deaconess Community of St Andrew

ANDREW, HERMITS OF ST

Defunct
RC (male) founded in Italy in c.1000 by Ludolf of Gubbio
Original habit: reputedly a white tunic, scapular and hood; hermits went unshod. By the 16th century this had changed to a short, white, knee-length cassock with a blue mantle, a white biretta and stockings.

Ludolf of Gubbio left home at the age of twenty-one intent upon living the life of a hermit in the valley of Fonte-Avellana, which lies between Mt Catria and Mt Corvo in the Apennines. With him went a companion, Julian, but they were soon joined by like-minded men. It is said that the hermits were visited by St Romuald (951–1027), who gave them a Rule which was characterized by its austerity, with fasting on bread and water on four days of each week, with a little fruit and some vegetables on the other days; meat was proscribed. A peculiarity of this Rule was the three periods of Lenten-like fast which preceded the feasts of the Resurrection, the Nativity, and that of St John the Baptist. Some extreme acts of penitence were part of the daily life of prayer and could include the wearing of chains and spikes. The psalter was to be recited before dawn each day, with arms outstretched and many genuflections. The first hermitage, founded around 1000, was dedicated to St Andrew; previous to this the hermits had been known as the Congregation of the Dove. It is alleged that Ludolf became bishop of Gubbio in 1009 but later resigned. St Peter Damian was a member of the Congregation, serving as prior from 1043 to 1072, during which time the Rule was modified. The membership increased greatly over the years, and the Congregation grew in importance, attracting many papal and diocesan privileges. By the end of the 14th century it had, however, grown lax, and it did not recover. A canonical visitation in 1569 led to its suppression, and the remaining members transferred to the Camaldolese Congregation of St Michael at Murano.

✠ Congregation of the Dove
  Hermits/Monks of Fonte-Avellana
  Monks of St Andrew

ANDREW, RELIGIOUS OF ST

Location: Belgium (Tournai)
RC (female) founded in Belgium in c.1231 (and again in 1857 by Flavie Delattre)
Abbr: RSA
Original habit: (second foundation) a black dress, cape and veil with a white crimped cap and collar. Lay Sisters wore an identical habit but without the collar.

The origin of the Order is probably found in a community, under the Rule of St Augustine, which came into existence at the time of the crusades to provide a hospital for crusaders and pilgrims. At the time of the French Revolution the community was disbanded and its property confiscated. In 1820 the convent of St Andrew was acquired by Flavie Delattre, who restored the community, which then adopted the Rule of St Ignatius. The Order continues, with an apostolate in education, parish ministry and retreat work. There are houses in Belgium, the United Kingdom, Brazil and the Republic of Congo.

ANDREW, SISTERS OF ST

Location: France (Poitiers)
RC (female) founded in France in 1806 by St André Hubert Fournet (canonized 1933) and St Elizabeth Lucie Bichier des Ages (canonized 1947)

A community of nuns devoting their lives to the care of the sick and dying and the education of children. The foundation received diocesan approval in 1817 and government recognition in 1819 and 1826. Other daughter foundations were made in the years that followed. The work of the Sisters today is in education, the care of churches and the nursing and care of the sick and dying. For their first five years with the community the Sisters take annual vows, and only then do they make their perpetual vows. A century after the foundation there were houses in France, Italy and Spain, but many were dispersed in 1905 following the enactment of the Association Laws in France, which removed education from the hands of the religious Orders.

✠ Daughters of the Cross

ANGELICALS OF ST PAUL

Location: Italy (Rome)
RC (female) founded in Italy in the 16th century by St Anthony Zaccaria (canonized 1897)
Abbr: ASSP

The Angelicals of St Paul were instrumental in helping with the reform of two female religious communities to a stricter observance of their Rule. This is a small Congregation largely concerned with teaching, catechetics and mission work. It is now represented in the USA, in Pennsylvania.

✠ Angelical Sisters of St Paul

ANGELO OF CORSICA, BROTHERS OF ST

Defunct
RC (male) founded in Italy at the end of the 14th century
Original habit: reputedly Franciscan in style, made from rough, coarse material.

The Order was founded by a group of tertiaries of St Francis who, through the generosity of Carlo di Malatesta, were given land upon which to build a hermitage. Other communities were formed in Italy, in Venice, Urbino, Novillara and Ferrara. In 1432 Pope Eugenius IV brought these tertiary hermits into the Hieronimite Congregation of Blessed Peter at Pisa.

ANNE, ORDER OF ST

Location: USA (Arlington, Massachusetts)
Anglican (female) founded in the USA in 1910 by Fr F. C. Powell and Mother Etheldreda Barry
Abbr: OSA
Original habit: a grey habit with a grey rope cincture and a black veil, with a scapular and ring for professed Sisters; a black wooden cross and a fifteen-decade rosary were also worn.

This Order follows an adaptation of the Benedictine Rule, and the foundation is said to date from the occasion of the clothing of the first four novices in 1910, with Mother Etheldreda serving as the first mother superior. The Rule is flexible enough to permit both a contemplative and an active vocation to coexist within the same community. The full divine office is recited daily, and each convent of the Order is autonomous. At one time there were eight houses, now reduced to two. The work of the Sisters is varied and includes the running of a boarding school for girls, homes for elderly women, nursing and convalescent homes for disabled children, and the provision of retreats and various parish ministries. In the past the work also included the running of schools on Indian reservations and mission work in the Far East. It was from this Order that nine Sisters left to become the nucleus of the Order of St Helena in 1945.

ANNE, SISTERS OF ST

Location: England (Wimbledon, London)
RC (female) founded in England in 1927 by Grace Gorden Smith (Mother Mary Agnes)
Abbr: SSA
Original habit: a blue habit with a blue scapular, a black veil and a white collar and wimple.

The Sisters devote themselves to various works of charity, especially social work and the nursing of the sick and dying, often in their own homes. General parish work is also undertaken.

ANNE, SISTERS OF ST – Lachine

Location: Canada (Lachine, Quebec)
RC (female) founded in Canada in 1850 by Esther Blondin (the Ven. Marie-Anne Blondin) and four companions

Esther Blondin and her companions became aware of the need for education among the rural poor of Quebec and set about establishing a Congregation to teach the young and nurse the sick. Their educational programme included religious education, reading, writing and arithmetic. By 1886 they were establishing missions in Alaska and the Yukon and were attracting postulants from all over Canada, the New England states, The Netherlands, Germany,

Belgium and Ireland. In 1887 a school was opened in Oswego, New York, and further foundations followed, in Boston and in some dioceses of the eastern states of the USA. In 1999, the Sisters were to be found in Florida, West Virginia, Missouri and Maryland, with missions established in Haiti in the West Indies, Chile, and Cameroon in Africa. A mission had also been sent to Japan, but this was later closed. The work is still heavily educational, and the Sisters also undertake campus ministries, retreat work, the care of the elderly and those who are housebound, various chaplaincies, some counselling services, and special ministries to those with AIDS and to the handicapped. In 1999 the Vatican accepted one miracle as authentic and it is possible that the Ven. Marie-Anne may be beatified early in the new millennium.

ANNE OF PROVIDENCE, SISTERS OF ST

Location: Italy (Rome)
RC (female) founded in Italy in 1834 by the Ven. Marquis Carlo Tancredi and his wife, the Marchioness Giulia Falletti di Barola
Abbr: SSA
Original habit: a dark tunic and veil with a neck cross.

The foundation of the Congregation was made in Turin, the founders being especially concerned about the plight of the children of poor families in terms of Christian education and formation. The Marquis died four years after the foundation was made and it was left to his wife to be the guiding hand and to see it through its early stages. Approbation was granted in 1846, and the Sisters began their work in education, which was later expanded to include social and health care ministries and the provision of retreats and pastoral ministries. The Order spread widely in Europe, Asia, Africa and the Americas, where the first

foundation was made in the USA in 1952 in Pennsylvania, followed by another in Texas.

ANNUNCIADES

Location: Brazil (Ponta Grossa)
RC (female) founded in France in 1501 by St Joan of Valois (canonized 1949)
Abbr: OBVM
Original habit: a grey habit, black veil and scarlet scapular and a white mantle and a waist cord with ten knots; a medal, on a blue ribbon, was suspended from the neck and a gold finger ring was worn.

St Joan of Valois (1464–1505; also known as St Joan of France) was the daughter of Louis XI of France and Charlotte of Savoy. After a loveless childhood, despised by her father for being female, sickly and deformed, she was married to the duke of Orleans, who continued the ill-treatment. A release from her misery came about through the annulment of the marriage, which was sought by her husband on the grounds that he had been forced into the marriage but rather more probably because he wished to marry Anne of Brittany. Joan was created duchess of Berry and was given a province to govern from Bourges in central France. Here she met Fr Gilbert Nicholas (also known as Gilbert Mary), a Franciscan, and together they founded the Order of the Annunciades. The Rule of the Order, which was known as 'The Ten Virtues of the Blessed Virgin', was Franciscan in spirit, with prayer rather than physical austerities characterizing the life of the Sisters. Abstinence was observed on four days of every week and there was no night office. The superior of each community was known as Ancelle (handmaiden), with extern members known as Sisters of Peace. Joan assumed the habit in 1504, a year before her death. Many miracles of healing were attributed to her, and she was beatified by Pope Benedict XIV (1740–58), who allowed her cult to spread throughout France, resulting in many foundations. With the outbreak of the French Revolution the various communities disbanded and the members fled to other countries. A house was established in England, at St Mary's-at-Cliffe, near Dover in Kent, but this has now gone. A sad note concerns the relics of St Joan, which were desecrated and burnt by Huguenots in 1562. St Joan was canonized in 1949. The Order is now restricted to houses in Brazil.

ANNUNCIATION, SISTERS OF THE BLESSED

Defunct
RC (female) founded in Italy in 1604 by the Blessed Maria Vittoria Fornari-Strata (beatified 1828)
Original habit: a white tunic and scapular with a blue mantle.

The desire of Maria Fornari-Strata to found a religious Order devoted to working for the Church did not have an auspicious beginning. Widowed, and left with the care of five children and a certain lack of money, she was counselled to be cautious. Enlisting the support and enthusiasm of four other women, who donated money for the building of the first convent, she made a beginning and received the habit from the archbishop of Genoa in 1602. The Constitution was approved by Pope Clement VIII in 1604, and the Order was placed under the Rule of St Augustine. Much of the work undertaken was in the making of vestments and altar linen. The life of the nuns was austere, and they were under strict enclosure, allowed the visit only of very close relatives three times a year. The Order spread throughout Europe.

✠ Blue Annunciades
　Caelestes
　Celestial Annunciades

ANNUNCIATION OF SAVOY, KNIGHTS OF THE

Defunct
RC (male Equestrian Order) founded in 1409 and revised in 1518
Original habit: a mantle that had many colour changes, at first white, then black and finally red, with an underlying doublet that also varied at times. The design of the collar also changed, but consisted mainly of four gold panels bearing the letters F.E.R.T. (Fortitudo Ejus Rhodium Tennuit – His Bravery Held Rhodes Fast), which refers to the founder's defence of Rhodes; the letters were intertwined with a knot, and each panel was separated from its neighbour by a smaller panel bearing a gold rose on a red and white enamelled base. From the centre of the collar was suspended a medallion bearing an engraving of the Annunciation, surrounded by knots of gold.

The Order had its origin in 1409 as the Order of the Collar, which had been instituted by Amadeus VIII of Savoy, who later became the anti-pope Felix V in 1434. It was he who dedicated the Order to the Blessed Virgin Mary. The knights looked for protection to the grand master, a position held by the counts of Savoy, and in return they were expected to give loyal service and to correct wrongdoing. The Statutes were recognized by Charles III 'the Good' in 1518. In 1627 the Order moved to Italy, to the Camaldolese hermitage near Turin, where the hermits served as the knights' chaplains.

ANTHONY, MISSIONARY SISTERS OF ST

Location: USA (San Antonio, Texas)
RC (female) founded in the USA in 1929 by Fr Peter A. Baque
Abbr: MSSA

A small Diocesan Congregation founded in San Antonio, Texas, and approved in 1956. The intention of the founder was that the Sisters would be involved in teaching, nursing, social service and home missions. The Congregation has houses only in Texas.

ANTHONY OF EGYPT, ORDER OF ST

Defunct
RC (male) founded in France in the 11th century by Gaston and Giroud de Valloire
Original habit: a long black tunic and mantle with a blue tau cross on the left hand side of each.

The Order was founded in 1095 at St Didier de la Mothe, near Vienne, France, as a community of canons regular who observed the Rule of St Augustine and cared for the sick. The foundation attracted particularly those pilgrims who were suffering from St Anthony's Fire (erysipelas), which was raging in the Rhone Valley towards the end of the 11th century. In 1040 a pilgrim named Jocelyn had brought the relics of St Anthony to the church of St Didier, and after praying before them his son was miraculously cured. In fulfilment of a promise, both Gaston and his son assumed a religious habit and established a hospital for those suffering from the disease. The priory at St Didier was established as an abbey, approved in 1297 by Pope Boniface VIII, and given to the Brothers, who were then known as the Canons Regular of St Anthony of Vienne. The Congregation spread throughout France, Spain and Italy, the black-robed hospitallers a common sight in western Europe as they collected alms and attracted attention by ringing small bells. Much wealth and many privileges were given to the Order, but with the wealth came a growing lack of discipline. Attempts at reform generally failed. There was a brief union with the Order of the Knights of Malta in 1776, but the Congregation was declared defunct in 1803.

✠ Antonines
  Canons Regular of St Anthony
  Hospitaller Brothers of St Anthony

ANTHONY OF ETHIOPIA, KNIGHTS OF ST

Defunct
Universal Church (male Equestrian Order) founded in Ethiopia in the 4th century by the Emperor John (but see below)
Original habit: a black woollen tunic with an unornamented blue cross whose vertical and horizontal bars terminate in fleurs-de-lis.

There are serious doubts about the authenticity of this Order. It was allegedly a Military Order, founded c.370 by an Ethiopian emperor named John for the dual purposes of maintaining the faith within the empire and the security of his own throne. Several authors suggest that the Order was approved by Pope Leo the Great (440–61) and that the grand master of the Order lived in great style on the island of Merole in the middle of the Nile, his council numbering about a dozen knights with the same number of clerics. The assets to support the Order, if it existed, are said to have come from the rich proceeds of gold- and silver-mining enterprises.

ANTHONY OF SYRIA, NUNS OF ST

Defunct
Universal Church (female) founded in Syria, possibly in the 4th century
Original habit: a black monastic dress.

When St Athanasius (296–373) was writing, he referred not only to the monks of St Anthony of the Desert, but also to some holy virgins who followed the Rule of St Anthony and who inhabited the region around and on Mount Lebanon in Syria in the early 4th century. These women were generally enclosed and practised works of penance and of charity. They were known to pray at set hours, were obliged to observe chastity, and were governed by a superior. In later years the community came under the direction of the Patriarchal and Maronite hierarchy once this had become established.

ANTONIAN ORDER

There are four Congregations of the Antonian Order, which each have their own superior-generals and councils but are subject to the same Rule:

1 The Maronite Order of the Blessed Virgin Mary (OMM) arose from the foundation made in 1695 by Archbishop Germanos Farhat of Aleppo and called the Congregation of St Eliseus, approved in 1732. The monks of the Order were called Aleppines. This split into two groups in 1757, the Baladites (or country monks) and those who remained as Aleppines. This division was confirmed by Rome in 1770. It was the Aleppines which gave rise to the present-day Maronite Order of the Blessed Virgin Mary.

2 The Order of Maronites of Lebanon (OLM) was formed following the split of the Congregation of St Eliseus into the Baladites and Aleppines. It was the Baladites who gave rise to the Order of Maronites of Lebanon.

3 The Order of the Maronite Antonians (OAM) dates from a Congregation of St Isaiah, founded in 1700 by Gabriel of Blauza, who later became the Maronite Patriarch. He established a monastic presence at the monastery of Mar Ishaya. Pope Clement XII granted approbation in 1740.

4 The Antonian Order of St Hormisdas of Chaldea (no abbreviation) was founded in 1808 by Gabriel Dembo, who took possession of the ruined monastery of Rabban Hormizd, named after its 7th-century Nestorian founder. The Rule observed by the Order is based on Maronite usage. The name of the monastery

was changed to that of St Hormisdas, who was martyred under Bahram of Persia in *c.*420. The Order was approved by Pope Pius VIII in 1830 and confirmed by Pope Gregory XVI in 1845. The members of the Order combine both active and contemplative lives in schools and in the mission fields.

✠ Disciples of St Anthony
   Maronite Antonians
   Maronite Order of St Anthony of Aleppo

APOSTLE BROTHERS OF THE POOR LIFE, THE

Defunct
RC (male) founded in Italy in 1431 by Alexander Grivelli, Antonio Petrasancta and Albert Besuzzi
Original habit: a brown tunic, scapular and cape; the Brothers were discalced.

There were many groups of hermits during the 13th and 14th centuries in Europe who were self-styled 'The Apostle Brothers', but the Apostle Brothers of the Poor Life must not be confused with these. This community of hermits, composed of both priests and laymen, was founded in Milan by three friends. Many like-minded men were attracted, and the foundation expanded throughout Italy, with hermitages opened in Rome, Lombardy and the Marches of Ancona in the north of the country. Pope Eugene IV (1431–47) insisted, in 1441, that they should unite with other, similar, communities. The union resulted in the formation of the Congregation of St Ambrose at Nemus. Before the Council of Trent this Congregation had the privilege of reciting the Ambrosian Breviary, but it was later decreed by Pope Pius V (1566–72) that the Roman Breviary was to be substituted. A lack of discipline within the Congregation caused its eventual demise and suppression.

✠ Congregation of St Ambrose at Nemus

APOSTLES, ORDER OF THE

Defunct
RC (male) founded in Italy at the end of the 15th
century by Giovanni Scarpa
Original habit: a tawny tunic with a leather girdle,
a scapular with hood attached and a cape or
mantle.

The Constitutions of the Order were
approved in 1496 under the Rule of St
Augustine by Alexander VI, with foundations made in Genoa and Ancona. In 1589
they were linked with the Ambrosian Apostle Brothers by Pope Sixtus V and later
confirmed by Pope Paul V in 1606, after
which the name of St Barnabas was added
to their title. The Order had four provincial
centres, with two houses in Rome. They
were dissolved in 1650 under Pope Innocent X.

✠ Apostolini
   Brothers of St Barnabas

APOSTOLATE, SISTERS AUXILIARIES OF THE

Location: USA (Mononagh, West Virginia)
RC (female) founded in Canada in 1903 by Francis
Olszewski and Emil Legal
Abbr: SAA (formerly AA)

This small diocesan Congregation was
founded in Krakow, Canada, but moved to
West Virginia in the USA in 1911. The
Sisters have been concerned with teaching
at their school of St Peter and St Paul in
Mononagh, West Virginia, and in the care
of the sick and those in need of convalescent care. The Congregation observes a
modified Rule of St Augustine.

APOSTOLIC OBLATES

Location: USA (Omaha, Nebraska)
RC (female) founded in Italy in 1947 by Bishop
Guglielmo Giaquinta of Tivoli (Rome)

This Secular Institute is linked with the Pro-
Sanctity Movement and is composed of
laywomen who witness in the world to the
universal call to holiness. There are two
types of membership, (a) internal oblates
who live inside a fraternal group and are at
all times available to the movement, and
(b) external oblates who take only simple
vows and live on their own to carry out
their own role in the world.

APOSTOLIC SODALES

Location: USA (Coronada, California)
RC (male) founded in Italy in 1992 by Bishop
Guglielmo Giaquinta

A Secular Institute designed to promote
fraternity among diocesan priests, who, in a
spirit of unity with their bishop, respond to
the call to holiness and fraternity.

APOSTOLINES, FRIARS OF THE ORDER OF THE

Defunct
RC (male)
Original habit: tawny tunic and hood with a
leather girdle.

An Order suppressed by Pope Urban VIII
(1623–44) for being of little use to the
Church; they were very similar to the
Barnabites.

ARROUAISIANS

Defunct
RC (male) founded in France in 1090 by two priests,
Conon and Heldemare

This eremitical community, founded by two
chapel masters at the court of William the
Conqueror, evolved into a more canonical
form in time and was confirmed by Pope
Blessed Urban II in 1097. Around 1126,
when the Order had degenerated to some
extent, a decisive turn of events took place,
which reformed the community with the
adoption of a new order, influenced by the

usages at Prémontré and Springiersbach. These usages were borrowed from the Rule of St Benedict, which governed matters such as daily life and liturgy. The community observed perpetual silence and abstinence from meat. The reforms succeeded in invigorating the Order, and new foundations were made throughout Europe and in England, Scotland and Ireland. Much of this success must be laid at the feet of the canons themselves, who farmed their land efficiently in the Cistercian manner. More problems arose in the 12th century, due in part to a growing lack of fervour among the communities as well as a lack of resources. The strong early bonds which united the houses failed, especially in England and Scotland, and the communities shrank in number so that by the 13th century these houses were strictly regional. An attempt to return the members to a strict observance of the vows, particularly those of chastity, abstinence and an acceptance of the customs of communal living, failed. A last attempt at reform was made in the late 17th century, but this, too, failed, and the Order became defunct.

ASSUMPTION, LITTLE SISTERS OF THE

Location: France (Paris)
RC (female) founded in France in 1865 by Antoinette Fage (Mother Marie de Jésus) and Fr Etienne Pernet, an Augustinian of the Assumption
Abbr: LSA
Original habit: a black habit, with a white linen coif, binder and wimple and a leather belt with a crucifix placed under the belt on the left-hand side.

It could not be overlooked by Etienne Pernet that there was gross poverty all around him in Paris, where he had gone to establish the first metropolitan house of the Augustinians of the Assumption. The plight of the poor, especially of those who were sick, was urgent and compelling, and he was joined in the work of finding a remedy by Mother Marie de Jésus, a member of the Association of Our Lady of Good Counsel in Paris, which had been founded by Mlle Gaillardin. At the time of their first meeting Mother Marie was in charge of a Dominican orphanage in Paris. Now placed in charge of this new community (1865), dedicated to nursing the poor in their own homes, she organized the taking over of domestic duties and the care of children where this was needed. The work today is both active and contemplative, and the Sisters prepare children and adults to receive the sacraments. The Little Sisters of the Assumption follow a modified Augustinian Rule. At their English foundation at Bow in London (founded 1880), people of all faiths were nursed, and the Sisters were known as the Nursing Sisters of the Poor, to distinguish them from the Sisters of the Assumption in Kensington Square, also in London. The Sisters remained at Bow until the house was bombed in 1940, during the Second World War. This necessitated a move across London to Hackney and then on to Stamford Hill, where they remained from 1944 to 1958. Today there are houses in France, Great Britain, Ireland and the USA, where the Sisters provide a supportive family ministry for the poor and underprivileged.

ASSUMPTION, MISSIONARY SISTERS OF THE

Location: South Africa (Grahamstown)
RC (female) founded in South Africa in 1850 by Amelie Henningsen (Mother Mary)
Original habit: a black tunic, with an embroidered cross, with a cord girdle, a black cloak, with the same design on the left-hand side, a black veil and a white headband and square-cut wimple.

This is a missionary branch of the Religious Sisters of the Assumption. Mother Mary, born in Brussels in 1822 of a good family, was also sometimes known as Sr Gertrude of the Blessed Sacrament, or simply as *Notre Mère*. She went to South Africa in 1849 and the Congregation was founded in the same year. With an apostolate in education the first school was opened there in 1850. The work of the Congregation expanded to include nursing and medical missions, with the building of hospitals, training schools and bush clinics. Mother Mary died in 1904. There are houses throughout South Africa and a school in Ireland, which was founded primarily as a contact centre for vocations.

ASSUMPTION, OBLATE MISSIONARY SISTERS OF THE

Location: France (Paris)
RC (female) founded in France in 1865 by Emmanuel d'Alzon
Abbr: OA
Original habit: a black habit and veil (white in the mission fields) with a white linen wimple and leather cincture.

Fr Emmanuel d'Alzon, who had previously founded the Augustinians of the Assumption, recognized the need for assistance in the mission fields and so founded the Oblate Missionary Sisters of the Assumption. Marie Correnson (later Mother Emmanuel Marie) became the first superior. In 1868 a group of Sisters was sent to the Balkans and Turkey to assist in the opening of schools, hospitals, free dispensaries and orphanages. A publishing venture in France, La Bonne Presse, was started by the Assumption Fathers, assisted by the Oblates, through which they produced books, periodicals and pamphlets, but it was to incur the disfavour of the French government, which feared it may also have been used to publish and distribute treasonable material aimed at helping a royalist overthrow of the Republic. When the near-eastern missions were closed down, new ventures were begun in Africa and later in England, mainland Europe and South America, where the Sisters now run

schools, guest houses and hospitals and continue with their work in publishing.

ASSUMPTION, SISTERS OF THE

Location: France (Paris)
RC (female) founded in France in 1839 by Anne-Eugenie Milleret de Brou (Blessed Mother Marie-Eugenie of Jesus; beatified 1975)
Abbr: RA
Original habit: a violet habit with a white cross on the breast, a violet cincture and a white cloak with a violet cross on the left shoulder.

Born into a wealthy but unstable family and used to the daily practice of what might be seen as unusual austerities for people of her rank, the young Anne-Eugenie Milleret found little taste for the luxuries of social life and a growing desire to devote her life to some form of service. Impressed by what she was learning from Lenten sermons she heard at the cathedral of Notre Dame in Paris, and encouraged by others, she began to envisage the sort of community she saw was needed, contemplative in character but dedicated to the education of women. She entered the novitiate of the Visitation Sisters of Coré Saint-André in the south of France in 1838 and began her own foundation, the Institute of the Religious of the Assumption, in 1839 with the help of five women. The beginnings were not auspicious, and the Sisters lived in great poverty, but slowly others were attracted to join them. A school was established and a novitiate opened in 1842. From 1850 the work went on apace, with schools and convents founded all over France, in England, the USA, where a foundation was made in 1919 in Worcester, Massachusetts, and in Spain, Italy, the Philippines and Central and South America. Mother Marie-Eugenie died in 1898. In 1972 the Sisters started an ecumenical centre, the Hengrave Community, in England, near Bury St Edmunds in Suffolk, where both Catholic and Reformed liturgies are celebrated. This centre for reconciliation is also used as a youth centre and for local parish events. In 1996 the Congregation numbered 1,500 distributed in 207 communities in 31 countries.

✠ Religious of the Assumption

ASSUMPTION OF THE BLESSED VIRGIN MARY, SISTERS OF THE

Location: Canada (Nicolet, Quebec)
RC (female) founded in Canada in 1853 by Fr Jean Harper (or Joseph-Calixte Marquis) with Léocadie Bourgeois, Mathilde Leduc, Hedwigge Buisson and Julie Héon
Abbr: SASV
Original habit: a black tunic and pleated veil for professed Sisters; postulants wore a grey habit and cape with a white muslin bonnet; novices had a black habit with a simple square white linen wimple and a fine white veil over a trimmed bonnet.

Although there has been much debate about the true founder of this community, the evidence appears to support Jean Harper, a priest, who worked with four of the co-founders. The Congregation was founded to teach poor girls of both town and country in and around the parish of St Gregoire-le-Grand in Nicolet, Quebec, which lies between Montreal and Quebec and was then a small colony of immigrant families who had come to Prince Edward Island following the capture of Louisburg by the English in the previous century, and of other settlers from Boston and New England. A religious community was needed to provide education, and the Congregation was founded. The usual three vows of poverty, chastity and obedience are taken by members, with an undertaking to dedicate themselves to the education of poor girls. The Sisters are now to be found teaching in Canada and the USA, where they made a foundation in 1891. They also undertake pastoral work, maintain campus ministries and organize missions to Japan, Brazil and Ecuador.

ASSUMPTIONISTS

Location: Italy (Rome)
RC (male) founded in France in 1845 by Fr Emmanuel d'Alzon
Abbr: AA
Original habit: a black habit, with wide sleeves, a black capuce and a leather cincture.

The Congregation of Augustinians of the Assumption was founded at Nîmes, France, when Fr d'Alzon took over the running of a boys' school and was encouraged to form a community of men who would live a community life under the Rule of St Augustine and dedicate their lives to teaching. The Constitutions were approved in 1864. Members see education as their principal apostolate, and they seek to evangelize through the media and mission work as well as providing retreats and various chaplaincies, which put them in touch with modern youth and its problems. The Assumptionists work throughout the world, divided into nine Provinces. Their work has taken them to Russia, the Near East, North and South America, Africa, New Zealand and Europe. In their missionary work in the Balkans and the Near East, the Fathers are helped by the Oblate Missionary Sisters of the Assumption.

✠ Augustinians of the Assumption

AUBERT, CANONS REGULAR OF ST

Defunct
RC (male) founded in France in the 7th century by St Aubert
Original habit: a violet cassock, cap and biretta with a white surplice.

St Aubert, who died in 669, was bishop of Cambrai-Arras. He enjoyed the reputation of being a founder of monasteries, although he was never a monk himself. His most famous foundation was that of the Abbey of St Vedast (St Vaast) at Arras. It was near Mont-Saint-Eloi, also in the region of Arras, that he dedicated a church to St Peter the Apostle and where he instituted the Congregation of Canons Regular of St Aubert. By 1066, according to the records of the thirty-second bishop of Cambrai, these canons were observing a modified Rule of St Augustine. John of Warneton (died 1130) had been a member of this community before he was made bishop of Thérouanne. This diocese was suppressed in 1559 and made into sees dependent on Reims.

✠ Canons Regular of St Autbert

AUGUSTINE, CANONESSES REGULAR OF ST – Neuilly-sur-Seine

Location: France (Neuilly-sur-Seine)
RC (female) founded in France in c.1634 (but see below)
Abbr: CSA
Original habit: a white habit with a white linen rochet, an unstarched wimple and a black veil. Lay Sisters wore a dark grey habit with a scapular and black veil.

The foundation of this Order is not clear. It may be a descendant of the Congregation of St Victor of Paris, which was founded in 1110 by William of Champeaux and was concerned with education. In 1634 a member of the Canonesses Regular of the Abbey of Beaulieu at Douai, Lady Mary Letitia Tredway, founded a community in Paris known as *Les Dames Anglaises*, who maintained a house for English nuns and also ran a school for girls. This was later to withstand the French Revolution, unlike so many religious houses. In 1860 the Congregation moved to the Paris suburb of Neuilly-sur-Seine. The Association Laws in France at the beginning of the 20th century

forced the Sisters to leave the country, and they settled in England, where they still maintain a day school for girls in the London suburb of Ealing.

AUGUSTINE, CANONESSES REGULAR OF ST – WINDESHEIM-LATERAN CONGREGATION

Location: Belgium (Bruges)
RC (female)
Abbr: CRL
Original habit: choir nuns wore a white habit with linen rochet with (in summer) a linen surplice or (in winter) a black cloak and an unstarched linen wimple with a black veil. Lay Sisters wore a black habit and scapular with a white veil.

The Order originated from the Brothers and Sisters of the Common Life, founded by Gerard Groote in the 14th century at Deventer in The Netherlands. On Groote's death, in 1384, some of the Brothers founded a monastery of canons regular at Windesheim (Utrecht). By 1400 the female foundation at Deventer had so flourished that a new one was made at Diepenveen, where the first twelve Sisters were professed as canonesses regular in 1408 and incorporated into the chapter of Windesheim in 1412. This was then known as the Windesheim-Lateran Congregation. The principal work of the Congregation was the education of the young. Other foundations were made, including that of St Ursula at Louvain, where a school was established. In 1548 an English nun, Elizabeth Woodford, was joined by others from England to form the English Augustinian Canonesses Regular at Louvain, dedicated to St Monica, which in turn founded the English Priory of Our Lady of Good Counsel, at Haywards Heath in Sussex, in 1886. This foundation, and that of another English contemplative house at Hoddesdon in Hertfordshire which is now closed, were affiliated to the Lateran but retained the Windesheim Constitutions. A Mission House was established in Rwanda in 1859, and in 1967 a House of Studies was opened in Rome, where the Canonesses can pursue higher studies. The Institute of St Agnes at Sion, Switzerland, provides a home for orphans and children with emotional and other difficulties.

AUGUSTINE, MISSIONARY SISTERS OF ST

Location: USA (Albany, New York)
RC (female) founded in India in 1897 by Mother Marie Louise de Meester
Original habit: a white tunic and scapular with a white wimple and headcover and a black veil with a peak over the forehead.

A Pontifical Institute, an active Order with simple vows. The Missionary Sisters' apostolate is in teaching, from kindergarten through to college level; in nursing in hospitals, leprosaria and maternity clinics; in social service ministries, including the administration of credit unions, co-operative schemes, hostels for children and the aged; and in foreign missions in Asia, Africa and the West Indies.

AUGUSTINE, ORDER OF ST

Location: Italy (Rome)
RC (male) founded in Italy probably in 1256 by Pope Alexander IV
Abbr: OSA
Original habit: a black tunic with wide sleeves, a hood, with a long, pointed capuce and a leather belt. At one time the habit was white, but this was worn outdoors only in areas where there were no, similarly garbed, Dominicans.

The Order was probably founded in 1256, when Pope Alexander IV united several groups of hermits who followed the Rule of St Augustine. Such semi-eremitical bodies included the Williamites, the Bonites, the Brittinians, the Hermits of the Holy Trinity and many more. The confusion arises because there were two successive unions of pre-existing groups, living mainly in Tuscany. An attempt to unite the several hermit groups was made by Pope Innocent IV. In 1256 Pope Alexander IV published a Bull creating an Order of Hermits that was exempted from episcopal jurisdiction, with the prior of the Bonites elected as first prior general. A uniform black habit was adopted, and the hermits gave their attention to pastoral work, teaching, study and the missions. Within a few years there were houses in Germany, France and Spain. Constitutions were produced, and the Order was approved by the Chapters of Florence in 1287 and Ratisbon in 1290. Much prosperity followed, but discipline became relaxed over the years, and the Reformation and the French Revolution both took their toll. At the end of the 19th century there was a renewal of activity, and the Order spread to Australia, Nigeria and the United States, and there has been a recent move to establish a house in Korea. The friars work mainly in education and foreign missions. An Augustinian friar is always selected to be the papal sacristan, and it is his duty to renew a consecrated host every week in readiness for the Pope should he become fatally ill; it is also the sacristan's privilege to administer the Last Rites to a dying pontiff.

✠ Austin Friars
  Hermits of St Augustine

AUGUSTINE, ORDER OF THE RECOLLECTS OF ST

Location: Italy (Rome)
RC (male) founded in Spain in 1588; an independent Congregation from 1622
Abbr: OAR
Original habit: a close-fitting black cowl with a small hood. White sandals made from cord could be worn.

The idea of founding an Order of discalced Augustinians in Spain came from Fr

Thomas of Jesus, an Augustinian friar since the age of fifteen. However, his untimely death in 1582 placed the work in the hands of a Fr Diaz, who, with the help of Philip II of Spain, established the first monastery at Talavera in 1588. It was not until 1622 that the Discalced Augustinians were permitted to be a separate Congregation with its own vicar-general. In 1912 the Congregation was raised to the status of a regular Order. Houses were established in Italy and later in the Philippines and Peru. In the early years of the Order, when the friars were living as hermits, members of the community would meet together only for Mass on Sundays, but between Palm Sunday and Low Sunday they were obliged to live in community. Strict silence was observed, together with total abstinence from flesh meat, fish and eggs.

✠ Order of Discalced Augustinians

AUGUSTINE, PENITENTS OF ST

Defunct
RC (female) founded in Italy in 1628
Original habit: a black tunic and knee-length mantle with a white scapular. The face was covered with a black veil.

A group of female Religious who chose to live a life of cloistered penance on the Flaminian Way in Rome in a monastery dedicated to St Mary Magdalen. The Order, which was established during the pontificate of Pope Urban VIII (1623–44), observed the Rule of St Augustine, with Constitutions modified to accommodate a penitential life. The nuns were cloistered to such an extent that they had no contact with the outside world and were allowed to meet only with their parents. They were governed by a superior who was answerable to a congregation of men under the chairmanship of a cardinal.

AUGUSTINIAN (DISCALCED) NUNS IN PORTUGAL

Defunct
RC (female) founded in Portugal in 1663
Original habit: a white tunic (with a black one added on feast days) with a black leather girdle, white scapular and black mantellum. On the head a rough white linen cloth which came down to the eyes in the front and reached the waist at the back was worn, to which a wide black cloth was attached.

The reputation of the Discalced Augustinians in Spain (see next entry) spread swiftly to Portugal and prompted many to follow this way of life. A monastery was founded in 1663 near the city walls of Lisbon, in the valley of Xabergras.

AUGUSTINIAN (DISCALCED) NUNS IN SPAIN

Defunct
RC (female) founded in Spain in the 16th century by Alphonse d'Orozco
Original habit: a black habit with a coarse white linen under-tunic and a white linen veil.

Alphonse d'Orozco, an Augustinian friar, was given money by a noblewoman of Madrid who wished to found a monastery dedicated to the Virgin Mary. The first Mass was celebrated there in 1589. The foundation was initially under the jurisdiction of the discalced Augustinians but became autonomous in 1600. With the help of Queen Margaret of Austria, who married Philip III of Spain by proxy in the presence of Pope Clement VIII in 1598, further foundations were made, one especially for the education of the daughters of the King of Spain's officers. The life of the nuns was very austere, with fasting from the feast of All Saints until Christmas Day and again from Septuagesima until Easter as well as on all Wednesdays and Fridays throughout the year.

AUGUSTINIAN RECOLLECTS OF THE HEART OF JESUS

Location: Venezuela (Los Teques, Edo, Miranda)
RC (female) founded in Venezuela in 1901 by Laura Evangelista Alvarado Cardoza (Blessed Mary of St Joseph – beatified 1995) and Fr Vincente Lopez Aveledo of Maracay
Abbr: OSA
Original habit: Augustinian style.

The Congregation was founded as the Sisters Hospitallers of St Augustine in 1901, changing to its present name in 1903. The work of the Sisters is to care for the sick, the orphaned and the elderly, for which the Congregation runs many orphanages and homes throughout the country. The founder, Blessed Mary of St Joseph, is the first beatified Venezuelan.

AUGUSTINIAN RELIGIOUS OF THE MONASTERY OF THE VIRGINS – Venice

Defunct
RC (female) founded in Italy in 1177 by Pope Alexander III (1159–81)
Original habit: a white habit with a black veil covering the face.

Julie, the daughter of the Emperor Frederick Barbarossa, joined this monastery together with twelve other noblewomen, and was its first abbess. The foundation was richly endowed through the generosity of the Doge of Venice, Sebastian Zani, who, together with his successors, was given the patronage of the monastery in perpetuity.

AUGUSTINIAN SISTERS – Meaux

Location: France (Meaux)
RC (female) founded in France in 1244
Abbr: OSA
Original habit: a black habit and veil and white linen under-veil and a white wimple; a silver cross was worn around the neck by professed nuns.

The sick of Meaux in the 13th century were cared for by the Trinitarian Fathers, helped by some women, who nursed the female patients, many of whom wished to take on the religious life. In 1250 a community of female religious was founded, following the Rule of St Augustine, known as the Religious of the Order of the Holy Trinity, and later as the Augustinian Sisters. They remained at Meaux, in charge of the Hôtel-Dieu, for over six hundred years, until 1845, when it was decided by the Commission for Hospitals to amalgamate the hospice at Meaux, run by the Sisters of Charity, with the Augustinian Hôtel-Dieu and the administration was placed in the hands of the Sisters of Charity. The Augustinians left the Hôtel-Dieu and became a Congregation of teaching and nursing religious, recognized by an imperial decree in 1854. The modified Rule, Statutes and Constitutions were approved in 1904. In the 1950s many fusions of the Augustinians of Meaux were undertaken and the number of houses increased from eight to fourteen over a period of three years, with the mother house remaining at Meaux. They were later linked formally with the Order of St Augustine, the Sisters becoming tertiary members of the Order. The present-day apostolate responds to the demands of the times and the needs of the people. In 1980 a small community was opened at Presteigne in Wales, with the aim of sharing the Augustinian way of life with others regardless of their faith or lack of it, but this closed after two years.

AUGUSTINIAN SISTERS – Pont de Beauvoisin

Location: France (Meaux)
RC (female) founded in France in 1818 by three religious from Mâcon

The Congregation is dedicated to nursing, especially of the aged, and teaching. It amalgamated in 1970 with the Augustinian Sisters of Meaux.

AUGUSTINIAN SISTERS OF CHARITY

Location: USA (Richfield, Ohio)
RC (female) founded in the USA in 1851 by Mother Bernardine
Abbr: CSA
Original habit: Augustinian style.

A diocesan Congregation, whose founding Sisters were Augustinians from Boulogne-sur-Mer, France. They were invited to Cleveland, Ohio, by its first bishop, Amadeus Rapp, in 1851 in order to make a new foundation whose members would provide health care in the area. The Sisters now carry on with this work and also undertake hospital staffing, teaching at all levels, an AIDS ministry, spiritual direction and parish ministries as required. At present the Congregation also maintains a missionary team in El Salvador.

AUGUSTINIAN SISTERS OF OUR LADY OF CONSOLATION

Location: The Philippines (Manila)
RC (female) founded in the Philippines in 1883 by Mother Rita Barcelo y Pages and Mother Consuelo Barcelo y Pages (blood sisters)
Abbr: OSA
Original habit: a white habit with a black cincture, white headdress and black veil and a wide white scapular. On special occasions a black habit and cincture were worn, with the same headdress.

The apostolate of the Congregation is concerned with the formal education of women, with social and pastoral ministry related to the needs of the poor and deprived, with catechesis, campus ministry, hospital chaplaincy, prison visiting and the conducting of retreats.

AUGUSTINIAN SISTERS OF THE HOLY HEART OF MARY

Location: France (Paris)
RC (female) founded in France in 1827 by Victoire Letellier (Mother St Angele)
Abbr: OSA
Original habit: a long black dress and a leather belt, with rosary, and scapular. A black veil, with a band of white linen, and a wimple was worn, with a crucifix and ring (for professed nuns); postulants wore a dark blue dress with a small veil; novices wore the same habit as professed nuns, but with a white veil.

Victoire Letellier, a member of the Augustinians at Saumur (Maine-et-Loire) from 1808, left there to start a foundation of her own when the upheavals at the time of the French Revolution affected the hospital administration in Saumur, which had been in the hands of the nuns. The first house of the new foundation was opened in Paris in 1828, with new Constitutions and with Victoire Letellier, now Mother St Angele, serving as the first superior-general. This first house, in rented property due shortly to be sold, was superseded by a house specially designed and built for the Congregation on the Rue de la Santé, which they eventually occupied in 1839. It is still the mother house of the Order. A sister house was founded at Nice in 1874. In 1880 some of the Sisters went to England, staying first in London before moving to St Leonard's-on-Sea in Sussex, where their work in nursing continues.

AUGUSTINIAN SISTERS OF THE HÔTEL-DIEU – Carpenteras

Location: France (Meaux)
RC (female) founded in France in 1736 by Jean-François Curnier and Malachie d'Inguimbert
Abbr: OSA

This Order was fused with the Augustinian Sisters of Meaux in 1954. The work of the

Sisters until then was concerned with the nursing of the sick in the Hôtel Dieu at Carpenteras.

AUGUSTINIAN SISTERS OF THE MERCY OF JESUS

Location: Canada (Sillery, Quebec, for the Canadian Federation) and France (Malestroit, for the French Federation)
RC (female) founded in France in the 13th century
Abbr: OSA
Original habit: white, with a white linen rochet and a black veil and mantle; a leather belt was worn beneath the rochet; lay Sisters wore the leather belt above the rochet.

A Congregation founded originally under the Rule of St Augustine for a group of women who lived in common and cared for the sick in the Hôtel-Dieu at Dieppe in the 13th century. They were known as the Hermit Sisters of St Augustine and did much work with the poor and needy. By the 16th century this had become a religious Order, and laxity later crept in, necessitating a reform which was undertaken by Cardinal Joyeuse of Rouen and which resulted in the granting of papal approval in 1665. Today, the hospitaller Sisters have communities in France, England, The Netherlands, Italy, Canada and Africa, where they continue to care for the sick in hospitals and nursing and convalescent homes, as well as running guest houses for priests and the laity.

✠ Canonesses Regular Hospitallers of the
   Merciful Heart of Jesus of the Order of
   St Augustine
   Hospital Sisters of the Mercy of Jesus

AUGUSTINIAN SISTERS OF THE MERCY OF JESUS

Location: England (Burgess Hill, Sussex)
RC (female) founded in Belgium in 1841 by Canon Peter John Maes

Abbr: OSA
Original habit: a black habit with a white scapular.

At the invitation of Cardinal Wiseman in 1866 a foundation for physically and mentally ill men and women, St George's Retreat, was made in the south of England, at Burgess Hill, Sussex, built in the Belgian style by men from Bruges. It was originally designed to cater for some 150 elderly and infirm men and women and was opened in 1868. Provision is now made at St George's Retreat for younger people who have special needs, particularly those with learning difficulties. Other houses are to be found in England, Ireland and Scotland. The Sisters running these homes are all qualified in general and psychiatric nursing.

AUGUSTINIAN SISTERS OF THE PRECIOUS BLOOD

Defunct
RC (female) founded in France in 1823 by Mgr Parisis
Original habit: a white habit with a black scapular and veil; a silver heart was suspended around the neck on a scarlet ribbon.

The Congregation arose from an attempt to amalgamate several Augustinian communities that had been running schools or hospitals as part of their apostolate since the 13th century and which had, for the most part, survived disbanding during the French Revolution. The amalgamation of these into a single Congregation was the work of Mgr Parisis of Arras, France, and the Sisters continued with their work in hospitals and schools, clinics, orphanages and parish ministries. Houses were opened in other parts of France and later in Belgium, Spain and Madagascar. There was also an English foundation at Hearnsey Manor, near Dover, Kent, at one time.

AUGUSTINIAN SISTERS SERVANTS OF JESUS AND MARY

Location: Italy (Rome)
RC (female) founded in Italy in 1827 by Maria
Teresa Spinelli
Original habit: a black tunic and veil with a white
linen wimple and headcover; a crucifix was worn
around the neck.

Maria Teresa Spinelli (1789–1850) had a
disastrous early life spent in caring for her
aged parents and enduring a physically abu-
sive husband. Once free of her problems
she became interested in the education of
young people and felt that God was calling
her to this work following a deeply spiritual
experience. Together with three other
women she opened the first state school for
girls at Frosinone in 1821 and later became
involved in running an orphanage and a
boarding school. Following her profession
in 1827, when her companions also took
the habit, the small community moved into
their first home, in buildings which had
belonged to the Augustinian Fathers, and it
was here that she died in 1850. The Sisters
have an apostolate in education and nursing. They also conduct retreats and undertake parish work. There are houses in the
USA, Brazil, Great Britain, Italy, India, the
Philippines, Malta, Africa and Australia.

AUSTRIA, CANONS REGULAR OF

Location: Austria (St Florian)
RC (male) founded in Austria in 1140 by King
Leopold of Austria
Original habit: a black cassock with a sleeveless
cotta and a grey fur hood.

A Congregation of Canons Regular,
founded in 1140 during the pontificate of
Pope Innocent II (1130–43), in honour of
the Blessed Virgin Mary. This was united,
in 1907, with other Augustinian foundations to form the Austrian Congregation.

✠ Assumptionists
Canons Regular of the Austrian Lateran
Congregation

AUSTRIAN CONGREGATION

An amalgamation made in 1907 of the
Canons Regular of Austria and the Con-
gregations of St Florian, Klosterneuberg,
Herzogenberg, Reichersberg, Voran and
Neustift.

AVIZ OF PORTUGAL, KNIGHTS OF

Defunct
RC (male Equestrian Order) founded in Portugal in
the 12th century by a group of knights
Original habit: a white mantle with a green fleur-
de-lis cross on the left shoulder; papal permission
for this was granted following a request by King
Alfonso IV of Portugal (1325–57).

The origin of this Order lies with a loose
group of Portuguese knights called the
Brethren of Santa Maria, who guarded the
open plains of the Almetejo Province
against the Moors in the mid-12th century
and who observed a revised Benedictine
Rule. In 1170, King Alfonso I of Portugal
(1139–85) legitimized this Military Order
as the Knights of Evora and established it
around the town of Evora, some twenty
miles south-east of Lisbon. But the group
was too weak to maintain this commandery, which was transferred to the Templars,
effectively placing the Knights of Evora
under the jurisdiction of the Knights of
Calatreve. In 1211, King Alfonso II, known
as The Fat, gave the town of Aviz to the
Master at Evora, Ferdinand Rodrigues
Monteiro, and the mother house was established here. The name of the Order now
changed to become the Knights of St
Benedict of Aviz. The Order of Calatreve
gave its Portuguese property to the Knights
of Aviz, who now became thoroughly inde-

pendent once more. But decline set in with a growing laxity. Vows were dispensed with in 1496, 'on account of concubinage', and the vow of poverty was dropped in 1505. All Portuguese Military Orders were dispersed in the 1830s and never fully recovered. Some survived as National Orders of Merit and on formal occasions the President of Portugal may wear an enamelled badge bearing three crosses, one of which is that of Aviz.

☦ Brothers of Santa Maria of Evora
Knights of Avis
Knights of Evora
Knights of St Benedict of Aviz

B

BANNABIKIRA SISTERS

Location: Uganda (Masaka)
RC (female) founded in Uganda by Sr Mechtilde and Mother St Foy

A native community of Sisters, founded and trained by the White Sisters, whose members now care for the sick at the Rubaga Hospital, Kampala, Uganda. This work was inherited from the Ladies of the Grail, who worked there from 1953 to 1974. The Bannabikira Sisters succeeded them and also achieved autonomous status with the added distinction of being the first female religious Congregation in Africa so to do.

✠ Daughters of Mary of Bannabikira

BAPTISTINES

Location: Italy (Parma)
RC (female) founded in Italy in 1730 by Giovanna Maria Baptista Solimani

A Congregation of Baptistines, which was founded at Moneglia, near Genoa, Italy, with the assistance of a Capuchin priest, Fr Athanasius, who helped with the drawing up of the Constitutions, with later co-operation from Fr Dominico Olivieri and a Barnabite priest, Mario Maccabei, who was responsible for getting papal approbation from Pope Benedict XIV in 1744. Giovanna and twelve companions made their profes-sions in 1746, following which she was elected as abbess. Houses were established in Rome (1755) and elsewhere throughout Italy. A strict cloister was observed and abstinence and penitence in the tradition of St John the Baptist was followed.

✠ Hermit Sisters of St John the Baptist

BAPTISTINES

Defunct
RC (male) founded in France in the mid-17th century by Michel de Saint-Sabine
Original habit: a brown tunic, cowl or capuce, and mantle with a black scapular and leather belt.

The founder of this now-defunct Order of Baptistine Hermits was a secular priest who reformed and united the hermits of various dioceses at the request of the diocesan bishops and drew up Statutes for an organization called the Hermits of St John the Baptist, also known as the Congregation of Brother Michel de Saint-Sabine. In 1673 he was made visitor to all the hermits in the diocese of Langres. The bishop of the diocese then added some new ordinanaces to the Constitutions and changed the colour of the habit from brown to white, so as to distinguish the hermits from vagrant Brothers.

✠ Hermits of St John the Baptist
    Hermits of St John the Baptist in France

BAPTISTINES

Defunct
RC (male) founded in Italy in c.1750 by Dominico
Olivieri

The purpose of this now-defunct Baptistine foundation was to form an association of priests who would evangelize people through missionary work in Italy, in both town and country. The Congregation was approved by Pope Benedict XIV in 1755. The vows that were taken were those of continuance in the Congregation and readiness to go to the missions as required. The missionary work in Italy was so successful that it was extended abroad, with members working in China, Bulgaria and Macedonia. The Congregation became defunct towards the end of the 18th century

✟ Missionary Priests of St John the Baptist

BAPTISTINES

Defunct
RC (male) founded in Spain, date uncertain
Original habit: a rough brown habit with a leather
girdle and a short mantle; around the neck a heavy
wooden cross was suspended.

An early foundation of Spanish Baptistines, which was established as a community near Pamplona (Navarre), with five hermitages each occupied by eight to ten hermits, some of whom may have been priests. The hermits led a life of penance and observed silence except for reciting the divine office in common; at all other times the silence was strictly observed. Solemn vows were taken but only after a considerable period of probation. Food was sparse, consisting of bread and vegetables with water the only drink allowed and flagellation performed at least three times a week and daily during Lent.

✟ Brothers of St John the Baptist of
    Penitence
  Hermits of St John the Baptist
  Penitents of St John the Baptist

BAPTISTINES

Location: Italy (Rome)
RC (female) founded in Italy in 1878 by Canon
Alphonso Maria Fusco and Mother Crociffisa
Caputo

An Italian Congregation with a wide apostolate. The Sisters work in nursing and in care for the aged, run day nurseries for children, give retreats and conduct foreign missions. The first American foundation was made in 1906, and the work has now expanded to include care not only for elderly women but also for men. The Sisters also pursue any ministry connected with the marginalized and with youth at risk. Foreign missions now include Korea, the Philippines, India and South America as well as work in Poland, Italy, Malawi, Zambia and Madagascar.

✟ Sisters of St John the Baptist

BARNABAS, BROTHERHOOD OF ST –
Pennsylvania

Defunct
Episcopal Church of the USA (male) founded in the
USA in 1913 by G. P. Hance
Abbr: SBB
Original habit: a grey cassock and hood with a
leather belt. A professed Brother would have a red
cross on the cassock, and a solemnly professed
Brother was entitled to wear a silver ring.

The founder of the Congregation, G. P. Hance, had been a member of the Church Army and a missioner in West Pennsylvania, USA. He opened a convalescent home for poor men, and later for incurables, at Carnegie, Pennsylvania, helped by the C. H. Pennington Brotherhood. The Congregation was formally recognized in 1913 and the Benedictine Rule was followed, adapted to the care and needs of the sick poor. The day office was recited together with matins and evensong, with vespers of the dead said on Fridays. The formation programme involved a six-month period as a visitor, followed by a further six months as a postulant. A two- or three-year novitiate led to a further year in junior vows followed by two years in senior vows before life vows were taken. The headquarters was at Gibsonia, Pennsylvania.

BARNABITE FATHERS

Location: Italy (Rome)
RC (male) founded in Italy in 1533 by St Anthony Zaccaria (canonized 1897)
Abbr: CRSP
Original habit: a black clerical tunic with a black cotton cincture and a biretta

A Congregation of secular clergy, named Barnabites from the church of St Barnabas in Milan which belonged to the Congregation in the 16th century. From here they operated their mission to revive the love of divine worship and a Christian life, through frequent preaching and administration of the sacraments, while at the same time living and working in the world. The brother of a founding member of this Congregation, Bartolomeo Ferarri, was a papal secretary, and it was he who brought the Congregation to the attention of Pope Clement VII (1523–34), who granted approbation in 1533, which was confirmed by his successor the following year. The Congregation soon spread throughout France and Germany. They were originally known as the Clerks Regular of St Paul Beheaded, but the last word was later removed. The work of the Congregation continues today with houses in Europe, Africa, South America and the USA, where

the first foundation was made at Buffalo, New York, in 1952

✢ Clerks Regular of St Paul

BARRATI

A name given at one time to Carmelites, because of the striped, or barred, garments they were compelled to wear by the Saracens; this is also the origin of the name of the Carmelite Convent des Barres, in Paris.

BARTHOLOMITES

Defunct
RC (male) founded in Italy in 1307 by refugee Basilian monks
Original habit: (at first) a tan-coloured robe with black scapular; (later) a habit resembling that of a Dominican lay brother, with a white tunic, black scapular, cloak and cowl.

In 1307 some refugee Basilian Armenian monks from Montenegro went to Italy and made a foundation there dedicated to the Virgin Mary and St Bartholomew, helped and encouraged by Archbishop Spinola of Genoa and Fr Martin. Houses were opened throughout Italy, at Siena, Pisa, Florence, Civita-Vecchia, Rome and Ancona. Mass was celebrated according to the Dominican rite, but the divine office was conducted as for the Roman use. The monks adopted the Rule of St Augustine, a change from that of St Basil, which was confirmed by Pope Innocent VI in 1356. Fr Martin has been credited as the founder, and following his death the Congregations seemed to lapse in the strictness observed in the early days. In 1650 Pope Innocent X sanctioned the remaining members to either enter other Orders or be secularised, and the Congregation became defunct

✢ Armenian Religious of Genoa

BARTHOLOMITES

Defunct
RC (male) founded in Austria in 1640 by
Bartholomew Holzhauser
Original habit: as for secular clergy.

A Congregation founded by Fr Holzhauser
at Tittmolning, near Salzburg, Austria, for
secular priests as role models living in community. Where communal living was not
possible, members would live in twos or
threes in parishes, where they would
observe a Rule of life which did not involve
the taking of vows but did require a sharing
of funds. A promise of obedience to the
superior was, however, taken and confirmed by oath. At the time of Fr Holzhauser's death in 1658 there were several
centres in Austria and Germany. The Institute spread to Poland, Sicily and Spain, with
papal approbation granted in 1680, but the
Congregation had died out by the end of
the 18th century.

✠ United Brethren

BASIL THE GREAT, ORDER OF ST

Location: Italy (Rome)

St Basil of Caesarea, a father of Eastern
monasticism, visited Egypt in 358, which
was at that time famous for its Pachomian
monasteries. St Gregory of Nazianzus
joined St Basil in living an ascetic life, while
his mother, St Emelia, and his sister,
Macrina, developed a community of nuns
at Pontus, on the Black Sea. To those who
placed themselves under his direction St
Basil gave two Rules, the Great and the
Little. From this start developed the Basilian
monastic family with its many branches.

1 Basilian Order of Grottaferrata
2 Basilian Order of St Josaphat
3 Basilian Order of the Most Holy Saviour
of the Melkites

4 Basilian Order of St John the Baptist of
the Melkites
5 Aleppine Basilian Order of Melkites

1. BASILIAN ORDER OF GROTTAFERRATA

Location: Italy (Grottaferrata)
RC Eastern Rite (male) said to have been founded
in Italy in the 10th century by St Neilos the
Younger, but a more recent date of 1579 is
generally taken as the date of foundation
Abbr: OSBI
Original habit: a dark, buttonless cassock, usually
black, with a belt and cloak. On the head is worn a
black *kamilavkion*, or hat, with an
epanokamilavkion, or veil; monks are usually
bearded.

This monastery of Basilian monks is dedicated to the Mother of God and was
founded by St Neilos the Younger, a Greek
from Calabria, Italy, who became a monk
in one of the many Byzantine monasteries
to be found in the south of Italy, following
the death of his wife and child. During his
lifetime, St Neilos undertook many journeys
and suffered at the hands of the Saracens.
In 981, at around seventy years of age and
in the company of some sixty monks, he
left the south of Italy and moved north to
Monte Cassino, where they were all well
received. Before his death in 1004 at Grottaferrata, St Neilos had a vision of Our Lady
telling him that this was where he was to
build a monastery. The Grottaferrata community faced many difficulties, including
occupation by soldiers in 1408. Many
attempts have been made to repair the
damage suffered over the centuries, and the
monastery underwent a great reform in the
19th century under Pope Leo XIII, when
the Byzantine Rite, which had become infil-
trated with Latin usages, was restored and a
college for the training of priests of the
Eastern Rite was opened.

2. BASILIAN ORDER OF ST JOSAPHAT

Location: Italy (Rome)
RC Eastern Rite (male) founded in Asia Minor in
the 4th century by St Basil the Great; centralized in
1617
Abbr: OSBM
Original habit: a dark, buttonless cassock, usually
black, with a belt and cloak. On the head is worn a
black *kamilavkion*, or hat, with an
epanokamilavkion, or veil; monks are usually
bearded.

By the 16th century many of the Basilian
monasteries were in communion with
Rome, and there was a recommendation
that they unite into Congregations. St Josaphat, from Vladimis in Poland, together
with Fr Rutski, worked to bring back the
Ruthenian churches into Catholic unity.
Reformed Basilian monasteries were organized distinctively into a Congregation under
a proto-archimandrite as superior-general,
and became known as the Congregation of
Lithuania, or of the Holy Trinity. The Congregation grew in size so that by the time
of a general chapter held in 1636 the number of participating houses had risen to
thirty. As recently as 1997 there were sixty-
nine houses belonging to this Order. The
life of the monks, who are in solemn vows,
is both active and contemplative, and they
work in education and the conducting of
retreats, as well as in parish and foreign
missions, especially among Eastern Rite
Catholics.

3. BASILIAN ORDER OF THE MOST HOLY SAVIOUR OF THE MELKITES

Location: Lebanon (Saida)
RC Eastern Rite (male) founded in the Lebanon in
1684/7 by Euthymios Saiffi, Metropolitan of Tyre
Abbr: BS
Original habit: a dark, buttonless cassock, usually
black, with a belt and cloak. On the head is worn a
black *kamilavkion*, or hat, with an

epanokamilavkion, or veil; monks are usually
bearded.

The Congregation was founded at the monastery of St Saviour near the village of Gun
in the Kharrub district of South Lebanon,
between Sidon and Beirut. The building of
the monastery was begun in 1708 by Fr
Na'amatullah, the superior, with several of
his monks. By 1743 the Constitutions and
the observance of an adapted Rule of St
Basil were confirmed. Today, students study
at St Saviour, the mother house, at the
Greek College in Rome, or at St Anne's in
Jerusalem, which is under the direction of
the White Fathers. The Fathers have established a seminary and novitiate in the USA,
at Methuen, Massachusetts. Priests of this
Congregation work mainly in parishes, conducting retreats and teaching. They are also
responsible for missions in Canada, Mexico
and South America.

✟ Basilian Salvatorian Fathers

4. BASILIAN ORDER OF ST JOHN THE BAPTIST OF THE MELKITES

Location: Lebanon (Khonchara)
RC Eastern rite (male and female) founded in the
Lebanon in 1697 by Gerasimos and Sulaiman
Abbr: BC
Original habit: a dark, buttonless cassock, usually
black, with a belt and cloak. On the head is worn a
black *kamilavkion*, or hat, with an
epanokamilavkion, or veil; monks are usually
bearded. Nuns wear a black habit and headdress.

Two former Jesuit missionary students,
Gerasimos, who later became the Melkite
metropolitan of Aleppo, and Sulaiman, who
became the archimandrite of Balamond,
had together gone to the monastery of Balamond near Tripoli, which was at one time
a Cistercian house but by then housed a
community of Eastern Orthodox monks.
Once there, they attempted to convert the
occupants to Rome and were in part suc-

cessful, resulting in their expulsion from the monastery, together with their converts. An appeal to Patriarch Cyril V resulted in his approval for their plans to build a monastery of St John the Baptist (Mar Hanna) near the village of Shuwair, between Beirut and Baalbek. Others joined them, but a later falling-out between Gerasimos and Sulaiman resulted in the latter returning to the monastery at Balamond, where he became its archimandrite. Gerasimos remained as superior of the monastery of St John and was later appointed metropolitan of Aleppo. Other monasteries wished to unite with the Shuwair Congregation, and new Constitutions were composed which were approved by Pope Benedict XIV in 1757. Attempts to unite the two original Congregations failed and the Shuwair monks eventually split into two groups, those of Aleppo and those of Lebanon; the latter were considered to be rustics. Two distinct Congregations emerged: the Country Shuwairites, who have kept the name Shuwairite Basilians, and the Aleppo Shuwairites, who are now called Aleppine Basilians. Monastic students attend their philosophy and theology courses at the Jesuit University of St Joseph in Beirut. There are also nuns of the Shuwairite Basilian Order who have a foundation at the Convent of Our Lady of the Annunciation at Zouk-Mikael Djounieh, Lebanon.

✠ Baladites
   Shuwairite Basilians

5. ALEPPINE BASILIAN ORDER OF MELKITES

Location: Lebanon (Sarba-Jounieh)
RC Easten Rite (male and female) founded in 1829 (and see previous entry)
Abbr: BA
Original habit: a dark, buttonless cassock, usually black, with a belt and cloak. On the head is worn a black *kamilavkion*, or hat, with an

epanokamilavkion, or veil; monks are usually bearded. Nuns wear a black habit and headdress.

The foundation of this Basilian Order dates from the separation of the monks of Aleppo from the Shuwairite Basilians (see previous entry). This separation was agreed upon in 1829 and came about because of bad feeling between the two communities which could not be resolved. Monastic students pursue their studies within the monastery. There are also Basilian nuns of this Congregation with a mother house at the Convent of St Michael at Zouk-Mikael Jounieh, Lebanon, close neighbours of the Shuwairite Basilian Sisters.

BASIL, PRIESTS OF THE COMMUNITY OF ST

Location: Canada (Toronto)
RC (male) founded in France in 1822 by some teachers
Abbr: CSB

As a result of the French Revolution, when so many religious communities were dispersed with a resulting loss of clergy numbers, the archbishop of Vienne, Mgr D'Aviau, set up a school in the mountains of Vivarais in the village of St Symphorien de Mahun. The venture was a success and expanded, housed in a former Franciscan monastery. In 1822 some teachers from the school sought permission to found a religious community, with the mother house at Annonay in the diocese of Viviers, whose bishop drew up the Rule for the Congregation. Approbation from Rome was granted in 1867. The members took four vows, of poverty, chastity, obedience and stability, but the vow of poverty in this case allowed each member to retain his own property, keep Mass stipends and spend whatever salary he earned, although he was not to speculate in investments. Colleges were founded throughout France, in Algeria, England (Plymouth) and in Canada, where

St Michael's College in Toronto was opened in 1852. Parochial work was later taken up in the USA, in Texas and New York. With the French Association Laws coming into effect at the start of the 20th century, when education was taken out of the hands of religious communities, the French colleges were closed.

BASIL THE GREAT, SISTERS OF THE ORDER OF ST

Location: Italy (Rome)
RC (female) founded in Italy in the 4th century
Abbr: OSBM
Original habit: a black Byzantine habit and headdress with veil.

The Sisters of St Basil the Great made a foundation in the USA in 1911, in Pennsylvania, where they observe the Byzantine Rite in their divine liturgy and office. The work of the Congregation is with teaching but the Sisters also run a nursing home for the elderly as well as helping with the administration of the Catholic (Ruthenian) archeparchy of Pittsburgh and in the Ruthenian eparchies of Parma, Ohio, Passaic, New Jersey and Van Nuys, Arizona. Some of the Sisters are involved in the making of vestments for use in the Catholic Byzantine Rite and in iconography.

BEAR, KNIGHTS OF THE

Defunct
RC (male Equestrian Order) founded in Switzerland in 1214 by the Emperor Frederick II, King of Sicily
Original habit: (insignia) a medallion with the image of a bear and a fleur-de-lis in each quarter of the circumference, suspended from a gold metal band which is decorated with oak leaves

The Order was founded by Frederick II, who, at the age of four, had been crowned king of Sicily, with his guardian, Pope Innocent III, as regent. When in later years trouble in Sicily arose because of the many local fighting feuds and the added threat of war-like action from Germany, Frederick was granted military assistance from Switzerland, and in gratitude for a successful outcome he founded the Order of Knights of the Bear. The Order enjoyed the support of the Benedictines of the Abbey of St Gall, in Switzerland, whose legendary association with the bear is well known.

BEC, MONKS OF

A Congregation of reformed Benedictines.

BEGHARDS

An association of laymen in The Netherlands which came into existence sometime in the 13th century. The men lived together in community in imitation of the Beguines (see next entry) and have sometimes been seen as their male counterpart, although there were many differences. They do not seem to have had an identifiable founder. Many of the Beghards took to the road to denounce clerical abuses, advocating that sinful priests should not celebrate the Mass and that there should be a form of lay-presidency which would allow anyone to celebrate Mass. Their belief that the sacraments were worthless did nothing to endear them to the Church, and the Beghards were suspected of heresy and their teaching condemned by the Council of Vienne in 1311. Some reforms followed, but the wandering preachers, who were scattered throughout the modern-day Low Countries and Germany, were distrusted by the Church as they had no ecclesiastical, or secular, masters. Many of the Beghards had organized themselves into stable communities, observing a Rule of life similar to that of Franciscan tertiaries, supporting themselves with their work and practising acts of charity which extended to the care of the dead during the time of the Black Death, for which they received some measure of civil protection. They were suppressed by Pope Innocent X in 1650.

BEGUINES

Defunct
RC (female) founded in the 12th century by Lambert le Beghe (uncertain)
Original habit: a black tunic with a long black cloak and a white veil covering the head and upper chest. A cap, resembling an upturned saucer, was worn over the veil.

The origin of the name is unclear, but a certain Lambert le Beghe of Liège was inspired to found an institution for women who wished to consecrate their lives to God, and the first house was opened in 1184. Beguines differed from nuns in that they took no religious vows. There was frequent opposition from the Church, which accused them of heresy (see also Beghards). The women, often well-born, lived in Beguinages, some extensive enough to be small villages, and worked with the poor and the sick. Beguinages were to be found throughout the Low Countries and in France, Germany and England, where there was a foundation at Norwich, in Norfolk. Some communities, including that of the well-known Beguinage at Bruges in Belgium, lasted into the 20th century.

 Beghines

BENEDICT, ORDER OF ST – ANGLICAN

There are many Anglican Benedictine communities, both male and female, within the Anglican communion in the UK, the USA, Australia and Korea. The earliest of these communities was founded in the mid-19th century. They all observe the Benedictine Rule, wear the Benedictine habit and use the post-nominal letters OSB For a history of the Order of St Benedict, see General Introduction at the beginning of the Benedictine Roman Catholic entry below.

The Benedictine habit

A black tunic, cincture, scapular and hood with a pleated cowl (the colour may vary). Benedictine nuns wear the same basic habit as the monks but in addition wear a black veil and white linen wimple and binder.

BENEDICT, ORDER OF ST – Alton Abbey

Location: England (Alton, Hampshire)
Anglican (male) founded in England in 1889 by Charles Plomer Hopkins
Abbr: OSB
Original habit: Benedictine style.

Originally called the Order of St Paul, the Congregation was founded to help seamen, both materially and spiritually. It was when Charles Plomer Hopkins was port chaplain in Rangoon, India, that the idea of such an Order began to develop in his mind, and on his return to England he joined the Society of St Paul, as Fr Michael, with a view to starting a maritime section of the Society. A priory of the Society of St Paul was subsequently opened in Calcutta, with others later set up in the ports of Barry, in South Wales (1894), and Greenwich, in London (1899). Land was also bought at Alton, in Hampshire, upon which Alton Abbey was built. By the time of Hopkins' death the community was reduced in number. The Constitution was revised to bring it into line with that of St Benedict's Rule and the Barry and Greenwich priories were closed. The Benedictine Rule was formally adopted in 1981 and the work among seamen abandoned in 1989. The monks of Alton Abbey are now concerned with printing, iconography, the making of incense and altar breads and the running of retreats and conferences.

BENEDICT, ORDER OF ST – Bartonville

Location: USA (Bartonville, Illinois)
Anglican (male) founded in Puerto Rico in 1985

Abbr: OSB
Original habit: Benedictine style.

The Abbey of St Benedict at Bartonville was founded as a Spanish-speaking Benedictine Anglican community. The full monastic life is observed. Before their move to Bartonville, Illinois, the community was affiliated to Alton Abbey (see entry above).

BENEDICT, ORDER OF ST – Burford Priory

Location: England (Burford, Oxfordshire)
Anglican (mixed community) founded in England in 1941
Abbr: OSB
Original habit: Benedictine style.

The Burford Priory Congregation was founded as the Priory of Our Lady by the Congregation of St Mary the Virgin, Wantage, for late vocations and for those women whose health might not be too robust but who felt that they had a religious vocation. The community at first observed the Rule of the Visitation Order, but this was later changed to the Benedictine Rule as it was found to be more satisfactory. Burford Priory had become vacant in 1949, and the community moved there from their first home, at the Bishop's Palace, Cuddesdon in Oxfordshire. Postulancy lasts for six months and is followed by a two-year novitiate leading to temporary and then solemn profession. In 1987, with the admission of two male novices, a step was made to convert the community into a mixed one, monks and nuns sharing life under the Benedictine Rule, and in 1996 the first prior was elected. The community works in iconography and printing, conducts retreats and offers hospitality through their guest house. This has been a mixed community since 1987.

BENEDICT, ORDER OF ST – Edgware

Location: England (Edgware, Middlesex)
Anglican (female) founded in England in 1866 by the Revd Henry Daniel Nihill and Hannah Skinner (Mother Monica)
Abbr: OSB
Original habit: Benedictine style.

The community began as a Sisterhood dedicated to caring for the poor and was prominent in its concern for the victims of the 1866 cholera outbreak in London, and the later smallpox outbreaks which followed. The Sisters, who lived at the Convent of St Mary of Nazareth in Shoreditch, London, opened a hospital there for the victims, with a second house outside London for those who needed convalescence. The property at Edgware, north of London, was bought in 1873, and a convent dedicated to St Mary of the Cross was built. In 1929 the Congregation was affiliated to Elmore Abbey, Nashdom (see below). The Shoreditch Hospital was closed in 1931, along with the convent, and the Sisters moved to the house in Edgware, at the same time changing the Congregation's name to that of St Mary at the Cross. A hospital block with an isolation unit was opened at Edgware, but during the Second World War the Sisters and their patients moved to the comparative safety of Elmore Abbey, in Berkshire. After the war a further foundation was made at Lancing, on the Sussex coast, where sick children could enjoy a seaside holiday. The work of the community is concerned with leading a Benedictine monastic life, caring for the sick, disabled and elderly, conducting retreats and providing conference facilities. Since 1926 it had been the tradition of the community to sing the divine office in Latin, but today it is mostly sung in English, with only vespers retained in Latin. The head of the community is styled as the Right Reverend Dame.

BENEDICT, ORDER OF ST – Elmore Abbey, Nashdom

Location: England (Newbury, Berkshire)
Anglican (male) founded in England in 1914 by Athelstan Riley and W. H. Hill
Abbr: OSB
Original habit: Benedictine style.

The community arose from the dissemination of the Caldey Island Anglican community when its abbot, Aelred Carlyle, and part of the community converted to Roman Catholicism in 1913. At the behest of Lord Halifax, premises were found at Pershore, in Worcestershire, to house those monks wishing to remain as Anglicans. The first superior was Dom Anselm Mardon, the last solemnly professed monk of Caldey Abbey, built on an island off the Welsh coast. He was installed in 1914 and postulants were admitted. The later conversion to Roman Catholicism of Dom Anselm led to Dom Denys Prideaux being raised to the status of abbot of Pershore by the former bishop of Bloemfontein in 1922. As the community enlarged, it was necessary to move to a larger property, and the community was housed at Nashdom Abbey. A small number of novices from the USA established a daughter house, dedicated to St Gregory, at Valparaiso, Indiana, which later moved to Three Rivers, Michigan. With numbers falling, Nashdom Abbey was closed and the community moved to Elmore Abbey in 1987. The life of the community is purely monastic, and the daily work is concerned with publishing, the preparation of incense and other community wares, hospitality and the giving of retreats.

BENEDICT, ORDER OF ST – Holy Cross Community

Location: England (Rempstone, Loughborough, Leicestershire)
Anglican (female) founded in England in 1857 by Elizabeth Neale
Abbr: CHC
Original habit: Benedictine style.

The Holy Cross Community observes the Benedictine Rule and life, but it is distinctive in that it does not use the normal post-nominal letters of OSB

BENEDICT, ORDER OF ST – Korea

Location: Korea (Yangssan-shi, Kyongnam-do)
Anglican (female) founded in Korea in 1993
Abbr: OSB
Original habit: Benedictine style.

The community was founded at the invitation of the Anglican bishop of Pusan, Bishop Bundo C. H. Kim. It is one of four Anglican religious communities in Korea which form a province of the Anglican Communion. At present the number of Sisters is very small. They observe the full Benedictine life.

BENEDICT, ORDER OF ST – Malling Abbey

Location: England (St Mary's Abbey, West Malling, Kent)
Anglican (female) founded in England in 1891 by Jessie Park Moncrieff
Abbr: OSB
Original habit: Benedictine style.

The Malling Abbey Benedictine community was founded by Jessie Moncrieff, a professed Sister of the Community of Holy Charity, Edinburgh, Scotland, which was concerned with parochial work among the poor and sick in an impoverished part of that city. Miss Moncrieff and one novice withdrew from the community, moved to Edmonton, in north London, and established the Community of the Holy Comforter. This community was drawn towards a contemplative rather than an active form of religious life, gradually adopting the Benedictine Rule, under the influence of Abbot Aelred Carlyle of Caldey Island, who later converted to Roman Catholicism. The community moved, in 1906, to Baltonsborough in Somerset, and from there to some vacated buildings at West Malling, Kent, when the previous community, the Sisters of Sts Mary and Scholastica, also converted to Roman Catholicism. The departure of the few remaining members of the original community was not without a legal wrangle.

BENEDICT, ORDER OF ST – St Gregory's Abbey

Location: USA (Three Rivers, Michigan)
Episcopalian/Anglican (male) founded in the USA in 1939 by three priest-novices
Abbr: OSB
Original habit: Benedictine style.

A small number of American priests, after having spent their novitiate at Nashdom Abbey in England, where they made their first simple profession, returned to the USA and set up a foundation dedicated to St Gregory at Valparaiso, Indiana. Two years later its status was changed to that of a priory, on the occasion of the first two solemn professions. In 1946 the community moved to Three Rivers, Michigan. The community has now been elevated yet again to the status of an abbey. The monks support themselves with retreat work and preaching.

BENEDICT, ORDER OF ST – St Mark's Priory

Location: Australia (Camperdown, Victoria)
Anglican (mixed community) founded in Australia in 1975
Abbr: OSB
Original habit: Benedictine style.

Initially founded in Melbourne, Victoria, the St Mark's Priory community moved to Camperdown, west of Geelong, when the members adopted the Benedictine Rule and began to observe the full monastic life. In 1993 the priory became a double community when two nuns from Malling Abbey in England went out to Australia. This has been a mixed community since then.

BENEDICT, ORDER OF ST – ROMAN CATHOLIC

Location: Italy (Rome)
RC (male and female) founded in Italy in the 6th century by St Benedict of Nursia
Abbr: OSB
Original habit: a black tunic, cincture, scapular and hood with a pleated cowl (the colour may vary). Benedictine nuns wear the same basic habit as the monks but in addition wear a black veil and white linen wimple and binder.

General Introduction

Benedictines are male and female religious who belong to different religious families but who have all adopted the Rule of St Benedict of Nursia, composed in the first half of the 6th century, as the basis of their religious life. St Benedict had taken to an ascetic life at Subiaco, fifty miles east of Rome, where he attracted many like-minded followers, but an attempt on his life persuaded him to move to Monte Cassino, near Naples, where in 529 he founded a monastery. According to legend his sister, St Scholastica, opened a convent at the foot of the same mountain and is generally thought of as the first Benedictine nun. St Benedict died in 547, having completed the writing of his Rule, which incorporated material from St Cassian and St Basil. There were later revisions, but in essence the Rule of St Benedict laid the basis for European monasticism. It is characterized by common-sense notions of moderation and flexibility and provides a sensible regulation of the lives and needs of all members of religious communities. Benedictine monks now undergo a novitiate of one year, followed by temporary profession for three years which concludes with solemn profession. Benedictine monasteries are to be found throughout the world, united into a Confederation which dates from 1893. The monks, who are addressed as Dom, and nuns work in every field, from the care of souls to missionary work, education, publishing and the arts as well as leading a full monastic life in community. There are Anglican as well as Roman Catholic Benedictine Congregations.

Individual Congregations of the Benedictine Confederation

For individual entries see below under BENEDICT, Order of St (name of Congregation).

American Cassinese Congregation
Annunciation Congregation
Austrian Congregation
Bavarian Congregation
Beuronese Congregation
Brazilian Congregation
Camaldolese Congregation
Cassinese Congregation
English Congregation
Hungarian Congregation
Netherlands Congregation
Olivetan Congregation
St Ottilien Congregation
Slavonic Congregation
Solesmes Congregation
South American Cono-Sur Congregation
Subiaco Congregation (Cassinese of the
    Primitive Observance)
Swiss Congregation
Swiss-American Congregation
Sylvestrine Congregation
Vallombrosian Congregation

BENEDICT, ORDER OF ST – American Cassinese Congregation

Location: USA (Newark, New Jersey)
RC (male and female)

There was a Benedictine presence in the United States as early as the 17th century, when some English monks are thought to have gone there as missionaries. It is more certain that towards the end of the 18th century an attempt was made by the bishop of Baltimore to settle some English Benedictines in his diocese, but the venture did not flourish. At the start of the 19th century immigrant settlers from Bavaria were catered for spiritually by a party of Bavarian monks who set up a mission in Beatty, Pennsylvania, in the erstwhile Franciscan foundation of St Vincent. A college was established there, and the Beatty foundation became an abbey in 1855 with two dependent priories. Other foundations followed, including that of St John's Abbey in Collegeville, Minnesota, and houses in the states of Kansas, New Jersey, Illinois, North Carolina, Florida and Washington. The head of the Congregation is known as the President.

Benedictine Nuns of the American Cassinese Congregation

The first Benedictine nuns to go to the USA did so at the invitation of Dom Wimmer, the leader of a party of Benedictine monks from Bavaria who cared for immigrant settlers. In 1922 this foundation received approbation as the Congregation of St Scholastica, and in 1974 was renamed as a Federation of some twenty-two monasteries in fifteen states and Mexico. The nuns work mainly in teaching and nurse training, but also conduct retreats and home missions and are active in publishing and parish chaplaincies.

BENEDICT, ORDER OF ST – Annunciation Congregation

Location: Ireland (Murrow, Co. Limerick)
RC (male and female)

The Congregation of the Annunciation of the Blessed Virgin Mary, also called the Belgian Congregation and which retains French as its spoken language, is an active foundation dating from 1920 with houses in Ireland, Germany, Poland, Portugal, Trinidad, Central Africa, India, the USA and Latin America. The members work in teaching, preaching, agriculture, writing and holding retreats, liturgical congresses and ecumenical gatherings. The head of the Congregation is known as the President.

Benedictine Nuns of the Annunciation Congregation

There are eight houses of nuns affiliated to the Congregation.

BENEDICT, ORDER OF ST – Austrian Congregation

Location: Austria (Gottweig)
RC (male and female)

The Austrian Congregation resulted from the union of existing Austrian monasteries in 1625, after an earlier attempt in 1470, which brought together nine abbeys, headed by that of St Peter at Salzburg. Problems arising in the 18th and 19th centuries, which affected the Austrian church badly, led to the suppression of many abbeys and forbidding the recruitment of novices. The situation later eased, and by the end of the 19th century there were twenty abbeys which were formed into two Congregations, that of the Immaculate Conception and that of St Joseph. The head of the Congregation is known as the President.

BENEDICT, ORDER OF ST – Bavarian Congregation

Location: Germany (Ebenhausen)
RC (male and female)

The Bavarian Congregation was created by the union of eighteen houses in 1684 as part of a reform movement in the wake of the Council of Trent. The union remained fairly stable until the start of the 19th century, when many foundations went into decline. King Ludwig I of Bavaria began to restore some of the old monasteries and to found new ones, such as those at Augsburg, Munich and Meltenburg. At present the Congregation has twelve monasteries and there is an upsurge in vocations. The head of the Congregation is known as the President.

Benedictine Nuns of the Bavarian Congregation

A Congregation of nuns was founded in 1970 and has six monasteries.

BENEDICT, ORDER OF ST – Beuronese Congregation

Location: Germany (Maria Laach)
RC (male and female)

The German Congregation of Beuron was founded in 1863 by two brothers, Maurus and Placid Wolter, both of whom subsequently became abbots of different foundations and who had taken their monastic training at the abbey of Solesmes. Helped by Princess Katharine von Hohenzollern, they took possession in 1863 of the old abbey at Beuron, near Sigmaringen, which had been founded in the 8th century and had once been the home of a community of canons regular but had stood vacant since 1805. Dom Maurus became its first abbot, while his brother, Dom Placid, was appointed first abbot of the abbey of

Maredsous, in Belgium. Other foundations followed, in England, Czechoslovakia, Germany, Belgium and Portugal. There are currently only five houses, all of nuns, of this Congregation. The head of the Congregation is known as the President.

Benedictine Nuns of the Beuronese Congregation

There are currently five houses of nuns of this Congregation.

BENEDICT, ORDER OF ST – Brazilian Congregation

Location: Brazil (São Paulo)
RC (male and female)

The Brazilian Congregation was formed in 1827 following the separation of Brazil from Portugal, with the abbot of Bahia presiding over the existing eleven houses. The number of vocations was badly affected in 1855 when Brazilian law forbade the recruitment of novices, and it was suggested by Pope Pius IX that the Benedictine Beuronese Congregation in Germany be approached for volunteers to enter the Brazilian houses. These arrived in 1895 and took over the abbey of St Benedict at Olinda. Monastic life there was resumed and a school for novices founded. Further foundations were made in Europe which would provide monks for Brazilian foundations. In recent years there has been an upsurge in numbers, and by 1997 there were fifteen foundations. The head of the Congregation is known as the President.

Benedictine Nuns of the Brazilian Congregation

There are thirteen houses of nuns of this Congregation, and the number of vocations is rising.

BENEDICT, ORDER OF ST – Camaldolese Congregation

Location: Italy (Camaldoli, Arezzo)
RC (male and female)
Original habit: white Benedictine habit; an ample white cowl is worn in choir.

The members of the Congregation are also known as Camaldolites, or Camaldulensians. They were founded in 980 by St Romuald to lead an eremitical and cenobitical life, but must not be confused with the Camaldolese Hermits of Monte-Corona, who are not Benedictines. There are houses in Italy and Brazil. The head of the Congregation is known as the President.

BENEDICT, ORDER OF ST – Cassinese Congregation

Location: Italy (Cesena)
RC (male and female)

Italian monasteries which had taken the Cluniac model in the 10th and 11th centuries had declined by the 14th century. The Monastery of St Justina of Padua, which was in a poor state, was given to Ludovic Barbo, a canon regular of St George in Alga, who became a Benedictine. He set about reforms which were taken up by other monasteries, including those at Subiaco, Monte Cassino and Farfa, which united together under the name of the Cassinese Congregation in 1504. The years of revolution in Europe affected monasteries adversely and resulted in a split in the Cassinese Congregation with the emergence of the Congregation of the Primitive Observance, which came to be called the Subiaco Congregation. What remains of the Cassinese Congregation is spread thinly among ten houses with a total of 146 religious (1997). The head of the Congregation is known as the President.

BENEDICT, ORDER OF ST – English
Congregation

Location: England (Ealing, London)
RC (male and female)
Original habit: Monks of the Congregation wear
the black Benedictine habit with a distinctive hood,
with its long flaps falling down in the front and
with a pointed end at the back; a black pleated
cowl is worn in choir. Nuns wear the black
Benedictine habit with an unstarched white linen
wimple and fillet, as well as a leather belt. A black
cowl with wide sleeves is worn in choir.

This is the oldest English Benedictine Congregation, formed in 1218 in Oxford, and has a sense of continuity with the earliest Benedictine foundation made by St Augustine at Canterbury in the 7th century. As early as 970, a charter of religious life had been drafted at Winchester which laid down the daily observance of Benedictine life. Members were sometimes known as Black Monks on account of the colour of the habit. By 1336 all the English Benedictine houses had united to form the English Benedictine Congregation (EBC). The dissolution of the monasteries in the 16th century scattered the Benedictines, but the houses were re-established and new foundations made in France following the French Revolution, when members of religious houses in the country were forced to flee into exile. The great flowering of new foundations in the 19th century gave England, among others, the now-famous abbeys and schools of Downside, Ampleforth and Douai. The head of the Congregation is known as the President.

Benedictine Nuns of the English Congregation

There are two houses of Benedictine nuns in England, at Stanbrook Abbey in Worcestershire and Colwich Abbey in Staffordshire. Stanbrook Abbey was founded in

1838 from an earlier house at Cambrai, Belgium, and there have been further foundations made from Stanbrook in South America. A second foundation from Cambrai, via a house in Paris, led to the formation of the contemplative community at Colwich Abbey. The nuns, addressed as Dame, work in a wide field which includes all kinds of artistic work, for which they are famous, as well as writing, printing and bookbinding, which expresses their devotion to the liturgy of the Church.

BENEDICT, ORDER OF ST – Hungarian
Congregation

Location: Hungary (Pannonhalma)
RC (male and female)

The Congregation was founded in the early 16th century with a characteristic centralized form of government. It forms a single monastic family under a single superior, or arch-abbot, who has full jurisdiction. The members are professed for the Congregation and not for a particular monastery. The picture today is one of decline, with the loss of two abbeys and a corresponding decline in members. The head of the Congregation is known as the Arch-abbot.

BENEDICT, ORDER OF ST – Netherlands
Congregation

Location: The Netherlands (Oesterhout)
RC (male and female)

The Congregation was founded in 1969. There are three abbeys, but the number of members is declining. The head of the Congregation is known as the President.

BENEDICT, ORDER OF ST – Olivetan
Congregation

Location: Italy (Siena)
RC (male and female)

Original habit: a white Benedictine habit; the nuns wear a black veil and white linen wimple.

The Benedictine Congregation of Our Lady of Mount Olivet was founded in 1313 by the Blessed Bernard Tolomei, who went with two companions to a place ten miles from Siena, his birthplace, where on top of Mount Oliveto he fulfilled a promise he had made to Our Lady, whose intercession had restored his eyesight, by leading the ascetic life of a monk. The men practised extreme austerities, were approved by the Church, and were clothed in white habits. For a time the monks occupied the monastery of St Justina of Padua until Cassinese monks moved in. It was not until 1960 that this Congregation joined the Confederation. An English foundation of Olivetan monks, at the monastery of Christ our Saviour, was founded in 1980. The head of the Congregation is known as the Abbot-General.

Benedictine Nuns of the Olivetan Congregation

There are five houses of nuns of the Olivetan Congregation, originating from a convent at Bari, Italy, founded in 1344. They have usually been enclosed, but a few undertook work in education, such as the Olivetan Benedictine Sisters in Jonesboro, Arkansas, USA, who were founded in 1887 by Mother M. Beatrice Renggli. The American nuns taught in Arkansas, Louisiana and Texas and also worked in nursing. Affiliated in 1904 with the Olivetan Congregation are the Sisters of the Immaculate Conception, founded at Rouen, France, in 1825, who moved to England and established a house at Strood, in Kent. There is also a convent of this Congregation at Turvey, Bedfordshire.

BENEDICT, ORDER OF ST – St Ottilien Congregation

Location: Germany (St Ottilien, Bavaria)
RC (male and female)
Original habit: in mission stations the members of the Congregation wear a white Benedictine habit.

The Congregation of St Ottilien was founded specifically for work in the foreign missions in what were once the German colonies in Africa, and the early missionary days were marked by several martyrdoms. The foundation dates from 1884, when the founder, Dom Andrew Arnheim, began the Congregation in the Abbey of St Ottilien under the title of the Congregation of the Sacred Heart. It later affiliated with the Cassinese Congregation and became part of the Confederation in 1904. Dom Andrew also founded the Tutzing Sisters in 1924, as the female branch of the Congregation. Today the members still work in the mission fields. The head of the Congregation is known as the Arch-abbot.

BENEDICT, ORDER OF ST – Slavonic Congregation

Location: Czech Republic (Prague)
RC (male and female)

The Congregation was founded in 1945 and currently has three abbeys, one priory and one dependent house. It is also known as the Slavonic Congregation of Sts Adalbert and Margaret. St Adalbert, the Apostle of the Slavs who was bishop of Prague at the end of the 10th century but unhappy about his work, went to Rome and became a Benedictine. The head of the Congregation is known as the President.

BENEDICT, ORDER OF ST – Solesmes Congregation

Location: France (Sable-sur-Sarthe)
RC (male and female)

The Solesmes Congregation was founded in 1837, brought together by Fr Prosper Gueranger, who had been urged to restore the Benedictine Order in France following the ravages on religious life caused by the French Revolution. He was able in 1833 to purchase the ruined priory at Solesmes, which had been founded in 1010. It was restored, and Benedictine life returned to Solesmes, which was raised to the status of an abbey. The abbey became a centre of the Liturgical Movement and played an important part in the revival and development of liturgical music. The foundation attracted many vocations, and daughter houses were opened. Following the Association Laws in France at the start of the 20th century, the Congregation scattered to form communities in other countries, all attracting vocations. New foundations were made in England, the Netherlands, Luxemburg, Canada, Argentina, Martinique and Senegal. There are eight monasteries in this Congregation. From the house in Liège, Belgium, a daughter house, Quarr Abbey on the Isle of Wight, was founded in England in 1882, and joined the Solesmes Congregation in 1950. Quarr Abbey founded a house in Bangalore, India, in 1967, which became an abbey in 1994 from which two further houses were founded in India. The head of the Congregation is known as the President.

Benedictine Nuns of the Solesmes Congregation

There are eight monasteries of nuns in this Congregation. From a foundation made in Liège, Belgium, in 1637, a daughter house was opened in England, on the Isle of Wight in Hampshire in 1882. It became an abbey and joined the Solesmes Congregation in 1950. From England further houses were founded in India. The nuns' work includes the making of altar breads and vestments, agriculture, art and writing.

BENEDICT, ORDER OF ST – South American Cono-Sur Congregation

Location: Argentina (Los Toledos, Buenos Aires)
RC (male and female)

The Congregation was founded in 1970 and approved six years later. There are five abbeys and four dependent houses, with rising vocations. The head of the Congregation is known as the President.

BENEDICT, ORDER OF ST – Subiaco Congregation

Location: Italy (Rome)
RC (male and female)
Original habit: monks of this Congregation wear the black Benedictine habit with the exception of those of Prinknash Abbey in England, originally derived from the Anglican Caldey Island foundation of Aelred Carlyle, who wear a distinctive white woollen habit, scapular and stockings, with a leather belt; a white cowl is worn in choir. Lay brothers of Prinknash Abbey wear the same white habit, with the belt outside the scapular and with a white cloak in choir.

The Congregation originated in 1872 with the uniting of several Italian monasteries of the Cassinese Congregation, whose members were intent upon a stricter observance of the Rule. Other monasteries became affiliated to Subiaco. Members are professed for the Congregation and not for a particular monastery. The head of the Congregation is known as the President.

Benedictine Nuns of the Subiaco Congregation

There are eleven houses in the UK, the first founded by nuns leaving France in 1792 at the time of the Revolution and settling at Fernham Monastery, Faringdon, near Oxford. Other monasteries and schools followed, and the nuns were affiliated to the Subiaco Congregation in 1979. The first house in the USA was opened at Petersham in Massachusetts in 1973 by some lay-women who had undergone monastic training at Stanbrook Abbey in the UK and who made their solemn profession in 1984. This community was aggregated to the Subiaco Congregation (English Province) in 1989. An initiative in 1849 by Archbishop Polding, OSB of Sydney, Australia, resulted in a foundation of Benedictine nuns at Jambaroo, near Wollongong, New South Wales, which is still flourishing. Other Australian foundations were made at Rockhampton in Queensland in 1978 and Melbourne, Victoria, in 1984, although the latter closed a few years later.

✠ Cassinese of the Primitive Observance

BENEDICT, ORDER OF ST – Swiss Congregation

Location: Switzerland (Disentis)
RC (male and female)

The Swiss Congregation was founded in 1602 when various Swiss monasteries united through the efforts of Abbot Augustine of Einsiedeln. Some of the monasteries could claim a continuity from the earliest foundation at Luxeuil (585) by St Gall and other followers of St Columbanus. The community was so large that it was possible to have continuous, or unceasing, singing of the divine office (*Laus Perennis*). At present there are seven constituent monasteries and it is the abbey at Disentis, which was founded in 612, plundered and destroyed in 1799 and restored in 1880, which serves as the headquarters today. The head of the Congregation is known as the President.

BENEDICT, ORDER OF ST – Swiss-American Congregation

Location: USA (St Benedict, Louisiana)
RC (male and female)

The Congregation was founded in 1881, deriving from the abbey of Einsiedeln in Switzerland. In 1854 monks from Switzerland set up a mission in Indiana, USA, together with a small school for boys, dedicated to St Meinrad. St Meinrad's Abbey was raised to the status of arch-abbey and served as a seminary and novitiate for the Order. Other foundations spread throughout the USA, in Missouri, Arkansas, Oregon, Louisiana and North Dakota. The activities undertaken include the giving of retreats, teaching, missionary work among the North American Indians, printing and publishing. The head of the Congregation is known as the President.

BENEDICT, ORDER OF ST – Sylvestrine Congregation

Location: Italy (Rome)
RC (male and female)
Original habit: the habit was originally dark blue, but is now black except in the Sri-Lankan mission, where white is worn.

The Congregation of Sylvestrine Benedictines was founded by St Sylvester Guzzolini in 1231 at Mount Fano, near Fabriano, in Italy, and received papal approval in 1248. The Congregation joined the Benedictine Confederation in 1973. Although St Sylvester adopted the Rule of St Benedict, he supplemented it with Constitutions which he devised and which had some added austerities. Later developments have included missions to Sri Lanka, the USA and Australia. The scope of work undertaken is largely concerned with teaching, parish and mission work. The head of the Congregation is known as the President.

BENEDICT, ORDER OF ST – Vallombrosian Congregation

Location: Italy (Vallombrosa, Florence)
RC (male and female)

Original habit: the habit underwent several colour changes, originally grey, then tawny, and now black.

The Congregation, which is also known the Congregation of the Order of St Benedict of the Shady Valley, was founded in Italy in 1093 by St John Gualbert. It suffered many difficulties and reforms and was responsible for introducing the Fratres Conversi, or lay Brothers, to the Benedictine Order. These Brothers wore a different habit, took simple but not solemn vows, were not allowed to vote in Chapter and undertook the manual duties of the house. During the reforms of the 15th and 17th centuries the Congregation briefly joined with the Sylvestrine Benedictines. The life of the monks was originally very austere and penitential, with perpetual silence, scourging for breaches of the Rule, strict poverty and enclosure. This has since become modified. The head of the Congregation is known as the Abbot-General.

Benedictine Nuns of the Vallombrosian Congregation

There is evidence of a group of lay Sisters under the charge of an elderly lay Brother which was attached to the monastery at Vallombrosa in the 11th century, and it is possible to date their foundation to *c.*1090. The founder is usually acknowledged as St Umilta (or St Humilitas, or Rosanna), an anchoress who lived close to the church where her former husband had become a Vallombrosan Benedictine. The duties of the nuns were largely domestic. Today there are four houses remaining, with a declining number of nuns.

BENEDICTINE NUNS AND SISTERS – ROMAN CATHOLIC

The usual difference between a nun and a Sister is that the former was enclosed and

in solemn vows, following a contemplative monastic life. Sisters were generally under simple vows pursuing an active ministry, However, since Vatican II these distinctions have been modified. The date of foundation is in parentheses. Those Congregations listed below which are members of the Confederation have further details included under the principal entry above.

BENEDICTINE NUNS

1. Annunciation Congregation (1920) with 3 houses, 9 affiliated houses and 13 houses of the Queen of Apostles Congregation (1921).
2. Bavarian Federation (1970) with 8 houses
3. Beuronese Congregation (1873) with 9 houses
4. Brazilian Congregation (1835) with 15 houses
5. Camaldolese Congregation (1074) with 10 houses
6. Cono-Sur (South American) Congregation (1976) with 7 houses
7. English Congregation (1623) with 3 houses
8. Immaculate Conception Congregation (Poland 1932) with 8 houses
9. Immaculate Heart of Mary Federation (France 1953) with 7 houses
10. Italian Federation with 49 houses
11. Netherlands Congregation (1969) with 1 house
12. Olivetan Congregation (1344) with 5 houses
13. Our Lady of Calvary Congregation (France 1621) with 5 houses
14. Our Lady of Peace Federation (France 1974) with 3 houses
15. Perpetual Adorers of the Blessed Sacrament (1653) with 47 houses
16. Solesmes Congregation (1837) with 8 houses

17 Spanish Federation (1960) with 30 houses
18 Subiaco Congregation (1851) with 18 houses
19 Swiss Federation (1976) with 9 houses
20 Vallombrosian Congregation (1090) with 4 houses
21 Vita et Pax (Olivetan Aggregated 1892) (1824) with 6 houses
Others – 75 houses

BENEDICTINE SISTERS

1 Oblates of St Frances of Rome (1433) with 1 house
2 Benedictine Adorers of Bellemagny (1851) with 17 houses
3 Sisters of the Good Samaritan (1857) with 88 houses
4 Olivetan at the Holy Cross (1862) with 6 houses
5 Servants of the Poor Oblates (1872) with 14 houses
6 Benedictines of Perpetual Adoration (1874) with 5 houses
7 Benedictine Missionaries of Tutzing (1885) with 124 houses
8 Olivetan Benedictines of Jonesboro (1887) with 9 houses
9 Adorers of the Sacred Heart of Montmartre (1898) with 5 houses
10 Benedictines of St Gertrude (1911) with 7 houses
11 Benedictine Missionary Sisters (1917) with 29 houses
12 Federation of St Lioba (1920) with 23 houses
13 Sisters of Our Lady of Loretto (1920) with 24 houses
14 Benedictines of St Bathilde (1920) with 8 houses
15 Benedictine Sisters of Charity (1926) with 20 houses
16 Federation of St Scholastica (1922) with 24 houses
17 Federation of St Benedict (1947) with 13 houses
18 Benedictine Samaritans (1927) with 14 houses
19 Guadalupe Missionaries (1930) with 31 houses
20 Benedictines of the Blessed Virgin Mary Montevergine (1930) with 4 houses
21 Benedictines of St Priscilla (1936) with 3 houses
22 Federation of St Gertrude (1937) with 24 houses
23 Benedictines of Oshikuku (1937) with 15 houses
24 Benedictines of Christ the King (1937) with 7 houses
25 Sisters of Jesus Crucified (1938) with 10 houses
26 Benedictines of St Agnes (1938) with 37 houses
27 Benedictine Oblates of St Scholastica (1944) with 6 houses
28 Benedictines of the Blessed Virgin Mary Help of Christians (1946) with 12 houses
29 Benedictines of Twasana (1947) with 7 houses
30 Benedictines of the Immaculate Heart of the Blessed Virgin Mary (1949) with 54 houses
31 Benedictines of St Alban (1957) with 3 houses
32 Federation of Swiss Benedictines (1975) with 5 houses
33 Benedictines of St Lioba (1951) with 4 houses
34 Eucharist King (1990) with 4 houses
35 Sisters of the Holy Family (1919) with 11 houses
36 Sisters of Grace and Compassion (1954) with 13 houses
37 Daughters of St Benedict (1927) with 4 houses
Independent – 5 houses
(Source: English Benedictine Congregation Trust)

BENEDICTINE SISTERS, MISSIONARY

Location: USA (Norfolk, Nebraska)
RC (female) founded in Germany in 1885 by Dom
Andreas Amrhein, OSB
Abbr: OSB
Original habit: Benedictine style.

Founded with a view to providing nursing
care and education and to conduct retreats
and missions both at home and overseas,
this Benedictine Congregation began in
Germany and spread to the USA, where
they run the Our Lady of Lourdes Hospital
and St Joseph's Nursing Home, in Norfolk,
Nebraska. They are also to be found in
other American dioceses and in Australia,
Angola, Brazil, Bulgaria, the Far East, South
Africa, Tanzania, India, the Philippines and
parts of Europe.

BENEDICTINE SISTERS OF OUR LADY OF
GRACE AND COMPASSION

Location: England (Brighton, Sussex)
RC (female) founded in England in 1954 by Mary
Garson
Abbr: OSB
Original habit: a dark blue tunic with a black veil.

A Congregation, since 1992 part of the
Benedictine Confederation, founded in
Brighton by Mary Garson, now its prioress-
general. It had been suggested to her that
she and her growing band of helpers, who
had opened a home for the sick and aged,
might form a Congregation with a lay community. The support of the laity, whether
as members of the lay community or as
oblates, has been essential for the success of
the community's work. Cardinal Cormac
Murphy O'Connor, now the successor to
Cardinal Basil Hume as archbishop of
Westminster, gave the community diocesan
recognition in 1992. The work of the Sisters, which involves the care of the poor,
the aged and the sick, has now extended
beyond England, and houses have been

opened in Kenya, India and Sri Lanka,
where all kinds of activities are undertaken
which help the local communities to support themselves.

BENEDICTINE SISTERS OF PERPETUAL
ADORATION

Location: USA (St Louis, Missouri)
RC (female) founded in the USA in 1874 by Mother
Mary Anselma Felber
Abbr: OSB
Original habit: Benedictine style.

This Congregation of Benedictine Sisters
was founded from the Maria Rickenbach
foundation in Switzerland when Mother
Mary Anselma went from there to begin a
new foundation in the USA at Clyde, Missouri. The Sisters devote their lives to the
perpetual adoration of the Blessed Sacrament. Their life is monastic, with the singing of the divine office, and their ministry
is in the contemplative apostolate of prayer
and meditation. The Congregation supports
itself through the production of altar
breads, church vestments, ceramics and artwork. The Sisters also edit and publish a bi-
monthly magazine, *Spirit and Life*, as well
as giving retreats and quiet days. The Congregation is restricted to the USA, with
houses in Missouri, Arizona, Wyoming and
Oklahoma.

BERNARDINE CISTERCIANS OF ESQUERMES

Location: France (St André, nr. Lille)
RC (female) founded in France in 1798 by three
Cistercian nuns
Abbr: OC or CBE
Original habit: a white habit with a black scapular
and veil and a sash which is worn over the
scapular; a white cowl was worn in choir.

The Congregation was founded by three
Cistercian nuns, Dames Hippolyte, Hom-
beline and Hyacinthe, who came from
ancient abbeys demolished during the

French Revolution when their communities dispersed. Arriving at Esquermes, near Lille, in 1798 after running schools in other parts of the country, they built a monastery and founded their Congregation, which was constituted in 1827 and confirmed by the Holy See in 1909. In 1897 the Congregation opened a house in England, at Slough in Berkshire, with another later at Carnforth, in Lancashire. Foundations in Japan and Africa have since been made. In 1982 the Bernardine Sisters went to Goma, Zaire, where another monastery was opened. While the Sisters follow the Rule of St Benedict and their observances are mainly Cistercian, these are modified to suit their Congregation, where many of the members are involved in an active apostolate embracing teaching, spiritual direction and the conducting of retreats.

✠ Bernardine Cistercians

BERNARDINE SISTERS OF THE THIRD ORDER OF ST FRANCIS

Location: USA (Philadelphia, Pennsylvania)
RC (female) founded in the USA in 1894 (but see below)
Original habit: a black habit with a square white wimple, a white under-veil and binder with a black outer veil; a cross was worn around the neck

The distant source of the Congregation is a group of Franciscan Tertiaries in Krakow, Poland, who lived in the monastery of St Agnes, from where they taught the poor children of the city and cared for the sick and elderly. When they later decided to lead the contemplative life, this work was abandoned. The present-day Congregation was founded by Mother Veronica Grzedowska, who left Krakow in 1894 with four other Sisters and went to New York before going on to Reading, Pennsylvania, where the foundation was made. Here the apostolate in education and nursing was resumed. It is

now a Pontifical Institute, an active Order with simple vows. The Sisters teach at Reading's state accredited Alvernia College, work in local schools, nurse, undertake social services and run foreign missions in Brazil, Mozambique, the Dominican Republic, Puerto Rico and Poland.

✠ Franciscan Sisters of St Bernard of Siena

BERNARDINES

A generic label used to describe those 16th- and 17th-century Cistercian nuns who aimed to restore the primitive observance of the Cistercian Rule. To that end a group of houses, which had been founded separately by Louise de Ballon and Mother de Ponconnas, joined together, and the union was recognized by the pope in 1634. Some of the reforms, which could differ from house to house, included great austerities, strict abstinence and fasting, silence and lengthy periods of meditation and the wearing of rough serge habits against the skin.

BETHANY SISTERS

Location: England (Southsea, Hampshire)
Anglican (female) founded in England in 1866 by Etheldreda Anna Bennett
Abbr: SSB
Original habit: a plain grey tunic and grey scapular with a white under-veil and black outer veil.

Etheldreda Bennett was much influenced by Dr Pusey and the other Tractarians active in 19th-century England. Following the death of her father in 1864 she entered the novitiate of the All Saint's Community, Margaret Street, London, and was professed in 1866. With another of the Sisters she went to work in a poor London parish, setting up home in Clerkenwell, from where they conducted retreats and founded the Society of the Sisters of Bethany, which soon expanded. In 1873 they took over an orphanage in Boscombe, on the English south coast, while work in London continued to grow, with the opening of the St Barnabas' Home to care for the sick-poor and a further home in Ramsgate, Kent. Some missionary work among the Nestorian Christians in the Near East followed, as part of the Archbishop of Canterbury's Mission to the Assyrian Churches. The Society is now much involved in ecumenical matters and the conducting of retreats.

✠ Society of the Sisters of Bethany

BETHLEHEM, BROTHERS OF

There is some confusion between two similarly named Equestrian Orders, both now defunct.

1 An Order, authorized by Henry III in c.1257 in England, housed on the outskirts of Cambridge, in Trumpington Street. Little is known about the Order's origin and purpose. The habit resembled that of the Dominicans and displayed a red star with five rays on the scapular, which was said to represent the Star of Bethlehem which had guided the Magi to the scene of the Nativity.

2 An Order of Bethlehemites, founded in 1459, called the Star Carriers, or Bearers. They were also known as the Knights of Our Lady of Bethlehem, and their origin lies with Pope Pius II (1458–64), who was anxious about the release of Europe from Turkish domination. His attempts to get a crusade organized met with little success. A papal Bull authorized the institution of the Order, the headquarters of which was to be on the Aegean island of Lemnos. Little more is known of the Order. Membership was made up of Brother knights, and priests under the direction of a grand master. The habit was white, decorated with a red cross.

The Rule adopted was that of the Knights of St John of Jerusalem

✠ Bearers of the Star
  Carriers of the Star

BETHLEHEM FATHERS

Location: Switzerland (Immensee)
RC (male) founded in Switzerland in 1921 by Pietro Bondolfi
Abbr: SMB
Original habit: as for secular priests.

The Congregation sprang from a theological college which was opened in Meggen, Switzerland, and which moved to Immensee in 1907, when the scope of education provided widened to include general studies. The Congregation was approved by Pope Benedict XV in 1921 as a Pontifical Institute whose members make solemn promises instead of vows. It is an active Order with the principal aim of providing missionaries, originally for China but now also for Japan, Africa, Taiwan and Colombia.

✠ Bethlehem Missionaries of Switzerland
  Foreign Mission Society of Bethlehem

BETHLEHEM SISTERS

Defunct
RC (female) founded in Guatemala in 1688 by Brother Anthony of the Cross and Marie Anne del Gualdo
Original habit: Franciscan style.

A Congregation with twelve initial members, who consecrated themselves to the nursing and care of sick women. The vows taken were the usual three of poverty, chastity and obedience with an additional one of hospitality. The Order was suppressed in 1820.

BETHLEMITA DAUGHTERS OF THE SACRED HEART

Location: Colombia (Santafé de Bogotá)
RC (female) founded in Guatemala in 1861 by
Maria Vincenta Rosal (Mother Maria Encarnación
of the Sacred Heart of Jesus)
Abbr: Bethl

The founder had become a Bethlehemite
Sister in Quezaltenango, Guatemala, in
1838 and was elected prioress in 1855. The
Congregation was failing, and although
Mother Maria attempted to breathe some
fresh life and reform into it, her efforts were
in vain. She then founded a new Congregation, the Bethlehemita Daughters of the
Sacred Heart, in Guatemala, which
attempted to preserve the charism of
Blessed Peter de Betancourt. This was subsequently recognized as a new Institute in
the Church and received its Decree of Praise
in 1891, with approbation granted in 1909.
The Congregation established a mother
house at Bogotá, Colombia, and made an
American foundation in Dallas, Texas. The
Sisters teach, undertake missions and work
in the care of the elderly in Central and
South America as well as in Italy and Africa.

BETHLEHEMITE FRIARS

There is mention made in the works of
Matthew Paris of some 'fraters Bethlehemite' who were given a house in Cambridge,
England, in 1257. They are described as
wearing a habit similar to that of the
Dominican Friars with the addition of a red
and blue star at the breast. There is nothing
more known about them, but it is thought
that they may have been a group of
reformed Dominicans.

BETHLEHEMITES

Location: Spain (Laguna, Santa Cruz de Tenerife)
RC (male) founded in Guatemala in c.1653 by

Blessed Peter of St Joseph (became defunct and
was restored in 1984)
Original habit: probably Franciscan Capuchin in
style, with a leather cincture, a cloak with a shield
on the right side bearing a representation of
Christ's nativity, and a hat.

The founder, a native of Tenerife and a
Franciscan tertiary, went to Guatemala to
study for the priesthood but abandoned his
plans and turned instead to the care of the
poor and the sick who came to his house
for help. Generous gifts from well-wishers
made it possible for him to build a hospital,
which he placed under the patronage of
Our Lady of Bethlehem. This dedication of
his house was inspired by his perception of
the message of love that the nativity of Our
Lord suggested. His efforts to care for those
who were poor and disadvantaged were far-
ranging, as he and his fellow-helpers
worked to educate the local children and
care for the welfare of prisoners. Other
hospitals were opened throughout Latin
America, in association with schools for
poor children, and the Congregation grew.
The members were originally under simple
vows, but Pope Blessed Innocent XI, in
1687, authorized them to make solemn
vows according to the Rule of St Augustine.
An extra vow was added later, that of caring
for the sick even at risk of their own lives.
A similar foundation for women was started
in 1668 under Peter's inspiration, but it
went through very difficult times and
eventually became defunct despite attempts
at reform by Maria Vincenta Rosal.

✢ Belemites
  Brothers of Bethlehem
  Hospitallers of Bethlehem

BLAISE AND ST MARY, KNIGHTS OF ST

Defunct
RC (male Equestrian Order) date of foundation
uncertain

Original habit: a cloak decorated on the left-hand side with a medallion enclosing a red cross in the centre of which was the figure of St Blaise wearing a stole, cope and mitre and carrying a crosier, all of western, medieval style.

The date of the origin of the Order of St Blaise and St Mary is uncertain but it is suggested it may have been at the time of the foundation of the Knights Templar of Jerusalem, in the 12th century, and that it was authorized by a king of Armenia, as St Blaise had been the bishop of Sebaste in Armenia in the 4th century. The Order had both religious and lay knights, whose duty it was to suppress any heretical uprisings in Armenia. The members initially observed the Rule of St Basil but later changed to that of St Augustine, in line with the observances of similar Equestrian Orders.

BLESSED SACRAMENT, FATHERS OF THE

Location: Italy (Rome)
RC (male) founded in France in 1856 by St Peter Julian Eymard (canonized 1962)
Abbr: SSS
Original habit: a black cassock decorated with the emblem of a monstrance.

A Congregation founded for the purpose of promoting adoration of the Blessed Sacrament. The Fathers lead a life of prayer and adoration as well as conducting retreats and working in the field of publishing. There are houses in many European countries, the Americas, India, Sri Lanka, Australasia, the Philippines and Africa.

✠ Congregation of the Blessed Sacrament Sacramentines

BLESSED SACRAMENT, MISSIONARIES OF THE

Defunct
RC (male) founded in Ireland in 1866 by Bishop Thomas Furlong of Fearns

Abbr: MSS
Original habit: as for secular priests.

An association of secular clergy living in community.

BLESSED SACRAMENT, OBLATE SISTERS OF THE

Location: USA (Marty, South Dakota)
RC (female) founded in the USA in 1935 by Fr Sylvester Eisenman, OSB
Abbr: OSBS

A diocesan Congregation founded for work which is largely concerned with providing various ministries to the American Indians.

BLESSED SACRAMENT, POOR VIRGINS OF THE

Defunct
RC (female) founded in Italy in the 17th century
Original habit: a dark, tawny tunic and cincture with a white head veil secured beneath the chin.

In 1650, a Holy Year, a pious lady attempted to care for poor, orphaned young women, dressing them in white tunics with red scapulars, but she lacked the money necessary to complete her work. Her needs were supplied when a Jesuit, Peter Caravita, and some noblemen came to her help. The Congregation was approved in 1665 and confirmed in 1671. The name of the Congregation derives from its devotion to the Blessed Sacrament, which was exposed daily.

BLESSED SACRAMENT, SERVANTS OF THE

Location: Italy (Rome)
RC (female) founded in France in 1858 by St Peter Julian Eymard and Mother Margaret Guillot
Abbr: SSS
Original habit: a white habit.

A foundation of religious women recognized as a Congregation by Pope Pius IX and approved by Pope Leo XIII. The foundation was made at Angers, France, where the Blessed Sacrament Fathers had a house. The purpose of the Congregation was to propagate devotion to the Blessed Sacrament through the People's Eucharistic League, a lay association whose members undertook a monthly hour of adoration before the exposed Blessed Sacrament, to recite daily the 'Tantum Ergo' or to say one Our Father and one Hail Mary; they were also obliged to have Mass said once a year for deceased members of the League. The apostolate of the Congregation is now extended to include the catechesis of children and their parents. Members of the Congregation are expected to make three adorations to the Blessed Sacrament in each twenty-four hour period, two during the day and one at night. They are best described as a contemplative and enclosed Congregation. Houses were set up throughout France, Belgium and Canada.

BLESSED SACRAMENT, SISTERS OF THE

Location: France (Valence)
RC (female) founded in France in 1715 by Pierre Vigne; revised in 1925 and 1962
Abbr: CBS
Original habit: a black tunic with a white wimple and black veil; a large rosary and crucifix were worn on the left-hand side and at the breast was a small silver monstrance – a privilege extended to the Congregation by Pope Pius IX.

Pierre Vigne (1670–1740), the founder of the Blessed Sacrament Sisters, was converted from Calvinism and after his ordination became a Vincentian for four years before becoming a diocesan priest. While he was preaching a mission in 1713 at Boucieu-le-Roi, he inspired Marguerite Rouveure to consider a religious life, to which end she began to teach a few village children. Her work quickly attracted the interest of several other young women. Fr Vigne had built a Way of the Cross in the

town which was attracting many pilgrims. The young women took to accompanying the pilgrims as they made their devotions here. They formed a small community in 1715 under the name of the Sisters of Calvary, for whom Pierre Vigne composed a Rule and a simple habit. In 1722, because of the importance of devotion to the Blessed Sacrament, they changed their name to the present one, and the foundation flourished and spread. The Sisters were much sought-after to care for the sick and teach the children in school. The French Revolution scattered the communities, but they were reunited as a Congregation in 1818, having been called upon to care for the sick in Valence and Tournon as early as 1795. A mother house was established at Romans, near Valence, which had once been the home of the Canonesses of St Just. Approbation was finally granted in 1869, and houses opened in Italy and England. The French Association Laws of 1901 once more scattered the Congregation, and it expanded overseas, opening houses in Brazil (1903), Ireland (1954) and Spain (1964). The apostolate is to give worship and to spread devotion to the Blessed Sacrament. The Sisters work mainly in the education of girls but also undertake nursing duties and the care of orphans and the infirm. The Rule that is followed is based on that of St Augustine. There are now foundations in France, England, Italy and Brazil, with many postulants being received from the African countries, especially Tanzania.

BLESSED SACRAMENT AND OF OUR LADY, RELIGIOUS OF THE

An Independent Order. Defunct in France, refounded in 1912 in the USA and still active
RC (female) founded in France in 1639 by Anthony le Quieu, a Dominican
Abbr: OSS
Original habit: a black habit with a white scapular;

a silver emblem of the Blessed Sacrament was worn over the heart and on the right arm, with a white veil and cloak worn in choir.

Founded at Marseilles, France, this was a Pontifical Institute, contemplative and enclosed. It represented a reform of the Dominican Order and was designed as an enclosed Congregation for the perpetual adoration of the Blessed Sacrament. It was while Fr Le Quieu was novice master at the Dominican Priory at Avignon that he laid the foundations of the Congregation, which faced many difficulties. Pope Innocent XII raised the Congregation to the status of an Order, whereafter the nuns, previously in simple vows, could now make solemn vows and observe the enclosure. The first daughter house was opened in 1724, at Bollene, where two choir Sisters from Marseilles were joined by five postulants. At the time of the Revolution in France the Marseilles convent was suppressed and only reopened in 1816. The convent at Bollene had suffered badly at the same time, with thirteen of the Sisters executed in 1794. Bollene was closed, to be re-established in the early 19th century when other convents were set up in France. Houses were opened in England but have since closed. The Order was re-established in the USA in 1912.

✠ Sacramentine Nuns

BLESSED SACRAMENT FOR INDIANS AND COLOURED PEOPLE, SISTERS OF THE

Location: USA (Bensalem, Pennsylvania)
RC (female) founded in the USA in 1889 by St Katharine Mary Drexel (canonised 2000)
Abbr: SBS

A Pontifical Institute and active Congregation with simple vows. It was founded in 1889 following the Third Plenary Council in Baltimore in 1884, which had urged action to aid the missionaries working with negroes and American Indians. With the approval of the archbishop of Philadelphia a Congregation was formed, dedicated to this type of missionary work. Katharine Drexel (1858–1955), who had inherited a fortune, part of which she used to fund the establishment of the Congregation, gathered together some like-minded women to undertake this work, which was not always popular with either her fellow citizens or the religious hierarchy. In 1892 a mother house and novitiate were opened at Maud, Pennsylvania, together with a training and boarding school for coloured children. The Congregation is marked for its devotion to the Blessed Sacrament. The Sisters founded both the Drexel University in Philadelphia and the Xavier University in New Orleans as well as special societies for the welfare of African-Americans and Native Americans. They also work with orphans and destitute children, care for the poor and aged and visit prisons.

✠ Blessed Sacrament Sisters

BLESSED TRINITY MISSIONARY INSTITUTE

Location: USA (Philadelphia, Pennsylvania)
RC (male and female) founded in the USA by Margaret Healy

A Pious Association founded by Dr Margaret Healy, who was inspired by the work of the late Fr Thomas Judge, CM. The purpose of the Association is to preserve the faith among people who are spiritually neglected, and to this end members dedicate themselves through private vows of poverty, chastity and obedience, which are taken after a period of training and professed annually for the first five years, and then for life. The members attend daily Mass, undertake a full prayer life and daily spiritual reading and also attend two weekend retreats annually.

BLESSED VIRGIN MARY, INSTITUTE OF THE

Location: Italy (Rome)
RC (female) founded in Flanders (Northern France) in 1609 by Mary Ward
Abbr: IBVM
Original habit: a long black dress with a full skirt and tight sleeves with white cuffs and a wimple which was fastened in front with narrow strings; a white forehead binder; and a girdle with a crucifix suspended; a silver ring was worn on the fourth finger of the left hand.

The Institute of the Blessed Virgin Mary is remarkable in that it was the first Congregation that was both active and unenclosed, both necessary for the fulfilment of its apostolate. The Council of Trent (1545–63) had declared that all female communities must observe solemn vows and strict enclosure. The founder, a Yorkshire-woman, left England to enter a convent of the Poor Clares at St Omer in Flanders, but she left within a year to found another community of Poor Clares, at nearby Gravelines, for English women, and this attracted both English and Irish aspirants. Mary Ward, still unprofessed, left the Gravelines community and returned to England, where she worked for prisoner relief, for the sick and for apostates. Returning to St Omer with some other women, they formed a community, opening a boarding school for English girls and a free school for local children in the town. The community was known locally as the English Ladies. By 1611 she was back in London, where she set up a house for the support and catechesis of Roman Catholics who were suffering public abuse, and because she decided to model the Congregation along Jesuit lines and to have a superior answerable only to the pope, many clergy named the community as Jesuitesses, with implied criticism, as it was considered by them to be a ploy to avoid direction by the English clergy. Considerable conflict followed and at one point the pope ordered the closure of the schools and the dispersion of the Congregation. Unaware of this and therefore seeming to be in defiance of the papal injunction, Mary Ward was arrested in Munich and imprisoned there in a Poor Clare convent. Her appeal to the pope against this action was successful and she was allowed to open another school, for the daughters of expatriates. The indefatigable Mary Ward finally returned to England and died there in York in 1645. Over the next two centuries more schools were opened. Approval of the Institute came only in 1703, with approbation following in 1877. The apostolate of the Sisters today is comprehensive and ranges from the running of schools and working with young people to the care of alcoholics, prison visiting, retreat-giving and parish work. The Institute is worldwide, divided into twenty Provinces and two Regions, or embryonic Provinces. Some progress has been made in gaining entry into Russia and China, and vocations are coming from India, Korea and some former Iron Curtain countries.

✟ English Ladies
 Institute of Mary

BLESSED VIRGIN MARY, INSTITUTE OF THE

Location: Italy (Rome)
RC (female) founded in Ireland in 1822 by Frances Ball (Mother Teresa Ball)
Abbr: IBVM
Original habit: as for the English Province (see previous entry).

Frances Ball, who had trained at the Bar Convent of the Institute of the Blessed Virgin Mary in York, England (see previous entry), where she was sent by Archbishop Murray of Dublin, returned to Ireland to open a school at Rathfarnham Abbey, near Dublin, in 1822, changing the name of the abbey to Loreto. It was Archbishop Murray's idea to introduce the Institute of the

Blessed Virgin Mary to Ireland in order to cope with the need for higher education for girls. From the Rathfarnham foundation others followed, in Europe, the USA, Australia, South Africa, India, Peru, Mauritius and Kenya. The work of the Sisters is largely educational and medical, concerned with the running of schools, orphanages and hospitals. Another Congregation of Loreto Sisters, founded from Rathfarnham, was made in North America with the headquarters in Toronto.

✚ Loreto Sisters

BLESSED VIRGIN MARY, INSTITUTE OF THE

Location: Canada (Toronto)
RC (female) founded in Canada in 1847
Abbr: IBVM
Original habit: as for the English Province.

This Branch of the Institute of the Blessed Virgin Mary originated from the Rathfarnham foundation (see above), from which further branch houses in North America were established. These were allowed to remain independent of the Irish mother house. The Sisters work mainly in education, at all levels, and also undertake social work and participate in an inter-branch mission in Bolivia.

✚ Loretto Sisters

BLESSED VIRGIN MARY, OBLATES OF THE

Location: Italy (Rome)
RC (male) founded in the USA in 1815
Abbr: OMV

A Congregation founded in the USA and approved in 1826. The priests and Brothers undertake the promotion of the Spiritual Exercises of St Ignatius through retreats and parish missions and through the production of Roman Catholic literature. They are represented throughout the USA and Canada as well as in their foreign missions in Argentina, Brazil, Mexico, Nigeria and the Philippines. The Congregation has a seminary at St Clement's Eucharistic Shrine in Boston, Massachusetts, and St Joseph's Novitiate in Milton, Massachusetts.

BLESSED VIRGIN MARY IMMACULATE, SONS OF THE

Location: France (Saint-Fulgent)
RC (male) founded in France in 1828 by Louis Baudouin
Abbr: FMI
Original habit: as for secular clergy.

A Congregation founded at Chavagnes-en-Paillers, Lucon, France, and concerned with teaching, especially in seminaries and through missions. Foreign missions have been undertaken to the West Indies, Canada and Venezuela. When the Association Laws began to operate in France, at the start of the 20th century, the Congregation fled to England and Belgium, but it is now back in France.

✚ Oblates of St Hilary

BLESSED VIRGIN MARY MOTHER OF MERCY, BROTHERS OF THE – Tilburg

Location: The Netherlands (Tilburg)
RC (male) founded in The Netherlands in 1844 by Joannes Zwijsen
Abbr: CMM

The Congregation was originally founded to cater for the needs of the poor and uneducated. The shortage of books and educational material led to the setting up of a printing press for the production of religious and school books. More schools followed, as well as a training course for teachers. The work extended to the care of the blind and the deaf and today the members work in many countries, caring as well for AIDS victims, refugees and the homeless. Houses are to be found in The Netherlands, Belgium, Indonesia, Namibia, Kenya, Brazil, Surinam and the USA.

BLIND SISTERS OF ST PAUL

Location: France (Paris)
RC (female) founded in France in 1851 by Anne Bergunion and the Abbé Henri Juge
Original habit: a black habit with wide sleeves and a cincture tied with three knots; a white headband, with lappets, and a starched white veil over the forehead with an outer black veil; a silver crucifix was worn at the breast and a copper rosary on the right-hand side with a crucifix of the same metal; a solemnly professed nun wore a silver ring; novices wore a white veil.

The Congregation dates from 1851, when Anne (her name in the baptismal register is given as Jeanne) Bergunion abandoned her novitiate with the Mother of God nuns at Versailles and set up a workroom where neglected children could have shelter and training. Some of the children were blind, and this decided Anne Bergunion to found a Congregation and to write a Rule, based on that of St Augustine, for blind Sisters. Both blind and sighted women were admitted, as it was necessary that the superior should be sighted although her assistant counsellors could include blind representatives. The Sisters now work in education, where they specialize in music training for both the blind and the partially sighted, and with the care of aged and infirm priests in their Marie-Thérèse hospital.

BLOOD OF CHRIST, SISTERS-ADORERS OF THE

Location: Canada (Saint-Hyacinthe, Quebec)
RC (female) founded in Canada in 1861 by Mother Caouette (Mother Catherine Aurelie of the Precious Blood)
Original habit: choir Sisters wore a white tunic and mantle with a red scapular and cincture, upon which were painted in white the instruments of the Passion. Lay Sisters wore the same habit except that the tunic was black.

A Pontifical Institute, an active Order with simple vows. The Sisters work largely in education but are also involved in health work and nursing care of the elderly, operate prison and hospital chaplaincies and outreach programmes for women and care for those who are marginalized by society. The Sisters also undertake domestic duties in seminaries and other religious institutions. Houses are found throughout the USA, and there are foreign missions in Europe, Africa, Bolivia and Guatemala.

✠ Sisters-Adorers of the Most Precious Blood of Our Lord Jesus Christ of the Union of St Hyacinthe

BON SECOURS SISTERS – Paris

Location: Italy (Rome)
RC (female) founded in France in 1822 by Hyacinthe Louis de Quelen, archbishop of Paris
Abbr: BSC
Original habit: a black tunic with a deep collar and cuffs and a crimped white wimple, a black leather belt and a black veil with a white headband, or sometimes a bonnet; a silver cross on a chain was worn around the neck.

Founded originally for the purpose of nursing the sick, rich and poor alike, in their own homes, the Congregation also played an indirect role in the religious regeneration in France, following the French Revolution, which had such a profound effect on communities. Houses were established throughout northern France and in Ireland (Dublin and Cork). The Congregation of the Sisters of St John of God arose from the Dublin foundation. Today, the Sisters specialize in all types of medical work and care for the aged and sick and for orphans and also undertake outreach programmes in inner city and rural areas. There are houses in Europe, the USA, Peru and Ecuador.

BON SECOURS SISTERS – Troyes

Location: France (Troyes)
RC (female) founded in France in 1840 by Paul Sebastian Millet
Abbr: SBST
Original habit: a black tunic with a white wimple, black veil and small black cape; a brass crucifix attached to a violet ribbon was worn around the neck.

The community was founded by a canon of Troyes cathedral for the purpose of nursing the sick in their own homes and was approved in 1863 after many difficulties. The Congregation spread to Italy, Spain, England, the USA and Africa.

BONI HOMINES

Several monastic brotherhoods have borne this name (see below). They must not be confused with the 'Bons Hommes'.

BONI HOMINES

An early Italian community of hermits. The date of the foundation is difficult to ascertain, but it followed the example set by Blessed John Buoni (*c.*1168–1249), who led an eremitical life at Cesena, Romagna, in the 13th century. Blessed John and his followers did not follow a definite Rule to begin with, as John tended to make *ad hoc* decisions about their way of life. It was not until the community of hermits became more settled that Pope Innocent IV agreed that they should follow the Rule of St Augustine. By the time of John Buoni's death there were eleven houses, which were united in 1256 by Pope Alexander IV, together with other similar foundations, to form the Hermit-Friars of St Augustine.

✠ Bonites
Boniti

BONI HOMINES – ORDER OF GRANDMONT

The Order was founded in France in the 11th century by St Stephen Grandmont, or Granmont. Their house at Vincennes was given to the Minims by Henry III of England. The main entry is under 'Grandmont'.

BONI HOMINES IN ENGLAND

Matthew Paris, in the 13th century, described some friars of a previously unknown Order as *fraters saccati* (friars of the Sack), and says that they were known also as Boni Homines. It is known that there was a house of the *fraters saccati* in Cambridge, on property owned by Peterhouse College. There is, however, no real evidence that these friars and the Boni Homines were one and the same, as the latter seem to have existed as a group of some twenty canons established at Ashridge, Hertfordshire, in 1257 by Richard, Earl of Cornwall, the brother of Henry III of England. The canons wore a blue habit, similar to that of the Augustinian canons, while the Friars of the Sack are described as wearing black and carrying a staff.

BONI HOMINES, CANONS 'CALLED' – Portugal

A Congregation of canons founded in Portugal in the 15th century by John Vincenza, bishop of Lamego. At its height there were some fourteen houses in Portugal, and foreign missions were undertaken to Ethiopia.

BONI HOMINES AS HERETICS

Roger de Hovedon, in an abstract from the Council of Lombers (Toulouse) in the 12th century, describes the examination and condemnation as heretics of men calling themselves Boni Homines. They seem to have resembled the Cathars and Paulicians in their heresies. The Albigensians have also been so called.

BONIFACE, BROTHERHOOD OF ST

Defunct
Anglican Church of Australia (male) founded in
Australia in 1911 by Bishop Goldsmith

The Congregation was part of the Bush
Brotherhood in Australia. It was formed in
the diocese of Bunbury, in Western Australia, with its headquarters at Williams, which
lies between Perth and Albany. The Congregation became defunct through a lack of
unmarried clergy who were willing to join
the Brotherhood.

BONS HOMMES

An alternative name for friars minims, who
were introduced into England at the time
of Henry III.

BRIDGE-BUILDING BROTHERHOOD

During the 12th and 13th centuries there
were various religious Associations whose
purpose was to help travellers and pilgrims
by constructing bridges, partly as an act of
piety but also for the common good. Indul-
gences were granted to those who contributed to this work either by their own labour
or by donating money. That these 'bridge-
builders' lived under vows and were ranked
as a religious Order is almost certainly a
myth and is now generally discounted. They
most closely resembled Confraternities, or
Third Orders, as the members could wear a
habit and a distinctive badge, but no vows
were made.

BRIDGET, KNIGHTS OF ST

Defunct
RC (male Equestrian Order) founded in Sweden in
1366 by St Bridget
Original habit: (insignia) a blue enamelled eight-
pointed cross, attached to the base of which was a
tongue of fire as a symbol of the Knights' ardour
for the Christian religion and for God.

St Bridget of Sweden was inspired by her
revelations to found this Military Order of
Knights in 1366. It was recognized by Pope
Blessed Urban V and attracted an enormous
amount of wealth, almost certainly because
of the deep reverence for the saint's visions
felt throughout Europe. Members of the
Order were obliged to live under the Rule
of St Augustine, to care for those in need
and in danger, to bury the dead, oppose
heretics and protect the Swedish realm from
invasion by barbarians.

⊕ Bridgettine Knights

BRIDGET, ORDER OF THE MOST HOLY SAVIOUR AND ST

There are two groups with almost identical
names:

1 Bridgettine Nuns
2 Bridgettine Sisters

⊕ Bridgettines

BRIDGETTINE NUNS AND MONKS

Location: Italy (Rome)
RC (male and female) founded in Sweden in 1344
by St Bridget of Sweden and St Catherine
Abbr: OSSS
Original habit: Choir nuns wore a grey habit and
cowl, with a grey mantle in choir, a black veil and a
white linen crown with white linen bands arranged
across the top of the head in the form of a cross,
upon which were sewn five pieces of red cloth in
honour of Christ's wounds. Lay Sisters wore the
habit and scapular and a white veil and wimple,
and a mantle decorated with a Maltese cross in
white with five red circles. Monks wore a grey
habit decorated with a red cross over the heart, in
the middle of which was a representation of the
Sacred Heart (for priests), a white circle with four
red tongues of fire coming from the Holy Spirit
(for deacons) or a white cross with five red spots
representing the holy wounds (for lay Brothers).

The Order was founded at Wadstena, south-west of Stockholm, by St Bridget and her daughter, St Catherine. Following her widowhood, and coming from a wealthy family, she was able to found her Congregation, which was built around the concept of a double monastery (see below). She spent most of her remaining years in Rome. St Bridget is credited with having many visions during her lifetime, which were held in great reverence in the Middle Ages. The Order was approved by Pope Urban V in 1378, a few years after the founder's death. From the foundation until the 16th century Bridgettine communities were run as double monasteries. The monks became defunct in 1875 but were recently resuscitated (1976). The English foundation of the Order was made in 1406, at the richly endowed Syon Abbey in Devonshire. In 1415 King Henry V, in thanksgiving for his victory at Agincourt, laid the first foundation stone of a monastery in London, at Syon, near Isleworth. Syon House was thus founded by a royal charter, only to be suppressed by another monarch, Henry VIII, in the 16th century. The community went to the Low Countries, returned briefly to England during Queen Mary's reign, and dispersed again after the accession of Queen Elizabeth I. At one time the Order had houses throughout Europe, with one foundation in Russia, at Reval.

The arrangement of a Bridgettine Double Monastery

A double monastery was so organized that monks and nuns lived in the same buildings and were ruled in temporal matters by the abbess, while the confessor-general, a priest, was in charge of spiritual matters; the monks attended to all external matters as the nuns were required to observe the rules of enclosure. The movement of food and clothing from the nuns to the Fathers and

Brothers was by way of a turnstile. In the convent a bier was set at the entrance to the choir to remind the nuns of their mortality, which was further underlined by the tradition of a perpetually open grave where the 'De Profundis' was recited daily. The numbers in a Bridgettine convent were limited to sixty choir nuns and four lay Sisters, and a community was also to include thirteen priests (in remembrance of the twelve apostles and St Paul), four deacons (for the Four Doctors of the Church) and eight lay Brothers.

✣ Order of the Most Holy Saviour
  Swedish Bridgettines

BRIDGETTINE SISTERS

Location: Italy (Rome)
RC (female) founded in Italy in 1911 by Marie Elizabeth Hesselblad
Abbr: OSSS
Original habit: Choir nuns wore a grey habit and scapular with a white wimple and black veil; a grey cloak was worn in procession and choir; on the head was a white linen crown with five pieces of red cloth arranged in the form of a cross across the top. Lay Sisters wore an identical habit but with a veil and a cloak decorated with a white Maltese cross with five red circles.

The Congregation was founded by a Swedish convert, Marie Hasselblad, who wanted to invigorate Roman Catholicism in Scandinavian countries. The apostolate pursues a life of prayer, work, silence and study. Originally in a strict enclosure, this was relaxed by Pope St Pius X, and the Sisters were encouraged to set up guest houses and be more available to people. The Congregation has houses in Europe and India.

BRIGID, CONGREGATION OF ST

Location: Ireland (Dublin)
RC (female) founded in Ireland in 1807 by Bishop Delaney of Kildare

Abbr: CSB
Original habit: a black tunic, scapular and veil with a white linen wimple and coif; a silver heart was suspended from the neck beneath the wimple; a white serge cloak was worn on feast days in the presence of the Blessed Sacrament.

The need for proper religious education for women and children in his diocese, which had become neglected by the end of the 18th century, led Bishop Delaney to enlist the help of six enthusiastic young women to undertake the work. A community was formed and the young women took vows but were precluded from wearing the habit until the repeal of the Penal Law in Ireland in 1829. The bishop drew up the Rule for the Institute, which he named after St Brigid (known in Ireland also as St Bride), the second patron saint of Ireland who lived in Kildare in the 6th century and had established the first Irish nunnery there. It is said that her parents had been baptized by St Patrick, but little is known in reality. There are now houses in Ireland, the United Kingdom, Australia and New Zealand, with the Sisters working mainly in education.

✠ Sisters of St Brigid

BRIGITTINE MONKS

Location: USA (Amity, Oregon)
RC (male) founded in the USA in 1976 by Benedict Kirby
Abbr: OSSS
Original habit: a dark grey habit as for Bridgettine monks.

A diocesan Institute founded at Amity, Oregon, with the aim of reintroducing a Bridgettine Congregation of monks which had existed in Europe from the 14th century until the time of its dispersal in 1856. The monks follow the Rule of St Augustine, and this is a small, fully monastic community engaged in an apostolate of prayer and contemplation. The monks support

themselves from the making of confectionery, and are especially famed for the quality of their fudge. The enclosure is maintained and prayers are offered for the unity of all Christians, for the souls in purgatory and for all sinners.

BRIGITTINES OF THE RECOLLECTION

Defunct
RC (female) founded in Spain in the early 17th century by Marina de Escobar
Original habit: similar to that of the Bridgettines.

A Congregation founded at Valladolid, Spain, by an ex-Carmelite nun, Marina de Escobar, and Fr Louis du Paul, her Jesuit spiritual adviser. Marina lived a very holy life and was well known for her great charity. For her Congregation she modified the Rule of St Bridget of Sweden to make it more suitable for Spain and for her contemporaries. She died before the first monastery was built and, like St Bridget, she did not take the habit of the Order herself. The Order received its approbation from Pope Urban VIII (1623–44).

BRITTINIANS

Defunct
RC (male) founded in Italy in the 13th century
Original habit: a grey habit, as for Franciscans, but with a leather belt instead of a knotted Franciscan cord. After their confederation with other penitential and semi-eremitical groups the habit was changed to black.

A Congregation of Augustinian monks living as hermits in Brittini, in the Ancona area of Italy. The foundation dates from the 13th century and was named after their first hermitage, which was built at St Blasius de Brittinis, near Fano in the Marches of Ancona. The hermits observed a most austere life, eating no meat and fasting from the Feast of the Holy Cross (14 September) until Easter, surviving on cheese and eggs three times a week, with only bread and water on the other days. In 1234 Pope Gregory IX ordered the hermits to adopt the Augustinian Rule, and later, under Pope Alexander IV in 1256, they were instructed to confederate with other semi-eremitical groups to form the Hermits of St Augustine.

BROOM, KNIGHTS OF THE

Defunct
RC (male Equestrian Order) founded in France in c.1234 by St Louis
Original habit: a white damask tunic with a violet silk cape and a collar composed of gold squares in the centre of which were engravings of lilies, the squares linked by gold broom flowers, with a pendant from the centre of which hung a plain gold cross with fleur-de-lis finials.

The origin of the Order has been attributed to St Louis, king of France (1226–70), but there has also been the suggestion that the founder was Charles VI of France (1380–1422). It is also a matter of dispute as to whether this was a full Equestrian Order, for even though membership was restricted to men of noble birth, they were referred to only as shield-bearers with the duty of guarding the king's person, and this may have been just a ceremonial position.

BUSH BROTHERHOOD

Inactive
Anglican Church of Australia (male) founded in Australia in 1902 by Aneurin Vaughan Williams

A Congregation founded to evangelize and work in remote parts of Australia. The term Bush Brotherhood was accidentally introduced at a public meeting at the Grosvenor Hall, London, in 1897 when the visiting speaker, Nathaniel Dawes, bishop of Rockhampton, Queensland, spoke of Australia as needing 'a bush brotherhood' as a missionary group. The name endured and many young Englishmen answered the call to go to Australia and become part of this Brotherhood, living and working together under a common Rule. Simple vows were taken for five-year periods. The apostolate was extended to include the running and managing of schools and work within the mining and agricultural communities. Bush Brotherhoods extended from Queensland to other states and were present in New South Wales, Victoria and South and Western Australia. Their work was concerned with evangelizing and bringing the sacraments to settlers and Aboriginies in the outback of Australia. The Bush Brotherhoods are no longer active.

✠ Brotherhood of St Barnabas

C

CAESARIUS, NUNS OF ST

Defunct
RC (female) founded in France in the 6th century
by St Caesarius
Original habit: a white, full-length tunic with
cincture and a black veil.

The community house at Arles was probably the first known double monastery, for
both men and women, in what was then
Gaul. St Caesarius (470–542) wrote separate Rules for the monks and nuns and
willed his property to the nuns. It was his
aim that every nun should learn to read
and write and that the Order had the right
to choose its own abbess. St Caesarius, one
of the greatest of the early French bishops,
had decided views about monastic life. Perhaps because, during his years in a monastery at Lérins, he had suffered a breakdown
in health which went largely unnoticed, he
forbade monks and nuns in his diocese to
have separate cells or to lead an exclusively
solitary life. His sister, St Caesaria, was the
abbess of the first convent of women at
Aliscamps, near Arles.

✠ Nuns of St Cesarius

CALATREVE, KNIGHTS OF – Toledo

Defunct
RC (male Equestrian Order) founded in Spain in
1158 by King Sancho III of Castile

Original habit: (dress) a white tunic with a
shortened hooded mantle; on active service the
knights wore a long, sleeveless surcoat and a fur-
lined cloak, or black armour; from c.1400 the
knights wore a short, dark grey or black tunic with
a red cross on the left breast; Order members all
wore a white mantle bearing a red cross in choir;
(insignia) from 1397 a red cross fleury was added
as an insignia, with the leaves curled to touch the
stem, forming the letter 'M' for Mary, Mother of
God.

This Military Order was founded to fight
the Moors in Spain. The Order was given
the use of the abandoned royal fortress at
Calatreve, on the road to Toledo, which
had been abandoned by the Knights Templars, leaving the area unprotected. Monks
from Navarre, led by Ramon Sierra, were
joined there by some soldiers in 1147, and
they defended the area successfully. Over
the next ten years the knights succeeded in
clearing the area of Moors and other raid-
ers. The Order was recognized in 1164, and
in 1179 a commandery was established at
Alcaniz, in Aragon, with the aim of fighting
the Moors at Valencia. The Moors eventually prevailed, and many of the Calatrevan
Brothers were captured. A new headquarters was founded in 1195, at which
time the Order underwent some name
changes, renamed first the Knights of Sal-
vatierra, and later known as the Knights of

Calatreve la Nueva. The Order grew in wealth and power, but later conflicts, especially with the king of Spain, led to many changes in the Constitutions which diminished the Order's importance, although it continued into the 19th century. The monastic vows originally taken by the knights were modified and then dropped, and in 1838 the Order was dispersed.

✠ Knights of the Order of Calatrava

CALATREVE, NUNS OF

Defunct
RC (female Equestrian Order) founded in Spain in 1219 by Maria Suarez
Original habit: a white tunic with black scapular, on the front of which was a red cross and a black veil with white under-veil. A white cowl with a red cross on the left-hand side was worn in choir.

A cloistered Order of nuns, observing the Cistercian Rule and under the general jurisdiction of the grandmaster of the Knights of Calatreve.

CALVARISTS

Defunct
RC (male) founded in France in 1633 by Hubert Charpentier
Original habit: as for secular clergy.

A group of secular priests who banded together to foster devotion to the Sacred Passion. They were later united with the Capuchin Fathers on Mount Valerian, near Paris, but were dispersed at the time of the French Revolution.

✠ Calvarians
  Missionary Society of Mount Calvary

CALVARY, DAUGHTERS OF MOUNT

Defunct
RC (female) founded in Italy in 1619 by Virginia Centurione Bracelli
Original habit: a grey habit, Franciscan in style.

During a time of famine in Italy, Virginia Centurione, the daughter of the Doge of Genoa and wife of Gasparo Grimaldi Bracelli, undertook the care of abandoned children. In time this led her, with many of her helpers, to begin a life of service to the poor and sick. The women lived together under the Franciscan Rule, but no vows were taken, only a solemn promise of perseverance in their work. Through the generosity of an early patron, Emmanuelle Brignole, they became known throughout Italy as the Brignole Sisters.

✠ Brignole Sisters

CALVARY, ORDER OF OUR LADY OF

Location: France (Orléans)
RC (female) founded in France in 1621 by Princess Antoinette of Orléans
Abbr: OSB
Original habit: a brown habit with a black scapular

Widowed and seeking a life in religion, Antoinette of Orléans entered the convent of the Feuillantines at Toulouse in 1599 and later moved to the convent at Fontevrault where she undertook a reform. In 1614, urged by Pope Paul V and assisted by Père Leclerc, a Capuchin friar and friend of Cardinal Richelieu, she left Fontevrault to found a new convent at Poitiers dedicated to Our Lady of Calvary, which observed a strict Benedictine Rule. The French Revolution took its toll, but the Order survived. The work today is mainly in education, with particular care for the deaf and dumb and the old and infirm. Of note is the orphanage and school which the Order established in

Jerusalem for the education and care of girls of the Greek rite.

✠ Calvarians
   Calvary Benedictines

CAMALDOLESE NUNS

Location: USA (New York)
RC (female) founded in Italy in 1086, possibly by the Blessed Rudolph
Original habit: a white habit with scapular and girdle and a white under-veil with a black outer veil.

The Congregation was founded at Mugello, near Florence in 1086, most probably by the Blessed Rudolph. There is a suggestion that houses of nuns were set up by St Romuald, founder of the male Camaldolese Order, although there is no evidence that any of them followed the Camaldolese Rule. There is a Camaldolese house in Windsor, New York, where the Sisters conduct retreats.

CAMALDOLESE ORDER

Location: Italy (Rome)
RC (male) founded in Italy in c.1012 by St Romuald
Original habit: a white habit with hood and girdle.

The killing of a relative by his father, over a question of property, made Romuald of Ravenna, a wealthy nobleman, seek a way of life which would in part expiate his father's sin. He entered the Benedictine monastery of St Apollinaris near Ravenna, where he rose to become abbot. Searching for a more austere life he left the abbey and wandered as a hermit in Italy and southern France, preaching and reforming as he went. A monastery was established at Camaldoli in Italy in the early years of the 11th century, which laid the foundation for a new form of monasticism, combining the solitary life of the hermit with the communal life of the monk. Many offshoots grew

from the Camaldoli foundation, some eremitical, some monastic. They divided into five Provinces:

1 Camaldolese (also called 'Holy Hermits')
2 Murano (Venice)
3 Mount Corona (Perugia)
4 Turin
5 French Province

The Order was reunited in 1935 and still exists today.

1 CAMALDOLESE MONKS – Benedictines

Location: Italy (Arezzo)
RC (male) founded in Italy in the 11th century by St Romuald
Abbr: OSB
Original habit: a white tunic with a hood, scapular and hooded over-robe.

The foundation of this Order is attributed to St Romuald, who was less a founder of an Order and rather more a reformer of existing Benedictine houses at the start of the 11th century. A date as early as 980 has also been recorded as the possible foundation of this Order. A hermitage was built at Campus Moldoli (Camaldoli) near Arezzo, in Tuscany, which became the mother house of the Congregation; a villa built two miles below, at Fonte Buono, served as the monastery, which allowed the members of the Order to choose between a cenobitical or an eremitical way of life. This diversity still applies today where there are hermitages as well as rural and urban monasteries. The reforms put in place by St Romuald were very severe, with an emphasis on austerity, simplicity, prayer and solitude. There was permanent abstinence from meat, and fasting on bread and water on three days of each week. Camaldolese hermitages are to be found near Naples and Lake Garda, and there is an urban monastery of St Gregory the Great in Rome. Foundations have also been made in Poland, France, India, Brazil, Tanzania and the USA, where a monastery was established at Big Sur, California, in 1958.

2 CAMALDOLESE MONKS – Murano

Defunct
RC (male) founded in Italy in 1212 by Guido, Prior of Camaldoli
Original habit: a white Benedictine-style habit with a scapular, cincture and a wide-sleeved, hooded cowl.

The Congregation was founded on Cemetery Island, between Venice and Murano, where the Order was given the use of a church dedicated to St Michael. The community began by being eremitical, but the large number of novices it attracted required the cenobitic life to be adopted. The Congregation at Murano became important when all the Venetian houses united with it in 1474, forming the Congregation of St Michael of Murano. Further affiliations followed during the 16th and 17th centuries. Differences between the demands for the cenobitic and the eremitical forms of religious life caused an inevitable split, and the revolutions and unrests of the 18th and 19th centuries took their toll, from which the Congregation was never to recover.

3 CAMALDOLESE HERMITS – Mount Corona

Location: Italy (Frascati)
RC (male) founded in Italy in the 15th century by Paolo Giustiniani
Abbr: ECMC.
Original habit: a shortened tunic with a short cloak, fastened at the neck with a wooden peg.

Intent on restoring the eremitical tradition of St Romuald, which had been abandoned except at the Camaldolese abbey itself, Paolo Giustiniani founded a new community, The Company of Hermits of St Romuald, with new Constitutions emphasizing penance and with a change in the shape of the Camaldolese habit. Approbation was granted in 1523. This reformed community, which was distinguished from the other Camaldolese Order by a Bull of Pope Clement IX in 1667, was from then officially known as the Congregation of Mount Corona. There were hermitages in Italy, France and Poland.

4 CAMALDOLESE HERMITS – Turin

Defunct
RC (male) founded in Italy in c.1600 by Alessandro Ceva
Original habit: a white habit with a hood and girdle.

The founder, Alessandro Ceva, a member of an aristocratic Piedmontese family, became prior-general of the Camaldolese Order in 1587. During his time as prior of the Camaldolese monastery at Puteo Strata, Turin, he was called to Milan during a time of plague which had struck the city of Turin. In an attempt to stop the spread of the plague, Ceva asked that Duke Charles Emmanuel of Savoy should make a vow to erect a hermitage in Turin. This was done, and its priests acted as chaplains to the Knights of the Annunciation of Savoy. In the 18th century this foundation became part of the Mount Corona Congregation.

5 CAMALDOLESE MONKS – Notre Dame de Consolation

Defunct
RC (male) founded in France in 1631 by Fr Boniface d'Antoine
Original habit: a white habit with hood and girdle.

Founded near Botheon, Lyons, and approved by the French king in the same year, and with six other foundations following with the approval of Pope Uraban VIII in 1634, this Congregation became tainted with the heresy of Jansenism and was suppressed at the end of the 18th century.

CAMILLUS, ORDER OF ST

Location: Italy (Rome)
RC (male) founded in Italy in 1582 by St Camillus of
Lellis (canonized 1746)
Abbr: OSCAM, or MI

Few founders of religious Orders had less to recommend them than the young Camillus, a soldier famed for his gambling, dissoluteness and very quarrelsome nature. His character led him into destitution, from which he was rescued by a Franciscan. In an effort to reform himself he applied to join the Franciscan Order but was refused partly because he was suffering from grave injuries to his feet but probably also because of his uncertain temper. He went to Rome and found work in a hospital for incurables, but was soon dismissed because of his unreformed ways. Another short spell in the army was followed by work as a builder's labourer for the Capuchins, and he was admitted as a lay Brother only to be dismissed when the condition of his wounds was examined. He returned to a hospital in Rome, where his wounds were treated and his character underwent a transformation. In time he rose to become director of the hospital. Influenced by his friendship with St Philip Neri, he became a priest and founded the Fathers of a Good Death, a company of priests and laymen who nursed incurables both in the hospitals and in their own homes. The Order is still in existence, with houses worldwide.

✠ Agonizants
  Camillans
  Clerks Regular Ministers of the Infirm
  Fathers of a Good Death
  Order of the Servants of the Sick

CANONESSES REGULAR

Religious women living together in communities attached to certain cathedrals, as, for example, the canonesses regular of the Lateran. They were bound by a Rule of poverty, unlike the canonesses secular, who were allowed to retain property. The duties of the canonesses regular were mainly concerned with the education of young girls and attention to decorative church arts, with much of the early decoration of manuscripts, vestments and church linen performed by these ladies.

CANONESSES REGULAR – Belgium

Defunct
RC (female) founded in Belgium in c.650 by Sts
Waldetrude the Widow and Aldegund the Virgin
Original habit: a black habit with white sleeves, a
peaked headdress, from the peak of which flew a
long pendant streamer, and a long silk mantle
lined with ermine; a full-length white linen surplice
braided with cord in ornamental knots and scrolls
was worn in choir. In some houses a rochet was
worn.

It was St Waldetrude who founded the first monastery of canonesses regular at Mons, while St Aldegund, her sister, became the first abbess of a house at Maubeuge (Meaux). The houses observed the Rule of St Augustine and there were many foundations in France and Germany.

CANONESSES REGULAR – Rouen

Defunct
RC (female) founded in France in the 13th century
by King St Louis of France (canonized 1297) and his
mother, Blanche
Original habit: a white, but later black, habit with
a black linen cincture and a black mantle lined and
edged with white fur; a black outer veil over a
white under-veil was worn.

The canonesses at first adopted the Rule of St Augustine. The original white habit was superseded by a black one when the Congregation later adopted the Benedictine Rule.

CANONESSES REGULAR HOSPITALLERS OF THE MERCIFUL HEART OF JESUS

Location: France (Malestroit)
RC (female) founded in France in the 13th century
Abbr: CROSA
Original habit: a white habit, with a white linen rochet and a leather belt, and a black veil for professed Sisters and a white veil for novices.

A Congregation of canonesses regular founded in Dieppe, France, and known originally as the Hermit Sisters of St Augustine. In the 17th century there was a revision of their Constitutions by the archbishop of Rouen, which was approved by Rome in 1664. Houses exist today in France, England, The Netherlands, Italy, Canada and Africa, with the members still working for the sick and the poor.

CANONESSES REGULAR OF THE ORDER OF ST AUGUSTINE OF THE CONGREGATION OF OUR LADY

Location: Italy (Rome)
RC (female) founded in France in 1597 by St Peter Fourier (canonized 1897) and the Blessed Alix le Clerc (beatified 1947)
Abbr: CND
Original habit: a black habit with a black veil and white wimple; no rochet was worn

The rise and spread of Calvinism in France, together with the general ignorance of his parishioners, led St Peter Fourier, an Augustinian canon regular of the Abbey of Chaumousy in Lorraine, to seek its remedy. Together with Blessed Alix le Clerc, who had spent a rather frivolous youth, they founded this Congregation at Mattaincourt with the purpose of providing free edu-

cation for local girls. Increasing vocations led to the establishment of further houses, and these spread into the USA and Canada during the 17th century. The Order later divided into two parts: the Roman Union with houses in France, Belgium, England, Italy and the Far East; and the Congregation of Our Lady of Jupille, France.

CANONESSES SECULAR

Groups of unmarried women, of proven noble birth but no fortune, who were offered shelter by the Church. They wore no particular habit but all wore purple clothes in the fashion of the day, and they were free to leave at any time. Their only duty seems to have been the daily recital of certain offices. There is some evidence that the canonesses were allowed to possess property, which distinguished them from nuns and canonesses regular, and were allowed to take vows of chastity and obedience. In Germany and France they became particularly numerous and the permission to hold private property led to much laxity.

CANOSSIAN DAUGHTERS OF CHARITY OF VERONA

Location: Italy (Rome)
RC (female) founded in Italy in 1808 by St Magdalen, Marchioness of Canossa (canonized 1988)
Abbr: FDCC
Original habit: a red-brown tunic with a black veil and shawl and a small neck medal.

Founded under the original title of the Servants of the Poor, the name of the Congregation was later changed to the present one. The founder, St Magdalen (1774–1835), had approached Antonio Rosmini, the founder of the Rosminians, with a view to establishing a society of the Daughters of Charity. There are many houses in Europe, the Americas, the Far

East, Africa and Australasia. With a special devotion to Our Lady of Sorrows, the Sisters work for the education of poor girls, administer and run hospitals, crèches and orphanages and maintain foreign missions.

✛ Canossian Sisters

CAPUCHIN POOR CLARE SISTERS

Location: autonomous
RC (female) founded in Italy in 1538 by the Ven. Maria Lorenza Longo
abbr: OSCCap
Original habit: Franciscan style.

The Congregation of the Capuchin Poor Clare Sisters was founded in Naples by Maria Longo, who had been a Franciscan Third Order Sister and was inspired to adopt the Rule of St Clare for her community. Members undertake to work among the homeless, preparing food for those in refuge shelters and repairing vestments and church linen. The Order has spread throughout Italy and has houses in France, Spain and the USA, where the Sisters may currently be found in Colorado and Texas.

CARACCIOLO FATHERS

Location: Italy (Rome)
RC (male) founded in Italy in 1588 by the Venerable John Augustine Adorno and St Francis Caracciolo (canonized 1807)
Abbr: CCRRMM (or CRM)
Original habit: secular in style

A contemplative and active Order, its members taking the three usual vows of religion, poverty, chastity and obedience, with the addition of a fourth vow which is not to aspire to ecclesiastical dignities either outside or inside the Order. The Fathers, who have a special devotion to the Blessed Sacrament, practise continual mortification and maintain perpetual adoration by rota, undertake parish work, conduct retreats, teach and run missions in the Congo and India. Further houses have been opened in Italy and Germany.

✛ Adorno Fathers
  Clerks Regular Minor

CARITAS CHRISTI

Location: France (Lourdes)
RC (female) founded in France in 1937 by Fr Perrin, OP

This Secular Institute was founded for the purpose of providing a community for women who desire to seek perfection in the world and at the same time to work for the glory of God. The members must be prepared to make a vow of chastity and promise to live in poverty and with a spirit of obedience. The probation of the novice lasts for up to five years. The first novitiate began in 1938 when the first superior, called the servant-general, was appointed. Despite the war years in Europe the numbers rose, and work continued to gain papal approval, which came in 1950, with diocesan rights following in 1955 when the Institute achieved pontifical status. By then there were over four hundred members spread throughout Europe, the Americas, the Near East and Asia. The formation of its members is maintained through frequent meetings with counsellors, the distribution of bulletins, days of recollection and annual retreats.

✛ Caritas Christi Union

CARITON, MONKS OF THE ORDER OF

Defunct
RC (male) founded in Italy in the late 3rd century by St Cariton (Chariton)
Original habit: a tawny tunic with a black hooded mantle.

An Order of monks, established in Italy in the reign of the Emperor Aurelian by St Cariton, a native of Lycaonia who was martyred in 165. The monks led a solitary and austere life, existing only on bread and herbs.

CARMELITES

A Roman Catholic male and female Order, the name deriving from the early Christian hermits who lived on Mount Carmel in the Holy Land. In 1154 they were organized into the Order of Our Lady of Mount Carmel by St Berthold. The Rule, written in the form of a letter and based heavily on Holy Scripture, had been given to the hermits by St Albert Avogadro, the Patriarch of Jerusalem. With the conquering of the Holy Land by the Saracens at the time of the crusades, the hermits fled to Cyprus, Sicily, France and England. Pope Innocent IV (1243–54) allowed a modification of the Rule in 1250 at the time of the election in England of St Simon Stock as prior-general, a result of a general chapter held there in 1247. The name of the Order was then changed to the Brothers of the Order of the Blessed Virgin Mary of Mount Carmel, and in 1287, at the general chapter held in Montpellier, France, the habit was also changed, substituting the striped mantle, composed of four white and three black vertical stripes, or rays, for a white one, thereby leading the communities to be known as the White Friars. From c.1413 reform movements began within the Order in an effort to return to the original eremitical spirit. Affiliation with some Beguines in Flanders in the mid-15th century led to the foundation of some strictly enclosed convents for Carmelite nuns. At the same time a papal Bull *Cum Nulla* sanctioned a Second Order of nuns and allowed for a Third Order for the laity. The influence of St Teresa of Avila, St John of the Cross and St Peter of Alcántara added weight to the proposed reforms, and new Constitutions were approved in 1581. A separation of the reformed (discalced, or unshod) Carmelites and the unreformed (calced, or shod) Carmelites came about following the general chapter at Cremona in 1593. The Order spread widely. In the USA there has been rapid growth of this Order, a development echoed in Europe, Latin America, Australasia, Asia, Africa and Oceania.

CARMELITES: CALCED

Location: Italy (Rome)
RC (male and female – for the history of the Order see entry under CARMELITES)
Abbr: OC or O.Carm
Original habit: a brown tunic with black leather belt, a scapular and hood; a white cloak (for friars); the habit was similar for the nuns, but with an additional white collar and black veil.

A Pontifical Institute, which is both active and contemplative. Fasting and abstinence are observed. Following a novitiate of one year, after which simple vows are taken for about three years and up to a maximum of six years, a period of pastoral placement leads first to simple profession and then to solemn profession for life. The active apostolate is in education, pastoral work, publishing and the conducting of missions. Carmelite nuns observe a strictly contemplative life within a strict enclosure under solemn vows.

CARMELITES: DISCALCED

Location: Italy (Rome)
RC (male and female – for the history of the Order see entry under CARMELITES)
Abbr: OCD
Original habit: as for the Calced Carmelites with the addition of sandals; choir nuns wore a black veil, lay Sisters a white one.

The friars and nuns observe a strict reform of the Carmelite Rule, and there is a strong emphasis on contemplation and reflection. The novitiate for men differs from that for women, the latter spending their time of training in their own convents whereas the male novices are sent to monasteries designed for training purposes. The novitiate lasts for one year, after which simple vows are taken and renewed over three years, and the taking of solemn vows follows. The communities are divided into Provinces, each one having a house known as the Desert, which is maintained for those seeking a contemplative life. The duties of the Second Order Carmelites include the recitation of the divine office as well as preaching, writing and the conducting of missions and retreats.

CARMELITES: TERTIARY REGULARS

Location: various
RC (male and female) founded in the mid-17th century (for the history of the Order see entry under CARMELITES)
Abbr: O.Carm
Original habit: Carmelite.

The Order, of which there is mention as early as the 15th century although the date of foundation is taken to be the mid-17th century, is composed of men and women who live in communities, wear the Carmelite habit, but observe a less austere Rule than the members of the First and Second Orders. The apostolate is usually active.

CARMELITES: CARMELITE COMMUNITY OF THE WORD

Location: USA (Ebensburg, Pennsylvania)
RC (female) founded in the USA in 1971 (for the history of the Order see entry under CARMELITES)
Abbr: CCW
Original habit: Carmelite style.

This Diocesan Institute was founded at Ebensburg, Pennsylvania. The members live in community and observe the traditional vows of religion, poverty, chastity and obedience. The apostolate is concerned with education at all levels, pastoral work and special ministries to the poor, the handicapped, the imprisoned and the homeless. The Sisters also operate soup kitchens and Family Life Support groups. At present the work is restricted to Pennsylvania.

CARMELITES: CARMELITE MISSIONARY SISTERS – Spain

Location: Italy (Rome)
RC (female) founded in Spain in 1861 by Fr Francisco Palau y Quer (for the history of the Order see entry under CARMELITES)
Abbr: CM
Original habit: a brown dress and veil with a white or beige blouse and a brown woollen cardigan; in hot climates the cardigan and veil are white or beige.

Following a mystical experience in the cathedral of Cuidadela on the Balearic island of Minorca, Francisco Palau, a discalced Carmelite, made the first foundation of the Carmelite Missionary Sisters in 1861. A year later a second house was opened in Barcelona, which is now the mother house of the Congregation. This Pontifical Congregation, which was granted approbation in 1907, undertakes missionary work in Spain, France, England, Italy, Poland, Portugal and the USA and throughout much of South America, Africa and Asia. The apostolate is in education, health care, catechesis and the concerns of the poor and needy.

CARMELITES: CARMELITE MISSIONARY SISTERS OF ST TERESA

Location: Mexico (Mexico City)
RC (female) founded in Mexico in 1903 by Srs.

Moreno, Leon, Bisurto and Mendez (for the history of the Order see entry under CARMELITES)
Abbr: CMST
Original habit: Carmelite style

An Institute affiliated to the discalced Carmelites and approved by the Holy See in 1938 and 1945. The work of the community is both active and contemplative and the Sisters observe the usual three vows of poverty, chastity and obedience. Their main work is among the poor, and in education and health care. Some Sisters also work in seminaries. Houses can be found in Mexico, Brazil, El Salvador, Peru, Bolivia and Texas.

✢ Missionary Carmelites of St Teresa

CARMELITES: CARMELITE SISTERS FOR THE AGED AND INFIRM

Location: USA (Germantown, New York)
RC (female) founded in the USA in 1929 by Teresa McCrory with Cardinal Hayes (for the history of the Order see entry under CARMELITES)
Abbr: OCarm
Original habit: Carmelite in style with a black veil, white linen collar and white cloak.

A Pontifical Institute which is an active Order with its members in simple, perpetual vows. The entire apostolate is confined to caring for the aged and infirm. After their training and religious profession the Sisters work in all branches of care, for which they receive both government and private funding. There is also a house in Dublin, Ireland.

CARMELITES: CARMELITE SISTERS OF CHARITY – Verdruna

Location: Italy (Rome)
RC (female) founded in Spain in 1826 by Blessed Joaquina de Vedruna (beatified 1940) (for the history of the Order see entry under CARMELITES)
Abbr: CCV or CaCh.
Original habit: Carmelite style.

The Sisters have an apostolate concerned with missions, nursing, education and social work among Hispanics and the homeless. There are many foundations throughout Europe, Asia, Africa and the Americas.

CARMELITES: CARMELITE SISTERS OF CORPUS CHRISTI

Location: Trinidad and Tobago (Tunapuna)
RC (female) founded in England in 1908 by Mother Mary of the Blessed Sacrament (for the history of the Order see entry under CARMELITES)
Abbr: OCarm
Original habit: Carmelite style.

A Pontifical Institute, active and with simple vows. The Sisters work in teaching, day nurseries, care of the sick, rescue homes and social welfare. There are houses in the Americas. The house in Leicestershire, England, is now closed.

CARMELITES: CARMELITE SISTERS OF MERCY

Location: USA (Newport, Washington)
RC (female) founded in the USA in 1990 (for the history of the Order see entry under CARMELITES)
Abbr: OCDH

A very small community founded as a Lavra of Hermits in accordance with Canon 603 (1983 revision). The hermits, who have had previous experience in communal living, observe the three traditional vows of religion, poverty, chastity and obedience, and accept direction from the diocesan bishop. They maintain a Carmelite 'desert' to which other Carmelite nuns can retreat for periods of solitude.

CARMELITES: CARMELITE SISTERS OF ST TERESA

Location: Mexico
RC (female) founded in Mexico in 1903 by Mother

Luisa Josefa of the Blessed Sacrament (for the history of the Order see entry under CARMELITES)
Abbr: OCDT

An active Order with simple vows. The Sisters work in education, nursing, and the provision of retreats. There are two other Congregations of a similar title, with head-quarters in India (Karnataka) and Italy (Turin).

CARMELITES: CARMELITE SISTERS OF ST TERESA OF FLORENCE

Location: Italy (Florence)
RC (female) founded in Italy in 1874 by Teresa Adelaide Manetti (Blessed Teresa Mary of the Cross – beatified 1986) (for the history of the Order see entry under CARMELITES)
Abbr: OCarm
Original habit: Carmelite style, with a white Carmelite habit for mission work.

There are other Congregations of the same name. This one was founded in Florence by Teresa Manetti, nicknamed Bettina, when she and two companions started an Insti-tute of Carmelite Tertiary Sisters at Campi Bisenzio, her home town, where they taught the children of the poor. The members were formally clothed in the Carmelite habit in 1888. The Sisters opened free schools for girls from poor families and provided care for orphans. The numbers grew quickly and approbation was granted in 1900, when the community was known as the Carmelite Sisters of St Teresa. Perpetual adoration of the Blessed Sacrament, which has always been an important part of the Congrega-tion's life, was formally permitted in 1902. The work expanded beyond Italy to the Middle East, when the first missionary Sis-ters, led by Sr Raffaela, left for the Lebanon in 1904. Missions have also been established in Beirut (1962 and 1976), Haifa, Israel (1907) and Brazil (1979 and 1984). In these mission foundations the Sisters undertake

catechesis and run free schools for rural children, they staff leprosaria and they care for the needy.

CARMELITES: CARMELITE SISTERS OF ST THÉRÈSE OF THE INFANT JESUS

Location: USA (Oklahoma City, Oklahoma)
RC (female) founded in the USA in 1917 by Mother Agnes Teresa Cavanagh
Abbr: CST
Original habit: Carmelite style.

A Diocesan Congregation founded in Bent-ley, Oklahoma, and concentrated in the archdiocese of Oklahoma City, where the Sisters work in education from pre-school to senior levels. They also undertake work in catechesis and provide various parish ministries as needed.

CARMELITES: CARMELITE SISTERS OF THE DIVINE HEART OF JESUS

Location: The Netherlands (Sittard, Limburg)
RC (female) founded in Germany in 1891 by Anna Maria Tauscher (Mother Mary Teresa of St Joseph) (for the history of the Order see entry under CARMELITES)
Abbr: DCJ
Original habit: a brown tunic and scapular with a leather cincture and a black veil and white cloak.

The work of the community is with the care of children and the aged, and the running of foreign missions. Perpetual pro-fession follows a period of postulancy and a novitiate lasting up to three years. Anna Tauscher, who was born in Sandow, Germany, now part of Poland, was a con-vert whose cause for beatification is cur-rently under consideration. The American foundation, made in 1912, has been most successful, and the Congregation there is divided into three Provinces. Foreign missions are also undertaken in Africa, Bra-zil, Nicaragua and Venezuela, and there are houses in The Netherlands, Germany, Croatia and South America.

CARMELITES: CARMELITE SISTERS OF THE INFANT JESUS

Location: Poland (Warsaw)
RC (female) founded in Poland in the 14th century (for the history of the Order see entry under CARMELITES)
Abbr: O.Carm
Original habit: Carmelite style.

The calced Carmelites in Poland date their foundation from the end of the 14th century and owe their origin to the Carmelite missionaries who made foundations as they travelled through Poland on their way to Persia (Iran). This Congregation has moved its mother house several times in recent years, from Czestochowa (Sisnowiec) to Krakow and most recently to Warsaw, as the number of houses and members has increased.

CARMELITES: CARMELITE SISTERS OF THE MOST SACRED HEART – Los Angeles

Location: USA (Alhambra, California)
RC (female) founded in the USA by Mother Luisa Josefa of the Blessed Sacrament (for the history of the Order see entry under CARMELITES)
Abbr: OCD
Original habit: brown with a black veil and white under-veil; scapular; white cloak.

Mother Luisa Josefa, who was active in Mexico, where she oversaw the building and running of hospitals, schools and orphanages, extended her work into California, where the Sisters today are engaged in education, retreat work and the care of the sick and aged. The postulancy lasts for nine months, during which time a blue uniform, but no veil, is worn. The novitiate is divided into two years; during the first year the Rule and Constitutions are studied with the novice now adding a white veil to her uniform. The second year is spent in gaining a knowledge and some experience of the various apostolates of the Institute. At profession the Sister will assume the brown habit and veil. Vows are made annually for six years, with perpetual vows following. Life in the community revolves around the recitation of the divine office, prayer, spiritual reading and the saying of the rosary. The Sisters provide staffing and administration for schools, nurse the sick and convalescent, and direct retreats.

CARMELITES: COMMUNITY OF TERESIAN CARMELLITES

Location: USA (Worcester, Massachusetts)
RC (male and female, single or married) founded in the USA in 1971 (for the history of the Order see entry under CARMELITES)
Abbr: O.Carm

This Congregation was founded in Massachusetts, USA, as a religious community which is part of the Order of discalced Carmelites. The members live in community and there is no distinction made between those who are clerics and those who are not. Members make a profession of vows, or promises, according to the secular Third Order Rule. The community is involved in providing a ministry of missions, and a youth and music ministry, and in arranging pilgrimages for various parish groups to visit the major shrines throughout the USA, Europe and the Near East.

CARMELITES OF MARY IMMACULATE

Location: India (Kerala)
RC (male) founded in India in 1831 by Blessed Kuriakose Elias Chavara
Abbr: CMI

This Congregation of Carmelite tertiaries of the Syro-Malabarese Rite were founded at Mannanam, India, and canonically approved in 1834, receiving their present Rule in 1906. The Brothers continue their work in India from their house at Ernakulam, Cochin, and have further houses in the USA and Canada, where they work in parishes and hospitals, undertake chaplaincies in universities and prisons, and maintain an active ministry among the Syro-Malabar Catholics.

✠ Karmilitha Nishpatkuka Munnam Sabha

CARMELITES OF OUR LADY OF PEACE

Location: USA (Somerset, Wisconsin)
RC (female) founded in the USA in 1998
Abbr: OCarm
Original habit: Carmelite style.

The members of this American Diocesan Institute live in community and observe the usual vows of religion, poverty, chastity and obedience, undertaking a contemplative way of life and offering opportunities for retreats and spiritual direction.

CARTHUSIANS, ORDER OF

Location: France (Grande Chartreuse, St Laurent-du-Pont)
RC (male and female) founded in France in the 11th century (men) and 13th century (women)
Abbr: OCart
Original habit: (male) a heavy white tunic, hood and scapular, the edges of which are joined by side bands; a large white cowl was used in choir; (male novices) a black cloak for use in church with a shorter scapular without bands; (female) as for the monks except that a black veil is substituted for the hood.

1 CARTHUSIAN MONKS

The Carthusians were founded by St Bruno of Cologne and six companions in 1084 at La Grande Chartreuse in France, 13 miles north-east of Grenoble. The monks are vowed to silence, and each maintains a semi-eremitical life housed in a small cell which consists of a small, two-storeyed house with a corridor which can be used for exercise in inclement weather. The rest is divided into three rooms, a work-room, antechamber and living cell. A small garden with walls high enough to preclude the sight of his neighbour completes the monk's living quarters and it is here that he can spend the hour each day set aside for manual work. In each cell there is a bed with a straw mattress, sheets and blankets, and a chest, table and chair. In the door of the cell is a hatch through which the monk receives his daily food from a lay Brother, for he must eat alone except on Sundays and feast days when the community eats together. Daily life revolves around the recitation of the daily office, which is said between 12 midnight and 2 am, the conventual Mass in the morning and vespers after 8 pm, for which the monks are present in chapel. On Sundays and feast days all the canonical hours except prime are chanted in chapel. Once a week the monks are permitted to walk together, usually in pairs. Each monk may write to his family four times a year and the family may visit the monastery once a year for a period of some three days. Carthusian foundations are known as Charterhouses and can be found throughout the world, with a combined membership of nearly four hundred monks.

2 CARTHUSIAN NUNS

The Carthusian Order for nuns was founded in France, at Salette on the Rhône, in c.1229 when the nuns from the abbey of Prebayon asked to be received as Carthusians. Their request was granted by Blessed John of Spain (1123–60), the prior of Montrieu (Mons Rivi), who adapted the Rule for nuns. A nun's cell consists of a workshop in one room, with a second room containing a bed, table, chair and oratory.

Each nun is required to work manually for an hour a day and this usually takes the form of typing and bookbinding, sewing and weaving, iconography and woodcrafts. The formation programme consists of a minimum six-month postulancy followed by a two-year novitiate. Profession of stability, obedience and conversion is made for three years and can be renewed for a further two years. Solemn profession then follows. There are also nuns in each Charterhouse who contribute to the running of the community; Converse nuns are those who deal with the needs of the house and also recite an office, while Donate Sisters are women who wish to consecrate their lives to God without making vows. For them, a period of temporary donation is followed by permanent status. Carthusian nuns, upon solemn profession or perpetual donation, have the privilege of receiving virginal consecration from the diocesan bishop. In this ceremony the nun is invested with a crown, ring, stole and maniple which is to be worn again only on the day of her Jubilee and, at her death, is laid upon her bier. At present there are five Charterhouses in France, Italy and Spain, with a population of some seventy-five nuns.

CASIMIR, SISTERS OF ST

Location: USA (Chicago, Illinois)
RC (female) founded in the USA in 1907 by Mother Maria Kaupas
Abbr: SSC

The Sisters form an active Order under diocesan control and they observe simple vows. Their work is with the education of the young, nursing and the care of the aged and poor. The ethnic background of the Sisters is Lithuanian, and the Order sent a group of members back to Lithuania in the early 1920s to continue their work there. They have also established a mission in Argentina. The group eventually became autonomous. The cause for beatification of the founder is currently under investigation.

CASSIAN MONKS

Defunct
RC (male) founded in France, in c.415 by St John Cassian

St John Cassian (360–435), the founder of monasticism in the West, lived as a child and young man in a monastery at Bethlehem, where he became a friend of the abbot, Germanus. Together they made a seven-year-long tour of monasteries in Egypt and went on to Constantinople, where Cassian was ordained deacon by St John Chrysostom. Cassian settled first in Rome and later in Marseilles after Rome was taken by the Goths in 410. He went on to found two monasteries, for men and women, in that town, that of the men dedicated to Sts Peter and Victor. The latter was martyred under Maximian and the monastery was built over the site of his tomb. John Cassian's many writings, which include his *Institutes* in which he set out the Rules for monastic life, and *Conferences*, which is an account of his meetings and conversations with Eastern monastics, were influential upon St Benedict when he was writing his Rule in the next century. Although never formally canonized in the Western Church, the founder was regarded as such by St Gregory the Great and is venerated in the Eastern Church as St John Cassian. Pope Urban V, who had been abbot of St Victor's monastery, had the word 'Saint' engraved on the silver casket that contained John Cassian's head.

CASSIAN NUNS

Defunct
RC (female) founded in the early 5th century by St John Cassian

Original habit: allegedly, a white tunic and rochet-like outer garment with a black veil.

The nuns' convent at Marseilles was dedicated to St Saviour. It is said to have observed the Rule of St Augustine.

CATECHISTS OF CHRIST THE KING, MISSIONARY

Location: USA (San Antonio, Texas)
RC (female) founded in 1989, when it achieved autonomy
Abbr: MCDP

Members of this Pontifical Congregation work with young people at all levels of education and provide counselling services, They also run a special ministry for Hispanics and are to be found in Texas, Arizona, Alaska, California, Nebraska and Nevada.

CATECHISTS OF THE HEART OF JESUS

Location: USA (Stamford, Connecticut)
RC (female, Ukrainian Catholic) founded in Brazil in 1940 by Christoforo Myskiv
Abbr: OSBM

A Secular Institute of women who are interested in religious instruction, helping clerics in missionary work and in the Church, and in maintaining the Ukrainian rite and culture. It was approved in 1971.

CATHERINE, KNIGHTS OF ST – Mount Sinai

Defunct
RC (male Equestrian Order) founded at Mount Sinai in 1067
Original habit: little is known beyond that a white mantle, decorated with a badge depicting a broken wheel traversed by a blood-stained sword (the instruments of martyrdom of St Catherine), was worn. Six rays, or tongues of fire, came from the outer border of the wheel.

A Military Order established for the help and protection of pilgrims to the Holy Land, which also undertook the repair of the roads used by the pilgrims and the care of the tomb of St Catherine. The knights observed the Rule of St Basil. The Order was abolished when it ceased to have a purpose. The monastery of St Catherine allegedly contains the relics of the saint, which were transported there from Alexandria by angels.

CATHOLIC FOREIGN MISSION SOCIETY OF AMERICA

Location: USA (Maryknoll, New York)
RC (female) founded in the USA in 1912 by Mary Joseph Rogers (Mother Mary Joseph)
Abbr: MM

A contemplative and active Order with simple vows. The Sisters have an apostolate in teaching, nursing, social work and home and foreign missions in Eastern Europe, Africa, India, Sri Lanka, the Far East, Asia, Oceania and South America. The Sisters are concerned with feminist issues and the building of communities, with a special interest in action for peace and justice in conflict situations.

✠ Maryknoll Sisters
   Missionary Sisters of St Dominic
   Sisters of St Dominic

CATHOLIC FOREIGN MISSION SOCIETY OF AMERICA, INC.

Location: USA (Maryknoll, New York)
RC (male) founded in the USA in 1911 by James Anthony Walsh and Thomas F. Price
Abbr: MM
Original habit: as for secular clergy.

This Congregation of secular priests and lay Brothers was founded to give expression to the missionary work of the Catholic Church in America, and the work is undertaken in thirty-two countries of the world, including the USA, Latin America, Asia, Africa, Russia and the Middle East. The apostolate includes a wide variety of activities, including parish ministries, social action issues, education, health care, aid to refugees and the establishment of Christian communities. It is an active Order, approved in 1930, whose members make solemn promises rather than vows.

✣ Maryknoll Fathers
  Maryknoll Society for Foreign Missions

CELESTINES

Defunct
RC (male) founded in Italy in 1294 by hermits together with Pope St Celestine V (canonized 1313)
Original habit: a grey Capuchin-style habit with sandals.

A defunct branch of the Franciscan Order. The foundation was established for the purpose of reforming the Franciscan Rule and returning it to the spirit of the original foundation. The founders were Pietro das Macerata, later called Liberato, and Pietro da Fossombrone, later known as Angelo Clareno, who lived as hermits with some others and were known together as the Poor Hermits of the Lord Celestine. Following the resignation of Pope St Celestine V and the loss of his patronage, the hermits left Italy. Many of them returned after the death of Liberato, but attempts to revive the community were suppressed by Pope John XXII in 1317, despite the efforts of Angelo Clareno, who defiantly made himself superior-general of the remaining hermits and opened novitiates for entry to his independent body known as the Brothers of the Poor Life. He was regarded as a demented heretic, but managed to avoid papal arrest. He died in 1337.

✣ Celestine Hermits
  Poor Hermits of the Lord Celestine
  Spiritual Franciscans of the Marches

CELESTINES

Defunct
RC (male) founded in Italy in c.1250 by Pietro di Murrone (Pope St Celestine V)
Original habit: a black cowl, hood and scapular bearing the badge of the Order, the letter 'S' entwined around a cross; white tunic.

The founder was a Benedictine priest who desired a more solitary life and lived for some years in the wooded hills in the Abruzzi region of Italy. Here he adopted a severe form of penitential life, subjecting his body to the wearing of a hair shirt, made even more painful because of knots which were made in the fabric, and with an iron chain around his waist. Others joined him in his rigorous way of life, with fasting, work and prayer their daily life. The Order was approved in 1264 as a branch of the Benedictines. The Celestine Order was administered along Cluniac lines in that all later foundations were subject to the mother house in Italy. The saintly reputation of the founder attracted the attention of the Sacred College in Rome at a time when it was failing to elect a successor to Pope Nicholas IV, who died in 1292. After an attempt to escape his fate Pietro di Murrone, by then almost eighty years of age, capitulated and agreed to his election as pope. He chose to ride to his coronation at Aquila astride an ass, with the ropes around the animal drawn by two monarchs. Thus was he elected and enthroned, but his career was both disastrous and short. A naive and incapable old man, he resigned after five months in office and was imprisoned by his successor, Boniface III. He died at the age of ninety-one. The Order became defunct in the 18th century.

✣ Hermits of Murrone
  Hermits of St Damian

CELESTINES – Provins

Defunct
RC (female) founded in France in 1836 by Mother Chantal Verrine and Fr Etienne Morey

The foundation was made in order to administer and run a clinic, an old people's home and a secondary school in the town of Provins, France. It later fused with the Congregation of the Augustinian Sisters of Meaux.

✠ Religious of Provins

CESARIUS, MONKS OF ST

Defunct
RC (male) founded in Germany in 1229 by Cesarius (Caesar)
Original habit: a grey tunic with a knotted cord, round hood and cape in the early Franciscan style.

Although sometimes incorrectly listed as a saint, Cesarius was a Franciscan monk at Speyer, Germany, who, together with some fellow monks who were unhappy with the laxity of their Order, established a separate Congregation noted for its austerity. Following reforms within the Franciscan Order, the monks returned to their original monastery and resumed the Franciscan way of life. Cesarius of Speyer (or Spires) must not be confused with St Caesarius of Arles.

CESARIUS, SISTERS OF ST

Defunct
RC (female) founded in France c.502 by St Caesarius (died 543)
Original habit: a white habit with a black veil.

A community of nuns founded by St Caesarius of Arles, a contemporary of St Benedict. The first convent, that at Aliscamps, was built outside the city walls of Arles but was destroyed by the Goths. A second convent was then built inside the city walls, with the bishop's sister, St Caesaria, serving as the first abbess. The Rule, drawn up by St Caesarius, imposed an austere way of life on the Sisters, with daily recitation of the divine office, much fasting and a certain amount of daily labour; their vows included one of perseverance until death. The Rule was copied by other female communities and, in an adapted form, by some male communities. The nuns maintained a school for girls from the age of six years, who were taught to appreciate a simple life.

CHAPEL, ORDER OF THE

(male Equestrian Order) founded in England in the 16th century

An Order of Knights instituted by King Henry VIII of England to assist at the funerals of English monarchs.

CHARITY, BROTHERS OF – Ghent

Location: Italy (Rome)
RC (male) founded in Belgium in 1807 by Pierre Triest
Abbr: FC
Original habit: a simple black tunic and scapular, with a belt and buckle worn outside the scapular and a rosary suspended on the right-hand side, tucked over the belt.

Canon Pierre Triest, a titular canon of the cathedral of St Bavon in Ghent, whose great dedication to works of charity has earned him the name 'St Vincent de Paul of Belgium', founded not only this Brotherhood, but also the Sisters of Charity of Jesus and Mary (1803), the Association of Maternal Charity (1822), the Brothers of St John of God (1825) and The Sisters of the Holy Childhood of Jesus (1835). The apostolate of the Brothers of Charity of Ghent was to relieve all aspects of suffering, both physical and moral, and to undertake the education of the young, particularly those with physical disabilities, and the educationally subnormal. Pierre Triest was honoured by his country and received three royal decorations for his work. It is of interest to note that the cathedral of St Bavon, or Bavo, in Ghent, is the home of one of the earliest known paintings in oil, by Jan van Eyck, depicting a naked Adam and Eve. At various times in history, as sensibilities rose and fell, the unfortunate pair have been alternately clothed or stripped, most notably the former on account of the prudery of the Holy Roman Emperor Joseph II (1765–90). The Brothers of Charity have an American mother house at Philadelphia, Pennsylvania, the foundation dating from 1877.

CHARITY, BROTHERS AND SISTERS OF

Location: USA (Berryville, Arkansas)
RC (male and female) founded in the USA in 1983 by Kohn Michael Talbot

An American Roman Catholic Public Association in the diocese of Little Rock, Arkansas. It is a mixed community of the monastic and domestic, men and women, married and single, with or without children. The monks live in community while the domestics stay in their own homes, attending monthly meetings and contributing to the upkeep of the monks. The aim of the community, which is Franciscan in style, is to help in the renewal of the Church. The formation programme involves a novitiate of one or two years, simple profession for three years with the final profession following. Groups are spread throughout the USA, with some five hundred members worldwide. The community runs an orphanage in Honduras, and some members work in a hospital in Jerusalem.

CHARITY, HANDMAIDS OF

Location: Italy (Rome)
RC (female) founded in Italy in 1839 by Paula di Rosa (St Mary di Rosa – canonized 1954)

A Congregation founded in Brescia, Italy. The founder, Paula di Rosa, was involved in nursing the sick during a cholera outbreak in 1836. When the crisis passed she agreed, with Gabriela Echenos-Bornati, who had helped her with the nursing, to take over a house for the care of some poor and abandoned girls. Problems arose, with the result that the two women left and established a similar home, caring for girls in need and those needing health care, using methods that would now be termed holistic. The Congregation received papal approbation in 1850. When Paula was professed in 1852, along with her fellow Sisters, she took the name in religion of Sr Mary of the Crucified, but was later canonized as St Mary di Rosa. The Congregation still has an apostolate in health care, with special ministries for the poor and abandoned and those who need help.

CHARITY, INSTITUTE OF

Location: Italy (Rome)
RC (male) founded in Italy in 1828 by Antonio Rosmini-Serbati
Abbr: IC
Original habit: secular, with a black mantle.

The Order was founded at Monte Calvario, Domodossola, in northern Italy and received papal approbation in 1838. Houses were opened throughout Italy, and the work spread into France, where an orphanage run by the Institute had to be closed in 1903 because of the Association Laws, and to England, Ireland and the USA. The first American foundation was made in 1877 at Galesburg, Illinois, with a mother house at Peoria, Illinois. Every type of charitable work is undertaken by the members, who include both priests and Brothers. Emphasis is placed on preaching, the conducting of retreats and missions, teaching and care of hospitals and prisons.

✠ Fathers of Charity
  Rosminians

CHARITY, MISSIONARIES OF

Location: India (Calcutta)
RC (female) founded in India in 1946 by Mother Teresa (Agnes Bojaxhiu)
Abbr: MC
Original habit: a white and blue sari, pinned with a crucifix.

A Congregation founded by Mother Teresa in Calcutta. She had completed her noviti-ate with the Irish Loreto Sisters at Darjee-ling, India, but later left that Congregation, adopted a new style of habit, and estab-lished the Missionaries of Charity to care for the abandoned, the homeless, the dying, as well as orphans and lepers in Calcutta. The fame of her work is known worldwide. Every type of social, physical and spiritual need is met by over four thousand members of the Congregation throughout India, the USA and most of the world, through soup kitchens, shelters, nursing homes, prison ministries, hospices for the dying and a very extensive foreign mission commitment.

CHARITY, MISSIONARY BROTHERS OF

Location: USA (Los Angeles, California)
RC (male) founded in 1975 by Mother Teresa of Calcutta
Abbr: MC

An Institute founded by Mother Teresa of Calcutta in an effort to express the charism of the Missionary Sisters of Charity through the expression of traditional vows and com-munal living by men. It is both active and contemplative, with opportunities for serv-ing the poor. Communities are found worldwide.

CHARITY, SERVANTS OF

Location: Italy (Rome)
RC (male) founded in Italy in 1908 by Blessed Louis Guanella (beatified 1964)
abbr: SC

The Congregation was founded by Louis Guanella (1842–1915) at Como, Italy. He began his priestly work in 1866, in a parish where he not only taught but also became actively involved in setting up a branch of Young Catholic Action, which had been founded in 1867 to help the local poor. Opposition to his work came from anti-clericals and the Freemasons. He went to Turin to join the Salesian Order, but was recalled to parish work by his former bishop and given a small mountain parish where a home for the elderly and infirm and an orphanage had been built. Louis, feeling that this work could be usefully expanded, gained permission to remove the operation to Como. Many were attracted to test their vocations, and in 1908, after many problems, the new Congregation of the Ser-vants of Charity was founded. In 1912 Louis travelled to the USA, concerned with the well-being of migrants travelling to Amer-ica, and he made a foundation there. The work continues still, with the care of the handicapped and disabled and those in need, in some nineteen countries through-out the world. The Congregation also administers the Association of St Joseph, as a ministry for the dying.

✠ Guanellians

CHARITY, SISTERS OF

Location: England (Plympton St Maurice, Plymouth, Devon)
Anglican (female) founded in England, in 1869 by Arthur Hawkins Ward
Abbr: SC
Original habit: a black tunic with a white muslin

cap; this later became a blue-grey French peasant style gown with a black veil and cloak

The Order was founded to provide care for the needy, with Elizabeth Lloyd, later Sr Elizabeth of the Ascension, chosen to be the first superior because of her experience among the poor at All Saints, Margaret Street, in London and her ability to manage the business side of the community. The Sisters observed a Rule similar to that which St Vincent de Paul had drawn up for his Sisters of Charity in France. In 1887 a request came from the bishop of Zanzibar that some Sisters might go out to Africa to continue their work as part of the Universities Mission to Central Africa, but it was a short-lived venture for the Sisters, all of whom returned to England a few years later. The Order continues, with the daily life of the Sisters revolving around meditation, spiritual reading, daily Mass, the divine office and retreats. At present the Order maintains a retreat house in the USA, at Boulder, Nevada, as well as houses in England.

CHARITY, SISTERS OF – THE FEDERATION

There are thirteen Congregations of Sisters of Charity which make up the Federation, which has currently over 7,000 members operating in the USA and Canada, the Far East, the Caribbean, and Central and South America.

1 Sisters of Charity of Cincinnati
2 Sisters of Charity of St Elizabeth
3 Sisters of Charity of St Vincent de Paul
4 Sisters of Charity of Leavenworth
5 Sisters of Charity of Nazareth
6 Sisters of Charity of New York
7 Sisters of Charity of Seton Hill
8 Vincentian Sisters of Charity of Bedford, Ohio
9 Sisters of Charity of Our Lady of Mercy
10 Les Religieux de Notre-Dame du Sacré-Coeur
11 Sisters of Charity of the Immaculate Conception
12 Daughters of Charity of St Vincent de Paul
13 Vincentian Sisters of Charity of Pittsburgh, Pennsylvania

CHARITY, SISTERS OF – Australia

Location: Australia (Sydney, New South Wales)
RC (female) founded in Australia in 1838 by Sr Mary John Cahill and others
Abbr: SC
Original habit: a black habit, cape and veil with a white linen collar and cap.

An offshoot of the Sisters of Charity, founded in Ireland by Daniel Murray and Mary Aikenhead to train novices for work in Australia. The first five Sisters arrived in Australia in 1838 and were the first professed religious in the country. One of their number, Mary Xavier Williams, a novice, was the first woman to take her vows in Australia, which she did in Sydney in 1839. The appalling plight of the deportees and their families, and of other early settlers in a hostile environment, made their work immediately necessary in an attempt to build something of a society from this misery. The Sisters nursed the sick, relieved the suffering of women and children in prisons and undertook to teach them the catechism while the priests set about regularizing marriages. After the initial problems were dealt with, the work extended into more general education and the care of the sick and orphaned. The first free hospital was opened at Pott's Point in Sydney in 1857, and schools and colleges followed in both Sydney and Melbourne. A separate foundation was made in Hobart, Tasmania. The Congregation was granted autonomous status in 1842.

CHARITY, SISTERS OF – Cincinnati

Location: USA (Mount St Joseph, Ohio)
RC (female) founded in the USA in 1809 by St
Elizabeth Seton (canonized 1975)
Abbr: SC
Original habit: a black habit, cape and veil with a
white linen collar and cap.

The origins of this community lie in
Emmitsburg, Maryland, where Elizabeth
Seton first set up a school, the Stone House.
In 1829, four Sisters went from here to
Cincinnati, Ohio, to found a school and
establish an orphanage for girls, but by 1850
the Emmitsburg community had taken the
decision to affiliate with the French Daughters of Charity, which led seven of the
Sisters, headed by Sr Margaret George, to
leave the community. Together they formed
the Sisters of Charity of Cincinnati, in 1852.
Their apostolate involved the setting up of
a Catholic hospital in Cincinnati, along
with an orphanage. The Sisters were also
active in nursing the wounded during the
Civil War. Schools of nursing were established towards the close of the 19th century,
as well as a boarding school for the deaf
and conventional schools in the area. In
1920 the College of Mount St Joseph was
founded near Cincinnati. The work of the
Sisters today is mainly in teaching, nursing
in hospitals and running orphanages and
infant homes, but they also conduct retreats
and run chaplaincies and missions. Houses
are found throughout the USA and in four
other countries, including England. The relics of St Elizabeth Seton lie below the altar
of the provincial house of the Daughters of
Charity in Emmitsburg.

CHARITY, SISTERS OF – Halifax, Nova Scotia

Location: Canada (Halifax, Nova Scotia)
RC (female) founded in Canada in 1856 by Mother
Basilia McCann
Abbr: SC
Original habit: a black habit, cape and veil with a
white linen collar and cap.

At the request of the bishop of Halifax,
Canada, to the Sisters of Charity in New
York, four Sisters from that community
went to Canada in 1849 to sow the seeds of
a new Congregation which was founded
some seven years later by Mother Basilia
McCann, who had been a pupil of St Elizabeth Seton, the founder of the Sisters of
Charity (later called the Daughters of Charity following their affiliation with the
French Order). The Sisters were then
engaged in education, health and the social
issues of the day. Today, the Congregations
extend throughout Canada, the USA, Peru,
the Dominican Republic and Ireland, with
an apostolate in religious education, home
visiting, pastoral care and teaching. The
Sisters, many of whom are medically qualified, also work as doctors, clinical specialists
and nurses.

CHARITY, SISTERS OF – Ireland

Location: Ireland (Sandymount, Dublin)
RC (female) founded in Ireland in 1815 by Mary
Frances Aikenhead and Archbishop Daniel Murray
of Dublin
Abbr: SSC
Original habit: black habit, veil and cape, with a
white linen cap and collar.

Mary Aikenhead, a Catholic convert, and
Alicia Walsh entered the novitiate of the
Institute of the Blessed Virgin Mary at the
Bar Convent in York, England, with the
view of establishing a new Congregation in
Ireland best suited to that country's needs.
With the help of Archbishop Murray the
two women were professed in Dublin in
1815 and set about visiting the sick in the
city's hospitals. Their Rule was based on
that of St Ignatius and the Constitutions
required a long period of probation, originally five and a half years with annual vows

being taken, and a fourth vow, that of devotion of their lives to the poor, added to the usual three vows of poverty, chastity and obedience. The Congregation spread throughout Ireland, and houses were also established in England and Australia. The present-day apostolate has now been extended to include running schools, orphanages and convalescent homes, caring for the blind, the sick and the dying, rescue work, prison visiting and the rehabilitation of discharged prisoners.

CHARITY, SISTERS OF – Leavenworth

Location: USA (Kansas City, Ohio)
RC (female) founded in the USA in 1858 by Mother Xavier Ross and fourteen companions
Abbr: SCL
Original habit: a black habit, cape and veil with a white linen collar and cap

The work of the Sisters includes education at all levels from elementary school to college, health care in many hospitals and clinics, pastoral ministry in parishes and retreat centres, and foreign missions to South America. Whatever spare time the Sisters have is spent in supporting Catholic charities and involving themselves in the problems of housing those in need.

CHARITY, SISTERS OF – Nazareth

Location: USA (Nazareth, Kentucky)
RC (female) founded in Kentucky in 1812 by Catherine Spalding and John Baptist David
Abbr: SCN

John Baptist David, a Sulpician, had left his native France to work in the Maryland Missions in the United States, moving later to Bardstown, Kentucky, where he set up St Thomas' Seminary and took charge of missions which were trying to educate the local children against a background of great hardship. The need for religious women to carry on with this work, and also to nurse the sick and provide for the poor, prompted a call for help. The first three women to come forward, Catherine Spalding, Teresa Carrico and Harriet Gardiner, were soon joined by others. With advice from St Elizabeth Seton of the Daughters of St Joseph, and a copy of the Rule of St Vincent de Paul, Fr David set about training the first novices, who took their vows in 1816. A convent was built for the new Sisters, much of the work being done by the seminarians, who felled trees and built a wooden structure known as Nazareth, a name retained in the title of the Congregation. This is an active Order with simple vows whose work includes the running of retreats and summer catechetical schools, teaching, nursing, working with the mentally sick and conducting foreign missions in India and Nepal. In 1990 the Sisters were asked by the Nepalese government to help in the education of poor women from rural areas, many of whom were turning to prostitution because of poverty and ignorance. To achieve success the Sisters are now running a training programme focused on home economics and agriculture.

CHARITY, SISTERS OF – New York

Location: USA (New York, New York)
RC (female) founded in the USA (from the Congregation at Emmitsburg, Maryland) in 1809 by St Elizabeth Seton
Abbr: SC
Original habit: a black habit, cape and veil with a white linen collar and cap.

It was Bishop Connolly of New York in 1817 who requested Elizabeth Seton to send some of her Sisters to care for the needy and dependent children in his diocese. In 1847 an independent New York mother house was established, providing Roman

Catholic education at all levels. The work of this Diocesan Congregation still includes education at all levels and the running of a nurse-training school, hospitals and orphanages. Foreign missions are maintained in the Bahamas, Guatemala and Puerto Rico.

✠ Sisters of Charity of St Vincent de Paul

CHARITY, SISTERS OF – Seton Hill

Location: USA (Greensburg, Pennsylvania)
RC (female) founded in the USA in 1870
Abbr: SC
Original habit: a black habit, cape and veil with a white linen collar and cap.

The origin of the Congregation may be traced to St Elizabeth Seton and the first American community of religious women founded in 1809. The Seton Hill Congregation was started in the diocese of Pittsburgh in 1870 followed by the opening of a house at Seton Hill, in Greensburg, Pennsylvania, in 1882. Subsequent foundations were made in Arizona in 1932 and South Korea in 1960, where currently some two hundred Korean Sisters now live and work. The apostolate is concerned with education, health care and social and pastoral ministry across the USA and in Korea and Israel.

CHARITY AND CHRISTIAN INSTRUCTION, SISTERS OF – Nevers

Location: France (Paris)
RC (female) founded in France in 1680 by Dom Jean-Baptiste de Laveyne
Abbr: SCN
Original habit: a black tunic and veil with a white bonnet which has two long white linen bands reaching the chest.

A Congregation founded for the purpose of serving the poor which began at the hospital in Nevers. Its rapid progress throughout France, with the growth of hospitals, schools, orphanages and homes for the elderly, suffered setbacks at the time of the French Revolution. The Association Laws in France in the early 20th century led the Congregation to spread into Italy, Spain, Switzerland, Belgium and the UK, with more recent expansion into Japan and Africa. St Bernadette of Lourdes was a member, from 1866 to her death in 1879.

CHARITY OF JESUS AND MARY, SISTERS OF

Location: Belgium (Brussels)
RC (female) founded in Belgium in 1803 by Pierre Triest
Abbr: SCJM
Original habit: a white tunic with a black scapular surmounted by a crucifix; in choir a white linen wimple and white cowl were worn.

Pierre Triest, later titular canon of the cathedral of St Bavon, or Bavo, in Ghent, and an indefatigable founder of Orders dedicated to the relief of suffering and the education of the least fortunate in his environment, began his work while still a curate by gathering together some pious women for the purpose of running an orphanage and teaching children who were greatly in need of guidance. His attempt to amalgamate this Order with that of the Sisters of Charity of St Vincent de Paul failed, and in 1805 a small group of six Sisters from his Order took up residence in the former Cistercian abbey at Terhaegen, where they established their community. Approval by the Holy See was granted in 1816. The Congregation today aims to unite the active and contemplative lives, and the Sisters are mainly occupied in the care of the elderly. In the past they maintained many fine day and boarding schools in the UK and foreign missions in India, Sri Lanka and Africa.

CHARITY OF OUR LADY MOTHER OF MERCY, SISTERS OF

Location: The Netherlands (Hertogenbosch)
RC (female) founded in The Netherlands in 1832 by Fr John Zwijsen and Mary Leijsen
Abbr: SCMM
Original habit: a black tunic with a cincture and rosary, black veil and scapular with a white linen cap and a circular wimple and a silver neck cross.

The Congregation was originally founded by John Zwijsen, later archbishop of Utrecht, to provide Roman Catholic education. In this he was aided by Mary Leijsen. Today the Sisters work in education at all levels including teacher training, the special education of the deaf, dumb and blind and those with special needs, the care of the elderly, the infirm and orphans, and mission work among the sick and those suffering from leprosy in Paramaribo, Guyana. In their work with the blind the Sisters welcome blind women to join the Congregation, at first as Oblates of Our Lady Mother of Mercy, which became a Congregation in its own right in 1946. There is provision for the Oblates to become professed Sisters if they wish, and their experience as blind women is invaluable in the training of the blind children. The Sisters pronounce the usual three vows of poverty, chastity and obedience, with an additional vow to practise works of charity. Their foundations are worldwide, with houses in The Netherlands, Belgium, England, the USA, Africa, Germany, the former Dutch colonies, Brazil and the Philippines.

CHARITY OF OUR LADY OF EVRON, SISTERS OF

Location: France (Evron)
RC (female) founded in France in 1682 by Madame Tulard
Abbr: SCE

Original habit: a black habit and veil with a white linen coif.

The Congregation of the Sisters of Charity of Our Lady of Evron was founded at La Chapelle-au-Riboul, France, with two aims in mind, the nursing of the underprivileged sick and the education of their children. Until the time of the French Revolution there were many convents of the Order throughout France, but the Sisters were then forced to disperse. They were reunited in 1803 at the Benedictine abbey at Evron, near Mayenne. Their revised Constitutions were approved by the Holy See in 1910. There are now houses in France, England and Canada.

CHARITY OF OUR LADY OF MERCY, SISTERS OF

Location: USA (Charleston, South Carolina)
RC (female) founded in the USA in 1829 by Bishop John England
Abbr: OLM

An American Diocesan Congregation, an active Order with simple vows, which is centred in the diocese of Charleston, South Carolina, where the Sisters serve in and staff several schools and hospitals as well as providing an Hispanic ministry. They also operate the Our Lady of Mercy Community Outreach Services in John Island, South Carolina.

CHARITY OF PROVIDENCE, SISTERS OF

Location: USA (Spokane, Washington)
RC (female) founded in Canada in 1843 by Bishop Ignatius Bourget and Emilie Gamelin
Abbr: FCSP
Original habit: a black habit and veil with a white frilled under-cap, secured beneath the chin; a crucifix is worn around the neck.

When Bishop Bourget of Canada failed in his efforts to bring any French Sisters of

Charity to help in his desire to provide food and shelter for the poor in his diocese, he turned to Emilie Gamelin and her companions, who were already working in this field. They agreed to undertake the work and received the habit in the chapel of the Asylum in Montreal. The name of the Congregation owes its origin to the label 'Providences' that were given to the first houses opened. The Sisters still work with the care of the poor, both physically and spiritually, provide shelter for the young and old, visit the needy sick in their own homes and care for the homeless.

CHARITY OF ST AUGUSTINE, SISTERS OF

Location: USA (Mt Augustine, Richfield, Ohio)
RC (female) founded in the USA in 1851 by Augustinian Sisters
Abbr: CSA

At the invitation of Bishop Amadeus Rappe, first bishop of Cleveland, four Augustinian Sisters, including two postulants who received training from Ursuline Sisters already in the area, arrived from France and set about caring for the poor in their own homes. By 1852 the French Sisters, having laid the foundations of the St Joseph Hospital in what is now Cleveland, wished to return home, and the bishop found an Ursuline novice, Ursuline Dissonette, who was professed as a Sister of Charity in 1852, to carry on with the work. During the next century and a half, as the Congregation assessed its usefulness in the community, hospitals and nursing schools have been opened and staffed and education at all levels undertaken. In 1971 the mother house of this Diocesan Congregation at Mount St Augustine opened its extensive grounds for cultural and educational activities and a House of Prayer and a hermitage were erected. In 1991 the Regina Health Centre was opened, providing innovative health care and assisted-housing for geriatric members of religious Orders.

CHARITY OF ST BARTOLOMEA CAPITANIO AND ST VINCENZA GEROSA, SISTERS OF

Location: Italy (Milan)
RC (female) founded in Italy in 1832 by Sts Bartolomea Capitanio and Vincenza Gerosa (both canonized 1950)
Abbr: CS

The Congregation was founded in Lovere, Lombardy, by two saintly women. Bartolomea Capitanio was concerned about the lack of education that many young people endured and felt that she wanted to found an active Congregation to remedy this. When she met up with Vincenza Gerosa, who had already founded a hospital for the poor, they decided to unite their apostolates. The foundation of this Congregation was effected in 1832, with Bartolomea drawing up the Constitutions, but she was to die the following year. The Congregation, then under the direction of Vincenza, accepted the Rule of the Sisters of Charity under the protection of St Vincent de Paul, which had been drawn up by St Joan Antide-Thouret. The first professions were made in 1841. Today, there are some six thousand Sisters of this Congregation, living and working in India, the Americas, Africa and England, with their apostolate still in education and health care.

✠ Capitanio Sisters
Sisters of the Infant Mary

CHARITY OF ST ELIZABETH, SISTERS OF

Location: USA (Convent Station, New Jersey)
RC (female) founded in the USA in 1859 by Mother Mary Xavier Mehegan
Abbr: SC
Original habit: a grey habit with wide sleeves and a long grey apron, white cap and black veil.

The founder of the Order, Mother Mary Xavier Mehegan, had been a Sister of Charity of St Vincent de Paul in New York. This foundation was at the behest of Bishop James Roosevelt Bayley, a nephew of St Elizabeth Seton who founded the Sisters of Charity in the USA. Appalled by the lack of care facilities and opportunities for education that were available in his diocese, he urged some Sisters to help him to remedy this. A hospital, and later a school, were opened and staffed by the fast-expanding community of Sisters. Their work included teaching from elementary to college standard, administering and staffing hospitals for the incurable as well as for the aged and infirm, setting-up and running orphanages and caring for the young in nurseries. Foreign missions were also undertaken to the Virgin Islands.

CHARITY OF ST HIPPOLYTUS, FRIARS OF

Defunct
RC (male) founded in Mexico in 1585 by Bernardin Alvarez
Original habit: a light brown habit.

A community founded in 1585 by a Mexican, Bernardin Alvarez, and approved by the Holy See in 1594. The work of the Brotherhood was concerned with the care of the sick, to which end many hospitals were built.

✠ Brothers of St Hippolytus

CHARITY OF ST JOAN ANTIDE, SISTERS OF

Location: Italy (Rome)
RC (female) founded in France in 1799 by St Joan Antide-Thouret (canonized 1934)
Abbr: SCSJA, formerly SdeC
Original habit: a grey habit with a black apron and veil and a large white wimple.

A Congregation founded at Besançon in France in 1799 by St Joan Antide-Thouret, who began her religious life before the French Revolution as a member of the community of the Daughters of Charity of St Vincent de Paul, in Paris. She felt drawn to the contemplative life of a cloistered nun, but after seeing a vision of hands reaching out to her through the cloister bars, she decided to leave and seek a community that combined prayer with ministry to the poor. The advent of the French Revolution shortly afterwards closed most of the convents and dispatched the nuns to their home towns. Joan Antide, by now back in her home village near Besançon, was invited by the vicar-general of that town to begin work among the needy people in his diocese. This work she undertook, which led to the opening of a free school for girls of the area, a soup kitchen for the needy and home visits to help alleviate the suffering of the sick. Others joined her in the work, and in ten years sixty-seven houses were opened. In 1810, at the request of the mother of the Emperor Napoleon I, Madame Laetitia, who was also known as Madame Mère, Joan Antide left Besançon and went to continue her work among the impoverished in Naples. This Italian foundation was not recognized by the archbishop of Besançon, although it was approved by the Holy See, with the result that St Joan remained with the Naples Congregation. She died rather suddenly there. After her death her mission prospered not only in Europe but also in Asia, Africa and in the USA, where the Sisters went in 1932 to minister to Italian immigrants at Milwaukee, Wisconsin, at the height of the economic depression. The Congregation now has houses in some twenty-five countries. St Joan Antide was canonized in 1934 and the Congregation was given its current name. The Sisters work in prison and social ministries, in teaching, nursing and the care of the elderly.

CHARITY OF ST LOUIS, SISTERS OF – Vannes

Location: Italy (Rome)
RC (female) founded in France in 1803 by Madame Mole de Champlatreux (Mother St Louis)
Abbr: SCSL
Original habit: a black habit and apron with a black veil, and a white wimple, binder and under-veil; a large crucifix was worn at the breast with a rosary suspended at the left side of the waist.

The Congregation was founded at Vannes, in Brittany, by Madame Mole de Champlatreux, whose husband, the Comte, was guillotined in 1794 during the French Revolution. The bishop of Vannes was anxious to have a community of the Sisters of Charity in his diocese to provide education for poor girls. This was undertaken and the Congregation founded. The founder did not live to see the Constitutions approved by Rome in 1840. Unusually for the time, there was no provision for lay Sisters in this Congregation, their work being done by the Oblates of St Louis. The work undertaken by the Sisters now includes education at all levels, as well as nursing in hospitals and clinics. There are houses in France, England, the USA and Canada.

CHARITY OF ST PAUL THE APOSTLE, SISTERS OF – Chartres

Location: Italy (Rome)
RC (female) founded in France in 1704 by four women under the direction of the Abbé Louis Chauvet
Abbr: SPC
Original habit: a black habit and starched linen headdress resembling the French cornette, with a white linen wimple and a small black cross around the neck; a rosary and crucifix are worn on the left-hand side; a black cloak could be worn out of doors.

The Congregation was founded to provide education for the children of the poor country parish of Leville-le-Chenard. The venture was successful and the small community was invited to Chartres, where they were given a Rule based on that of the Daughters of Charity of St Vincent de Paul. The community stayed in the ancient convent of St Maurice until the advent of the French Revolution, which led to the dispersal of its members and the confiscation of their property. The Congregation was restored by Napoleon I and continued to spread, opening houses in Belgium, Italy, Switzerland, England and Canada, as well as throughout France. It has now extended its work to the Philippines and Thailand.

CHARITY OF ST PAUL THE APOSTLE, SISTERS OF – Selly Park

Location: England (Selly Park, Birmingham)
RC (female) founded in England in 1847 by Sisters from the Chartres Congregation (see entry above)
Abbr: SCSP

An English branch of the Order of the Sisters of Charity of St Paul the Apostle (see previous entry), which subsequently became independent of the Chartres community when, in 1847, Dr William Tandy, encouraged by Cardinal Wiseman, invited two Sisters to come from Chartres to open and run a community school at Banbury, Oxfordshire. Joined by others from Chartres and with financial assistance from their community, the Sisters were able to buy part of the Hospital of St John the Baptist, formerly St John's Priory, which had been suppressed by Henry VIII. Here they stayed until 1864, when they bought property at Selly Park in Birmingham which they dedicated to St Paul. Here the Sisters began their work of educating the poor. There are many houses in England, with three in Ireland, one in Scotland and four in South Africa. The work of the Sisters still includes education at all levels as well as nursing and community care, catechesis and parish duties, social work and guild and club activities. There is a postulancy of six months followed by a novitiate of one year at Selly Park, then six years under temporary profession leading to a final profession for life.

CHARITY OF ST VINCENT DE PAUL, DAUGHTERS OF

Location: France (Paris)
RC (female) founded in France in 1633 by St Vincent de Paul (canonized 1737) and St Louise de Marillac de Gras (canonized 1934)
Abbr: DC
Original habit: a 17th-century French peasant's dress in blue-grey, with an apron and a linen collar; the headdress was a white cornette with wings (the Sisters were familiarly known as Butterfly Nuns); a rosary and crucifix were suspended from the waist.

A Society of Apostolic Life in Community. The Congregation evolved from the Confraternity of Charity, also known as the Dames de Charité, whose members lived in the world and undertook charitable works among the sick and poor in their own homes, usually by offering the help of their servants. St Vincent de Paul, seeing an enthusiasm for the same work among the peasant girls who were precluded because of their lowly social status from joining the Dames de Charité, formed a community of the Sisters of Charity which he put under the direction of Louise de Marillac, whose position in life bridged the gap between the Dames and the lower-born women, for she was the illegitimate daughter of a nobleman. The initial apostolate was to accompany the Dames on their charitable errands, but as numbers expanded, so too did the scope of their work. Initially, four young women underwent training in the home of Louise de Marillac, but as others came forward to join, larger premises had to be found. In 1655 St Vincent drew up a Rule and Constitutions for the Congregation, which was approved in 1668. Members of the community retain their family name but take that of a saint as their first name. Their vows of poverty, chastity and obedience, with a fourth one of charity, are taken annually. The communities are now worldwide, and the members are involved in every type of work. Accepting no boundaries, the Sisters are active in their work with AIDS victims, drug addicts, and the care of the physically handicapped and those needing rehabilitation. They also run schools and centres for the blind, the deaf and the dumb, for abandoned children and for the illiterate, organize refugee camps and run soup kitchens where there is need.

CHARITY OF THE BLESSED VIRGIN MARY, ORDER OF

A defunct Order of Augustinian nuns founded in 1290 and confirmed by Popes Boniface VIII and Clement VI. Their habit was Augustinian in style.

CHARITY OF THE BLESSED VIRGIN MARY, SISTERS OF

Location: USA (Dubuque, Iowa)
RC (female) founded in the USA in 1833 by Fr T. Donoghue and Mother Mary Frances Clarke.
Abbr: BVM

The Order began in Dublin, Ireland, in 1831 as a Congregation of five young Irishwomen who undertook the education of children and opened a school for this purpose. Needing a greater challenge and the chance to dedicate their lives to what they saw as a more urgent need for their services, the five women sailed for America in 1833, heading for Philadelphia. Their cause was treated sympathetically by the archbishop of Philadelphia and permission was granted for the opening of a school where the Irishwomen could work as teachers. In 1843 they moved to Dubuque, Iowa, at the urgent request of the bishop at a time of violent anti-Roman Catholic action, with churches and convents being attacked. The boarding school which they started at Dubuque, for the education of girls, later went on to become Clarke College. Further schools were set up along the Upper Mississippi valley in Iowa and further west. The work of the Sisters continues today and they are concerned with running schools, a senior college (in Dubuque) and a college in Chicago, Illinois, as well as pastoral work, which includes concern for handicapped children and adults, drug addicts, the elderly, the homeless and those afflicted with AIDS

♱ Blessed Virgin Mary Sisters
  BVM Sisters

CHARITY OF THE IMMACULATE CONCEPTION, SISTERS OF

Location: Canada (St John, New Brunswick)
RC (female) founded in Canada in 1854 by Honora Conway (Sr Mary Vincent) and Bishop Thomas Connelly

The Congregation came into existence following a visit to the Sisters of Charity in New York by the bishop of St John, New Brunswick, when he requested that a daughter foundation might be set up in Canada. Sr Mary Vincent and four other Sisters went to Canada and set up a house at St John. Both Sr Mary Vincent and Bishop Thomas Connelly are regarded as the co-founders of this Congregation.

CHARITY OF THE INCARNATE WORD, SISTERS OF – Houston

Location: USA (Houston, Texas)
RC (female) founded in the USA in 1866 by Claude Marie Dubuis
Abbr: CCVI
Original habit: a black tunic and scapular, which bore an embroidered crown of thorns in red silk,

and a black outer veil over a white cap and wimple.

The urgent need for nursing care in the early days of Texan history led to the formation of this American community. The first Sisters to join were recruited from France, where they had been members of the Community of the Incarnate Word and Blessed Sacrament, in Lyons, experienced in nursing and the care of the needy and dying. They brought with them the Constitutions of that Order, which were adapted to their new needs. The first hospital was opened at Galveston in 1867 and the headquarters was in the same city. Other foundations in Texas followed, in Houston (see next entry), Beaumont and Temple. By the start of the 20th century there were foundations throughout the USA. An Irish house, in County Clare, was opened in 1925, in which year the mother house was transferred from Galveston to Houston, where there is now a convent, a convalescent home and a *Ruah*, which serves as a centre of spirituality for those seeking a retreat. Sisters from the community have continued their work in Guatemala, El Salvador and Kenya, where a novitiate was established at Nairobi in 1993.

CHARITY OF THE INCARNATE WORD, SISTERS OF – San Antonio

See previous entry. This Congregation was seeded from the Houston foundation and is independent. The habit was almost identical, except that the under-veil and wimple were not starched and a crucifix was worn on the left-hand side.

The San Antonio Congregation was founded in 1869 and has foundations in the USA, Mexico and Peru. The Sisters are involved in education and nursing, with one of their earliest foundations being that of the Santa Rosa hospital in San Antonio.

CHARITY OF THE MOST PRECIOUS BLOOD, DAUGHTERS OF

Location: Italy (Rome)
RC (male) founded in Italy in 1872
Abbr: DCPB

A Congregation founded at Pagani, Italy, from which an American foundation was made in Connecticut in 1908. The Sisters work in the care of the young, the elderly and the sick and also maintain missions in Brazil, Nigeria and India. The Congregation has retained a presence in Italy.

CHARITY OF THE SACRED HEART OF JESUS, DAUGHTERS OF

Location: France (Montgeron)
RC (female) founded in France in 1823 by Fr Jean-Maurice Coutroux and Rose Giet (Mother Marie)
Abbr: FCSCJ

The Congregation of the Daughters of Charity of the Sacred Heart was founded at La Salle de Vihiers, France, to provide teaching and nursing for those in need. Following the Association Laws in France at the beginning of the 20th century, a foundation was made in 1905 in the USA, at Newport, Vermont. At present the Sisters are to be found in France, the USA and Canada, South Africa and several African countries as well as Madagascar, Tahiti and Brazil. They provide day care for children and adults, staff schools from elementary to secondary level and undertake work in catechesis, care for the aged, hold retreats and give spiritual direction.

CHARLES BORROMEO, MISSIONARIES OF ST

Location: Italy (Rome)
RC (male) founded in Italy in 1887 by Blessed John Baptist Scalabrini (beatified 1997)
Abbr: CS

Bishop Scalabrini, distressed at the plight of so many Italian immigrants leaving Milan for the United States, many of them without having made adequate preparation for their new life, was encouraged to establish the Christopher Columbus Apostolic Institution, to provide care and advice. The Congregation was founded in Milan in 1887 and approved in 1888. In time the name was changed to the present one, the Missionaries of St Charles (Borromeo), and the work was extended to the United States and South America, where support could be given to recent arrivals. A further Congregation, the Society of St Raphael, was founded in New York, staffed by two priests and one lay Brother, with five other priests and three lay Brothers going to Brazil to undertake similar work there. Female immigrants were cared for at St Raphael's by the Pallottine Sisters. The Missionaries then began to establish Italian parishes and schools wherever the immigrants settled. In the USA today the Congregation is to be found in two provinces, one based in Oak Park, Illinois, the other in New York City, and further foundations have been made in Mexico, Haiti and some South American countries. The work is still heavily committed to the care of immigrants and with the provision of homes for the elderly, seminaries and seamen's clubs.

✠ Missionaries of St Charles
  Pious Society of the Missionaries of St Charles
  Scalabrini Fathers
  Scalabrinians

CHARLES BORROMEO, MISSIONARY SISTERS OF ST

Location: Italy (Rome)
RC (female) founded in Italy in 1895 by Blessed John Baptist Scalabrini (beatified 1997)
Abbr: MSCS (or MSSCB)

Several years after he had founded the Missionaries of St Charles Borromeo for men, Bishop Scalabrini established a similar foundation for women. The Sisters undertake missionary work in over twenty countries worldwide. Their European and American work is concerned with service to immigrants, migrants and refugees. They provide catechesis, education, pastoral care for the sick and social service advice to newcomers into a country.

✠ Scalabrini Sisters

CHRIST FOR POLISH EMIGRANTS, SOCIETY OF

Location: Poland (Poznan)
RC (male) founded in Poland in 1932 by Fr Ignacy Posadzy
Abbr: SChr (or TChr)
Original habit: secular style.

The Congregation was founded in Poznan, Poland, and approved in 1964, to provide care for Polish emigrants leaving to begin new lives in other countries and to help them to settle into their new homes. It is represented throughout the USA and Canada, with some houses in the UK. The members have the care of many parishes and pastoral centres and also aim to care for Polish families through ethnic radio programmes and other media apostolates.

CHRIST, MISSIONARY SERVANTS OF

Location: USA (Ocean City, Maryland)
RC (male) founded in the USA in 1979 by Brother Edwin Baker
Abbr: MSC

A Diocesan Institute founded by Edwin Baker with a view to forming a community of men under vows who would be willing to work with the poor and the elderly. The Brothers also work in the maintenance of church buildings, raise funds for the parishes and undertake catechesis.

CHRIST, ORDER OF

Location: Italy (Rome)
RC (Equestrian Order) a papal award; founded in 1319 with the approbation of Pope John XXII

This present-day Papal Order of Knighthood's provenance is derived from the Order of Christ the King and as the highest of the Pontifical Orders it is reserved for Christian heads of state.

CHRIST JESUS, MISSIONARIES OF

Location: Spain (Madrid)
RC (female) founded in Spain in 1944 by Maria Camino Sanz Orrio (1896–1991)

A Congregation of missionary Sisters whose work is concerned with the care of the poor, the sick and those in need of catechesis. They are to be found in Spain, Japan, India, the Philippines, throughout South America and in Zaire.

CHRIST THE KING, KNIGHTS OF

Defunct
RC (male Equestrian Order) founded in Portugal in 1318 by King Diniz
Original habit: a white mantle, or cloak, with a double cross in red and silver.

The Order was Instituted by King Diniz for defence against the Moors and to curtail the growing influence in Portugal of the Order of St John following the dissolution of the Knights Templar in 1312. By 1321 there were nearly one hundred knights and other brethren in the new Order. At the beginning of the 15th century, Henry the Navigator became the grand master and the Order flourished under his control, becoming a foremost maritime power and colonizing Madeira and the Canaries, the Azores and parts of the west coast of Africa. The explorer Vasco da Gama was a knight of the Order when, in 1499, he sailed to India by way of the Cape of Good Hope. The

Order later declined in importance, and by the early 16th century lax practices had crept in, even allowing the brethren to marry. An effort at reform was made and the Order continued into the 19th century before becoming defunct.

CHRIST THE KING, MISSIONARY SISTERS OF

Location: Canada (Ville de Laval, Quebec)
RC (female) founded in Canada in 1928 by Mgr F. X. Ross
Original habit: a black tunic with a large white wimple and cap and a black outer veil; a crucifix was worn around the neck; on missions the habit was entirely white.

The Congregation was founded by Mgr Ross, bishop of Gaspe within the archdiocese of Rimouski, for the purpose of spreading the Christian message, especially in pagan countries. The members of the community also participate in social, educational and health care work. There are houses in Canada, Japan, Africa and India.

CHRIST THE KING, MISSIONARY SISTERS OF

Location: Poland (Poznan)
RC (female) founded in Poland in 1959 by Fr Ignacy Posadzy
Abbr: MSCK

This growing Diocesan Congregation was founded in Poland and went to the USA and Canada in 1978. The work of the Sisters is to help Polish immigrants and to try to keep alive the Polish culture wherever there are Polish communities.

CHRIST THE KING, SCHOOL SISTERS OF

Location: USA (Lincoln, Nebraska)
RC (female) founded in the USA in 1976
Abbr: CK

A Public Association whose members live in community under vows of poverty, chastity and obedience and whose work is largely educational. There is a deep foundation of prayer and a special devotion to the Blessed Sacrament, the Passion and Our Lady.

CHRIST THE KING, SERVANTS OF

Defunct
Anglican (male) founded in England in 1919 by Joseph Gardner
Original habit: a grey tunic, scapular, hood and girdle, Benedictine in style.

The Congregation of the Servants of Christ the King was founded by Brother Joseph Gardner at Staithes, near Whitby, in Yorkshire. The work of the community was to care for mentally defective boys. Always ultramontane, with a crown resting on top of the tabernacle and the sacrament reserved as a symbol of their devotion to Christ the King, the whole community converted to Rome in 1936 and the members became Benedictine Oblates but were allowed to retain their habit. The Brothers continued in their work, but vocations failed to appear and the Congregation was disbanded

CHRIST THE KING, SISTER-SERVANTS OF

Defunct
RC (female) founded in the USA in 1936

An active Order with simple vows, now defunct. The work undertaken was entirely that of domestic service.

CHRISTA SEVA SANGHA

Defunct
Anglican (male) founded in India in 1922

The Christa Seva Sangha was a Franciscan-type community of laymen and clergy attempting to adapt an Indian lifestyle and worship to the more traditional Anglo-Roman Catholic framework of worship, and as such was an early attempt at inculturation. A novice, Fr Algy (W. S. A.) Robertson, who joined the Poona Community in 1929, was forced by ill-health to return to the UK, where he started an English branch of the Christa Seva Sangha at St Ives in Huntingdonshire. The community was known as the Brotherhood of the Love of Christ. In India, the Congregation maintained an orphanage and dispensary as well as providing social and educational support for those in need, but it is now defunct.

CHRISTIAN BROTHERS

Location: Italy (Rome)
RC (male) founded in Ireland in 1802 by Edmund Ignatius Rice
Abbr: CFC
Original habit: a black soutane and cincture with a clerical collar.

Edmund Ignatius Rice, who as a young widower had been interested in joining a contemplative Order such as the Augustinians, where his brother was already a member, turned instead to a more active expression of his vocation when he was encouraged to open a school house at Mount Sion, Ireland. Others joined him in his work and foundations followed in Waterford and Tipperary. The Rule was a modification of that observed by the Presentation Sisters, and the Congregation was then known as the Society of the Presentation, but in 1817, with a change of Rule, they became known as the Irish Christian Brothers. The Constitutions were approved in 1820. The various communities later united, except for that at Cork City. This community, under Austin Reardon, led later to the establishment of the Presentation Brothers. The work of the Christian Brothers is almost entirely educational, at all levels from primary to vocational, and extends to the care and training of the deaf, blind and dumb, as well as the running of orphanages and residential care institutions.

The Brothers also work with the homeless and unemployed. Foundations have been made in the USA (1906), Australia, New Zealand, Canada, Gibraltar, India, South America and the UK.

✝ Brothers of the Christian Schools in Ireland

CHRISTIAN CHARITY OF THE BLESSED VIRGIN MARY, SISTERS OF

Location: Italy (Rome)
RC (female) founded in Germany in 1849 by Pauline von Mallinckrodt
Abbr: SCC

Pauline von Mallinckrodt, the daughter of an evangelical father and a Roman Catholic mother, and sister of the political leader Herman von Mallinckrodt, spent much of her early working life caring for the blind in her native Paderborn, and she founded an Institute for their care. Her efforts to put her Institute under the care of the Society of the Sacred Heart of Jesus took her to Paris, where she sought the help of Sr (later St) Mary-Magdalen Sophie Barat, but the Prussian government refused permission for a French Congregation to be established in Prussia. This action provoked her to form her own Congregation at Paderborn in 1849, and she became its first superior. Political troubles in Prussia forced the Institute abroad, initially to New Orleans in 1873, where a community and school were established. Other foundations followed throughout America, ranging from colleges, schools and orphanages to vocational training centres. The Sisters work in education, catechesis, nursing and the care of children and the elderly. They also conduct retreats and have a special ministry to native American Indians.

✝ Daughters of the Blessed Virgin Mary of the Immaculate Conception
Sisters of Christian Charity

CHRISTIAN DOCTRINE, FATHERS OF
Two Orders at least have shared this name:

1 FATHERS OF CHRISTIAN DOCTRINE (extant)

Location: Italy (Rome)
RC (male) founded in Italy in 1592 by the
Venerable Cesar de Bus
Abbr: DC

After a self-indulgent past, Cesar de Bus took up studies for the priesthood and devoted himself to works of charity, preaching and catechesis. He founded a Congregation of priests, the Fathers of Christian Doctrine, whose members taught and worked in these fields, papal approval being granted in 1597. The Congregation at times seemed to fluctuate between being a religious Order and a secular organization, in which members made no vows and did not observe a precise Rule of life. Cesar de Bus also founded the Daughters of Christian Doctrine.

2 FATHERS OF CHRISTIAN DOCTRINE (defunct)

RC (male) founded in Italy in 1560 by Marco de
Sadis-Cusani

The Congregation was founded in Milan, Italy, by Marco de Sadis-Cusani, who may have been a disciple of St Philip Neri, for the purpose of teaching both children and adults, instructing them in Christian doctrine. Pope Pius IV gave them the use of the church of St Apollinaire as their headquarters. The work was carried out in the streets and in private houses and it spread from Italy to France and Germany. Associated with this Congregation was the Confraternity of Christian Doctrine (founded 1562), which was open for the laity to join. In a Bull of 1571, Pope St Pius V urged his bishops to establish these confraternities in every diocese.

✠ Doctrinarians
  Priests of Christian Doctrine

CHRISTIAN DOCTRINE, SISTERS OF

Location: France (Nancy)
RC (female) founded in France in 1718 by the Duke
of Lorraine and Fr Jean-Baptiste Vatelot.

Three Congregations shared this name at some time, two of which have become defunct, with only the one surviving. The defunct Congregations were those of Meyruis, which was founded in France in 1837, and Montpellier, founded in France in 1853. Neither of these Congregations survived the effects of the French Association Laws at the start of the 20th century. The only Congregation of Sisters of Christian Doctrine to survive was that of the Vatelottes, named after Fr Vatelot, one of the founders. The Sisters are largely concerned with health care and nursing, but they also teach and bring catechesis to both children and adults.

✠ Vatelottes

CHRISTIAN EDUCATION, RELIGIOUS OF

Location: France (Saint-Maur)
RC (female) founded in France in 1817 by Louis
Lafosse and Marie-Anne Dutertre
Abbr: RCE
Original habit: a black habit; choir Sisters wore a black habit and cape and had a small cloth heart embroidered with the lily of St Joseph and the Sacred Hearts of Jesus and Mary attached at the breast; lay and co-adjutor Sisters wore a black shawl over the habit instead of the cape.

The founders of the Institute, the Abbé Louis Lafosse and Marie-Anne Dutertre, together with three companions, opened their first house at Echauffor in Normandy in 1817, with a second house at Argentan in 1818, with the aim of educating girls. Diocesan approval was granted in 1821.

Following troubles in France with the implementation of the Association Laws at the turn of the 20th century, which removed education from the hands of the Church and the religious Orders and Congregations, the Sisters moved to England and opened a school at Farnborough, in Hampshire, which still exists although it is no longer administered by the Sisters. The school is housed in the former mansion of the Empress Eugénie of France, the widow of Napoleon III, who spent the last part of her life in Farnborough and is buried, together with her husband and son, the Prince Imperial, at St Michael's Abbey, a Benedictine house close to her home in Farnborough. Later foundations, including many schools, were made in Belgium, Ireland and the USA, with missions to Benin, Peru and South America.

✠ De La Mennais Brothers

CHRISTIAN INSTRUCTION, BROTHERS OF – St Gabriel

Location: Italy (Rome)
RC (male) founded in France in (possibly) 1585 by Cesar Bianchetti or (probably) in 1705 by St Louis Grignon de Montfort (cannonised 1947)
Abbr: SG
Original habit: a black cassock.

Some claim that this foundation dates from 1585, when Cesar Bianchetti established a house at Boulogne, France, but it is more generally thought that the Congregation was founded at Saint-Laurent-sur-Sèvre, France, by St Louis Grignon de Montfort, in 1705. The present Congregation arose from the union of the Brothers of the Holy Ghost with another Congregation in 1821. Progress was rapid throughout France and Germany, but in 1853 some of the members formed an independent Institute to be known as the Brothers of St Gabriel, the name possibly taken from a small chapel at

Boulogne which the Brothers had used and which was dedicated to St Gabriel. The new Institute was concerned solely with education, and approbation was granted in 1910. The work, which includes the running of technical schools and agricultural training centres, spread to Canada and encompassed the training and education of children and young people with special problems, particularly the blind, deaf and dumb. The Brothers take no vows, but they make a long novitiate and take a promise of obedience

CHRISTIAN INSTRUCTION, SISTERS OF

Location: France (Redon)
RC (female) founded in France in 1807 by Gabriel Deshayes and Michelle Guillaume
Abbr: SCI
Original habit: a black tunic and white bonnet without a veil, and a large crucifix around the neck; for chapel and outside wear there was a black, hooded cloak.

After the French Revolution, which had forced the closure of many religious houses and scattered their members, the Abbé Deshayes encouraged Michelle Guillaume to undertake the education of the children in the area. Together with five other women she formed a religious community in 1820. To house the community, the Sisters were given the old Benedictine abbey of St Gildas-des-Bois, near Redon. The work expanded to include nursing, especially of the poor in their own homes. The Association Laws at the start of the 20th century in France forced the Sisters either to become laicized or to go into exile. They went to England and are still working there. The Sisters maintain a presence in France and throughout Europe, with missions to Africa.

✠ Sisters of St Gildas

CHRISTIAN INSTRUCTION, SISTERS OF – Flone-lez-Amay

Location: France (Amay)
RC (female) founded in Belgium in 1823 by Mother Agatha Verhelle
Abbr: RCI.
Original habit: choir Sisters wore a black dress and shawl with a white muslin cap, frilled at the edge, and a black veil; lay Sisters wore the same habit but with a pleated cap and an apron.

Mother Agatha Verhelle, and four other women, were given permission to occupy the vacant Bernardine abbey at Dooresele, near Ghent in Belgium. Here they lived and worked, concentrating on the education of girls. The Constitutions and Rule are based on those of St Ignatius and were approved in 1827. The Congregation spread to England in 1891, with the opening of schools for girls.

✟ Religious of Christian Instruction of Ghent

CHRISTIAN INSTRUCTION OF PLOERMEL, BROTHERS OF

Location: Italy (Rome)
RC (male) founded in France in 1817 by Jean-Marie-Robert de La Mennais
Abbr: FICP or FIC.
Original habit: a black cassock, buttoned to the hem, with a short black mantle and a copper crucifix.

The lack of local schools for the poor children of Saint-Brieuc in Brittany encouraged the Abbé de La Mennais to remedy the situation. His aim was to provide teachers who could run small, local schools. Education at this time was mainly in the hands of the De La Salle Institute, whose Rule obliged members to live in communities of not less than three, which would not allow them to supply trained teachers to what in many cases were single-teacher schools. The

Brothers took simple vows. Approbation was granted in 1891 and foundations were made throughout France and in the UK, the USA, Africa, Asia, South America, the West Indies and Oceania.

CHRISTIAN RETREAT, SISTERS OF

Location: France (Le Russey)
RC (female) founded in France in 1789 by Abbé Antoine-Silvestre Receveur
Abbr: CR
Original habit: a cream serge tunic, cape and scapular and a white cap which was worn in place of a veil; a crucifix was worn at the breast and a large rosary at the waist; the outdoor habit was black, with a black cloak.

The work of the Order is in teaching, at both primary and secondary level, and the conducting of retreats. Established in troubled times because of the French Revolution and its aftermath, the Sisters were forced for the sake of safety more than once to go into exile, and they established houses in Switzerland, Belgium and England as well as France. An unusual custom with this Order was that at midnight a bell was rung to arouse the Sisters to thank God for their vocations, and on November 19th each year a special midnight service was held in memory of their entry at midnight into their first convent. A spiritual service is held daily, called the Adoration of the Cross, because their founder had a great devotion to the cross and declared 'it is a cross to be without one'.

CHRISTIAN SCHOOLS, BROTHERS OF THE

Location: Italy (Rome)
RC (male) founded in France in 1680 by St Jean Baptist de la Salle (canonized 1900)
Abbr: FSC
Original habit: a black tunic with a white collar, which had two wide, hanging white linen bands, and cloak with a black and wide-brimmed hat.

A member of a wealthy Reims family, Jean Baptist de la Salle rose to be a canon of the cathedral in that city. His friendship with a minim priest, Nicolas Barre, who had founded a teaching Order of nuns known as the Dames de Saint Maur, persuaded him that there was a great need for an appropriate education for the poor, and with the help of a friend, Adrian Nyel, he opened the first free school. The movement grew as they were joined by other interested teachers, and the members formed themselves into the Brothers of the Christian Schools, with the revolutionary idea, for the times, of teaching in French rather than the more usual Latin, which had served to limit education to the families of the wealthy. Sunday schools were also established, bringing knowledge and training to many of the poor. A training college, with its own novitiate, was opened to provide staff for the schools, which achieved such a reputation for excellence that they were able to survive suppression at the time of the French Revolution, being allowed to reopen again in 1801. The De La Salle Brothers now have foundations throughout Europe, Asia, Africa, Australia, New Zealand and the USA.

✠ De La Salle Brothers

CHRISTIAN SCHOOLS, SISTERS OF THE

Defunct
RC (female) founded in France in 1698 by Jacques-Nicolas Colbert

The Congregation was founded, because of falling standards in clerical education, by Jacques-Nicolas Colbert, archbishop of Rouen, France, who achieved some adverse publicity because of suspected Jansenism. The Sisters were concerned with teaching and caring for the sick in their own homes.

✠ Bonnes Capotes
  Hospitallers of Ernemont

CHRISTIAN VIRGINS, INSTITUTE OF

Defunct
RC (female) founded in China in 1782 by Blessed John Martin Moye (beatified 1954)
Original habit: no distinctive habit was worn.

Blessed John Martin Moye (1730–93) was the founder not only of this Institute, but of the Sisters of Divine Providence (founded 1762). Part of his life was spent as a missionary in China, for which he volunteered in 1771 and was posted to Macao. Here, despite serious problems in adjusting to the Chinese culture, he managed to form the Institute of Christian Virgins, to care for the sick and to provide instruction to mothers and their children in their own homes. He encountered many difficulties in China, and this precipitated his return to Europe in 1784.

CHURCH, SISTERS OF THE

Location: England (Richmond, Surrey)
Anglican (female) founded in London in 1870 by Emily Ayckbowm
Abbr: CSC
Original habit: a black tunic and veil with a square white linen collar; a crucifix is attached to the girdle.

The growing plight of the poor in London in the mid-19th century gave rise to many efforts to improve their lot in practical ways. Emily Ayckbowm came to London to run a Sunday school for the children of the streets, where they were given their catechism and some practical skills as well as hot tea and buns, to make their existence a little easier. By 1870, having attracted others to the cause, the first community was established, with Emily as the first novice. The Sisters initially cared for the sick and the poor of the parish, but this soon grew until they were also running convalescent homes and rest houses throughout the country. More houses were established overseas, in Canada, India and Australia, New Zealand, Burma and South Africa, where teaching was the main work. The Rule was composed by Mother Ayckbowm. Today the Sisters also conduct retreats and run workshops and chaplaincies.

CISTERCIANS (ANGLICAN)

An Anglican Cistercian foundation was made in England at Ewell Monastery, West Malling, Kent in 1966 by Fr Aelred Arnesan and was recognized by the Church of England in 1977. The Rule is based on that of St Benedict, modified according to the Cistercian reform. This is a small community in spiritual affiliation with the Cistercian order. The abbreviation is OCist. For details of the Cistercian Order, see the following entries.

CISTERCIANS (ROMAN CATHOLIC)

Cistercians are members of either the Sacred Order of Cistercians (O.Cist), or the Cistercian Order of the Strict Observance (OCSO). There are Congregations of Cistercians, both male (monks) and female (nuns). The following general notes apply across the Congregations.
Habit: Monks wear a white tunic with a black scapular, with a leather belt buckled over the scapular; a white cowl is worn in chapel. In pre-Second Vatican Council days the habit for a lay Brother was brown with a white cloak, but lay Brother status has now been discontinued and all members profess as monks. Nuns wear a white tunic with a black veil and scapular and an unstarched linen headband and wimple; a leather girdle is worn outside the scapular; a white woollen cowl with wide sleeves is worn in chapel. Lay Sisters, now largely discontinued, would wear a brown habit with a white cloak. Trappist and Trappistine: these are popular expressions which respectively describe the male and female

members of the Order of Cistercians of the Strict Observance.

CISTERCIANS, ORDER OF (MONKS)

Location: Italy (Rome)
RC (male) founded in France in 1098 by Sts Robert of Molesme (canonized 1222), Alberic and Stephen Harding (canonized 1623)
Abbr: OCist
Original habit: see general notes above.

The Order began with the desire for reform of growing laxity within the Benedictine Order and a wish to return to an earlier, more ascetic way of life which would include manual labour and a stricter form of poverty. Robert of Molesme and some other monks went to Cîteaux to establish their new community. Some of the monks, including Robert, who had been abbot at Cîteaux, later returned to Molesme on the order of the pope, and Alberic continued as abbot. Lay Brothers were introduced to handle the material affairs of the monastery. With Alberic's death, in 1109, the Englishman Stephen Harding became abbot and wrote the Charter of Charity, which detailed the life of Cîteaux, and insisted that the Rule of St Benedict was to be observed with provision for regular visitations to ensure that this was correctly maintained. This charter was approved by Pope Gelasius II in 1119. St Bernard of Clairvaux had entered the Congregation at Cîteaux with some thirty of his friends and relatives in 1113, and in 1115 he became the founding abbot at Clairvaux. Through his efforts the Cistercian Order saw phenomenal growth throughout Europe and into the wider world by the end of the Middle Ages. With its growth of influence within the Church and its economic importance there was an inevitable decline in spiritual vigour, and attempts at another reform arose, leading to the founding of the Cistercians of the Strict Observance (see below).

CISTERCIANS, ORDER OF (NUNS)

Location: Italy (Rome)
RC (female) founded in France in 1125 by
Benedictine nuns aided by St Stephen Harding
Abbr: OCist
Original habit: see general notes above.

The first Cistercian nuns were usually Benedictines who had accepted many of the reforms that Cîteaux represented, and some were actual sisters of the Cistercian monks. The first foundation was made in 1125 by Benedictine Sisters from the monastery at Juilly, in the diocese of Langres, France, with the help of St Stephen Harding. Many other European foundations followed. As with the Cistercian monks, certain lax practices slowly crept in and reforms were attempted. Following the French Revolution, during which the nuns became scattered when the religious houses were closed, Dom Augustine de Lestrange, a monk of La Trappe, reassembled many of the Cistercian Sisters and they went to a Trappistine convent of the Cistercians of the Strict Obervance in Valais in Switzerland, where they lived the austere life. Houses were again founded in France as well as in many other European countries. An English house was opened at Wimborne, Dorset, in 1801 and one in Ireland, at Glencairn, Wicklow, in 1932. The English nuns moved from Dorset in 1989 and eventually settled in Whitland, South Wales, while the Glencairn foundation established a monastery in the USA at Wrentham, Massachusetts, in 1949, from which further daughter foundations have been made. The approval of the Constitutions in 1925 brought the Trappistines into full membership of the Trappist Order, although the nuns retain their autonomous Rule. The daily life is similar to that of the monks but with less hard, manual work undertaken. Today there are houses throughout Europe, the USA, Canada and Japan.

CISTERCIANS OF THE STRICT OBSERVANCE

Location: Italy (Rome)
RC (male) founded in France in 1682 by Armand
Jean Le Bouthillier de Rancé
Abbr: OCSO
Original habit: see general notes above.

The Congregation was founded at the abbey of Notre Dame de la Trappe, giving the alternative name of Trappists for monks, or Trappistines for the nuns, to Cistercians who chose to move away from the main Cistercian Order when they perceived a growing lack of austerity in their monasteries. The French Revolution caused the Trappists to leave France and open houses in Switzerland and Germany. They returned to France in 1814. In 1892 three separate Orders which had accepted the reforms of La Trappe were united to form a single, autonomous Order called the Order of Reformed Cistercians of Our Lady of La Trappe, which is now known as the Order of Cistercians of the Strict Observance. Their austere practices, including the Rule of Silence, were relaxed following Vatican II, but the daily life of the monks is hard. Fish and eggs have been added to the previously vegetarian diet, with meat allowed for the sick and for visitors. Cistercian monks are now found throughout the world.

✠ Trappists
Trappistines

CLARETIAN FATHERS

Location: Italy (Rome)
RC (male) founded in Spain in 1849 by St Anthony
Mary Claret (canonized 1950)
Abbr: CMF
Original habit: secular clerical dress with a short cape and fringed sash; Lay Brothers had the same dress but with an unfringed sash.

Although drawn to a religious life and contemplating joining the Carthusians or Jesuits, Anthony Claret (1807–70) suffered from too much ill-health for this to be possible. Ordained as a priest in 1835, and with a great devotion to the Heart of Mary, he was one of the first to see how the media could be harnessed to achieve his aim of spreading devotion to the Virgin Mary. A man of acknowledged spirituality and devotion, who survived several attempts on his life, he was appointed archbishop of Santiago in Cuba in 1852 at the young age of forty-five years. He left Cuba in 1857 and returned to Spain to be confessor to Queen Isabella II and was a strenuous defender of papal infallibility at the First Vatican Council in 1870. His involvement in printing and publishing led to the establishment of lay societies whose members still participate in the writing and publishing of relevant material and maintain libraries. There is also a Secular Institute for women, the Daughters of the Most Holy Heart of Mary. Claretians are expected to have a special devotion to the Immaculate Heart of Mary and to the pope and to pursue an active apostolate in the media. There are houses in Europe, Asia, Africa and the Americas.

✠ Missionary Sons of the Immaculate Heart of Mary

CLERKS REGULAR

Roman Catholic clergy who live in community, under religious vows, while engaging in pastoral work. Dating from the 16th century in Europe they embraced the ordered, disciplined life of the religious. Clerks regular must not be confused with monks and other religious. They can be distinguished in four ways:

1 They devote their lives to the sacred ministry.

2 They are obliged to cultivate the sacred sciences.
3 They wear clerical dress and not a monastic habit.
4 The life is less austere.

See under the following entries:

Camillans, Order of St
Jesuits, Society of
Marian Fathers of the Immaculate Conception of the Blessed Virgin Mary, Congregation of the
Mother of God, Clerks Regular of the
Piarist Fathers
Somasca, Clerks Regular of
Theatine Fathers

CLOTHILDE, SISTERS OF ST

Location: France (Paris)
RC (female) founded in France in 1821 by Sophie Antoinette Aubrey-Desfontaines (Mother Marie-Thérèse)
Abbr: SC
Original habit: a black dress with a white linen collar, a black veil and cape with a cap which had crimped edges.

Sophie Aubrey-Desfontaines had been a member of a religious community which was dispersed at the time of the French Revolution. Through her friendship with Jean Baptiste Rauzan, founder of the Fathers of Mercy, she was encouraged to found a community with an apostolate for the education of girls. The French Laws of Association at the start of the 20th century, which precluded religious communities from running schools, drove the Sisters to England, where they continued their work in education, bringing a distinctive style of their own in that the Sisters and pupils shared their domestic life instead of the more usual separate arrangement. The school they opened was at Lechlade, in Gloucestershire, in a house which had been a gift from Henry VIII to his first wife, Catherine of Aragon, and later belonged to Catherine Parr, his widow. The community has now returned to France.

CLUNY, ORDER OF (MONKS)

Defunct
RC (male) founded in France in 909 by Duke William of Aquitaine
Original habit: a black tunic, scapular and wide-sleeved cowl with hood and girdle.

Duke William of Aquitaine, who founded and built the abbey of Cluny, in Burgundy, a model of reformed monasticism, placed at its head St Berno of Gigny, the first abbot. In following the reformed Rule, which contained many changes from that followed by houses which had adopted the Rule of St Benedict, the practice at Cluny differed widely in many ways from that of the Benedictine Order. The time spent in choir was extended, upsetting the Benedictine balance of prayer, work and study and changing fundamentally the way the Cluniac houses were administered. Whereas the Benedictine houses were all independent, with the abbot as the father of his community, the Cluniac houses were headed by priors, each appointed by the abbot of Cluny, who remained in overall charge with the priors answerable to him. This system has been described as 'patriarchal and quasi-feudal' (Dom David Knowles). The influence of Cluny was extensive, with two of the early abbots, St Odo (879–942) and St Odilo (962–1049) responsible for much of this growth. There were foundations throughout Europe, and at one time forty-five houses for men and three for women in England and Wales alone. Several of these houses were suppressed in the 13th century. The centralized administrative structure was in time to lead to its downfall. With everything answerable to the abbey at Cluny, there was the inevitable loss of the monastic family spirit which safeguarded the Benedictine houses. Efforts made to reform the Order, particularly by Cardinals Richelieu and Mazarin in the 17th century, came to naught. The abbey of Cluny, after suffering during the 16th-century religious wars, was suppressed at the time of the French Revolution and closed in 1790.

✠ Cluniac Monks

CLUNY, ORDER OF (NUNS)

Defunct
RC (female) founded in France in 1055 by Hugh, abbot of Cluny
Original habit: as for the monks, with a black head veil.

The first abbey of Cluniac nuns was founded in 1055 on land at Marcigny, near Cluny, and was subject to the centralized structure which governed the male houses, with each house ruled from the abbey of Cluny. It would seem that this house at Marcigny was built to house the female relatives of the founder, with a male member of his family being given the position of prior over the community. The nuns made their profession to the abbot of Cluny and therefore became members of the major male community. Enclosure was strictly observed, and the way of life was very similar to that in the male houses. Other monasteries for women were established in Italy, Belgium and Spain. Suppression followed at the time of the French Revolution.

✠ Cluniac Nuns

CLUNY SISTERS

Location: France (Paris)
RC (female) founded in France in 1807 by the Blessed Anne-Marie Javouhey (beatified 1950) and her three sisters
Abbr: SJC
Original habit: a blue tunic with a black scapular

and cape, a white coif and a small black veil; lay Sisters wore a similar habit, but with an apron and black shawl.

The Congregation was founded at Cabillon, France, to provide education for girls, but other work was also undertaken and the Sisters cared for the sick and the poor, and provided employment for girls by setting up a silk-spinning venture. Anne-Marie Javouhey had begun her religious life with the Sisters of Charity but felt that her vocation lay elsewhere. In 1812 she moved her Congregation to Cluny. They were active in undertaking missionary work in far-flung parts of the world, in Réunion (1817), where the Sisters opened schools for indigenous and white children, in Senegal (1819) and Senegambia, the old name for the territory between the Senegal and Gambia rivers in West Africa. It was here that the founder's strong opposition to slavery became evident. Other foundations followed, in Africa, Canada, Ireland, the USA and India. The early years of the 20th century saw the first Sisters in Australia, where they undertook both teaching and nursing. The Australian undertaking was withdrawn by the French mother house, but the Sisters returned to Melbourne in 1950. Today the apostolate includes teaching, nursing, domestic work, care of orphans, home missions and retreat work.

♰ St Joseph of Cluny Sisters

COLETTINES

Defunct
RC (female) founded in France in the early 15th century by St Colette Boellet (canonized 1807)
Original habit: Franciscan in style, as for the Poor Clares.

St Colette Boellet (1381–1447) of Corbie, France, having tried her vocation with both the Beguines and the Benedictines, finally joined the Franciscan Order. A vision, in 1406, of St Francis telling her to begin a reform of the Franciscan nuns, started her on a new enterprise. By the time of her death, in Ghent, Belgium, she had carried out her reform in twenty-two convents, modifying the Rule of St Clare with Constitutions and Ordinances of her own devising. These received papal approval in 1434 and later confirmation in 1458. The reforms enforced the strict enclosure of the communities, a stricter observance of the rule of poverty, the insistence that all members were to work within their own communities and also ordained that all communities were subject to the authority of the Franciscan First Order of Friars

♰ Colettans

COLLEGE OF FOOLS, KNIGHTS OF THE

Defunct
RC (male Equestrian Order) founded in Germany in 1381 by Rudolph, Count of Cleves
Original habit: (insignia) a fool, or a man dressed as a jester, all in red with gold lace, wearing black shoes and carrying a tray filled with fruit. This was worn on the left-hand side of a short cloak.

Little is known of the Order, which was founded in Westphalia. On the first Sunday after the feast of St Michael (29 September), the Knights would come together and distribute as much as they could to the poor. There is no further mention of this Order beyond 1671.

COLORITO, HERMITS OF

Defunct
RC (male) founded in Italy in 1530 by Bernardo di Rogliano
Original habit: a long black tunic with a round hood, a mantle and woollen girdle.

A Congregation of hermits founded on Mount Colorito near Morano in Lower Calabria by Bernardo di Rogliano, who had been given the land by the duchess of Bisagnano and went there to live the life of a hermit. In 1567 Pope St Pius V ordered the hermits to adopt the Rule of St Augustine and allowed them to retain the name of Coloriti. Their independence continued until 1600, when they were absorbed into the Order of Augustinian Friars.

COLUMBAN, MISSIONARY SISTERS OF ST

Location: England (Birmingham); Ireland (Wicklow)
RC (female) founded in Ireland in 1922 by John Blowick
Abbr: SSC
Original habit: a black tunic with a white collar and a white, peaked headband making a heart-shaped border around the face, and a black outer veil; a crucifix was worn around the neck.

The Congregation was founded in Cahiracon, County Clare, by John Blowick, the superior of the Society of St Columban. The purpose of the Congregation was to help the priests of the Society in all their missionary undertakings. Education was provided for Christians and non-Christians alike, and medical and nursing care given to the sick, the infirm and to lepers. In 1926 the Congregation made its first foundation in China, at Hanyang. Houses were later opened in the USA, South America and the Philippines.

✙ Columban Sisters
  Sisters of St Columban
  Sisters of St Columban for Missions
    among the Chinese

COLUMBAN, MISSIONARY SOCIETY OF ST

Location: Ireland (Dublin)
RC (male) founded in Ireland in 1917 by E. J. Galvin and John Blowick
Abbr: SSCME
Original habit: as for secular clergy.

Founded in Maynooth, Ireland, for missionary work overseas, the Congregation established its first house in China at Hanyang. It was approved in 1925 and 1932. Fr E. J. Galvin was later appointed as vicar apostolic of Hanyang. The Society made foundations in the Far East, Fiji, South America, the USA, Australia and New Zealand. Fr John Blowick was the founder of the Missionary Sisters of St Columban. One of the Columban Missionary priests in the Philippines, Fr Shay Cullen, has been nominated for the Nobel Peace Prize on account of founding the People's Recovery Empowerment and Development Association, in 1974, initially to help child drug addicts and more recently to help children move away from organized paedophile sex rings.

✙ Columban Fathers
  St Columban's Missionary Society

COLUMBANUS, ORDER OF ST

Defunct
RC (male and female) founded in France in the 6th/ 7th century by St Columbanus
Original habit: a tunic of undyed wool, with a large cowl of the same material.

St Columbanus, an Irishman, lived and worked with fellow monks in England and later in Brittany, where he founded a Congregation at Annegrai, in the Vosges district of France, in an old castle which the community soon outgrew. He then founded the abbey at Luxeuil but was forced into exile on account of his denunciation of the Frankish court. He died in the abbey of Bobbio, in Italy, which he had also founded. The Rule Columbanus imposed on his Congregation was noted for its austerity and penitential system but was observed by many monasteries until the reign of Charlemagne, when, for the sake of uniformity, the Rule of St Benedict was adopted. St Columbanus founded only single, male, monasteries, but his successors extended his concept of monastic life and founded double monasteries to house both men and women.

COMMON LIFE, BRETHREN OF THE

A community of Brothers and Sisters, also called the Devotio Moderna, established in the Low Countries in the 14th century with the aim of leading lives of the highest Christian calibre. The founder, Geert de Groote (1340–84) was a revered mystic despite problems with the Church authorities, who did not appreciate the open criticism, through his preaching, of the lax conditions of the clergy of his day, and withdrew his preacher's licence. His answer was to withdraw into a semi-monastic way of life, where he was joined by friends. This group in time became known as the Community of the Brethren of the Common Life. No vows were taken, and their work was largely devoted to providing a free education of the highest quality. Brethren with appropriate skills produced written, later printed, copies of manuscripts. After the death of the founder some of the Brothers branched away from the community, adopted a Rule and became Augustinian canons. Thomas à Kempis and Jan Busch were Brethren, the latter writing a history of the community at Windesheim.

COMMON LIFE, ORATORY OF THE

An ecumenical community presently being formed in the United States by Joel Retzloff, based on that of the Brethren of the Common Life (see previous entry).

COMPANIONS OF JESUS THE GOOD SHEPHERD, COMMUNITY OF THE

Location: England (Clewer, Windsor, Berkshire)
Anglican (female) founded in England in 1920 by

W. E. P. Hogg and members of the Guild of the Good Shepherd
Abbr: CJGS
Original habit: a brown tunic with girdle and a brown veil

The community, founded by the Revd W. E. P. Hogg and a small group of teachers who belonged to the Guild of the Good Shepherd, came into existence through the desire to form a religious community for women which would engage in educational work. This was established as the Congregation of Jesus the Good Shepherd and adopted its present name when the Constitution was revised in 1943. The original mother house was at Wantage, in Berkshire. The Sisters follow the Rule of St Augustine, which involves a daily Mass, and the saying of the divine office according to the Sarum Diurnal. Their principal work is in education, with overseas missions to Guyana, Antigua, Barbados, Belize and Honduras. The mother house, since 1996, is now in Windsor, Berkshire, where the Sisters live alongside the Community of St John the Baptist. The Sisters also involve themselves in giving retreats, in running training programmes for the laity and for local non-stipendiary ministers and also in care for the elderly and those in need.

COMPANY OF MARY OUR LADY, SISTERS OF THE

Location: Italy (Rome)
RC (female) founded in France in the 17th century by St Jeanne de Lestonnac (canonized 1949)
Abbr: ODN
Original habit: a black dress and girdle with a white wimple, black veil, crucifix and rosary; the cross has the monogram JM engraved on it; a long black mantle was worn in choir.

St Jeanne de Lestonnac (1556–1640), after being widowed, tried her religious vocation with the Cistercians but without success.

She felt drawn to found an Institute dedicated to the education of girls, and was helped to achieve this by a Jesuit priest, Jean de Bordes, who drew up a Rule which was approved by Pope Paul V in 1607. There is a strong Benedictine influence in the customs of this Congregation, probably because St Jeanne did her novitiate with the Feuillantine Benedictines at Toulouse and because the pope affiliated the Sisters to the Order of St Benedict so that they could share the privileges of that Order. The work of the Congregation is largely educational and catechetical but has also included nursing and the care of orphans, as well as extending to both domestic and foreign missions. There are houses in France, Spain, Italy, the USA, England and the Far East

✠ Company of Mary
   Company of the Daughters of Mary Our Lady
   Notre Dame Nuns

COMPANY OF ST PAUL

Location: USA (White Plains, New York)
RC (male and female) founded in Italy in 1920

A Secular Institute which was founded for priests and laity under the auspices of Cardinal Ferrari of Milan. It became a Secular Institute of Pontifical Right in 1950, designed to promote the practice of evangelism in the faithful.

COMPASSION OF JESUS, COMMUNITY OF THE

Defunct
Anglican (female) founded in England in 1892 by Mother Mary Margaret
Original habit: a grey tunic, with a black veil for outside wear and a white veil indoors.

The Community of the Compassion of Jesus was founded in Deptford, London, for work among the poor and neglected in the south-east of the city. Later moves took the

Sisters across the city, first to Maida Vale and finally to Hampton Court. As members joined, the work expanded into caring for neglected and abandoned young women and the reclamation of girls who were at risk, training them for domestic service, and also working with homeless children. After 1935 the Sisters took in homeless children and accommodated them in St Agnes' Home, at Thames Ditton. Despite their very active apostolate the Sisters strove to observe a fairly enclosed and contemplative life, following an adapted version of the Rule of St Benedict.

COMPASSIONISTS

Defunct
RC (female) founded in the USA in 1886 by Mgr Thomas S. Preston and Mother Mary Veronica
Abbr: RDC

A teaching Congregation founded in New York with its headquarters at White Plains, New York. The original idea in Mgr Preston's mind was to rescue poor children, especially girls, from a life on the streets, for which purpose he opened the House of the Holy Family. It was supported by donations and assistance from the Association for Befriending Children and Young Girls, notably by Mrs Mary C. D. Starr, who later became Mother Mary Veronica. It was soon apparent that a religious community would be best able to administer this work, and a Rule was devised by Fr Preston in 1873 which received a cautious approval from the archbishop of New York. Full approbation followed in 1900, and other foundations were made which added a vocational training school for girls at White Plains, New York, as well as a hostel for working girls in New York.

✠ Sisters of Divine Compassion

CONSOLATA FATHERS

Location: Italy (Rome)
RC (male) founded in Italy in 1901 by the Blessed
Joseph Allamano (beatified 1990)
Abbr: IMC
Original habit: as for secular clergy.

An Institute whose members are under simple vows, founded as a missionary Congregation with the purpose of converting non-believers to Christ; its Constitutions were approved in 1923. The members work mainly in Africa and South America, where there are many foundations and where many missions have been made.

✠ Consolata Society for Foreign Missions

CONSOLATA MISSIONARY SISTERS

Location: Italy (Nepi, Viterbo)
RC (female) founded in Italy in 1910 by the Blessed
Joseph Allamano (beatified 1990)
Abbr: MC

The Congregation was founded in Turin by Joseph Allamano, who was rector of the Consolata Shrine in Turin. The Sisters were trained to co-operate with the efforts of the Consolata Missionary Fathers in their missionary work, the aim of which was to convert non-believers to Christ. The Sisters have been particularly active in Africa, Europe and the Americas, with their mission extending to teaching, nursing and social reform. The first house in England was established in 1951, in the diocese of Brentwood.

CONSTANTINIAN ORDER OF ST GEORGE

Defunct
RC (male Equestrian Order) founded in the 16th
century
Original habit: the choir mantle was sky blue with
the cross of the Order on the shoulder; the grand
master's bonnet featured a black ostrich feather
and was made of crimson velvet lined in white

satin and caught up at four points with the Chi-Rho monogram embroidered in gold; (insignia) a gold-edged red cross fleury with a gold Chi-Rho monogram; (collar) there were to be fifteen medallions of blue and gold enamel, with the middle one bearing a four-cornered cross and the letters I.H.S.V. (In Hoc Signo Vinces – In This Sign you will Conquer); Christ's name, as the Chi-Rho, is inscribed between the cross bars and on either side of the Greek letters alpha and omega; the centre of the medallion bears the image of St George in gold, astride a horse and killing a dragon.

The Order was founded in the 16th century by a Greek family from Albania, the Angeli (which gave rise to the alternative name of the Order). Some of the knights were recruited by King John Sobieski of Poland to fight against the Turks for the relief of Vienna in 1680. The grand mastership of the Order was sold in 1699 to the duke of Parma, Francesco Farnese, and to his successors. This was confirmed in the same year by Pope Innocent XII. The knights saw brief action at the start of the 18th century, but by 1734 the grand mastership of the Order had passed to the Royal House of the Two Sicilies.

✠ Angelics of St George

CRESCENT MOON, KNIGHTS OF THE

Defunct
RC (male Equestrian Order) founded in Italy in
1268 by the King of Naples and Sicily
Original habit: (insignia) from a central fleur-de-lis
hung a crescent moon with the motto 'Donec
Totum Impleat' (Until Everything is Fulfilled)
engraved on it. The insignia was worn on the left-hand sleeve of the knight's tunic and was also
suspended from a collar of gold composed of
linked fleurs-de-lis and starbursts.

The Order was founded for the defence of the faith, the protection of pilgrims and the burial of the dead. It received papal approval from Pope Clement IV (1265–68).

The right to wear the distinctive insignia was awarded to recognize the bravery of the knights and nobles of Messina, Sicily.

CROSS, DAUGHTERS OF THE - Liège

Location: Belgium (Liège)
RC (female) founded in Belgium in 1833 by Jean-Baptiste-Guillaume Habets and Johanna Haze (Blessed Mary-Theresa of the Sacred Heart – beatified 1991)
Abbr: FC
Original habit: a black habit and scapular with a white wimple and binder and a black veil lined with white; a cross bearing a white crown was suspended from a black neck ribbon. Lay Sisters wore the same habit, but with a white veil.

The apostolate of the Order is to educate, house and nurse those in need, especially the aged and the handicapped, the deaf and epileptics. There is daily recitation of the offices of the Blessed Virgin Mary and the annual renewal of vows on Our Lady's birthday (8 September). The Sisters live under a modified version of the Rule of St Ignatius. There are houses in Belgium, England, Ireland, Germany, Italy, the USA, Brazil and India.

CROSS, DAUGHTERS OF THE - Torquay

Location: England (Torquay, Devon)
RC (female) founded in France in 1625 by Françoise Vallet, Marie Samier, Charlotte and Anne de Lancy
Abbr: FDLC
Original habit: a black tunic and veil with a double-pointed wimple and a bonnet whose ends tied under the chin to form a bow; a small silver cross was worn around the neck with rosary beads at the waist, on the left-hand side.

The foundation of this Congregation really started in Roye, a small town in Picardy in the diocese of Amiens, in 1625, when four pious women agreed to the suggestion made by the Abbé Pierre Guérin that they provide education and training for those girls of the area who came from families unable to pay for this. While in Paris arranging for the necessary permits a new Congregation would need, Marie Samier met St Vincent de Paul and Madame Marie l'Huillier de Villeneuve, a widow, whose spiritual director was St Francis de Sales. Marie de Villeneuve bought a house at Vaugirard, and the Sisters moved there, together with Marie, who made her profession there in 1641. The Congregation followed a Rule written by St Francis de Sales. In 1636 they all removed to Paris, on account of war. Some five weeks later their vows were renewed, on the feast of the Exaltation of the Holy Cross, on which day the Sisters still renew their vows. New foundations were made in France, Belgium and Canada. The French Revolution dispersed the Congregation until 1804. Nearly a century later four Sisters left the Belgian foundation at Teguier and went to England, where they opened a house and school in Torquay, in Devon, in 1903, with others following; but today the lack of vocations has forced the closure of some of these, with only the schools at Tremough and Stoodley Knowle still operating.

CROSS, DAUGHTERS OF THE HOLY

Location: France (Saint-Pierre-de-Maille)
RC (female) founded in France in 1811 by St André-Hubert Fournet (canonized 1933) and St Elizabeth Bichier des Ages (canonized 1947)

The founders met when André-Hubert Fournet returned to France in 1801 from exile in Spain in the years following the French Revolution. Together they founded a Congregation at Guinetiere, near Bethines in the diocese of Vienne, and a mother house was later opened at Maille in 1811. Diocesan approval was granted in 1817. The work spread quickly through France, with many houses founded. The dispersal of the French religious Orders at the start of the

20th century because of the Association Laws sent the Sisters into Italy, Spain and Canada, where new houses were opened. The principal occupation of the Congregation is education, especially for children in country areas, social welfare of the young and care for the dying.

✠ Sisters of St Andrew

CROSS, KNIGHTS OF THE

Defunct
RC (male Equestrian Order) founded in Bohemia in the 13th century
Original habit: (insignia) a simple red cross with a red six-pointed star; the colour and composition of the collar was left to the monarch, or prince, awarding the knighthood.

There have been several Orders with this name. The most famous was that founded in Bohemia in the 13th century, the knights forming a fraternity attached to a Prague hospital and under the jurisdiction of the Poor Clares. This Congregation was formally reconstituted as an Order in 1238 by Pope Gregory IX, under the Rule of St Augustine. The Order was active in its charitable work and in education until the start of the 20th century, but is now defunct.

CROSS, RELIGIOUS OF THE

Defunct
RC (female) founded in France in 1625 by Abbé Pierre-Hubert Guérin
Original habit: a black tunic and veil with a shoulder cape and a linen cap with a pleated frill.

The foundation was made by the Abbé Guérin in Picardy when he brought four young women together to form a society of Sisters, without vows, for the purpose of educating and training young girls to enable them to earn a living. The community went to Paris, where, with the help of St Vincent

de Paul and Madame de Villeneuve, a widow, they set up a house in 1651, with diocesan approval. At this point the introduction of vows was thought necessary and this resulted in a split, with those who took vows (the Daughters of the Cross) and another group who felt they could not take the vows. Both groups flourished until the French Revolution, when the members were dispersed. At the end of the Revolution the group who felt they could not take vows established a community at Saint-Quentin, which included Mother Hunegonde Duplaquet, who had been imprisoned in her own convent during the time of the Terror. This group then affiliated with some other nuns, but they were allowed to retain their title of *Dames Religieuses de la Croix*. When the Association Laws in France took effect at the turn of the 20th century, the mother house was moved to La Louvière in Belgium, returning to Saint-Quentin in 1939. Convents and schools had been established in England, France and Belgium, but the Order became defunct.

✠ Sisters of the Cross

CROSS OF JESUS, BROTHERS OF THE

Defunct
RC (male) founded in France in 1820 by Fr C. M. Bochard

The Congregation was founded in Lyons by the vicar-general of the Lyons archdiocese, Fr C. M. Bochard. From the start they were under the direction of priests, but as these were needed for parochial duties the Congregation eventually became composed only of Brothers. Their work, largely concerned with education, spread throughout France and into Switzerland but the Association Laws in France at the start of the 20th century destroyed most of the foundations. A fresh beginning was made in Canada, at Rimouski, Quebec.

CROSS OF SAINT ANDREW, DAUGHTERS OF THE

Location: France (Poitiers)
RC (female) founded in France in 1807 by St André-Hubert Fournet (canonized 1933) and St Elizabeth Bichier des Ages (canonized 1947)

The founders of the Order had colourful stories, played out against the background of the French Revolution. André-Hubert Fournet, a simple rural parish priest at the time of the Terror in France, was forced into exile and spent some time in Spain. On his return to France in 1797, forced to wander the country for several years in an effort to avoid arrest, he met the indefatigable Elizabeth Bichier and some years later assisted her to found her Institute. So great was her determination to found her *Filles de la Croix de Saint André* that she managed to overcome all official obstacles placed in her way, and this leads us to see in her a woman of heroic proportions. The Congregation flourished, working in education and nursing, but was forced to leave France in 1905 at the time of the Association Laws. The Sisters established houses in Spain and Italy, and a provincial house was set up in Manitoba, Canada. The members of the Congregation at one time numbered nearly two thousand professed Sisters.

CRUSADERS OF ST MARY

Location: USA (McLean, Virginia)
RC (male) founded in Spain in 1960 by Fr Tomas Morales

A Congregation founded by a Jesuit priest, who was born in Macuto, Venezuela, in 1908. It was recognized as a Secular Institute of Diocesan Right in 1988, and its intended focus is on young people, to help them integrate the spiritual with the secular, achieved through Ignatian Spiritual Exercises. The overall emphasis is on Marian devotions. Fr Morales was also responsible for founding the Homes of Mary, which is a movement for married couples, and the Militia of Mary, an apostolic youth movement.

CRUTCHED FRIARS

Defunct
RC (male) foundation uncertain, see below
Original habit: a black habit decorated with a red cross (but see below).

The foundation of the Crutched Friars is uncertain. There is an early claim that they were founded by St Cletus, a 1st-century pope, and were reconstituted in the 4th century by St Cyriacus, Patriarch of Jerusalem. There were two groups of friars, one a group of mendicants who first appear in Italy in the 12th century, when they were given a Rule by Pope Alexander III (1159–81). This group was numerous in Italy and was said at one time to have had over two hundred monasteries divided between the five provinces of Bologna, Venice, Milan, Rome and Naples. From their mother house at Bologna an English foundation came into being in the 13th century, when a number of the friars sought permission to settle in England. Ten English monasteries were opened, the first probably at Colchester in Essex, while in London it was this Congregation which gave the name to a locality near the Tower of London called Crutched Friars. The habit of this English group was originally brown, or black, but was changed to blue by Pope Pius II (1458–64). The habit had a red cross sewn on to the breast, and each friar carried a wooden stave surmounted by a wooden, later silver, cross. The second group of similarly named friars, who also claimed a similar origin, went to France and the Low Countries, where they are reputed to have been organized in 1211 by Theodore of Celles. Their habit was black with a red cross. They became defunct at the time of the French Revolution.

✟ Brothers Crossbearers
  Crossed Friars
  Fratres Cruciferi

CULDEES

There has always been much controversy and speculation about the Culdees. They appear to have started as groups of men in Ireland who sought solitude and manual work and who lived an almost Carthusian way of life, living in individual cells under obedience to their superior and meeting together only for daily Mass. St Aengus of Tallaght followed a Rule, composed by both St Maelrun and himself, called the Rule of Celidhe De, in which every detail of Culdee life was outlined. The Rule was not observed in any other Congregation. In Armagh a community of Culdees persisted and maintained a communal type of existence, responsible for the daily service and the administration of church property. Many of the Culdees were secular canons and could be married. By the end of the reign of Elizabeth I (died 1603) these Culdees had died out and were replaced in 1628 by a new body, the priors and vicars-choral of the Cathedral of Armagh, to whom the Culdees' land and property was transferred. In Scotland the many Culdee establishments had almost disappeared by the 13th century, probably as a result of growth in wealth, laziness and corruption. The Metropolitan Church of St Andew had been founded by Angus, king of the Picts, and was first served by the Culdees, but by 1144 they had been replaced by canons regular on the authority of the bishop. The Culdees of St Andrews had certainly disappeared by the time of the Reformation.

CYRIL AND METHODIUS, SOCIETY OF STS

Location: USA (Danville, Pennsylvania)
RC (female) founded in USA in 1909 by Fr Matthew Jankola
Abbr: SSCM

A Congregation of Sisters and lay associates, founded by an immigrant priest, Fr Jankola, with the help of Mother Mary Cyril, which is to be found throughout the USA. Mother Mary, a member of the Sisters-Servants of the Immaculate Heart of Mary, directed the formation of the first three Sisters of this new Congregation, Mary Mihalik, Mary-Joseph Bartek and Mary-Emmanuel Pauly, with the first professions taking place in Scranton, Pennsylvania. The Sisters work in education at all levels, from elementary to college and university. They have a special ministry to those who have impaired hearing and for the old and those in retirement. The Congregation also supports a music conservatory and provides both spiritual direction and a retreat ministry.

D

DAMIANITES

An alternative title for the Poor Clares which derives from the fact that St Clare of Assisi and her sister, Agnes Offreduccio, lived at St Damian's Church, which had been rebuilt by St Francis of Assisi himself. It was here that the austere Order of Poor Clares, originally called the Order of the Poor Ladies, originated, when other women joined St Clare and her sister in order to live the Franciscan life.

✠ Damianissines
  Damianistes
  Poor Clares

DEATH, BROTHERS OF

Defunct
RC (male) founded in France in c.1620 by Guillaume Callier
Original habit: a white habit with a black capuce and scapular which has a skull and crossbones on the front panel.

A short-lived Congregation of hermits who lived in solitary cells built outside various towns in France; those hermits who were not solitaries visited the sick and dying. Theirs was a life of extreme penitence, with flagellation and the wearing of a hair shirt mandatory, and the *memento mori* ever present in their daily life; the greetings, one to another, of 'My dear Brother, remember death' and 'Remember your last end and sin no more', served to underline their mission. Those who were granted permission to live as solitaries were obliged to join the rest of the community at choir offices and on Sundays and feast days. The motif of skull and crossbones embroidered on the scapular was echoed in the cells and on the refectory tables with the use of actual skulls and bones as grotesque ornamentation. Thirteen years after its foundation this Congregation was suppressed.

✠ Order of St Paul the First Hermit

DENIS, CANONS REGULAR OF ST

Defunct
RC (male) founded in France in the 9th century, re-established in the 11th century
Original habit: a white cotta, with wide sleeves, reaching almost to the ankles, and a black biretta; a white mantle with fur-lined sleeves was worn in winter.

A Congregation founded in the 9th century at Reims by Archbishop Hincmar (808–82), who had been educated at the abbey of St Denis and was a frequent visitor there. He was made archbishop in 845. By the 11th century the abbey had fallen into disrepair and was re-established by Gervase, archbishop of Reims.

DENMARK, KNIGHTS OF

Defunct
RC (male Equestrian Order) revived in 1672 by King Christian V of Denmark
Original habit: a white tunic, on the breast of which was a green ribbon from which hung a cross with diamond-shaped insets, bearing the motto 'Pietati et Justitiae' (For Piety and Justice) and a white fur-lined, rose-coloured cape and plumed hat.

When King Christian V wished to celebrate the birth of his firstborn son, Frederick, he revived the Order of the Knights of Denmark, which had become defunct. It seems to have had no particular purpose beyond the ceremonial.

DENYS, COMMUNITY OF ST

Location: England (Warminster, Wiltshire)
Anglican (female) founded in England in 1879 by Canon Sir James Erasmus Philipps
Abbr: CSD

The community came into being when women who had trained at a college established for this purpose by Canon Phillips wished to enter the religious life. A novitiate was set up and the new Sisters were professed in the community, dedicated to St Denys the Areopagite, in 1879, which marks its foundation. The Rule they followed was based on that of St Augustine. The Sisters have worked in India, Burma and South Africa, where they have undertaken teaching and the care of orphans. Three members of this community were ordained as priests in 1995.

✠ Missionary Community of St Denys

DIJON AND LANGRES, HOSPITALLERS OF

Defunct
RC (female) founded in France in 1685 by Benigne Joly

A foundation made at Dijon, France, by the Venerable Benigne Joly while he was canon of St Etienne. He also founded a local Congregation of women known as the Sisters of the Good Shepherd.

DIOCESAN LABORER PRIESTS

Location: USA (Washington, DC)
RC (male) founded in Spain in 1885

A Secular Institute of Pontifical Right, approved in 1952 for the purpose of gathering together priests who would be able to promote and cultivate vocations to the secular priesthood and to the religious life.

DISCIPLINE AND THE WHITE EAGLE, KNIGHTS OF THE

Defunct
RC (male Equestrian Order) founded in Austria in the 16th century
Original habit: (insignia) a white crowned eagle with outstretched wings; a badge with the same motif was suspended from the neck over the tunic. Knights wore a blue mantle and a helmet decorated with the eagle motif in metal.

An Austrian Order awarded to those who defended the Roman Catholic faith against its enemies, notably the Turks. The obligations that were attached to this honour were that the bearer would hold himself ready to take up arms on behalf of the Church, obey the head of state, guard the realm and live under the Rule of St Basil.

✠ Knights of the Whip and the White Eagle

DIVINE CHARITY, DAUGHTERS OF

Location: Italy (Grottaferrata)
RC (female) founded in Austria in 1868 by Mother Mary Franciska Lechner
Abbr: FDC
Original habit: a black habit with a black cape, a white frilled cap with a bow and a short, black silk veil.

An active Order with simple vows which received papal approval in 1897. The Sisters work with the poor and the homeless and help to find work for unemployed women and girls. They also conduct foreign missions, teach catechetics and care for children in need and for the elderly. The Congregation is widespread, with houses in Austria, Hungary, Poland, former Yugoslavia, England, Brazil and the USA.

DIVINE COMPASSION, SOCIETY OF

Defunct
Anglican (male) founded in England in 1894 by Revd the Hon. J. G. Adderley
Abbr: SDC

A society founded in Plaistow, London, but which had its origins in the chapel of Pusey House in Oxford, where the novitiate was conducted. The founders were James Adderley, Henry Chappell and Ernest Hardy, who went to London and there began their missionary work among the poor, their venture gaining the approval of Edward White Benson, the archbishop of Canterbury. The work of the Society, the members of which observed the Franciscan Rule, was much involved in conducting missions, preaching and the general relief of the poor in this disadvantaged area of London. They also opened workshops for the unemployed, where they set up printing presses and taught the skills necessary for the repair of clocks and watches. An attempt at missionary work in Southern Rhodesia was less successful, and it closed inside a year.

DIVINE HEART, HANDMAIDS OF THE

Location: Spain (Madrid)
RC (female) founded in Spain in 1885 by Blessed Marcello Spinola y Maestre (beatified 1987) and Velia Mendez (Mother Teresa of the Sacred Heart)
Abbr: ADC.

Original habit: a very dark blue tunic with a black scapular bearing the initial 'M' intertwined with the symbol of a heart surmounted by a cross and the motto 'Servir es Reinar' (To Serve is to Reign) above a crescent moon; a black veil was tightly gathered at the front over a white cap, with a cross around the neck and a chain-like cincture.

The Congregation was founded at Coria, in the Alagon Valley in Spain, and approved in 1909. Celia Mendez, the widow of the Marquis dela Pueblo de Obando, wanted to try her religious vocation with an established Order, but was persuaded by a Jesuit, Fr Mon, and Mother Angela de la Cruz, the founder of the Sisters of the Cross, to try to gather together a group of women who would be willing to teach young girls. For this purpose a school was opened. In 1885, with the encouragement of Fr Spinola, who was to become auxiliary bishop of Seville and who wrote the Rule for the new Congregation, the women received the habit and their names in religion, dedicating themselves to the Christian education of the young. The work of the Sisters is still concerned with the young but has extended into the running of youth clubs, educational centres, missions, adult literacy programmes and parish catechesis. There are houses in Spain, Italy, South America, Japan, the Philippines and Angola.

✠ Spinola Sisters

DIVINE MASTER, PIOUS DISCIPLES OF THE

Location: Italy (Rome)
RC (female) founded in Italy in 1924 by Giacomo Alberione
Abbr: PDDM

A Pontifical Institute with simple vows, the Congregation was founded at Alba by Fr Alberione. In 1947 some of the Sisters went to New York, and their first house, on Staten Island, later became the centre for the religious formation programmes for intending members. The Congregation is both active and contemplative. The Sisters work in social and domestic work, participate in health care programmes and undertake secretarial work. On the creative side they are involved in the making of vestments, iconography, printing, sculpture and music.

✝ Sisters-Disciples of the Divine Master

DIVINE MERCY, INSTITUTE OF

Location: USA (Dallas, Texas)
RC (female) founded in the USA in 1995 by Charles V. Grahmann, bishop of Dallas
Original habit: a blue tunic with a white veil.

A cloistered contemplative community founded by Bishop Grahmann, who had been moved by the writings of St Maria Faustina Kowalska (canonized 2000) and especially by her book 'Divine Mercy in My Soul'. Maria Faustina, a Polish woman and a Sister of the Congregation of the Sisters of Our Lady of Mercy, had received some visions, the first being in 1935, when Our Lord revealed that a foundation was to be made as soon as possible to honour his divine mercy. She did not live to see her vision accomplished, dying in 1938 in Krakow, Poland. A new house was opened in Cagua, Peru, in 1999, to which two novices from Dallas travelled and met up with eight postulants there to form a new cloistered Divine Mercy Convent. Pope John Paul II has always been impressed by St Faustina and her writings, which allegedly influenced his 1980 encyclical *Dives in Misericordia*.

DIVINE MERCY, INSTITUTE OF THE SERVANTS OF

Location: USA (Jerome, Arizona)
RC (male) founded in the USA in 1989
Abbr: SDM

A Diocesan Institute of Brothers who observe the Benedictine Rule, but take the three traditional vows of poverty, chastity and obedience, with an emphasis on hospitality and eucharistic adoration. The Brothers' other activities include the conducting of retreats and missions, publishing, and working with those who are in need of care and feel themselves outcast from society

DIVINE MERCY, SOCIETY OF

Location: USA (Roslindale, Massachusetts)
RC (male) founded in the USA in 1993

A Society geared to the spiritual renewal of diocesan priests. The apostolate includes the conducting of missions, retreats and conferences, as well as the provision of counselling and formation programmes for clergy and members of religious Orders.

DIVINE PROVIDENCE, SISTERS OF – San Antonio

Location: USA (Helotes, Texas)
RC (female) founded in the USA in 1868 by Blessed John Martin Moye (beatified 1954) and Mother St Andrew Feltin
Abbr: CDP

A Congregation founded because of the need for uncloistered nuns to teach in the local community. To this end, two volunteer Sisters, led by Mother Feltin, left their convent at St Jean-de-Bassel, in Lorraine, France, and travelled to Texas, where the new foundation was made at Castroville. In time other Sisters came from France to join the new community. It became independent of the mother house in France in 1886 and received papal approval in 1907 and 1912. The administration centre was moved in 1896 to Our Lady of the Lake convent in San Antonio, and a college, now a university, was built. The work of the Congregation is not entirely occupied with education but also extends to health care, pastoral ministry and the care and rehabilitation of the disadvantaged from various ethnic and minority groups.

DIVINE PROVIDENCE, MISSIONARY CATECHISTS OF

Location: USA (San Antonio, Texas)
RC (female) founded in the USA in the 1920s by Sr Benitia Vermeersch
Abbr: MCDP

A Congregation founded in Houston, Texas, for the purpose of working mainly with Mexican Americans. The founder was a member of the Sisters of Divine Providence of San Antonio. The Sisters are currently engaged in providing catechesis, care and rehabilitation for those in need throughout the San Antonio diocese as well as in Mexico. Papal approval was granted in 1946, and full autonomy as a Pontifical Congregation was gained in 1989.

DIVINE PROVIDENCE, POOR SERVANTS OF

Location: Italy (Rome)
RC (male and female) founded in Italy in 1907 by St John Calabria (canonized 1999)
Abbr: PSDP

A Congregation founded by a secular priest, St John Calabria (1873–1954), who was concerned about the needs of the poor. He opened an orphanage for neglected and homeless children and homes for the elderly and the sick. To staff these foundations and to address the needs of the poor, he founded the Congregation of the Poor Servants of Divine Providence, which was approved in 1956. The Congregation is made up of priests and lay Brothers and Sisters, assisted by a distinctly lay Order known as the Family of Extern Friars.

DIVINE PROVIDENCE, SISTERS OF

Location: France (St Jean-de-Bassel, Fenetrange)
RC (female) founded in France in 1762 by Blessed John Martin Moye (beatified 1954)
Abbr: CDP

The Blessed John Martin Moye was very aware of the need to relieve poverty and to educate and catechize in his community, and he made this foundation in Metz, Lorraine, for this purpose. The work began by sending young women out into the parish to help correct the twin evils of poverty and ignorance. They were not to be cloistered nuns but unenclosed women who followed four Virtues, rather than the vows of a nun. The Virtues were abandonment to divine providence, simplicity, poverty and charity through works of mercy. It was only in 1839 that the Sisters were to take the traditional religious vows of poverty, chastity and obedience. The founder joined the Paris Mission Society in 1771 and left for China, where he worked in Sichuan. While there he was instrumental in forming The Chinese Christian Virgins, a version of his French Congregation. The coming of the French Revolution resulted in the suppression of the French Congregation. Fr Moye himself went into exile in Trier, Germany, where he died in 1793. The Congregation eventually re-formed in France and three of the Sisters went from there in 1889 to Kentucky, where St Anne's Convent was built for them. The enterprise has expanded and now includes orphanages, homes for the aged, and education with particular attention to those from rural areas.

DIVINE PROVIDENCE, SISTERS OF

Location: Switzerland (Baldegg)
RC (female) founded in Switzerland in 1831 by Josef Widmer, Josef Leu and Fr Josef Leonz Blum
Original habit: a black tunic with a white blouse

and a black veil and cincture; a simple Greek-style cross was worn on a cord around the neck.

Founded in an old castle at Baldegg, Switzerland, 1829, the purpose of the Congregation was the education of young women. Seven young women from the same family, Hartmann, were recruited and were joined, in 1831, by two more. The community was recognized in 1844 as a Diocesan Congregation whose first mother superior was Sr M. M. Jodoka Ruffieux. The community observes a Franciscan Third Order Regular Rule and the practice of Franciscan spirituality. The Sisters have missions in Tanzania, Papua New Guinea and Ethiopia, hospitals, several schools and a house of formation at Hertenstein, in Switzerland.

DIVINE PROVIDENCE, SONS OF

Location: Italy (Rome)
RC (male) founded in Italy in 1903 by Blessed Don Luigi Orione
Abbr: FDP

A Congregation founded in his home town of Tortona when Don Orione opened a school for the poor boys of the town and established other works of mercy in an effort to overcome the poverty present all around him. Other houses were opened throughout Italy and spread to the rest of Europe and South America. A lone priest, Fr Paul Bidone, travelled to England in 1949 and started a home for the aged in Streatham, London, and this led to further expansion to Hampton Wick, Kingston-upon-Thames, which is now the headquarters of the Sons of Divine Providence in England. Other communities arose as needed, with homes for learning-disabled men in Surrey and Norfolk, care centres for the aged and a house for homeless children in Dublin, Ireland. The Sons of Divine Providence, whose members include priests,

clerics, lay Brothers and hermits, received its approbation in 1954. The first hermitage which Don Orione established was in 1897, near Alesandria in Piedmont, Italy, for blind hermits, who had to be lay Brothers, with a sighted priest in charge of each community. They wore a grey habit, hood, cape and scapular with a girdle.

✠ Don Orione Congregation

DIVINE PROVIDENCE OF RIBEAUVILLE, SISTERS OF

Location: France (Strasbourg)
RC (female) founded in Germany in 1851 by Bishop Wilhelm von Ketteler and Mother Maria de la Roche
Abbr: CDP

Founded in Finthen, near Mainz in Germany, this is a Congregation with an arrangement for its formation programme made with the Sisters of Divine Providence at Ribeauville, Alsace. The Sisters worked originally in the field of education, but this later expanded to include the running of an orphanage at Neustadt which they opened in 1856. After the German *Kulturkampf* in 1876, the Congregation turned away from being fully involved in education and undertook work in hospitals, asylums, vocational training schools and the care of the aged. American provinces were opened from Germany in 1876 when some of the Sisters left Mainz for the USA. The work undertaken in the USA includes teaching, nursing, home missions and foreign missions in Puerto Rico, Peru and Korea. The Sisters also work with single mothers, Mexican immigrants, AIDS sufferers and homeless children.

✠ Finthen Sisters

DIVINE PROVIDENCE OF ST ANDREW OF PELTRE, SISTERS OF

Location: France (Marly, Metz)
RC (female) founded in France in 1806 by Fr Anton Gapp

The original work of the Congregation was the education of young children and the secondary education of girls. After official state authorization was received, the mother house was moved from Forbach, in Lorraine, to Peltre. Fire destroyed this foundation, but it was later re-established. The Congregation spread throughout Lorraine and into Belgium

DIVINE PROVIDENCE OF ST MAURITZ, SISTERS OF

Location: Germany (Münster)
RC (female) founded in Germany in 1842 by Fr Eduard Michelis

A Congregation founded by the private secretary of the archbishop of Cologne, following a spell of imprisonment which he shared with the archbishop from 1837 to 1841. Fr Michelis returned to his birthplace of St Mauritz, where, with the help of two priests, he founded an orphanage which had special responsibility for poor and neglected children, and was administered by the Congregation of Sisters of Divine Providence. The work of the Sisters was extended to include all manner of care for those in need, from nursing and social welfare to education and help with pastoral matters. In 1876, during the *Kulturkampf* in Germany, the Sisters moved to Steyl, in The Netherlands, and continued their work there. The Congregation later spread into South America, where the Sisters worked in Brazil, and to Cameroon in Africa. Many of the Sisters in The Netherlands were taken as prisoners in 1916, during World War I. Later expansion took the Congregation to Indonesia (1934), Aruba (1955) and East Africa (1995).

DIVINE REDEEMER, SISTERS OF THE

Location: Italy (Rome)
RC (female) founded in France in 1849 by Elisabeth Eppinger (Mother Alphonsa Maria)
Abbr: SDR (previously DDR)
Original habit: a black tunic, veil and short cape, with a black cincture and rosary; a crucifix was worn around the neck.

The Congregation, originally known as the Daughters of the Divine Redeemer, was founded at Niederbronn, in Alsace, France. From this foundation a new one was made at Odenburg in 1863, which was declared independent by 1867 with a mother house at Sopron (Odenburg). The first superior-general was Mother Basilissa, and approbation of the Constitutions was confirmed in 1940. From this foundation several new provinces have been established, in Hungary, Austria, Slovakia and the USA. The Sisters are committed to charity, especially in serving the sick, the poor and the elderly, in teaching and in providing parish ministries as they are needed.

DIVINE SAVIOUR, DAUGHTERS OF THE

Location: Austria (Vienna)
RC (female) founded in Austria in 1866

The Daughters of the Divine Saviour was established in Vienna in 1857, as a branch of the Sisters of the Divine Redeemer foundation at Niederbronn and became independent in 1866, adopting its present name. From this foundation other houses were established in Austria, Germany, The Netherlands and Argentina. Another branch, from the mother house in Vienna, was developed in Bratislava (Pressburg) in 1916, which became the Daughters of the Most Holy Saviour, and spread into Germany, Hungary and Slovakia. The Vienna community has since reverted to the Nieder-bronn foundation and has been granted a name change to that of the Sisters of the Divine Redeemer. This was effected in 1984 and confirmed again in 1999. The work of the Sisters is concerned with the care of the sick and education for girls at all levels, including vocational schooling.

DIVINE SAVIOUR, SISTERS OF THE

Location: Italy (Rome)
RC (female) founded in Italy in 1888 by Fr Francis Jordan
Abbr: SDS
Original habit: a black habit with a black waist cord, a white coif and wimple; a white habit was worn in hospitals, day nurseries and kitchens.

A Congregation, initially of four women, founded in Rome in 1888 by the founder of the Salvatorians who had also formed an association of religious and lay missionaries called the Apostolic Teaching Society, with the assistance of Baroness Teresa von Wue-lenweber (later Blessed Mother Mary of the Holy Apostles; beatified 1968). By 1890 the Sisters were working in India, China and Latin America, teaching at all levels, caring for minority groups in bilingual schools and clinics and for the poor and elderly, and working for justice and peace. Their work is now undertaken throughout the world, with missions in North and South America, Africa, Asia, the Holy Land and Europe, frequently working alongside the Salvatorian priests and Brothers.

✧ Salvatorian Sisters

DIVINE SHEPHERD OF DIVINE PROVIDENCE, SISTERS OF THE

Location: Poland (Jablonowo Pomorskie)
RC (female) founded in Poland in 1894 by Blessed Mother Maria Karlowsky (beatified 1997)
Original habit: a black tunic with cincture and rosary and short black cape with a square white

wimple, a white head cap and a black veil with a central depression, and a crucifix worn around the neck beneath the wimple.

The Congregation was founded by Maria Karlowsky (1865–1935) at Winiary, near Poznan, Poland. She was deeply concerned by the number of young women who had moved to the city from the country in search of work and had ended up in prostitution. In her efforts to found a Congregation that would work for the rehabilitation of these young women, Maria was helped by Klementyna Jaworsky and Countess Aniela Potulicky, who provided a property near Poznan for their purposes. The work soon attracted many offers of help and postulants who were ready to try their vocation. The first professions took place in 1906, and a new foundation was made in Wiktoryn, a suburb of Lublin. The Sisters' work expanded and a foundation was made in Torun, where they nursed those stricken with venereal diseases. Further foundations followed, and in 1933 a castle was bought at Jablonowo Pomorskie, where the generalate of the Congregation and a school for girls were established. The work continues in education, the care of prostitutes and the treatment of those who are diseased on account of their lifestyle.

DIVINE WORD, SOCIETY OF THE

Location: Italy (Rome)
RC (male) founded in The Netherlands in 1875 by Blessed Arnold Janssen (beatified 1975)
Abbr: SVD
Original habit: a black soutane with a cincture and crucifix.

Founded at Steyl, in The Netherlands, the Society of the Divine Word served as a missionary centre for Germany. Following his ordination in 1861, Arnold Janssen became diocesan president for the Apostleship of Prayer for the diocese of Münster, and founded the Mission House of St Michael at Steyl, from which grew the Society of the Divine Word, receiving papal approbation in 1901. Fr Janssen also founded the Society of the Servants of the Holy Ghost, and the Society of the Sister Servants, who would help the Divine Word Missionaries in their work. Early missionary foundations were made in China, Togo in West Africa, New Guinea and some of the Pacific Islands, with a later expansion into South America. Houses were also opened throughout Europe and the USA.

✠ Divine Word Missionaries
  Steyl Missionaries

DOMINIC, MISSIONARIES OF ST

Location: Spain (Madrid)
RC (female) founded in Spain in 1887
Original habit: a white tunic and scapular with a black cincture and a short black veil.

A Congregation founded in Toledo, Spain, which became independent within the Dominican Order in 1933. Its apostolate is concerned with teaching the young and caring for the aged and sick. The work of the Congregation now extends to Italy, Spain, Portugal, the Philippines, Taiwan, Japan, Korea, Chile, China and the USA.

DOMINIC, ORDER OF ST – Anglican

Defunct
Anglican (male and female) founded in England in 1925

Founded in 1925 as the Anglican Third Order of St Dominic, the Congregation was made up of priests and laymen observing the Rule of the Third Order and receiving guidance from a council of priest-tertiaries. They undertook to recite the Dominican office of compline daily. Priests in Holy Orders could recite either the Roman or the Dominican Breviary.

DOMINIC, ORDER OF ST – Roman Catholic

Location: Italy (Rome)
RC (male and female) founded in France in the 13th century by St Dominic Guzman (canonized 1234)
Abbr: OP
Original habit: (monks) a white tunic and scapular, cape and hood with a leather cincture and a black cape. Dominican nuns and Sisters wear the same habit with a white unstarched wimple and binder and a black veil. Lay Sisters and Brothers wore the white tunic with a black scapular.

GENERAL INTRODUCTION

St Dominic Guzman (1170–1221), who was born at Calaruega in Spain, was ordained at the age of twenty-four and became an Augustinian canon regular of the cathedral of Osma. This was a time of much change in the Roman Catholic world, with the general ignorance of the average believer unable to cope with the great heresies of the Albigensians and the Waldenses which were starting to make serious inroads among the faithful of Lombardy and Languedoc. Pope Innocent III tried to recruit preachers to improve the quality of sermons and catechesis, and St Dominic, together with his bishop, Blessed Diego de Azevedo, went to southern France, where the Albigensians were flourishing. In 1206 at Prouille, in the diocese of Toulouse, St Dominic founded his first monastery for women who had converted from the Albigensian heresy. The women were placed under the Augustinian Rule, with special constitutions drawn up for them by St Dominic. The First Order of Preachers was founded from a group of diocesan missionaries at Toulouse in 1215, whose main occupation was to combat the Albigensian heresy. These preachers, or friars, were sent out to oppose heresies, with the approval of Pope Honorius III. Lay defenders of the Church, known as the Militia of Jesus

Christ, were also recruited and joined with another lay group, the Brothers and Sisters of the Penance of St Dominic, to form the Third Order of St Dominic.

The Dominican family today is divided into the following:

1 The First Order of Friars Preachers
2 The Second Order of St Dominic (nuns)
3 The Third Order of St Dominic (Sisters)
4 Secular Institutes and Third Order Seculars affiliated to the Order
5 Lay fraternities – in addition there are fraternities of priests and Associations, such as those of the Holy Name of Jesus and of the Most Holy Rosary, attached to the Order

The First Order of Friars Preachers (the Order of Preachers)

The First Order was founded in 1215 by St Dominic, and approved in 1216, from a group of diocesan missionaries in order to preach against the heresies, particularly the Albigensian, which were making much progress in southern France. The Order is now both active and contemplative, its members involved in teaching at all levels, in preaching, writing and conducting retreats and missions. Dominican friars are to be found throughout the world, divided into various provinces.

The Second Order of Contemplative Nuns (Nuns of the Order of Preachers)

From its foundation the Second Order of St Dominic spread rapidly throughout Europe, and many houses were opened in Germany, France and Italy. There were houses in England and Scotland before they were suppressed by Henry VIII in 1539. Today the Order is strictly enclosed, with the members observing a fully contemplative way of life revolving around the conventual Mass and the divine office.

The Third Order of Dominican Sisters (the Conventual Third Order; the Sisters of Penance)

Originally deriving from male and female secular members of the Militia of Jesus Christ and another lay group, the Third Order is now of Sisters only. The Sisters are grouped into many autonomous Dominican Congregations.

DOMINICAN CONGREGATION OF OUR LADY OF THE ROSARY OF FATIMA

Location: Puerto Rico (Ponce)
RC (female) founded in Puerto Rico in 1949 by Mother Dominic Guzman
Abbr: OP
Original habit: Dominican style.

A Congregation founded to evangelize, care for the sick and undertake social action. In 1954 it was affiliated to the Dominican Order, and it received papal approbation in 1965 and 1983.

DOMINICAN CONGREGATION OF OUR LADY OF THE SACRED HEART

Location: USA (Grand Rapids, Michigan)
RC (female) founded in the USA in 1871 by Mother Aquinata
Abbr: OP
Original habit: Dominican style.

A Congregation founded in Traverse City, Michigan. The Sisters work in education and maintain Aquinas College, founded in 1886, and several academies. They also nurse and have concern for the social needs of the disadvantaged.

✠ Dominican Sisters of Marywood

DOMINICAN CONGREGATION OF THE SINSINAWA CONGREGATION OF THE MOST HOLY ROSARY

Location: USA (Sinsinawa, Wisconsin)
RC (female) founded in the USA in 1847 by Fr Samuel Mazzuchelli
Abbr: OP
Original habit: Dominican style.

The Sinsinawa Congregation, which combines both the active and the contemplative lives, is concerned with prayer, study, ministry, sponsoring Roman Catholic schools and colleges, running retreats and maintaining a care centre for needy women. There are houses in the USA, Bolivia, Guatemala and Trinidad.

✦ Sinsinawa Dominicans

DOMINICAN MISSIONARY SISTERS OF THE MOST SACRED HEART OF JESUS

Location: Zimbabwe (Harare)
RC (female) founded from Germany in 1877
Abbr: OP
Original habit: Dominican style.

The foundation dates from 1877, when six Dominican Sisters from the convent of St Ursula in Augsburg, Germany, went to South Africa and settled at King William's Town, Cape Colony. The community became independent in 1905 with a new set of Constitutions. The Congregation now operates in Zimbabwe and Zambia, in South America (Colombia) and in England and Germany. The main area of work is in health care programmes, especially for those with AIDS and TB, hospital chaplaincies, general parish work, counselling, and teaching at all levels.

DOMINICAN NUNS – Farmington Hills

Location: USA (Farmington, Michigan)
RC (female) founded in 1966

Abbr: OP
Original habit: Dominican style.

The house in Farmington was opened when this community moved there from Detroit, Michigan, in 1966. The original Dominican nuns had left Europe and settled in Newark, New Jersey, in 1906, later opening the house in Detroit. The nuns are cloistered and contemplative. They support themselves through alms, the baking of altar breads and the making and selling of small gift items.

DOMINICAN NUNS – Menlo Park

Location: USA (Corpus Christi Monastery, Menlo Park, California)
RC (female) founded from the Dominican Nuns of the Bronx (see below)
Abbr: OP
Original habit: Dominican style.

It was largely due to the unfailing enthusiasm of a Dominican priest, Fr A. L. McMahon, that eight Dominican nuns left their monastery in the Bronx, New York, in 1921 to travel to California, where they lived in rented buildings. A few years later they were able to buy the property at Menlo Park, where they give their lives to Eucharistic devotion, maintaining perpetual adoration of the Blessed Sacrament in their convent chapel.

DOMINICAN NUNS – Oslo

Location: Norway (Lunden, Oslo)
RC (female) founded from the Dominican monastery at Lourdes
Abbr: OP
Original habit: Dominican style.

These contemplative Dominican nuns were founded from the Dominican monastery in Lourdes, France, arriving in Oslo in 1951. The new foundation became independent in 1959 and the buildings were completed in 1966. The full monastic life is followed.

DOMINICAN NUNS – The Bronx

Location: USA (Hunt's Point, Bronx, New York)
RC (female) founded in the USA in 1889 by Julia Crooks (Mother Mary of Jesus)
Abbr: OP
Original habit: Dominican style.

Mother Mary of Jesus, from St Dominic's Monastery in Newark, New Jersey, which was the first Dominican house in America, left to found the Corpus Christi Monastery in the Bronx district of New York. She was accompanied by six nuns and an extern Sister. The life of the nuns today is purely enclosed and contemplative.

DOMINICAN SISTERS – Amityville

Location: USA (Amityville, New York)
RC (female) founded in the USA in 1853 by Mother Josepha
Abbr: OP
Original habit: Dominican style.

A Congregation founded in Brooklyn, New York. The Sisters work in education, nursing, domestic service and home and foreign missions. Their work takes them into eight other American states and to Puerto Rico and Colombia.

DOMINICAN SISTERS – Bethany

Location: France (St Sulpice-de-Favières)
RC (female) founded in France in 1866 by Fr M. Jean-Joseph Lataste
Abbr: OP
Original habit: Dominican style.

This Dominican Congregation was founded as a contemplative community by Fr Lataste, who had been deeply moved by the effect that a retreat had on some women prisoners. The purpose of the Congregation is to help those who are in trouble and to

offer counselling and spiritual direction as necessary. There is another house in England and several in Europe and the USA.

DOMINICAN SISTERS – Caldwell

Location: USA (Caldwell, New Jersey)
RC (female) founded in the USA in 1912
Abbr: OP
Original habit: Dominican style

The origin of the Congregation lies with the Second Order of Dominican nuns, or Contemplative Dominicans, who had left Ratisbon, in Bavaria, for New York in 1853. Mother Catherine Muth and some other Sisters established their first house – the Convent of St Dominic – in Jersey City in 1881. A move to Caldwell was made in 1912, when the Congregation changed to the more appropriate active Third Order, which accommodated a teaching apostolate. Other foundations were made, at Tacoma, Washington and Akron, Ohio. The work of the Congregation has now expanded from teaching and includes parish catechesis, working for social justice, care for the aged and infirm and running the Genesis Farm, a reflection centre.

DOMINICAN SISTERS – Malta

Location: Malta (Rabat)
RC (female) founded on Gozo in 1880 by Caroline Cauchi
Abbr: OP
Original habit: Dominican style.

A Congregation founded on the island of Gozo, Malta, and which has now spread to other countries, including in the Far East. The Sisters work with the aged and the sick; they also teach, take care of orphans and undertake various forms of missionary work.

DOMINICAN SISTERS – Maryknoll

Location: USA (Maryknoll, New York)
RC (female) founded in the USA in 1912 by Mother
Mary Joseph Rogers
Abbr: OP
Original habit: Dominican style.

This is both an active and contemplative
Congregation with simple vows. The apostolate includes teaching, nursing, social and
domestic service, home missions, and foreign missions to Africa, the Caroline
Islands, Ceylon, Japan, Hong Kong, the
Philippines, Taiwan and South America.

✠ Maryknoll Sisters

DOMINICAN SISTERS OF HOPE

Location: USA (Ossining, New York)
RC (female) founded in the USA in 1981
Abbr: OP
Original habit: Dominican style.

A foundation formed from the close collab-
oration of three earlier Congregations, the
Dominican Sisters of St Catherine of Siena
(Fall River, Massachusetts), of the Most
Holy Rosary (Newburgh, New York) and of
the Sick Poor of the Immaculate Conception (Ossining, New York).

DOMINICAN SISTERS OF ST CATHARINE OF SIENA

Location: USA (St Catharine, Kentucky)
RC (female) founded in the USA in 1822 by Fr
Samuel Thomas Wilson
Abbr: OP
Original habit: Dominican style.

An active Congregation with simple vows
and now concerned with the conducting of
retreats, teaching, nursing and maintaining
missions to Puerto Rico.

DOMINICAN SISTERS OF ST CATHERINE DE RICCI

Location: USA (Elkins Park, Philadelphia)
RC (female) founded in the USA in 1880 by Mother
Catherine de Ricci
Abbr: OP
Original habit: Dominican style.

The mother house of the Congregation,
originally in Glen Falls, New York, was later
moved to Philadelphia. The Sisters combine
active and contemplative lives by conducting retreats, teaching, maintaining residences for women, particularly for those in
need or in danger, and other social service
concerns.

DOMINICAN SISTERS OF ST CATHERINE OF SIENA – King William's Town

Location: South Africa (Crown Mines 2025)
RC (female) founded in South Africa in 1877 by
Sisters from Augsburg, Bavaria
Abbr: OP
Original habit: Dominican style.

A Congregation of Dominican Sisters
founded at the request of the vicar apostolic
of the East District of the Cape of Good
Hope. Six Dominican Sisters went from
Bavaria to the Cape Province and opened a
school there in 1878. Further foundations
were made in East London, the Transvaal
and Natal. In 1905 the Congregation
became independent of the German mother
house and pontifical approbation was
granted in 1926. Throughout South Africa
this Congregation runs schools for children
of all races, as well as hospitals, institutes
for the disabled and for the deaf and dumb,
and centres for the training of African
teachers. Separate independent foundations
were made in Rhodesia (Zimbabwe) and
also at Oakford, Natal, from which was
founded the Congregation at Newcastle,
Natal. In the 1930s further houses were
opened in England and Ireland. The latest

developments are excursions into South America, in Bolivia and Ecuador.

DOMINICAN SISTERS OF ST CATHERINE OF SIENA – Newcastle

Location: England (Watford, Hertfordshire)
RC (female) founded in South Africa in 1896 by Mother Rose Niland
Abbr: OP
Original habit: Dominican style.

This independent Congregation was founded in Newcastle, Natal, from the Oakford Congregation as a rescue operation when Oakford was threatened with closure. The Sisters work in education, retreat-work and the care of convalescents.

DOMINICAN SISTERS OF ST CATHERINE OF SIENA – Oakford

Location: South Africa (Bedfordview, 2008)
RC (female) founded in South Africa in 1890
Abbr: OP
Original habit: Dominican style.

A Congregation founded by six Sisters from the Dominican King William's Congregation in Natal, which became autonomous within a year of its foundation. The Congregation created many houses throughout South Africa and has convents in England, Germany, the USA and Argentina. At one stage in its history the Congregation was on the verge of closure, but Mother Rose Niland, founder of the Newcastle Congregation, came to its rescue. The Sisters work in counselling, care of the elderly, parish catechesis and the giving of retreats.

DOMINICAN SISTERS OF ST CATHERINE OF SIENA OF RACINE

Location: USA (Racine, Wisconsin)
RC (female) founded in the USA in 1830 by Mother M. Benedicta Bauer and Sr Thomasina Gincker

Abbr: OP
Original habit: Dominican style.

The Congregation was founded by two Sisters from the Holy Cross Convent in Ratisbon, Bavaria. From the time of foundation the Congregation has always been occupied with education at all levels and has also taken up hospital work and chaplaincies. The Sisters provide retreat facilities, work with social issues and maintain missions in Mexico and Kenya. There are houses throughout the USA.

✠ Racine Dominican Sisters

DOMINICAN SISTERS OF ST CECILIA

Location: USA (Nashville, Tennessee)
RC (female) founded in the USA in 1860
Abbr: OP
Original habit: Dominican style.

A Congregation of Dominican Sisters, founded in Nashville as an active community to provide a Roman Catholic education for young women, from primary to college level. The Sisters now work in Tennessee, Ohio, Virginia, Maryland and Alabama.

DOMINICAN SISTERS OF ST DOMINIC – Akron

Location: USA (Akron, Ohio)
RC (female) founded in the USA in 1929
Abbr: OP
Original habit: Dominican style.

A Congregation of Dominican Sisters who are involved in teaching, running summer camps, home missions and catechesis.

DOMINICAN SISTERS OF ST MARY OF THE SPRINGS

Location: USA (Columbus, Ohio)
RC (female) founded in the USA in 1830 by Mother Angela Sansbury

Abbr: OP
Original habit: Dominican style.

The Congregation was founded in Ohio by Mother Sansbury, who came to Ohio in 1830 with three other members from the Dominican foundation in Kentucky, which had been founded in 1822. From the Columbus foundation two others were made, in Galveston, Texas, and West Springfield, Illinois. The Sisters, who have houses throughout the USA, work in a variety of fields. They teach, provide home health care, nurse in hospitals, conduct parish and campus ministries, care for the elderly and have a concern for social issues. Foreign missions are maintained in Puerto Rico, Bolivia, Peru and China.

DOMINICAN SISTERS OF THE CONGREGATION OF BROOKLINE

Location: USA (Brookline, Massachusetts)
RC (female) founded in France in 1853 by Mother Marie de St Rose Lejeune
Abbr: OP
Original habit: Dominican style.

The apostolate of the Congregation is in teaching, social service, nursing and the conducting of retreats, and in home and foreign missions, which have taken the Sisters to Japan, North Africa and Sweden.

DOMINICAN SISTERS OF THE CONGREGATION OF OUR LADY OF THE ROSARY

Location: USA (Sparkhill, New York)
RC (female) founded in the USA in 1876 by Alice Thorpe (Mother Antonius Thorpe)
Abbr: OP
Original habit: Dominican style.

The foundation dates from 1876, a few years after Alice Thorpe, a convert, and her sister Lucy went to New York as missionaries. They were anxious to work among the poor and needy and were encouraged

in their venture by Fr John Antonius Rochford. With the approbation of the cardinal archbishop of New York, Fr Rochford was able to receive the simple vows of both Alice Thorpe and Ellen Higgins. The community grew and moved in 1884 to Sparkhill to found an orphanage for boys. As the community increased, so too did their work as it extended into teaching, and supporting a foreign mission to Pakistan and a care centre for women in need.

✠ Sparkhill Dominicans

DOMINICAN SISTERS OF THE CONGREGATION OF ST CATHERINE OF SIENA – Kenosha

Location: USA (Kenosha, Wisconsin)
RC (female) founded in Portugal in 1866
Abbr: OP
Original habit: Dominican style.

A Dominican Congregation founded in Portugal and introduced into the USA in 1912. It became an independent Congregation in 1952. The apostolate includes teaching in parish schools, nursing the sick in hospitals and caring for the aged and infirm.

DOMINICAN SISTERS OF THE CONGREGATION OF THE HOLY CROSS

Location: USA (Edmunds, Washington)
RC (female) founded in the USA in 1923
Abbr: OP
Original habit: Dominican style.

A Congregation of Dominican Sisters who teach and work in health care, especially through nursing.

DOMINICAN SISTERS OF THE CONGREGATION OF THE MOST HOLY ROSARY

Location: USA (Adrian, Michigan)
RC (female) founded in the USA in 1853 by nuns from Bavaria

Abbr: OP
Original habit: Dominican style.

This Congregation is descended from a group of Bavarian Dominican nuns who went to Williamsburg, New York, from Regensburg in 1853, and went on to Michigan in 1877, where they were joined by six Dominican Sisters from New York. Their initial work was to establish schools, and these were followed by hospitals and homes for the elderly and an academy for young women. The Adrian Congregation became independent in 1923 and received papal approval in 1937.

✠ Adrian Dominicans

DOMINICAN SISTERS OF THE ENGLISH CONGREGATION OF ST CATHERINE OF SIENA

Location: England (Stone, Staffordshire)
RC (female) founded in England in 1859 by Mother Margaret Hallahan
Abbr: OP
Original habit: Dominican style.

A Congregation of Dominican Sisters which was founded to teach, care for the sick and minister to the poor. It received papal approval in 1859. The English Congregation, as it is today, was formed in 1929 by the union of the following Congregations with that of Mother Hallahan's Congregation at Stone, Staffordshire:

1 The Congregation of St Rose of Lima (founded 1855)
2 The Congregation of the Holy Rosary (founded 1871)
3 The Congregation of St Vincent Ferrer (founded 1909)
4 The Congregation of Our Lady Help of Christians (founded 1866)

The Sisters still work in education, preaching and care of the sick, infirm and handicapped, as well as in parish ministries.

DOMINICAN SISTERS OF THE MOST HOLY NAME OF JESUS – San Rafael

Location: USA (San Rafael, California)
RC (female) founded in the USA in 1851 by Sister Mary Goemaere
Abbr: OP
Original habit: Dominican style.

An active Congregation founded from the Convent of the Holy Cross in Paris in response to a request from the first bishop of San Francisco, Joseph Sadoc Alemany, OP. Other foundations followed in both California and Nevada. The Sisters work in health care, parish ministry, the conducting of retreats, the care of the elderly and welfare for the poor

DOMINICAN SISTERS OF THE PRESENTATION OF TOURS

Location: Italy (Rome)
RC (female) founded in France in 1696 by Marie Poussepin
Abbr: OP
Original habit: a white serge tunic with a black apron; a cornette-style headdress and a fifteen-decade rosary.

A Congregation founded in Sainville, France, in the 17th century. The Sisters now work throughout Europe, North and South America, India and Africa with an apostolate in teaching, nursing the elderly and poor, and other charitable works.

✠ Dominican Sisters of Charity of the Presentation of Our Lady
Dominican Sisters of the Presentation

DOMINICAN SISTERS OF THE QUEEN OF THE MOST HOLY ROSARY

Location: USA (Mission San Jose, California)
RC (female) founded in the USA in 1888 by Mother Pia
Abbr: OP
Original habit: Dominican style.

A Congregation founded as a combined active and contemplative community with simple vows. Its members work in education and in the care of abandoned and orphaned children, undertake social services and conduct home missions

DOMINICAN SISTERS OF THE RELIEF OF INCURABLE CANCER

Location: USA (Hawthorne, New York)
RC (female) founded in the USA in 1896 by Rose Hawthorne (Mother M. Alphonsa)
Abbr: OP
Original habit: Dominican style, with a white veil worn when attending the sick.

Rose Hawthorne worked in a New York tenement, attending the sick who were suffering from cancer. With Alice Huber and others she was later able to buy the tenement which then became known as St Rose's Free Home for Incurable Cancer. The community was received into the Third Order of St Dominic in 1899 and in 1901 opened a second Home in Sherman Park, now known as Hawthorne.

✠ Congregation of St Rose of Lima

DOMINICAN SISTERS OF THE ROMAN CONGREGATION

Location: Italy (Rome)
RC (female) founded in 1959
Abbr: OP
Original habit: Dominican style.

The Congregation was formed when five Congregations, each with a long Dominican tradition, joined together in 1956–7 to form a single, large foundation. The Sisters' work is varied and the apostolate chosen depends on the need of the local church, but they are all heavily involved in poor relief, peace and justice projects, and education at all levels including literacy programmes and special needs teaching. The members are also concerned with ministries among non-Caucasian populations and the provision of retirement homes, retreats and spiritual renewal centres. The Congregation is represented in the USA and Canada, Europe, Japan, Brazil, Chile, Benin and Haiti.

DOMINICAN SISTERS OF THE SACRED HEART

Location: USA (Houston, Texas)
RC (female) founded in the USA in 1882 by Mother Agnes Mageveney
Abbr: OP
Original habit: Dominican style.

The Congregation of the Sacred Heart was founded at Galveston, Texas, with the encouragement of Bishop Sylvester Rosecrans. Mother Mageveney and Mother Rose Lynch, members of the Congregation of St Mary of the Springs in Columbus, went to Galveston to open a school. With some twenty other Sisters accompanying them, the party arrived in Galveston in 1882 to begin their foundation. In 1902 it was affiliated to the Dominican Order and became a Pontifical Congregation in 1943. Following Vatican II, ministries such as parish catechesis, campus ministries and social work were taken up, together with a mission to Guatemala. In 1987 the Sisters offered public sanctuary to refugees from El Salvador and Guatemala.

DOMINICAN SISTERS OF THE THIRD ORDER – Great Bend

Location: USA (Great Bend, Kansas)
RC (female) founded in the USA in 1902 by Mother Antonina Fischer
Abbr: OP
Original habit: Dominican style.

A Dominican Congregation founded at Great Bend, Kansas, with an active apostolate in teaching, home and foreign missions and the conducting of retreats.

DOMINICAN SISTERS OF THE THIRD ORDER – Springfield

Location: USA (Springfield, Illinois)
RC (female) founded in the USA in 1873
Abbr: OP
Original habit: Dominican style.

A Dominican Congregation founded in Springfield, Illinois, whose work includes teaching, nursing and domestic service.

DOMINICAN SISTERS – Western Australia

Location: Western Australia (Doubleview, Perth)
RC (female) founded in Western Australia in 1899 by Mother Mary Gabriel Gill
Abbr: OP
Original habit: Dominican style.

In 1899 a Dominican foundation was made from Dunedin, New Zealand, in the Western Australian diocese of Geraldton. Six professed Sisters went to Australia and set up schools at Greenough and Back Flats, Western Australia. A mother house was later established at Dongara. Some controversies arose over the status of this Congregation and what were seen as certain irregularities in the Constitution, such as the substitution of the little office for the divine office. After the death of Mother Gill, Sisters from Ireland and New Zealand as well as from other parts of Australia joined the Congregation and new foundations were made. The Sisters have an active apostolate in education, counselling, chaplaincy and hospital visitation, parish work and catechesis. There are houses in Sydney, Melbourne and Geraldton in Australia, and another in California.

DON BOSCO INSTITUTE

Location: USA (Peterson, New Jersey)
RC (male) founded in Italy in 1917

The origin of this Institute is to be found in the Don Bosco Volunteers, founded by the Blessed Philip Rinaldi (beatified 1990) in Rome in 1917. The Institute's approval as an Association of Faithful was granted in 1994. The aim of the members is to improve society by observing the precepts of the Gospels and by living a life of witness according to the Salesian spirit.

DON BOSCO VOLUNTEERS

Location: Italy (Rome)
RC (female) founded in Italy in 1917 by Blessed Philip Rinaldi

Blessed Philip Rinaldi, the founder of this Secular Institute of pontifical right, was successor to St John Bosco, the founder of the Salesians. The original intention of the Volunteers was to help young people by imitating the spirituality of Don Bosco, and this was achieved by the members taking the three traditional vows of religion, those of poverty, chastity and obedience, but not wearing any identifying habit or badge, allowing them to work in many areas. The Volunteers can be found in all sectors of society, in business and in office management, as health workers, in education as teachers, or as social workers. They also act as ministers of the Eucharist in parishes. The Church gave its approval to Secular Institutes in 1947.

DOROTHY, ORDER OF ST

Location: Italy (Rome)
RC (female) founded in Italy in 1834 by St Paula Frassinetti (canonized 1984)
Abbr: SSD
Original habit: a black tunic with a white crimped headband partially encircling the face, and a black veil.

A Congregation founded at Quinto, near Genoa, in Italy, the birthplace of the founder, Paula Frassinetti (1809–82). It started with a small group of young women who wanted to live a religious life, help in the parish and educate girls. They banded together, with the encouragement of the founder's brother, Fr Giuseppe, who drew up a Rule of life for them. The Congregation was at first known as the Daughters of Holy Faith. Two priests, Frs Luca and Marco Passi, were forming little groups of religious foundations to further parish work in Italy, especially targeting young people, which were known as the Apostolic Work of St Dorothy. Paula Frassinetti was offered the leadership of this, which she accepted with a view to amalgamating the various groups into one Congregation. As they all had different apostolates, this was not to be, but it has resulted in more than one Italian Congregation today known as the Sisters of St Dorothy, others being in Venice and Brescia. The Congregation of St Dorothy, as it evolved, underwent many difficulties and privations. The Sisters still work in education, which now includes catechesis. There are missions throughout the world and houses in Italy, England, Portugal, the USA, Taiwan, Africa and Brazil.

DOROTHY OF CEMMO, SISTERS OF ST

Location: Italy (Cemmo di Capo di Ponte, Brescia)
RC (female) founded in Italy in 1843 by Blessed Annunziata Cochetti (beatified 1991)
Original habit: a dark tunic with a small white collar and a black veil over a white head cap which is gathered at the edge but does not completely surround the face.

The Congregation was founded in Cemmo by Annunziata Cochetti (1800–82), who had trained as a teacher. Following the death of her parents she decided to offer herself to teach in a school for country girls at Cemmo, which had experienced many problems. Together with the help of a friend, she greatly improved the standard of the school. Feeling that she may have a vocation in this field, Annunziata completed a novitiate with the Sisters of St Dorothy (see previous entry), with a view to founding her own Congregation, the Sisters of St Dorothy of Cemmo, which was achieved in 1843. The Congregation now has houses in Europe, Argentina, Burundi and Zaire, where the Sisters undertake work with a special emphasis on teaching and the provision of retreats.

DRAGON, KNIGHTS OF THE

Defunct
RC (male Equestrian Order) founded in Germany in the 15th century
Original habit: (insignia) a dead dragon hanging from a gold-linked chain with a green knot signifying victory over heretics and infidels.

The newly elected German king and king of the Romans, Sigismund, was crowned as Holy Roman Emperor in 1433. He revived an earlier tradition of emperors by convening Ecumenical Councils at Constance (1414–18) and Basle (1431). In order to reward those who were prepared to protect Christendom against the infidel he erected the Most Noble Military Order of the Dragon, whose members wore the insignia described above.

E

EAR OF CORN, KNIGHTS OF THE

Defunct
RC (male Equestrian Order) founded in France in the mid-15th century by Francis I, Duke of Brittany
Original habit: (insignia) the image of a white ermine on a gold thread field with the motto 'A Mia Via' (From My Way) held between its front and hind paws; (dress) a white damask robe lined in royal purple silk with the insignia on the left-hand side and a gold collar with crossed ears of corn from which the insignia is suspended.

The Order was founded in honour of the Blessed Sacrament. It was suppressed by King Charles VIII of France in the late 15th century.

EDITH STEIN COMMUNITY, THE ST

Location: USA (Lubbock, Texas)
RC (male and female) founded in the USA in 1998

A Public Association whose members may take vows but do not live in community, maintaining their lives and professions in the world. Membership is open to all, male and female, married and unmarried, and an undertaking is made to attend daily Mass when possible, to recite the prayer of the Church, to meditate for at least one half hour a day and to wear the brown scapular of Our Lady of Mount Carmel under the outer clothes.

EDMUND, SOCIETY OF ST

Location: Italy (Rome)
RC (male) founded in France in 1843 by Jean-Baptiste Muard
Abbr: SSE

A society founded at Pontigny, France, the name deriving from the fact that the original foundation was made in the ruined Cistercian Abbey, where St Edmund (Rich), an archbishop of Canterbury in the 13th century, had retired and died as a Cistercian. The Fathers' work is mainly concerned with parish missions, education in seminaries and colleges, and conducting foreign missions. The Congregation arose in the wake of the French Revolution, and its priests preached missions and tried to counter the effects of Jansenism, a heresy widespread in France at the time. Houses were later opened in the USA, where the society settled in Colchester, Vermont. The Jesuit-inspired Rule and Constitutions were approved by the Holy See in 1911. Fr Muard left this community in order to found the Missionary Benedictines of La Pierre-qui-Vire, from which Buckfast Abbey in England was founded in 1882.

⊕ Edmundite Fathers
   Edmundites
   Society of Oblate Fathers of St Edmund

and of the Sacred Heart of Jesus and the Immaculate Heart of Mary

ELEPHANT, KNIGHTS OF THE

Defunct
RC (male Equestrian Order) founded in Denmark in the 16th century
Original habit: (insignia) a gold collar from which hung an elephant with a castle turret. Beneath the elephant was a medallion bearing the image of the Blessed Virgin Mary, surrounded by rays. The insignia later changed when two patriarchal crosses were added to the collar; (dress) a silk cloak, worn only on days of great solemnity, with a jewelled clasp and a white cross with radiating rays decorating the left-hand side. Beneath the cloak and on the right-hand side of the chest was worn a pendant with the elephant insignia, held in place by interwoven silk cords.

A 16th-century Danish Equestrian Order dedicated to the Blessed Virgin Mary and more properly known as the Order of St Mary and the Elephant. It is not clear whether the foundation was made by King Frederick I of Denmark, or his son, Christian III. The elephant insignia was chosen because of the animal's reputation for fortitude and prudence.

ELIGIUS IN FRANCE, THE NUNS OF ST

Defunct
RC (female) founded in France in 6th century by St Eligius (Eloy)
Original habit: a black tunic and white mantle with a black veil.

St Eligius (or Eloy) had trained as a goldsmith and rose to be the mint master of Paris, attracting the attention of the French court of Clothaire II and his son, Dagobert I, and he was rewarded with considerable wealth. The saint used this money and property he had acquired to establish an Order of nuns, first at Solignac and later at Paris. The Order was strictly contemplative and enclosed, and perpetual abstinence was observed. Although St Eligius was only in deacon's orders, he was persuaded with some reluctance to accept the bishopric of the united and vacant sees of Noyon and Tournai. Legend has it that he once took the devil by the nose with his goldsmith's tools.

ELIZABETH, SISTERS OF ST

Location: Italy (Rome)
RC (female) founded in Germany in 1842 by Klara Wolff

The Congregation of the Sisters of St Elizabeth was founded in Neisse, Silesia, by Klara Wolff with the help of two sisters, Mathilde and Maria Merkert and Franziska Werner. They did not want to adopt a definite Rule and were content to remain an association of itinerant nurses. This lack of organization almost caused the downfall of the community, and many left to join the Sisters of St Charles Borromeo. When both Mathilde and Maria Merkert died, the remaining Sisters resolved to renew their efforts to put the Congregation on a more traditional footing, dedicating their enterprise to St Elizabeth. The work then began to prosper, and ecclesiastical approbation was given in 1859 by the prince-bishop Heinrich Forster of Breslau (Wroclaw), which was then part of German Silesia. A novitiate was started, and a year later the first twenty-four Sisters made their profession. Papal approbation came in 1887 and 1898. The Congregation spread to Italy, Sweden and Norway. The Sisters now work with the care of the poor, especially those who are sick or who may be living in isolated circumstances and without home assistance.

EPIPHANY, COMMUNITY OF THE

Defunct
Anglican (female) founded in England in 1883 by George Wilkinson and Mother Julian Warrender

An Anglican religious community founded in Truro, Cornwall, in 1883 by George Wilkinson, bishop of Truro, and Miss (later Mother) Julian Warrender. The two had met while George Wilkinson was running a mission in London. Miss Warrender and some companions, who all wished to embrace a religious life, came together and moved to Truro at the invitation of George Wilkinson, who composed a Rule and Constitutions for the new Congregation, and a mother house was established there. A (lay) Second Order was founded in 1910 to provide an opportunity for laywomen who felt they had a vocation to join in with the work of the Congregation. The Sisters worked in many fields, from arranging and running quiet days for young people to making and maintaining church vestments and altar-bread making. For some time there was also a convalescent home, a boarding home for schoolchildren and a rehabilitation centre for girls at risk. The influence of the community was also felt in the outside world through foreign missions. Foundations were made in Japan, at Kobe (1927), St Hilda's Mission (Tokyo, 1919) and the Community of Nazareth (Tokyo, 1938); the latter is now an independent community with its own Rule and Constitutions, but the other Japanese houses closed with the outbreak of the Second World War.

EPIPHANY, OXFORD MISSION BROTHERHOOD OF THE

Location: India (Calcutta)
Anglican (male) founded in India in 1880
Abbr: BE

A Congregation founded in Calcutta, India, but now also found in a second centre at Barisal, Bangladesh. The work of its members, who do not take formal vows but only a solemn promise of obedience, is to maintain Christian hostels for students and to work for the care of the sick, including sufferers from leprosy.

EPIPHANY, OXFORD MISSION SISTERHOOD OF THE

Defunct
Anglican (female) founded in India in 1902

A community of women, founded on Benedictine lines, who could co-operate with the Oxford Mission Brotherhood of the Epiphany (see previous entry) in their work. The Sisters, who worked at the two centres in Calcutta and Barisal, Bangladesh, taught Indian Christian women, provided a boarding school for girls at Barisal, and a home for widows, orphans and single mothers, and helped with medical care, especially as midwives. The two Epiphany communities worked closely together.

✤ Sisterhood of the Epiphany

EPIPHANY, SOCIETY OF THE

Defunct
Anglican (female) founded in the USA in 1897 by Herbert L. Satterlee

A Society founded by the bishop of Washington. The Sisters ran a school for girls in that city.

EUCHARIST, RELIGIOUS OF THE

Location: Belgium (Watermael)
RC (female) founded in Belguim in 1856 by Anna de Meeus and Fr Jean-Baptiste Boone, SJ
Abbr: RE
Original habit: a black dress, cape and bonnet with a black veil, white coif and binder and starched collar; a long veil was worn in chapel during adoration; a silver cross with the image of the

Sacred Heart on one side and a chalice sumounted by a host on the reverse, was worn after final vows had been taken.

Motivated by the sad state of repair of many churches and their fabric, Anna de Meeus decided to form an association in Brussels in 1848 which would make reparation for the insults to the Blessed Sacrament, and undertake the repair of vestments and church linen. This Association led to the formation of The Religious of Perpetual Adoration, which received papal approbation in 1872. The Sisters now work in catechetics, especially for First Communicants, give retreats and spread devotion to the Blessed Sacrament through such exercises as the Forty Hours Devotion and Exposition.

✠ Religious of the Perpetual Adoration of the Most Holy Sacrament

EUCHARIST, SOCIETY OF THE DAUGHTERS OF THE

Defunct
RC (female) founded in the USA in 1909 by Mother Katharine A. Dietz
Abbr: SDE

An active Order concerned with visiting the sick and running a convalescent home for aged and infirm women.

EUCHARISTIC FRANCISCAN MISSIONARIES

Location: USA (Los Angeles, California)
RC (female) founded in Mexico in 1943 by Mother Maria Gemma de Jesus Aranda.
Abbr: EFMS

This Diocesan Congregation was founded in Mexico City, with a later foundation made in California, where the Sisters undertake missionary work through the adoration of the Blessed Sacrament and provide catechesis. They are also involved in outreach programmes, retreats and diocesan work throughout California.

EVORA AND AVIZ, KNIGHTS OF

Defunct
RC (male Equestrian Order) founded in Portugal in the 12th century
Original habit: a white woollen mantle with a green fleur-de-lis cross outlined in gold on the left-hand side

Alfonso I, the first king of an independent Portugal, having won a great victory over the Moors at Ovrique in 1139, left a small company of knights, known as the Brethren of St Mary, to guard the open plains of Alemtejo Province. The knights were given a foundation at Evora, south-east of Lisbon, embraced a Benedictine life modified along Cistercian lines and became known as the Brethren of St Mary of Evora. When Evora was returned to the more powerful Knights Templar, the community was handed over to the Templars and came under the jurisdiction of the Order of Calatreve. In 1190, following invasion by a Muslim sect from North Africa, Evora held out, gaining as a prize the town of Aviz, and the monks were afterwards known by both titles. The community separated into knights, who were dispensed from their vow of celibacy in 1492, and monks. By the 15th century the Order had declined and became defunct.

F

FAITH OF JESUS, CLERKS REGULAR OF THE

Defunct
RC (male) founded in Italy in 1798 by Nicholas
Paccanari

The founder, Nicholas Paccanari, was a native of Valsugnana in Italy, and had a remarkable life although the details of his death remain a mystery. He was a soldier, the sergeant of a garrison, and belonged to a pious association at the Oratory of the Caravita in Rome, which was under the direction of an ex-Jesuit. Paccanari, in his enthusiasm to reconstitute the Society of Jesus (Jesuits), which had been suppressed by Pope Clement XIV in 1773, won over the support of some priests who belonged to the same association. After drawing up a Rule, Paccanari went on an eleven-month retreat to Loreto and on his return to Rome was granted approval for his project. At the Oratory, in August 1797, Paccanari and his companions made the usual vows of poverty, chastity and obedience with an additional one of obedience to the pope. The new Congregation, known as the Society of the Faith of Jesus, was approved and moved into a country house near Spoleto to begin the communal life. Many men joined the Society and houses were opened in France, Germany, The Netherlands and England, but as the prospects for the suppressed Order brightened, members of Pac-canari's community began to leave to join the Jesuits. Fr Paccanari was undaunted and continued in his enthusiasm for his Society, but unsavoury details of his private life began to emerge and he was instructed to retire. A canonical trial took place and he was imprisoned by the Holy Office. He later disappeared, released when the French army opened the pontifical prisons, and it has been suggested that he went in disguise to Switzerland, although there are also suggestions that he was murdered and his body thrown into the Tiber. The few remaining members of his community lingered on until 1814, but had to relinquish the habit. By then the Society of Jesus had been restored and most of the remaining Paccan-arists became Jesuits.

 Baccanarists
Paccanarists

FAITHFUL COMPANIONS OF JESUS

Location: England (Broadstairs, Kent)
RC (female) founded in France in 1820 by Marie
Madeleine Victoire de Bengy, Viscountess de
Bonnault d'Houet
Abbr: FCJ
Original habit: a black habit and veil with a white
wimple.

Widowed within a year of her marriage, Marie Houet was encouraged to found a female community for those women called to the Jesuit way of life. She bought a house in Amiens, France, where the new community undertook the education and care of poor girls entrusted to them. Another house was founded at her birthplace, Chateauroux near Bourges, which became a boarding school for the daughters of wealthy families and also gave free education to those unable to pay. Another school, catering for the daughters of middle-class families, was later opened. The Society was approved in 1826 and confirmed in 1837, with Marie Houet remaining superior for life. The Institute was established in London in 1830 and the first Irish house was opened, in Limerick, in 1845. The Association Laws of France at the beginning of the 20th century encouraged the opening of more schools in Switzerland and Belgium. In 1882 the Society responded to a call from Australia, and twelve Sisters arrived in Melbourne to open and run schools which would provide a Roman Catholic education. Other foundations were made in the state of Victoria, including a nursing home for Jesuits and members of other religious Orders. Canadian and American foundations followed. The Madonna High School for Girls was opened in Toronto in 1963, and to date there are three foundations in that city. The Sisters went to Sierra Leone in 1979, where they work as part of a team with the Holy Ghost Fathers serving the whole of West Africa. Work is also carried out in Cordoba, Argentina, where the Sisters have set up a mission for pastoral, parish and retreat purposes.

FAITHFUL VIRGINS, DAUGHTERS OF THE

Location: France (Douvres La Délivrance)
RC (female) founded in France in 1831 by Henriette de Forrestier d'Osseville (Mother Saint Mary)
Abbr: OLF

Original habit: a white tunic and scapular with a black veil; a cruciform silver medal was worn around the neck, on which were engraved the words 'Virgo Fidelis'; lay Sisters wore the same habit with a brown scapular.

The Congregation of the Daughters of the Faithful Virgins was founded at La Délivrance, near Caen in Normandy and underwent many name-changes. Papal approval was granted in 1896, and today the Sisters are a presence in France, Belgium, Italy and England. The apostolate is the care of abandoned children, education in primary and secondary schools, the running of hostels for students, the conducting of retreats and the care of young women.

✠ Congregation of Our Lady of Fidelity
  Society of Our Lady of Charity of the
    Orphans
  Society of the Faithful Virgins

FATHER KOLBE MISSIONARIES OF THE IMMACULATA

Location: Italy (Bologna)
RC (female) founded in Italy 1954 by Fr Luigi Faccenda, OFMCap

A female Secular Institute founded in Bologna, Italy, and approved in 1992. Its members live out their baptismal consecration as fully as possible and seek to be charitable and to promote the knowledge and veneration of Our Lady. The members do not profess the vows of poverty, chastity and obedience.

FELIX, SISTERS OF ST

Location: Italy (Rome)
RC (female) founded in Poland in 1855 by Maria Angela Truszkowska (Blessed Mary Angela) and Blessed Honorat Kozminski (beatified 1988)
Abbr: CSSF
Original habit: brown, with a black veil and white cord girdle.

The Congregation of the Sisters of St Felix, also known as the Felicians, was founded in Warsaw under the spiritual direction of Fr Kozminski, a Capuchin. The name derived from the Sisters' practice of taking children to the shrine of St Felix, a 15th-century Franciscan saint who was especially devoted to children. In the 1860s, with civil unrest in the country, the Sisters moved to Krakow, then under Austrian control. In 1874 the Felicians established their first house in the USA, settling at Polonia, Wisconsin. There are now provinces throughout Poland, the USA, Canada and Brazil, and houses in England, France, Italy, Kenya, Mexico and Estonia. The work of the Sisters is extensive and covers all levels of education from primary school to senior college. They are also involved in health care programmes, social service issues, evangelization, pastoral and youth ministries, retreats, and domestic and diocesan administrative work.

✠ Congregation of St Felix of Catalice of the
　Third Order of St Francis
　Felician Sisters
　Felicians

FEUILLANTS, ORDER OF

Defunct
RC (male and female) founded in France in c.1145
Original habit: (male) a white Benedictine-style habit; the monks were initially discalced, but this was later restricted to the houses in France, and in Italy black wooden sandals were permitted; (female) a white woollen robe with large hanging sleeves and a black veil over a white under-veil; sandals were worn.

This was a Cistercian foundation made in the mid-12th century in a shady valley called Fuliens, near Toulouse, from which the members became known as Feuillants. In response to laxity which had developed within the community, a commendatory abbot, Jean de la Barrière (1544–1600), introduced a reform programme in 1577; the resident monks either could accept it, or would have to leave the abbey. Most of them chose to leave, settling in other Cistercian foundations, leaving just five monks at Fuliens. The reforms introduced many austerities. Wine, fish, eggs, butter and salt and other seasonings were proscribed, the monks were to go barefoot and they were to sleep on the floor with a stone for a pillow, with only four hours of sleep a night allowed. These austerities had the effect of stimulating recruitment rather than the opposite. The new Constitutions were approved by Rome in the 1580s and new communities were created in both Paris and Rouen. Jean de la Barrière also created a female version of this austere reform, the Feuillantines, membership of which was much sought after by pious women. It was Pope Urban VIII, in 1630, who divided the Feuillants into two distinct branches, the French branch under the title of *Notre Dames des Feuillants*, and an Italian branch known as the Reformed Bernardines, or more simply as the Bernardoni. Both Congregations modified their Constitutions during the 17th century. The reformed Bernardines united with the Cistercians at Cîteaux. All Feuillants and Feuillantines suffered suppression at the time of the French Revolution.

FIDELITY, ORDER OF

Defunct
RC (male Equestrian Order) founded in France in 1416
Original habit: (insignia) a cross, similar to that worn by the Bavarian Knights of the Order of St Hubert, except that on the reverse of the medallion was the insignia of the Duchy of Bar with the words (in Latin) 'The Noble Order of St Hubert of Bar, Founded in 1416'.

An Order under the patronage of St Hubert, but not to be confused with the Bavarian foundation, the Knights of the Order of St Hubert. The origins of the Order of Fidelity lay in a way of resolving conflict between the duchies of Bar and Lorraine, uniting them under René of Anjou. When the duchies were ceded to France in the 18th century, King Louis XV confirmed the Order. During the time of the French Revolution the headquarters were moved to Frankfurt, and although it returned to France in 1815, the Order failed to survive the revolution of 1830.

✠ Order of St Hubert of Lorraine

FILIPPINI RELIGIOUS TEACHERS

Location: Italy (Rome)
RC (female) founded in Italy in 1692 by St Lucy Filippini (canonized in 1930)
Abbr: MPF

The lack of education for girls from the poorest families, and the subsequent moral problems which stemmed from this, led to the foundation of this Congregation by St Lucy Filippini and Cardinal Mark Anthony Barbarigo at the end of the 17th century. The work started with the training of schoolmistresses at Montefiascone and spread throughout the world. The Sisters are now found in Europe, the USA (1910), Brazil, Ethiopia and India, and their work, still concerned with religious education, has been extended to include the care of the elderly and general parish work. The emphasis of their work in the Third World is among the very poor and deprived.

✠ Pontifical Institute of the Religious
  Teachers Filippini
  Sisters of St Lucy

FINDING OF JESUS IN THE TEMPLE, SISTERS OF THE

Location: France (Vernon, Eure)
RC (female) founded in France in 1858
Abbr: JT
Original habit: a blue tunic with a white wimple, cap and veil; a cincture with a rosary and a silver medal with the image of the Holy Family. A cross of silver and mother-of-pearl was worn around the neck, inscribed with the words 'Jesus-Mary-Joseph – His sick and His Poor'. A black veil was worn over the white one out of doors, together with a brown cloak.

Originally founded at Dorat, in France, the Congregation was invited by Cardinal Manning in 1860 to open a house in England. They settled first in London, but moved to Bristol in 1861. The Sisters observe the Rule of St Ignatius, and although not exclusively a nursing Order, they nurse the sick in their own homes and care for the poor as well as providing nursing care for elderly and sick priests.

✠ Sisters of Jesus in the Temple
  Sisters of the Temple
  Blue Nuns

FLEURY, ABBEY OF

Defunct
RC (male) founded in France (possibly) in the 7th century by Leodebaldus

The abbey was founded in Fleury-Saint-Benoit, a small village on the banks of the River Loire, the founder said by tradition to have been Leodebaldus, the abbot of St Aignan, Orléans. Two churches were erected at the abbey, one dedicated to St Peter and the other to the Virgin Mary. The abbey was famous for being the place to which the relics of St Benedict were transferred in 672, when the Lombard invasion of Italy made their removal prudent. This claim, however, has been contested. In the

10th century, with the revival of monasticism, monks from England are known to have gone to Fleury, and it was the Fleury tradition which was later taken back to England. Under the guidance of St Dunstan and St Aethelwold, many monastic centres, including those at Winchester, Abingdon and Glastonbury, were established along Fleury lines. Fleury itself was drawn into the Congregation of St Maur in the 17th century.

FONTEVRAULT, ORDER OF

Defunct
RC (male and female) founded in France in 1099 by Blessed Robert of Arbrissel
Original habit: (male) a black girded tunic, scapular and hood; (female) a black tunic with white gremial and veil; the nuns of the reformed Order wore a black veil over a white under-veil and a black mantle.

An Order founded in north-west France by Robert of Arbrissel, a noted preacher who attracted many to take up the religious life. He had made an earlier foundation of canons at La Roe, in 1096, but took little interest in them. His main concern was with those marginalized by society, especially those driven by poverty and lack of education into prostitution, and with lepers. The new foundation at Fontevrault was designed as a double monastery, with separate living areas for male and female, the members living under the Benedictine Rule. Reformed prostitutes and those in need of care and nursing were housed in their own quarters, away from the community. The overall command of the monastery was in the hands of the abbess, most likely a woman with royal or aristocratic status, for as many as fourteen of the early abbesses were princesses, five of them from the royal family. The monks were to be of service to the nuns, acting as their chaplains and spiritual directors but otherwise subser-

vient. Abstinence from flesh-meat and wine was observed, with strict enclosure and silence. The Order spread throughout France, with control exercised from Fontevrault. Three foundations were made in England, at Westwood, Nuneaton and Amesbury, all enjoying aristocratic patronage. Later reforms in France led to a new foundation in the 15th century at La Madeleine-lez-Orléans, another double house with its own Rule, which attracted many vocations. This reformed Order was dispersed during the French Revolution and later attempts to revive it did not meet with diocesan approval. The Order then became defunct. Fontevrault Abbey is the resting-place of Richard I, the Lionheart, and of Henry II of England and his wife, Eleanor of Aquitaine.

FOREIGN MISSION SOCIETY OF QUEBEC

Location: Canada (Ville de Laval, Quebec)
RC (male) founded in Canada in 1921 by the bishop of the Province of Quebec
Abbr: PME
Original habit: secular style.

A Society, with Constitutions approved in 1929, which undertakes missions in foreign countries.

FOREIGN MISSIONS, INSTITUTE FOR – Yarumal

Location: Colombia (Medellín)
RC (male) founded in Colombia in 1927
Abbr: MXY

An Apostolic Life Society approved in 1939 and 1945, founded for the purpose of undertaking missions according to need.

FOREIGN MISSIONS OF PARIS, SOCIETY OF

Location: France (Paris)
RC (male) founded in France in 1660 by Mgr Pallu and Mgr De la Motte

Abbr: MEP
Original habit: as for secular clergy.

An Apostolic Life Society founded in Paris by the vicars apostolic of Tongking (now North Vietnam) and Cochin China (now South Vietnam) to evangelize non-Christian countries and run training programmes for native clergy. The first house was set up in Paris in the Rue de Bac and was known as the Seminary of Foreign Missions, once also called the Seminary for the Conversion of the Infidels in Foreign Lands. The Society is composed of secular priests, who are not bound by vows but are committed to community life and make a promise to devote themselves to the foreign missions until death. Much of the Far East was evangelized, many native clergy ordained and an Order of nuns established to take care of the thousands who had been baptized. In the 18th century the mission field widened to include India, where the Society took over missions abandoned by the Jesuits following their suppression by the Portuguese, and China. The legacy of the French Jesuits in China, where they had begun a movement of liturgical inculturation which had been roundly condemned by Rome, led to the expulsion of the Society from China. The growth and success of the Society was halted by the French Revolution but survived to continue its work today with missions maintained throughout the Far East and India.

FRANCES OF ROME, OBLATES OF ST

Location: Italy (Rome)
RC (female) founded in Italy in the 15th century by St Frances of Rome (canonized 1608)
Original habit: a black girded tunic with rosary beads, white veil and full mantle.

St Frances of Rome (1384–1440), with a reputation for being an exemplary wife and mother and with a love for ministering to the poor and performing other works of charity, joined together in 1425 with some other women to form a Society which in time became a type of Benedictine Oblate community associated with the monks of Mount Oliveto. The small community was known as the Oblates of the Tor de'Specci, which was the name of the community house. After the death of her husband in 1436, St Frances joined the community, became its superior and remained with them for the rest of her life, during which time she experienced many visions and many miracles were attributed to her. The community, which is sometimes referred to incorrectly as the Collatines, is still in existence but with very reduced numbers. The generalate in Rome is a place of pilgrimage.

✠ Oblates of St Frances of Rome in Tor de'Specci
  Oblates Regular of St Benedict

FRANCIS DE SALES, MISSIONARIES OF ST

Location: France (Annecy)
RC (male) founded in France in 1838 by Fr Mermier
Abbr: MSFS
Original habit: secular style.

A Congregation, with simple vows, founded originally as a society of missionary priests who would counteract the destruction caused to religious life by the French Revolution. This work was later extended into the foreign mission fields, and in 1845 some members went to India. Further missions were undertaken in England, where several foundations were made which offered care for orphans as well as education for boys and young men in schools and seminaries. Members are distributed among five provinces, in England, Switzerland, Brazil, India, and the USA, with another foundation made in Africa (Tanzania).

✠ Fransalians

FRANCIS DE SALES, OBLATE SISTERS OF ST

Location: France (Troyes)
RC (female) founded in France in 1871 by Mother
Mary de Sales Chappuis
Abbr: OSFS (previously OSFrS)
Original habit: a black tunic with a shortened veil
and a velvet cape.

A Congregation founded in Troyes by
Mother Mary de Sales Chappuis, a former
Visitation Sister who was famous for her
particular brand of spirituality known as
The Way, with the co-operation of Fr Louis
Brisson. The purpose of the Congregation
was to help and support the male Oblates
of St Francis de Sales in their work in
education. The Sisters are to be found in
many countries.

FRANCIS DE SALES, OBLATES OF ST

Location: Italy (Rome)
RC (male) founded in Italy in 1871 by Louis
Alexander Alphonse Brisson
Abbr: OSFS

A Congregation founded in Troyes, France,
by Fr Louis Brisson, a seminary professor,
with the co-operation of Mother Mary de
Sales Chappuis. The foundation flourished
in France but was forced to spread into
other countries when its members had to
leave because of the Association Laws in
France in 1903. Foundations were also
made in the USA and South America, Canada and the Virgin Islands. The work of the
Oblates is mainly concerned with education, both in schools and in seminaries,
and with parish work and foreign missions.
They work closely with the Oblate Sisters of
St Francis de Sales (see previous entry).

FRANCISCANS – ANGLICAN

Anglican male and female Franciscans are
divided into:

1 First Order Friars – the Society of St
  Francis; First Order Sisters – The Community of St Francis
2 Second Order of Nuns – the Community
  of St Clare
3 Third Order of the Society of St Francis

THE FIRST ORDER FRIARS OF THE SOCIETY OF ST FRANCIS

Location: England (Dorchester, Dorset)
Anglican (male) founded in England in 1921 by
three laymen
Abbr: SSF
Original habit: a brown Franciscan habit with a
knotted cord, hood and sandals.

An Anglican Franciscan Society founded by
three laymen, Edward Kelley Evans, who
had been with the Divine Compassion
Society and was known as Brother Giles,
Roger Fox, and Charles Boyd, an Australian. When they were offered the lease
on some property in Dorset, the three men
opened a refuge for tramps and wayfarers.
A farm was started, which did not flourish,
and the community turned to market-gar-
dening, the production of various handicrafts and the running of a small printing
unit. The purpose of the Society was to help
the poor and marginalized, and the
Brothers work in the same field today,
offering shelter throughout England and
Scotland to homeless men, as well as providing residential retreats and conducting
preaching missions. The Society is divided
into various provinces, with houses in
Europe, the USA, Australasia and the
Pacific Islands.

THE FIRST ORDER SISTERS OF THE COMMUNITY OF ST FRANCIS

Location: England (Stepney, London)
Anglican (female) founded in England in 1905 by
Rosina Rice
Abbr: CSF

Original habit: a brown Franciscan habit with a knotted cord, black veil and sandals.

The founder, Rosina Rice, had been a Sister of Bethany and was encouraged to leave them in order to make a new foundation. Three other Bethany Sisters joined her, and in 1906 they went to Hull, in the north of England, to work in a parish. In 1908 they returned to London and a novitiate was started. By now Sr Rosina was feeling the call of Rome at a time when news was reaching them of the submission to Rome of the Anglican Franciscan Society of the Atonement in the USA. Three of the community joined her in her journey to New York with the intention of joining the Graymoor Sisters of Atonement. But another change of mind overtook Sr Rosina, and she entered instead the Franciscan Missionary Sisters of the Sacred Heart at Peekskill, New York, a Roman Catholic Congregation. Those left behind in England persevered, and a home for the aged and for incurables was opened. Today, the community has grown and there are several foundations throughout England, with others in New Zealand and the USA.

THE SECOND ORDER NUNS OF THE COMMUNITY OF ST CLARE

Location: England (Witney, Oxfordshire)
Anglican (female) founded in England in 1950 by five Oblates of St Clare
Abbr: CSCL
Original habit: brown, with a black veil and white cord girdle and sandals

The Community was established by the Oblate Sisters who were given permission to form a separate, contemplative community. After several moves they settled at Witney in Oxfordshire, where today the Sisters live the contemplative life observing the Benedictine Rule with certain modifications, conduct retreats and run a guest

house with retreat facilities. Manual work is also performed by the Sisters, who make altar breads, run a printing press and practice various arts and crafts.

THE THIRD ORDER OF THE SOCIETY OF ST FRANCIS

A Society open to laity and ordained Anglican clergy alike. Members are called tertiaries and aim to follow a modified Franciscan Rule in their homes and workplaces in the world, but no vows are taken. Members meet regularly and receive counselling and spiritual direction from members of the First Order of Friars. The headquarters of the Society, which is worldwide, is in Lochwinnoch, Renfrewshire, Scotland.

FRANCISCAN SERVANTS OF JESUS AND MARY

Location: England (Crediton, Devon)
Anglican (female) founded in Scotland in 1926 (but see below)
Abbr: FSJM
Original habit: a brown habit made from handwoven material, a scapular with a red cross and a white Franciscan cord. A white coif and brown cornette were worn as a substitute for a veil; sandals were worn.

The community began in Paisley, Scotland, as an experiment in communal living. Of the four women involved, only two persevered and went to London, where the first Sisters made their life vows in 1935 with the permission of the bishop of London. They made a temporary move to Whitwell, on the Isle of Wight, and then a final move to Crediton, in Devon, where they were able to live the Franciscan way of life. The apostolate encompasses missions in villages for both adults and children, providing hospitality for retreats and conferences, catechesis and prison visiting with some after-prison care and assistance. The Sisters also work to produce handicrafts, which include weaving and the printing of posters and illuminated cards.

FRANCISCANS – ROMAN CATHOLIC

Friars

Members of the Franciscan Order all regard St Francis of Assisi (1181–1226) as their founder. As a young man he had enjoyed a wealthy and indulgent lifestyle, but he underwent a religious conversion, made a pilgrimage to Rome, and on his return to Assisi lived as a lay hermit in the run-down chapel of San Damiano. He regarded himself as a penitent, a member of the laity who took on a life of penance, austerity and almsgiving. Others joined him, and they became known as the Fratri Minores (lesser brothers, or friars minor). A visit to Rome in 1209 gained for the group the verbal approval of the Pope, and Francis was ordained deacon. Of the original Rule nothing has remained, but it is thought to have included the three vows of religion, poverty, chastity and obedience, together with some passages from the Gospels to be used as examples of how they should live. The friars returned to Assisi, living first in an abandoned house from which they were later evicted, and then in the Portiuncula chapel, where they lived a life of preaching, fasting and manual labour, working among the lepers and begging for their food. Many joined them, and by 1217 Francis had to divide the group into smaller provinces, with provincial ministers in charge of each smaller group. Within a year or two there were friars working in Hungary, Spain and France as well as throughout Italy. St Francis, who bore the stigmata, died in Assisi in 1226.

✠ Grey Friars

Franciscan Sisters

A sermon preached by Francis in 1212, which was heard by a young woman, Clare, resulted in her receiving the religious habit from him in 1215. St Francis appointed St Clare as the first abbess of the new Congregation of Poor Ladies, or Lesser Sisters, which we now call the Poor Clares. The Sisters were given the Benedictine Rule to follow at first, but St Clare rewrote much of this and her Rule was approved in 1253, only days before her death.

Franciscan Tertiaries

In 1221 the foundation of the Brothers and Sisters of Penance, now known as the Franciscan tertiaries, was made, designed for those who were unable to leave the world but wanted to follow the Franciscan way of life as much as possible, wearing the Franciscan cord and, at certain times, the habit. They could observe a Rule of prayer and fasting according to their state of life.

The Franciscan Order

The story of the Franciscan Order, with its distinctive feature of poverty, is one of reform and reuniting which is beyond the scope of a dictionary, but it has resulted in its division into the following Orders:

1 *The First Order*
   (i) Friars Minor of the Regular
       Observance (OFM)
   Location: Italy (Rome)
   Original habit: a brown tunic with a separate hood and capuce, a white knotted cord with a seven-decade rosary (the Seven Joys of Our Lady), sandals and a short cloak.

   (ii) Friars Minor Conventual
       (OFMConv)
   Location: Italy (Rome)
   Original habit: a grey/black habit (more recently black) with a separate hood, capuce and cape

and a white knotted cord with a seven-decade rosary (the Seven Joys of Our Lady); sandals may be worn.

(iii) Friars Minor Capuchin (OFMCap)
Location: Italy (Rome)
Original habit: a brown tunic with an attached hood, a white knotted cord with the seven-decade rosary (the Seven Joys of Our Lady) and sandals. Capuchin friars wear beards.

2 *The Second Order*
  (i) The Poor Clares and their derivatives

3 The Third Order (Tertiaries. TOR)
  (i) Third Order Regular – male and female Congregations
  (ii) Third Order Secular – secular clergy and laity living in the world

FRANCISCAN CONGREGATIONS

1 DAUGHTERS OF ST FRANCIS OF ASSISI

Location: USA (Lacon, Illinois); now Slovakian Republic (Bratislava)
RC (female)
Abbr: OSF

This began as a Hungarian Congregation, founded in 1892 by Mother Mary Anna Brunner at Esztergom, which went to the USA in 1946, where the Sisters worked in Illinois, Missouri and Ohio, caring for the sick in hospitals and nursing homes. The Congregation has recently returned to Europe and is now to be found in Bratislava, Slovakian Republic.

2 FRANCIS, BYZANTINE BROTHERS OF ST

Location: USA (Redlands, California)
RC (male)
Abbr: BBSF

A Diocesan Institute founded in 1992 which operates within the eparchy of Van Nuys of the Eastern Catholic Church. The Brothers take the three monastic vows of poverty, chastity and obedience. This is a mainly contemplative community but has an active apostolate concerned with education and the needs of the poor.

3 FRANCIS, LITTLE BROTHERS OF ST

Location: USA (Roxbury, Massachusetts)
RC (male)
Abbr: LBSF

A Diocesan Institute founded in 1970 by Brother James Curran as a contemplative group of Brothers who observe the three monastic vows of poverty, chastity and obedience and follow both an active and a contemplative life of liturgical prayer, Eucharistic devotion and the *lectio divina*. Their active apostolate is concerned with homeless men and women and those who have been marginalized by society. The head of this Institute is known as the servant-general.

4 FRANCIS SERAPHICUS, POOR BROTHERS OF ST

Location: Italy (Rome) and Germany (Aachen)
RC (male)
Abbr: CFP

The founder of the Congregation, Philip Hoever, was influenced by Blessed Mother Frances Schervier of the Franciscan Sisters of the Poor, and with four companions from Aachen, dedicated himself in 1857 to the care of homeless men. The association was approved in 1861 and again in 1910 by Pope St Pius X. From Germany the Congregation spread to the USA, and houses were opened in Illinois, Michigan, Kentucky and Ohio. When the *Kulturkampf* in Germany forced many religious to leave the country, the mother house was moved from Aachen to Blyerheide in The Netherlands. After 1888 the communities were able to return to Germany, and new houses were opened in Upper Silesia, with others in Belgium and The Netherlands.

5 FRANCISCAN BROTHERS – Brooklyn

Location: USA (Brooklyn, New York)
RC (male)
Abbr: OSF

Two Franciscan tertiary Brothers, John McMahon and Vincent Hayes, from the Irish Congregation of the Third Order Regular Franciscans at Roundstone Monastery, Galway, Ireland, founded the Congregation in Brooklyn in 1859. It is an active Order with simple vows, approved in 1989, and undertakes teaching, catechesis and running summer camps for young people.

6 FRANCISCAN BROTHERS OF CHRIST THE KING

Location: USA (Peoria, Illinois)
RC (male)
Abbr: OSF

7 FRANCISCAN BROTHERS OF PEACE

Location: USA (St Paul, Minnesota)
RC (male)
Abbr: FBP

A Public Association founded in 1982 and currently seeking canonical status as a Diocesan Institute. Its charism is to give service to the poor, especially to those suffering from AIDS.

8 FRANCISCAN BROTHERS OF THE HOLY CROSS

Location: Germany (Hausen Wied)
RC (male)
Abbr: FFSC

An Institute, founded in Germany in 1862 by Peter Wirth (Brother Jacob – 1830–71) together with Anton Weber in the Chapel of the Cross, which was part of a ruined hermitage. Peter Wirth was by training a shoemaker and repairer, skills he was able to use in his care of orphans and abandoned children, who were able to learn the trade from him. The Congregation, which was approved in 1923, undertakes works of charity, including the care of orphans, the aged and infirm, as well as providing vocational training for artisans and craftsmen. The Brothers run several institutes in the USA, with their headquarters at Springfield, Illinois.

9 FRANCISCAN BROTHERS OF THE SACRED HEART

Location: USA (Fargo, North Dakota)
RC (male)
Abbr: OSF

A Diocesan Institute founded in 1986 under the direction of Bishop Sullivan, which has as its main aim the education of the young through religious education programmes, diocesan and parish retreats and missions, chaplaincies and catechesis. The Brothers wear the habit of the Franciscan Third Order when in community and observe a structured life of prayer involving daily Mass, meditation, the divine office and other devotions.

10 FRANCISCAN BROTHERS OF THE THIRD ORDER REGULAR

Location: Ireland (Mount Bellew)
RC (male)
Abbr: OSF

The Congregation was founded in Ireland in 1818 by Archbishop MacHale of Tuam, not only as a revival of the Franciscan Third Order Regular in Ireland, but also to provide agricultural education, which the Brothers still offer, and to counteract proselytism that was threatening Roman Catholicism in Ireland at the time. It was a lay Institute of the Third Order Regular of St

Francis, whose members were Brothers solely, unlike the earlier Third Order Regular model which was composed of both priests and Brothers. In 1918 Pope Benedict XV brought all the Franciscan Brothers in Ireland under a single superior-general, with the Constitutions confirmed and approved in 1930 and 1938. The Congregation at Mount Bellew has undertaken foreign missions in Africa.

11 FRANCISCAN FRIARS MINOR

Location: Italy (Rome)
RC (male)
Abbr: OFM; OFM Conv; OFM Cap

The Friars Minor, who were founded in 1209 when Pope Honorius III verbally sanctioned the original Rule drawn up by St Francis, still maintain a Franciscan witness, either as Friars of the Regular Observance or as Conventuals, or Capuchins (founded 1525). Found throughout the world they are engaged in every type of Christian apostolate. The total membership is in excess of thirty thousand.

12 FRANCISCAN FRIARS OF MARY IMMACULATE – Massachusetts

Location: USA (New Bedford, Massachusetts)
RC (male)
Abbr: OSF

A Pontifical Institute, founded in 1990, which is affiliated with the Franciscan Friars and Sisters of Mary Immaculate in Rome. Their aim is to live the Rule of St Francis but to emphasize a Marian bias, after the style of St Maximilian Kolbe. To demonstrate this, the profession of a member involves the usual three monastic vows of poverty, chastity and obedience but with an additional vow which consists of a total consecration to the Immaculate Virgin Mary. While some community members live a contemplative life, others have made themselves available to be used by the Church wherever a need arises.

13 FRANCISCAN FRIARS OF MARY IMMACULATE – North Dakota

Location: USA (Pisek, North Dakota)
RC (male)
Abbr: OFMI

A Public Association currently seeking diocesan status. It was founded in 1983 and is primarily concerned with the conversion of youth through missions, publications and preaching in schools and at summer camps. The community has a strongly Marian bias and their devotion to and promotion of the Blessed Virgin Mary is in the tradition of St Maximilian Kolbe, while their life of penance and austerity is strongly Franciscan.

14 FRANCISCAN FRIARS OF THE ATONEMENT

Location: USA (Graymoor, Garrison, New York)
RC (male)
Abbr: S.A

This Congregation started as an Anglican community known as the Society of the Atonement, founded in 1898 at Graymoor, New York, by the Revd Lewis T. Wattson (1863–1940), who later became known as Fr Paul James Francis, and co-founded by Sr Lurana White (1860–1935), who had been an Anglican nun. The Congregation is composed of priests and Brothers living in community. Their work involves many ministries such as conducting retreats, running shelters for the homeless and the poor, working with AIDS victims, staffing alcohol and drug dependency rehabilitation units, and maintaining prison and hospital chaplaincies. The members also work in publishing and man the Catholic Central Library in London, England. Foreign missions have been undertaken to Canada, Brazil and Japan.

15 FRANCISCAN FRIARS OF THE IMMACULATE

Location: Italy (Frigento, Avellino)
RC (male) founded in Italy in 1970 by Stephano Maria Pio Manelli and Gabriel Maria Pelletieri
Abbr: OFM Conv

The Franciscan Friars of the Immaculate was founded by two priests as a Franciscan reform. It was Fr Stephano Manelli who submitted the *Tracia mariana* – a Marian plan for the Franciscan life – which was approved by the superior-general of the Conventual Franciscans in 1970. The reform is heavily Marian in character and is seen as a return to the ideals and life of St Maximilian Mary Kolbe (1894–1941) which he began at his Niepokalonow foundation, west of Warsaw, Poland, where he sought to return the Franciscan Order to the Marian spirit of St Francis. The friars were recognized as a Diocesan Institute in 1990 and received papal approbation in 1998. The life is very frugal and austere. In addition to the usual three vows of religion, poverty, chastity and obedience, there has been added a fourth, a Marian vow of total consecration to the Immaculate. The friars are very involved in media work and are to be found in Italy, the USA, Brazil, Benin, Nigeria, Asia and Australia.

16 FRANCISCAN FRIARS OF THE RENEWAL

Location: USA (Bronx, New York)
RC (male)
Abbr: CFR

A Capuchin Franciscan-type Public Association founded in 1987, started by Capuchin friars. The members observe the three monastic vows of poverty, chastity and obedience and work for both personal and communal renewal as called for by Second Vatican Council. The community works among the poor, the marginalized and the abandoned in society.

17 FRANCISCAN HANDMAIDS OF THE MOST PURE HEART OF MARY

Location: USA (New York City)
RC (female) founded in the USA in 1916 by Fr Ignatius Lissner and Mother Mary Theodore Williams
Abbr: FHM
Original habit: Franciscan in style

A Diocesan Congregation founded in New York City by a priest of the African Missions Society. The Sisters conduct a summer camp, Camp St Edward, and a nursery and day care centre at St Benedict's Day Nursery. They are also available for teaching, parish ministries and the conducting of retreats. At one time the Congregation also provided hostel accommodation for young working women and undertook mission work in North and South Carolina.

18 FRANCISCAN HOSPITAL SISTERS

Location: Germany (Münster)
RC (female)
Abbr: OSF

A foundation made at St Mauritz, Germany, in 1844 by Christopher Behrensmeyer, a Franciscan, and which went in 1875 to the USA, where the Sisters settled in Springfield, Illinois. This foundation became the American mother house. The Sisters are concerned with nursing, nurse training and education. They also conduct missions to the Far East.

19 FRANCISCAN HOSPITALLER SISTERS OF ST ELIZABETH,

Location: Luxemburg (Luxembourg City)
RC (female)
Abbr: OSF

It was through the generosity and inspiration of Marie Zorn of Luxemburg that this Congregation came into existence. It began as an idea of hers to bring some Sisters of

Charity to her city to nurse the sick. She was prepared to donate a house and lands towards the founding of such a community. Obtaining the necessary letters patent from the French king, she looked to the Hospitaller Sisters of Aix-la-Chapelle to send some Sisters to Luxemburg. Three Sisters went from there to make the Luxemburg foundation in 1672. Numbers increased and the Congregation flourished but the French Revolution a century later obliged the Sisters to abandon their religious habit, although allowing them to continue to serve the sick and the poor. Twelve Sisters remained, wearing lay clothes and trying to observe as far as possible the religious life. When the Revolution ended there was an attempt to unite this now ageing community with the new Congregation of St Chrétienne which had been founded in France in the city of Metz. When Luxemburg became separated from France, the Sisters of St Elizabeth wanted to resume their previous observances and regain their independence, for which permission was granted in 1816. A succession of very able superiors from 1847 to 1920 brought about a re-birth of the community. The Constitutions were revised and approved in 1915 and 1919. Today, the Congregation is thriving and its members are still concerned with their apostolate to the sick and the poor.

20 FRANCISCAN MINIMS OF THE SACRED HEART

Location: Italy (Caiano)
RC (female)

The founder, who even as a child had been moved by the plight of the poor, entered the Congregation of Sisters of St Maximus, but left again, dissatisfied with the life it was offering. Together with some companions, she opened a school for homeless children. This soon grew into a community of five, and by 1902 had expanded into a community house with an oratory, dedicated to the Sacred Heart. The work of the community attracted many vocations, and the Order spread to other parts of Italy, with twelve of the houses reputed to have been established by the founder herself. Today, the Franciscan Minims of the Sacred Heart have fifty-four houses accommodating some five hundred members, with the work now extended into foreign missions, where they are a presence in Egypt, Israel and Brazil.

21 FRANCISCAN MINORESSES

Location: England (Melton Mowbray, Leicestershire)
RC (female)
Abbr: FSM

A Diocesan Congregation, approved in 1910, founded in London in 1888 by Sr Mary Francis Murphy with the approval and encouragement of Cardinal Manning. Their work began with the very poor in London and spread to Nottingham and Oakham, Rutland, where the Sisters undertook child care, education from elementary to adult level, nursing and care for the terminally ill, pro-life issues, catechesis, parish ministries and youth work. There are houses in Ireland, the USA, South Africa and Ethiopia.

22 FRANCISCAN MISSIONARIES OF JESUS CRUCIFIED

Location: USA (Albany, New York)
RC (male and female)
Abbr: FMJC

A Public Association, founded in 1987 and now seeking papal approbation, composed of many communities of Franciscan tertiary men and women, many of whom have disabilities. The Association provides opportunities for the members to contribute to the life of the Church and to help others with disabilities.

23 FRANCISCAN MISSIONARIES OF MARY

Location: Italy (Rome)
RC (female)
Abbr: FMM

A truly international Institute, founded in Ootacamund, India, in 1877 by Hélène de Chappotin de Neuville (Mother Mary of the Passion), a Breton. There are now some nine thousand members spread between sixty-five nationalities. The principal aim of the Congregation is to provide spiritual and material care for those in need, Christian and non-Christian alike. Work is therefore undertaken in hospitals, pharmacies, day and boarding schools, orphanages and day nurseries and in homes for the elderly and convalescent. The Institute has a special devotion to Mary Immaculate, Queen of the Apostles, and a tradition of veneration of the Blessed Sacrament.

24 FRANCISCAN MISSIONARIES OF OUR LADY OF SORROWS

Location: USA (Beaverton, Oregon)
RC (female)
Abbr: OSF

An indigenous Congregation founded in China, in 1939, and wholly dedicated to the missions. The founder was Bishop Raphael Palazzi, an Italian tertiary. When Communism overtook China, the Sisters left for Hong Kong and the USA, where they opened houses in California and Oregon, with a mother house in Los Angeles and a novitiate in San Fernando, California. In 1985 the Sisters returned to Hong Kong and went on to open a house in Taiwan.

25 FRANCISCAN MISSIONARIES OF ST JOSEPH

Location: England (Manchester)
RC (female)
Abbr: FMSJ

A Congregation founded in 1883 by Cardinal Vaughan and Alice Ingham (Mother Mary Francis) in order to help the Mill Hill Missionary Fathers (the Society of St Joseph), which had been founded by Cardinal Vaughan some years before. The work of the Sisters covers education, domestic service, social work and the care of the elderly. Houses are to be found in Europe and the USA, with novitiates in England, South America and East Africa.

26 FRANCISCAN MISSIONARIES OF THE DIVINE MOTHERHOOD

Location: England (Godalming, Surrey)
RC (female)
Abbr: FMDM

The origin of the Congregation lies with a group of lay Franciscan tertiaries who worked to ease the condition of the underage cotton mill workers in Rochdale, Lancashire in the 1870s. Following a move to Aldershot, in Hampshire, in 1892 of a branch of the Franciscan Missionaries of Littlehampton, some of the Rochdale tertiaries joined this community. In 1896 the community was recognized as one of religious Sisters. They became independent of the Littlehampton community in 1911. The Sisters work in every aspect of health care, having opened the famous Mount Alvernia General and Maternity Hospital at Guildford, Surrey, in 1936 and many others. Communities now exist in Europe, Africa, the Middle and Far East, Australia and New Zealand.

27 FRANCISCAN MISSIONARIES OF THE IMMACULATE CONCEPTION

Location: Mexico (Mexico City)
RC (female)
Abbr: OSF

Founded in 1874 in Mexico City by Miss Dolores Vasquez and Fr Refugio Morales, this is a Pontifical Institute with simple vows and an active apostolate in the education of children and adults, health care, home visiting and the care of the elderly. The Sisters are also represented in New Mexico and California.

28 FRANCISCAN MISSIONARY BROTHERS OF THE SACRED HEART OF JESUS

Location: USA (Eureka, Missouri)
RC (male)
Abbr: OSF

A small Diocesan Congregation founded in 1927 by Bronislaus Luszcz, a Franciscan Third Order Regular Brother, and concerned mainly with nursing.

29 FRANCISCAN MISSIONARY SISTERS –
Littlehampton

Location: England (Littlehampton, Sussex)
RC (female)
Abbr: FMSL

A Congregation founded in 1895 when a small group of tertiary Sisters undertook to work with orphans and the poor in the parish of Hampstead, in north London. A later foundation at Aldershot, Hampshire was the start of the Franciscan Missionaries of the Divine Motherhood. Since 1980 the Congregation has taken up missionary work in Lima, Peru.

30 FRANCISCAN MISSIONARY SISTERS FOR AFRICA

Location: Ireland (Sandymount, Dublin)
RC (female)
Abbr: OSF

A Congregation which came into independent existence in 1952, before which they had been part of the African Province of the Franciscan Sisters of Mill Hill. The work of the new foundation was then expanded to include all aspects of medical and nursing care, midwifery, health care programmes, care of lepers and AIDS victims, as well as AIDS research. Teaching is also undertaken at all levels, and the Congregation now has houses throughout Africa, in the UK, and in the USA.

31 FRANCISCAN MISSIONARY SISTERS OF THE DIVINE CHILD

Location: USA (Williamsville, New York)
RC (female)
Abbr: FMDC

A Diocesan Congregation which was founded at Buffalo, New York, by Bishop William Turner in 1927. The Sisters have undertaken ministries which include religious education, catechetics, parish surveys and teaching at all levels.

32 FRANCISCAN MISSIONARY SISTERS OF THE IMMACULATE CONCEPTION

Location: Scotland (Glasgow)
RC (female)
Abbr: OSF

In 1847 a foundation of Franciscan Regular tertiaries was made in Glasgow by Sr Mary Francis, from a Congregation at Tourcoing, France, to care for orphans and to teach the local children. The Sisters work in nursing and teaching, social work, counselling and the giving of retreats. Houses are to be found in all parts of the UK, Ireland, the

USA and Canada, South America, Egypt, Australia and New Guinea.

33 FRANCISCAN MISSIONARY SISTERS OF THE INFANT JESUS

Location: Italy (Rome)
RC (female)
Abbr: FMIJ

A Pontifical Congregation founded at L'Aquila, Italy, in 1879 by Sr Maria Giuseppa Micarelli, as the Franciscan Sisters of the Infant Jesus. An American foundation was made in New Jersey in 1961. The Sisters are involved in education, health care, care for the elderly and the young, catechesis and parish ministries. They also maintain foreign missions throughout the world.

34 FRANCISCAN POOR SCHOOL SISTERS

Location: Austria (Vocklabruck)
RC (female)
Abbr: OSF

A Congregation founded in 1842 by the prince-bishop of Seckau, a Benedictine, who had been dispensed from his vows and became a canon in Vienna prior to becoming bishop. He introduced the Poor School Sisters into his diocese as part of a process of renovation through education. The Sisters were also made very welcome in the USA, where they settled around Pittsburgh, Pennsylvania, to work with immigrant families. Members of the Congregation were later to work in foreign missions to South America and to extend the apostolate into nursing.

35 FRANCISCAN SCHOOL SISTERS

Location: Austria (Vienna)
RC (female)
Abbr: OSF

A foundation made by Fr Sebastian Schwarz and Mother M. Francesca in 1850 to work in education and nursing.

✠ Savannah Franciscans

36 FRANCISCAN SCHOOL SISTERS OF CHRIST THE KING

Location: Italy (Rome)
RC (female)
Abbr: OSF

An Austrian Congregation founded at Graz in 1843 when a small group of Franciscan tertiaries wanted to undertake teaching among the poor and uneducated. The moving force within the group was Sr Francis Lampel. The Congregation became independent in 1869. Foundations were made in the USA, in Lemont, Illinois, where the Sisters have undertaken the care of dependent children, the elderly and orphans and have also worked in liturgical and pastoral ministries and in education.

37 FRANCISCAN SERVANTS OF JESUS

Location: USA (Prescott, Wisconsin)
RC (female) founded in the USA in 1993
Original habit: Franciscan style.

This Public Association was founded in 1993 and follows a Franciscan pattern, aiming to combine the active and contemplatives lives. The Shekinah House of Prayer, at Brownsville, is maintained for days of recollection and retreat as well as providing opportunities for hospitality. The Sisters support themselves through a printing enterprise, making illuminated manuscripts, gift cards and memorial stationery.

38 FRANCISCAN SISTERS – Allegany

Location: USA (Allegany, New York)
RC (female)
Abbr: FSA

The Congregation began in 1859 when a Franciscan priest, Pamfilo de Magliano, gave the tertiary habit to three women, Mary Jane Todd, Ellen Fallon and Mary Anne O'Neill. The active work of the Sisters was concerned with the education of women in the diocese. The enterprise was so successful that many others were attracted to the Congregation. In 1860 the St Elizabeth Academy was opened in Allegany, with other schools established later. The Sisters now work in education and health care and run homes for the elderly and the very young, as well as having parish duties. Missionary work took them to Jamaica and the British West Indies in 1879, and to Brazil in 1946 and Bolivia in 1965.

39 FRANCISCAN SISTERS – Little Falls

Location: USA (Little Falls, Minnesota)
RC (female)
Abbr: OSF

This Congregation owes its origin to the Franciscan Sisters of the Immaculate Conception in Belle Prairie, Minnesota, and was founded in 1890 by Mother Mary Ignatius of Jesus. Today, the Sisters are present throughout the USA as well as in Ecuador, Honduras and Tanzania. The apostolate is in teaching, health care, social services, pastoral care, parish ministries, retreats and spiritual direction. The members are also active in promoting peace and justice.

40 FRANCISCAN SISTERS – Mill Hill

Location: England (Mill Hill, London)
RC (female)
Abbr: OSF

The Congregation was founded at Mill Hill, north of London, in 1868 by Mother Francis Basil and five other Sisters who had been members of an Anglican community. They had completed their novitiate in Calais, France, before moving to Mill Hill to set up a novitiate and mother house of the Congregation, with the encouragement and approval of Cardinal Manning.

41 FRANCISCAN SISTERS – Oldenburg

Location: USA (Oldenburg, Indiana)
RC (female)
Abbr: OSF

A Congregation founded in 1851 by Francis Joseph Rudolf, a missionary priest who invited Sr (later Mother) Theresa Hackelmeier to leave Vienna, Austria, and travel to the USA to found a American religious Order dedicated to the teaching of German-speaking children and to care for the many orphans of the area which had suffered badly in the cholera epidemic of 1847. With the help of three other Sisters, schools were opened in Oldenburg and elsewhere in Indiana, followed later by others in Kentucky (1861), Cincinnati (1876), Ohio and Kansas (1890). At the end of the 19th century the Sisters tackled the difficult task of opening schools for African-American children. They now work among the North American Indians and have undertaken missions to Mexico, China, Papua New Guinea and Korea.

42 FRANCISCAN SISTERS – Peoria

Location: USA (East Peoria, Illinois)
RC (female)
Abbr: OSF

A Congregation founded by five Sisters, led by Mother Mary Frances Krasse, from the Franciscan Sisters of the Holy Family, at Dubuque, Iowa, in 1876. Lacking money, but with the help and encouragement of Bishop John Lancaster Spalding, a foundation was made. The Sisters now run seven hospitals and two nursing homes in the area and are also involved in education and the support of young women at risk.

43 FRANCISCAN SISTERS OF BLESSED ANGELINA

Location: Italy (Rome)
RC (female)
Abbr: OSF

This Congregation has had a long career, founded by Blessed Angelina (1377–1435; beatified 1825) after the death of her husband. In 1392 she assumed the habit of a Franciscan tertiary and became renowned locally for her preaching and calls to repentance. She had a vision in which she was told to found an enclosed community of Franciscan tertiaries in Foligno, which she did, becoming the superior of a group of twelve women. This move to found a community of enclosed tertiaries was very popular, and similar houses were opened throughout Italy, with Angelina founding at least sixteen during her own lifetime. The popularity did not wane, and more such houses were founded throughout the 15th and 16th centuries. The work of the community was always educational, but since the rule of enclosure was mitigated at the start of the 20th century, this has widened to include a variety of apostolic works.

44 FRANCISCAN SISTERS OF CHRISTIAN CHARITY – Manitowoc

Location: USA (Manitowoc, Wisconsin)
RC (female)
Abbr: OSF

A Congregation founded at Manitowoc in 1869 by five religious Sisters from Germany, with the teaching of the children of German immigrants as their aim. The work later extended into nursing and health care programmes. The Sisters still work in all forms of nursing care, teaching and parish mission work throughout the USA and in Peru.

45 FRANCISCAN SISTERS OF MARY IMMACULATE – Joliet

Location: USA (Joliet, Illinois)
RC (female)
Abbr: OSF

Founded in 1865 this was the first Franciscan Sisterhood in Illinois, whose main apostolate is teaching, although the Sisters also work in catechesis, domestic and secretarial work, home missions, retreats and the care of the elderly. This Congregation later gave rise to the Franciscan Sisters of Our Lady of Perpetual Help at St Louis, Missouri. The founders were Mother Mary Alfred Moes and Fr Pamfilo de Magliano, who founded the Franciscan Sisters of Allegany. Mother Moes went on to found the Franciscan Sisters of Our Lady of Lourdes (1878), which in turn provided the founding Sisters for the Congregation of Our Lady of Lourdes at Sylvania, Ohio (1916).

46 FRANCISCAN SISTERS OF OUR LADY OF LOURDES – Ohio

Location: USA (Sylvania, Ohio)
RC (female)
Abbr: OSF

When the Diocese of Cleveland, Ohio, was divided into Cleveland and Toledo in 1910, the first bishop of Toledo, Bavarian-born Joseph Schrembs, collaborated with Mother Mary Adelaide from the Franciscan Sisters of the Immaculate Conception at Rochester, Minnesota, to lay the foundations of this Congregation at Sylvania. The Sisters work in teaching, nursing and maintaining convalescent homes.

47 FRANCISCAN SISTERS OF OUR LADY OF PERPETUAL HELP

Location: USA (St Louis, Missouri)
RC (female)
Abbr: OSF

A Congregation of Sisters concerned with education, especially of Polish immigrants, founded in Missouri in 1901, by Mother Mary Solna, Mother Mary Hilaria and Mother Mary Ernestine, who had come from the Franciscan Sisters of Mary Immaculate in Joliet. The Sisters also undertake nursing care and run missions to bring catechesis to marginalized groups.

48 FRANCISCAN SISTERS OF OUR LADY OF SORROWS

Location: USA (Brown Deer, Wisconsin)
RC (female)
Abbr: OSF

A Congregation established informally in Rome in 1883 when Amelia Streitel (Mother Frances) left the Franciscan Sisters of Maria Stern in Augsburg, Germany, feeling attracted to a contemplative Carmelite life. However, she left the Carmelites in 1882 and went to Rome, where, with others, she formed the Sisters of the Sorrowful Mother. In an effort to provide themselves with funds, some of the Sisters went to the USA in 1888 and established St Francis' Hospital in Wichita, Kansas, with other foundations soon following. Misunderstandings and jealousies arose, and Mother Frances was deposed. She went back to Rome and worked for a time in a child-care institute, dying in 1911. The American Congregation flourished and has many houses in the USA, in Europe, Brazil, the West Indies and the Dominican Republic. The range of the apostolate is wide and encompasses education, literacy programmes, youth work, health care, counselling, conducting retreats and concern with social issues.

49 FRANCISCAN SISTERS OF PEACE

Location: USA (Haverstraw, New York)
RC (female)
Abbr: FSP

An institute which sprang from a Congregation, the Franciscan Missionaries of the Sacred Heart, founded in 1858 in Italy. Three members from that Congregation left Italy in 1865 to work with Italian immigrant families in the USA. The first house was opened in New York, and foundations later extended to Philadelphia and New Jersey. In 1985, 112 professed Sisters of the Order co-founded an institute, the Franciscan Sisters of Peace, which was heavily committed to the promotion of peace. To this end, the Sisters work through education, spirituality, the visual arts and media studies.

50 FRANCISCAN SISTERS OF PENANCE AND CHARITY

Location: USA (Tiffin, Ohio)
RC (female)
Abbr: OSF

A Congregation, founded in 1869 at Tiffin, Ohio, by Fr Joseph Bihn and Mother Francis Schaeffer. The apostolate of the Sisters is concerned with education, nursing and parish ministries.

51 FRANCISCAN SISTERS OF PENANCE AND CHRISTIAN CHARITY

Location: Italy (Rome)
RC (female)
Abbr: OSF

A Congregation, founded at Heythuizen in The Netherlands in 1835 by Mother Catherine Damen, which went to the USA and made a foundation at Lewiston, New York. The work of the Sisters is divided between organizing retreats, parish ministries, teaching, nursing and operating foreign missions to the Far East.

52 FRANCISCAN SISTERS OF PERPETUAL ADORATION – La Crosse

Location: USA (La Crosse, Wisconsin)
RC (female)
Abbr: FSPA

This is a very large Congregation, which was founded at Nojoshing, now in Milwaukee, in 1849 when a group of men and women who were Franciscan secular tertiaries emigrated there from Bavaria. The women went on to found the Congregation, which has now increased to such an extent that it is divided for administrative purposes into three regions, with foreign missions in Canada, Mexico, the Caroline-Marshall Islands, Zimbabwe, Guam and El Salvador. The work of the Sisters is concerned with education, health care, various pastoral ministries and chaplaincies, particularly in prisons and immigrant centres, and social service. They also have a special interest in ecological issues.

53 FRANCISCAN SISTERS OF ST ELIZABETH

Location: Italy (Rome)
RC (female)
Abbr: FSSE

A small Congregation founded in Italy in 1862 by Fr Louis of Casoria, a Franciscan. The Sisters are dedicated to teaching and catechesis, nursing and the manning of day nurseries. Houses have been opened in Italy, Poland, Panama, India and the Philippines.

54 FRANCISCAN SISTERS OF ST GEORGE THE MARTYR

Location: Germany (Thuine, Osnabruck)
RC (female)
Abbr: OSF

A German foundation dating from 1869. In 1923 five of the Sisters set out for the USA and settled in Alton, Illinois, where they set up schools, a hospital and nursing homes. The Sisters also run day care and pre-school programmes and have daily Exposition of the Blessed Sacrament.

55 FRANCISCAN SISTERS OF ST JOSEPH – New York

Location: USA (Hamburg, New York)
RC (female)
Abbr: FSSJ

Founded in 1897 by the Very Revd Hyacinthe Fudsinski, a Franciscan, and Mother M. Colette Hilbert, the Congregation is committed to the education of young people at all levels and to teacher training. The Sisters also run nurseries, work in hospital administration and with medical technology and care for the aged and chronically ill.

56 FRANCISCAN SISTERS OF ST JOSEPH – Wisconsin

Location: USA (Stevens Point, Wisconsin)
RC (female)
Abbr: SSJ-TOSF

The Congregation was founded in 1901 at South Bend, Indiana, by Mother Mary Felicia and Mother Mary Clara, and specializes in the conducting of retreats, in teaching, nursing and providing home missions.

57 FRANCISCAN SISTERS OF ST MARY

Location: USA (St Louis, Missouri)
RC (female)
Abbr: FSM

The purpose of the Congregation, which was founded in 1872, is to promote justice, peace and non-violence. When the founding Sisters left Germany they went to St Louis, Missouri, where they undertook the care of the sick in their own homes together with the protection of young women, including those in single-parent pregnancies, and orphans. They formed themselves into the Sisters of St Mary of the Third Order of St Francis (abbr: SSM). In 1894 seven of the Sisters, who felt the call to commit their lives to a Franciscan way of life, left to found the Sisters of St Francis at Maryville, Missouri. The two communities continued independently until 1987, when they were reunited to form the Congregation of the Franciscan Sisters of Mary. Today, their ministries include parish work, the staffing of hospitals, hospices and clinics, the running of retreats and women's centres and the care of marginalized women and children. Houses are to be found throughout the USA, in South Africa and in Brazil.

58 FRANCISCAN SISTERS OF THE ATONEMENT

Location: USA (Graymoor, Garrison, New York)
RC (female)
Abbr: SA

A Congregation founded by two converts from Anglicanism, the Revd Lewis T. Wattson (Fr Paul James Francis) and Sr Lurana White, at Graymoor, New York. The apostolate is varied and includes catechesis, the conducting of retreats and social work in the USA, Canada, Europe and the Far East.

59 FRANCISCAN SISTERS OF THE BLESSED KUNEGUNDA

Location: USA (Lemont, Chicago)
RC (female)
Abbr: OSF

The members of the Order, which was founded in Chicago by Mother Mary Theresa Dudzik and Mother Mary Ann Wisinski and approved in 1939, are concerned with the education of the young and of children in nurseries, care of the aged and sick in hospitals and the provision of a counselling and advisory centre for girls who may be at risk. The Blessed Kune-

gunda, or Cunegundes, was the 13th-century wife of Boleslaw the Chaste, king of Poland, who took a vow of perpetual chastity and gave herself up to austerities and to works of charity. On the death of her husband, Kunegunda sold everything she had and gave the proceeds away for the relief of the poor, entering the convent of the Poor Clares at Sandeck for the rest of her life.

60 FRANCISCAN SISTERS OF THE EUCHARIST

Location: USA (Meriden, Connecticut)
RC (female)
Abbr: FSE

A community of women, founded in 1973, and dedicated to a love of the Eucharist and to striving to develop a Franciscan spirituality. The Sisters work in education, the care of the aged, pro-life issues and the nursing of the terminally ill in hospices.

61 FRANCISCAN SISTERS OF THE FIVE WOUNDS

Location: USA (Baltimore, Maryland)
RC (female)
Abbr: OSF

A Congregation which arose from the Franciscan Sisters of Mill Hill. In 1861 some of the community were invited to go to the USA to work among coloured and marginalized people, helping them through teaching and catechesis, and caring for orphans. The Congregation has now extended its work into the African mission field, in particular to Uganda, where the Sisters run hospitals and schools.

62 FRANCISCAN SISTERS OF THE HEART OF JESUS

Location: Malta (Victoria, Gozo)
RC (female)
Abbr: OSF

The foundation of this Congregation dates from 1877, when some twelve young girls met for prayers of reparation to the Sacred Heart and formed a group known as the Twelve Stars of the Sacred Heart. They were later professed as Franciscan Regular tertiaries. The Congregation members aim to be of service to the world and to make reparation to the Sacred Heart of Jesus through their work for the Church, through catechizing, teaching the young and caring for the poor. There are now houses in Malta, Italy, Greece, Poland, Israel, parts of Africa, Australia, Pakistan and Brazil.

63 FRANCISCAN SISTERS OF THE HOLY FAMILY

Location: USA (Dubuque, Iowa)
RC (female)
Abbr: OSF

A Congregation which owes its origins to the late 19th-century *Kulturkampf* in Germany which resulted in many members of religious Orders leaving the country. Mother Mary Xaveria Termehr fled with others to the USA, settling at Dubuque, Iowa, where the Sisters worked in education, nursing and social service. From this community was founded the Franciscan Sisters of East Peoria in 1876. The Sisters maintain missions in El Salvador and Africa.

64 FRANCISCAN SISTERS OF THE HOLY VIRGIN MARY OF THE ANGELS

Location: Germany (Waldbreitbach)
RC (female)
Abbr: OSF

A foundation, made in Germany in 1863 by Mother Mary Rose Flesch, whose members are mainly concerned with nursing. They are present in the USA, where the Sisters run St Mary's Home in St Paul, Minnesota.

65 FRANCISCAN SISTERS OF THE IMMACULATE CONCEPTION – Belle Prairie

Location: Italy (Rome)
RC (female)
Abbr: OSF

A Congregation founded in the USA at Belle Prairie, Minnesota, in 1872 by Elizabeth Hayes (Sr Ignatia), who had been born into an Anglican family on the island of Guernsey in the English Channel. After the death of her parents she moved to London, became influenced by the Oxford Movement, and entered the Anglican Community of St Mary the Virgin at Wantage in Oxfordshire. But she was to leave the Anglican Church and became a Roman Catholic, joining the Franciscans of the Immaculate Conception at Greenwich, London, a community largely composed of Anglican converts and affiliated to the Franciscan Regular tertiaries which had been established in Glasgow in 1847 from Tourcoing in France. Sr Ignatia, intent on the mission field as her vocation, left England for Jamaica, but the conditions of life she found there persuaded her to return to England. Once more she set out, this time to the USA, where she and another from her community settled at Belle Prairie and founded the Missionary Franciscan Sisters of the Immaculate Conception in 1872, where the Sisters worked with the Indian population. Missionary work has also been undertaken to the Far East, Papua New Guinea and Queensland, Australia. A group of Sisters from this foundation later formed a separate house at Little Falls, Minnesota.

66 FRANCISCAN SISTERS OF THE IMMACULATE VIRGIN MARY

Location: USA (Pittsburgh, Pennsylvania)
RC (female)
Abbr: OSF

A Franciscan Congregation founded in 1855 by St John Nepomucene Neumann, a Bohemian who became bishop of Philadelphia, for the purpose of educating the young. The activities of the Sisters include teaching, nursing and foreign missions to Puerto Rico.

67 FRANCISCAN SISTERS OF THE POOR

Location: USA (Brooklyn, New York)
RC (female) founded in Germany in 1851 by
Blessed Frances Schervier (beatified 1974)
Abbr: SPF (originally SPSF)
Original habit: Franciscan style

The Congregation was founded in Aachen in Germany. From an early age Frances Schervier (1819–76) had been concerned about the welfare of the poor and the sick, and as she grew she became particularly worried about the plight of abandoned children and young women at risk. She had undergone some training in nursing with the Sisters of St Charles Borromeo in Aachen and had helped relieve the plight of the poor through work she undertook with the curate of her parish who had set up a soup kitchen in 1841. These experiences gave her a liking for social work. She became a Franciscan tertiary in 1844 and, together with four other tertiaries, began to live a community life, caring for the sick and poor. Within a few years the numbers had swelled to twenty-three, and Frances was elected leader of the group. In 1851 the members received the habit, and the Congregation of the Sisters of the Poor of St Francis was founded. Seven years later some of the Sisters went to the USA, where they established a house in Cincinatti, Ohio, caring for German immigrants and others in need of assistance. Hospitals were later established in other parts of the USA. The Sisters now maintain a presence in Italy, Brazil, Senegal and the USA. Their apostolate includes special ministries for gypsies and refugees and for the handicapped, maternity care, training for girls in vocational skills, the provision of retirement homes and refuges, the running of soup kitchens and rehabilitation programmes. They also have a special ministry to provide and care for AIDS sufferers and those who are addicted to drugs and alcohol.

✠ Schervier Sisters
  Sisters of the Poor of St Francis

68 FRANCISCAN SISTERS OF THE PROVIDENCE OF GOD

Location: USA (Pittsburgh, Pennsylvania)
RC (female)
Abbr: OSF

This American Congregation was founded by Bishop M. L. Krusas to provide teaching and nursing care for the immigrant German population of Pittsburgh. The community also runs foreign missions, particularly to Brazil

69 FRANCISCAN SISTERS OF THE SACRED HEART

Location: USA (Frankfort, Illinois)
RC (female)
Abbr: OSF

A Congregation founded in Avilla, Indiana in 1876, for the purpose of educating the children of German immigrant families. Mother Anastasia Bischler, together with several other Sisters, left Germany at the time of the *Kulturkampf*, which was at its height in the late 1870s, waging a severe struggle against Roman Catholic education and compromising the position of members of religious Orders. The Sisters came to the USA well experienced. They had lived and worked through the horrors of the aftermath of the Franco-Prussian War and had known the distress caused by epidemics of typhoid and smallpox. Today, the apostolate includes working in clinics and hospices, caring for pregnant teenagers, social service programmes, religious education and the running of retreats and youth work.

70 FRANCISCAN SISTERS, DAUGHTERS OF THE SACRED HEARTS OF JESUS AND MARY

Location: Italy (Rome)
RC (female)
Abbr: OSF

A Congregation founded in Salzkotten, Germany, by Mother Mary Pfaender in 1859, with an apostolate to care for the sick in hospitals and private homes, and to teach from elementary to secondary level. The Sisters also maintain orphanages and provide hostels for young women at risk.

✛ Franciscan Sisters of Jesus and Mary

71 FRANCISCAN SISTERS OF THE THIRD ORDER REGULAR OF THE SORROWFUL MOTHER

Location: Italy (Rome)
RC (female) founded in Italy in 1882 by Fr Francis Jordan
Abbr: SSM
Original habit: Franciscan style.

The Congregation, which was initially strictly enclosed and contemplative, was founded in Rome by Francis Jordan, the founder of the Salvatorians, following the failure of a similar enterprise in Germany. The first superior, Mother Francisca Streitel, a former Franciscan, imposed a very strict ethos upon her community. By 1885 Rome had taken the Congregation out of Francis Jordan's control, and it continues to operate independently. The first American foundation was made in 1889. The Sisters now work actively in education as well as running nursing homes, staffing hospitals and providing social workers.

There are many foundations in the USA as well as in Grenada and the Windward Islands.

72 FRANCISCANS OF ST MARY OF THE ANGELS

Location: France (Angers)
RC (female)
Abbr: FSMA

The Congregation was founded in 1871 at Angers, France, by Caroline Rurange (Mother Mary Chrysostom) and a Capuchin priest, Ferdinand Potton (Fr Chrysostom) and arose from a Franciscan tertiary group which cared for children orphaned by the Franco-Prussian War. The work of the Sisters is to serve the poor, the sick and the young through education and to help the aged and those in need of counselling. The charism of the Congregation is decidedly Marian, with Eucharistic Adoration forming an important part of the Sisters' daily life. There are houses in Europe, the USA, India, Guadalupe and Ethiopia.

73 FRANCISCANS OF THE PRIMITIVE OBSERVANCE

Location: USA (New Bedford, Massachusetts)
RC (male)
Abbr: FPO

This Public Association was founded in 1995 with the aim of following the strict observance of Franciscan life in the Capuchin tradition. The life followed is austere, and members engage in preaching, organize retreats for people of all ages and offer to serve the poor and disadvantaged.

74 MINOR CONVENTUALS – Syracuse

Location: USA (Syracuse, New York)
RC (female)
Abbr: OSF

A Congregation founded in 1860 by Sr (later Mother) Mary Bernardine Dorn from Philadelphia with the help of six other Sisters, who went to the German parishes at Syracuse and Utica at the invitation of the Franciscan Fathers in order to teach religion and work with the poor. As a result of their work, hospitals were opened in both Syracuse and Utica. In 1883 some of the Sisters went to Molokai, Hawaii, to take over a ministry which worked with lepers and their families. Today the Sisters are a presence throughout the USA and Peru, working in retreat centres, schools of nursing, rehabilitation centres, hospices for the dying, parish ministries and day care and drop-in centres.

75 POOR CLARES – See main entry under POOR CLARES

76 SCHOOL SISTERS OF ST FRANCIS – Milwaukee

Location: USA (Milwaukee, Wisconsin)
RC (female)
Abbr: OSF

A foundation made in 1873 by Mothers Alexia, Alfons and Clara, who left Germany in order to staff local schools and teach the children of German immigrants. The demand was so great that by 1895 the Congregation had houses in seventy-four towns in the USA and opened a mission school for the children of the Chippewa Indian tribe in North Wisconsin. Other schools and colleges followed. At present their work continues throughout the USA, and in Germany, Switzerland and The Netherlands, where the Sisters teach, run hospitals and asylums and continue missionary work at home and abroad.

77 SISTERS OF ST FRANCIS OF ASSISI

Location: USA (Milwaukee, Wisconsin)
RC (female)
Abbr: OSF

An American Congregation founded in 1849 when five laymen and six female Franciscan tertiaries led by two priests, Franz Keppeler and Matias Steiger, went to the USA to form a community at Nojoshing, Milwaukee. Their purpose was to teach and nurse the sick. In 1995 the apostolate was extended, and the Sisters now undertake work with the poor and oppressed, and with orphans. Their teaching programme runs from elementary to college level, and they are active in teacher training and schools of music throughout the USA and in Japan and Taiwan.

78 SISTERS OF ST FRANCIS – Philadelphia

Location: USA (Aston, Pennsylvania)
RC (female)
Abbr: OSF

Three women, experienced in caring for the sick and helping the poor in their home villages in Bavaria, went to the USA and founded this Congregation in 1855, where they continued their work with the German immigrant families. They were given diocesan permission by St John Nepomucene Neumann, the bishop of Philadelphia and a Redemptorist, to found the Sisters of St Francis. In 1896 the mother house moved to Glen Riddle, Pennsylvania. The Congregation was divided into provinces and other daughter-foundations followed, at Buffalo, New York, which led to further foundations at Millvale, Pennsylvania (1896), and Mount Hope, Westchester County, New York (1893), with another at Syracuse, New York (1862).

79 SISTERS OF ST FRANCIS OF OUR LADY OF LOURDES

Location: USA (Rochester, Minnesota)
RC (female)
Abbr: OSF

This Pontifical Congregation, which observes the Third Order Regular Rule of St Francis, was founded in the USA in 1877 by Mother Mary Alfred Moes. The Sisters are engaged in serving the poor, the young and the elderly in hospitals and schools in both urban and rural areas. In addition to their work in the USA, the Sisters have foreign missions in Thailand, Colombia, Peru and South Africa.

80 SISTERS OF ST FRANCIS OF PERPETUAL ADORATION

Location: Germany (Olpe, Paderborn)
RC (female)
Abbr: OSF

A Congregation founded in 1860 which began in Germany but moved to the USA as anti-clericalism grew in Germany. The Sisters established a community at Lafayette, Indiana, where they took over the running of an orphanage. A hospital was opened in 1876, dedicated to St Elizabeth, together with many schools and homes for the care of the aged. In 1962 a mission was opened in the Philippines. There is a foundation at Colorado Springs.

81 SISTERS OF THE THIRD ORDER OF ST FRANCIS – Maryville

RC (female)
Abbr: OSF

A Congregation founded in 1894 when seven Sisters left the community of the Sisters of St Mary of the Third Order of St Francis to lead a different Franciscan way of life. The two Congregations were reunited in 1987 as the Franciscan Sisters of St Mary.

FRISIA, KNIGHTS OF

Defunct
RC (male Equestrian Order) founded in France in 802 by the emperor Charlemagne
Original habit: (insignia) the Imperial Crown in gold; (dress) a white tunic.

The Order was founded by Charlemagne to celebrate a victory over the warlike Frisii, an ancient Germanic tribe who lived in the area of the present-day Netherlands and, for whatever reason, were constantly waging battles against the peoples of present-day Denmark and Sweden.

FRUCTUOSUS, ORDER OF ST

Defunct
RC (male and female) founded in the 7th century, possibly by St Fructuosus
Original habit: a grey tunic with a hooded cowl and cloak and a black girdle; the nuns were discalced in summer, but shoes were worn in winter.

According to a well-founded tradition St Fructuosus (died 665) founded a monastery at Compludo, in Spain, assuming the monastic habit and the running of the house until he could appoint another to take over, while he retired to a place of solitude where he exercised great austerity. Other foundations followed, some as double monasteries where entire families could follow the religious life, the children, when they had reached the age of reason, housed in a community of oblates. One of the monasteries he established was for some eighty virgins, which was presided over by the saintly Abbess Benedicta. St Fructuosus drew up two monastic Rules, the Regula Monachorum and the Regula Communis. The latter contained the form of profession and entry to the religious life and was used in Spain and Portugal until the close of the first millennium.

G

GABRIEL, BROTHERS OF ST

Location: Italy (Rome)
RC (male) founded in France in 1821 (but see below)
Abbr: FSG

There is a tradition that the Order was founded in 1585 by Caesar Bianchetti and arose from a group of laymen in Boulogne who worked together for the purpose of improving Christian knowledge, but it is more likely that the Order dates from 1821, in the aftermath of the French Revolution, when two groups united in order to provide education for young boys and men and were renamed the Brothers of St Gabriel. The first of these groups was the Brothers of the Holy Ghost, founded by St Louis-Marie Grignion de Montfort (1673–1716), the second a small community founded by Gabriel Deshayes in 1816. The new Congregation, which adopted its name from the chapel of St Gabriel at Boulogne which had been used by the Brothers of the Holy Ghost, spread throughout France and Germany, the Brothers dedicated to teaching. At the end of the 19th century houses were opened in Canada and later in Asia. Today the Congregation is spread throughout the world. Members take no vows, but make a promise of obedience to their Superior and an undertaking that they will dedicate themselves to the work of the insti-tution, which now includes the care of orphans, blind and deaf young men and those with other special needs.

GENEVIEVE, CANONS REGULAR OF ST

Defunct
RC (male) founded in France in 1634 by Charles Faure
Original habit: a white tunic and linen rochet with a black biretta and a fur almuce; in winter a black hooded cloak was worn.

A Congregation of canons regular which was founded by Charles Faure, a canon from the abbey of St Victor at Senlis, at the request of Cardinal François de la Roche-foucauld, who had been appointed abbot of the existing foundation of St Genevieve by King Louis XIII of France. St Genevieve (419–512) was patroness of Paris. She had built a church dedicated to Sts Peter and Paul at Mont-les-Paris with the assistance of Clovis (481–511), king of the Salian Franks. When the saint died in 512, her body was interred in the church, which was then in the care of Benedictine monks. By the 9th century it had been given over to some secular canons, but in time lax prac-tices crept in which prompted the founda-tion of the Order of Canons Regular in 1634. Charles Faure and some twelve com-panions took control of the church of St

Genevieve in 1634. The Order spread throughout France.

✠ Sleeping Fathers

GENEVIEVE, DAUGHTERS OF ST

Defunct
RC (female) founded in France in 1636 by Francesca de Blosset
Original habit: a white tunic and surplice with a black fur scarf, ornamented with white spots, which was worn over the left arm, a white wimple and headdress and a black veil.

The Congregation was founded in Paris by Francesca de Blosset, who was a co-worker with St Vincent de Paul, for the purpose of nursing the sick, teaching young girls, training rural teachers and caring for the poor. Approval of the Congregation was granted in 1658. In 1665 they joined with a group known as the Miramiones, an Institute dedicated to the Holy Family which had been founded in 1611 by Marie Bonneau de Rubella Beauharnais de Miramion, a widow. Following the union, the name of the Congregation changed to the Daughters of the Holy Family. The members were much respected for their work with the sick during epidemics.

✠ Daughters of the Holy Family

GEORGE IN ALGA, CANONS REGULAR OF ST

Defunct
RC (male) founded in Italy in 1400 by Angelo Correr (later Pope Gregory XII)
Original habit: a white cassock, blue mantle with ample sleeves, and a biretta; an almuce was worn in winter.

A Venetian Congregation founded in Alga in the old, unoccupied monastery of the Canons Regular of St Augustine by Angelo Correr and his nephew, Gabriel Condulmaro (later Pope Eugenius IV). The members observed a Common Life Rule and were distinguished from the secular clergy by their style of dress. The Order was suppressed by Pope Clement IX in 1668.

GEORGE, ORDERS OF KNIGHTS OF ST

1 KNIGHTS OF THE GARTER

Equestrian Order
Abbr: KG
Insignia: the Garter ribbon with the motto 'Honi Soit Qui Mal Y Pense' (Evil Be to him who Evil Thinks); a star with the Cross of St George and a collar with a badge representing St George and the dragon.

The Order was founded by King Edward III of England (1327–77) in 1348. It is now the highest British civil and military honour that can be awarded, but its original aims and purposes are not easy to decide as early records were destroyed by fire. Membership was originally restricted to the sovereign and his heir, the Prince of Wales, each with twelve companions. In 1805 this was expanded to allow twenty-five companions and remains unchanged. At the beginning of the 19th century other members of the royal family were admitted, known as Royal Knights Companions. Distinguished foreigners can also be admitted and are known as Extra Knights.

2 KNIGHTS OF ST GEORGE OF ALFAMA

Defunct Equestrian Order
Insignia: (dress) a white habit; (insignia) no insignia was worn until the Order united with the Order of Montesa.

A Spanish Order founded in Aragon around 1200 by King Pedro II, which received papal approbation in 1363. Members followed the Augustinian Rule and accomplished very little. They were brought under the aegis of the Order of Montesa in 1400.

3 KNIGHTS OF ST GEORGE IN AUSTRIA

Defunct Equestrian Order

An Order founded by the Emperor Frederick III of Austria in the mid-15th century and approved in 1464. The purpose of the foundation was to defend the frontiers of Austria against the Turks. The Order, severely lacking in funds, did not oblige members to take a vow of poverty. By the end of the century it had become defunct, the founder, who died in 1493, outliving his foundation.

4 KNIGHTS OF ST GEORGE IN GENOA

Defunct Equestrian Order
Insignia: a plain red cross against a white background.

An Order of knights created in the mid-15th century, following the crowning of Frederick III, the first Habsburg emperor, by Pope Nicholas V in 1452.

5 KNIGHTS OF ST GEORGE IN RAVENNA

Pontifical Order
Insignia: a red cross with the arms slightly divided at their extremities, the whole surmounted by a red crown.

An Order instituted by Pope Alexander VI (1492–1503); a similar award was made by Pope Paul III (1534–49) to those from Ravenna who were active in defending the Adriatic coast against the Turks.

6 KNIGHTS OF ST GEORGE IN GERMANY

Equestrian Order
Insignia: a plain red cross surmounted by a gold crown.

The founder of the Order was Maximilian I, Holy Roman Emperor, who at the end of the 15th century wished to honour those whose valour was outstanding in the defence of the Roman Catholic religion

against the Turks. Members of the Order were to observe the Rule of St Augustine, and their vows at profession were those of conjugal chastity, obedience and defence of the Roman Catholic religion.

GEORGE OF ALFAMA, KNIGHTS OF ST

Defunct
RC (male Equestrian Order) founded in Aragon (probably) c.1200 by King Pedro II of Aragon (1196–1213)
Original habit: reputedly a plain white habit, later bearing the insignia of the cross after the union with the Order of Montesa in 1399.

The Order most likely dates from the early 13th century, when the kingdom of Aragon was under the protection of St George. In 1363 it received the approbation of the Blessed Pope Urban V. Union with the Order of Montesa came in 1399 when they were thereafter known as the Order of Montesa and St George of Alfama. The members observed the Rule of St Augustine.

GEREON IN THE EAST, KNIGHTS OF ST

Defunct
RC (male Equestrian Order) founded in the 12th century
Original habit: (insignia) a white (or red) patriarchal, double-barred cross standing on a green hill.

The origin of the Order is obscure but it may have been founded by the German emperor Frederick I Barbarossa in c.1190 as he set out on the third crusade, in which he was to die, or by his nephew, Frederick II, who was later crowned king of Jerusalem, in 1228.

GILBERT OF SEMPRINGHAM, CANONS REGULAR AND NUNS OF ST

Defunct
RC (male and female) founded in England in the

12th century by St Gilbert of Sempringham (1083–1189 – canonized 1202) Original habit: (canons) a black cassock and hood, with a white surplice lined with lamb's wool, long stockings and shoes; a white linen cape was worn in chapel; (nuns) a black tunic, mantle and hood, lined with lamb's wool, and a coarse black head veil.

St Gilbert was rector of Sempringham, in Lincolnshire. He had studied in England and France, became a teacher and was later ordained by the bishop of Lincoln in *c*.1123. When his father died, Gilbert inherited the position of squire and with it the care of his small rural community. When seven pious women from his village wanted to live a communal religious life, Gilbert built them a cloister and convent and drew up a revision of the Cistercian Rule for Women for them to follow. The community grew, and lay Brothers and Sisters were introduced who could manage the manual and labouring work for the nuns. St Bernard of Clairvaux, who met Gilbert at the General Chapter of Cîteaux in 1147, helped him draw up the Institutes of Sempringham. On his return to England, Gilbert was placed in charge of the Order, appointing canons to serve the community as priests. The Congregation then became a double monastery, the religious living under the Rule of St Augustine while the lay brethren still observed the Cistercian Rule. The Order spread throughout England, and at its height it is said to have numbered seven hundred canons and fifteen hundred Sisters. Many of the later foundations were for men only, as in Cambridge. Leper hospitals and orphanages were established as the members cared for the communities in which they lived. Towards the end of his life, and it is claimed that he lived to 106, Gilbert handed over control of the Order to his successor, Roger, prior of the single-sex Malton Priory in Yorkshire. Only at this point did Gilbert, by now very ill and nearly blind, make his religious profession. By the end of the 15th century the Order had fallen upon hard times and the houses were dissolved, without acrimony and with the consent of the canons and nuns, who each received a reasonable annual pension.

✠ Gilbertines

GIRDLE, LADIES OF THE

A group of pious women, gathered together in the 15th century for the purpose of practising various penances and saying prayers for the overthrow of heretics, by Anna, duchess of Brittany, the wife of King Charles VIII of France. The women vowed their chastity to God and came together three times daily for communal prayer so that 'God might give victory over the enemies of the Catholic faith' (Bonanni, *Catalogus Ordinum Religiosarum*, 1707). The name derives from the girdle, or knotted white cord, which the women wore around their waists as a testimony of their chastity.

GLORIOUS ASCENSION, COMMUNITY OF THE

Location: (male) England (Kingsbridge, Devon); (female) France (Fayenne, Var)
Anglican (male and female) founded in 1960
Abbr: CGA

A group of religious Brothers and Sisters who have committed themselves to working in ordinary jobs and living a communal life in small groups in order to witness to the faith among their neighbours and colleagues. The inspiration for this way of life came from the Little Brothers of Charles de Foucauld. At present the community in Devon, England, offers facilities for retreats and opportunities for quiet reassessment.

GOLDEN FLEECE, KNIGHTS OF THE

Location: Spain (Madrid)
RC (male Equestrian Order) founded in France in
1430 by Philip the Good, Duke of Burgundy
Original habit: (insignia) a golden fleece suspended
from an enamelled flintstone, from which flames
arise, with the motto 'Pretium Laborem Non Vile'
(The Reward of Labour is not Cheap). The robes
worn by a knight have varied at different times
and could include a scarlet mantle trimmed at the
edge with embroidered gold crosses of St Andrew
with a plain cap for the head. A collar could also
be worn, made from gold and representing the
arms of Philip the Good with flaring flintstones,
from the centre of which was suspended the
golden fleece, and with the same motto.

An Equestrian Order, still awarded in Spain,
founded by Philip the Good, duke of Burgundy, at Bruges on the occasion of his
marriage in 1430 to Isabella of Portugal.
The Order received papal approbation in
1433 and 1516, and Spanish kings were
given authority to grant the honour from
the 16th century. It is thought that the
foundation was made to add to the splendour of the Burgundian court. No vows
were taken.

GOLDEN SPUR, ORDER OF THE

Location: Italy (Rome)
RC (Equestrian Order), a papal award; date of
foundation uncertain; restored in 1905
Original habit: (insignia) an eight-pointed yellow
enamelled gold cross from the base of which is
suspended a gold spur. The cross is worn around
the neck on a white ribbon bordered in red. In the
centre of the cross is a white medal with the
inscrption 'Maria' encircled in gold, and on the
reverse side the date '1905' in Roman numerals is
surrounded by the inscription 'Pius X Restituit'.

The Order was restored by Pope Pius X in
1905 to mark the Golden Jubilee of the
definition of the dogma of the Immaculate
Conception and is given as an award to
those who through either their bravery or
their writings have safeguarded, or spread,
the Roman Catholic faith.

GONZAGA, HERMITS OF

Defunct
RC (male) founded in Italy, possibly in the 15th
century, by Jerome Raigni di Castelgioffre with
Francesco di Gonzaga
Original habit: a rough brown woollen tunic

An Order of Hermits co-founded in the late
15th or early 16th century by Jerome Raigni
di Castelgioffre and Francesco di Gonzaga,
a nobleman. Francesco fell from his horse,
and he believed that his life had been spared
through the intercession of Our Lady. In
return, he vowed to live a life of penance.
He and Jerome decided to leave the world
and live as solitaries. This attracted many
followers, and it was necessary to have a
Rule of Life, which was provided for them
by the bishop of Reggio. The Constitutions
were approved by Pope Alexander VI. The
form of life was austere, the accommodation was bare and the diet was unremit-
ting with just bread and vegetables allowed.
Scourging was the norm, at least three times
a week and daily during Lent.

✠ Hermits of Our Lady of Gonzaga

GOOD SAMARITAN, SISTERS OF THE

Location: Australia (Glebe Point, Sydney, New
South Wales)
RC (female) founded in Australia in 1857 by
Archbishop Polding, OSB, assisted by Geraldine
Gibbons (Mother Scholastica), a Sister of Charity

Originally founded as the Good Shepherd
Sisters in Sydney, New South Wales, the
name was changed to its present one
because of fear of encroaching on other
Good Shepherd Congregations in Europe.
The Sisters were specifically introduced into
Australia from Europe by the French Insti-

tute of the Good Shepherd, which was already established in Melbourne. The Sisters work in teaching, with both boarding and day schools in their care, and run orphanages and homes throughout Australia. Their Rule is that of the Regular Oblates of St Benedict, with certain additions and modifications. The Sisters established missions in Japan in 1948, with the Japanese Sisters sending their missionaries to the Philippines in 1990. More recently a Good Samaritan novitiate has been opened (1997) in Kiribati in the Pacific Ocean. Other work undertaken now includes the running of liturgical and retreat centres, hospital and prison chaplaincies, and parish ministries directed at the elderly, the homeless, the sick and the dying and aboriginal families in the outback.

GOOD SAVIOUR, DAUGHTERS OF THE

Location: France (Caen)
RC (female) founded in France in 1720 by Anne Leroy and the Blessed Pierre François Jamet (beatified 1987)
Abbr: BS
Original habit: a black tunic and veil with a white linen under-cap covered by a black silk veil which ends in two wide bands over the breast.

After trying her vocation with the Ursulines and other Orders, Anne Leroy, with the help of her friend Mme. Lecouvreur de la Fontaine, rented two small houses in Caen, and from there they began their work of teaching the young and visiting the sick and destitute in the neighbourhood. A mental asylum was opened in 1731, by which time the community was formalized as the Association of Mary, changing later to its present title. The Order survived the French Revolution, despite the small numbers, helped by their chaplain Fr Jamet, who is regarded as their second founder, and further houses were opened throughout France. With the coming of the French

Association Laws at the start of the 20th century, which led to the dispersal of many religious communities, new houses were established in Ireland, Italy, Spain, the United Kingdom and Madagascar. The Rule is that of St Augustine, and there is a special devotion to the Holy Trinity. Choir Sisters recite the whole of the little office of the Blessed Virgin Mary, and a daily silence is kept from 2 to 3 pm, in honour of Our Lord's agony on the Cross. The Sisters are now involved in various works of charity, including Institutes for the deaf and dumb, nursing homes for those with nervous complaints, and schools.

GOOD SHEPHERD, LITTLE BROTHERS OF THE

Location: Canada (Hamilton, Ontario)
RC (male) founded in Canada in 1951
Abbr: BGS

A Congregation founded to provide a ministry to poor and destitute men, women and children, and to care for the elderly and for those who are mentally ill or physically handicapped. The Brothers also conduct an AIDS ministry and care for the victims of abuse by providing sheltered accommodation, and run an orphanage in Haiti. The Congregation was approved in 1983.

GOOD SONS, CONGREGATION OF THE

Defunct
RC (male) founded in France in 1615 by Henri Pringuel
Original habit: a black soutane, as for French secular clergy; this changed after 1626 to a grey Franciscan habit with a knotted cord and a grey mantle.

The Congregation was founded at Armentières by five pious working men led by Henri Pringuel, who had been unsuccessful in his desire to become a Capuchin. The five men came together and formed a small community, adopting the dress of a secular priest. They helped the members of their parish, teaching reading and writing, and nursing the sick. In 1626 the men became Franciscan tertiaries, taking their religious vows of poverty, chastity and obedience. Houses were established in the dioceses of Arras and Tournay.

GOSPEL OF CHARLES DE FOUCAULD, LITTLE SISTERS OF THE

Location: France (La Courneuve)
RC (female) founded in France in 1963
Abbr: LSG

A Diocesan Congregation, founded by René Voillaume, for work among the poor and the marginalized in the community, with a special ministry to those in prison. Considerable emphasis is placed on community life and the value of contemplative prayer. A foundation was made in the USA in 1972.

GRANDMONT, HERMITS AND THE ORDER OF

Defunct
RC (male) founded in France in the 11th century by St Stephen of Muret (canonized 1189)
Original habit: a coarse brown tunic with scapular and hood; the colour later changed to black and a rochet and biretta replaced the scapular and hood.

The founder, St Stephen of Muret, having spent some time as a hermit in Calabria, returned to his native France determined to introduce the eremitical life in his own country. He lived as a hermit at Muret, in the mountains near Limoges, gathering around him some disciples, praying together and reciting the offices, allowed to beg for food only when their supplies had run out and then only with the permission of the bishop. A Rule was drawn up based largely on the example of St John the Baptist, on whom the hermits were to model themselves. St Stephen, although leader of the group, refused to be styled abbot, preferring the title of corrector. After Stephen's

death the Brothers moved to Grandmont in Normandy, and other foundations were made, including one in England in the 12th century. Life at Grandmont was not without its problems, centred mainly around disputes between the choir monks, who wished to continue as recluses, and the lay Brothers, who did most of the work and sought some respite. The Order began to decline and an attempt at reform was made in 1643 when Dom Charles Fremon founded the Strict Observance of the Order of Grandmont, which returned to the early austerities and a life of penitence; this now formed a separate branch. A relaxation of the Rule of poverty at Grandmont, which led to the acquisition of considerable wealth by the lay Brothers, who then regarded themselves as equals of the choir monks, ensured that the decline continued. The two branches of the Order survived until the time of the French Revolution, which saw their demise. There were by then only two surviving monks, and they were expelled from the mother house in 1787. Today, all that remains of the abbey of Grandmont is a line of stones.

GREEN SHIELD, KNIGHTS OF THE

Defunct
RC (male Equestrian Order) founded in France by King Charles VI
Original habit: (insignia) a shield in green, of the type used by foot soldiers, with lines radiating from the centre.

An Order created by Charles VI, king of France (1368–1422), for a reason lost in obscurity but possibly related to the defence of the noblewomen at his court.

GREGORY THE GREAT, ORDER OF ST

Location: Italy (Rome)
RC (Equestrian Order), a papal award; instituted in 1831 by Pope Gregory XVI

Original habit: (insignia) an eight-pointed red enamelled cross in the centre of which is a blue medal with a distinctive image of St Gregory in gold, showing the saint with a dove near his right ear, surrounded by the words 'S. Gregorius Magnus'; the reverse of the medal is inscribed with the words 'Pro Deo et Principe' (for God and the State) and 'Gregorius XVI PM Anno 1', marking the first year of the pontificate.

Pope Gregory XVI (1831–46), who endured many troubles and uprisings in the Papal States, instituted the Order in 1831. It has two divisions, to reward both civil and military achievements of the citizens of the Papal States. The Order was reformed in 1905 by Pope St Pius X. The image of St Gregory with the dove is drawn from the tradition that the saint was seen with a dove, the emblem of the Holy Spirit, whispering in his ear by John the Deacon, his secretary, while St Gregory was dictating his Homilies.

GREY NUNS – Beauport

Location: Canada (Beauport, Quebec)
RC (female) founded in Canada in 1849
Abbr: SCQ

The Congregation was founded in Quebec City when four Grey Nuns from the Sisters of Charity of Montreal arrived there in 1849 and began to work in education and the care of the elderly, which they maintain today. There is an American house in Massachusetts which was founded in 1890. Missions are working in Japan, Uruguay, Paraguay and Argentina.

✠ Sisters of Charity of Quebec

GREY NUNS – St Hyacinthe

Location: Canada (St Hyacinthe, Quebec)
RC (female) founded in Canada in 1840
Abbr: SCSH

This Congregation was founded at the request of the local bishop when several Grey Nuns arrived to serve the poor and needy in the diocese. The Sisters continue their work, running homes for the elderly and a child care centre, staffing hospitals and involving themselves in catechetics and pastoral work. They have a foreign mission in Haiti.

✠ Sisters of Charity of St Hyacinthe

GREY NUNS OF THE CROSS

Location: Canada (Ottawa, Ontario)
RC (female) founded in Canada in 1845 by Sr Elizabeth Bruyère
Abbr: SCO

In 1845 four Grey Nuns from the Sisters of Charity of Montreal, led by Elizabeth Bruyère, made the foundation at Bytown, Ottawa, for the purpose of serving the poor. A further foundation was made, in the USA, in 1857. The work is now concerned with nursing the sick and elderly as well as staffing schools and providing catechesis in parishes where it is needed, together with foreign missions in Brazil, Japan, Central Africa, Haiti and New Guinea. In 1926, seventy-seven Grey Nuns from this Congregation founded the Grey Sisters of the Immaculate Conception.

GREY NUNS OF THE SACRED HEART

Location: USA (Yardley, Pennsylvania)
RC (female) founded in the USA in 1921 indirectly by St Marie d'Youville
Abbr: GNSH

This is an autonomous group, and the only Congregation of Grey Nuns with an American mother house, which has its origins in the Grey Sisters of Montreal. Houses are found throughout the USA and Canada and the pastoral work includes rehabilitation, care for the aged, catechetical instruction in parishes, a prison ministry and care for the homeless. The Sisters also help with the provision of housing, run nursing homes and are involved in education at all levels.

GREY SISTERS – Melbourne

Location: Australia (Surrey Hills, Melbourne)
RC (female) founded in Australia in 1930 by Cecily Mary Maud O'Connell
Abbr: FCS
Original habit: a grey habit.

A Diocesan Congregation founded in Daylesford, Victoria, by Maud O'Connell (as she preferred to be called) with the help of William Collins, a priest. Following the death of her mother, Maud became interested in training to be a teacher and also became involved with women's rights and the social issues of the day, including equal pay for equal work and industrial and political reforms. Her interest took her into rescue work. Together with Mary Glowry she founded a home for unemployed women who had lost their jobs because of a lock-out at a local chocolate factory and were in urgent need of help. Maud's interests now turned to nursing and Labour Party social politics. She saw a great need to provide support for mothers in their own homes at time of childbirth and illness, and was able to set up a rest home at Daylesford where she also started a training centre for home nursing. On Christmas Day 1930, Maud and a companion, Mary Bannon, dedicated themselves privately and independently to caring for women in need. Fr Collins drew up a Rule for the new community, which was set up formally and with diocesan approval under the name of the Little Company of Our Lady of the Blessed Sacrament. The word 'Little' was later dropped and members soon became known as the Grey Sisters from the colour of the grey nurses' uniforms the Sisters wore. As well as courses in nursing and motherhood

at Daylesford, a clinic was set up at Prahan, Melbourne, in 1932 and in Surrey Hills, Melbourne, in the following year. Members of the Congregation make annual vows. Despite many difficulties and delays, papal approval was finally granted in 1949.

✠ Company of Our Lady of the Blessed Sacrament

GREY SISTERS – Montreal

Location: Canada (Montreal, Quebec)
RC (female) founded in Canada in 1737 by St Marie Marguerite Dufrost de la Lammerais d'Youville (canonized 1990)
Abbr: SGM
Original habit: a distinctive grey habit.

After the death of her husband, Marie d'Youville was still a young woman, and she resolved to spend the rest of her life caring for the poor and needy. To that end she worked as a volunteer visiting prisoners and the sick and elderly in their homes and in hospitals. It was not long before other women wanted to join her in the work, and with the enthusiastic support of the Church authorities in Montreal, particularly that of Fr Louis Normand du Faradon of the Montreal Seminary, Marie d'Youville and three others made their profession on New Year's Eve 1737 and adopted a simple Rule. The new Congregation, known as the Sisters of Charity of the General Hospital of Montreal, was given diocesan approval in 1754 and papal approbation in 1880. The Sisters wore a distinctive grey habit, thus earning them the familiar name by which they are still known. In addition to the usual three vows of religion, poverty, chastity and obedience, the Sisters undertook to dedicate themselves to the service of suffering humanity. In 1747 Mother Marie took over the administration of the Charon Brothers' General Hospital, which had fallen into disrepair. This had been built by François

Charon, the founder of the Hospitaller Brothers of the Cross and of St Joseph, an Order which was by then defunct. The hospital was repaired and is still caring for the sick and needy today. Mother Marie was beatified by Pope John XXIII in 1958 and given the title 'Mother of Universal Charity'. She was canonized in 1990 by Pope John Paul II, the first saint of Canadian origin. The work of the Congregation today is still mainly with the sick, but also includes the care of orphans and homeless and abandoned people.

✠ Sisters of Charity of the General Hospital of Montreal

GREY SISTERS OF THE IMMACULATE CONCEPTION

A foundation made in Canada in 1926 by seventy-seven Grey Nuns. The Congregation works in Canada, the Bahamas and the Dominican Republic.

GUARDIAN ANGEL, SISTERS OF THE

Location: Spain (Madrid)
RC (female) founded in France in 1839 by Fr Antonio Rosa Ormieres and Mother St Pascual
Abbr: SAC
Original habit: a black tunic and veil with a simple white wimple, under-veil and cap.

A Congregation which was founded in Quillan, France, receiving state approval in 1852 by a decree of Napoleon III. Mother St Pascual had been a member of the Congregation of Christian Instruction of St Gildas, which had been founded by Fr Gabriel Deshayes in 1820. It was Fr Deshayes who supplied the first Sisters for this new Congregation. The work of the Sisters is now largely concerned with the needs of the poor and making the Church more accessible to them. An American foundation was made in Sapin, Los Angeles.

GUASTALLA, VIRGINS OF

Defunct
RC (female) founded in Italy in 1557 by Countess Luigia Torelli
Original habit: a black secular-style dress with a veil folded loosely over the hair, and a ring, engraved with the emblem of a hand holding a cross.

Luigia Torelli, Countess of Guastalla, had been twice widowed by the age of twenty-five and turned to religion to give her life a purpose. In 1530 she had founded the Congregation known as the Angelicals, which she entered in 1536 taking the name in religion of Sr Paola Maria. The Angelicals were intended to be an active Order, given to charitable works and especially to the care of the sick and of orphans, but Pope Paul III (died 1549) imposed a strict enclosure on the Congregation and brought their charitable work to an end. Paola Maria built another house, in Milan, known as the College of Guastalla. Members were placed under the care of the Barnabite Fathers and were known as the Daughters of Mary. The female orphans they cared for were to be nobly born and to remain with the Congregation for twelve years, after which they could return to the world with a dowry provided, or join the community. After the death of Paola Maria in 1559 it was again decided, this time by Pope Urban VIII on the advice of St Charles Borromeo, that this community must also be strictly enclosed with the members making solemn vows, attending choir and observing the monastic routine of prayer, silence and work. Both Congregations are now defunct.

✠ Daughters of Mary
Guastallines

H

HATCHET, ORDER OF THE

Defunct
RC (female Equestrian Order) founded in Spain, in
1149 by Raymond Berengar, Count of Barcelona

An Order founded in memory of the
defence of the city of Tortosa against the
Moors by women armed with hatchets, or
axes.

HEART OF JESUS, INSTITUTE OF PRIESTS OF
THE

Location: France (Paris)
RC (male and some laity) founded in France in 1791
by Fr Peter Joseph de Clorivière
Abbr: ISPCJ (for clergy)
Original habit: secular style.

The Institute of Priests of the Heart of Jesus
was founded in Paris along the lines of the
Daughters of the Heart of Mary (see entry
below) by Peter de Clorivière. It became
defunct but underwent a renewal in 1918
when David Fontaine, Charles Viennot and
Leon Bois renewed the original commitment made by Peter de Clorivière and committed themselves to the Institute. It
received approval in 1952. Although originally recognized as a society of diocesan
priests, constituted by and for priests, some
mixed lay groups have recently been admitted. The members maintain contact with
each other by way of reunions, journals,
study groups and retreats. The Institute has
spread from France through Europe and
into the USA, Africa and India.

HEART OF JESUS, MISSIONARIES OF THE

Location: Italy (Rome)
RC (male) founded in Italy in 1867 by Bishop Daniel
Comboni
Abbr: MCCJ
Original habit: as for secular clergy.

Upon his return to Italy from Central Africa
because of ill-health, Daniel Comboni
founded the Institute of Missionaries for
Negroes, in Verona in 1867, with a second
foundation, the Institute of the Holy
Mother, for women who could help in the
mission fields. At the same time he opened
Institutes in Cairo where members could
gain some experience of the life ahead of
them in Africa. A seminary in Verona, given
over to the Congregation, underwent reorganization under Jesuit guidance, with a
new Rule approved in 1900 and a change
of name to the Sons of the Sacred Heart
of Jesus. Associated with the Congregation
was the College for the Central African
Missions. In 1923 the Congregation split
into two branches along lines of language,
into the Sons of the Sacred Heart of Jesus,
restricted to German-speaking members,
and the Congregation of the Sacred Heart
of Jesus, for the Italian-speakers. The two

branches were reunited in 1979 and today the priests and Brothers are found in mission stations around the world, where they work among the poorest and most disadvantaged people and exercise a pastoral ministry for minority groups.

✠ Comboni Fathers
  Verona Fathers

HEART OF MARY, DAUGHTERS OF THE

Location: France (Paris)
RC (female) founded in France in 1790 by Fr Peter Joseph de Clorivière
Abbr: DHM
Original habit: no religious habit has ever been worn.

The congregation was founded during the French Revolution, which in part may explain its traditional lack of habit, since its founder, a former Jesuit priest (the Jesuits were suppressed by Pope Clement XIV in 1772), had thought of a way for pious women to form an association to perform charitable works without attracting attention to themselves during this time of persecution of religious Orders in France. Members could live either in community, or alone, or in a family, and those who wished to take vows could do so. This Society, whose spirituality has been described as Ignatian in character, follows a flexible but firm Rule of life and has spread throughout the world. Houses have been established in most parts of Europe, North and South America and Africa, and in India, Pakistan and Japan. The American foundation was made in 1851. The Sisters work in education, run hostels and orphanages and conduct retreats.

HEDWIG, SOCIETY OF ST

Location: Germany (Berlin)
RC (female) founded in Germany in 1859 by Canon R. S. Spiske

A Society which began as a pious Association for women and young girls in Breslau, Germany, in 1848, becoming a Congregation of Sisters in 1859. The Sisters observe the Rule of St Augustine, and their work is largely educational, covering vocational training as well as teaching in schools at all levels and the care of orphaned and abandoned children. In their work the Sisters reflect the spirit of St Hedwig (1174–1243), a Bavarian aristocrat who was deeply involved in the catechesis of the uneducated.

HELENA, ORDER OF ST

Location: USA (Vails Gate, New York)
Anglican (female) founded in the USA in 1945
Abbr: OSH

When nine Sisters from the Anglican Order of St Anne left the foundation at Versailles, Kentucky, where they were running Margaret Hall School, they went on to found the Order of St Helena in New York. The last of the founding Sisters, Catherine Buchanan Remley (Sr Josephine) died recently. They had been encouraged in the move and in the foundation of a new Order by the bishop-visitor and by the superior of the Order of the Holy Cross, Fr Alan Whittemore. In this new foundation the Sisters adopted the modern Rule of the Order of the Holy Cross, which has some Dominican-like features in its Constitutions. The Order of St Helena remained affiliated to the Order of the Holy Cross until 1970, when the Sisters became autonomous. Houses are to be found in the states of New York, Washington and Georgia, where the Sisters work in organizing conferences, running retreats and workshops, conducting pilgrimages and the practice of psychotherapy, in which field some of the Sisters have qualified.

HIPPOLITES

Defunct
RC (male) founded in Mexico in 1585 by
Bernardino Alvarez

The Order was founded originally as a Brotherhood to care for the sick and was responsible for the building of three hospitals, the first dedicated to St Hippolytus, the second to the Holy Spirit and the third to the king of Spain, who had helped to finance the enterprise. Pope Gregory XIII (1572–85) granted the first approbation, later confirmed by Pope Sixtus V (1585–90), and it was Pope Clement VIII (1592–1605) who granted a further approbation and also the privilege of being an Order of Hospitallers. A new Constitution was confirmed in the 18th century by Pope Innocent XII, who authorized the addition of a fourth vow, that of dedication to the care of the sick, to the usual three vows of poverty, chastity and obedience.

✠ Brothers of Charity of St Hippolytus

HOLY AND UNDIVIDED TRINITY, SOCIETY OF THE

Defunct
Anglican (female) founded in England in 1851 by
Marian Rebecca Hughes
Original habit: contemplative Sisters wore a blue habit and active Sisters a brown one, but this was later changed to a simple black habit with blue facings on the sleeves and a blue girdle for all Sisters.

The Society was founded at Witney, in Oxfordshire, with the assistance of Samuel Wilberforce, bishop of Oxford and later of Winchester. Marian Hughes had been inspired by John Henry Newman's work, *Church of the Fathers*, to explore the possibility of a religious life. Her vows were taken privately, at the home of the Reverend Charles Seager, after which she went to receive holy communion at the Church of St Mary the Virgin, the celebrant being Newman himself. By the time of the founding of the Society, Newman had left the Anglicans and been received into the Roman Catholic Church. Marian Hughes went on a tour of religious communities in France and returned to England with clear ideas of how her community was to be structured. She helped Dr Pusey, the Tractarian leader, to draw up a Rule. Following the death of her father, she went with her mother to live in Oxford, where her brother had the living of the church of St Thomas the Martyr. Some women of the parish had formed a sisterhood, its members caring for the poor and for girls wishing to be trained for domestic service. Two of the women, Catherine Fraser and Augusta Landon, joined Mother Marian, as she was now known, and the small community received the approval of Bishop Samuel Wilberforce in 1849, which marks the foundation date. The work undertaken was largely that of service to the poor and sick, to children, prisoners and those in need, together with teaching, the making of altar breads, church embroidery and printing.

HOLY CHILD JESUS, SOCIETY OF THE

Location: Italy (Rome)
RC (female) founded in England in 1846 by
Cornelia Connelly
Abbr: SHCJ
Original habit: a black habit with a white cap and collar and a black veil.

The founder, Cornelia Connolly, was born in Philadelphia in 1809 and after her marriage both she and her Episcopalian clergyman husband, Pierce Connolly, became Roman Catholics. This became a problem when, in 1840, Pierce wished to become a priest, which would involve his wife in entering a religious Order herself. Papal permission was granted for this, but despite having made a public vow of chastity in order to clear the way for her husband's ordination, Cornelia entered the Congregation of the Sisters of the Sacred Heart in France with reluctance. Her life had been one of great tragedy. One of her three children, John, had died after falling into a vat of boiling maple syrup when only two years old, and her other children, a boy and girl, led tempestuous lives and were always to give their mother great anguish. Pierce Connolly was ordained as a priest in Rome, but later lost his faith and reverted to Protestantism, demanding that his wife should rejoin him, which she would not do. Unable to settle with the Sisters of the Sacred Heart it became clear that she should leave to found a Congregation. She was instructed to draw up a Rule and Constitutions for such a foundation with the help of a Jesuit priest. Although she thought at this point to return to the USA, Cornelia was persuaded to accept the invitation of Cardinal Wiseman to go to England, and it was here that the first convent was opened, in Derby in 1847, but the upkeep proved too expensive for the small community and they moved to St Leonard's-on-Sea in Sussex. The Society prospered, and further foundations were made in England, with others in the USA in both Pennsylvania and New York. The work of the Sisters, which was later to spread to Ireland and France, was always largely educational, and they now teach at every level, develop spiritual and pastoral ministries and participate in justice and compassion programmes. There are foreign missions to Africa and Chile. Cornelia Connolly died at the Congregation's convent at Mayfield in Sussex in 1879. This Society must not be confused with the Congregation of the Holy Child Jesus (Les Dames de Saint-Maur).

HOLY CHILD JESUS OF THE THIRD ORDER REGULAR OF ST FRANCIS, SERVANTS OF THE

Location: Germany (Zell am Main, Würzburg)
RC (female) founded in Germany in 1855 by Antonia Werr
Abbr: OSF
Original habit: Franciscan style

The Congregation was founded at Oberzell, near Würzburg, in Germany, for the care of girls and young women at risk and who were socially disadvantaged. The Sisters also undertook nursing and work in kindergartens and elementary schools. In 1929 foundations were made in the USA, on Staten Island and Yardville, New Jersey, where the Sisters now undertake the care of retarded women at St Elizabeth's Home. More recently, a house was established to carry on with this work in Kwazulu-Natal.

HOLY CHILDHOOD OF JESUS, INSTITUTE OF THE

Location: France (Metz)
RC (female) founded in France in 1807 by Anne-Victoire Mejanes
Abbr: SSCH

A Congregation founded for the education of young children and the care of the sick. It began with a group of women, led by Anne-Victorie Mejanes, who worked locally in these areas and who were invited by Bishop Jauffret of Metz to come to his city to take over the disused abbey of St Glossinde, there to continue their work. The congregation was approved in 1888 and 1899. Sisters of the Institute are now found throughout Europe, the USA and Canada with nearly sixty houses opened. It should be noted that there are two defunct societies of the same name. The first was founded in France in 1835, in the diocese of Frejus-Toulon, and had its mother house at Draguignan. These Sisters were also concerned with education and the care of the sick.

Another foundation was made in France, at Sens, in 1838 with a mother house at St Colombe-les-Sens and with the same apostolate.

✙ Sisters of St Chrétienne

HOLY CROSS, BROTHERHOOD OF THE

Defunct
Anglican (male) founded in England in 1924 by Fr George Potter
Original habit: a dark grey, double-breasted cassock with a Franciscan knotted cord from which was suspended a small cross.

The Brotherhood of the Holy Cross was founded at Nunhead, London, and canonically established in 1932 when the community moved to a large house known as St Francis' Friary. Here the Brothers were able to help young men from deprived backgrounds, who were often homeless and descending into crime. The life of the Brotherhood was distinctly Franciscan, with a Rule and Constitutions approved by the bishop of Southwark.

HOLY CROSS, CONGREGATION OF

Location: Italy (Rome)
RC (male) founded in France in 1837 by Fr Basil Anthony Moreau
Abbr: CSC

The foundation of the Congregation came about through the union of two French societies, the Auxiliary Priests of Le Mans (founded 1835) and the Brothers of St Joseph (founded 1820). The Auxiliary Priests were founded by Canon Moreau to enable priests to live in community and be of assistance to the diocesan priests, while the Brothers of St Joseph was a diocesan community which trained its members to become teachers and work where they were needed. The union was made in order to combine the novitiate facilities, with Canon

Moreau elected as the first superior. The congregation took its name from the Church of the Holy Cross in Le Mans. In the early days the priests were known as Salvatorists and the Brothers as Josephites, but these titles were discarded in 1872. The Order was approved in 1855 and 1857. The apostolate of the Congregation is to provide Christian education for the poor and to preach in rural areas and in foreign missions. Houses were opened in Europe, Algeria, elsewhere in Africa, East Bengal and the USA, where the members arrived in 1841 to establish a small college in North Indiana, at Notre Dame-du-Lac, which later became Notre Dame University. Much of the overseas expansion, especially to Canada, Bengal and the USA, was in consequence of the French Association Laws of 1901. A new Constitution adopted in 1986 was an attempt to return more closely to the ideals of the founder.

✙ Holy Cross Fathers

HOLY CROSS, MARIANITES OF

Location: USA (Washington, DC)
RC (female) founded in France in 1841 by Fr Basil Anthony Moreau and Leocardie Gascoin (Sr Mary of the Seven Dolours)
Abbr: MSC
Original habit: a black tunic, with a white collar and a distinctive large, white, disc-like concave headdress surrounding the face, which was covered with a black veil.

Leocardie Gascoin, together with three other women who wished to enter the religious life, was sent to the Good Shepherd house in Le Mans, France, to begin studies for religious formation. They made their profession in 1841, after which they went, as a community, to help the Brothers and priests of the Congregation of Holy Cross. Fr Moreau placed the new Congregation under the protection of Our Lady of Sorrows. In 1843, four members of the Congregation went to the USA at the invitation of Bishop de la Hailandière of Vincennes, Indiana, to help the community at Notre Dame-du-Lac. By 1861 the Sisters were running schools and orphanages in Indiana, Illinois, Michigan, Kentucky, Louisiana, New York, Pennsylvania, Maryland and Washington, DC. The Indiana province of the Marianites became autonomous in 1869, its Constitutions approved in 1896 and the Congregation renamed as the Sisters of the Holy Cross. A Canadian foundation made near Montreal in 1847 became independent in 1883.

HOLY CROSS, ORDER OF THE

Location: Belgium (Denderleeuw)
RC (male) date of foundation unknown (possibly 13th century)
Abbr: OSC
Original habit: a white tunic with a black scapular and short black mantle with a small black hood; a cross is sewn on to the upper part of the scapular, the upright beam in red with the cross beam in white.

The origin of this Order is uncertain, but it is known that an Order of the Brethren of the Holy Cross was founded in the early 13th century when four canons, under the leadership of Blessed Theodore de Celles, founded a monastery at Liège in Belgium. It is possible, therefore, that the first Brethren, also known as Crosiers, were canons regular. The Blessed Theodore had met Mary of Oignies, a woman in close contact with many pious people, and she was probably a great influence in his decision to leave the Liège Cathedral chapter. The canons were given the first house of their new Order together with the church of St Theobald at Clair-Lieu, near Huy. The Order spread to France, The Netherlands, Germany and England. The Crosiers spoke against the Albigensian heresy then flourishing in France. The Albigenses taught that Christ was an angel, and that he neither suffered nor rose again from the dead. Members of this heretical cult led a severely ascetic life, believing that all matter was evil, condemning marriage and abandoning the sacraments. Salvation, they believed, could only come through strict adherence to Christ's words and teachings. The heresy was to last until the late 14th century, despite energetic and at times violently cruel action against the heretics. The Order of the Holy Cross, which was noted for hospitality towards the poor, the sick and travellers, continued to flourish, but with the Reformation many houses in England and The Netherlands were destroyed, and again at the French Revolution, French and Belgian houses were laid to ruin. Foundations were made in the USA, in Indiana, New York, Minnesota, Maryland, Michigan and Arizona, and there is now a mission at Agats in Indonesia. The Brothers work in publishing and education, conduct retreats and run home and foreign missions.

✚ Crosier Fathers
  Crosiers

HOLY CROSS, SERVANTS OF THE

Defunct
Anglican (female) founded in Australia

This defunct community began as a foundation in the country diocese of Bathurst, New South Wales, made by the remnant of a small Sisterhood which had set out from Australia to work in New Zealand but which has been disbanded on the death of its superior. Bishop Long of Bathurst agreed to a proposal, in 1922, to restore the Servants of the Holy Cross so that the Sisters could work among the children of the outback. The community moved to Port Elliott, South Australia, in 1933, where they continued their work in education with some parish responsibilities, but the community later closed.

HOLY CROSS, SISTERS OF THE - USA

Location: USA (Notre Dame, Indiana)
RC (female) founded in France in 1841 (but see below)
Abbr: CSC

The Congregation was the result of a split inside the Marianites of the Holy Cross, an Order which came to the USA in 1843. Because of certain administrative difficulties and strains between the foundation in Indiana and the mother house in France, a separation was agreed to, and in 1869 they were recognized as an independent foundation, with Fr Sorin as superior-general. Final approbation was granted in 1896. The Sisters work in the USA, Bangladesh, South America and Africa, where they have recently opened a mission in Ghana. Their ministry is very wide and embraces parochial work, education, health care, drop-in and day care centres for women and children and social work with refugees and immigrants.

HOLY CROSS, SOCIETY OF THE

Location: South Korea (Seoul)
Anglican (female) founded in Korea in 1925 by Bishop Mark Trollope
Abbr: SHC

The Sisters of the Community of St Peter, Woking, England, had been missionaries in Korea since 1892, and it was they who initiated the founding of this society, in 1925, and which was approved by Bishop Mark Trollope of the Anglican Church of Korea. Phoebe Lee was admitted as the first postulant. The Sisters observe the Rule of St Augustine and take the usual vows of religion, of poverty, chastity and obedience. Their work includes a range of activities, from parish ministries, care for elderly women, counselling, university chaplaincies and the running of retreats and guest houses to the making of altar breads and vestments.

HOLY CROSS, TEACHING SISTERS OF THE - Menzingen

Location: Switzerland (Lucerne)
RC (female) founded in Switzerland in 1844 by Fr Theodosius Florentini

Deeply worried about the future welfare of the Roman Catholic Church in Switzerland, a Capuchin priest, Fr Florentini, founded a small community of three Sisters at Altdorf, known as the Institute of the Franciscan Sisters of the Holy Cross. From this there emerged a group, the Teaching Sisters of the Holy Cross, with their mother house at Menzingen. The Congregation received papal approval in 1901, by which time their work in education had widened to include the care of the aged and infirm and of orphans. The congregation spread from Switzerland into Italy, Germany, England, South Africa, South America and India. The apostolate now includes the running of leper colonies, care of the terminally ill, catechesis and parish ministries.

✟ Sisters of the Holy Cross

HOLY FAITH, SISTERS OF THE

Location: Ireland (Glasnevin, Dublin)
RC (female) founded in Ireland in 1856
Abbr: CHF
Original habit: a black habit and veil with a white wimple and binder.

The Congregation of Sisters of the Holy Faith was founded in Dublin, under the guidance of a Vincentian priest, Fr John Gowan, aided by Miss Margaret Aylward and with the support of Cardinal Cullen of Dublin. It arose from a Ladies' Association of Charity which founded an orphanage in the city in 1850, and the new Congregation was approved in 1897 and 1910. The Sisters' main work is with the care of orphans but includes teaching and the care of the poor. Many foundations were made throughout Ireland with other houses opened in the USA (1953), the West Indies, Australia and New Zealand.

HOLY FAMILY, ASSOCIATION OF THE – Bordeaux

Location: Italy (Rome)
RC (male and female) founded in France in 1820 by the Abbé Pierre Bienvenue Noailles
Abbr: HFB.

Although this Association was founded in 1820, it arose from several earlier foundations made by Fr Noailles which came together under this new name. The abbé had started a series of Catechism of Perseverance classes in his parish of St Eulalie, in Bordeaux, to which young women came, some of them expressing an interest in joining a religious community. This resulted in the founding of the Institute of the Holy Family Sisters. Others of the group, wishing to live active religious lives while remaining in the world, formed the Ladies of the Holy Family, more recently renamed the Holy Family Secular Institute. Following an authenticated miraculous experience during a Benediction service, the Institute of the Holy Family attracted great interest and membership was extended to include laymen and clerics, who were enrolled as associates. In 1868, the Oblate Sisters of Mary Immaculate joined with the Institute, exchanging their blue Oblate habits for the black habit of the Holy Family Sisters. The Association, which it had now become, was divided into three groups, originally known as 'branches':

1 The Branch of Jesus – composed of clerics who either took an active role in the association or were united with it by prayer;
2 The Branch of Mary – which included all women, divided into active and simple groups, the latter being united by prayer;
3 The Branch of Joseph – which was composed of lay men, married or single.

By the time of Fr Noailles' death the Association had extended throughout France and was established in Spain, Belgium and Algeria. Since Vatican II, the Congregation has been divided into four new groups:

1 The Religious Apostolic Sisters, who live in community and take vows;
2 The Contemplative Sisters, also called Solitary Sisters, who live a contemplative community life with vows;
3 The Lay Associates, male and female, married and single, who live in the world and make promises, but not vows;
4 The Consecrated Seculars, who are single women who live in the world and take vows.

Until the 1950s the Congregation was further divided, each with apostolates suited to the needs of society. These included the Sisters of St Joseph (orphanages), the Sisters of Hope (nursing), the Agricole Sisters (agricultural work – these no longer exist), the Sisters of St Martha (care for aged and infirm priests and seminary work) and the Daughters of God Alone (a group at the disposal of their superiors to go wherever and whenever they are needed). Today, the Association undertakes a wide range of ministries and service, from teaching and health care to social service, the running of hostels for the disabled and residential homes, and chaplaincy work. Members are to be found worldwide, throughout Europe, Asia, Africa and America.

HOLY FAMILY, BROTHERS OF THE - Belley

Location: Italy (Rome)
RC (male) founded in France in 1827 by Brother
Gabriel Tabourin
Abbr: FSF

A lay religious Institute, founded at the
second attempt by Brother Gabriel in order
to provide chanters and sacristans for the
churches, and to instruct the young men,
in the diocese of Saint-Claude (Lons le
Saunier). The congregation was approved
in 1841 and 1936. The ministry today is
largely educational, at all levels, but is still
concerned with the training of sacristans.
The Institute is strictly composed of lay
Brothers and teachers. Priests are permitted
to be members only in such numbers as are
needed to administer the sacraments, but
the offices of superior and procurator-gen-
eral can be held by priests.

HOLY FAMILY, COMMUNITY OF THE

Location: England (West Malling, Kent)
Anglican (female) founded in England in 1898 by
Mother Agnes Mason
Abbr: CHF

Agnes Mason had been educated at Newn-
ham College, Cambridge, and she
responded to the need for providing secondary education for girls in those
countries which were then British colonies.
Together with three other young women,
who had been members of the Guild of the
Epiphany for Teachers, a foundation was
made with the Rule drawn up by Mother
Agnes herself. This allowed members of the
community to work in small groups of
never fewer than three under the authorization of the local diocesan bishop. The
first mother house was in London, but is
now at West Malling, in Kent. Schools were
established and the Sisters also opened a
house of studies in Cambridge, where both
community members and laywomen can

study for various degrees, including theology. Almost from the outset it was in the
mind of the founder to set up a house
where those Sisters who felt drawn to a
more contemplative way of life could live.
This was started in 1929 at Monmouth, and
a second house was established in 1937 at
Peakirk, near Peterborough. The community is the possessor of a magnificent
collection of books, which has become an
educational resource centre, with accommodation for retreats, conferences and
guests who may like to stay.

HOLY FAMILY, INSTITUTE OF THE SISTERS OF THE

Location: Italy (Comonte di Seriate, Bergamo)
RC (female) founded in Italy in 1856 by Blessed
Paula Cerioli (beatified 1950)

Paula Cerioli (1816–65) had been married,
but on the death of her husband and the
untimely demise of her three children she
decided to put her wealth to good use,
caring for orphans and country children.
She created a congregation of women who
would undertake these works of charity in
a more structured way, making her own
vows in 1857. Not content to restrict herself
to dealing with the problems of country
girls, she then oversaw the creation of a
similar Congregation which would care for
boys in rural areas. A suitable training
in horticulture and agriculture was made
available for them all, and this work continues today.

HOLY FAMILY, LITTLE SISTERS OF THE

Location: Italy (Castelletto di Brenzone, diocese of
Verona)
RC (female) founded in Italy in 1892 by Blessed
Joseph Nascimbeni (beatified 1988)

The founder, who served for almost all of
his priestly life in the parish of Castelletto,
founded the Congregation on the advice of

Bishop Baciliri of Verona and with the help of the future first superior of the Order, Mother Maria Manovani. There are many foundations of this Congregation today throughout Italy, and its members undertake a wide range of activities involving education and health care.

HOLY FAMILY, LITTLE SISTERS OF THE – Sherbrooke

Location: Canada (Sherbrooke, Quebec)
RC (female) founded in Canada in 1874 by Blessed Mary Paradis (beatified 1984) and Fr Camille Lefèbvre
Abbr: PSSF

The founder, Blessed Mary Paradis, was a professed member of the Marianites of Holy Cross. She founded the Little Sisters of the Holy Cross at Memramcook, New Brunswick, in 1874. The work soon spread throughout several Canadian and American dioceses and American archdioceses and the foundation was recognized as a Diocesan Congregation in 1896. The Sisters work in seminaries and colleges as well as episcopal residences. They also teach domestic skills to young women. There was a foundation made in the USA in 1900.

HOLY FAMILY, MISSIONARIES OF THE

Location: Italy (Rome)
RC (male) founded in The Netherlands in 1895 by Fr John Baptist Berthier
Abbr: MSF
Original habit: as for secular clergy.

A Congregation founded in The Netherlands by Fr Berthier, a member of the Missionaries of Our Lady of La Salette. The members of the Congregation are prepared to undertake any apostolate that will help the Church meet current needs. Houses are also to be found in Canada (Ottawa), Mexico (Saltillo) and the USA (Texas, Virginia and Missouri), where the priests and Brothers care for the aged and undertake help with late vocations and various parish missions.

HOLY FAMILY, MISSIONARY SISTERS OF THE

Location: Poland (Komorow, Warsaw)
RC (female) founded in 1905 by Blessed Boleslawa Lament (beatified 1991)

The founder of the Congregation, Blessed Boleslawa Lament (1862–1946), was inspired to make her own foundation by the example of Blessed Honoratus Kozminski (beatified 1988), a Capuchin Franciscan who had founded the Congregation of Mary, of which Boleslawa was a member. The apostolate of the Congregation of Mary was to work in Russia with a view to the conversion of members of the Russian Orthodox faith. Boleslawa was persuaded to found the Congregation of the Missionary Sisters of the Holy Family, and she established a mother house in St Petersburg in 1907. The Sisters' work was in education, which extended into Finland, and this came to a stop with the Russian revolution. The congregation returned to Poland, changing its apostolate to the relief of poverty rather than conversion to the Roman Catholic faith. Many foundations were made throughout the country. The Second World War destroyed much of the Congregation's work in eastern Poland, but there has been a recovery, with more schools and orphanages opened.

HOLY FAMILY, SISTERS OF THE – New Orleans

Location: USA (New Orleans, Louisiana)
RC (female) founded in the USA in 1842 by Henriette Delille
Abbr: SSF

An American congregation founded by a free woman of African descent who became, in 1989, the first American-born black person whose cause for canonization was officially opened in Rome. With a friend, Juliette Gaudin, who was born in Cuba of Haitian parents, Henriette dedicated herself to the education of the children of slaves. They catechized both the children and the adults, preparing them for first communion and confirmation. Because of the social customs of the day and the laws concerning peoples of African descent in the USA, the Congregation was not officially recognized until 1842, although they had come together many years earlier. Despite all prejudices and difficulties, the work of the Sisters expanded into teaching, the care of orphanages, especially those catering for coloured children, and the running of an Old People's Home which is the oldest Roman Catholic home for the elderly in the USA. The Sisters also operate two independent facilities for retired people on low income in New Orleans. The teaching programme runs from pre-school child development through to high schools. Missions are staffed in Texas, California, Washington DC, Nigeria and Belize.

HOLY FAMILY, SISTERS OF THE – San Jose

Location: USA (Mission San Jose Fremont, California)
RC (female) founded in the USA in 1872 by Elizabeth (Lizzie) Armer (Mother Dolores Armer) and Mgr John J. Prendergast

An active congregation, whose members observe simple vows, providing catechesis for neglected children unable to attend Roman Catholic schools. The Sisters also run sewing classes and sodalities and provide crèche care for working mothers. Their general mandate is to care for the underprivileged and those marginalized in society.

HOLY FAMILY, SISTERS OF THE – Villefranche-de-Rouergue

Location: France (Villefranche-de-Rouergue)
RC (female) founded in France in 1816 by St Emilie de Rodat (canonized 1950)
Abbr: RHF
Original habit: a black tunic with a black veil and a black cloth cincture and a large white wimple, which was unstarched; a small silver crucifix on a black cord was worn around the neck.

The Congregation was founded as a teaching Institute to combat the damage done to religious education, especially in the poorer classes, by the French Revolution. The Sisters also cared for the sick in their own homes, looked after prostitutes and the housebound, and visited those in prison. Today, the Sisters run orphanages and health care centres. Houses are to be found in France, England, Switzerland and Spain, in the Near East, Africa, Bolivia and Brazil.

HOLY FAMILY, SONS OF THE

Location: Spain (Barcelona)
RC (male) founded in Spain in 1864 by Blessed Joseph Manyanet y Vives (beatified 1984)
Abbr: SF
Original habit: secular style.

A Spanish Congregation with an apostolate in the provision of residential care for young men. The members are also involved in parish ministries.

✠ Holy Family Fathers

HOLY FAMILY OF NAZARETH, SISTERS OF THE

Location: Italy (Rome)
RC (female) founded in Italy in 1875 by Blessed Frances Siedliska
Abbr: CSFN
Original habit: a black tunic with a collar and a black veil, with a distinctive cream-coloured, multi-pleated silk wimple and a silver crucifix suspended from the neck; a black cloak was worn outdoors.

Lay Sisters wore the same black tunic with plain white collars and used a black shawl instead of the cloak.

A devout child, Frances Siedliska decided very early in her life that she wanted to spend her life in religion, to the dismay of her father, although he later relented. It gradually became clear that she should found an Order, and in 1873 she visited Rome to seek the pope's approval, which was forthcoming. A house was bought in Rome in 1875 and the Congregation of the Holy Family of Nazareth was officially founded. Frances, taking the name of Mother Mary of Jesus the Good Shepherd, became the first mother-general. The Sisters cared for abandoned and destitute children and provided opportunities for women to come together to share their problems and seek solutions. This was later extended into teaching and visiting the sick and the poor. The first Polish foundation was made at Krakow in 1881 and others followed, with a house opened in the USA in 1885, where the Sisters helped the new Polish immigrant families, and other foundations made in England and France. Today there is a large Congregation in Australia, at Marayong, in New South Wales, which was opened in 1954. Here the Sisters care for the elderly, run a child care centre, a Polish nursing home and a Polish immigrant apostolate. There are now houses throughout Europe, in Israel, Australia, the Philippines, the USA (1885), Puerto Rico, the Ukraine and Belarus.

HOLY GHOST, HOSPITALLERS OF THE

Defunct
RC (female) founded in France in 1180

The Hospitallers of the Holy Ghost was a branch of a male Order of the same name, founded at Montpellier in 1180. The female branch was established at Neufchâteau and moved to Rouceaux in 1842. The convent at Rouceaux then became the mother house of the Order. Earlier German foundations at Memmingen and Wimpfen survived until the start of the 19th century. The work of the Congregation was with abandoned children and orphans.

HOLY GHOST, ORDER OF THE – CLERKS REGULAR

Defunct
RC (male) founded in Italy in the 12th century
Original habit: a black cassock with a double white cross on the breast and a black cloak with the same cross on the left-hand shoulder.

An Order of clerks regular hospitallers which was given papal approbation by Pope Innocent III and which came into being partly in response to the successful creation, in 1145 in Montpellier, of a lay community founded by Guy de Montpellier which observed the Rule of St Augustine and which attended to the needs of the sick. There had been an Anglo-Saxon hospice in Rome since 715, which had fallen into ruin but was able to be repaired. The pope invited Guy de Montpellier to oversee the reorganization of the newly rebuilt hospital, which was renamed the 'Santo Spirito in Sassia'. The hospital attracted many papal privileges, and other houses sought affiliation with the new foundation in order to boost their own resources. Wealth was poured into the hospital, from land revenues and handsome donations. With the wealth came the opportunity to make other foundations throughout Italy and France, but the Hospital of Santo Spirito in Sassia was removed from the control of the Order by Pope Sixtus IV (1471–84). There were also nuns of the Order (see next entry). An Order of knights, the Militia of the Holy Ghost, was created and led to a further equestrian foundation, the Knights of Our Lady of Bethlehem. In time these became defunct. There was an attempt in France in the early 17th century to recreate the Militia of the Holy Ghost, but it met with little success.

✠ Clerks Regular of the Order of the Holy
    Ghost
    Hospitallers of the Holy Ghost

HOLY GHOST, ORDER OF THE – NUNS

Defunct
RC (female) founded in Italy in the 12th century by Pope Innocent III
Original habit: a black tunic and veil with a double white cross on the upper left-hand side of the tunic. An uncloistered nun would wear the same with a white veil.

An Order of nuns founded to assist the clerks regular of the Order of the Holy Ghost. They helped in the running of the Hospital of Santo Spirito in Sassia, where they also cared for the orphans and foundlings. German foundations at Memmingen and Wimpfen survived until the start of the 19th century. The same Order also had a foundation in Poland which cared for the sick and needy.

✠ Hospitallers of the Holy Ghost

HOLY GHOST, SISTERS OF THE – Ohio

Location: USA (Garfield Heights, Ohio)
RC (female) founded in Italy in 1890 by Mother Mary Josephine
Abbr: CSSp

The Sisters work largely in education, both elementary and secondary, and in nursing, especially in the fields of physical and occupational therapy and nursing home administration.

HOLY GHOST, SISTERS OF THE – Pittsburgh

Location: USA (Pittsburgh, Pennsylvania)
RC (female) founded in the USA in 1913 by Bishop Francis Canevin
Abbr: SHS

A Congregation with diocesan status founded at Donora in the diocese of Pittsburgh and concerned with education and nursing. This work was of particular importance at the time of the foundation because of the many different ethnic and language groups settling in the area, when education was to provide a future for the immigrants.

HOLY GHOST AND OF THE IMMACULATE HEART OF MARY, CONGREGATION OF THE

Location: Italy (Rome)
RC (male) founded in France in 1848
Abbr: CSSp

The Congregation is the result of the union of two existing Orders, the Congregation of the Holy Ghost, which had been founded in Paris in 1703 by Fr Claude-François Poulart, and the Society of the Immaculate Heart of Mary, founded at Amiens in 1842 by the Venerable Francis Paul Libermann. The Congregation of the Holy Ghost, which had been an attempt to provide hostel accommodation in Paris for students for the priesthood who were poor, had suffered badly at the time of the French Revolution, despite its earlier success when at its height it was sending missionaries to the French colonies and the Far East. The Revolution all but destroyed the Congregation, with only one priest, Fr Berout, surviving. The Society of the Immaculate Heart of Mary, which had been founded by a Jewish convert, had a similar apostolate and, on advice from Rome, the two Congregations joined together. Fr Libermann, who was made superior-general of the new Order, is regarded as its founder. African missions were started by two Americans, Bishop England of Charleston and Dr Barron, vicar-general of Philadelphia. After many mishaps, Dr Barron, who had been on the African missions, died from yellow fever. There are now missionaries working in many countries and throughout the USA. The Congregation, as well as supplying the mission fields and caring for homeless boys, runs the French Seminary in Rome, the Duquesne University in Pittsburgh, Pennsylvania, and various other colleges and novitiates in the USA, Canada and Europe.

✠ Holy Ghost Fathers
   Holy Ghost Missionaries
   Spiritans

HOLY HEART OF MARY, DAUGHTERS OF THE

Defunct
RC (female) founded in Senegal in 1858 by Mgr Kobes

A Congregation founded at Dakar, the capital of present-day Senegal, for the indigenous native women, who were ideally suited through their familiarity with local culture and language to work in catechizing and preparing adults and children for the sacraments. Their immunity from yellow fever made the Sisters very valuable in the nursing of Europeans, who contracted the fever very easily. The Congregation is no longer in existence.

HOLY HEART OF MARY, SISTERS-SERVANTS OF THE

Location: Canada (Montreal, Quebec)
RC (female) founded in France in 1860 by Fr Francis Delaplace
Abbr: SSCM
Original habit: a voluminous black tunic with a knotted, tasselled girdle, a short elbow-length cape, a small wimple with a white cap and a small black veil; a crucifix is worn around the neck and a rosary at the waist.

Fr Delaplace, a Holy Ghost Father, was much concerned for the abandoned children in Paris, and with the help of Marie-Jeanne Moison he established a house for a Congregation of Sisters who would care for these children. The Sisters also visited the sick in their homes and in hospitals. In 1889 they were invited to go to the USA, to open a boarding school for girls at Bourbonnais, Illinois. Hospitals and parochial schools quickly followed. The Sisters still continue in the same ministries as before, but they have brought various business skills to their work and are deployed in parishes and college campuses. The Congregation has also worked in Canada, Africa, the Argentine, Cuba, Mexico and Chile.

HOLY HUMILITY OF THE BLESSED VIRGIN MARY, SISTERS OF THE

Location: USA (Villa Maria, Pennsylvania)
RC (female) founded in France in 1854 by Fr John Joseph Begel and Marie-Antoinette Poitier
Abbr: HM (previously HHM)
Original habit: a blue woollen tunic with a white headdress and band, a black veil for professed nuns and a white veil for novices.

Aware of the great need around them for education, three French women came together and offered to teach the poor children of their area. From this the Congregation was founded in Donmartin-sous-Amance in 1854, with Marie-Antoinette Poitier, one of the original three, as co-founder with Fr Begel; diocesan approval followed in 1858. The original apostolate included the education of country children, the care and education of orphans and the maintenance of churches. Fr Begel had the reputation of being outspoken against the government, and this prejudiced the future of the community with the result that the Sisters were not given the necessary licence to teach. In 1864 the entire community, with Fr Begel included, was invited to go to the USA by Bishop Rappe of Cleveland, Ohio. They went to live in a very poor, uncultivated property known as the Villa Maria, in New Bedford, Pennsylvania, which had been vacated by the Sisters of Charity of St Augustine. Undaunted by their circumstances and serious lack of funds, the Sisters eventually enlarged the house, built a hospital, cared for orphans and resumed their teaching apostolate. Their work today continues in the major fields of education and nursing as well as various parish ministries and work for justice and peace. They are largely represented in Ohio and Pennsylvania but have houses in many other states.

✠ Sisters of the Humility of Mary

HOLY INFANCY, BROTHERS OF THE

Defunct
RC (male) founded in the USA in 1853 by Bishop John Timon

The foundation of the Brothers of the Holy Infancy in order to care for homeless and delinquent boys was made by the bishop of Buffalo, New York. Homes were set up at Lachawanna, near Buffalo, but financial difficulties prevented further development at that time. There was a later expansion, with the building of orphanages and vocational training schools, where a variety of trades were taught, from printing to plumbing and gas-fitting. The Congregation did not survive.

HOLY MARTYRS IN PALESTINE, KNIGHTS OF THE

Defunct
RC (male Equestrian Order) founded in c.1032
Original habit: (insignia) a plain red cross in the centre of which, on a circle, were the images of the martyr saints Cosmos and Damian.

An Order founded during the pontificate of Pope Benedict IX as a reward for services to the Roman Catholic faith and the redemption of Christian captives from the infidel during the crusades. Before his death in 1056, Pope Benedict IX made a generous donation to the monastery of Sts Cosmos and Damian which may in part account for the nature of the insignia of this Order. The Order was later suppressed, but the date of suppression is not known.

HOLY NAME, COMMUNITY OF THE

Location: Australia (Cheltenham, Victoria)
Anglican (female) founded in Australia in 1888 by Emma Caroline Silcock (Sr Esther)
Abbr: CHN

The Community of the Holy Name was founded in a Melbourne suburb by Emma Silcock, who had been a novice in England at the Community of St Mary the Virgin, at Wantage. She emigrated to Australia in 1885 and met up there with women who were working among the poor in Melbourne. Emma Silcock made her religious profession in 1894, with others of the group following soon after. The new Congregation, which received its charter from Archbishop Clarke in Melbourne in 1914, was active among the poor and disadvantaged and the work extended into New South Wales, where the Sisters ran homes for boys and girls in and around Newcastle. Today, in addition to their work with children, the Sisters are also involved in prison and court work, youth hostels, retreat centres, AIDS ministry and counselling, drug and alcohol abuse programmes, and chaplaincies in both general and psychiatric hospitals.

HOLY NAME, COMMUNITY OF THE

Location: England (Oakwood, Derby)
Anglican (female) founded in England in 1865 by Sr Frances Mary
Abbr: CHN

The Congregation grew out of a parochial Association of women who banded together for mission work in the parish of St Peter, Vauxhall, London. It became known as the St Peter's Mission Sisterhood, the first Sister being professed in 1865. The moving force behind the formation of the sisterhood was George Herbert, the vicar of St Peter's. A growing need for a fuller religious life soon became evident, and two of the members of the Mission Sisterhood, Sr Ellen and Sr Frances Mary, were sent to stay with the Community of St Margaret, at East Grinstead in Sussex, where they could learn what was needed in the setting-up of a convent. On their return to London Sr Frances Mary was elected as mother superior and the Mission Sisterhood underwent a change of name to become the Mission Sisters of the Holy Name of Jesus. Property was obtained at Malvern Link in Worcestershire, in 1879, and there they established the Good Shepherd Home, a refuge for women who had been in trouble and were in need of help. Within the space of eight years the property had expanded and became the Convent of the Holy Name. More expansion followed and the community now has houses at Oakham in Rutland, Keswick in Cumbria and Radford in Nottingham, and a Retreat Centre in Chester. The Sisters are involved in parish ministries, prison visiting and counselling. There are also foundations in Lesotho and KwaZulu-Natal Province.

✟ Mission Sisters of the Holy Name of Jesus

HOLY NAME, COMMUNITY OF THE – Lesotho

Location: Lesotho (Leribe)
Anglican (female) founded in Lesotho in 1962
Abbr: CHN

In 1923 the Community of St Michael and All Angels, in Bloemfontein, South Africa, made a daughter foundation, the Community of St Mary at the Cross, at Leribe in Lesotho, but in 1959 it was decided that the work being done there should be undertaken by the Community of the Holy Name Sisters, who began their work at Leribe in 1962, at the Convent of the Holy Name. The Sisters of St Mary at the Cross were invited to join them, and a full union was effected in 1964. The Sisters were deeply involved in the anti-apartheid movement and now provide an important pastoral witness in their work in prisons and with youth counselling.

HOLY NAME, COMMUNITY OF THE – Zululand

Location: Kwazulu-Natal, South Africa (Melmoth)
Anglican (female) founded in Zululand in 1969
Abbr: CHN

This community is justified in tracing its foundation to the 1865 beginning of the Community of the Holy Name, in England, but the Zululand community was founded in 1969 when three Sisters, who had begun their religious life at Leribe, Lesotho (see previous entry), made a settlement at Melmoth. The Sisters undertake an active apostolate which includes teaching and nursing as well as the making of altar linen and vestments. There are other houses in Kwazulu-Natal (Durban, Nongoma), Transkei (Umtata) and Swaziland (Luyengo).

HOLY NAME COMMUNITY

Location: Zimbabwe (Penhalonga, Mutare)
Anglican (female) founded in Zimbabwe in 1935 by Fr Baker and Mother Isabella
Abbr: CZR

The founder of the Holy Name Community, Fr Baker, was a member of the Community of the Resurrection, at Penhalonga, whose convent at Grahamstown in South Africa was of great assistance as the new community grew. Mother Isabella was elected as the first mother superior, and help with the foundation was supplied by the Sisters of the Order of the Holy Paraclete. The work of the community involves the running of clinics and primary and secondary schools, home visiting, catechesis and the making of altar breads and church vestments. The community underwent a division in 1982, when half the members, including some novices, left Penhalonga to create another community, that of the Holy Transfiguration, at Bonda, Mutare. Six months later some of these Sisters went to Harare and founded the Community of the Blessed Lady Mary. More recently, in 1989, some of the Bonda community went to Gokwe and formed yet another community, that of the Gifts of the Holy Spirit.

HOLY NAME OF JESUS, CONGREGATION OF THE

Defunct
Anglican (female) founded in the USA in 1910

An American foundation with its headquarters in Brooklyn, New York. The Sisters undertook parochial duties and worked in education.

HOLY NAME OF JESUS, SISTERHOOD OF THE

Defunct
Anglican (female) founded in the USA in 1884

The Sisterhood was founded at Boston, Massachusetts, but spread away from the east coast to Tyler, Texas, where the Sisters ran a small hospital, and a parochial school at Marshall, also in Texas. The Boston Sisters were occupied with parish visiting and the care of the sick poor.

HOLY NAMES OF JESUS AND MARY, SISTERS OF THE

Location: Canada (Longueuil, Quebec)
RC (female) founded in Canada in 1844 by Blessed

Mary-Rose Durocher (Eulalie Melanie Durocher; beatified 1982)
Abbr: SNJM

A teaching Congregation founded at Longueuil by Eulalie Durocher and approved in 1877 and 1901. The founder and two other Canadian women, Henriette Cere and Melodie Dufresne (Srs Marie-Madeleine and Marie-Agnes) had trained for the religious life with the French teaching community of the Congregation of the Holy Names of Jesus and Mary, at Marseilles, France, and made their profession in 1844. It was the Marseilles Congregation which gave the title and a modified Rule and habit to the Canadian Sisters. In 1859 some of the Sisters were invited to go to Oregon, and this began the division of the Congregation into various provinces:

1 The New York province – extends its missionary work to Africa, Haiti and South America. The Sisters are involved in parish ministries to the elderly, counselling, health care, migrant welfare and teaching at all levels. They are present in many parts of the East Coast of the USA.

2 The province of Oregon – has Sisters working in Brazil, Africa, Haiti and Canada as well as in many parts of the USA. Their work embraces working for the disadvantaged, the care of the elderly, teaching from elementary to college level, retreat ministries, pastoral care and family education and counselling.

3 The Californian province – has Sisters involved in teaching, pastoral work and campus ministries, health care and community service as well as missionary work in Central and South America, South Africa, Haiti and Canada. The Sisters are to be found in the archdioceses of San Francisco and Los Angeles as well as in many West Coast American dioceses.

4 The province of Washington – has no foreign mission undertakings. The houses are concentrated in the archdiocese of Seattle and the dioceses of Spokane and Yakima. The Sisters undertake teaching and various pastoral ministries.

HOLY NATIVITY, SISTERHOOD OF THE

Location: USA (Fond du Lac, Wisconsin)
Anglican (female) founded in the USA in 1882 by Fr Grafton and Sr Ruth Margaret Vose
Abbr: SHN
Original habit: a black tunic with a black woollen cincture, a white headdress with a black veil, and a silver crucifix around the neck.

The co-founders of this Congregation had both withdrawn from religious societies. Fr Grafton, later bishop of Fond du Lac, had been a member of the Society of St John the Evangelist, and Sr Ruth Margaret Vose had been with the Society of St Margaret at East Grinstead in Sussex, England, before moving to the USA, where she had worked since 1873. They came together to inaugurate the Sisterhood of the Holy Nativity. The Rule observed by the Sisters is a modification of that of St Augustine. Today the Sisters work in parishes preparing candidates for confirmation, form guilds, organize retreat centres and church camps and run an outreach ministry for those in need. Other houses are to be found in California and West Virginia. At one time there were houses in many other parts of the USA, but many of these have now been closed.

HOLY PARACLETE, ORDER OF THE

Location: England (Whitby, Yorkshire)
Anglican (female) founded in England in 1915
Abbr: OHP

The Order of the Holy Paraclete was founded as a teaching Order whose members follow a Rule based on that of St Benedict. The Constitutions were drawn up for the Sisters by Fr Walter Frere. The Community of St Michael and All Angels (founded 1895), which lacked new members, was affiliated with the Order of the Holy Paraclete in 1946. This explains the daily emphasis within the communities of the divine office and the Eucharist, in addition to whatever active ministry the Sisters are engaged upon. Today, the work of the Order embraces hospital and university chaplaincies, and the Sisters also conduct retreats and missions, organize conferences and participate in parish work as well as running a school at Whitby and a children's hospice at Wetherby, West Yorkshire. The Order also has houses in South Africa, Ghana and Swaziland in addition to their foundations in the United Kingdom at Leicester, York, Rievaulx, Dundee and Boston Spa.

HOLY PARACLETE, SERVANTS OF THE

Location: New Mexico (Jemez Springs)
RC (male) founded in New Mexico in 1952 by Fr Gerald Fitzgerald
abbr: sP
Original habit: a grey habit, scapular and hood with a dark cincture.

A Congregation of priests and Brothers founded with a view to helping clergy who are experiencing difficulties, whether physical, psychological, emotional or spiritual, or who have drug dependency problems. The members are trained in counselling and various therapeutic skills, and they maintain a residential setting for those priests and Brothers in need of their help. The Congregation was affiliated with the Discalced Carmelites in 1956 and received its decree of praise in 1970. Houses can be found in the USA in St Louis, Missouri, and Cherry Valley, California, with an English house at Stroud in Gloucestershire.

✠ Paraclete Fathers

HOLY REDEEMER, CONGREGATION OF THE – Bologna

Defunct
RC (male) founded in Italy in 1136

A Congregation, also called 'the Renana', which became affiliated to the Congregation of Canons Regular of the Lateran.

HOLY REDEEMER, SISTERS OF THE

Location: USA (Huntingdon Valley, nr. Philadelphia, Pennsylvania)
RC (female) founded in France in 1849 by Elizabeth Eppinger
Abbr: CSR

The Congregation was founded in Nieder-bronn in Alsace Lorraine and later spread to the USA. Its founder, Elizabeth Eppinger (later Mother Alphonse Maria), had a vision of the religious life she wanted to found, an active community which cared for the needy sick in their own homes. To realize her vision of such a religious life she founded the Sisters of the Holy Redeemer, whose members today minister to the needs of the poor, the sick, the aged and destitute as well as one-parent families in and around Philadelphia and New Jersey. The Sisters run transitional housing and services for homeless women and their children, and care for pensioners and disabled adults in low-income housing. They also work in hospitals and hospices.

✠ Daughters of the Most Holy Redeemer

HOLY ROOD, COMMUNITY OF THE

Location: England (Chichester, Sussex)
Anglican (female) founded in England in 1858
Abbr: CSC

The community owes it origins to an explosion at the Snowden and Hopkins Iron-works at Middlesborough, in the north of England, which injured many of the men who worked there. The health care of the day was not adequate to cope with the range of injuries they suffered and, while some of the men were sent to hospitals for treatment, others had to stay in their own homes for their families to care for them in far from ideal surroundings. At Coatham, some miles away, a group of ladies, known as The Christ Church Sisterhood, had been formed some time previously to help in the parish and a simple kind of sisterhood was started, led by Miss Jacques (later Sr Mary) who had undergone some training with the Lutheran Deaconesses of Kaiserwerth. Some property was acquired and a hospital set up in Middlesborough. Others were to follow. The name was then changed to The Community of the Holy Rood, and in 1871 Mother Teresa Newcomen and another Sister made their life vows at Oxford. When it became clear that some of the Sisters wanted a more contemplative life, a new convent and chapel was built at Erdeley where the Sisters continued to work in the parishes. A later move took the Congregation to The Convent of the Holy Rood at Lindfield, in Sussex, but in 1997 the older members of the community moved to a retirement home in nearby Chichester. The remaining Sisters joined The Community of St Peter at Woking, in Surrey.

✠ Servants of the Cross

HOLY ROSARY, MISSIONARY SISTERS OF THE

Location: Ireland (Blackrock, Dublin)
RC (female) founded in Ireland in 1924 by Bishop Joseph Shanahan
Abbr: MSHR
Original habit: a white habit and scapular with a black veil; a cross is worn around the neck.

The founder of the Congregation, a member of the Order of the Holy Ghost (Spiritans) was vicar-general of Southern Nigeria. The purpose of his foundation was to provide missionary Sisters, trained in Ireland, who would work among the native women and help to foster their dignity. The training, which took place at the Cabra Dominican Convent in Dublin and which showed a strong Dominican influence, attracted seven initial postulants, five of whom were professed and arrived in Nigeria to begin their work in 1928. From these beginnings the Congregation has spread throughout Africa, with other houses in South Africa, the United Kingdom, Ireland, South America and the USA, where a foundation was made in Philadelphia, Pennsylvania, in 1954. The Sisters work in health care, which ranges from clean water projects and care of the under-fives and of lepers, to the provision and staffing of maternity units, dispensaries and counselling centres for AIDS sufferers and their dependants. On the educational front there is provision of teacher training, vocational training and adult education. The Sisters have also started credit unions and co-operatives, which has led to the development of local industries.

✠ Missionary Sisters of Our Lady of the
   Holy Rosary

HOLY SAVIOUR, KNIGHTS OF THE ORDER OF THE – Aragon

Defunct
RC (male Equestrian Order) founded in Aragon in 1118 by King Alfonso I, 'The Battler'
Original habit: possibly a white tunic bearing a pectoral image of the Saviour and a cape with a white (or red) cross on the left-hand shoulder.

Little is known of this Order, but it is reputed to have been founded by Alfonso I of Aragon to reward selected nobles for their Christian virtues and generosity. The recipients of the Order were to observe conjugal chastity, promise obedience to the grand master and be prepared to defend the Roman Catholic faith.

HOLY SEPULCHRE, CANONESSES REGULAR OF THE

Location: each house is autonomous; the English HQ is at Chelmsford, Essex.
RC (female) foundation uncertain (but see below)
Abbr: CRSS
Original habit: a black tunic over which was worn a white, sleeveless surplice reaching to the knees, with a white veil surmounted by a black veil on the head and a cloak with a double barred cross in red on the left-hand shoulder. A girdle made from two crimson woollen ropes, tasselled at the ends and knotted together with five knots to signify the five wounds of Christ's Passion, was tied around the waist.

The origins of this Order are obscure, but the earliest date mentioned is when a convent was founded at Saragossa, Spain, in 1276 by Doña Marquesa, the daughter of the king of Navarre. There are records which show that other foundations were made in Flanders and Germany, and firm evidence of a house established in 1622 in France, at Charleville, by the wife of the Marquis de Chaligny, who later entered the community as Mother Claude of St Francis. The Constitutions were approved in 1631 by Pope Urban VIII. An Englishwoman, Susan Hawley (1622–1706), underwent her novitate with the Canonesses at their house at Tongres in Belgium, on the strict understanding that following her profession she would be permitted to form an English community. In 1642, having been professed as Mother Mary of the Conception, she went with a small number of English nuns to Liège, where they established a new convent, and in the early 18th century this was expanded to include a school which was run by the prioress, Mary Christine Dennett. The French Revolution sent the nuns in France into exile, and they opened houses in England, at Holme Hall in Yorkshire, Dean House in Wiltshire (1796) and New Hall, Chelmsford (1799). The Order continues, and today the canonesses, who follow a monastic regime, work in education. There are other houses in Belgium, The Netherlands, Germany, Spain and France. All houses of the Order are autonomous.

✠ Order of the Resurrection

HOLY SEPULCHRE, CANONS REGULAR OF THE

Defunct
RC (male) foundation uncertain (see below)
Original habit: a black tunic with a double barred red cross on the breast, a black cape, with a Greek cross embroidered on the left-hand side, a white rochet and almuce and a black, biretta-type cap. In the four quarters of the crosses were smaller crosses in red. The Canons Regular in Bohemia, Poland and Russia wore a black tunic with a rochet and with a second, sleeveless, rochet-like garment which was open at the front and reached to just above the knee. It bore a double barred cross on the left-hand side.

There are two possible origins for this Order. It may have been a foundation dubiously attributed to the apostle St James the Less, the first bishop of Jerusalem, who is supposed to have established some clerics living in common, but the earliest historical reference mentions some canons regular, living under the Rule of St Augustine, who were introduced to the Holy Land by Godfrey de Bouillon. He went to the first crusade in 1096 and was made defender of the Holy Sepulchre, in Jerusalem. The canons were driven out of the Holy Land by the Muslims and set up houses in Italy, where they were later suppressed by Pope Innocent VIII (1484–92), and in France, Spain, Poland, Russia and England. They con-

tinued to thrive in Europe until the time of the French Revolution.

HOLY SEPULCHRE OF JERUSALEM, KNIGHTS/DAMES OF THE

Location: Italy (Rome)
RC (male and female Equestrian Order) founded at the beginning of the 12th century by Godfrey de Bouillon
Abbr: vary according to the rank of membership; KHS (for a knight)
Original habit: (insignia) a Jerusalem cross, composed of a large red cross with four small inset crosses representing the five wounds of Christ's Passion; this emblem decorated a white cloak.

The first Knights of the Holy Sepulchre were founded by Godfrey de Bouillon at the time of the re-establishment of the Latin patriarchate in Jerusalem following its recapture from the Muslims in 1099 in the first crusade. The Order's Constitution was given by King Baldwin I of Jerusalem in 1103. The knights maintained a presence in the Holy Land, remaining there even after Jerusalem fell again to the Muslims in 1243, until the fall of the port of Acre (now Akko, on the coast of Israel) in 1291 persuaded them to flee to various parts of Europe, where they established Augustinian priories of the Holy Sepulchre. Various attempts were made to reorganize the knights as a Papal Order, with the pope as grand master, or to amalgamate them with other Orders, without success. In the 15th century some noble ladies, the Dames of the Holy Sepulchre, were admitted to join the knights. The Order has now expanded, and national lieutenancies have been established in many countries. The work undertaken by the members continues to be concerned with the upkeep of the Holy Places and the protection and conservation of the practice of the Roman Catholic faith in the Holy Land.

HOLY SOULS, HELPERS OF THE

Location: France (Paris)
RC (female) founded in France in 1856 by Blessed Eugenie Smet (beatified 1957)
Abbr: HHS
Original habit: a black dress and cape with a black fluted bonnet which was secured under the chin with a large black bow; a silver crucifix was worn around the neck; and for outdoors, a long black cloak and black gloves.

Eugenie Smet, who even as a young girl had a great concern for the holy souls, decided that there was need for a Congregation devoted to their cause. She looked for five proofs that such a Congregation was needed, and soon found them. She had already started an Association of prayer for the dead, which was both successful and had papal approval, two of the needed proofs. Others followed, including a prediction from the Curé d'Ars, St John Baptist Vianney, that such a Congregation was needed. Difficulties and uncertainties presented themselves, but Eugenie received the approval of Archbishop Sibour of Paris. The problems were slowly overcome and, established as Mother Mary of Providence, she led her little community. The Sisters financed themselves through their handiwork, taught, nursed the sick, visited the poor and did housework for the elderly. Their Rule was a modified version of that of St Ignatius. Two further foundations were made in France, at Nantes and Clamart, and a lay Association for the Holy Souls flourished. From here the Congregation expanded, with a house established in China by six of the Sisters. During the Franco-Prussian war the Congregation was busy working in military hospitals and organizing ambulances. Today the Helpers of the Holy Souls have houses in the United Kingdom, mainland Europe, the USA and Canada, Mexico, Japan, Indonesia and Africa.

HOLY SPIRIT, COMMUNITY OF THE

Location: USA (San Jose, California)
RC (female) founded in the USA in 1970
Abbr: CHS

A Congregation founded as a religious community of women who are engaged in teaching, health care and social services. The members of this community observe the traditional three vows of religion, poverty, chastity and obedience.

HOLY SPIRIT, CONGREGATION OF DAUGHTERS OF THE

Location: France (St Brieuc)
RC (female) founded in France in 1706 by Marie Balevenne and Renée Burel
Abbr: DHS (previously FSE)
Original habit: a white habit with a black cloak and hood for outside wear; a small silver dove on a dark cord. was worn around the neck,

The Congregation of the Daughters of the Holy Spirit was founded in Brittany, near Saint-Brieuc, by two local women, with the assistance of a priest and an influential layman, who were given diocesan approval to form a community dedicated to the Holy Spirit and Mary Immaculate. They worked locally, teaching and catechizing children and caring for the poor and the sick. The Sisters observed a Rule that was designed to combine the active and contemplative lives. After the French Revolution, which destroyed so many religious foundations, the Congregation recovered well and underwent a remarkable expansion, but the French Association Laws at the beginning of the 20th century caused the Sisters to disperse abroad, to England, Belgium and the USA, where they arrived at Hartford, Connecticut, in 1902. Their work today is still concerned with women and young people and also with those marginalized by society, for whom they run health care programmes. The Sisters maintain several foreign missions, to Haiti, Nigeria, Cameroon, Chad, Chile and Peru. In Europe their communities are to be found in England, France, Belgium, Romania and The Netherlands. Houses have been set up in many states across the USA, in Alabama, California, New England, Pennsylvania, Virginia, and New York.

✠ White Sisters.

HOLY SPIRIT, MISSION SISTERS OF THE

Location: USA (Saginaw, Michigan)
RC (female) founded in the USA in 1932 by Bishop Joseph Schrembs
Abbr: MSSp
Original habit: a dark blue street dress with a hat; a veil was worn in choir

A Diocesan Congregation which was founded in Cleveland, Ohio, by the Bavarian-born first bishop of Cleveland, Joseph Schrembs. The Constitutions and spirituality of the Congregation are Benedictine in form. The original purpose of the foundation was to bring social welfare and health care to American Indians. The Sisters now engage in religious education and work with the mentally handicapped and the deaf, with some pastoral ministries also undertaken.

HOLY SPIRIT, MISSIONARIES OF THE

Location: Mexico (Mexico City)
RC (male) founded in Mexico in 1914
Abbr: MSpS

A missionary Congregation founded to provide spiritual direction for priests, members of religious Orders and the laity. For this purpose the members conduct retreats and provide houses of rest and renewal. They are to be found in Mexico, Peru, Italy, Germany, Spain, Canada and the USA (California).

HOLY SPIRIT, MISSIONARY SISTERS OF THE

Location: Italy (Rome)
RC (female) founded in The Netherlands in 1889 by Blessed Arnold Janssen (beatified 1975)
Abbr: SSpS
Original habit: a dark blue habit and scapular with a white girdle, a linen wimple and dark blue veil; a crucifix on a red ribbon was worn around the neck.

A Congregation founded at Steyl in The Netherlands by the founder of the Society of the Divine Word, who had also founded the Holy Spirit Adoration Sisters. The Missionary Sisters of the Holy Spirit are to be found worldwide, with houses in North and South America, Europe including the Ukraine and Russia, Australia, West Africa, the Far East, the Philippines and New Guinea. The Sisters help the Divine Word Missionary priests, particularly in health care programmes, where they work as physicians, nurses, administrators, dieticians and technicians, and also in education, social work, catechesis and the running of retreats.

✠ Holy Ghost Missionary Sisters
   Missionary Sisters-Servants of the Holy
   Ghost

HOLY SPIRIT, ORDER OF THE

Defunct
RC (male Equestrian) founded in France in 1578 by Henry III of France
Original habit: a black silk mantle with a black silk or velvet bonnet, which sported a feather.
(Insignia) the cross of the Order was a deep blue Maltese cross outlined in gold, in the centre of which was a descending dove as a symbol of the Holy Spirit; the cross was suspended from a fleur-de-lis held in a gold collar with a crowned 'L' (for Louis) on either side of the cross (this was later changed to 'H', for Henry).

A French Equestrian Order founded to mark the accession to the throne of Henry III on Pentecost Sunday, 1578. The Order was intended to replace the Order of St Michael, which had been created by King Louis XI, and was restricted to one hundred members of the nobility.

HOLY SPIRIT AND MARY IMMACULATE, SISTERS-SERVANTS OF THE

Location: USA (San Antonio, Texas)
RC (female) founded in the USA in 1888 (1893) by Mother Margaret Mary Healy Murphy
Abbr: SHSp

An American foundation established at San Antonio and granted papal approbation in 1938, designed for the exclusive benefit of American Indians and negroes who were in need of schools, orphanages, and homes for the elderly. The Sisters currently minister in parishes and are engaged in catechesis and social services. Houses have been opened in Mexico and Zambia.

✠ Sisters of the Holy Ghost

HOLY SPIRIT OF PERPETUAL ADORATION, SISTERS-SERVANTS OF THE

Location: Germany (Bad Driburg)
RC (female) founded in The Netherlands in 1896
Abbr: SSpSdeAP
Original habit: a rose-pink tunic, white scapular and wimple with a long white veil; a crucifix was worn around the neck.

A contemplative Congregation, a branch of the Missionary Sisters of the Holy Spirit, which was founded in 1889 by the Blessed Maria Virgo (Helena Stollenwerk) and Blessed Arnold Janssen, the founder of the Society of the Divine Word at Steyl, in The Netherlands. Helena Stollenwerk, then known as Mother Maria, had become the first superior-general of the Missionary Sisters of the Holy Spirit Congregation, but when this new and completely cloistered branch of the Holy Spirit Adoration Sisters was founded she transferred there as a nov-

ice, taking the name of Sr Maria Virgo. Her health was not robust, and on 3 February 1900, when she was dying, she was permitted to make her religious profession. She was beatified in 1995. The Congregation was introduced into the USA at Techny, Illinois, in the early years of the 20th century. There are houses now in the Philippines, Argentina, Germany, The Netherlands, India, Brazil, Poland, Togo and Indonesia.

✠ Holy Spirit Adoration Sisters
  Pink Sisters

HOLY STIGMATA, CONGREGATION OF THE

Location: Italy (Rome)
RC (male) founded in Italy in 1816 by St Caspar Bertoni (canonized 1989)
Abbr: CSS (formerly CPS)

Ordained as a priest at a time of great trial for the Church, when the French Napoleonic occupation of northern and central Italy interfered with any kind of religious work, St Caspar Bertoni developed a devotion to the stigmata, the miraculous wounds of Christ. When the French were finally defeated, in 1816, he founded a group which was nicknamed the Stigmatines, the name deriving from the nearby Church of the Stigmatics of St Francis. The group opened a free school, where they taught poor children, and were active in encouraging religious vocations. The Congregation of the Holy Stigmatics of Our Lord Jesus Christ, as it came to be called, received papal approbation in 1890, after a long delay. There are houses in Europe, the USA, Brazil, the Philippines and Thailand. The priests and Brothers run parishes, give retreats and conduct missions. The founder was beatified in 1975 and canonized in 1989.

✠ Stigmatines

HOLY TRINITY, SOCIETY OF THE

Defunct
Anglican (female) founded in England in 1848 by
Lydia Sellon, Anne Terrot and Catherine Chambers
Abbr: SHT
Original habit: a black woollen dress with long,
flowing sleeves, a woollen girdle from which was
suspended a small ebony cross, and a white cap
with long black strings. For outside wear there was
a black cloak and bonnet with a black crêpe veil.

The Society of the Holy Trinity is now
virtually defunct, its last member now living
with the Community of the Holy Name, at
Oakwood, Derby. It was originally called
the Church of England Sisterhood of Mercy
at Devonport and Plymouth, naval towns
on the south coast of England, and was
designed to take care of the orphaned
daughters of sailors. Miss Sellon made the
start of her foundation in 1848 at Devonport, with a small school for boys and two
for girls. She visited the Sisterhood of the
Holy Cross at Park Village West in London,
to gain further insight into the religious life,
returning to Devonport in October 1848
when the Sisterhood officially came into
existence, with the blessing of Bishop Phill-
pott of Exeter. The habit and Rule were
decided upon, and many institutions,
including a soup kitchen, orphanages, a
place of refuge, an industrial school and
accommodation for the poor, were set up
in and around Devonport. The growth of
the Sisterhood was rapid, and by 1852 it led
to the development of three Orders, or
'Rules'.

1 The Sisters of Mercy of the Holy Communion, which had a mixed active and
contemplative life and whose members
wore a black serge habit with a black veil
which sometimes covered the face. They
were dedicated to God the Father, the
First Person of the Trinity.

2 The Sisters of the Sacred Heart, who were
dedicated to God the Son, the Second
Person of the Trinity, were contemplatives and retained the title 'of the Sacred
Heart' until 1861 when it was changed to
'of the Love of Jesus'. This Order, or
Rule, practised a most austere life and
observed watches of intercession and reparation throughout the night. Their habit
was white at first but later a brown habit
with a black veil was adopted. The Order
was discalced. This group was the last to
be closed and existed until 1995.

3 The Sisters of Charity, dedicated to the
Holy Ghost, the Third Person of the
Trinity, were concerned with caring for
orphans, the homeless, the sick poor and
others in need. In 1856 this group split
into the Blue Sisters, who lived a semi-
conventual life, and the Grey Sisters, who
lived in their own homes.

By 1854, which marked the start of the
Crimean War, the Sisterhood of the Holy
Cross at Park Village West was almost
defunct, and Mother Lydia (Sellon) took it
over. She sent some of the Devonport Sisters to Scutari to work under Florence
Nightingale. After that war, the remains of
the Sisterhood of the Holy Cross and the
Sisters of Mercy of Devonport and
Plymouth were united, in 1856, to form the
Society of the Holy Trinity. New Rules were
drawn up and the distinction between the
three Orders, or Rules, referred to earlier,
was redefined. The foundation of the
mother house at Ascot in Berkshire was the
result of a legacy and generous gifts. Mother
Lydia died at Ascot in 1876 and is buried
there.

✠ Society of the Most Holy Trinity

HOLY UNION OF THE SACRED HEARTS OF JESUS AND MARY, SISTERS OF THE

Location: Italy (Rome)
RC (female) founded in France in 1833 by Louise Mennecier
Abbr: SUSC
Original habit: a black habit with a black veil and apron, a white starched linen cap, and a small silver cross around the neck. A black cloak could be worn out of doors.

A Congregation which was formed from a group of women in Douai, led by a linen draper, Louise Mennecier, with the help of Fr Jean-Baptiste Debrabant, who had concern for the education and catechesis of poor village children. From this very simple beginning the community soon evolved, and by 1833 the new Congregation had a habit and Rule, although diocesan approval and permission to make a profession of vows only came in 1843, with papal approval granted in 1877. By this time the Congregation had opened many schools in France and Belgium. The Sainte-Union, as it came to be called, spread to Ireland, the UK, the USA, South America and Africa. The work is heavily educational, at all levels including adult education and parish religious education, but also encompasses health care, nursing and hospital chaplaincies, ministry and services for the needy, for immigrants, refugees and prisoners, AIDS ministry and foreign missions.

✠ Congregation of the Holy Union of the
    Sacred Hearts of Jesus and Mary
  Holy Union Sisters
  La Sainte Union

HOME MISSION SISTERS OF AMERICA

Location: USA (Owensboro, Kentucky)
RC (female) founded in the USA in 1941 by Fr William Howard Bishop
Abbr: GHMS

The Home Mission Sisters were founded in 1941, just three years after Fr Bishop had founded the Home Missioners of America for men (see next entry). The community, which was canonically recognized in 1952 by the archbishop of Cincinnati, has a similar apostolate to that of the Home Missioners, in spreading the faith especially in those parts of the United States where there are few Roman Catholics, working with those in need, catechizing children and adults and addressing issues of injustice and poverty. The Glenmary Sisters, as they are also known, are found in the Appalachians and the deep south of America.

✠ Glenmary Sisters

HOME MISSIONERS OF AMERICA, THE

Location: USA (Cincinnati, Ohio)
RC (male) founded in the USA in 1939 by Fr William Howard Bishop

The Society was founded in Ohio in 1939 for priests and Brothers who see their work as preaching and evangelizing poor and marginalized Roman Catholics in the deep south, the Appalachians and the south-west of America. To this end they maintain currently some seventy-one mission stations in Georgia, Ohio, Alabama, Arkansas, Oklahoma, Tennessee, Virginia, West Virginia and Washington DC The Missioners are helped in their work by the Home Mission Sisters of America, known also as the Glenmary Sisters (see previous entry).

✠ Glenmary Home Missioners

HOPE, SISTERS OF

Location: Italy (Rome)
RC (female) founded in France in 1820 by the Abbé Pierre Bienvenu Noailles

The Congregation is one of the branches, or groups, of the Holy Family Institute founded by Pierre Noailles to provide Sisters who were not only dedicated to the care of the sick and poor but who were also skilled in that care. Before the reorganization of the Institute there were many foundations established by the Sisters of Hope, in England, Ireland, Spain, Italy, France, Belgium, Canada, Brazil and Poland. Today, the same care and help is provided, but under the blanket-title of the Association of the Holy Family at Bordeaux.

HUBERT, KNIGHTS OF ST

Defunct
RC (male Equestrian Order) founded in Bavaria in the 15th century by Gerard V, duke of Julich
Original habit: (insignia) a gold collar from which hung a gold cross enamelled in white, in the centre of which was an image of St Hubert in an attitude of veneration before a deer between whose antlers is a crucifix. The head of St Hubert's horse can just be seen in the upper right hand corner of the medallion. This image is an allusion to the legendary account of the saint's conversion on Good Friday while out hunting. The motto 'In Fide Sta Firmiter' (Firm in Fidelity) is on the reverse side. The gold collar was composed of forty-two links which alternate the image of the conversion of St Hubert with the letters I.T.V., for the Gothic 'In Traw Vast' (Firm in Fidelity). A round sun-burst badge was also worn on the mantle, on the left-hand side, which bore the same motto, probably in its Gothic version.

The Order is said to have been founded in 1445 to commemorate a victory that had been won on St Hubert's Day (3 November). The award was limited to men of noble birth and was known as the Military Order of St Hubert. It was still in existence at the start of the 18th century, although it had at one time become almost redundant and had been revived in 1708 by the Prince Elector Johann Wilhelm of Neuberg. Those courtiers who received the Order were expected to make over a tithe of the pensions they received when they were granted

the honour and also to make a generous donation to the poor on their day of reception. In 1800 Maximilian of Bavaria confirmed the Order and fixed the number of knights to be limited to twelve. Another Order of St Hubert existed in Lorraine, founded in 1416, but that was generally known as the Order of Fidelity.

HUMILIATI

Defunct
RC (male) founded in Italy in the 12th century
Original habit: a grey, later white, tunic, scapular and short mantle with a hood; a cloak could be worn beneath the mantle, open in front, and a beret-like cap, which gave the Order the alternative name 'Barettini'.

The founding of this Order has been variously dated back to the beginning of the 12th century, under the Holy Roman Emperor Henry V. Noblemen who returned to Milan following a humiliating defeat by the Germans were given to works of penance and charity, and many were persuaded to withdraw from the world, having first secured their wives' consent. A monastery was set up for them in Milan. St John of Meda joined the Humiliati in 1134 and advised the Congregation to observe the modified Benedictine Rule which he had composed, which advice they followed. Papal approbation was received in 1200 from Pope Innocent III. The Order expanded rapidly; with success came wealth, and before long abuses crept in. Pope St Pius V asked St Charles Borromeo of Milan to reform the Order, which was resisted by some who went so far as to plot his murder. These conspirators were executed. The Order was suppressed in 1571 by Pope St Pius V.

✠ Order of Humility
  Barettini

HUMILIATI

Defunct
RC (female) founded in Italy in the 12th century
Original habit: a white, or grey, girded tunic with a
loose white scapular and white veil; in some houses
the veil was black.

An Order founded in Milan at the same
time as the male Humiliati Order (see previous entry). When some of the noblemen
took to the cloister following their defeat by
the Germans, a number of their wives followed the same route, under the leadership
of Clara Blassoni. The Order became so
successful that other convents were opened.
The nuns occupied themselves in caring for
those in need and for the sick, especially for
lepers. Within their houses the nuns
observed a very penitential regime, and they
were unaffected by Pope St Pius V's Bill of
Suppression of 1571 which dissolved the
male branch of the Order. Some houses of
Humiliati nuns persisted into the early part
of the 20th century.

✠ Hospitallers of the Observance
   Humble Ladies

I

IDENTE MISSIONARIES OF CHRIST CRUCIFIED

Location: USA (Briarwood, New York)
RC (female) date of foundation unknown
Abbr: MId

The Sisters of this American Association have undertaken the running of retreats and campus ministries as well as providing spiritual direction and parish work. There are only a few Sisters remaining, to be found today in Europe, the Far East and some South American countries.

✠ Idente Association of Christ the Redeemer

IMITATION OF CHRIST

Location: India (Kottayam, Kerala)
RC (male and female) founded in India in 1918–19 by Fr George Geevarghese
Abbr: OIC
Original habit: (male) a yellow gown, or sanyasin, with a wooden cross around the neck and a close-fitting black cap; on profession a cap with seven crosses embroidered on the upper side is worn; (female) a white or black tunic and black veil for professed Sisters.

The community was founded originally as a Jacobite brotherhood by Fr George Geevarghese, a scholar who wanted to revive the spiritual and monastic life of Indian Orthodoxy according to the Syriac rite. He named the foundation 'Bethany'. It is a religious brotherhood for both missionary and educational work. The Rule originally observed was an amalgamation of the Rules of St Basil, St Benedict and St Francis of Assisi. The monastery proper is known as an ashram. It was at a Synod in 1925 that Fr George was authorized to investigate the possibility of a union with the Holy See. This was granted and accepted by Fr George, who was later consecrated as a bishop under the name of Mar Ivanios. The activities pursued by the Religious of the 'Imitation of Christ', include the running of schools, colleges, hospitals and orphanages.

✠ Bethany Fathers and Sisters

IMMACULATE CONCEPTION, CANONS REGULAR OF THE

Location: Italy (Rome)
RC (male) founded in France in 1866 by Dom Adrien Grea, OSB
Abbr: CRIC
Original habit: a white cassock and linen rochet with a black hooded cloak and mozetta.

Founded at Saint-Antoine in France by Dom Adrien Grea, the vicar-general of St Claude, the Congregation was approved by Popes Pius IX and Leo XIII during the 1870s and admitted into the Confederation of Canons Regular of St Augustine in 1961. The canons regular live as secular priests except that they do so within a community, following the Rule of St Augustine. Their life is marked by a spirit of penitence and perpetual abstinence together with the observance of very strict fasts and of devotion to the liturgy, especially in the celebration of the divine office. The original mother house was at Saint-Antoine (Isère), but with the coming of the French Association Laws of 1901 the Congregation moved to Italy, first to Genoa and then to Rome. There are foundations in England, France, Italy, Peru, Brazil, Canada and the USA (California).

IMMACULATE CONCEPTION, KNIGHTS OF THE ORDER OF THE

Defunct
RC (male Equestrian Order) founded in Italy in 1625
Original habit: (insignia) a pectoral medallion featuring a gold cross (Maltese style) in the centre of which was a blue enamelled panel with an image of the Immaculate Conception, the whole surrounded by a Franciscan knotted cord; on the opposite side of the cross was an image of St Michael the Archangel. The ribbon from which the cross was suspended was of intertwined blue and golden silk. The same emblem was worn on the left shoulder of the mantle with additional tongues of fire issuing from the four corners of the cross.

Ferdinand, duke of Mantua, Charles of Nivers and Adolphus, count of Altham all wanted Pope Urban VIII to approve the establishment of a Christian military Order for noblemen prepared to defend the Roman Catholic religion on land or sea, under the title of the Order of the Immaculate Conception, and under the patronage of St Michael the Archangel. The approval was granted and the Rule and habit prescribed. The knights took vows of poverty, chastity and obedience along with an oath

of fidelity to maintain and profess the faith. Discord within the Order caused its decline after a very brief time. Under Charles III of Spain (1759–88) a revival was approved by Pope Clement XIV, but the Order later became defunct.

IMMACULATE CONCEPTION, LITTLE SERVANT-SISTERS OF THE

Location: Poland (Krosnienskie)
RC (female) founded in Poland in 1850 by Fr Teofil Baczynski
Abbr: LSIC

The founder, a Jesuit priest, saw the need for a Congregation of Sisters prepared to teach, nurse and care for the aged, which work the members still maintain in many countries, including the USA. The Sisters run nursery and elementary schools, provide religious education, offer home nursing and care in nursing homes, senior day centres and homes for the aged. Pastoral work, youth ministry and social services are also undertaken, as well as the maintenance of a mission in Mexico. The Sisters are to be found in many countries of Europe, including Russia, Moldavia and the Ukraine, in South Africa and Zambia. The American foundation dates from 1926.

IMMACULATE CONCEPTION, LITTLE SISTERS OF THE

Location: Brazil (São Paulo)
RC (female) founded in Brazil in 1895 by Amabile Wisenteiner (Blessed Pauline of the Suffering Heart of Jesus, beatified 1991)

This Congregation, which is devoted to the care of the sick and poor, had its beginnings when an Italian immigrant family from northern Italy went to Brazil in 1875. A daughter of the family, Amabile Wisenteiner, who was ten years old when the family moved to Brazil, was a particularly pious child, and from this early age she taught catechism to young children in the town of Nova Trento, near her family home. She and a companion visited the sick and performed other acts of charity, and it came as little surprise when Amabile decided upon the religious life. At the age of twenty-five she left her parents' home and, with a friend, set up a small community where their first patient was a woman suffering from cancer. In 1895 they moved back to Nova Trento and received diocesan approval for their foundation. Amabile was permitted to take her vows and receive her new name in religion. The Congregation was guided along Ignatian lines, since its spiritual director was a Jesuit. In 1903 the Sisters moved to São Paolo and a period of rapid expansion began. Many new houses were founded and today these number nearly six hundred. Papal approbation was received in 1933. The Congregation still works with the poor and the sick and also undertakes the usual parish ministries and catechesis, mainly in Brazil. The founder died in 1942.

IMMACULATE CONCEPTION, MISSION PRIESTS OF THE

Defunct
RC (male) founded in France in the early 19th century by Jean-Marie-Robert de La Mennais

A Congregation founded at St Meen, Rennes, for the care of diocesan seminaries and missions. Jean-Marie de La Mennais was also the founder of the Brothers of Christian Instruction of Ploermel, a Congregation which still flourishes today. The Mission Priests of the Immaculate Conception did not survive for very long, despite a reorganization in 1837.

✠ Missionaries of Rennes

IMMACULATE CONCEPTION, MISSIONARIES OF THE – Lourdes

Location: France (Monleon, Magnoac)
RC (male) founded in France in 1848

A Congregation approved in 1876 and 1956. The members undertake the usual parish ministries and preach at retreats. They are also involved in teaching the young and caring for the poor.

IMMACULATE CONCEPTION, MISSIONARY SISTERS OF THE

Location: Canada (Outremont, Quebec)
RC (female) founded in Canada in 1902 by Mother Mary of the Holy Spirit
Abbr: MIC

The Sisters, who are under simple vows, organize retreats, teach, nurse and run social work programmes. They maintain missions to Africa, South America and the Far East.

IMMACULATE CONCEPTION, SISTERS OF THE

Defunct
RC (female) founded in France in 1853

A French Congregation, no longer in existence, which provided teaching and nursing service. The mother house was at La Laye Maheas (Nantes).

IMMACULATE CONCEPTION, SISTERS OF THE

Location: USA (Los Angeles, California)
RC (female) founded in the USA in 1873 by Fr Cyprien Venissat
Abbr: CIC

A Diocesan Congregation with simple vows, the Congregation was founded at Labadieville, Louisiana, to provide education and assistance with their problems for children of families impoverished by the American Civil War (1861–65).

IMMACULATE CONCEPTION, SISTERS OF THE

Location: Spain (Madrid)
RC (female) founded in Spain in 1892
Abbr: RCM

The Sisters of this Congregation undertake missionary work in many parts of the world, maintaining a presence in Spain, Italy, Japan, Zaire, South Korea, the Philippines, the Dominican Republic, Equatorial Guinea, Brazil and Venezuela. Houses have also been established on the west coast of the USA, where the Sisters work in catechesis, social parish work and youth ministry.

IMMACULATE CONCEPTION, SISTERS OF THE

A foundation made by the Pierre Noailles at Bordeaux in 1820. The Congregation has been defunct since the 1950s.

IMMACULATE CONCEPTION, SISTERS OF THE – Armenian

Defunct
RC (female) founded in Turkey in 1847 by Mgr Hassun

A Congregation founded to provide education for girls and young women. Houses were set up at Trebizond, Angora and Marash. During World War I nearly fifty of the nuns were either murdered or kidnapped and the remainder were amalgamated with the Sisters of Constantinople, which has also since become defunct.

IMMACULATE CONCEPTION, SISTERS OF THE – St Meen

Location: France (St Meen)
RC (female) founded in France in 1831 by Abbé Courvoisier and Pelagaie le Breton de Maisonneuve (Mother St Felix)
Abbr: IMC
Original habit: a black habit, cape and veil with a small square white linen wimple; a large crucifix was tucked into a black corded cincture.

This Congregation of Sisters was founded at St Meen-le-Grand in Brittany. Fr Courvoisier was a member of the Missionary Society of Rennes, which had the care and education of youth as one of its aims. Following the French Revolution, which destroyed much of religious education in France, it was apparent that a great deal needed to be done and the Sisters set up small communities where their work was needed and where they could also care for the sick. The Congregation extended into the field of foreign missions, and the Sisters opened houses in Zaire and the Congo. The Congregation is also to be found in England, where the members engage in pastoral work, catechesis, the care of the homeless and handicapped as well as prison aftercare ministries and hospital chaplaincies.

IMMACULATE CONCEPTION OF OUR LADY OF LOURDES, SISTERS OF THE

Location: Italy (Rome)
RC (female) founded in Belgium (later in France) in 1863 by Eugénie Ducomb (Mother Marie de Jésus Crucifié)
Original habit: a white habit with a blue sash and white veil; lay Sisters wore a blue tunic and white veil.

Eugénie Ducomb set up a small community at Tournai, in Belgium, but on a visit to Lourdes she was able to purchase some land adjacent to the grotto, where she built the first mother house. The Constitutions were approved in 1910. The original purpose of the Congregation was to take charge of the grotto at Lourdes, together with its sanctuary, and to provide assistance for pilgrims. Today, the emphasis has changed, and the Sisters provide education for girls, conduct retreats and undertake catechesis for both adults and children. Their lives are devoted to the adoration of the Blessed Sacrament. Houses are maintained in Belgium, Turkey and South America.

IMMACULATE CONCEPTION OF THE BLESSED VIRGIN MARY, CONGREGATION OF THE

Location: Italy (Rome)
RC (female) founded in 1484 by St Beatrice de Silva (canonized 1976)
Original habit: a white habit with a white scapular and blue mantle.

A Congregation founded by St Beatrice de Silva (1424–90). She was the sister of the Franciscan Brother Amadeus, who was responsible for the reform of his Order known as 'of Marignano'. Well connected at the court of Princess Isabel, the daughter of Prince John of Portugal, Beatrice incurred the displeasure of the princess at the time of the latter's marriage to John II of Castile, mainly because of Beatrice's beauty, which inspired much jealousy. After a short period of incarceration, Beatrice was allowed to retire for the next thirty years to the Dominican convent at Toledo, in Spain. It was while she was here that she was inspired by a vision to found an Order in honour of the Virgin Mary's Immaculate Conception. In 1484, together with some other women, she established the Congregation of the Immaculate Conception of the Blessed Virgin Mary, known also as the Conceptionists, who observed a modified Cistercian Rule and wore a habit the style and colour of which was dictated in the vision. In 1489 Pope Innocent VIII authorized the foundation of a convent set up in the Castle of Galliana, which came as a gift from Queen Isabella the Catholic (1474–1504). The Rule was approved, and later modified by Pope Julius II in 1511. After Beatrice's death in 1490 the Order came under the Franciscan influence of Cardinal Ximenez de Cisneros of Toledo and the Rule was changed to a modification of that observed by the Poor Clares. Expansion of the Order into Europe and to North America followed.

IMMACULATE CONCEPTION OF THE BLESSED VIRGIN MARY, SISTERS OF THE – Lithuania

Location: USA (Putnam, Connecticut)
RC (female) founded in Lithuania in 1918 by Archbishop George Matulaitis
Abbr: MIC
Original habit: a black habit with a small white collar and a black veil.

The Congregation was originally founded at Marijampole in Lithuania. In 1936 the first American foundation was made, and the Sisters are now involved in catechesis, spiritual renewal programmes and the education of pre-school children and young people, especially at their Camp Neringa in Marlboro, Vermont. They undertake care for the sick and aged in their nursing home at Putnam, Connecticut, and are also much involved in media-style ministry. Other foundations were made in the USA, as well as in Toronto and Montreal, Canada.

IMMACULATE CONCEPTION OF THE MOTHER OF GOD, MISSIONARY SISTERS OF THE

Location: USA (West Paterson, New Jersey)
RC (female) founded in Brazil in 1910 by Amando Bahlmann, OSF and Mother Mary Immaculata of Jesus
Abbr: SMIC
Original habit: a white habit with a blue scapular

The work of the Congregation is concerned with teaching, from elementary grades through to graduate colleges, and with health and social care services, retreat work and care for the aged. Missions have also been established in Brazil, Africa and the Far East. Since their foundation in the USA in 1922 there has been a rapid expansion into many dioceses across America.

✠ Immaculata Sisters

IMMACULATE HEART OF MARY, BROTHERS OF THE

Location: USA (Steubenville, Ohio)
RC (male) founded in the USA in 1948
Abbr: IHM

The Brothers of the Immaculate Heart of Mary was organized in Steubenville, Ohio, where the members carry out parish ministries, provide counselling for drug and alcohol addiction, teach, and undertake general administrative work within the diocesan chancery office and in the residence of the bishop.

IMMACULATE HEART OF MARY, CONGREGATION OF THE

Location: Italy (Rome)
RC (male) founded in Belgium in 1862 by Fr Theophile Verbist
Abbr: CICM

A Congregation founded at Scheut, near Brussels, in order to evangelize through foreign missions. In 1861, after the Treaty of Peking, it was possible for the first time for missionaries to go to China. In order to prepare priests for their work, Fr Verbist founded a seminary, Scheutveld College, where missionaries could study and learn the skills they would need in the mission field. The first missionaries went to Mongolia in 1863 and the work spread throughout Asia and Africa. Papal approval was received in 1900. The Congregation has had many martyrs, notably during the period of the Boxer Rebellion in China. The missionaries, who at first were mainly Belgian or Dutch nationals, now include members from many other countries and are to be found throughout the Far East, including China, Mongolia, Hong Kong, Singapore, Japan, Taiwan, Indonesia and the Philippines. 'Sheutists', as they are sometimes called, are also to be found in the USA, where their work is largely confined to hospital and parish ministries especially among poor and marginalized people, as well as in Europe, South America and Africa. There are plans to send missionaries to Cuba, Papua New Guinea and Mozambique.

✣ Congregation of Scheutveld
 Missionhurst Congregation of the
  Immaculate Heart of Mary
 Scheut Fathers

IMMACULATE HEART OF MARY, DAUGHTERS OF THE – Rennes

Defunct
RC (female) founded in France in 1640 by Morel du Verger

The Daughters of the Immaculate Heart of Mary originated as an Association in Rennes, France, whose members were in charge of a home for incurables. The Association survived the French Revolution and in 1841 was organized into a religious community. Its members did not take the usual vows of religion and were bound only by a bond of mutual charity, observing tacit obedience to the eldest Sister.

IMMACULATE HEART OF MARY, HERMITS OF THE

Location: USA (Williamsport, Pennsylvania)
RC (male) founded in the USA in 1994
Abbr: HIHM

A small, contemplative Diocesan Congregation whose members undertake at least three hours of Eucharistic devotion daily.

IMMACULATE HEART OF MARY, MISSIONARY SISTERS OF THE

Location: Italy (Rome)
RC (female) founded in India in 1897
Abbr: ICM

The Congregation was founded with a view to providing education for Indian girls. The work expanded, and in 1910 a new foundation was made in the USA. The work of the Sisters is largely educational, but they also maintain parish ministries and work in the field of health care and in leprosaria. They have a large representation in Africa, Hong Kong, India, Taiwan, the Philippines, Europe and Latin America in addition to their houses in the USA.

IMMACULATE HEART OF MARY, SISTERS OF THE – Arizona

Location: Italy (Rome)
RC (female) founded in the USA in 1871
Abbr: IHM

The Congregation was founded originally in Spain, by Dr Joaquin Masmitja y de Puig, with a later foundation made in the USA, in Arizona, in 1871. The Sisters are involved in education at all levels, catechesis and other parish ministries. Houses of the Congregation are found in Arizona and Florida, with foreign missions conducted in Europe, Cuba, Chile and Brazil.

IMMACULATE HEART OF MARY, SISTERS OF THE – Blon

Location: France (Caen)
RC (female) founded in France in 1842 by the Comtesse de Saint-Leonard (Mother Marie du Sacré Coeur)
Original habit: a black tunic and veil with a cloth girdle, a square white wimple and a large metal crucifix.

The few Sisters that remain of this Congregation undertake teaching, nursing and all kinds of charitable work. They are also known as the Sisters of Blon.

IMMACULATE HEART OF MARY, SISTERS OF THE – Porto Alegre

Location: Brazil (Porto Alegre, RS)
RC (female) founded in Brazil in 1843 by Barbara Maix

A Brazilian Congregation with an apostolate in the care of orphans.

IMMACULATE HEART OF MARY, SISTERS OF THE – Wichita

Location: USA (Wichita, Kansas)
RC (female) founded in the USA in 1979
Abbr: IHM
Original habit: a dark blue habit with a scapular, bearing a badge of the Immaculate Heart, and a black veil.

This is a small Public Association which follows the Carmelite tradition and is a combined active and contemplative community. Although founded in the USA in 1979 the Congregation has claim to an earlier date of foundation when, in Spain in 1848, the Daughters of the Immaculate Heart of Mary began to catechize the young. By 1871 the founder, Fr Joaquin Masmitja, was persuaded by the rapid growth of the Congregation to accept an opportunity to go to California, where the Sisters opened schools. In 1924, the Californian province became independent and built schools, a college, a retreat house and a general hospital. It was in 1976 that five of these Sisters founded the house in Wichita, Kansas, to provide religious education. This foundation became an independent and Public Association in 1979. The Sisters live in community, take the traditional vows of religion, chastity, poverty and obedience, and are actively involved in teaching and conducting retreats as well as in praying for the conversion of sinners and for the welfare of the Church and its clergy. On the first and third Fridays of each month the

Sisters observe an all-night vigil before the Blessed Sacrament.

IMMACULATE HEART OF MARY, SISTERS-SERVANTS OF THE – Immaculata

Location: USA (Immaculata, Pennsylvania)
RC (female) founded in the USA in 1856
Abbr: IHM

The Congregation was an independent house, derived from the Congregation of the Sisters-Servants of the Immaculate Heart of Mary which had been founded in 1845 at Monroe, Michigan (see next entry). The Sisters at Immaculata fulfil the original vision of Fr Gillet, the founder, in running a college, several academies and many parish schools. Houses are to be found throughout the USA, in Philadelphia, Miami, Atlanta, Hartford and San Francisco as well as in Peru and Chile.

IMMACULATE HEART OF MARY, SISTERS-SERVANTS OF THE – Michigan

Location: USA (Monroe, Michigan)
RC (female) founded in the USA in 1845 by Mother Theresa Duchemin, Mother Mary Joseph Walker and Fr Louis Gillet
Abbr: IHM

The Congregation was founded in Monroe, Michigan by Theresa Duchemin, an Oblate of the Sisters of Providence, a Congregation to which she had belonged since 1829. Theresa Duchemin had an inauspicious start in life, being the offspring of an unmarried, coloured mother. She went to Michigan in 1845 as one of the first four members of the new foundation and became its superior. Mother Mary Joseph Walker, who succeeded as superior in 1859, is regarded as a true founder along with Fr Louis Gillet. Independent foundations followed, at Immaculata, and Scranton, Pennsylvania, both established in the 1870s from the mother house at Monroe, Michigan.

The work today includes education, the care of the sick and aged, hospital and chaplaincy work as well as counselling services. The apostolate has been extended into the provision of foreign missions to Brazil, Ghana, Honduras, Mexico, Nicaragua, Puerto Rico, South Africa and Zimbabwe. This is a large Congregation with houses throughout the USA.

IMMACULATE HEART OF MARY, SISTERS-SERVANTS OF THE – Scranton

Location: USA (Scranton, Pennsylvania)
RC (female) founded in the USA in 1856
Abbr: IHM

A Congregation, founded as an independent house in the same year as that at Immaculata (see above), and deriving from the Congregation of the Sister-Servants of the Immaculate Heart of Mary at Monroe, Michigan (which also see). The Sisters engage in many aspects of education from this centre, from the specialist care of the mentally disturbed and of physically disabled children to a full range of school and college programmes. Added to this, they work in health care in hospitals and clinics, particularly for those with AIDS, and run parish ministries. Houses are to be found throughout the USA and in Peru.

IMMACULATE HEART OF MARY AND OF THE GOOD SHEPHERD, SISTERS-SERVANTS OF THE

Location: Canada (Ste-Foy, Quebec)
RC (female) founded in Canada in 1850 by Marie Fitzbach Roy (Sr Marie du Sacré Coeur)
Abbr: SCIM

Founded in Quebec by Marie Fitzbach Roy with the encouragement and assistance of the archbishop of Quebec, Mgr (later Archbishop) Turgeon, the Congregation is dedicated to the care and rehabilitation of prostitutes and degenerate women and the Christian education of their children. The

Sisters also undertake missions to Africa, and work in catechesis, nursing, social service and teaching. They are usually known as the Good Shepherd Sisters. An American foundation of this Congregation was made in 1882.

✠ Good Shepherd Sisters

INCARNATE WORD, INSTITUTE OF THE

Location: USA (Brooklyn, New York)
RC (male) founded in the USA in 1984

A Public Association, founded to evangelize culture along the lines of Vatican II. To this end the members, who take the usual three vows of religion, poverty, chastity and obedience, and a fourth one of 'Devotion to Mary Most Holy', preach missions and conduct a programme of the Spiritual Exercises of St Ignatius of Loyola. There is another house in the USA, in Philadelphia, and the Institute is also represented in many other countries.

INCARNATE WORD AND THE BLESSED SACRAMENT, SISTERS OF THE

Location: USA (Cleveland, Ohio)
RC (female) founded in France in 1625 by Jeanne Chezard de Matel
Abbr: SIW

A French foundation concerned mainly with the education of the young. Houses were set up at Paris, Avignon and elsewhere in France. The Congregation was confirmed by Pope Innocent X in 1644. The French Revolution did not deal too kindly with the Order, but it survived, was revived at Azerables, near St Sulpice in central France, and began to grow once more. In 1853 some Sisters went, at the request of the French-born first bishop of Galveston, Texas, to the United States and made the first American foundation at Brownsville, Texas, with subsequent houses following. Today, this Diocesan Congregation is concerned with education, the conducting of retreats, spiritual direction and a pastoral ministry. The Sisters also work in hospitals and nursing homes and in the care of the mentally disabled.

INCARNATE WORD AND THE BLESSED SACRAMENT, SISTERS OF THE

Location: USA (Victoria, Texas)
RC (female) founded in the USA in 1866 by Mother St Claire
Abbr: IWBS

This Pontifical Congregation had its origins in the foundation made by Jeanne Chezard de Matel in Lyons, France, in 1625 and subsequently in Ohio in 1853 (see previous entry). In 1866 a further foundation was made at Victoria, Texas, with Mother St Claire, the leader of the group of pioneer Sisters from Lyons, as the first American superior. Today, this large community continues the founder's concern for education by teaching at every level, as well as providing chaplaincies and parish ministries, retreat work and spiritual direction. The Sisters have also undertaken mission work in Kenya.

INCARNATE WORD AND THE BLESSED SACRAMENT, SISTERS OF THE

Location: USA (Houston, Texas)
RC (female) founded in the USA in 1873
Abbr: CVI

A further foundation from that made by Jeanne Chezard de Matel in Lyons, France, in 1625 (see entries above). The Houston Congregation derives from that made at Victoria, Texas, in 1866. The apostolate is in teaching, but also in providing a ministry for the local Hispanic community, caring for the aged and needy, nursing and visiting the housebound. The work of this smaller community of Sisters is currently confined to the state of Texas.

INCARNATE WORD AND THE BLESSED SACRAMENT, SISTERS OF THE – Corpus Christi

Location: USA (Corpus Christi, Texas)
RC (female) founded in the USA
Abbr: IWBS

The Congregation is another descendant of the original Lyons foundation made by Mother St Claire in 1853 (see above). The Corpus Christi foundation was made as a daughter house and its members are concerned with education at most levels, also having a language school. The Sisters also run parish ministries throughout Texas and missions to Nakuru in Kenya.

INCARNATION OF THE ETERNAL SON, SOCIETY OF THE

Defunct
Anglican (female) founded in England in 1894 by Mother Gertrude Clare

The work of this Anglican community, which was founded as a Franciscan-style Sisterhood at Plaistow in London, was concerned with the welfare of boys and unemployed young men. The founder, Miss Bromby, was professed as Mother Gertrude Clare in 1898, having been joined there by novices in 1894. In 1900, Mother Gertrude moved to the Marylebone area of London, where her friend and fellow Christian Socialist, Fr Adderley, had charge of the parish of St Mark. After a few years she was persuaded to move her Congregation again, this time to Birmingham, where Fr Adderley had also moved. Here she opened foundations known as the Homes of the Incarnation, which housed children from the workhouses and gave them a good education. There was a Third Order of the Congregation, and Oblates associated with

the Society of the Incarnation. The Oblates were women who could take the vows of poverty and obedience, while the Third Order was for both men and women.

INFANT JESUS, CONGREGATION OF THE

Location: USA (Brooklyn, New York)
RC (female) founded in France in 1835 by Désiré Routel (Sr Mary de Gonzaga)
Abbr: CIJ

A Diocesan Congregation, with a very varied apostolate, which came to the USA from France in 1905. The Sisters work mainly in the medical field, as technicians and therapists, and with disabled people. Pastoral and hospice care and the management of day nurseries as well as catechesis are all undertaken. Some of the Sisters work in education and the provision of social service care.

✟ Nursing Sisters of the Sick Poor

INFANT JESUS, SISTERS OF THE

Location: Italy (Rome)
RC (female) founded in France in 1682 by Fr Nicolas Barre
Abbr: SIJ
Original habit: a black tunic with a long black train and veil.

A Pontifical Institute founded at Rouen, France, by Nicolas Barre, a Minim friar who wanted to ease the plight of poor girls and young women through education. Several schools were opened in Paris and its surrounding suburbs. The women who undertook the teaching felt that they would like to form a religious community. They were allowed to proceed, although limited to making simple promises rather than the vows of religion, because the nature of their work broke the strict enclosure which the hierarchy insisted was mandatory for fully professed nuns at the time. After the French

Revolution, which scattered most of the religious communities in the country, the Congregation was reorganized, and by the 1850s some of the Sisters were engaged in foreign missions in the Far East. Initial papal approval was received in 1866 and in 1872. The title 'Les Dames de Saint-Maur' derives from a school opened in the Rue Saint-Maur in Paris, which was for a time the mother house of the Congregation. The first American foundation was made in California in 1950. The work today is still confined to helping those educationally deprived through poverty. There are houses in the USA, the UK and Ireland.

✛ Dames de St-Maur
  Sisters of the Holy Child Jesus
  Charitable Mistresses of the Holy Infant Jesus

INFIRMARIANS OF ST FRANCIS, SISTERS

Location: Germany (Münster)
RC (female) founded in Germany in 1844 by Christopher Behrensmeyer
Abbr: OSF
Original habit: Franciscan style.

A Franciscan Third Order Regular Congregation founded in Münster, Germany, whose members work in education, catechesis and nursing, with a special care for those who are drug or alcohol dependent. The Sisters run AIDS clinics and home missions. In the past they were also involved in foreign missions to Japan and China. In 1875 the Congregation extended into the USA, and houses were opened in Chicago and Milwaukee.

INSTRUCTION OF THE INFANT JESUS, SISTERS OF THE

Defunct
RC (female) founded in France in 1667 by Fr Louis Tronson

A Congregation founded by Fr Louis Tronson, a Sulpician priest who became director of the Society of St Sulpice, with responsibility for some ten seminaries. With his co-founder, Mlle Martel, he created this Congregation of Sisters dedicated to teaching.

ISIDORE, NUNS OF ST

Defunct
RC (female) founded in Spain in the late 6th century by St Isidore
Original habit: probably a grey, or black, tunic with a hooded cape; the nuns were discalced.

St Isidore (c.565–636), who became archbishop of Seville in c.600, was responsible for strengthening the Church in Spain by organizing various councils and places of learning. He gathered some pious women together into a community which observed the Benedictine Rule, but little more is known about them.

J

JAMES, BROTHERHOOD OF ST

Defunct
Anglican (male) founded in England in 1835 by
Edward Steere

A short-lived Brotherhood whose founder later became a missionary bishop in Africa. Together with three other companions, all of whom had belonged to the Anglo-Catholic Guild of St Alban, in London, he founded a semi-monastic community at Tamworth, north of Birmingham, but the group failed after some six months.

JAMES, SISTERHOOD OF ST

Defunct
Anglican (female) founded in England in the late
19th century

This small Sisterhood was founded at Kilkhampton, in Cornwall, where the Sisters had created orphanages for boys and girls and were nursing in the local area and maintaining other parish duties. In 1892 they went to London, where the Sisters started some innovative work at Clapham, establishing a Hostel of God, a type of hospice for the dying. This was later taken over by the Sisters of the Society of St Margaret, from East Grinstead in Surrey, when the Sisterhood of St James became defunct in 1896. The hospice was later to prove inadequate and larger premises were found at Clapham Common in London. It was described by Sr Magdalen, who was in charge for thirty-seven years, as 'a clearing house for Heaven'. The Sisterhood of St James was not in existence for very long, but it achieved much.

✠ Servants of the Poor

JAMES OF ALTOPASCIO, ORDER OF ST

Defunct
RC (male Equestrian Order) founded in Italy in the
10th century
Original habit: a dark grey habit with a Tau, or truncated cross, of the Order worn on the left-hand side of the chest. The hood was red with a Tau cross in white.

The Order has its origins in a hospital built by Augustinian friars at Altopascio, near Lucca, in north-west Italy, for the care of pilgrims on their way to Rome or to Santiago de Compostela. Originally a non-military Order, this changed of necessity when it was vital that the pilgrims be accompanied by armed escorts because of the dangers they were facing on the roads. Pope Gregory IX (c.1148–1241) gave his approval for the Order, which later made other foundations in Europe, including one in England with a house opened somewhere near Islington, London, in c.1626. In 1585 the Order of St James of Altopascio became part of the Order of the Knights of St Stephen of Tuscany.

✚ Order of the Tau

JAMES OF HAUT-PAS, ORDER OF ST

Defunct
RC (male) founded in France probably in the 13th century

The origin of the Order is not clear, but it is known that the members were hospitallers and that in 1330 some of the Brothers were accused of making false claims to having grants of indulgence-privileges that were more extensive than they really were. As a result, the offending Brothers were rounded up and imprisoned by order of Pope John XXII.

JAMES OF THE SWORD, CANONS REGULAR OF ST

Defunct
RC (male) founded in Spain possibly in the 9th century
Original habit: a white woollen tunic and rochet.

Although the origins of the Order are obscure, it may date from the reign of King Ramiro of Leon in the 9th century. A more certain origin can be traced from a Bull of Pope Alexander III in 1175 (5 July) and confirmed by many of his successors, in which there was a reference to a clerical class within the Order of St James of the Sword. The clerics were obliged to live a communal life under obedience to a prior, and to observe the Rule of St Augustine. There was a later union with a monastery of canonesses in Lisbon, Portugal.

JAMES OF THE SWORD, KNIGHTS OF ST

Location: Spain (Madrid)
RC (male Equestrian Order) founded in Spain in the 11th or 12th century
Original habit: a white habit with a red cross on its upper part whose central shaft terminates in a sword, with a scallop shell (an association with the pilgrimage at Santiago) on its hilt and the remaining arms of the cross extended to a fleur-de-lis finial; (insignia) a gold shield with a lily-hilted, cruciform sword (motto); 'May the Sword be Red with Arab Blood'.

Although some sources claim that the Order originated in 1030, it is safer to date its origins to the 12th century, when Pope Alexander III confirmed the foundation in 1175, recognizing it as a religious Order and giving the Congregation the title of the Knights of St James of the Sword. The Order, which is still awarded, had several classes:

1 The canons, who had the care of the spiritual welfare of the members.
2 The canonesses, who were concerned for the material welfare of the pilgrims.
3 The religious knights, who lived in community.
4 The married knights, who were regarded as full members of the Order.

There was rapid expansion of the Order, which extended into Palestine and had a foundation in England. The knights were very successful against the Muslims, both on land and at sea. One strange requirement of aspirant members was that they must have at least six months experience at sea, in galleys, although exemption from this could almost certainly be purchased. The knights lived under the Rule of St Augustine and observed the three vows of religion, poverty, chastity and obedience, with married knights enjoined to observe conjugal chastity and expected to live apart from their wives during Lent and Advent and to spend part of these seasons in retreat. The vows of poverty and obedience made the families and property of married knights technically part of the Order. The headquarters of the Order was at Ucles, in the province of Cuenca, until 1869 when the archives were transferred to Madrid.

✠ Order of St James of Compostela
    Order of Santiago

JAMES OF THE SWORD, NUNS OF ST

Defunct
RC (female) founded in Spain in 1312 by Don Pelayo Perez and Maria Mendez, his wife
Original habit: a black girded tunic with a red cross (as for the Knights of St James of the Sword, see above) worn on the upper right-hand side, with a white, full-length cape and a black veil, with a white under-veil.

A congregation of pious women, including daughters of the nobility, who observed the Rule of St Augustine and lived in the House of the Holy Spirit in Salamanca, dependent on the grand master of the Knights of St James of the Sword. Their principal occupation was serving in the hospitals established for poor pilgrims visiting the shrine of St James at Compostela. The nuns were under the protection of St Anne.

JAMES THE APOSTLE, MISSIONARY SOCIETY OF ST

Location: USA (Boston, Massachusetts)
RC (male)
Original habit: as for secular clergy.

An Association of diocesan priests who have volunteered to be sent by their bishops to work as missionaries in Ecuador, Peru and Bolivia. The priests are recruited from Great Britain, Canada, the USA, Australia and New Zealand.

JEROME, HERMITS OF ST – LUPO OLMEDO REFORM

Defunct
RC (male) founded in Italy in 1424 by Lupo de Olmedo

Original habit: a white tunic with a black leather girdle, a scapular with a small, round hood and a tawny-coloured cowl; a black biretta could be worn indoors.

A reform movement of hermits, begun by Lupo de Olmedo, a man noted for his erudition, which resulted in the Congregation of Monk-Hermits of St Jerome of the Observance. Their style of life resembled that of the Carthusians, with constitutions taken directly from the writings of St Jerome. The Congregation was approved by Pope Martin V (1417–31). The Italian foundations created by Lupo de Olmedo retained their independence and were known collectively as the Hermits of St Jerome of Lombardy.

✠ Monk-Hermits of St Jerome

JEROME, MONKS OF THE ORDER OF ST

Location: Spain (Segovia)
RC (male) founded in Spain possibly in the 14th century
Abbr: OSH
Original habit: a white tunic with a brown scapular, a habit granted by Pope Gregory XI in 1373.

There have been many groups known as Jeronimites, but it is thought that this Order was made by a Franciscan tertiary hermit, Bishop Tomasuccio, and a group of disciples who were inspired to make a foundation in Spain. Two such foundations were made, one at Taxuna and the other at Nuestra Señora de Castanel, near Toledo. In 1379 the hermits transferred to the monastery of San Bartolome de Lupiana, changing from an eremitical to a cenobitic way of life at a time when they were being suspected of heresy. The first prior of the monastery was Pedro Ferdinando Pecha, bishop of Jaen, who secured approval for these hermits and is often regarded as the founder of the Order. The Order thrived and received royal patronage, especially during the reigns of King Philip II and his successors. Today, the monks observe a monastic life with the divine office and the celebration of the divine liturgy as the centre of their day. They also engage in charitable works and run guest houses.

✛ Hermits of St Jerome
  Hieronymites
  Jeronimite Monks (Hermits)

JEROME, NUNS OF THE ORDER OF ST

Defunct
RC (female) founded in Spain at the end of the 14th century
Original habit: a white tunic and grey scapular with a black head veil and cloak.

An Order of nuns founded by Maria Garcias Alvarez, a member of the duke of Alba's family. Houses were opened in several locations in Spain, including the monasteries of St Paula in Toledo, St Paula in Seville (1473) and La Concepción Jeronima (1504) in Madrid, with other foundations made in Cordoba and Granada.

✛ Hieronymite Nuns

JEROME OF BLESSED PETER OF PISA, HERMITS OF ST

Defunct
RC (male) founded in Italy in the 15th century by Blessed Peter of Pisa (Pietro Gambacorti) (beatified 1693)
Original habit: a tawny tunic with a leather girdle and a cape and cowl of the same colour. The hermits were originally discalced, but when they adopted the cenobitic life the habit changed slightly and they eventually became calced. A black biretta was worn indoors.

Pietro Gambacorti (1355–1435) was a young nobleman whose father was ruler of the republic of Pisa. In 1380, leaving his wealth behind him, Pietro lived as a hermit

on Monte Bello, relying on alms to keep him alive. Here he built an oratory and, by tradition, converted some dozen highwaymen who abandoned their lawless way of life to live in cells on the mountain. The life was especially hard as the small community observed four Lents in each year, fasted on all Mondays, Wednesdays and Fridays and lived on bread, fruit and vegetables at all other times. The hermits subjected themselves to the wearing of hair shirts and underwent all manner of privations. The Order was approved in 1421 by Pope Martin V and again by Pope Eugenius IV. Its rapid success in spreading throughout Italy led to outbreaks of jealousy from other communities, together with accusations of heresy, but the Order continued to thrive. The hermits gradually moved to a cenobitic way of life, a change approved by Pope St Pius V in 1568. The remnants of other eremitical congregations were united with the Hermits of St Jerome of Blessed Peter. These included:

1 The Hermits of St Jerome of Fiesole (united in 1668 – see next entry)

2 The Hermits of Blessed Nicolas di Furca-Palena – with houses in Naples, Rome and Florence. The founder, Blessed Nicolas, had begun his religious life as a hermit under the direction of Rinaldo of Piedmont, who had a hermitage near the church of San Salvatore in Rome. These hermits are thought to have observed the Rule of the Third Order of St Francis. Nicholas and Peter of Pisa were good friends, and their two foundations were similar in nature.

3 The Hermits of Pietro di Malerba (united in 1531) – largely concentrated in the north of Italy.

4 The Hermits of Monte Segestre (united in 1579) – who came together in the middle of the 14th century when the founder, Brother Lorenzo, came to Italy

from Spain with several companions and began a hermitage on Mount Segestre, near Genoa, where the hermits erected a chapel dedicated to the Annunciation. By 1460 they had abandoned the eremitical life in favour of monastic life.

5 The Hermits of Fra Angelica of Corsica (united *c.*1430) – a congregation of Franciscan tertiaries headed by Fra Angelica which had been founded near Rimini in the 14th century. As their numbers grew, new foundations were made at Venice, Urbino, Pesaro and Ferrara.

6 The Hermits of Bavaria and the Tyrol (united *c.*1695) – groups of hermits from the mountains. The Holy Roman Emperor, Leopold I (1658–1705) petitioned that they would be allowed to join the Hermits of Blessed Peter of Pisa, a request granted by Pope Innocent XII. Despite the affiliation, however, these hermits continued to live as before, being discalced, wearing short beards and eschewing meat at all times.

✠ Hermits of Monte Bello

JEROME OF FIESOLE, HERMITS OF ST

Defunct
RC (male) founded in Italy in 1406 by Carlo di Montegraneli
Original habit: Franciscan style in grey cloth, but this changed, in 1461, to a white habit.

A group of hermits who came together in 1406 when a Florentine nobleman, Carlo di Montegraneli, with some companions who may have been Franciscan tertiaries, retired to an isolated hillside near Fiesole, north of Florence, where Cosimo de Medici built a small church for them, dedicated to St Jerome. The Order, which observed Constitutions based on the Augustinian Rule, spread throughout Italy, and gained the approvals of Popes Innocent VII, Gregory XII and Eugenius IV. By the start of the

17th century the population was, however, in serious decline and the Order was suppressed by Pope Clement IX in 1668, incorporating the few Brothers who remained with the Hermits of St Jerome of Blessed Peter of Pisa. The small monastery and chapel of St Jerome at Fiesole is currently used by the Sisters of the Little Company of Mary. The site is also notable for an amount of Etruscan remains which have been found there.

JESUATS

Defunct
RC (female) founded in Italy in 1367 by Blessed Catherine Colombini
Original habit: a white tunic with a brown scapular and cape, the latter worn during services in chapel, and a white under-veil with a black outer one.

Blessed Catherine Colombini was the cousin of Blessed John Colombini, the founder of the Jesuats. He prompted her to gather together at her home some pious, well-born women in order to form a small community. The women later made their first foundation at Florence, under the title of the Community of the Visitation of Mary. The members observed monastic enclosure and adopted the Rule of St Augustine, leading an austere life, with stringent fasting, perpetual silence and flagellation. Despite these hardships, the Congregation spread rapidly throughout Italy and survived until 1872.

✠ Jesuatesses
   Sisters of the Visitation of Mary

JESUATS, CONGREGATION OF

Defunct
RC (male) founded in Italy in 1354 by Blessed John Colombini
Original habit: a white tunic and leather girdle with a square white hood secured around the neck; this was later changed to a grey hood. A

reddish-brown mantle was also worn, with white, sleeve-like appendages; sandals were worn.

After a life of almost total pleasure and financial success, John Colombini (1305–67) was converted to a penitential and charitable way of life after reading an account of the life of St Mary of Egypt, whose early years had also been self-indulgent but who had turned away from this to practise penance. His conversion was characterized by great philanthropy, caring for the poor and the sick in his own home. Having made a substantial settlement on his wife for her maintenance, John Colombini and some friends from other noble families began to lead the lives of hermits near Siena and to attract the attention of the locals, who accused them of becoming an unofficial Order, or Fraticelli. In the face of this derision they left Siena and travelled throughout Italy, continuing to carry out their charitable works as they went. They later petitioned Pope Blessed Urban V to recognize them as a Congregation of lay Brothers, which he did, approving both their use of the Rule of St Augustine and their habit. The initial constitution adopted Statutes from the Rule of St Benedict. The name 'Jesuati' was applied to the group because of the Brothers' constant use of the cry, 'Praised be Jesus Christ' as they went about their work of caring for the sick, burying the dead, prayer and various mortifications. Following the death of John Colombini in 1367 the Congregation went into gradual decline, and efforts at reinvigoration, which included the admission of priests in 1606, came to little. Abuses and lack of fervour forced Pope Clement IX to suppress the Jesuats in 1668.

✠ Apostolic Clerics of St Jerome
  Jesuati

JESUS, CONGREGATION OF THE DAUGHTERS OF

Location: France (Paris)
RC (female) founded in France in 1834 by Fr Pierre Noury and Mother Sainte Angèle (Perrine Samson)
Abbr: FJ (also DJ)
Original habit: a black tunic, veil and apron with a starched white head binder and a small linen wimple. A large ebony crucifix was worn around the neck and a black rosary at the waist.

The Congregation was founded at Kermaria, in the diocese of Vannes, France, for the education and care of the poor in their area. A rural school was opened by the first members of the community, and the sick were cared for in their own homes and in local hospitals. Since then, the work has spread to many countries, and foundations have been made in England, throughout Canada and in the USA (1903), with missions conducted in the West Indies and Africa.

JESUS, DAUGHTERS OF

Location: Italy (Rome)
RC (female) founded in Spain in 1871 by Candida Maria de Jesus
Abbr: FI

A Pontifical Institute, founded in Spain, and now present in the USA in the diocese of Baton Rouge, where a house was opened in 1950. The work of the Sisters is concerned with teaching and the provision of retreats.

JESUS, FRATERNITY OF THE LITTLE BROTHERS OF

Location: England (London)
RC (male) founded in the Sahara Desert in 1933
Original habit: none

The Brotherhood was founded in an oasis in the Sahara Desert and received papal approval in 1968, as a Pontifical Institute of men, some of whom may be priests. They take as their inspiration the example of Brother Charles of Jesus (Charles de Foucauld, 1858–1916). The members of the fraternity live in small community units, leading a contemplative life with great emphasis on Eucharistic adoration and prayer, but at the same time working in the local community and observing its standards.

JESUS, FRATERNITY OF THE LITTLE SISTERS OF

Location: Italy (Rome)
RC (female) founded in the Sahara Desert in 1939 by Sister Magdeleine
Abbr: LS (or LSJ)

A congregation closely in line with that of the Fraternity of the Little Brothers of Jesus (see previous entry), founded in the Sahara Desert and inspired by the life of Charles de Foucauld. Today, the Sisters are to be found throughout the world, where they manage to combine a contemplative life centred around the Blessed Sacrament with an active life, sharing in the lifestyles of the communities in which they live. As much of their work is with the poor and marginalized, the Sisters can suffer many privations.

JESUS, MISSIONARIES OF

Location: USA (Brownsville, Texas)
RC (female) founded in the USA in 1975 by Sr Juliana Garcia

A Diocesan Institute founded for the purpose of helping the poor and educating those in need, especially in the Hispanic community. The Sisters live in community under the usual vows of poverty, chastity and obedience.

JESUS, SOCIETY OF

Location: Italy (Rome)
RC (male) founded in Spain in 1534 by St Ignatius Loyola (canonized 1622)
Abbr: SJ
Original habit: a black habit, sash and biretta.

Members of the Society of Jesus are more familiarly known as Jesuits. They belong to a collective group of clerics called the clerks regular, priests who live in community, observe a Rule and make the usual three vows of religion, poverty, chastity and obedience, to which the Jesuits have added a fourth, that of a willingness to go wherever the pope feels that they can be of use. The Society was founded in 1534 but did not receive official approval from the Holy See until it was granted by Pope Paul III in 1540. Ignatius Loyola was a wealthy courtier and soldier, with no thought of embracing a religious life or founding an Order until he underwent a conversion experience which led him to give away his possessions and enter a period of meditation and self-denial, with the most severe fastings and austerities. He came under the scrutiny of the Inquisition in Spain and was temporarily imprisoned. Feeling himself in need of formal education, he went to Paris and completed his studies at the university, at the same time gathering around him some companions, including (St) Francis Xavier, who were like-minded. Together they took a conditional vow to spend their lives in the service of men. Their plan was to go to Jerusalem, but this was not to be. With the pope's approval they were ordained in Venice and stayed in that city to begin the work of preaching, teaching, working in hospitals and giving instruction in the Spiritual Exercises which Ignatius Loyola had composed at Manresa, near Barcelona. The companions now set about drawing up the Constitutions, called the Formula, which was made up of five chapters and incorporated their special obedience to the pope. The Formula was approved and a papal Bull (1540) was promulgated, giving formal approval of the Society of Jesus. By the time of the founder's death in 1556, the Society was established in Europe and had extended its missions to Africa, especially Ethiopia, to China, India and Japan. The first Jesuit foundation in England was made in 1578. Later expansion, in the 17th and 18th centuries, took the Jesuits to America and into other parts of Asia. The Society has faced many problems during its history, suffering banishment in Portugal and Spain in the 18th century and suppression under Pope Clement XIV in 1773, to be restored again by Pius VII in 1814. They have maintained a presence over vast areas of the globe and today continue their work in almost every field, from academic and pastoral apostolates to health care, home and foreign missions, chaplaincies and retreats.

✠ Jesuits
Company of Jesus

JESUS AND MARY, CONGREGATION OF

Location: Italy (Rome)
RC (male) founded in France in 1643 by St John Eudes (canonized in 1925)
Abbr: CJM

The Congregation was founded at Caen, France, in 1643. Its founder, St John Eudes (1601–80), had always been unimpressed by the parochial catechesis that he had experienced as a child in his small village. When the Oratorian Congregation opened a house at Caen in 1622, the young John Eudes was so impressed that he went to Paris, joined the Oratorians and was ordained as a priest in 1625. He was then inspired to found a society of priests, and having left the Oratory in Paris he opened a seminary at Caen where, despite opposition from the Oratorians, he founded the

Society of Jesus and Mary, whose members were to teach in the seminaries and conduct missions. St John Eudes was indefatigable in missionary work and is said to have conducted more than a hundred missions throughout Normandy, each one lasting from six to eight weeks. The Society was not a religious Order as such, and the members took no vows and wore no habit. The French Revolution took its toll, with some Eudists losing their lives, and it was not until the middle of the 19th century that the Society began to develop again after this setback, only to suffer once more under the French Association Laws at the start of the 20th century. The work in college education and the foreign missions continued as before, and today members of the Society of Jesus and Mary are to be found in the USA, Italy and France, with missions established in Africa, Canada, South America, Cuba, the Dominican Republic and Mexico.

✠ Eudist Fathers

JESUS AND MARY, LITTLE SISTERS OF

Location: USA (Salisbury, Maryland)
RC (female) founded in the USA in 1974 by Sr Mary Elizabeth Gintling
Abbr: LSJM
Original habit: a plain blue cotton dress without a collar, a plain cross around the neck, a dark cincture and a short black veil.

The Little Sisters of Jesus and Mary was founded in Maryland in the basement of the rectory of the Church of the Immaculate Conception in Baltimore. Sr Mary Elizabeth had been a member of the Community of the Little Sisters of the Poor, which she left in 1964 in order to care for the elderly and poor. In 1966 she founded Joseph House as a centre from which she and some volunteer lay people could form a Christian community to help the poor and assist with the social services they needed. With the aid of finances they were able to raise from their books and art store – Joseph House Gifts – the work could proceed. In 1974 it was resolved to form a religious community, and permission was granted. The Diocesan Community came into existence to serve the poor and promote social justice. The members received the religious habit in 1974 at a ceremony at the Trappist abbey of Our Lady of the Holy Cross, at Berryville, Virginia. This is a growing community whose members follow the example of Charles de Foucauld in caring for the disadvantaged. Joseph House Villages were opened in 1991 in Salisbury, Maryland, to provide practical help in the form of transitional housing for homeless families. In 1998 they opened Joseph House II in Salisbury, in which small local industries are able to train people in useful employment skills.

JESUS AND MARY, RELIGIOUS OF

Location: Italy (Rome)
RC (female) founded in France in 1818 by St Claudia Thévenet (Mother St Ignatius; canonized 1993)
Abbr: RJM

St Claudia Thévenet (1774–1837), with the help of her parish priest, Fr Coindre, organized a group of young women to engage in charitable work and education in Lyons, France. Elected as their superior, she took the name in religion of Mother St Ignatius. The Constitutions were approved in 1847. In order to carry out their work, the Sisters created two establishments at Fourvière, one for educating middle-class girls and the other for orphans and abandoned children, who were taught useful trades so that they might be able to find employment. By 1842 the Sisters were able to send missionaries to India and make new foundations in Spain and Mexico. A North American house was opened at Sillery, Quebec, which led on to

the foundation of the first US house at Falls River, Massachusetts, in 1877. The Association Laws in France at the beginning of the 20th century, which closed many religious houses, led to the expansion of the Congregation into other parts of Europe. The Sisters now work in education, catechetics, health care, counselling, retreat work and the running of many lay Associations. They also maintain missions in Africa, Asia, South America and parts of Europe.

JESUS CARITAS FRATERNITY

Location: USA (Yonkers, New York City)
RC (female) founded in France in 1952

This Secular Institute can be found today in over twenty countries around the world. The members follow in the contemplative tradition of Charles de Foucauld in order to bring God's love to his most neglected children, living their ordinary secular lives, and not wearing a habit. Monthly meetings are held locally for a period of adoration, when members attend the divine liturgy and meditate. Once a year the local fraternities meet for a week's retreat together.

JESUS CHRIST, POOR HANDMAIDS OF

Location: Germany (Dernbach, Westerwald)
RC (female) founded in Germany in 1851 by Katharina Kasper (Blessed Mary Kasper; beatified 1978)
Abbr: PHJC
Original habit: a black tunic and veil with a white linen wimple and cap; a rosary was suspended from a black rope cincture; the veil, which was waist-length, was secured beneath the chin.

A spiritual experience, while she was engaged in the harsh occupation of breaking stone for the building of roads, led Katharina Kasper (1820–88) to found her Congregation which was to care for the needy. In her mind's eye she had seen every detail, including the design of the habit, of the life of her future Sisters. In 1851 the first Sisters were professed, with Katharina taking the name of Mary. The new congregation attracted many postulants, and many foundations were set up throughout Germany. By 1854 it became clear to them that there was a great need for teachers, and the Sisters took up the new challenge with enthusiasm. Their work expanded, and houses were established abroad, the first American house opening in 1868 where the Sisters ran an orphanage and hospital in Indiana. Foundations followed in England, initially for the care of German immigrants, and boarding and day schools, some since closed, were established. The Sisters have also undertaken foreign missions, to India, Mexico and Brazil, where their work continues to be a mixture of teaching and caring for orphans and the sick.

✠ Ancilla Domini Sisters

JESUS CHRIST CRUCIFIED AND THE SORROWFUL MOTHER, POOR SISTERS OF

Location: USA (Brockton, Massachusetts)
RC (female) founded in the USA in 1924 by Alphonsus Maria, CP
Abbr: CJC

A Diocesan Congregation founded by a Lithuanian priest, a member of the Congregation of the Holy Cross and Passion of Our Lord Jesus Christ (Passionists), in Scranton, Pennsylvania. He was inspired to make the foundation in order to cope with the many physical, social and spiritual difficulties which new immigrants to the USA from Lithuania faced. The Sisters followed a modified Passionist Rule. In 1945 a house was opened at Brockton, Massachusetts, at the invitation of Cardinal Cushing of Boston, and this is now the mother house. The work of the Sisters is now in nursing, teaching at elementary to high school level and

conducting retreats. They also operate pastoral centres.

JESUS CRUCIFIED, CONGREGATION OF

Location: France (Brou-sur-Chantereine)
RC (female) founded in France in 1930
Abbr: OSB

A Benedictine Congregation which was innovative in that it was willing to accept postulants with physical impediments which would normally preclude them from seeking a community religious life. The charism of this foundation is essentially contemplative and Benedictine. There are houses in The Netherlands and Japan, with an American mother house at Devon, Pennsylvania. The American foundation was made in 1955.

JESUS ETERNAL PRIEST, MISSIONARY SISTERS OF

Location: Italy (Varallo Sesia)
RC (female) founded in Italy in 1953 by Mother Margharita Maria Guaini (Sr Elizabeth)
Original habit: a black tunic with a white, high-necked blouse and a white cap with a black veil.

The founder of this Congregation had entered the novitiate of the Sisters-Servants of Charity, in Brescia, Italy, in 1925, receiving her name in religion of Sr Elizabeth. She was solemnly professed in 1932 and qualified as a nurse, but she felt drawn to the contemplative life. With the permission of Bishop Ernesto Pasini of Brescia, she entered the largely contemplative monastery of the Visitation Sisters in 1938, where she was professed and given the name of Mother Margharita Maria. By 1947 she had become inspired to found a new community, dedicated to the reparation of offences against the pope and clergy and to pray for their sanctification, and in 1953 she received approval for the foundation of the Missionary Sisters of Jesus Eternal

Priest. The first Sisters made their profession in 1954. The congregation expanded to Bolivia, Peru and the Philippines, where the work now encompasses health care, catechesis and religious formation.

JESUS, MARY AND JOSEPH, MISSIONARY SISTERS OF

Location: Spain (Madrid)
RC (female) founded in Spain in 1942 by Mother Maria Dolores de la Cruz Domingo
Abbr: MJMJ

A Spanish Congregation which spread quickly to the USA, where the first American foundation was made in 1956. The Sisters work among the Hispanic poor and provide crèche accommodation and a preschool programme at Joseph of the Valley Pre-School in El Paso, Texas, for the children of working mothers. They also participate in delinquency prevention work. The work in Spain continues, and has now extended into Chile, Mexico and Africa.

JESUS OF CHARITY, SISTERS-SERVANTS OF

Location: Italy (Rome)
RC (female) founded in Spain in 1871 by St Maria Josefa de Corazón de Jesus (canonized 2000)
Abbr: Sde J.
Original habit: a dark, full-length tunic and shoulder cape with a white wimple, a dark veil and a cincture with a rosary on the right-hand side. In the tropics a white habit, cape, veil and headband was worn.

A Congregation founded in Vitoria, Spain, with houses now in Europe, Central and South America and the Philippines. St Maria (1842–1912) began her religious life as a Sister of the Institute of the Servants of Mary, in Madrid, bearing the name of Sr Maria of Health. Her spiritual director was St Anthony Mary Claret. She and two of the other Sisters of this Congregation felt that they needed to make a new foundation,

and with their confessor's approval they left Madrid to set up the new community and began their work by visiting the sick in their own homes. Their work expanded to Castro Urdiales, Valladolid and Burgos, where the Sisters helped staff hospitals and care for girls in orphanages. The work continued to expand throughout Spain, and the Decree of Approval was granted by Rome in 1846. Further expansion to Chile followed during St Maria's lifetime. Today, the work of the Congregation continues among the sick, the poor and the needy in society.

JESUS OF NAZARETH, COMMUNITY OF

Defunct
Anglican (female) founded in England in 1928

The founders, a group of women guided by Bishop Gore, saw their mission in evangelization and preaching, especially in parish missions and at meetings of women and young girls, and it was to this end that the community was established. Several branch houses were set up from their headquarters at Kingham, near Oxford, mostly in England, at Plymouth, Tewkesbury, Birmingham and Deal, and with one house in Scotland, at Perth. The houses are now all closed.

✠ Evangelical Sisters of Jesus of Nazareth

JESUS THE ETERNAL PRIEST, HERMITS OF

Location: USA (North Brookfield, Massachusetts)
RC (female) founded in the USA in 1993
Abbr: HJEP

An American Congregation founded for women who want to live under vows. The life is one of contemplation, silence and penance. Its members pray for priests and priestly vocations.

JESUS THE GOOD SHEPHERD, COMMUNITY OF THE COMPANIONS OF

Location: England (c/o St John the Baptist
Community, Clewer, Windsor, Berkshire)
Anglican (female) founded in England in 1920
Abbr: CJGS
Original habit: a brown habit.

This community developed from the Guild for Holy Innocents, which had been founded specifically for primary and secondary school teachers and which in turn gave rise to the Guild of the Good Shepherd, whose members wanted to form a religious community but still continue to teach. This was made possible, the members of the Congregation coming together in the school holidays to live the communal life. A house was made available from the Community of St Mary the Virgin, at Wantage in Berkshire, which became the headquarters. The Sisters opened a church secondary school at Mill Hill, London, and by 1939 had their own mother house, St Agnes' House, at Wantage in Berkshire. The Augustinian Rule was followed. Originally known as 'Companions', it was later decided by the Advisory Council on Religious Communities that the members would be better termed 'Sisters'. The community came to consist of two main types of member, those who were conventuals, who lived in a communal house and wore the habit and who had a novitiate of two and a half years, and tertiaries, who lived in the world but maintained their contact with the community by returning each year to spend some time with them. The training period for tertiaries lasted for about eighteen months. In 1943 the Sisters moved to Newton Abbot, in Devon, and also opened schools and a kindergarten at Newbury, in Berkshire. Since then their work has extended overseas, to Barbados, New Guinea and Antigua. An independent branch was established in East Malaysia in

1978, which today forms the Community of the Good Shepherd (CGS). Like their mother congregation, the members observe the Rule of St Augustine and do similar parish and mission work. In 1966 the Newton Abbot community in Devon moved to Clewer, Windsor, Berkshire, where they have been involved in lay and local training for the non-stipendiary ministry as well as spiritual direction and the conducting of retreats.

JOAN OF ARC, CONGREGATION OF SISTERS OF ST

Location: Canada (Sillery, Quebec)
RC (female) founded in the USA in 1914
Abbr: SJA

A Congregation which combines an active and contemplative mission, especially in the domestic services of the Church, caring for seminaries, bishops' residences and presbyteries as well as undertaking various parish ministries when required. The Sisters are to be found in Massachusetts and Rhode Island in the USA, as well as in Canada.

JOHN, CONTEMPLATIVE SISTERS OF ST

Location: USA (Laredo, Texas)
RC (female) founded in the USA in 1982

A Diocesan Congregation affiliated to the Congregation of St John, in Autun, France. It is one of the four categories of a family, or community, of St John. The others are the Brothers, the Apostolic Sisters and the Oblates. The Contemplative Sisters are devoted to solitary evening prayer and community daily prayer, with adoration of the Blessed Sacrament and daily Mass. The usual three vows of poverty, chastity and obedience are made.

JOHN, SOCIETY OF ST

Location: USA (Elmhurst, Pennsylvania)
RC (male) founded in the USA in 1998

A Public Association founded as a means
for priests and clerics to restore some of the
traditional rites within the Roman Catholic
Church, especially through the daily celebration of a solemn Mass and offices
according to the Latin rite, with the permission of the diocesan bishop.

JOHN AND THOMAS, KNIGHTS OF THE ORDER OF STS

Defunct
RC (male) founded in Syria in the 13th century
Original habit: (insignia) a red 'Jerusalem'-style
cross, in the centre of which was a medallion
depicting the images of both St John and St
Thomas, worn on the left shoulder of the mantle.

An Order, instituted at Accone, in Syria, to
care for the pilgrims who passed en route
to the Holy Land and were in need of
hospitality and what then passed for medical care. The Order was probably an imitation of the Knights Hospitallers of St John
of Jerusalem. Members observed the Rule
of St Augustine and the Order was confirmed by Pope Alexander IV (1254–61)
and Pope John XXII (1316–34).

JOHN LATERAN, CANONS REGULAR OF ST

Location: Italy (Rome)
RC (male) founded in Italy in the 4th century
Abbr: CRL
Original habit: a white woollen cassock and linen
rochet with a black biretta. From the feast of All
Saints until Easter the canons wore a long black
cloak and mozetta, giving them the popular name
of 'Black Canons'.

A very old Congregation of canons regular
which claims an origin dating back to a
disciple of St Augustine, Pope St Gelasius
(492–96), who allegedly established a com-

munity of clerics who lived the common
life. This example was followed by other
popes, notably Gregory the Great, Eugenius
II, Sergius III and Alexander II, all of whom
tried to maintain the observance of the
regular life which had become established
at the Lateran Basilica of St John in Rome.
As time went by, laxity developed and it
was necessary to call for a reform, which
was asked for by St Peter Damian in the
11th century. Some canons from the church
of St Frigidian at Lucca were brought to
Rome to establish a less relaxed lifestyle,
and this reform spread. Canons regular
served in the basilica until 1391, when secular canons were introduced by Pope Boniface VIII. There was a temporary return of
the canons regular in 1445, but the basilica
was finally handed over to the secular canons in 1483. There are two major divisions
of this Congregation.

1 The canons whose motherhouse is in
  Rome and who are known as the Canons
  Regular of the Lateran of the Most Holy
  Saviour, which comprises those canons
  in Italy, France, Belgium, Poland, Eng-
  land and South America.
2 The canons whose headquarters is at St
  Florian in Austria, who are known as the
  Canons Regular of the Lateran in Austria.
Both Congregations are subject to an abbot
general and were at times called 'Black
Canons' because of their custom of wearing
a black cloak and mozetta over their ordi-
nary white choir habit from the Feast of All
Saints until Easter.

✠ Black Canons
   Canons Regular of St Saviour
   Fathers of the Shirt

JOHN OF CHARTRES, CANONS REGULAR OF ST

Defunct
RC (male) founded in France in 1092 by St Ivo
(canonized 1347)

Original habit: a white cassock and rochet with a fur hood.

The Order of Canons Regular of St John of Chartres was founded in that city by the bishop of Chartres, St Ivo, who had been the provost of the Augustinian canons regular of St Quentin. The abbey at Chartres was destroyed in 1562, and it was not until 1624 that the canons were reinstated. They observed the Rule of St Augustine.

JOHN OF GOD, BROTHERS HOSPITALLERS OF ST

Location: Italy (Rome)
RC (male) founded in Spain in 1538 by St John of God (John Cuidad; canonized 1690)
Abbr: OH or OSJD.
Original habit: a black habit, hood and scapular with a leather belt. The habit may at one time have been grey with a rounded hood, which distinguished the wearer from Franciscan Capuchins.

John Cuidad (1495–1550) was born in Montemor-o-Novo in the diocese of Evora in Portugal, and after a life of adventure, during which he fought in various armed conflicts, he turned to selling books from door to door and at one time opened a bookshop in Granada. He underwent several mystical experiences and was converted to an extreme and penitential way of life by St John of Avila (1500–69). In 1538 came the opportunity to open a hospital in Granada, with some forty-six beds, which John maintained in immaculate condition and supported through his own begging. The bishop of Tuy, Sebastian Ramirez, clothed him in a habit and confirmed that he should be called John of God, on account of a vision that John had experienced. Other hospitals were established throughout Spain, and the Congregation of the Hospitaller Brothers was founded. It was approved by Pope St Pius V in 1571, who placed the Brothers under the Rule of St Augustine. The Constitutions, which were approved by Pope Paul V in 1617, provided for the Brothers to take the usual three vows of religion, poverty, chastity and obedience, but also to add a fourth, that of caring for all illnesses even at the risk of their own lives. The Order experienced great success initially, especially in Spain and Italy, where the Brothers were know as 'Fate Bene Fratelli', but was later to undergo many trials. Hospitals in France were confiscated during the French Revolution, and the Brothers expelled from over forty houses. From such setbacks the Order went on to recover and is now present throughout the world. There are over two hundred hospitals and schools run by the Hospitallers in the Far East, Australasia, Africa, South America and the Holy Land as well as in Europe. The work of the Brothers includes all types of general nursing, with special facilities for alcohol rehabilitation and acute care. There are also vocational centres and schools, especially for those with special needs and those who require counselling.

✠ Fate Bene Fratelli

JOHN OF GOD, SISTERS OF ST

Location: Ireland (Wexford)
RC (female) founded in Ireland in 1871 by Thomas Furlong
Abbr: SJG
Original habit: a black dress and veil with a white wimple, a leather belt and a black rosary with a metal crucifix.

Impressed by the work of the Bon Secours Sisters, who had come from France to nurse the sick in hospitals in Ireland, Bishop Furlong was anxious to see an extension of this work which would take nursing care into the home, where the poor could be better cared for. Sr Mary Visitation Clancy and four other Bon Secours Sisters decided not to renew their vows but instead to form the type of Diocesan Institute that the bishop had in mind. Their apostolate of nursing began at Sallyville, Wexford, in 1890. Five years later the work had spread to Australia, where the aftermath of the gold strikes in Western Australia left so many in need of nursing care. Two of the first Sisters to arrive there died as a result of typhoid infection. By 1907 the work had extended, with a mission set up at Broome, Western Australia, to care for the aboriginal community. In 1924 the independent foundations of the Sisters of St John of God amalgamated and papal approbation was granted, with the Australian province having its mother house at Perth. A new foundation was made in Nigeria in 1960, where local girls could be trained as teachers and nurses, and from 1964 to 1966 secondary schools for girls were opened in Awka and Agula. Nursing care continued, with some of the Sisters working at the hospital in Axhi, in the Enugu diocese. Since 1974 work has also been undertaken in the Cameroon.

JOHN OF JERUSALEM, CANONESSES OF THE ORDER OF ST

Defunct
RC (female) founded in Jerusalem in c.1048
Original habit: a red (later white) habit with a white cotta, a black cloak bearing a white, eight-pointed cross, and a black veil. A distinctive rosary was worn, made from beads divided by eight tiny silver shields on which were engraved the emblems of the Passion of Christ.

In order to become a canoness of the Order of St John of Jerusalem a woman was required to prove noble birth, as were men of the Order. The canonesses followed a contemplative life within the enclosure, observing the Rule of St Augustine, and also worked in hospitals in Jerusalem until the fall of the city to the Muslims.

JOHN THE BAPTIST, CANONS REGULAR OF ST

Defunct
RC (male) founded in England in 1425
Original habit: a black tunic, scapular and hooded mantle with a black cross on the left-hand side.

The Canons Regular of St John the Baptist were established in Coventry during the pontificate of Pope Martin V (1417–31). They lived in community and provided assistance to the poor as well as fulfilling their round of offices in the cathedral.

JOHN THE BAPTIST, COMMUNITY OF ST

Location: England (Clewer, Windsor, Berkshire)
Anglican (female) founded in England in 1852 by Thomas Thelluson Carter
Abbr: CSJB
Original habit: a black tunic and veil with a white linen wimple and head cap. A silver cross, bearing an engraving of the Agnus Dei (Lamb of God), was worn around the neck.

Thomas Carter, the rector of Clewer, in Berkshire, anxious to help some local women who had been abandoned and were living in great difficulty, turned to a clergyman's widow, Mrs Tennant, to help him in this undertaking. She took some of the women into her own home and helped to reform their way of life, but the numbers outgrew her resources. Some land was bought and a House of Mercy was built in which the work continued. One of the helpers who came to the House of Mercy to continue the work started by Mrs Tennant, who had by then become ill, was the widowed sister-in-law of Mr Carter, Harriet Monsell, and she was professed in 1852 by Bishop Samuel Wilberforce of Oxford, becoming the first superior of the community, which quickly grew and expanded. Other foundations were made at Clewer, including almshouses (1868), St Stephen's College, a boarding school for girls (1867), St John's Home, for children of 'respectable parentage' (1882) and many more missions, refuges and homes in and around London and elsewhere in England. Some of the Sisters went to India in 1881 and set up the Presidency Hospital in Calcutta, several schools and orphanages and a sanatorium in Darjeeling. The Sisters at Clewer have now made a Spirituality Centre for group and individual retreats and quiet days, and they also provide hospitality, care for the elderly and for mentally handicapped women, work with the deaf and blind, run a hospice and participate in parish work.

JOHN THE BAPTIST, COMMUNITY OF ST

Location: USA (Mendham, New Jersey)
Anglican (female) founded in the USA in 1949 (but see below)
Abbr: CSJB

The Community of St John the Baptist in America owes its origins to the English community of the same name which was founded at Clewer in Berkshire (see previous entry) but became autonomous in 1949. The two founding Sisters of the American Community were Fanny Paine (Sr Frances Constance) and Helen Stuyvesant Folsom (Sr Helen Margaret) of New York. The Community had affiliated, but independent, status with the Clewer Community from 1881. The familiar pattern of work in schools, colleges, penitentiaries and refuges was undertaken. The first houses were opened in the New York area, but in 1915 the Sisters moved to New Jersey, from where they continue to teach in schools and undertake parish work.

JOHN THE BAPTIST, HERMITS OF ST

Defunct
RC (male) founded in France in c.1630 by Brother Michael de Saint-Sabine
Original habit: a brown tunic and hooded mantle with a black scapular and a leather girdle.

A group of French hermits who came into existence in the 1630s, organized by a secular priest who took the religious name of Brother Michael de Saint-Sabine. He had travelled widely and become acquainted with the eremitical way of life and its organization. He later drew up the Statutes for the Hermits of St John the Baptist, and the Congregation was approved in 1634. The life of the hermits was well organized. Aspirants were required to live as hermits for twenty-five years and be at least forty-five years of age before they were allowed make the profession of four vows, those of perpetual chastity, poverty, obedience and stability.

JOHN THE BAPTIST, SISTERS OF ST

Location: Italy (Rome)
RC (female) founded in Italy in 1878 by Canon Alfonso Maria Fusco and Mother Crocifissa Caputo
Abbr: CSJB

A Pontifical Congregation which was founded to care for neglected children and the elderly. The first American foundation was made in 1906. The Sisters are involved in education, especially religious education, social work, health care for elderly women and the care of poor and abandoned young people. They also maintain foreign missions in Africa, India, South America, the Philippines, Poland, Korea, South Africa and Madagascar.

JOHN THE BAPTIST OF PENITENCE, HERMITS OF ST

Defunct
RC (male) founded in Spain in the late 16th century
Original habit: a rough brown serge tunic with a short cloak and scapular and a brown leather cincture; a large wooden cross was suspended over the chest; the hermits usually went barefoot.

In the kingdom of Navarre, near the city of Pamplona, approbation was given at the time of Pope Gregory XIII (1572–85) to a community of hermits who inhabited five hermitages in the area, named after St Clement, St Mary of Montserrat, St Bartholomew, St Martin and St Fulgentius, bishop of Carthage. Not more than ten men were allowed in each community, where they lived in cells surrounding a chapel. The hermits practised many austerities, being continually barefoot and wearing a rough, heavy tunic. They also observed continual silence, ate no meat and took just water and vegetables as their food. The discipline, or scourge, was used three times a week and daily during the season of Lent as an act of penance. The men slept on bare boards with a stone for a pillow and carried a large, heavy wooden cross around their necks at all times. It is not known when they became defunct.

✠ Hermits of St John of Penance

JOHN THE BELOVED, ORDER OF ST

Defunct
Anglican (female) founded in England in 1904 by the Revd J. L. Davids

An Order of Anglican nuns which aimed to combine the active and the contemplative life. The Sisters ran the John Lenthal Memorial Home as a guest house, as well as operating a church supplies store at Westcliff-on-Sea, in Essex. The Order became defunct in 1925.

JOHN THE DIVINE, NURSING SISTERS OF

Location: England (Birmingham)
Anglican (female) founded in England in 1848 by Bishop Bloomfield
Abbr: CSJD.

In the mid-19th century a need was felt for nurses who were able and willing to care for the poor, staff hospitals and visit families in need of care in their own homes. With these objectives in mind, Bishop Bloomfield of London, encouraged by and with the approval of the archbishop of Canterbury, decided to found an Institution of Sisters who would not be required to take vows. By the end of 1848, four such women had presented themselves. A Rule was approved and a house set up in Fitzroy Square, London, known as St John's House and Sisterhood. The Sisters did not wear a religious habit but adopted a simple uniform, and began the work of caring for their patients in their own homes. They had been trained as nurses at the Middlesex and Westminster Hospitals in London and, in turn, trained others. Florence Nightingale took twenty-six nurses trained by the Nursing Sisters of St John the Divine with her to the Crimean War. The Sisterhood grew, and in 1880 extended to Canada, when Sr Anna Lomas went from London to found the Canadian Sisters of St John the Divine, an independent community. A small hospital and training school for nurses was opened in Lewisham, London, and a hospital for women and children, together with a crèche, was founded in the London suburb of Poplar. Further London foundations were made, including St John's Hospital at Lewisham, a district home in Deptford, a home for sick nurses and private patients and a convalescent home for women and girls on the south coast at Littlehampton in Sussex. The need for a more structured life was apparent and the Cowley Fathers revised and constructed the Rule and Statutes of the community, which now permitted vows to be taken. Following this revision, postulants and novices began to arrive, and new houses and developments were made. The Sisters now provide guest house and retreat facilities and a special ministry to the bereaved, AIDS counselling, hospital chaplaincy work and various paramedical services. The Congregation is associated with the Royal Foundation of St

Katharine in London, where with others they form a community which offers retreat and conference facilities.

JOHN THE DIVINE, SISTERHOOD OF ST

Location: Canada (Willowdale, Ontario)
Anglican (female) founded in Canada in 1884 by Mrs Hannah Grier Coome and Sr Anna Lomas
Abbr: SSJD

This Sisterhood was founded in Canada with the help of Sr Anna Lomas, who was sent over from the St John's House Nursing Institute in London, England (see previous entry). The members nursed and cared for the wounded in the North West Rebellion in Canada in 1885. Many foundations have followed which include a home for unmarried mothers, care homes for elderly women and a home for mentally retarded children. The Sisters also run a guest house and mission facility as well as a school at Regina, Saskatchewan, and a convalescent hospital at Newtonbrook, Ontario.

JOHN THE DIVINE, SOCIETY OF ST

Location: South Africa (Durban)
Anglican (female) founded in South Africa in 1887
Abbr: SSJD

The Society was founded in Durban, Natal, where the Sisters cared for children who had been abandoned, in both the white and black communities. The Sisters worked in a native mission dedicated to St Christopher, near Pietermaritzburg, and also in the Mission of St Luke. Their work was supported through prayer by another group of Sisters who were given to the contemplative life within the same community. A falling membership, however, has made a material difference to the work undertaken. An orphanage for boys in Durban has been closed and a school for girls is now administered by the diocese. Apart from child welfare and teaching, the Sisters also made

the altar breads which were used throughout South Africa and in former Rhodesia (Zimbabwe). The few remaining Sisters now provide a parish ministry within a small Durban parish.

JOHN THE EVANGELIST, SISTERS OF ST

Location: Ireland (Ballsbridge, Dublin)
Church of Ireland – Anglican (female) founded in Ireland in 1912 by Fletcher Sheridan Le Fanu
Abbr: LCSJE or CSJE.

A Church of Ireland foundation whose members specialize in church embroidery and needlework, and who also run the All Saints Home for young girls in Dublin, visit hospitals and prisons and provide retreat facilities. The community was controversial at the time of its foundation, when the founder drew upon the Visitation Rule (Roman Catholic) as the basis of the Rule and Constitutions for the new Sisterhood, which encountered opposition and dismay from some Protestants. The first Sister to enter made her novitiate with the Sisters of the Society of St Margaret, at East Grinstead in West Sussex, England, where she was also taught many practical skills, including church embroidery. Upon her return to Ireland she was joined by several other women, and a small community was formed. A Third Order, known as the Company of St John of the Cross, was founded for those who wish to be associated with the community but who have commitments in the world.

✠ Sisters of the Love of Jesus

JOHN THE EVANGELIST, SISTERS OF THE COMMUNITY OF ST

Defunct
Episcopalian Church – Anglican (female) founded in the USA in 1888 by Bishop Abram N. Littlejohn and Srs Julia and Emma

The Sisterhood began as a deaconess society on Long Island, New York, founded in 1872 and transformed into a religious community in 1888. The Sisters ran an orphanage, a home for the elderly, and St John's Hospital for the elderly and the blind. They also worked with the poor and those in need of education.

✠ Sisterhood of St John the Evangelist

JOHN THE EVANGELIST, SOCIETY OF ST

Location: England (Westminster, London)
Anglican (male) founded in England in 1866
Abbr: SSJE
Original habit: secular.

This Society is one of mission priests and Brothers who work in parishes, with both groups and individuals, wherever a need is perceived. The original name, the Society of Mission Priests, was later changed to the present one. Its programme of foundation has recently been changed, so that a postulant is now called a seeker. After a minimum of one year, vows may be taken as an internal oblate Brother. These must be renewed annually and can lead on to life vows after a further period of at least two years, dependent on the discernment of both the candidate and the community. The members observe a daily service schedule of matins, Eucharist, terce, a midday office, evensong and compline, and a programme of work which includes spiritual direction, counselling, the conducting of retreats and a ministry of care for sufferers from ME. There is a special ministry to those people with various learning difficulties due to dyslexia and autism. Some of the members also work in the fine arts, depending on their skills. An American Congregation was established in 1872 and is currently to be found in Massachusetts. This became an independent province in 1914 and was formally constituted as an American Congregation in 1921. Close links between the two communities have been maintained.

✠ Cowley Fathers

JOSEPH, CONGREGATION OF SISTERS OF ST – Annecy

Location: France (Annecy)
RC (female) founded in France in 1835 by Bishop Reys of Annecy
Abbr: SSJA
Original habit: a black tunic and veil with a black cincture and rosary and a white linen binder, coif and, later, wimple; a crucifix, originally of brass but later of silver, was worn around the neck.

The Congregation was founded with a view to providing teachers for the young and to staff hospitals, care for orphans and visit the sick and poor in their homes. Papal approbation was granted in 1901, but the Association Laws in France at this time, which closed religious communities, sent the Congregation to England, where the first foundation was made at Devizes, in Wiltshire, in 1880. Other Sisters went from Annecy to Switzerland.

JOSEPH, CONGREGATION OF SISTERS OF ST – Baden

Location: USA (Baden, Pennsylvania)
RC (female) founded in the USA in 1869
Abbr: CSJ
Original habit: a black tunic and veil with a black cincture and rosary, and a white linen binder and coif and, later, wimple; a crucifix, originally of brass but later of silver, was worn around the neck.

A Pontifical Congregation founded from the community at Flushing, Long Island, when Mother Austin O'Keane and two others from the Congregation of Sisters of St Joseph went to Ebensburg, Pennsylvania. The venture was so successful that many wished to join, and the mother house was moved to Baden in 1901. The Sisters by then had staffed many schools and had founded a hospital in Pittsburgh. Today, there are Sisters in many of the eastern and southern states of the USA, and they are represented in foreign missions in Brazil and Jamaica. Their work ranges from prison ministries to housing management, but education remains an important part of the Sisters' lives, as well as health care, social and pastoral ministries, Family Life ministry and Outreach projects.

JOSEPH, CONGREGATION OF SISTERS OF ST – Bordeaux

Defunct
RC (female) founded in France in 1840 by Mother St Joseph Chanay
Abbr: SSJB.
Original habit: a black tunic and veil with a black cincture and rosary, and a white linen binder and coif and, later, wimple; a crucifix, originally of brass but later of silver, was worn around the neck.

This Congregation was based on the model of that at Le Puy (see below), which had been founded in 1650 by Fr Medaille, SJ The Sisters undertook all kinds of charitable work including teaching. They maintained a boarding school for girls in England, at Tamworth in Staffordshire.

JOSEPH, CONGREGATION OF SISTERS OF ST – Boston

Location: USA (Brighton, Massachusetts)
RC (female) founded in the USA in 1873
Abbr: CSJ
Original habit: a black tunic and veil with a black cincture and rosary, and a white linen binder and coif and, later, wimple; a crucifix, originally of brass but later of silver, was worn around the neck.

Some Sisters from the Congregation of Sisters of St Joseph, at Brentwood, went to Jamaica Plain, Boston, in 1873 and opened their first school there. Other foundations followed in Massachusetts, in Cambridge (1885) and Brighton and Canton (1902).

The Sisters undertook some innovative work with deaf children and also organized an industrial school where useful trade skills were taught. They are now involved in various ministries in education, health care, social services, counselling and retreat work.

JOSEPH, CONGREGATION OF SISTERS OF ST – Brentwood

Location: USA (Brentwood, New York)
RC (female) founded in the USA in 1856
Abbr: CSJ
Original habit: a black tunic and veil with a black cincture and rosary, and a white linen binder and coif and, later, wimple; a crucifix, originally of brass but later of silver, was worn around the neck.

When Bishop Loughlin of Brooklyn was in need of some Sisters to take over the running of schools, to care for the sick and to organize an orphanage in his diocese, he applied, in 1856, to the Congregation of Sisters of St Joseph, at Chestnut Hill, Philadelphia. Two of the Sisters from this foundation, and one from the Buffalo Congregation, went to Williamsburg, where they established a school. From here, an interim foundation was made at Flushing, Long Island, from where in 1873 some Sisters went to Rutland, Vermont, in the diocese of Burlington. It was not until 1903 that a mother house was set up at Brentwood, New York, where another school was also established. The Sisters are now involved in all levels of education, in religious education, health care, retreat work and the running of sheltered accommodation for women at risk.

JOSEPH, CONGREGATION OF SISTERS OF ST – Buffalo

Location: USA (Buffalo, New York)
RC (female) founded in the USA in 1854
Abbr: SSJ
Original habit: a black tunic and veil with a black

cincture and rosary, and a white linen binder and coif and, later, wimple; a crucifix, originally of brass but later of silver, was worn around the neck.

In 1854 three Sisters left the Congregation of St Joseph at Carondelet to establish a new house at Canandaigua, New York. Two years later, one of the Sisters went to Buffalo to look after an Institute for deaf-mutes, a ministry the Sisters still continue today. With an increase in the number of postulants, a novitiate that had been set up at Canandaigua proved too small, and a new one was opened at Buffalo in 1861. By 1868 the foundation was sufficiently established to declare itself independent. The Sisters provide education at all levels, including specialized teaching for the deaf, staff orphanages and maintain hospital and prison chaplaincies and a spirituality centre.

JOSEPH, CONGREGATION OF SISTERS OF ST – Burlington

Location: USA (Rutland, Vermont)
RC (female) founded in the USA in 1873
Abbr: SSJ
Original habit: a black tunic and veil with a black cincture and rosary, and a white linen binder and coif and, later, wimple; a crucifix, originally of brass but later of silver, was worn around the neck.

A Diocesan Community founded by Sisters from the interim community at Flushing made by the Sisters of St Joseph from the Brentwood Congregation. The Sisters have maintained an active interest in teaching at all levels, as well as taking part in parish ministries.

JOSEPH, CONGREGATION OF SISTERS OF ST – Canada

Location: Canada (Hamilton, Ontario)
RC (female)
Abbr: CSJ
Original habit: a black tunic and veil with a black cincture and rosary, and a white linen binder and

coif and, later, wimple; a crucifix, originally of brass but later of silver, was worn around the neck.

The French Revolution destroyed the communities of the Sisters of St Joseph founded at Le Puy, France (see below), and it was through the efforts of Mother St John Fontbonne, who had narrowly escaped execution, that the remnants of that Congregation were reorganized, with the establishment of a house for the Sisters at Lyons. In 1836, some Sisters from the Lyons foundation went to the USA, where they established the Sisters of St Joseph of Carondelet in Missouri, from which other foundations were made, including a Canadian foundation at Hamilton, Ontario, which grew quickly. It was decided to unite the Congregations into the Federation of the Sisters of St Joseph of Canada. The Canadian Congregations that are federated are:

1 THE SISTERS OF ST JOSEPH OF HAMILTON (Ontario)

The Sisters started their work with an orphanage, and they taught in parish schools. With the establishment of the separate diocese of Hamilton in 1856 they became a separate Diocesan Congregation.

2 THE SISTERS OF ST JOSEPH OF LONDON (Ontario)

A foundation established by five Sisters from the Toronto Congregation in 1868, when an orphanage was opened. In 1870 this became an independent congregation, and by 1880 the Sisters had established a hospital in London and were involved in running refuges for women at risk, and homes for the elderly.

3 THE SISTERS OF ST JOSEPH OF PETERBOROUGH (Ontario)

This Congregation was established in 1899 from the Toronto Congregation, with education as its main focus. The Sisters also ran orphanages and homes for the elderly.

4 THE SISTERS OF ST JOSEPH OF PEMBROKE (Ontario)

The Pembroke Congregation was founded from the Peterborough Congregation in 1921. The Sisters set up schools and cared for orphans, the elderly and the sick poor.

5 THE SISTERS OF ST JOSEPH OF SAULT STE MARIE (Ontario)

The Congregation was established in 1881 by four Sisters from Toronto, at Prince Arthur's Landing, in the city of Thunder Bay at the head of Lake Superior and began with a ministry in Northern Ontario. It was here that the missions at Sault Ste Marie, Sudbury and North Bay were opened.

6 THE SISTERS OF ST JOSEPH OF TORONTO (Ontario)

The Congregation at Toronto has been a constant source of missionary Sisters throughout Ontario. It was founded from Chestnut Hill, Pennsylvania, in 1851. The Sisters have set up many schools and provide education at all levels as well as running charitable institutions and hospitals.

JOSEPH, CONGREGATION OF SISTERS OF ST – Carondelet

Location: USA (St Louis, Louisiana)
RC (female) founded in the USA in 1836
Abbr: CSJ
Original habit: a black tunic and veil with a black cincture and rosary, and a white linen binder and coif and, later, wimple; a crucifix, originally of brass but later of silver, was worn around the neck.

A Pontifical Institute, founded at Carondelet, Missouri, from the French congregation at Lyons. In just a few years further foundations were made throughout the USA,

with a general chapter arranged in 1860 which resulted in a revision of the Constitutions. These were approved by the Holy See in 1867 and 1877. The independent Congregation is now divided into four provinces, St Louis-Missouri, St Paul-Minnesota, Albany-New York and Los Angeles-California, and one vice-province, Hawaii. There are nearly two and a half thousand Sisters in this Congregation, and although the Provinces are autonomous, interchange between them is allowed. The apostolate is extremely varied, encompassing education, nursing and health care, the care of children and geriatrics as well as specialized teaching for the deaf, and social ministries. The Sisters also maintain foreign missions in Peru, Chile and Japan and are present in nearly two hundred American dioceses.

JOSEPH, CONGREGATION OF SISTERS OF ST – Chambéry

Location: Italy (Rome)
RC (female) founded in France in 1816
Abbr: CSJ
Original habit: a black tunic and veil with a black cincture and rosary, and a white linen binder and coif and, later, wimple; a crucifix, originally of brass but later of silver, was worn around the neck.

Following the upheaval of the French Revolution the remnants of the Order of St Joseph was re-formed at Lyons, France. By 1816 some of the Sisters had been sent to Chambéry, south-east of Lyons, where they began to teach, nurse the sick and care for the elderly. The Congregation experienced tremendous growth and was accorded the status of Pontifical Congregation, approbation being granted by Pope Pius IX in 1874. A foundation was made in the USA in 1885.

JOSEPH, CONGREGATION OF SISTERS OF ST – Chestnut Hill

Location: USA (Philadelphia, Pennsylvania)
RC (female) founded in the USA in 1861

Abbr: SSJ
Original habit: a black tunic and veil with a black cincture and rosary, and a white linen binder and coif and, later, wimple; a crucifix, originally of brass but later of silver, was worn around the neck.

A Congregation founded from the one at Carondelet when four Sisters went to Philadelphia to take charge of an orphanage which had been under the care of the Sisters of Charity. There was some initial trouble in the city, with the Sisters suffering from bigotry and misunderstanding, and in 1858 they moved away to a farmhouse, which became the Mount St Joseph Convent. There was much need for education at this time, especially for the children of immigrants. The Congregation became independent of the Carondelet foundation in 1861, and papal approval was granted in 1895. Today, the Sisters undertake many ministries, in health care, religious and academic education, the care of the elderly, hospice and hospital work, and drug and alcohol rehabilitation programmes. They are also committed to justice issues and are active in campaigning against the death penalty and racial discrimination.

JOSEPH, CONGREGATION OF SISTERS OF ST – Cleveland

Location: USA (Cleveland, Ohio)
RC (female) founded in the USA in 1872
Abbr: CSJ
Original habit: a black tunic and veil with a black cincture and rosary, and a white linen binder and coif and, later, wimple; a crucifix, originally of brass but later of silver, was worn around the neck.

A Diocesan Congregation, founded at Painesville, Ohio, by Mother Saint George Bradley. The Sisters now undertake a variety of ministries, including pastoral and hospital chaplaincy work, nursing, education, campus ministries, a special apostolate for the deaf, the use of the media for book publishing and broadcasting, the provision of legal advice, business administration and holistic health programmes.

JOSEPH, CONGREGATION OF SISTERS OF ST – Cluny

Location: France (Paris)
RC (female) founded in France in 1807 by Blessed Anne Marie Javouhey (beatified 1950)
Abbr: SJC
Original habit: a blue tunic with a black scapular and cape.

A Pontifical Congregation which began when its founder, Blessed Anne Marie Javouhey (1779–1851), after trying her vocation with both the Sisters of Charity at Besançon and the Trappists at La Val, decided that neither were what she required. With three other young women she opened a school in Chamblanc and formed the Association of St Joseph with civil permission and encouragement from the Church. In 1807 she was clothed in the habit of the new Congregation, which marks the date of foundation. In their enthusiasm, the first Sisters founded workshops, a hostel for the poor and a boys' school. Financial ruin was only averted when the founder's father paid their bills and bought the Sisters a former friary at Cluny. Their successful method of teaching attracted the attention of the authorities, and the Congregation was persuaded to send some Sisters to Réunion to start a school there, a mission which met with such success that other schools were set up in Senegal, Guadalupe, Guiana, Sierra Leone and the Gambia. At the same time, further houses were opened in France and the founder was appointed superior-general, although not without some problems with the bishop of Autun. Today, the Congregation has houses throughout Europe, the USA, Canada, Asia and Africa.

JOSEPH, CONGREGATION OF SISTERS OF ST – Concordia

Location: USA (Concordia, Kansas)
RC (female) founded in the USA in 1884
Abbr: CSJ
Original habit: a black tunic and veil with a black cincture and rosary, and a white linen binder and coif and, later, wimple; a crucifix, originally of brass but later of silver, was worn around the neck.

A Pontifical Congregation founded in the USA by some Sisters from Rochester, New York, who went to Newton in Kansas in 1883, a town just a little north of Wichita, and moved in 1884 to Concordia, where they established their mother house. The apostolate is now centred on the care of those who can do little for themselves, especially refugees, the homeless, the handicapped and those suffering from drug dependence.

Location: USA (Erie, Pennsylvania)
RC (female) founded in the USA in 1860 by Mother Agnes Spencer
Abbr: SSJ
Original habit: a black tunic and veil with a black cincture and rosary, and a white linen binder and coif and, later, wimple; a crucifix, originally of brass but later of silver, was worn around the neck.

A Diocesan Congregation founded by Mother Spencer, who went from the Congregation of St Joseph at Carondelet, together with two others, to administer an academy already existing at Corsica, Pennsylvania. After a few years they opened a hospital and took charge of parish schools in the area. In 1892 the Sisters opened the Villa Maria Academy, which still functions, and which in 1987 became the novitiate and mother house of the Congregation. The Sisters provide sheltered accommodation for women at risk, as well as working in liturgical ministries, catechesis, fine art work and publishing. Although most members of the congregation are still in North West Pennsylvania, others work in Kentucky, Wisconsin, Tennessee, Texas, Florida and Washington, DC

JOSEPH, CONGREGATION OF SISTERS OF ST – Lafayette/Tipton

Location: USA (Tipton, Indiana)
RC (female) founded in the USA in 1888
Abbr: CSJ
Original habit: a black tunic and veil with a black cincture and rosary, and a white linen binder and coif and, later, wimple; a crucifix, originally of brass but later of silver, was worn around the neck.

A Diocesan Congregation founded by the Sisters of St Joseph from Carondelet, Missouri, who went to Tipton in response to a request from the priest of St John's Church, Tipton, who needed some Sisters to open and run a school there. More women joined the community, and other schools in the neighbourhood were established. The need for health care was apparent, and hospitals were built in Kokomo and Elwood, Indiana, and at Bend, Oregon. After Vatican II, further ministries were undertaken, especially in the social services, and in 1989 the Sisters went into partnership with the diocese of Lafayette-in-Indiana, and a hospice was sponsored in Port-au-Prince, Haiti. Here the staff can dispense food and some medical care as well as providing accommodation for retreat groups.

JOSEPH, CONGREGATION OF SISTERS OF ST – La Grange

Location: USA (La Grange Park, Illinois)
RC (female) founded in the USA in 1899/1900
Abbr: CSJ
Original habit: a black tunic and veil with a black cincture and rosary, and a white linen binder and coif and, later, wimple; a crucifix, originally of brass but later of silver, was worn around the neck.

A Congregation founded by Mother Stanislaus from the Diocesan Community at Rochester, New York. The work of the Sisters covers some modern innovative missions, especially in encouraging creative expression through music and the arts, as well as seeking the reconciliation of conflict through works of peace, justice and education. Other work undertaken by the Congregation includes an outreach enterprise to the poor.

JOSEPH, CONGREGATION OF SISTERS OF ST - Le Puy

Location: There are now many independent Congregations derived from this parent foundation. Their mother houses appear in the entries listed below.
RC (female) founded in France in 1650 by Fr Médaille, SJ
Abbr: CSJ
Original habit: a black tunic and veil with a black cincture and rosary, and a white linen binder and coif and, later, wimple; a crucifix, originally of brass but later of silver, was worn around the neck.

The Le Puy Congregation, founded in Haut-Loire, France, was the originator of the many congregations of St Joseph that followed later. Fr Médaille was enthusiastic in his work of creating sodalities of people who would perform acts of charity, instruct the young, visit the sick and help the poor. He realized that a more solid framework was needed, and the idea of a Sisterhood appealed to him as a way of best providing for this. The first Congregation of the Sisters of St Joseph emerged, and six women, Frances Eyraud, Claudia Chastel, Marguerite Burdier, Anna Chayler, Anne Vay and Anna Brun, were professed and began their work by taking charge of an orphanage for girls. The Congregation received diocesan approval in 1655 together with royal confirmation from Louis XIV, and soon spread through many French dioceses. The French

Revolution caused the closure of many convents of the Congregation and the martyrdom of at least five Sisters. One who narrowly escaped death by execution was Mother St John Fontbonne, who was diligent in reorganizing the Congregation after the Revolution and in making a new foundation, the Convent of St Joseph, at Lyons in 1816, from which many daughter houses sprang. By the time of the French Association Laws at the start of the 20th century, the Congregation had spread to many countries, and many independent congregations were being formed.

JOSEPH, CONGREGATION OF SISTERS OF ST - Lyons

Location: France (Lyons)
RC (female) founded in France in 1816 and the USA in 1906
Abbr: CSJ
Original habit: a black tunic and veil with a black cincture and rosary, and a white linen binder and coif and, later, wimple; a crucifix, originally of brass but later of silver, was worn around the neck.

An American foundation of the Sisters of St Joseph was made directly from the Lyons Congregation in 1906 in Jackman, Maine. The principal foundation of the Maine Province is now at Winslow, where the Sisters are involved in running a nursing home at Waterville and also taking charge of a children's day care centre at Auburn. Catechesis and pastoral ministries, especially in several foreign missions, also form part of the Sisters' apostolate.

JOSEPH, CONGREGATION OF SISTERS OF ST - Medaille

Location: USA (Cincinnati, Ohio)
RC (female) founded in France in 1650 and the USA in 1855
Abbr: CSJ
Original habit: a black tunic and veil with a black

cincture and rosary, and a white linen binder and coif and, later, wimple; a crucifix, originally of brass but later of silver, was worn around the neck.

The work of this Congregation has been brought to public notice because of its prison ministry in the USA and in particular the involvement with prisoners on death row, with a Sister ready to offer solace and comfort right up to the moment of execution. The main emphasis of the apostolate is the care of the underprivileged poor and minority groups in society. The Sisters provide retreats, health care and literacy programmes in addition to their work in education at all levels, including efforts on behalf of adults who are mentally handicapped, and rehabilitation programmes for the victims of drug abuse. A mission to Nicaragua is also maintained.

JOSEPH, CONGREGATION OF SISTERS OF ST – Nazareth

Location: USA (Nazareth, Michigan)
RC (female) founded in the USA in 1889
Abbr: SSJ
Original habit: a black tunic and veil with a black cincture and rosary, and a white linen binder and coif and, later, wimple; a crucifix, originally of brass but later of silver, was worn around the neck.

A Pontifical Congregation founded by some Sisters of St Joseph from the Ogdensburg (Watertown) community in New York, who made a settlement at Kalamazoo, Michigan, from which a novitiate was founded at Nazareth, Michigan. The Sisters are involved in many parish and church-related ministries, as well as health care for the handicapped in a day-care centre and for the mentally sick in an outpatient health clinic. Their foreign mission work is at present conducted in Peru, Africa and Japan.

JOSEPH, CONGREGATION OF SISTERS OF ST – Orange

Location: USA (Orange, California)
RC (female) founded in the USA in 1912
Abbr: CSJ
Original habit: a black tunic and veil with a black cincture and rosary, and a white linen binder and coif and, later, wimple; a crucifix, originally of brass but later of silver, was worn around the neck.

A Congregation of the Sisters of St Joseph, founded through the efforts of Mother Bernard Gosselin, from the La Grange Congregation, at Eureka, California. The Sisters devote their lives to teaching and nursing in numerous schools and hospitals throughout California and at St Mary of the Plains Hospital in Lubbock, Texas. Catechesis and foreign missions to Hungary, Mexico, El Salvador, Israel and Australia are also part of the apostolate.

JOSEPH, CONGREGATION OF SISTERS OF ST – Rochester

Location: USA (Rochester, New York)
RC (female) founded in the USA in 1854
Abbr: SSJ
Original habit: a black tunic and veil with a black cincture and rosary, and a white linen binder and coif and, later, wimple; a crucifix, originally of brass but later of silver, was worn around the neck.

A Pontifical Congregation founded from the Carondelet foundation. The Sisters of this large community maintain many different apostolates. They work in education at all levels, including the Trinity Montessori School, they work with children who have special educational needs, and teach in academies, colleges and graduate schools. Other Sisters work in the field of health care and with the elderly, the emotionally disturbed and those with drug dependencies. Social service and prison ministries are undertaken, and the Sisters are also responsible for sponsoring a programme of foster care homes and a food kitchen for the poor, as well as a mission to Brazil.

JOSEPH, CONGREGATION OF SISTERS OF ST – St Augustine

Location: USA (St Augustine, Florida)
RC (female) founded in the USA in 1866
Abbr: SSJ
Original habit: a black tunic and veil with a black cincture and rosary, and a white linen binder and coif and, later, wimple; a crucifix, originally of brass but later of silver, was worn around the neck.

The Congregation at St Augustine was founded from the French Le Puy Congregation (see above) when eight Sisters were sent to Florida at the invitation of Bishop Verlot. The Sisters were expected to teach the coloured children and adults following the Civil War (1861–65). It soon became apparent that there were many white people who also lacked any useful skills, and the Sisters widened their teaching programme. In 1899 the Congregation became independent of the parent Congregation at Le Puy and some of the Sisters returned to France. Today, the Congregation works solely within Florida, where the Sisters maintain schools and provide religious and academic education as well as other ministries in prison visiting, AIDS counselling, and care for the elderly, for unmarried mothers and for those who are physically disabled.

JOSEPH, CONGREGATION OF SISTERS OF ST – St Vallier

Location: Canada (Quebec)
RC (female) founded in Canada in 1683
Abbr: CSJ
Original habit: a black tunic and veil with a black cincture and rosary, and a white linen binder and coif and, later, wimple; a crucifix, originally of brass but later of silver, was worn around the neck.

The Canadian foundation at St Vallier dates from 1683, when two Sisters from the French Congregation at Le Puy (see above) responded to the request of Jean Baptiste de la Croix Chevrière, later bishop of Quebec, who needed help to staff a hospital he had founded at St Vallier. As time went by, the work of the Sisters expanded to include teaching. The Sisters are still involved in teaching and caring for the sick.

JOSEPH, CONGREGATION OF SISTERS OF ST – Springfield

Location: USA (Holyoke, Massachusetts)
RC (female) founded in the USA in 1883
Abbr: SSJ
Original habit: a black tunic and veil with a black cincture and rosary, and a white linen binder and coif and, later, wimple; a crucifix, originally of brass but later of silver, was worn around the neck.

A Diocesan Congregation founded by seven Sisters from the community at Flushing, Long Island, who went to take over a small parish school at Chicopee Falls, Massachusetts. The numbers swelled, and by 1883 the community was asked to move to the parish of Springfield, where they opened their mother house. Today, the Sisters teach at all levels and provide special education. They also work in prison ministries, hospital chaplaincies and health care. Foreign missions are maintained in Guatemala and Tanzania.

JOSEPH, CONGREGATION OF SISTERS OF ST – Watertown

Location: USA (Watertown, New York)
RC (female) founded in the USA in 1880
Abbr: SSJ
Original habit: a black tunic and veil with a black cincture and rosary, and a white linen binder and coif and, later, wimple; a crucifix, originally of brass but later of silver, was worn around the neck.

A Diocesan Congregation founded by Sisters from the Congregations of St Joseph at Buffalo, New York and Erie. The Sisters were initially engaged upon largely educational and orphanage work, but today the apostolate is more varied, still involved in education, but also in pastoral work, health care and hospital ministries. The Sisters also maintain a conservatory of music.

JOSEPH, CONGREGATION OF SISTERS OF ST – Wheeling

Location: USA (Wheeling, West Virginia)
RC (female) founded in the USA in 1860
Abbr: SSJ
Original habit: a black tunic and veil with a black cincture and rosary, and a white linen binder and coif and, later, wimple; a crucifix, originally of brass but later of silver, was worn around the neck.

A Diocesan Congregation which began as a small community started by some Sisters from the Carondelet foundation in 1853, when they opened an orphanage and hospital in Wheeling, West Virginia. By 1860 it was obvious that this community should be independent, and a separate foundation was made. During the Civil War the hospital was commandeered by the government and the Sisters provided nursing care. Today, members are to be found in the Wheeling-Charleston diocese, where they provide most forms of education from elementary to college level, as well as health care programmes, spiritual direction and retreat facilities. The Sisters run the hospitals of St Francis at Charleston and St Joseph at Parkersburg, West Virginia.

JOSEPH, CONGREGATION OF SISTERS OF ST – Wichita

Location: USA (Wichita, Kansas)
RC (female) founded in the USA in 1887
Abbr: CSJ
Original habit: a black tunic and veil with a black cincture and rosary, and a white linen binder and coif and, later, wimple; a crucifix, originally of brass but later of silver, was worn around the neck.

A Pontifical Congregation founded by four Sisters from the Concordia community who were sent to open a small parish school at Abilene, Kansas. A little later a sanitorium was opened at Del Norte, Colorado, now known as St Joseph's Convent. The work of the Sisters encompasses religious and academic education as well as distance learning in adult religious education. They are also involved in programmes for helping those with physical handicaps and those in need of special education. Homes for the aged, pro-life programmes, language schools, pastoral ministries and health care programmes in hospitals and clinics all are undertaken. The Sisters have now opened St Joseph's Hospital and St Mary's School for the Handicapped, in Japan, together with a kindergarten and a home for the elderly.

JOSEPH, HOSPITALLERS OF ST

Location: Canada (Montreal, Quebec)
RC (female) founded in France in 1636 by Marie de la Ferre

A Congregation which began in France but spread to Canada. Marie de la Ferre established the first convent at Lafleche, France, and this was soon followed by others at Laval, Bauge and Beaufort. The Congregation was approved by Pope Alexander VII in 1666. One of its earliest houses was that at Montreal, Canada, and in this foundation Jeanne Mance (1606–73) had a pivotal part to play. She was inspired to join the Society of Montreal, otherwise known as the Society of Notre Dame of Montreal for the Conversion of the Savages of New France, a nursing sisterhood. Despite her very limited nursing experience, gained during a plague epidemic in her native France, Jeanne Mance sailed for Montreal, where she set up a small dispensary, a hospital with two wards, six beds for men and two for women, and a small chapel. This was the beginning of the Hôtel-Dieu of Montreal, which was founded in October 1645. Financial problems and frequent attacks by warlike Iroquois in 1651 did not stem her resolve. She returned briefly to France to recruit some Hospitaller Sisters of St Joseph from Lafleche to return with her to Montreal. Jeanne Mance faced many more perils and difficulties before her death, in Montreal, in 1673. The Hospitallers today manage many hospitals, dispensaries, sanatoria and leper hospices and run a training school for nurses as well as orphanages and schools. They now work in many Canadian and American dioceses and conduct missions to Africa and Peru.

JOSEPH, LITTLE DAUGHTERS OF ST – Canada

Location: Canada (Pierrefonds, Quebec)
RC (female) founded in Canada in 1857 by Fr Antoine Mercier

A Congregation founded by Fr Mercier, a Sulpician priest, in Montreal, Canada, which received diocesan approval in 1897. The work of the Sisters is to help the clergy through the making of altar vestments and equipment, especially for priests in missionary situations. They also work in parish ministries.

JOSEPH, LITTLE DAUGHTERS OF ST – Italy

Location: Italy (Verona)
RC (female) founded in Italy in 1893 by Blessed Joseph Baldo (beatified 1989)

The Congregation was founded in Verona by Joseph Baldo to help remedy the rural poverty in Italy at the time. He embarked on a programme of creating vocational schools for boys and girls to give them skills which would be useful in their adult life, and opened a rural savings bank to stop the poor from falling into the hands of the moneylenders who impoverished them even more. Some local women were organized

into a sodality called the Sisters of Charity of Our Lady of Succour, and by 1888 a hospital for the sick and elderly had been opened. The Sisters still maintain the same apostolate, working in education and with the sick.

JOSEPH, MEDICAL SISTERS OF ST

Location: India (Kerala)
RC (female) founded in India in 1946 by Mgr Joseph C. Panjikarran
Abbr: MSJ

A Congregation founded in Kothamangalam, Kerala, Southern India. The Sisters provide medical care by staffing hospitals, clinics and dispensaries in ten dioceses in India. They are also present in the USA, in the diocese of Wichita, Kansas. The Congregation received pontifical approbation in 1990.

JOSEPH, OBLATES OF ST – Asti

Location: Italy (Rome)
RC (male) founded in Italy in 1878 by Blessed Bishop Joseph Marello (beatified 1993)
Abbr: OSJ

A Congregation of oblates founded by Joseph Marello (1844–95) in Turin, Italy, which received its approbation in 1909. The apostolate of the Congregation is concerned with youth work, catechesis and parish ministries. The priests also run the St Joseph's Oblate Seminary for the Congregation at Pittston, Pennsylvania, as part of its eastern province mission, as well as a house of studies and the Mount St Joseph Seminary in California. The Congregation also conducts foreign missions to India, the Philippines, Poland, Romania, Slovakia and several countries in South America.

JOSEPH, ORDER OF ST

Defunct
Anglican (male) founded in England in 1866 by the Revd R. Tuke (later Fr Basil)
Original habit: Franciscan style.

When its founder converted to Roman Catholicism in 1867, less than a year after its foundation, the Order of St Joseph became defunct. The Congregation began in some rented cottages in East Grinstead, Sussex, opposite the entrance to St Margaret's Convent. Many men applied to join, with some taking up the communal life while others continued with their daytime work, returning to the community in the evenings. The members followed the Rule of St Augustine, even though the habit was distinctly Franciscan, and ran classes for men and boys. They were also responsible for opening a small orphanage.

JOSEPH, POOR SISTERS OF ST

Location: Argentina (Buenos Aires)
RC (female) founded in Argentina in 1880
Abbr: PSSJ

A Pontifical Congregation which had its beginnings in Argentina and now has an American presence in Bethlehem and Reading, both in Pennsylvania, and in Alexandria, Vermont. The work of the Sisters is concerned with parish ministries, hospital work and day care centres.

JOSEPH, RELIGIOUS DAUGHTERS OF ST

Location: Mexico (Mexico City)
RC (female) founded in Spain in 1875
Abbr: FSJ

A Pontifical Congregation founded in Gerona, Spain, which has undertaken an apostolate among working people and labourers. There are houses in Spain, Portugal, Italy, the USA and Africa.

JOSEPH, SERVANTS OF ST

Location: Italy (Rome)
RC (female) founded in Spain in 1874
Abbr: SSJ

A Pontifical Congregation founded at Salamanca, Spain, in an effort to help the poor and marginalized working classes, especially through teaching and helping with social services, missions and the provision of hostels for young working women. An American foundation was made in 1957, but the majority of members work in Spain and Italy, with missions in the Philippines, South America, Cuba, Africa and Papua New Guinea.

JOSEPH, SISTERS OF ST – St Hyacinthe

Location: Canada (St Hyacinthe, Quebec)
RC (female) founded in Canada in 1877 by Louis-Zephirin Moreau

A Congregation founded by the bishop of St Hyacinthe to provide Sisters for teaching and catechesis in schools within his diocese and to work with the sick. Its diocesan status was confirmed in 1882.

JOSEPH, SISTERS OF ST – Tarbes

Location: France (Cantaous, Tarbes)
RC (female) founded in France in 1844
Abbr: SJT

A Congregation which came into being when six young women in the town of Cantaous simultaneously felt the call to the religious life. Their first thought, that they should all become contemplatives, changed as they realized that they were called to an active life which was fuelled by the contemplative model. They undertook both teaching and nursing responsibilities, and in 1886 the Venezuelan government persuaded the Congregation to send some of its Sisters to Venezuela, where they worked in hospitals and established several schools, especially at Caracas, Valencia and Puerto Cabello. Sisters from this Congregation have worked in Peru and Colombia, and also in India, from which community some Sisters went to England in 1957 to help staff parish schools in the Wolverhampton area, where they have now set up an independent Roman Catholic primary school dedicated to St Joseph. Missionary work has now been expanded to Africa, where the Sisters work in Kenya.

JOSEPH, THE WORKING BROTHERS OF ST

Defunct
Episcopalian Church – Anglican (male) founded in the USA in 1935 by Br Francis Anthony
Original habit: a black tunic, scapular and hood with a black leather belt; a rosary was worn at the waist.

A defunct Brotherhood founded at Peekskill, New York, as a community of laymen who were interested in an active religious life through manual labour, which encompassed the care and renovation of Church property, music and liturgical artwork of all kinds as well as parish visiting. The Brothers followed the Rule of St Benedict.

✠ Brothers of St Joseph

JOSEPH CALASANZIO, CONGREGATION OF THE CHRISTIAN WORKERS OF ST

Location: Austria (Vienna)
RC (male) founded in Austria in 1889 by Fr Anton Maria Schwartz
Abbr: C.Op.

The members of the Congregation, which was founded in Vienna, work principally with the care of those in need, running associations for working men, elementary and trade schools, catechetical centres and oratories.

JOSEPH OF MURIALDO, CONGREGATION OF ST

Location: Italy (Rome)
RC (male) founded in Italy in 1873 by St Leonard Murialdo (canonized 1970).
Abbr: CSJ

A Congregation founded in Turin by Leonard Murialdo. The initial name was the Society of St Joseph, but this later changed to its present name. Papal approbation was received in 1904. The founder had always been interested in providing help for young people who needed to acquire skills that fitted them for the workplace. The Congregation soon spread to other places in Italy, and an American foundation was made in 1951 with houses in Cleveland, Ohio and Los Angeles, California. Associated with the priests and Brothers of this Congregation are the Murialdine Sisters, who work with the children of underprivileged families. Mission work is carried out in South America and India, and the Congregation continues its work in Italy, Albania and Romania.

JOSEPH OF NAZARETH, SISTERHOOD OF ST

Defunct
Episcopalian – Anglican (female) founded in the USA in 1892

This community was based in Bronxville, New York, and was incorporated in 1892. It had as its principal object the performance of works of charity, especially through the teaching and training of young people. To this end the Sisters ran St Martha's Training School, for girls 'of good character'.

JOSEPH OF PEACE, SISTERS OF ST

Location: USA (Washington, DC)
RC (female) founded in England in 1884
Abbr: CSJP
Original habit: a black tunic and scapular with a

white wimple, black veil and leather cincture. A rosary is worn and a silver ring, which is given at final profession.

A Pontifical Congregation founded by Margaret Anna Cusack in Nottingham, England. Miss Cusack was a convert from Anglicanism and had been for a long time a member of the Poor Clares Congregation in Kenmare, County Kerry, Ireland. She was a prolific writer of spiritual works, including many biographies, but she became interested in issues of reform and justice, especially for the people of Ireland who had suffered in the great famines of the 1840s. Her writings attracted some unwelcome attention, and she was persuaded to leave Kenmare and found her own community, the Congregation of St Joseph of Peace. The purpose of the Congregation was to provide training for young women so that they could secure employment in domestic situations, but the apostolate widened to include catechesis and instruction for potential converts, visiting the sick, caring for orphans and the blind and general teaching. The American Bishop Wigger of Newark, New Jersey, was very interested in the training of young women for useful work and invited the Sisters to Newark in order that they could help with the work. The Congregation has set up many houses throughout the USA, where the Sisters undertake many education, health and care ministries as well as conducting retreats. They also have houses in Canada, England, Ireland and Haiti.

JOSEPH OF ST MARK, SISTERS OF ST

Location: France (Colmar)
RC (female) founded in France in 1845 by Fr Peter Blank and Mother Mary Xavier (Salomea Neff)
Abbr: SJSM

A French Diocesan Congregation which went to the USA in 1937 and became estab-lished at Louisville, Ohio. The superior-generalate is in France, with an American mother house at Euclid, Ohio. There are few Sisters working in the USA, their work being concerned with nursing, dietetics, health technology, social service and general administration in their special fields.

JOSEPH OF THE APPARITION, SISTERS OF ST

Location: France (Fontenay-sous-Bois)
RC (female) founded in France in 1832 by St Emily de Vialar (canonized 1951)
Abbr: SJA
Original habit: a black tunic, veil and cloak with a tight-fitting white, frilled cap, a large white collar and a silver cross around the neck.

The founder of the Congregation, the well-born Emily de Vialar, thought that she might have a religious vocation, and when she received an inheritance from her grandfather she bought a house at Gaillac, in the Languedoc, for herself and three companions, and from here they began to care for the sick and the poor and teach young children. The archbishop of Albi granted permission for the postulants, by now twelve in number, to be clothed in a religious habit and to be known as the Congregation of St Joseph of the Apparition. The term 'apparition' refers to St Joseph's vision and the angelic message. The Congregation with its Rule was approved in 1835, with papal approbation following in 1862. Houses were founded in Algiers, Bône, Tunis, Malta and Constantine, but the Algerian missions had to be abandoned because of difficulties with the local bishop. Foundations were made in England, Ireland, North America, the Near and Far East and Australia. The Sisters continue to be concerned with education, and with helping the poor, the sick and the dying as well as caring for orphans.

JOSEPH OF THE SACRED HEART, SOCIETY OF ST

Location: USA (Baltimore, Maryland)
RC (male) founded in England in 1866 by Fr (later Cardinal) Vaughan; American foundation made in 1892
Abbr: SSJ
Original habit: as for secular clergy, but with a sash into which a crucifix is tucked.

The origin of the Congregation lies in England, in the area of Mill Hill, London. Members were to be secular priests and lay Brothers who wanted to undertake foreign missionary work. Four young priests from Mill Hill went to America in 1871, where they established a house at Baltimore, Maryland, and began to care for the spiritual needs of the coloured Roman Catholic parish of St Francis Xavier's Church. Further foundations were made and missions conducted in the southern states. The American branch became independent of the Mill Hill foundation in 1892. The Congregation now works within the Afro-American community, through educational, pastoral and social ministries. They are represented in nearly seventy parishes and missions.

✠ Josephites
   St Joseph's Society for Coloured Missions

JOSEPH OF THE SACRED HEART OF JESUS, SISTERS OF ST

Location: Australia (North Sydney, New South Wales)
RC (female) founded in South Australia in 1866 by Fr Julian Tenison Woods and Blessed Mary MacKillop (Mother Mary of the Cross; beatified 1995)
Original habit: a brown habit and veil, with a dark blue monogram embroidered on the habit.

Mary MacKillop (1842–1909) was employed as a governess at Penola, South Australia, when she became aware of the growing need for the religious education of young children in the country districts, an

opinion shared by Fr Woods. He drew up the first Rule of the Congregation in 1867, the year in which Mary made her profession, taking the name of Mother Mary of the Cross. Numerous difficulties presented themselves, not least from the hierarchy, but the Congregation survived and grew and the Sisters, affectionately known as Brown Joeys, became a legend in Australia. Indefatigable in their efforts and enthusiasm, the Sisters cared for orphans, ran hospitals, housed women at risk and undertook numerous other works of charity. Their work knows no denominational boundary and the Sisters are found today throughout Australia.

✠ Brown Joeys (Australian usage)
   Bush Sisters
   Josephites

JOSEPH OF THE THIRD ORDER OF ST FRANCIS, SISTERS OF ST

Location: USA (South Bend, Indiana)
RC (female) founded in the USA in 1901 by Mother Mary Felicia and Mother Mary Clare
Abbr: SSJ(TOSF)
Original habit: Franciscan in style.

A Pontifical Congregation founded at Stevens Point, Wisconsin. The Sisters provide education at all levels from elementary to college, and work in health care and pastoral ministries throughout the USA. They also have missions in Peru, Puerto Rico and Brazil.

JOSEPH THE WORKER, SISTERS OF ST

Location: USA (Walton, Kentucky)
RC (female) founded in the USA in 1973
Abbr: SJW
Original habit: a black, calf-length dress with a half scapular, a black veil with a white turn-back and a white collar; a crucifix is worn on a chain over the scapular.

A Diocesan Congregation founded in the diocese of Covington, Kentucky, and approved by the Holy See in 1974. The Congregation began with eighteen professed Sisters from another Congregation who, after a period of reflection lasting some three years, decided to make a new foundation. Within the dioceses of Covington and Lexington the Sisters are responsible for the education of young people, the care of the elderly, catechesis, social services, domestic and dietary work in community institutions and secretarial functions. The Sisters also maintain a nursing facility in Versailles, Kentucky. The mother house and novitiate, together with an elementary school, are in Walton, Kentucky.

JOSEPHITE FATHERS

Location: Belgium (Melle, Ghent)
RC (male) founded in Belgium in 1817 by Canon Konstanz van Crombrugghe
Abbr: CJ
Original habit: a black cassock and sash.

A Congregation founded at Grammont, in the diocese of Ghent, Belgium. The first house, known as 'Jerusalem', was set up under the patronage of St Joseph. The aim of the Congregation was to work among the poor on account of the great poverty that was around them. The members taught people how to weave in order that they might use the skill to support their families. So successful was their work that the Congregation attracted many members and had to expand. The enterprise was interrupted by Dutch governmental red tape (Belgium was at that time united with The Netherlands) and the Brothers dispersed. It was not until Belgium's independence in 1830 that the work was resumed. Under Fr Ignatius van den Bossche, the first superior-general, the Congregation expanded and schools and colleges were opened, the two main ones at Louvain and Melle, where a grant of land enabled the establishment of

a commercial education college. A foundation was made in England, in 1869, with the opening of St George's College at Croydon, which later moved to Weybridge, in Surrey. The American foundation, with a headquarters at Santa Maria, California, dates from 1963, and its members work in parishes, schools and hospitals. An African mission is also maintained, in Kenya.

✠ Sons of St Joseph

JULIAN OF NORWICH, ORDER OF

Location: USA (Waukesha, Wisconsin)
Episcopalian (male and female) founded in the USA in 1982 by Fr John-Julian Swanson
Abbr: OJN
Original habit: long black tunic, blue hooded scapular for monks and a wimple and long veil for Sisters.

This semi-enclosed, contemplative Order was legally founded in 1982 in the USA, in Norwich, Connecticut, following its founder's pilgrimage to the Julian Shrine in Norwich, England. Fr Swanson drew up a Rule based on that of the Benedictines, and with his bishop's permission to profess life vows before the Visitor Bishop and to receive postulants. This rule provided for double communities, whose members practise and teach silent and intercessory prayer while observing the usual three vows of religion, poverty, chastity and obedience, with an additional fourth vow which binds them to a life of prayer. The communities occupy themselves additionally with gardening, housework and the provision of hospitality for guests as well as spiritual direction for affiliated Oblates and Associates. A move was made from Norwich, Connecticut, to Racine, Wisconsin, in 1988, and a monastery was later founded at Waukesha, Wisconsin, in 1991, with a branch house established in Eastman, Wisconsin, in 1999.

K

KAISERSWERTH ALLIANCE

Location: Germany (Kaiserswerth, Düsseldorf)
Lutheran (female) founded in Germany in 1836 by
Pastor Theodore Fliedner

The Lutheran Alliance of Deaconess Communities, which is now spread throughout the world, was founded in the German Rhineland by Theodore Fliedner (1800–64), the Lutheran pastor of Kaiserswerth who acted as prison chaplain in Düsseldorf and became most concerned about the prisoners' welfare. His first wife, Friederike, was of great help in getting a society started whose members not only could argue for better prison conditions, but, as women, could help especially with the rehabilitation of female ex-prisoners. During a trip to England, Pastor Fliedner met the prison reformer Elizabeth Fry, who encouraged his interest in prison reform and visited Kaiserswerth in 1840. The work extended into visiting and nursing the poor in their own homes and caring for destitute children. The plight of the very poor, faced with the harsh and inadequate hospital conditions of the day, worsened during the outbreaks of cholera which reached Europe in the early 19th century and made the work all the more necessary. A training school for nurses was later opened in Kaiserswerth, and in 1845 a trained matron and several nurses were sent to staff the German Hospital in London at a time when such training was unknown in England. The community gradually took shape, and foundations were made in Berlin, Hamburg, Dresden and Frankfurt. Fliedner visited the Middle East in 1851 following the death of Friederike, exploring the possibilities for making more foundations there. The Kaiserswerth influence was growing, and their good medical practice was continued with great success. The Second World War broke up many of the foundations, but there has been much recovery and today the Alliance exists throughout the world. The work undertaken by the Deaconesses is varied and includes parish ministries, hospital work, the care of the elderly, the administration of hostels and guest houses, the making and selling of church furnishings and the running of bookshops.

✠ Kaiserswerth Deaconess Community

KATHARINE OF EGYPT, COMMUNITY OF ST

Defunct
Anglican (female) founded in England in 1879 by
Pauline Mary Grancille (Sr Pauline Mary)
Abbr: CSK

The founder, Pauline Grancille, made her novitiate with the Community of St Mary the Virgin, at Wantage, in Oxfordshire and was clothed there as a novice with a view to founding her own community. She was professed in 1880 and formed a very small community of three, at Earls Court, London. Their first major work was to begin an orphanage, followed by a House of Rest, which they opened at Tunbridge Wells in Kent. As their numbers increased, other houses were opened, at Bexhill-on-Sea, Sussex and Padstow, Cornwall. After the Second World War, which dispersed many of the Sisters, they reassembled in 1945 at Haslemere, Surrey, where a Boarding House for Ladies (in reduced circumstances) was opened. As this work grew, larger premises were found at Henley-on-Thames, where retreats were also undertaken. The attempt to rebuild the community was not successful, however, and it is now defunct.

✠ Community of St Katharine of Alexandria
Community of St Katharine of Fulham

KINGSHIP OF CHRIST, MISSIONARIES OF THE

Location: USA (Dittmer, Missouri, for males; Silver Spring, Maryland, for females)
RC (male and female) founded in Italy in 1919 by Fr Agostino Gemelli
Abbr: SIM

A Secular Institute based on Franciscan spirituality, with separate provision for male and female members. Originally designed just for women, it was founded at Assisi, Italy, by Agostino Gemelli, a Franciscan, and Armida Barelli, who was very active in the female branch of Catholic Action, where she organized places for Italian women in politics. Fr Gemelli, her spiritual director, had worked to reconcile the Roman Catholic faith with modern culture and went on to found the Catholic University at Milan in 1921. The apostolate of the Institute is to work in the field of Catholic action by promoting the doctrine of the kingship of Christ, the cultivation of Eucharistic devotion, the publication of spiritual works and the provision of protective housing for women at risk. There is no community life, members fulfilling their apostolate in their daily lives and maintaining a presence in some twenty countries worldwide. Approval from Rome was granted in 1953, the same year in which the first five American missionaries were professed.

KNOT, KNIGHTS OF THE

Defunct
RC (male Equestrian) founded in the 14th century
Original habit: a dark red-purple, floor-length gown, which was open and sleeveless, with a dark red cap. A cord of purple and gold intertwined threads was wound around the left arm, above and below the elbow, and tied with a knot.

This Chivalric honour was granted by one of the Avignon Popes, Clement VI, to commemorate the coronation in Naples, by the papal legate, of King Louis (Prince of Taranto and Achaia) and his wife, Queen Joan I, in 1352. Membership was limited to sixty (some authorities say seventy) noblemen, who undertook to observe the Rule of St Basil, defend the faith and promise obedience to the king of Naples.

L

LA SALETTE FATHERS

Location: Italy (Rome)
RC (male) founded in France in 1858
Abbr: MS

The apparition of Our Lady at La Salette, near Grenoble, in 1845 to two little shepherds, Melanie Calvat (Mathieu) and Maximin Giraud, began pilgrimages to the shrine and to the church which had been built where the visions took place. By 1852 the number of pilgrims making the journey called for the formation of a group of priests to take care of them. A group was formed and a small community was established which received diocesan approval in 1876 and papal approval in 1890. Some five missionaries and fifteen students for the priesthood from this Congregation went to the USA in 1892, initially to Hartford, Connecticut, but later spreading to other parts of America. In 1902 the La Salette Fathers opened houses in Canada, in Quebec, and Saskaatchewan, and foreign missions were set up in Burma, the Philippines, Argentina, Madagascar and Bolivia. The Missionaries of La Salette also undertake parish duties, run retreats and chaplaincies and provide counselling.

✠ Missionaries of Our Lady of La Salette

LAMB OF GOD, KNIGHTS OF THE

Defunct
RC (male Equestrian Order) founded in Sweden in the 16th century
Original habit: a silk girdle secured above the right hip and an elaborate collar made up of alternating images of the Seraphim and of crowned wreaths. At the centre of the collar was a medallion showing the risen Christ with the words 'Deus Protector Noster' (God Our Protector), supported on either side by a pair of angels. From the medallion hung a pendant of the Lamb of God.

An Order of Chivalry bestowed on some members of the court of King John III of Sweden to commemorate his coronation. John III, who had married a Polish Catholic, Catherine Jagellon, was anxious to reconcile the Swedish Lutheran Church with the Holy See, as well as to revive the use of some of the discarded parts of the Roman Catholic liturgy in Sweden. He succeeded in this, introducing what has become known as the 'Red Book', containing a liturgy of his own, in 1577.

LAMB OF GOD, SISTERS OF THE

Location: France (Brest)
RC (female) founded in France in 1945
Abbr: AD

A Diocesan Congregation, its members mainly in France but also present in Kentucky, USA, where a foundation was made in 1958 as a house of formation for future American Sisters. The Congregation is innovative in that it provides a possibility for women with physical disabilities to consider a vocation to the religious life, which is denied by most other Orders. The work of the Sisters varies according to each one's abilities and the needs of the diocese.

LAUDUS, CANONS REGULAR OF ST

Defunct
RC (male) founded in France in the 12th century by Hugh of Amiens
Original habit: a full-length violet cape, with violet mozetta and hood in winter, worn over a white cassock and rochet.

The priory of the Order of the Canons Regular of St Laudus was in the centre of the city of Rouen, its erection attributed to St Mellonius, the reputedly Welsh-born first bishop of Rouen who died in 314. The original priory church was dedicated to the Holy Trinity, but its name was later changed to that of St Laudus, the 6th-century bishop of Coutances, Normandy, because his relics were enshrined in the church. The canons regular were established there by the archbishop of Rouen, Hugh of Amiens, in 1144, and later confirmed in a Bull of Blessed Pope Eugenius III (1145–53).

✠ Canons of St Laudo
   Canons of St Lo

LAURENCE, BROTHERHOOD OF ST

Defunct
Anglican (male) founded in Australia in 1930
Original habit: secular.

The St Laurence Brotherhood, part of the Australian Bush Brotherhood which has become inactive, originated in Newcastle, New South Wales, and moved to Fitzroy,

Victoria, where the Brothers managed hostels for single unemployed men as well as a foundation in the country where they provided opportunities for training unemployed men in skills that would allow them to become self-supporting. It is now defunct.

LAURENCE, COMMUNITY OF ST

Location: England (Belper, Derbyshire)
Anglican (female) founded in England in 1874 by the Revd E. A. Hilyard
Abbr: CSL

An Anglican community which was founded in Norfolk, in the parish of St Laurence at Norwich. The founder was a well-known conductor of retreats and a mission priest, who saw a need for a religious community which would help the poor. Some like-minded women, including Ellen Lee, who later became the first superior, answered his call and went to Belper, in Derbyshire, there being much poverty in this cotton mill area. The community was approved by the bishop of Lichfield, who helped in the drawing up of the community's Rule and Statutes. The Sisters' work expanded to include the care of the elderly and of incurable invalids. They also run retreats for associates of their community, members of the Guild of the Good Shepherd, and for any women who wish to make a retreat. A rest home which was opened for the benefit of clergy and their families in Scarborough, Yorkshire, has since closed. The community's motto, 'Christo in Pauperibus' (With Christ Among the Poor), succinctly describes the ethos of the community, whose work is now mainly in the parish, but the Sisters continue to conduct retreats and quiet days.

LAZARUS AND OUR LADY OF MOUNT CARMEL, KNIGHTS OF ST

Defunct

RC (male Equestrian Order) founded in France in 1608

Original habit: (insignia) a purple cross in the centre of which is a small medallion of the Virgin Mary. The cross is embroidered on the mantle, and a similar cross in metal is worn around the neck.

An Equestrian Order founded by Henry IV of France (1553–1610) as a Military Order under the name of the Order of Our Lady of Mount Carmel, its members sworn to defend Roman Catholicism and to fight heresy. Aspiring knights had to be of proven nobility by descent and be free to marry. The income of the Order was drawn from ecclesiastical properties. In 1608 the Order united with that of St Lazarus of Jerusalem (see next entry), an arrangement which fused the name, prestige and property of the Order of St Lazarus of Jerusalem with the impeccable status of the Knights of Our Lady of Mount Carmel. When the union was effected, the octagonal cross of the Order of St Lazarus was quartered with the colours of each Order, purple and green, and remained like this until 1778, when it changed back to green alone.

LAZARUS OF JERUSALEM, ORDER OF ST

Location: Worldwide

RC (male Equestrian Order) founded in Jerusalem in the 12th century

Original habit: a black habit with a green, eight-pointed cross on the left-hand side (the cross does not appear to have been adopted until the 16th century).

A Military Order which evolved from the Hospital for Lepers in Jerusalem in the 12th century, possibly created by a Bull of Pope Paschal II in 1115, and which cared for and defended lepers. It was made mandatory for leprous knights to enter the Order, whether willing or not, and their wives, sick or healthy, had to follow their husbands; these couples were then obliged to observe chastity. By the start of the 13th century, the Order had been transformed into a knightly militia although the hospitaller role remained the most important part of their activities. In 1243, with the fall of Jerusalem, the Order moved its headquarters to Acre, where it had its Tower of Lazarus in the northern suburb of Montmusard, from which the Order defended that area of the city. Acre fell in 1291, and the Order moved to Cyprus, abandoned its military activities and kept only to the hospitaller role. The Order continued until the late Renaissance, when it underwent a revival in Savoy and France. The French branch was united in 1608 with the newly created Order of Our Lady of Mount Carmel to become the Order of Our Lady of Mount Carmel and St Lazarus. The union prospered and there were at one time over one hundred and forty commanderies of knights, who were prepared to do battle against the English and had warships at the ready. In 1790 the Order was virtually suppressed, and by the time of the French Association Laws at the start of the 20th century, it had become, with the approval of Pope Pius XI, the Association of Hospitallers of St Lazarus, a Congregation noted for its charitable rather than its martial ethos. Today, the Order is still in existence, still involved in the care of lepers, especially in New Zealand, where it is directly involved in Pacific area programmes against leprosy, and in working on many humanitarian projects. In Europe the Order maintains a presence as a volunteer ambulance corps. Other valuable work is carried on in the USA, targeting leprosy sufferers in South America, and the Order recently contributed medical aid to earthquake victims in Italy and Central America. The Order runs a hospice for the terminally ill in Edinburgh and is recognized by the EU as a humanitarian organization.

✠ Hospitallers of St Lazarus
　Knights of St Lazarus

LEGIONARIES OF CHRIST

Location: Italy (Rome)
RC (male) founded in Mexico in 1941 by Fr Marcial Maciel
Abbr: LC
Original habit: secular.

A Congregation founded in Mexico in 1941, while the founder was still a seminarian, and in the USA in 1965. It has attracted many priests and recruited some two and a half thousand seminarians. The Legionaries are found throughout the USA, South America, Canada, much of Europe, and Australia. Their work is to involve the lay apostolate with the education of the young, to conduct missions, work for the needs of the poor, provide catechesis and work with the media.

LÉRINS, THE ABBEY OF

Location: France (Îles de Lérins, Cannes)
RC (male) founded in France in the 5th century by St Honoratus
Abbr: OCist
Original habit: this varied at different times, but a Cistercian habit is now worn.

The present abbey, which is in the hands of the Congregation of the Cistercians of the Immaculate Conception, was founded in the 5th century on the Îles de Lérins in the Mediterranean. Its founder, St Honoratus, was a pagan who converted to Christianity, eventually becoming archbishop of Arles. He had once lived as a hermit at Lérins, attracting many followers. A foundation of monks living in community, together with some anchorites living in cells, was established and became an important influence

on the area, with such a good reputation for its schools of mysticism and theology that many later bishops, including St Hilary and St Caesarius at Arles, Eucherius at Lyons and Maximus at Riez, had all at one time been members of the Lérins Congregation. From the 7th century, the monks at Lérins observed the Benedictine Rule. By the 11th century the foundation, which had suffered setbacks from Saracen action, began to grow in prosperity, receiving gifts and privileges from the popes and the French kings. Reform in time became necessary because of a growing laxity, but the decline continued and led to suppression at the end of the 16th century. Restoration was undertaken in 1868, when the abbey of Lérins became part of the Cistercian Congregation of Senanque of the Mean Observance. They are now known as the Congregation of the Immaculate Conception, approved in 1867.

LIFE, SISTERS OF

Location: USA (The Bronx, New York City)
RC (female) founded in the USA in 1991 by Cardinal O'Connor of New York
Abbr: SV
Original habit: a white tunic with a cincture and a rosary worn on the left-hand side, a black scapular and shoulder cape and a white veil and collar; a medallion is worn around the neck.

A Public Association whose members observe the Rule of St Augustine and undertake the usual vows of poverty, chastity and obedience, with an extra vow to protect the sanctity of human life. The community observes a mixed contemplative and active religious life. In order to fulfil the charism of the community, the Sisters aim to provide housing and shelter for pregnant and vulnerable women, to run clinics along pro-life lines, provide counselling for those who have had abortions and make available educational packages from the Dr Joseph R. Stanton Human Life Issues Library and Resource Center. At present the community is restricted to the archdiocese of New York.

LILY, KNIGHTS OF THE

Defunct
RC (male) Equestrian Order founded in Navarre in the 10th century by Garcia the Great
Original habit: (insignia) a double chain in gold from which hung a pendant engraved with a crowned Lily of the Valley.

An Order of knights founded under Garcia the Great (992–1035) in thanksgiving for the prosperity which came to Navarre, largely through the efforts of his father, Garcia Sanchez the Trembler, who had set the Moors to rout. The knights had the privilege of wearing a special lily-of-the-valley medallion and were expected to observe the Rule of St Basil, and to recite the rosary of the Blessed Virgin Mary. Little is known about this Order.

✠ Knights of the Lily of the Valley

LITTLE ONES, SISTERS OF THE

Location: Belgium (Antwerp)
RC (female) founded in Belgium in 1910 by Madame Adelin van de Werve and Canon Edward Moeremans
Abbr: SLO
Original habit: a blue habit with a blue veil lined with white and a white wimple and bonnet. A double-sided silver medal with an engraving of Our Lady of Sorrows on one side and a chalice and host on the other is worn on a chain around the neck.

A small Congregation founded in Antwerp, when Canon Moeremans realized the value of Madame van de Werve's existing charitable work in caring for the young, which had started some years before. He gained approval for the foundation, which is dedi-cated to the care of little children from a few days old to around seven years of age. Madame van de Werve and the first postulants travelled to England in 1910 to stay with the Sisters of Charity of Jesus and Mary in Bury, Lancashire, and began their religious formation with them. It was not until 1919 that the Congregation was able to establish its mother house in Borgerhout, near Antwerp, and in 1926 was officially approved by Rome. The Sisters run two residential homes and a day centre for abandoned children in Belgium, and they are also established in Liverpool, England, where the Sisters work in co-operation with the Social Services Department to care for mentally handicapped people, the deaf and children in need.

LITTLE SCHOOLS, SISTERS OF THE

Location: France (Parame, Rennes)
RC (female) founded in France in 1853 by Amélie Fristel
Original habit: a black habit and veil with a white collar and coif, a woollen girdle with attached rosary, and a crucifix around the neck.

The Sisters of the Little Schools was founded at Paramé by Amélie Fristel, who had gathered together some companions a few years before to care for elderly men, opening a home, Notre Dame des Chênes, for the purpose. The work expanded, and the Sisters now teach in elementary and junior schools as well as still caring for the elderly in Belgium, The Netherlands, the Channel Islands and Canada, where they have houses at Halifax and Ste Marie.

✠ Sisters of the Junior Schools
  Sisters of the Oaks
  Sisters of the Sacred Hearts of Jesus and
    Mary

LIVING WORD, SISTERS OF THE

Location: USA (Arlington Heights, Illinois)
RC (female) founded in the USA in 1975 by
Annamarie Cook
Abbr: SLW

The purpose of this Diocesan Institute, which was founded by Annamarie Cook and some ninety other women, was to try to re-examine the nature and charism of the religious life. The founding meeting, in August 1975, produced an outline, or proposed Constitution, followed by an interim Constitution. Five members of the leadership team lived at St Gregory's Convent, Chicago, but in 1985 new premises were acquired at Arlington Heights, which is now the Congregation's headquarters. Approval by Rome was granted in 1995, and the Congregation is now to be found in many parts of the USA, including Chicago, Los Angeles, New Orleans, St Louis, St Paul and Minneapolis. The Sisters worked initially in education, but it was later felt that other ministries should be sought that were in keeping with the talents and experience of members of the community. Their apostolate has now extended to encompass work with the poor and oppressed, the homeless, the illiterate, the elderly and the housebound.

LOCHES, HOSPITALLERS OF

Defunct
RC (female) founded in France in 1621

A group of hospitallers, drawn together by Susanne Dubois, a member of the Hôtel-Dieu of Paris. The foundation was made at Loches, a town north of Poitiers in the west of France. The hospitallers were to be of both sexes, living a communal life under the Rule of St Augustine and vowed to perpetual chastity and the service of the sick and poor. From this foundation some seventeen other convents were derived, at Cler-mont, Riom and elsewhere in France, but the Congregation is now defunct.

LORD JESUS CHRIST, DISCIPLES OF THE

Location: USA (Channing, Texas)
RC (female) founded in the USA in 1972
Abbr: DLJC

A Diocesan Institute, founded in 1972, whose members follow a Franciscan community life of contemplation and support for an active apostolate of retreat work, parish missions and youth retreats as well as providing opportunities for Bible study in vacation schools. The Sisters also undertake mission work in Alexandria, Louisiana.

LORETTO AT THE FOOT OF THE CROSS, SISTERS OF

Location: USA (Nerinx, Kentucky)
RC (female) founded in the USA in 1812
Abbr: SL

The Loretto community was founded in the USA by the Belgian-born priest Charles Nerinckx, often called 'the apostle of Kentucky', with the help of Fr Stephen Badin. At first the community was known as the Little Society of the Friends of Mary at the Foot of the Cross, and it arose from the perceived need for Roman Catholic education for the children of the colonists of Kentucky. Three young women in the area, Mary Rhodes, Christina Stewart and Anne Havern, had opened a log-cabin school, and they were encouraged by Charles Nerinckx to adopt the religious life, clothed as the first novices of the new Congregation in April 1812. Two others, Anne Rhodes and Sarah Havern, followed, the former becoming the first superior until her early death in December 1812, having been given permission to pronounce her vows just three days earlier. She was succeeded by Mary Rhodes. The Sisters observed a fairly austere Rule of life but attracted more postulants.

The Congregation was approved in 1907, and branch houses were founded. Today, the Sisters are heavily involved in education at all levels, including that for children with special needs; they teach in seminaries, conduct pastoral ministries, care for the elderly and aged, nurse, run conflict resolution and justice and peace ministries and conduct retreats. As well as a strong presence in the USA there is a mission in Ghana and participation in an ecumenical partnership of men and women who share ministries in many American States and in six foreign countries.

✠ Loretto Community

LOUIS, SISTERS OF ST

Location: Ireland (Rathgar, Dublin)
RC (female) founded in France in 1842 by Abbé Louis-Eugène-Marie Bautain and the Baroness de Vaux (Mother Thérèse of the Cross)
Abbr: SSL
Original habit: a black habit and cape, with a black veil over a headdress, and a black cord girdle; a small black cross is worn around the neck on a black silk ribbon.

This Congregation, which is often confused with that of the Sisters of Charity of St Louis, was founded at Juilly, near Paris, and approved in 1844. Some young women from Ireland went to France and joined the Congregation, some of them returning to Ireland in 1859 at the request of the bishop of Clogher, who needed teachers for the schools in his diocese. The Irish foundations later became independent, with their own Constitutions approved in 1938. Boarding and day schools were opened as well as a poor school, orphanages and a vocational training school. The Sisters have expanded their work in education and are also concerned with nursing, the giving of retreats, parish ministries and chaplaincy work in hospitals and prisons. Houses are

to be found in France, Belgium, England, California, Nigeria, Ghana and Brazil. The American foundation, in California, dates from 1949.

✠ Sisters of St Juilly
   Sisters of St Louis – Monaghan

LOVE OF CHRIST, THE BROTHERHOOD OF THE

Defunct
Anglican (male) founded in England in 1929 by the Revd W. S. A. Robertson
Original habit: secular.

This Brotherhood was founded by Fr Algy Robertson as the English branch of the Christa Seva Sangha, a Franciscan-style community in India. Fr Algy had been forced by ill-health to return to England from India, where he had been a novice at Poona. His aim in founding the English branch was that men could train there for work in India. Fr Robertson made his life profession in the Society of St Francis, at Cerne Abbas, in Dorset, England, in 1937.

LOVE OF GOD, COMMUNITY OF SISTERS OF THE

Location: England (Fairacres, Oxford)
Anglican (female) founded in England in 1906
Abbr: SLG
Original habit: a brown Carmelite habit with a black veil.

A contemplative Anglican community which is reminiscent of a Carmelite foundation but with certain differences. It owes its origin to Fr George Seymour Hollings, SSJE The first foundation was made in 1906 in Oxford, in a small terraced house in Leopold Street, but was later housed at Fairacres, off the Iffley Road, Oxford, where the Sisters observed a simple Rule of life. After the death of Fr Hollings a new Rule was drawn up by his successor, Fr Lucius Cary, which received the approval of the bishop of Oxford, Charles Gore. The building of the convent at Fairacres was completed in 1923, and other foundations were made, at Hemel Hempstead, Hertfordshire, in 1928, and Burwash, Sussex, in 1935. Plans to establish a foundation at Ain Karim, the birthplace of St John the Baptist, did not come to fruition because of the political and military troubles that followed after 1939. Today, the community continues its contemplative life and provides opportunities for retreats. The Sisters also produce pamphlets and books on spirituality and prayer.

LOVE OF GOD, SISTERS OF THE

Location: Spain (Madrid)
RC (female) founded in Spain in 1864 by Fr Usera

A Congregation founded at Toro, Spain, inspired by the experiences of Fr Usera from his time in the West Indies, when he realized that in order to teach the poor and needy from childhood through to adulthood a band of dedicated Sisters was needed. With the help of St Mary Michaela Desmaisières (1809–65), who had founded the Handmaids of the Blessed Sacrament and of Charity, the foundation was made, with St Mary Michaela training the first

postulants. The work today is largely in education and the running of children's homes, but the Sisters are also involved in social work, day care centres, hospitals and nursing homes, missions to immigrants and foreign missions.

LOVERS OF THE HOLY CROSS SISTERS

Location: USA (Gardena, California)
RC (female) founded in South Vietnam (Cochin China) in 1670
Abbr: LHC

A Diocesan Congregation originally founded by Bishop Pierre Lambert de la Motte, who also founded the Society of Foreign Missions of Paris in 1658. The name Annamite, or Annamites, is sometimes attached to members of this Congregation and refers to the geographical area then known as Annam, which lay east of Kampuchea, and from which the members largely came. A foundation was made in the USA in 1976 and houses are to be found in the dioceses of Los Angeles, Orange and New Orleans, where the Sisters are involved in various parish ministries, in nursing, teaching and social services.

☩ Votaries of the Cross

MACARIUS, HERMITS OF ST

Defunct

RC (male) founded in Egypt in the 4th century by St Macarius the Elder

Original habit: according to tradition the hermits wore a violet tunic with a black scapular and a small cowl and a cap covering the hair, forehead, temples and ears.

St Macarius (*c.*300–90), sometimes called 'the Elder' or 'the Egyptian', was a desert monk and a disciple of St Antony of the Desert. He gathered together a group of eremitical followers in Skete, or Sketis, in the Nitrian desert of Egypt, some sixty miles south of Alexandria, in around 330. He spent the next sixty years there, and as he was an ordained priest he was able to offer Mass for his many hermits. Legend tells us that the life of the community was very austere, with the nearest source of water several miles away, and only caves in which to sleep on beds made of rushes and reeds. The water was described by Palladius as being 'of dire colour as it might be bituminous, yet inoffensive to taste'. St Macarius the Elder should be distinguished from St Macarius of Alexandria.

MACARIUS IN EGYPT, NUNS OF ST

Defunct

RC (female) founded in Egypt (probably) in the 4th century

Original habit: by tradition a tawny tunic tied with some rope, like a cincture, with a black cape, or sheepskin, around the shoulders and some sort of head covering. A white tunic may have been worn at times, according to St Athanasius.

That there were female hermits, or nuns, attracted by the lifestyle of St Macarius in Egypt, is attested to by St Athanasius, writing in the 4th century. Little is known about them.

MADONNA HOUSE

Location: Canada (Combermere, Ontario)

RC (male and female) founded in Canada in 1947 by Catherine de Hueck Doherty

A Public Association of clerics and lay people whose members seek personal sanctification through complete dedication to Christ and to witnessing to Christ through a life of prayer and sacrifice and through acts of mercy, with a special apostolate to those most neglected by society. It was founded in Toronto, Ontario, and approved by Bishop William Smith of Toronto in 1956.

MAESTRE PIE VENERINI SISTERS

Location: Italy (Rome)

RC (female) founded in Italy in 1685 by the Blessed Rose Venerini (beatified 1952)

Abbr: MPV

Rose Venerini (1656–1728) had entered a convent intent on becoming a nun, but left in order to care for her widowed mother. Their home soon became a centre for a group of pious women from the neighbourhood who gathered there as a sodality in order to recite the rosary together. A Jesuit, Fr Ignatius Martinelli, encouraged Rose to open a free school for girls in Viterbo, her birthplace, and her success was so great that she became an adviser to the bishop when he was trying to organize education in his diocese. Despite this success, there was considerable conflict and opposition from Rome. It was only after the founder's death, in 1728, that her sodality was accorded the status of a religious Congregation. The Sisters today still work in education as well as running day nurseries. There are houses in Italy and the USA.

MAGDALEN, NUNS OF ST

Defunct
RC (female) with various foundations (see below)
Original habit: a white tunic and veil.

Magdalens were members of communities dedicated to the reform of their lives which had previously been sinful, although the group of Madgalens known as 'The White Ladies', who wore a white habit, had never been public sinners. There were several such houses, the earliest being at Metz in Germany, which is traditionally given a date of foundation of 1005, but was most likely founded in 1452. There were other German foundations, at Naumberg and Speyer, which date from the 13th century. Members of these communities observed the Rule of St Augustine, but later became affiliated with the Franciscans and Dominicans. There were Magdalen communities in Naples (14th century), Paris (16th century), Rome (16th century) and Seville (16th century). The purpose of the Magda-

len communities was later carried on in Congregations such as the Sisters of the Good Samaritan in Sydney, Australia, which was founded in 1857 and provided accommodation for penitent women, while the Sisters of Our Lady of Charity of the Good Shepherd cared not only for voluntary penitents but also for those who were sent to them by the legal authorities.
See also: MARY MAGDALEN, THE ORDER OF ST

✠ Magdalens
   White Ladies

MALTA, KNIGHTS (and DAMES) OF THE SOVEREIGN MILITARY ORDER OF

Location: Italy (Rome)
RC (male and female Equestrian Order) founded in the Holy Land in the 11th century
Original habit: knights wore a black cloak with an eight-pointed Maltese cross as decoration. Dames wore a black tunic and scapular with a white under-veil covered by a black one, and a very long black cape decorated with a white Maltese cross. The dames also wore a black and white silk chain around the neck which supported wooden images of the instruments of the Passion. (This Order must not be confused with the Venerable Order of St John, which despite wearing the same insignia and using the old priory of the Knights of Malta at Clerkenwell, London, was chartered by Queen Victoria in 1888 and is a voluntary paramedical ambulance service, its black and white uniformed members maintaining a presence at most large gatherings in the UK.)

The Knights of Malta were hospitallers attached to the hospital of St John of Jerusalem at the end of the 11th century. They were originally known as the Knights of the Order of the Hospital of St John of Jerusalem, but the Order underwent two name changes, to the Knights of Rhodes (after

1330) and the Knights of Malta (from 1530). Members took the usual three vows of religion, poverty, chastity and obedience, and their mission was to care for pilgrims in the Holy Land. Many foundations were made in Europe during the 12th century. The knights were also a military presence in the Holy Land during the times of the crusades and were defeated by the Ottomans at the fall of Jerusalem in 1187. In 1290, with the fall of Acre, they left the Holy Land and went to Cyprus, conquering Rhodes in 1309. By now the character of the Order was more military than religious in nature, and the knights were renowned for their bravery. The Order became very rich, benefiting from the dissolution of the Templars in 1312 by inheriting their wealth. A further move was made to Malta, in 1530, giving the Order the name it still bears. Today, the knights form both a religious community and an Order of Chivalry. It is organized into five grand priories and several national associations, and members are active in many fields, including representation on the Council of Europe and UNESCO; they also maintain hospitals and first-aid centres and care for war victims and refugees. The dames of the Order, whose history runs parallel to that of the knights, are now eligible to be elected to the hospitallers' governing body.

MARCELLINA, SISTERS OF ST

Defunct

RC (female) founded in Italy in 1408

A Congregation founded in Pavia, Italy, by three local women, Dorothea Morosini, Eleanora Contarini and Veronica Duodi. They were moved by the plight of the poor and sick to provide some relief. Houses were established in Lombardy and Venetia, the members following the Rule of St Augustine.

✣ Annunciates of Lombardy
  Nuns of St Ambrose

MARCELLINA, INTERNATIONAL INSTITUTE OF SISTERS OF ST

Location: Italy (Milan)

RC (female) founded in Italy in 1838 by Mgr Luigi Biraghi and Sr Marina Videmari

Abbr: MS

The Congregation was founded at Cemusco sul Naviglio, Milan, for the purpose of providing an education for young girls. The work continues today, with the Sisters working in education at all levels from kindergarten to university as well as undertaking catechesis and parish ministries and working with the elderly and those in need, including those suffering from leprosy. Mission stations are maintained, and work is carried out in hospitals in Italy, France, England, Switzerland, Brazil, Canada and Mexico.

MARGARET, SOCIETY OF ST

Location: England (East Grinstead, Surrey)

Anglican (female) founded in England in 1855 by John Mason Neale

Abbr: SSM

Original habit: a dark grey habit (since the 1960s a lighter grey habit has been adopted).

The Revd John Mason Neale, then warden of Sackville College, East Grinstead, a 17th-century foundation for the care of the old, had dreamed of forming a Sisterhood which would be able to help the sick and poor. His vision was shared by Ann Gream, the daughter of a rector, who went to the college to nurse the sick inmates. Neale drew up a Rule of life, based on that of the Visitation Order of St Francis de Sales. The training was initially taken at the Westminster Hospital in London, and in 1855 Ann Gream took her first vows and became the first mother superior of the new Congregation. The first house was opened in her home town of Rotherfield to allow Ann Gream to nurse her sick father, but the small community of just six Sisters moved back to East Grinstead following his death. Here they took charge of some orphans who had previously been under the care of John Mason Neale's sister. The work expanded, with some members working in London among the poor. A branch House, St Saviour's Priory, was opened in the Haggerston area of the city in 1866. This foundation became autonomous and is still operating, the Sisters working for people in need, especially those with AIDS and HIV. Some of the members of this community have now been ordained to the priesthood, undertaking parish ministries and giving spiritual direction. A house of refuge was opened near Aldershot, in Hampshire, in 1862, the same year seeing the start of a Scottish daughter house, St Margaret's in Aberdeen, which also became autonomous. Constitutionally, what Dr Neale had done in making this foundation was innovative. He had made two types of foundation, the mission houses and the affiliated houses. The mission houses were supplied with Sisters from East Grinstead who could be recalled at any time by the mother superior and remained members of the mother house. Affiliated houses were independent from East Grinstead and had their own superiors, novitiate and chapter. The first American affiliated house was opened in Boston, Massachusetts, in 1873, with others following. Expansion into other parts of the world took the Society of St Margaret to Sri Lanka in 1887, where schools were opened, and to South Africa in 1898. Since 1967 the term affiliated has been dropped. In 1994 a further autonomous community was established in England, at the Priory of Our Lady in Walsingham, Norfolk.

MARIAN FATHERS OF THE IMMACULATE CONCEPTION OF THE BLESSED VIRGIN MARY, CONGREGATION OF THE

Location: Italy (Rome)
RC (male) founded in Poland in 1673 by Fr Stanislaus Papczynski
Abbr: MIC

A Congregation founded at Puczcza, Korabiewska, in the diocese of Poznan by Fr Papczynski of the Clerks Regular of the Mother of God (founded 1574), as an independent branch of this Order, which was recognized in 1677 and approved in 1723 and 1787. The Rule adopted was based on that of the Annunciades. The Congregation grew quickly and its members spread throughout Poland and into Lithuania, Portugal, Spain and Italy. Political upsets in Middle and Eastern Europe had a serious effect on the Order, which declined, especially in Lithuania and Eastern Poland, until only one member survived, but with the timely intervention of Archbishop George Matulewicz at the start of the 20th century it was reconstituted and in 1910 received approbation from Pope St Pius X. Now vigorous throughout the USA, its members work in publishing, organizing retreats, arranging Marian pilgrimages, providing counselling and spiritual direction as well as undertaking foreign missions, especially to Eastern Europe, where the members work in Lithuania, Estonia, Belarus, Ukraine and Kazakhstan, and to Austria, Poland, Portugal, Germany, England, France and Rwanda.

✠ Marian Fathers

MARIAN INSTITUTE OF ST FRANCIS DE SALES

Location: USA (Fairfax, Virginia)
RC (male and female) founded in Austria in 1943 by Fr Franz Reisinger, OSFS

This Secular Institute of Pontifical Right was founded in Vienna and approved in 1964. The Institute provides for women to be professed while married, and for single males and females to become associates. The members seek their own personal sanctification within their parishes and dioceses by following the application of the spirituality of St Francis de Sales as outlined in his *Spiritual Directory*.

MARIAN SISTERS OF THE DIOCESE OF LINCOLN

Location: USA (Waverly, Nebraska)
RC (female) founded in the USA in 1954
Abbr: MS
Original habit: a grey habit and veil.

A Diocesan Congregation which was founded in Lincoln, Nebraska, when two Sisters, Sr Martha and Sr Theresa of the Mercy Sisters of St Francis in Brno, Czechoslovakia, who had taken refuge in Austria after the communist takeover of their country, responded to an invitation by the bishop of Lincoln to run St Thomas's Orphanage in the city. They were at first known as the Mercy Sisters of St Francis of the Diocese of Lincoln, but in 1961 the title changed to their present one. The Congregation soon attracted other young women, and the work was extended to include teaching. The Sisters moved from the orphanage to Waverly and their work continues in education at all levels including the teaching of mentally handicapped children, and the nursing and care of the elderly and handicapped adults.

MARIAN SOCIETY OF DOMINICAN CATECHISTS

Location: USA (Boyce, Louisiana)
RC (female) founded in the USA in 1954
Abbr: OP
Original habit: Dominican style.

The Sisters of this Diocesan Congregation, which today has fewer than ten members, work in the field of catechesis in St Margaret's Convent, Boyce, which acts as a catechetical centre.

MARIANIST SISTERS

Location: USA (San Antonio, Texas)
RC (female) founded in France in 1816 by Adèle de Batz de Trenquelleon
Abbr: FMI
Original habit: a black tunic and veil with a white head cap and a white cloak secured by means of two thin dark cords crossed over a white linen square wimple; a crucifix was worn around the neck.

This Congregation grew out of the Association formed by Adèle de Batz de Trenquelleon and several of her friends in Condom, France, and extended throughout France from 1804 to 1814. The members of the Association visited and cared for the sick, undertook catechesis of children in the area, ran a small school in the family home and cared for orphans, finding them places in foster homes and later employment. Adèle and three of her friends decided to form a religious community at Agen, France, in 1816 in an historic convent called 'The Refuge', which they rented, with other women who shared the vision joining them. Permission to wear the religious habit was granted on Christmas Eve 1816, and the Congregation of the Daughters of Mary, or Marianists, was founded. Despite many difficulties new convents were opened at Tonneins, Condom and Arbois in France. The Sisters are now to be found in France, Spain, Italy, the USA, Latin America, Japan, Korea and Africa, working in the fields of education, catechesis, parish and campus ministries, the giving of retreats and the care of the elderly.

✟ Daughters of Mary

MARIANNHILL, CONGREGATION OF MISSIONARIES OF

Location: Italy (Rome)
RC (male) founded in South Africa in 1909
Abbr: CMM
Original habit: as for secular clergy.

The Mariannhill Congregation was formed as a missionary offshoot of a Trappist (Cistercians of the Strict Observance) foundation made in Cape Colony, South Africa, in 1880 by Abbot Alfred Pfanner with members from the Maria Stern Congregation from Bosnia. Their first settlement had to be abandoned because of droughts, wind and baboon activity, and the community transferred to Mariannhill, some few miles from Durban, in Natal. The foundation here was so successful that it expanded, and other missions were set up in South Africa. It was soon clear, however, that the Cistercian Rule and missionary work were incompatible. Mariannhill became an independent Congregation in 1909 and separated from the Trappists. The abbey at Mariannhill became a collegiate church under a provost, and members of the Congregation were put under simple, but perpetual, vows. The Mariannhill Missionaries have houses throughout Europe, in the USA and Canada and still maintain their missions in South Africa, Zimbabwe, Zambia, Papua New Guinea and Mozambique.

✠ Mariannhill Brothers
  Mariannhill Fathers

MARIE, CONGREGATION OF SAINTE

Defunct
RC (female) founded in France in 1843 by Marie-Joseph Vesnat (Sr Mathilde).
(This Congregation should not be confused with that of the Sisters of St Mary of Namur)

A Congregation founded in Paris by one of the many nuns who left the Congregation of Saint Mary in Paris, which had been founded from Port Royal in the 18th century and which had become embroiled in the Jansenist heresy. The Sisters were given every encouragement to form a new Congregation of Sainte-Marie, living under the Rule of St Augustine, to care for the sick and to teach in some schools in Paris. The foundation developed well, receiving approbation in 1875, and the work expanded throughout France until the early years of the 20th century, when the Association Laws in France drove the Sisters to leave France and make fresh foundations in England and Mexico.

MARIE-AUXILIATRICE, SOCIETY OF SISTERS OF

Location: France (Paris)
RC (female) founded in France in 1854 by the Blessed Marie-Thérèse de Soubiran (beatified 1946)
Abbr: MA
Original habit: a black habit, scapular and veil with an unstarched, square-cut wimple and a black knotted cord girdle; an ebony and brass crucifix was worn over the scapular. In choir a long black veil was worn.

A Congregation founded in Castelnaudary, near Carcassonne, in south-west France. Its founder was of a well-connected, aristocratic family who began her religious life at a Beguinage in Belgium. When this proved unsatisfactory, because of the laxity she found there, she returned to France and founded a reformed Beguinage, where a life of great austerity was observed, its members giving up all rights to property and observing all-night vigils before the Blessed Sacrament. Still in search of the religious life she desired, Marie-Thérèse left Castelnaudary with some companions and opened the first convent of her new foundation, the Society of Marie-Auxiliatrice, at Toulouse, which was approved by the Holy See in 1868. Further houses were opened at Amiens and Lyons. The Franco-Prussian War of 1870 caused some of the Sisters to leave France for England and settle for a time in Kennington, London. They later returned to France to continue their work of educating the poor and opened a hostel for young working women and an orphanage in Toulouse. One of the Congregation, Mother Mary Francis, who was responsible through chicanery for the expulsion of the founder from her Order, usurped her position. Following the death of Marie-Thérèse in 1889, the Toulouse Congregation turned against Mother Mary Francis, and it was discovered, although not until after her death, that she was never validly a nun since she was legally and secretly married and had been at the time of her profession. The expulsion of Marie-Thérèse from the Congregation was, therefore, invalid. Today, the Sisters are to be found in Japan, England, Ireland, France, Italy, West Africa, the Caroline Islands and Korea and they continue to provide help for young and vulnerable women as well as teaching in schools and running orphanages.

✠ Society of Mary the Helper

MARIE-MAGDALEN POSTEL, SISTERS OF ST

Location: France (Saint-Sauveur-le-Vicomte)
RC (female) founded in France in 1807 by Julie Françoise Catherine (St Marie-Magdalen Postel; canonized 1925)
Abbr: SCS

The founder was born in Barfleur, near Cherbourg, in 1756, and while still at school in a Benedictine convent at Valonges, made a private vow of virginity. The Benedictines hoped that she would join them, but she returned to Barfleur to open a school for girls. At the height of the French Revolution she was instrumental in hiding priests and reserving the Sacrament for the use of the sick and dying in the area. Moving later to Cherbourg, she founded a house and was

joined there by three other teachers. In 1807 they all made their religious vows together. By the end of 1807 there were some two hundred young girls in their care and the community grew. In 1832 the Congregation moved to the Abbey of St-Sauveur-le-Vicomte, where they continued their work, adopting the Rule which had been approved for the Brothers of the Christian Schools. The name of the Congregation changed then to the 'Sisters of the Christian Schools of Mercy', but following Vatican II this was changed again to the 'Sisters of St Mary Magdalen Postel'. Their work continues to prosper and there are over six hundred Sisters in seventy-five houses throughout the world, in Europe, Africa and Asia, nursing the poor and elderly and involved in education.

MARIE REPARATRICE, INSTITUTE OF

Location: Italy (Rome)
RC (female) founded in France in 1857 by Emilie d'Oultremont (Mother Marie de Jésus)
Abbr: SMR
Original habit: a white tunic and shoes with a blue veil and scapular and a pale blue girdle, from which a white rosary was hung. Over the scapular there was a heart-shaped copper medallion, engraved in Latin on both sides with a verse from Luke 12.49 and another from the Song of Songs. In choir a long white serge cloak with a pale blue border and a white choir veil was worn.

The Institute was founded in Paris by Emilie d'Oultremont following the death of her husband, and was inspired by a vision of Our Lady she had experienced in 1854. The purpose of the Institute is to make reparation to Our Lord in the Blessed Sacrament through his mother, Mary. The Sisters now have a combined contemplative and active apostolate, and they follow the Rule of St Ignatius. Their work includes various forms of retreat work, counselling and parish ministries. Houses are to be found throughout

Europe, with foundations made in England (1863) and in the USA (1908), and with foreign missions in South America, Africa and Mexico.

✠ Society of Mary Reparatrice

MARIST BROTHERS

Location: Italy (Rome)
RC (male) founded in France in 1817 by St Marcellin Champagnat (canonized 1999)
Abbr: FMS (or PFM)
Original habit: a black cloth tunic with a black cord girdle and a divided white collar.
(This Institute is not to be confused with the Brothers of Mary, or Marianists, founded by Fr Chaminade in Paris in the same year.)

The founder of the Institute decided early in life that he would become a priest, despite difficulties he was having with his schooling. Overcoming these problems he entered the seminary for training and, with some fellow seminarians, founded a society placed under the patronage of Mary, dedicated to parish mission work and to the Christian education of the young. Mindful, perhaps, of his own difficulties, he was anxious that this group would teach country children who were disadvantaged in their schooling. When the dream became a reality, beginning with just two young men, they took the name of the 'Marist Brothers of the Schools'. By the time of his death in 1840, St Marcellin Champagnat had personally founded forty-five schools and placed Marist Brothers in charge of them, and the Institute was approved in 1863. The keynotes of the Institute are the three Marian virtues of humility, simplicity and modesty. The expansion of the Congregation continued in France, and with the coming of the Association Laws in France at the start of the 20th century, which dispersed many religious communities and in particular those concerned with edu-

cation, there was further expansion throughout the world. Houses are now to be found in Canada and the USA, South America, most European countries, Australasia, Africa, the Pacific Islands and the Far East. The apostolate is varied and includes education at all levels, from pre-nursery and pre-school centres to postgraduate work, the care of the handicapped and work with apostolic youth movements and in young offenders' establishments, counselling, catechesis, the conducting of foreign missions and work with refugees.

✠ Little Brothers of Mary
   Marist Brothers of the Schools

MARIST FATHERS, THE

Location: Italy (Rome)
RC (male) founded in France in 1816 by the Venerable Jean-Claude-Marie Colin and others
Abbr: SM
Original habit: a black secular cassock with a black cashmere sash, a small black, elbow-length cape and a biretta.

A Society founded by the Venerable Jean Colin and others, including Blessed Benedict-Marcellin Champagnat, the founder of the Marist Brothers (see previous entry), while they were still seminarians. The day following their ordination the young priests went to the shrine of Our Lady of Fourvière and pledged themselves to found the Marist Society and work as missionaries in country districts. By 1823 their work was so successful that the missionaries were placed in charge of a seminary. Pope Gregory XVI approved the Society of Mary in 1836 on condition that they accepted a mission-vicariate in Western Oceania, where priests were needed. One of their number, St Peter Chanel, went to Oceania as superior of the first band of Marist Fathers, and was martyred on Futuna Island by the native king in 1841.

Oceania, divided into different dioceses because of its geographical vastness, was placed under the care of Marist bishops, and further foundations were made in the separate provinces of New Zealand and Australia. The Marists made a foundation in England in 1850, at the request of Cardinal Wiseman, with an Anglo-Irish Province erected in 1889. In 1863 a request for Marists to go to North America to take charge of largely French-speaking parishes was made by Archbishop Odin of Louisiana. In the USA today, the Marists are represented in eleven states and in Mexico. The first American province was established in 1889 and has since been subdivided into three separate provinces, the most recent being that of San Francisco in 1962. Members take the usual three vows of religion, poverty, chastity and obedience, as well as a declaration of a spirit of special devotion to Our Lady, of absolute loyalty to the pope, reverence for the hierarchy and the love of a hidden life. The work of the Society is concentrated in missions, both at home and in foreign fields, and in the running of colleges and seminaries.

✠ Society of Mary

MARIST MISSIONARY SISTERS, THE

Location: Italy (Rome)
RC (female) founded in France in 1857 by the Venerable Jean Colin
Abbr: SMSM
Original habit: a black tunic with a small white collar, a black shoulder cape and veil and a white peaked head cap; a small crucifix was worn around the neck.

The Congregation was founded in France by the founder of the Marist Fathers (see previous entry), with an American foundation made at Boston, Massachusetts, in 1922. The work of the Sisters is worldwide, and they maintain a presence in Asia, Africa, the Caribbean, Europe, Oceania and South America as well as in the USA, where they undertake the usual missionary work as well as pastoral care, the formation of native Sisterhoods, medical education and the maintenance of leprosaria.

✠ Missionary Sisters of the Society of Mary

MARIST SISTERS, THE

Location: Italy (Rome)
RC (female) founded in France in 1824 by the Venerable Jean-Claude-Marie Colin and Jeanne Marie Chavoin (Mother Saint-Joseph)
Abbr: SM (previously MS)
Original habit: a dark blue habit with a dark blue veil and a white cape which extended to the waist and a brass crucifix on a white cord around the neck.

A Pontifical Congregation co-founded by Mother Saint-Joseph, who was born in 1786 in Coutouvre in the Beaujolais region of France and became its first superior-general. There was a difference of opinion as to what Fr Colin, founder of the Marist Fathers, and Mother Saint-Joseph expected of the Marist Sisters, as they became known. Fr Colin seemed to see them as a semi-contemplative branch, praying for Marist Fathers and Brothers in the field and without any active apostolate outside the convent, which ran counter to Mother Saint-Joseph's view of her mission. Unable to reconcile these differing ideas, Mother Saint-Joseph resigned in 1853, to pursue her view of her vocation. The Marist Sisters went on to open conventional schools in France, England and Ireland, but the missionary spirit did not die. Despite much official opposition, because it was supposed at the time that women were not suited to the hardships and dangers of missionary life, but encouraged by the requests from the Marist Brothers and Fathers in the mission fields, Marist Sisters finally joined them in their work. Today, the Sisters are to be found worldwide. The earliest American foundation was made at Dearborn Heights, Michigan, in 1956. Their extensive work now includes teaching, parish ministries, counselling, working in hospitals with an emphasis on pastoral care, and administering infirmaries and orphanages.

✠ Sisters of the Holy Name of Mary

MARK, CANONS REGULAR OF ST

Defunct
RC (male) founded in Italy in 1194 by Bishop Enrico
Original habit: a white woollen tunic and cloak, with a mozetta and white biretta worn in choir and a sheepskin scarf.

Bishop Enrico, who had the title of Imperial Vicar in Italy, was given authority from the Holy See to erect a college of Canons Regular of St Mark in Mantua, Lombardy, whose members would observe the Rule of St Albert. This was approved by Pope Innocent III in 1204 and confirmed by Honorius III in 1218. The foundation received many benefits and privileges from successive popes and flourished for many years, but gradually declined until it became defunct. Its foundation, the Monastery of St Mark, was given over to the Camaldolese monks.

MARK OF VENICE, KNIGHTS OF ST

Defunct
RC (male Equestrian Order) founded in Italy in 1332
Original habit: (insignia) a gold medallion on a chain, engraved with a winged and crowned lion with an open book on which is written 'Pax Tibi Marce Evangelista Meus' (Peace Be to Thee, O Mark My Evangelist).

An Equestrian Order which was bestowed as a reward on those who had defended Venice against its enemies and for defending the Roman Catholic faith against the Turk.

MARTHA, SISTERS OF ST – Périgueux

Location: France (Tresillac)
RC (female) founded in France in 1643 by Jeanne and Antoinette Juillard
Abbr: RSM
Original habit: a black tunic with a white coif and veil and a silver crucifix

The Congregation was founded at Périgueux, in the Dordogne, and dedicated to St Martha because the town has a special devotion to the saint. Many foundations were made, each retaining its independence but observing a similar Rule. During the French Revolution, which caused the break-up of religious Congregations, the Sisters worked incognito in the markets, selling vegetables and fruit. Through this they would hear of those who were ill, and were able to care for the people in need and take the sacraments to them. The Council of Bordeaux in 1850 authorized the various 'Martha' communities to unite and federate, with Périgueux as the headquarters of the superior-general. The Sisters have an apostolate of nursing and teaching and have opened houses in France, England (Rottingdean), Scotland (Falkirk), Argentina, Spain and the Cameroon. The apostolate is concerned with domestic service. There are also communities of St Martha in Canada, where the foundation in Nova Scotia has given up domestic service to concentrate on work in education, but is now in decline. Following Vatican II vocations were in short supply, and in 1969 two Congregations of St Martha, those of Angoulême and Rome, united with the Congregation of Perigueux. In 1971, two more, La Doctrine Chrétienne and Le Bon Pasteur, joined the others.

MARTHE, SISTERS HOSPITALLERS OF ST

Location: France (Beaune)
RC (female) founded in France in 1687

The Congregation was founded at Portarlier, to the east of the present mother house at Beaune. The Sisters care for the sick and poor and undertake the education of girls and young women. The Hôtel-Dieu at Beaune, built in 1450, once enjoyed a reputation for wealth, mainly because of its fine vineyards.

MARTIN, CANONS REGULAR OF ST

Defunct
RC (male) founded in the early 12th century
Original habit: a white tunic, above which was worn a curious garment called a sarrocium, resembling a short, tight-fitting, buttonless waistcoat with puffed sleeves.

The Congregation took its name from the abbey of St Martin at Epernay, in the Champagne district of France, which is famous for its sixteen-mile-long cellars of Moët & Chandon champagne. The Congregation, which was founded around 1128, was under the leadership at one time of a Dean of Canons called Galerant. The canons observed the Rule of St Augustine and were approved by the archbishop of Reims. They were later replaced by secular canons.

MARTIN OF TOURS, CONGREGATION OF SISTERS OF ST

Location: France (Bourgeuil)
RC (female) founded in France in 1824 by Canon Besnard
Original habit: a black habit, cape and veil with a projecting linen bonnet and a frilled collar.

Founded in the wake of the French Revolution by the vicar-general of Tours, with the help of some Carmelite lay tertiaries, the Congregation of the Sisters of St Martin of Tours undertakes teaching and caring for

the sick and those in need, especially in their own homes. The Congregation extended into other parts of France and has opened houses in England, Belgium and Switzerland.

MARY, EVANGELICAL SOCIETY OF – Darmstadt

Location: Germany (Darmstadt)
Interdenominational – Ecumenical (female)
founded in Germany in 1947 by Dr Klara Schlink (Mother Basilea) and Erika Madauss (Mother Martyria)
Original habit: a long white, sometimes black, tunic with a deep yoke and a white cord cincture; a soft white close-fitting bonnet is secured under the chin.

An international evangelical group of women formed within the framework of the German Evangelical (Protestant) Church at Darmstadt, Germany. The founders had started a residential Bible course for future clergy wives during the years of the Second World War at a time when religious gatherings were forbidden by the Nazis. This idea did not succeed, and the two women started instead a Bible class for girls at the Schlink family home outside Darmstadt. In the post-war years a fellowship began to develop within this group, and the need for a community life began to arise. The Ecumenical Community of the Sisters of Mary began in an attic flat in Mother Basilea's house, with seven young Sisters and the two founders. A gift of land on the outskirts of the city was used to build a chapel and convent, and here the Sisters began their evangelization programme through the use of religious plays, or Rufer-Spiele, which they performed. The themes of the plays were taken from the Bible and introduced with a short address, with the audience invited to join in with hymn-singing. The community grew, and more space was required. A block of nearby land, which they called Canaan, was the inspiration of the Kanaan Rule drawn up by Mother Basilea after her visit to Mt Sinai in 1963. Each postulant had to wait six months to begin her two-year novitiate. The first profession, as a Sister of the Cross, was marked by the reception of a small white cross which was sewn on to the habit; after five years the reception of a ring and a white girdle marked the profession of life vows. The Sisters have worked in Israel since 1957, in a hospital near Tel Aviv and a convalescent home for Jews in Jerusalem, the Beth Abraham. An ecumenical centre for pilgrims, the Beth Gaudia Dei, has also been set up. The apostolate includes work in an outreach ministry through various media outlets.

✠ Evangelical Sisters of Mary

MARY, HANDMAIDS OF

Location: Italy (Rome)
RC (female) founded in Spain in 1851 by Manuela Torres Acosta (St Mary Soledad; canonized 1970)
Abbr: S. de M. (also SM)
Original habit: a black habit and veil and white linen wimple and binder; a small crucifix was worn over the wimple on a string of black beads. For outdoor use a large veil, which reached to the hem of the habit, was worn.

A Pontifical Congregation founded in Madrid by Manuela Acosta, who as a child had become deeply concerned about the plight of the poor, especially when they were sick and dying. With the help of her parish priest, Fr Miguel Martinez y Sanz, a Servite priest, and some volunteers she founded the Congregation, but not without difficulty. The intervention of the queen of Spain on their behalf helped their cause, and the Congregation received diocesan approval in 1861. Today, the Sisters are to be found in most parts of the world, where they provide not only care for the dying but

some respite for those families who are trying to care for patients in their own homes.

✠ Ministers of the Sick
 Sisters-Servants of Mary
 Spanish Nursing Sisters

MARY, LITTLE COMPANY OF

Location: England (Tooting Bec, London)
RC (female) founded in England in 1877 by the Venerable Mary Potter
Abbr: LCM
Original habit: a black habit and scapular with a red wool cincture and rosary and a crucifix around the neck on a red cord; a wimple and binder of white linen was worn with a blue veil indoors, or with a black veil edged with blue for outdoor wear. A white cloak was worn in choir.

The founder, Mary Potter, had begun her religious life as a Sister of Mercy in Brighton, Sussex, following a broken engagement. Her interest in entering a convent was possibly sparked by reading some literature given to her by her erstwhile fiancé. She stayed with the Mercy Sisters for eighteen months before returning home, when grave illness took her to the brink of death and provided the impetus she needed to found a Congregation whose members would care for the sick and dying. The Little Company of Mary was founded by Mary, together with two companions, in a dilapidated factory in Nottingham with the assistance of Bishop Bagshawe, who suggested that they could help themselves financially if a little teaching was also undertaken. The Rule which he wrote for the new Congregation put much control into his hands and caused Mary Potter much difficulty, and by 1893, when the Congregation was given Papal approbation, she had changed and modified much of it. The Sisters are devoted to the care of the sick and dying and have a special devotion to the Heart of

Mary at Calvary. Throughout the world today, the Sisters are to be found running hospitals and health care clinics, outreach programmes and social work and prison ministries. There are houses in Australia, Africa, Europe, the USA and Asia. The first foundation in Australia was made in Sydney in 1885, at the invitation of Cardinal Moran. There the Sisters opened a soup kitchen for the poor in William Street, and went on to found the famous Lewisham Hospital in 1887, which started as a hospital for blind children but later became a general hospital. There is also a specialized Aboriginal Health Care programme. From the Sydney foundation others were made in South Africa, at Port Elizabeth in 1904, and in New Zealand, at Christchurch in 1914. Further expansion within Australia continued, and a mission to Korea was made in 1963. Their popular name of Blue Nuns came from the long, blue veil the Sisters wore with the original habit, which became a familiar sight.

✠ Blue Nuns

MARY, LITTLE FRANCISCANS OF

Location: Canada (Baie-St-Paul)
RC (female) founded in the USA in 1889
Abbr: PFM
Original habit: a brown tunic and scapular with a white hood and wimple, a white woollen cord and a silver crucifix.

An American Pontifical Congregation founded in Worcester, Massachusetts, with the mother house later moving to Canada, to Baie St Paul, Quebec, in 1891. The Constitutions were approved in 1903. The Sisters observe the Rule of the Third Order of St Francis and are concerned with teaching, pastoral care, nursing and caring for the elderly, catechesis and mission work in Madagascar. There are houses in the USA,

in Worcester, Massachusetts, and Portland, Maine, as well as in Quebec in Canada.

✠ Little Franciscan Sisters of Mary

MARY, MEDICAL MISSIONARIES OF

Location: Ireland (Blackrock, Dublin)
RC (female) founded in Ireland in 1937 by Mother Mary Martin
Abbr: MMM
Original habit: a simple grey tunic with a collar with a grey veil.

A Congregation founded to provide personnel who can take medical care and expertise to those in need in deprived parts of the world. Mary Martin had experienced the trauma of war injuries when she had gone as a volunteer VAD (Voluntary Aid Detachment) nurse to France, Belgium and Malta during the First World War. After the war she trained in Dublin as a midwife and went to work in Africa, where her experiences in the field showed her that there was a great need for trained nurses who were also religious Sisters, but canon law made this a difficult undertaking as there was a ban against religious Sisters training in obstetrics, which was not lifted by Rome until 1936. The Congregation of the Medical Missionaries of Mary was founded a year later in a large private house in Drogheda, Ireland, which was converted into a hospital and mother house, and this came in time to be recognized as a general training hospital. Further developments followed, with foundations made in Africa and Italy, and in 1950 Mother Mary Martin went to the USA to open a house in Boston, which was later followed by one at Winchester, Massachusetts. Many of the Sisters are qualified medical practitioners and nursing sisters, some receiving their training after entry to the Congregation. Sisters are now to be found in ten African countries,

Brazil and Honduras as well as in Ireland, England and North America.

MARY, MISSIONARIES OF THE COMPANY OF

Location: Italy (Rome)
RC (male) founded in France in 1705 by St Louis Grignon de Montfort (canonized 1947)
Abbr: SMM
Original habit: a black cassock, with girdle and rosary.

St Louis de Montfort (1673–1716), a priest in Paris, saw the need for a company of like-minded priests who would conduct retreats and preach missions to bring greater devotion to the Sacred Heart and the Blessed Virgin Mary. In 1713 he devised a Rule for his Company of Missionaries, but the initial response was poor and few recruits presented themselves to him. By the time of his death in 1716, only two young priests, Fr Vatel and Fr Mulot, had joined him, along with a few lay Brothers. His success in drawing others to his cause had never met with the response he had hoped for and his methods of recruitment could be bizarre. His attempt to recruit women in Poitiers to form a religious community to help the poor and beggars was a disaster. He dragooned some twenty female hospital patients, some physically handicapped, and organized them into some sort of Congregation under a superior who was blind, bringing upon himself the understandable disapproval of the hospital authorities. He managed, however, to found the Daughters of Wisdom, who were dedicated to caring for the poor and running schools for the children of poor families. But although the numbers within his Society were few at the start, the Montfortian preaching was successful, converting, among others, many Calvinists. Schools were opened for poor youth in La Rochelle. The French Revolution destroyed many of the communities, but they were later reor-

ganized, and the Society was approved in 1825. Foreign missions were undertaken, initially to Haiti, but with the French Association Laws at the start of the 20th century, which sent many religious communities into exile, houses were established in England, The Netherlands, Denmark, Iceland, Canada and Africa. The American foundation was made in 1904.

✛ Montfort Fathers
 Montfortian Society of Mary
 Montfortians
 Society of Mary of Montfort

MARY, MISSIONARY SOCIETY OF

Location: USA (Framingham, Massachusetts)
RC (male) founded in the USA in 1952 by Fr Edward F. Garesche, SJ
abbr: FMSI

A Society, founded at Framingham, Massachusetts, to provide medical care and attention as well as help with catechetics. The members address social issues both in the USA and currently also in Manila, in the Philippines.

✛ Sons of Mary Health of the Sick

MARY, SERVANTS OF

Location: Italy (Rome)
RC (male) founded in Italy in 1233 by seven Florentine men
Abbr: OSM
Original habit: a black tunic, scapular, belt, hood and cloak.

Following a vision of the Blessed Virgin, seven wealthy young men who were members of the Confraternity of Our Lady set up a community at Monte Senario, north of Florence, where they lived as hermits adopting the Rule of St Augustine and dedicating themselves to Our Lady of Sorrows. The original white habit is said to have been changed to black following another vision of the Virgin Mary, who wished that her sorrow on the death of her Son should be remembered. The Order experienced considerable growth, and by the 13th century there were houses throughout Europe. An early prior-general of the Order was St Philip Benizi (1233–85), a man of great learning and wisdom who held doctorates in medicine and philosophy from Padua and Paris. He had first joined the Order as a lay Brother in 1255 and worked for some years as a gardener, until his remarkable talents were revealed. He was ordained as a priest and elected as prior-general in 1267. Much of his life was spent preaching in Italy and France, and he sent missionaries to India. When Philip Benizi was beatified in the 16th century, the artist Andrea del Sarto was asked to paint frescos for the cloisters of the Order's Santissimo Annunziata convent in Florence. There is some evidence that del Sarto was paid very little for his efforts as it is recorded that the convent's sacristan, Fra. Mariano, declared that the exhibition of one's work where the faithful could view it in prayerful remembrance was recompense for the poor pay. St Philip Benizi was canonized in 1671. The Servite Order was not established in England and America until the 19th century. It is still an active Order with solemn vows.

♦ Order of Servites

MARY, SERVANTS OF

RC (female)

There are two branches of the female Congregation of the Servants of Mary.

1 The Second Order of Contemplatives
2 The Third Order, or Mantellate Sisters

1 The Second Order of Contemplatives

Abbr: OSM
Original habit: a black habit, scapular and veil with a short black cape, a leather belt and rosary of the Seven Dolours; sandals are worn.

The Congregation was founded in Florence in 1233. The nuns are enclosed and live a contemplative life of devotion to Our Lady's Sorrows and the Passion of Our Lord. The Order originated in Todi, in the Umbria region of Italy, when two penitents of St Philip Benizi (1233–85), himself a prominent Servite, began to form a community. Its present form did not take shape until 1619, when Blessed Benedicta di Rossi founded a convent in Venice where a most austere version of the Rule was observed. She called her community the Servite Hermitesses under the Rule of Monte Senario. A foundation from here was made at Arco, north of Riva, Italy, and another in Munich, Germany. It was from the Arco foundation that some nuns came to England in 1888, led by Louisa Rauchenneger, and settled in Bognor Regis, Sussex. Nearly a century later, in 1976, the nuns moved to Begbroke in Oxfordshire, where the Robertson family had bequeathed land to the Roman Catholic Church and where a priory was built. Here the nuns led a contemplative life until 1999 when the priory was sold.

2 The Third Order Servite Sisters (Mantellate Sisters)

Location: England (Solihull, West Midlands)
Abbr: OSM
Original habit: a black habit and veil with a white pleated linen wimple, a leather belt and a rosary of the Seven Dolours; the scapular at one time had a large image of a Host embroidered on the left-hand side.

The Congregation was founded in Florence, Italy, in 1306 by St Juliana Falconieri (1270–1341), a niece of St Alexis Falconieri, one of the seven founders of the Servite Order. St Juliana had been clothed in the Servite habit by St Philip Benizi while still

in her teens, and she organized other tertiaries to live a communal life in the Palazzo
Grifoni in Florence. She drew up a Rule for
the Mantellate Sisters which was formally
recognized by Pope Martin V (1417–31).
The Mantellate Sisters were so called on
account of the habit having capacious but
short sleeves, which gave the appearance of
a mantle but left the hands free for work.
St Juliana's special devotions to Our Lady
of Sorrows and the recitation of the Rosary
of the Seven Dolours as well as her devotion
to the Blessed Sacrament find echoes in
today's Servite Sisters, who wear and recite
the Rosary of the Seven Dolours. Servite
houses are to be found in Europe, the USA,
and Canada, where the Sisters provide education at all levels and conduct parish ministries, counselling services and chaplaincies
in hospitals and prisons. There are ministries to cancer and AIDS patients which
operate from the Congregation's foundation in Omaha, Nebraska. The Sisters also
give support to unwed mothers, care for the
mentally and physically handicapped and
support foreign missions in Jamaica and
Zaire.

✝ Mantellate Sisters
  Servites

MARY, SISTERS OF ST – Namur

Location: Belgium (Namur)
RC (female) founded in Belgium in 1819 by Fr
Nicholas Joseph Minsart
Abbr: SSMN
Original habit: a black habit and apron, a white
headdress and coif and a square-cut linen wimple
and binder; a leather belt with a rosary suspended,
and with a brass crucifix and medal of Our Lady.
(This Congregation must not be confused with the
Sisters of Notre Dame de Namur.)

The founder, Nicholas Minsart, had been a
Cistercian monk from the abbey of Boneffe
but had been expelled from his community

during the French Revolution. Working as
the parish priest of Saint-Loup, Namur, he
was anxious that the young girls should be
given some training in needlework skills,
which would enable them to seek employment. Two local women agreed to help, and
a workroom was opened. They were known
as the Associates of Saint-Loup, and soon
increased in number, evolving into a religious community. Diocesan approval was
granted in 1834, when sixteen Sisters
received the habit and eight of the early
members made their profession, with
Mother Claire de Jésus becoming the first
superior-general a short time before the
founder's death. Other houses were opened
in Belgium and the first American convent
was founded in 1863 at Lockport, New
York, which is now part of the Eastern
Province of the American Congregation,
with its headquarters in Kenmore, New
York. The Western Province of the American Congregation has its headquarters in
Fort Worth, Texas. The Order is divided
into six provinces worldwide, with the Sisters mainly occupied with academic and
religious education, parish ministries, refugee assistance and health care. They also
care for young children with AIDS, conduct
prison ministries, run Hispanic pastoral
services and care for the elderly. Within the
UK, boarding and day schools were opened
and missions have been established in Zaire,
Rwanda, Cameroon and Brazil.

MARY, SISTERS-HOME VISITORS OF

Location: USA (Detroit, Michigan)
RC (female) founded in the USA in 1949
Abbr: HVM

Designed to meet the needs of people living
in a completely urban situation, this Diocesan Congregation was founded in Detroit,
Michigan, and provides opportunities for
retreats at the Sojourner House for Retreats.
The Sisters maintain a prison ministry and

some members work in seminaries and in their African-American Spirituality Centre.

MARY, SOCIETY OF

Location: Rome (Italy)
RC (male) founded in France in 1817 by William Joseph Chaminade
Abbr: SM
(This Society must not be confused with the Marists, who use the same post-nominal initials.)

The Society of Mary was founded in the aftermath of the French Revolution by Fr Chaminade, a priest who had tried to continue his priestly work during the years of the Revolution but had finally been driven into exile in Spain, where he remained in Saragossa until 1800. Returning to France, he went to Bordeaux and gathered together some men and women who were anxious to revive the Church in France. Sodalities were formed which evolved into the Daughters of Mary Immaculate, or Marianist Sisters (founded 1816) and the Society of Mary (founded 1817). The Society was approved in 1865. The main work of the Society was in education, and it included both ordained and non-clerical members, taking the same three vows of religion, to which was added a fourth, that of stability in the service of the Blessed Virgin Mary. The French Association Laws enacted at the beginning of the 20th century necessitated the removal of the headquarters from Paris to Nivelles in Belgium before moving to Rome. The first American foundation was made in Cincinnati, Ohio, in 1849 with other foundations following, arranged into provinces. Overseas missions were established in Ireland, Japan, Africa, Korea and Puerto Rico. The work of the Society is still largely educational at every level, but the members also undertake parish ministries, work with the poor and disadvantaged, run peace and justice centres, retreats, AIDS ministries, drug and alcohol clinics and counselling centres.

✠ Brothers of Mary
   Marianists

MARY, THE LADIES OF

Location: Italy (Rome)
RC (female) founded in Belgium in 1817 by Canon Constant Guillaume van Crombrugghe.
Abbr: DMJ
Original habit: a black habit with a black veil and white under-veil and a blue scapular and belt, both embroidered in blue with a monogram of the intertwined letters 'A.M.'. On special occasions a long blue veil was worn in choir. Lay Sisters wore black scapulars which were embroidered in the same way.

The Ladies of Mary Congregation was founded at Alost, Belgium, to provide catechesis for young, poor children and to teach useful crafts, such as lacemaking and needlework. Some years later the Sisters opened a fee-paying school, and their interest in education continues today, extending from local parish schools to grammar and high schools. On the west coast of the USA the Sisters have opened a detention centre, where they care for offenders. There are houses in England, Ireland, Uganda, Ghana, Burundi and Cameroon. As well as their work in education, the Sisters are also concerned with a prison ministry and with health care, in both nursing and dispensing.

✠ Daughters of Mary and Joseph

MARY, XAVERIAN MISSIONARY SISTERS OF

Location: Italy (Parma)
RC (female) founded in Italy in 1945
Abbr: XMM

The Society of Xaverian Missionary Sisters of Mary, founded in Italy, opened its first American House in 1954. Their work is concerned with missions to non-Christians, but the Sisters also exercise a special ministry to the Hispanic community, teaching as well as undertaking the care of the elderly and running clinics for those who are drug or alcohol dependent. The Society is represented in many parts of Africa, Japan and Mexico as well as in Italy and the USA, where houses are to be found in the archdiocese of New York and in Worcester, Massachusetts.

MARY HEALTH OF THE SICK, DAUGHTERS OF

Defunct
RC (female) founded in the USA in 1935 by Fr Edward F. Garesche and Mother Mary Angela
Abbr: FMSI
Original habit: a black tunic and veil with an angular white starched wimple and a white binder. A crucifix was worn around the neck.

A Diocesan Congregation which combined the active and contemplative life, founded in New York. The mother house and novitiate was in Cragsmoor, New York, from where the Sisters were prepared and formed for the religious life. The apostolate of the Congregation included religious instruction and nursing as well as social service work. A mission in Okinawa, Japan, was opened after the Second World War.

MARY HELP OF CHRISTIANS, DAUGHTERS OF

Location: Italy (Rome)
RC (female) founded in Italy in 1872 by St John Bosco (canonized 1934) and St Mary Dominic Mazzarello (canonized 1951)
Abbr: FMA
Original habit: a black habit and veil with white linen wimple and a shawl for use outdoors.

Founded in Mornese, near Genoa, Italy, this Pontifical Congregation was founded by St Mary Mazzarello under the guidance of St John Bosco. She had been a member of a Marian sodality organized by her parish priest, who had been very impressed with

the work of St John Bosco in Turin. An outbreak of typhus saw the sodality members volunteering to work among the victims. Mary caught the disease and nearly died, and as a result of this her health never fully recovered and she took up dressmaking, opening a small business which employed local girls. She realized that, with the help of others, she could train and educate young girls along similar lines to those followed by St John Bosco for boys. Under his guidance, and with others having joined her, the Congregation was founded, with Mary as superior. The first professions were made in 1872. There are houses now throughout Europe, in Asia, Africa, Australia, and in North and South America. The Sisters work with young people, especially the poor and abandoned, in schools, youth centres and summer camps; they also conduct retreats and work in catechesis.

✠ Salesian Sisters of St John Bosco

MARY IMMACULATE, DAUGHTERS OF

Location: Italy (Rome)
RC (female) founded in Spain in 1876 by Vincenta Maria Lopez y Vicuna
Abbr: RMI (also FMI)
Original habit: a black habit and veil with a black cape bound with blue, and a white wimple which is in part covered by the cape; a silver crucifix on a blue cord was worn around the neck.

The founder of this Congregation had been very moved by the plight of young women who had left their homes in order to find work and who were often then in need of care and protection. With help and encouragement from the bishop of Madrid she opened the first hostel in her aunt's home. Others joined her in the work, which led to the opening of further hostels in major cities throughout Spain. Papal approval for the Congregation was granted in 1888, two years before Vincenta's death. The Sisters are still concerned with the welfare of young women who are working or studying away from home, and those who are in need of advice, or help with employment. They also organise cultural centres where adult educational programmes and recreational activities can be enjoyed. Missions have been established in twenty-one countries throughout Europe, Asia, Africa and North and South America.

✠ Daughters of Mary Immaculate for the
    Protection of Working Girls
    Religious of Mary Immaculate

MARY IMMACULATE, OBLATE MISSIONARIES OF

Location: Canada (Trois Rivières, Quebec)
RC (female) founded in Canada in 1984

A Secular Institute for women which received approbation in 1984. The members aim to be an integral part of the Church's missions to the poor and to reflect the charity of Christ through service to and solidarity with the poor. As well as in Canada, houses of the Institute are also to be found in Africa, Europe, the USA and Asia.

MARY IMMACULATE, OBLATES OF

Location: Italy (Rome)
RC (male) founded in France in 1816 by Blessed Charles Joseph Eugène de Mazenod (beatified 1975)
Abbr: OMI
Original habit: a clerical cassock with a black cincture which has a large missionary cross tucked into it; a black ferreola was worn.

A Congregation founded at Aix-en-Provence. The founder, Blessed Charles de Mazenod (1782–1861), came from a noble family which was forced into exile in Italy at the time of the French Revolution. During his stay there, Charles de Mazenod trained for the priesthood and was ordained in December 1811. Returning to France, he worried about the level of ignorance of the Roman Catholic faith there, a legacy of the French Revolution, and gathered together a number of like-minded priests. In 1818 they made their religious profession to form the Missionary Society of Provence, which was later renamed the Congregation of Oblate Missionaries of Mary in 1826, when papal approval was received. The members worked in country parishes, catechizing and preaching by means of local retreats and missions in which devotion to the Sacred Heart and to Mary Immaculate was emphasized. Charles de Mazenod was the nephew of the bishop of Marseilles, succeeding him in 1837. The Congregation prospered and spread throughout Europe and into the USA, South Africa, Sri Lanka and South America. In the USA, where the Missionaries have been most active, the Congregation is divided into five provinces, the earliest (Eastern American Province) having been founded in 1883. It is in America that the priests and Brothers run many media enterprises, parishes, seminaries, retreat houses, hospital and prison chaplaincies, and outreach programmes for the poor and marginalized. Foreign missions have taken them into French Polynesia, Canada, Mexico, Puerto Rico and Zambia. Today, the Missionaries are also to be found in Asia and Oceania, including Australia.

✠ Missionary Oblates of Mary Immaculate
    Missionary Society of Provence

MARY IMMACULATE, PARISH VISITORS OF

Location: USA (Monroe, New York)
RC (female) founded in the USA in 1920 by Mother Mary Teresa Tallon
Abbr: PVMI
Original habit: a navy blue dress with a white collar, a dark veil and a finger ring, which was received at the time of perpetual profession; a

medallion of the Immaculate Conception was worn around the neck.

A Congregation, founded in New York and concerned with serving the Church through its pastoral ministries. The Sisters provide religious education and catechesis through their parish and catechetical centres, visit the sick, care for the neglected members of society and also provide a specialized Korean Centre. The Parish Visitors have missions in New York City and upstate New York, as well as in Connecticut, Pennsylvania and New Jersey. A new mission has also been started in the diocese of Okigwe, Nigeria.

MARY IMMACULATE, SISTERS OF

Location: India (Krishnagar, West Bengal)
RC (female) founded in India in 1948 by Bishop Louis La Ravoire Morrow of Krishnagar
Abbr: SMI

The Sisters of Mary Immaculate undertake the teaching of religious education and the provision of catechesis for children and adults in India. An American foundation was made at Leechburg, Pennsylvania, in 1981, where the Congregation maintains the Bishop Morrow Personal Care Home, for those in need of health care.

✠ Catechist Sisters of Mary Immaculate
　Help of Christians

MARY IMMACULATE, SISTERS-SERVANTS OF

Location: Italy (Rome)
Eastern Catholic – Ukrainian (female) founded in the Ukraine in 1892 by Fr Jeremiah Lomnitsky and Michaeline Hordashevska (Sr Josaphata)
Abbr: SSMI

The Congregation, founded in Zuzel, Ukraine, is of the Ukrainian Byzantine Rite. Michaeline Hordashevska underwent a formation programme with the Sisters of St Felix in Zhovkva, in readiness to become the first member of the new Congregation, which was the inspiration of her spiritual director, Fr Jeremiah Lomnitsky, and was approved in 1932. An American foundation was made in 1935 at Stamford, Connecticut. During the Communist takeover of Western Ukraine in the 1940s, the then superior-general, Sr Veronica Gargil, escaped to Rome together with another member of the community, and in 1947 the generalate was transferred there. With the downfall of Communism, the Sisters emerged from their underground existence and re-established mission work once more. The Sisters work in Ukrainian-Byzantine-Rite parishes and also provide nursing care for the elderly, undertake various parish ministries and make and repair church vestments. There are houses throughout Europe, including former Yugoslavia, and in the USA and Canada, Brazil, Argentina and Australia.

MARY IMMACULATE AND THE SACRED HEART, THE HANDMAIDS OF

Location: Spain
RC (female) founded in Spain in 1902 by the Blessed Marcellus Spinola y Maestre (beatified 1987)

A Spanish Congregation, founded in Seville and dedicated to education at all levels and to addressing social concerns, especially those affecting the working classes. Much of the apostolate is inspired by the writings of Blessed Marcellus when he was bishop of Malaga and later archbishop of Seville.

MARY-JOSEPH AND OF MERCY, SISTERS OF

Location: France (Le Dorat, Limoges)
RC (female) founded in France in 1841 (but see below)
Abbr: DMJ (also SMJ.)
Original habit: a black habit and veil with blue

under-veil and a white wimple; a metal crucifix was worn.

A Congregation which can trace its origins back to the foundation of the Sisters of St Joseph, at Le Puy in 1650. After the French Revolution, Cardinal Fesch of Lyons began to reunite the Sisters who had been scattered when religious houses were closed, and it was found that some of these women had used their time to exercise a prison ministry and wanted to continue with this work. It was felt that this work required special training and a separate Institute was needed. This was founded as 'Le Congréga-tion de Marie-Joseph', which separated from its parent foundation in 1841. The work of the Sisters not only includes the traditional prison visiting, but provides nursing, counselling and catechesis for the inmates and has now further extended into providing care and counselling for discharged prisoners and hostels for girls who may be at risk. The Sisters also run orphanages and homes for the elderly with foundations in France, England, The Netherlands and elsewhere in Europe.

✠ Sisters of Mary and Joseph

MARY MAGDALEN, THE ORDER OF ST

Defunct
RC (female) founded in France in 1618 by Fr Athanasius Mole

An Order of nuns founded in Paris for women who wished to rehabilitate themselves and enter the religious life. The Constitutions were approved in 1640 and some foundations made in Paris, Rouen and Bordeaux. There were three types of member, who were accommodated in separate buildings and followed different Rules. The first were those who had been sufficiently reformed to be capable of taking solemn vows and these were known as the Magdalens. Second, there were those who were

unable to take more than simple vows, and they were known as the Sisters of St Martha; they had the option after training and formation to progress to become Magdalens. The third group comprised those who were imprisoned within the convent against their will because they were public sinners, and these were known as the Sisters of St Lazarus. The Order became successively part of the Visitation and Ursuline Congregations, the Sister Hospitallers of the Mercy of Jesus and, from 1720, part of the Religious of Our Lady of Charity.

✠ Madelonnettes

MARY MOTHER OF GOD, SISTERS OF

Defunct
RC (female) founded in the USA in 1953 by Cardinal McIntyre and Mother Francis Xavier
Abbr: SMMG

A Diocesan Congregation founded in the USA at Long Beach, California. A mother house and novitiate were established at Marycrest Manor, Culver City, California, and from here the Sisters were trained to undertake nursing, teaching and home missions. The Congregation is now defunct.

MARY MOTHER OF THE CHURCH, DAUGHTERS OF

Location: USA (Greenbrae, California)
RC (female) founded in the USA in 1993
Abbr: DMMC

A small contemplative community of women who live a Carmelite style of life. Its members aim to undertake spiritual programmes such as retreats, days of reflection and missions in parishes. One of the community's aims is to foster Eucharistic devotion and to provide a resource for catechesis which may be called upon by parishes as the need arises.

MARY MOTHER OF THE CHURCH, SISTERS OF

Location: England (Brownshill, Stroud, Gloucestershire)
RC (female) founded in England in 1982
Original habit: a dark blue and white dress with a dark blue veil.

A recently founded Congregation for mature women who have a vocation for the religious life. There are foundations in and around Stroud and a residential home for the elderly in Cork, Ireland. The Congregation combines the active and contemplative life with an emphasis on the recitation of the divine office and adoration of the Blessed Sacrament, which is exposed daily. The Rule followed is Ignatian, and the Spiritual Exercises of St Ignatius feature large in the formation and spiritual life of the Congregation and its members. The Sisters undertake to visit the sick and lonely and to bring them Holy Communion, as well as preparing children by catechesis for their first Holy Communion.

MARY MOTHER OF THE EUCHARIST, SISTERS OF

Location: USA (Ann Arbor, Michigan)
RC (female) founded in the USA in 1991

A Public Association founded when Cardinal O'Connor, archbishop of New York, established the foundation with the first four Sisters. A former prioress, Mother Assumpta Long, came from the Congregation of St Cecilia's Dominicans at Nashville, Tennessee, to become prioress-general of the new Association. The Congregation is both contemplative and active within the Dominican mould, although currently following the Rule of St Augustine, with plans to amalgamate with the Dominican Order. It is primarily a teaching Congregation and was moved to the diocese of Lamsing,

Michigan, to start running a small, multigrade school of fewer than a hundred pupils. The Sisters also undertake more traditional schooling and support the Catholic Evidence Guild, which provides a public forum for Roman Catholicism within the University of Michigan.

MARY OF GUADALUPE FOR FOREIGN MISSIONS, INSTITUTE OF ST

Location: Mexico (Mexico City)
RC (male) founded in Mexico in 1949
Abbr: MG
Original habit: secular style

The Institute was founded in 1949 and approved by Pope Pius XII in 1953. The purpose of the foundation is to undertake missions abroad and to educate the indigenous clergy. Missions are maintained in the USA, Japan, Korea, Hong Kong, Peru, Brazil, Cuba, Angola and Italy.

✠ Missionaries of Guadalupe

MARY OF JERUSALEM, ORDER OF TEUTONIC KNIGHTS OF ST (Teutonic Order)

Location: Austria (Vienna)
RC (male Equestrian Order) founded in the Holy Land in 1190
Original habit: a knight wore a white mantle with a black cross outlined in silver; a priest member wore a black tunic under the same mantle; a sergeant wore a grey mantle bearing a three-armed cross.

The Order was founded during the fourth crusade, after the siege of Acre, by some German merchants from Bremen and Lübeck who built a field hospital in St Nicholas' Gate at Acre for the care and treatment of their sick and wounded countrymen. This became a permanent institution, financially supported by Frederick of Schwaben and the Holy Roman Emperor, Henry VI (1190–97). Soon established as a religious Order, the members followed the Rule of St Augustine and were divided into three classes, each distinguished by its habit.

1 Knights, who were to be well born and would take a vow to defend the Christian Church and the Holy Land as well as protecting German pilgrims
2 Priests
3 Sergeants

By the start of the 13th century the Order had houses in Palestine, Greece, southern Italy and Germany. Expansion in the Holy Land was not possible as all the important castles and lands were already in the hands of the Hospitallers of St John and the Templars. The Teutonic Knights fought in many battles in north-east Germany and the Baltic lands at the time of the Christianizing of these lands, but their power and influence began to wane over the centuries. The Order was abolished by Napoleon in 1809 and their land and property redistributed. A revival was made in Austria in 1834 under Emperor Franz I, but the Order's activities were restricted then to charitable work. After the fall of the Habsburgs in 1918, the Teutonic Order changed itself into a mendicant Brotherhood, headed by a priest, and in 1929 it underwent a complete reformation with the restoration of a religious discipline. The Order was apparently dispersed by Adolf Hitler during World War II, but twelve surviving members were hanged in July 1944 after the failure of a plot to assassinate him. The Order is now re-established as the 'Deutsche-Orden' and has houses in Austria, Italy and Germany; its members undertake various charitable roles and have established a mission in Sweden.

MARY OF NAZARETH AND CALVARY, COMMUNITY OF ST

Location: Tanzania (Masasi)
Anglican (female) founded in Tanzania in 1946 by Bishop William Vincent Lucas
Abbr: CMM

The founder, a former Anglican bishop of Masasi, established the Community of St Mary of Nazareth and Calvary to undertake the care and education of young women and girls. The work has now expanded to include parish work, the running of development groups for girls, nursing, serving the needy and visiting the sick and those in prison. Other houses are found throughout Tanzania, and the community maintains the Ndola Convent, at Ndola, Zambia.

✠ Chama Cha Maria Mtakatifu

MARY OF OREGON, SISTERS OF ST

Location: USA (Beaverton, Oregon)
RC (female) founded in the USA in 1886 by William H. Gross, archbishop of Oregon City
Abbr: SSMO

A Pontifical Congregation, founded in Sublimity, Oregon, and placed under the patronage of St Francis Xavier, which received papal approbation in 1927. The work of the community, which runs the St Mary of the Valley convent and school, is largely educational, with some nursing care at the Maryville Nursing Home. Other work includes parish ministries, catechesis and an Hispanic ministry. The Sisters are represented not only in Oregon, but also in the archdioceses of Los Angeles and Chicago.

MARY OF PROVIDENCE, DAUGHTERS OF ST

Location: Italy (Rome)
RC (female) founded in Switzerland in 1881 by Blessed Aloysius Guanella (beatified 1964)
Abbr: DSMP

Original habit: a black, or sometimes white, tunic with a veil; a crucifix was worn around the neck.

A Pontifical Congregation founded in Como, Switzerland, with an apostolate in care for the poor and sick. The founder had been ordained as a secular priest but later joined the Salesian Order after some antagonism from local Freemasons had forced the closure of a school which he had opened in his first parish at Sovogno. He was recalled to parish work in Traona, where he was again to see Masonic interference, which resulted in his removal to a tiny parish in the mountains where there was an orphanage and a small hospice. The premises were inadequate, and in 1886 the Little House of Divine Providence was founded at Como. In the space of four years the newly formed Congregation of the Daughters of Mary of Providence was caring for nearly two hundred people. Papal approval for the Congregation was granted in 1917. The Sisters have now developed an extensive apostolate which includes caring for physically and mentally handicapped children and adults, youth group work, the care of the elderly, help with the housing of those in need and general hospital and hospice work together with catechesis and parish ministries. Members of this Congregation are to be found in Switzerland, Italy, Spain, Romania, India, the Philippines, South America, Mexico, Canada and the USA.

✠ Guanellians

MARY OF THE IMMACULATE CONCEPTION, DAUGHTERS OF

Location: USA (New Britain, Connecticut)
RC (female) founded in the USA in 1904 by Bishop Lucian Bojnowski
Abbr: DM
Original habit: a dark blue habit and scapular with a black outer veil over a white under-veil and a simple white collar; a white cincture and rosary; a medallion is worn around the neck.

A Congregation founded in New Britain, Connecticut, to honour the Immaculate Conception and to help, through a Marian apostolate, those in need. The work was started by six young women who were members of the sodality of the Children of Mary, and who began by caring for orphans. The work expanded, and a community was formed, with papal approval in 1929 and 1939, when it became a Pontifical Congregation. Following Vatican II, revised Constitutions received approval in 1982. The Sisters work largely in the eastern States of New York and Massachusetts, in education with specialist work in a reading clinic as well as assistance at several catechetical centres, in care for the aged and child day care at the Our Lady of Rose Hill day care centre and in social service provision for women at risk and in need of care.

MARY REPARATRIX, SOCIETY OF ST

Location: Italy (Rome)
RC (female) founded in France in 1857 by Emily d'Outremont d'Hooghvorst
Abbr: SMR

The Society of St Mary Reparatrix was founded originally as a contemplative Congregation, but its work from the New York foundation (1908) now includes organizing retreats, spiritual direction, pastoral care of the needy and catechetics. Missions, originally just in the Holy Land and the Near East, are now maintained in Africa and South America.

MARY THE VIRGIN, COMMUNITY OF ST

Location: England (Wantage, Oxfordshire)
Anglican (female) founded in England in 1848 by Elizabeth Lockhart and Mary Reid
Abbr: CSMV

The community had its beginnings in 1848 when the vicar of Wantage, William John Butler, realized there was a need for a Sisterhood to provide an education for the children of the parish. Elizabeth Lockhart and Mary Reid began the work in two small cottages, but by the end of the same year larger premises were needed. Elizabeth Lockhart by then felt convinced that her vocation lay rather in the rescue and care of women and girls who were at risk because of their lifestyles, and a home for penitents was opened there in 1850. When Elizabeth went on to adopt a religious habit, this was not well received by Bishop Wilberforce of Oxford. Unable to see their way forward in the Anglican Church, the two founders converted to Roman Catholicism, and the Wantage foundation was put in the hands of Harriet Day. Parochial work and teaching continued, a foundation course for pupil teachers was initiated, and schools, including the boarding school of St Mary's, Wantage, were opened. Rescue work continued as before and more hostels were opened. The Sisters also founded a school for embroidery, for the making of church linen and vestments, altar frontals and falls, and initiated the printing of books of plain chant. Their interest in foreign mission work developed, and houses were opened in India and South Africa, where the members worked in hospitals and dispensaries as well as in education. This work continues today. Much of the Community's earlier work in schools and branch houses has now ceased, but they still operate a vigorous printing press, run studios and workshops at Wantage, care for the elderly and undertake parish work.

MAUR, CONGREGATION OF ST

Defunct
RC (male) founded in France in 1618
Original habit: Benedictine style.

This was a branch of the reformed Benedictine Congregation of St Vannes, which lasted until 1818. The Congregation of St Vannes, which met for its general chapter in 1616, decided that an independent Congregation for all the reformed French houses was needed, and with the support of the king, Louis XIII, and that of the influential Cardinals de Retz and Richelieu, the Congregation of St Maur was established and received its approval from Pope Gregory XV in 1621 and Pope Urban VIII in 1627. By the close of the 17th century there were so many monasteries joining this Congregation that it was divided into six provinces throughout France. The daily life of the monks was noted for its austerities, which included total abstinence from meat and unusually long periods of silence. Many of the houses attracted scholars, and heresy crept in, especially Jansenism, which continued until the outbreak of the French Revolution when the monasteries were closed and the monks were scattered. An attempt to reverse the dispersal of members after the Revolution was not successful and the Congregation became defunct.

✠ Maurists

MAURICE, CANONS REGULAR OF THE ABBEY OF ST

Defunct
RC (male) founded in France in the the 8th century by Charlemagne
Original habit: a black cassock and rochet with a purple cape, or mozetta, and a biretta

A Congregation founded in Savoy, in the diocese of Tarentaise (present-day Chambéry) as a chapter of canons regular, who would live in common in an abbey dedicated to St Maurice of Agaunum (Augine), now Saint-Maurice-en-Valais. It was here that the relics of St Maurice and his companions in the Theban Legion were enshrined. The abbey, which evolved from the church built at Agaunum in the 4th century, was the first in the Western Church to have a *laus perennis*, or 24-hour constant recitation of the divine office by a relay of choirs.

MAURICE AND LAZARUS, KNIGHTS OF ST

Defunct
RC (male Equestrian Order) founded in France (see below)
Original habit: an ash-grey tunic with a gold cincture and a grey cloak decorated with a golden cross.

An early tradition alleges that the Order was founded by Amadeus, first duke of Savoy, in the late 10th century as an Order of knights under the Rule of St Augustine, but more reliable sources date its foundation to Amadeus III of Savoy, later to become 'Pope' Felix V (anti-pope, 1439–49), who eventually withdrew to a chateau near Thonon on Lake Geneva. The Order was of hermit-knights and was composed, in the main, of noblemen.

MECHITARISTS, ORDER OF

Location: Italy (Rome) and Austria (Vienna)
RC–Catholic Armenian (male) founded in the 18th century
Abbr: CMV
Original habit: a black tunic and hooded cape decorated with a red cloth cross, which was worn as a symbol of the readiness of members to die for the faith. Members are bearded.

There are two Congregations of these monks:

1 The Mechitarists of Venice, with their headquarters on the island of San Lazarro, Venice.
2 The Mechitarists of Vienna, with their headquarters in Vienna, Austria.

The founder of the Order was Peter Manuk Mechitar, who established the first Congregation in Constantinople in 1701 and the first monastery at Modor, in the Morea peninsula in Greece, which since 1687 had been under Venetian rule. The original members, twelve priests and three postulants who formed the nucleus of the Congregation, observed a common life, followed, at first, the Rule of St Antony and took the traditional vows of religion, of poverty, chastity and obedience, with an additional vow to undertake missionary work. As they were Roman Catholics, the pope was anxious that a more usual Western Rule be used, and the monks adopted the Rule of St Benedict. Peter Mechitar was elected abbot for life. The capture of Morea by the Turks in 1715 resulted in a move to Venice, eventually to the island of San Lazarro, where the Congregation remains today. In 1773 the Mechitarists from Venice set up a house in Trieste, which later transferred to Vienna in 1811, becoming an independent Congregation which was approved in 1852 and 1885. Mechitarists are noted for their literary output in the Armenian language and in works relating to the Armenian culture. The members work in education wherever there is a sizeable Armenian population. They conduct foreign missions in Russia, Turkey, Iran, Egypt, former Yugoslavia, Greece and Romania. New Constitutions were proposed and conditionally approved in 1987.

MEDICAL MISSIONARY SISTERS, SOCIETY OF

Location: England (Acton, London)
RC (female) founded in the USA in 1925 by Anna Dengel (Mother Anna)
Abbr: MMS
Original habit: a simple grey habit with a blue veil.

The Congregation was founded in Washington, DC, by the Austrian-born doctor Anna Dengel (Mother Anna), receiving diocesan approbation from the archbishop of Baltimore, Mgr Curley. She had been inspired by the example of Dr Agnes Mc-Laren, a Scottish convert doctor who had gone to Rawalpindi, India, to work in the hospital for women which had been set up by Bishop Dominic Wagner. Anna Dengel went there as a volunteer in the early 1920s. It was clear that there was a need for many female medical professionals to work in the field of medical care for women, especially for those who were unable to receive treatment from male physicians because of various religious or cultural laws. The Sisters work not only in mission stations in Asia and Africa, but also across the USA, in Europe and in South America, where they are engaged in many health promotion programmes, including nutrition, providing a low-cost alternative to existing health care systems.

✠ Society of Catholic Medical Missionaries

MERCEDARIAN SISTERS OF THE BLESSED SACRAMENT

Location: Mexico (Mexico City)
RC (female) founded in Mexico in 1910
Abbr: HMSS

The Congregation was founded in Mexico, from which an American foundation was made in 1926. The Sisters teach at all levels, from elementary to junior college level, as well as providing ministries to Hispanics, the sick and elderly and, in true Mercedarian tradition, to the imprisoned. There are houses in Texas and California, many South American countries and Spain.

✠ Sisters of Mercy of the Blessed Sacrament

MERCY, BROTHERS OF

Location: Germany (Niederelbert)
RC (male) founded in Germany in 1856 by Brother Ignatius Loetchert

Abbr: FMM
Original habit: a black tunic and cincture with a rosary and a short, black, hoodless cape.

The Brothers of Mercy are involved solely in nursing and health care. They work in hospitals, infirmaries and private homes in Germany and The Netherlands. The work has taken the Congregation to Africa, and they are also represented in the USA, where there are several nursing homes in their care in Clarence, New York.

MERCY, PRIESTS OF

Location: USA (South Union, Owensboro, Kentucky)
RC (male) founded in France in 1808
Abbr: CPM (or SPM)

A Congregation of priests founded in Lyons, France, in 1808 and then reorganized in Paris in 1814 by Fr Jean-Baptiste Rauzon, later vicar-general of Bordeaux. He intended that members of his society should be good preachers and they came to be called the Missionaries of France, but at one point lost favour with the authorities, mainly through the falling-out of Napoleon with Pope Pius VII, and were suppressed. Despite this setback, they managed to continue with their preaching around the country. During the revolution of 1830 and the destruction of their house in Paris, the members went into exile in Rome, where they were encouraged by Pope Gregory XVI to found a new society, the Fathers of Mercy. Approval of the new Congregation, which incorporated the Missionaries of France, was granted in 1834. The first American foundations were made in 1839, where the members worked among the French immigrants to the USA in Louisiana, Alabama and New York. Their work continues as in the past, with preaching missions and the conducting of retreats.

MERCY, SISTERS OF

Location: various; each community is independent
but may belong to a Union, or one of eight
Federations.
RC (female) founded in Ireland in 1831 by the Ven.
Catherine Elizabeth McAuley
Abbr: RSM
Original habit: a black habit and veil and a leather
belt, into which is tucked a large crucifix, with a
rosary.

The numerous Congregations of Sisters of
Mercy began with the endeavour of Catherine Elizabeth McAuley (declared Venerable
in 1990), whose portrait currently appears
on the front of the Irish Five Punt note, the
daughter of a devoutly committed Roman
Catholic father and a less than committed
mother. When her father died, Catherine
received little by way of encouragement from
her mother to practise her faith. Following
the death of her mother, Catherine and her
younger brother and sister, James and Mary,
were cared for by Protestant friends of her
father. As a beneficiary of her Protestant
guardians she inherited a fortune upon their
death and resolved to use it to help poor
women and girls, nurse the sick and catechize
in the Poor Schools in Dublin. To this end
she bought a piece of land in the city and
built a house which contained a small oratory, school rooms and dormitories. In this
work she was helped by Anna Maria Doyle,
who had planned to become a Presentation
nun. In 1827 the house, dedicated to Our
Lady of Mercy, was opened and received two
homeless women and a handful of pupils.
As the work increased, volunteer helpers
joined them. Gradually and unconsciously
religious practices began to develop. The
workers in the house began to wear identical
clothes, a black dress with a plain lace cap
and a grey outdoor cloak with a little black
bonnet. They even referred to each other as
'Sister'. In 1828 the archbishop of Dublin
asked Catherine to choose a name for her
community and she decided upon the Sisters
of Mercy. The path was not smooth, however, and there was much criticism that these
women, however pious, were not real nuns.
Anxious to put her small community on a
secure footing, Catherine and two other
members entered the novitiate of the local
Presentation convent at George's Hill, Dublin, and by 1831 they were able to return as
professed Sisters of Mercy. Their convent
and House of Mercy was formally blessed on
13 December 1831. The Sisters helped during the cholera outbreak in the city, working
in shifts to help the sick and dying victims
in a temporary hospital which had been put
at their disposal. A Decree of Praise was
received from Rome in 1835 and papal
approval was granted in 1841. The Rule
followed was that of the Presentation Order,
modified by St Augustine's Rule, which in
part explains the independence of the Mercy
Congregations, each having the right to
found other communities, which in turn are
also independent. Through this, the foundations spread rapidly throughout the
world. The Irish Communities founded during Mother Catherine's lifetime began with
that established at Dun Laoghaire (Kings-
town) in 1835, where there was a school for
two hundred children, followed by one at
Tullamore (1836), Charleville (1836) and
Carlow (1837). Others were opened at Naas,
Waterford, Cork, Booterstown and Limerick. Two English Sisters who had gone to
Ireland in 1835 were invited to return to
England to make further foundations, and
they went, in the company of Mother Catherine and their Irish superior, Mother Clare,
to open a house in Bermondsey, London, in
1839. More and more foundations followed
throughout the world.

MERCY, SISTERS OF – Australia

The Institute was founded when many
of the Mercy Congregations aggregated

together in 1981, building upon the foundations made by the arrival of Sr Mary Ursula Frayne and three professed Sisters, three novices and one postulant in Perth in 1846. They had come from Ireland at the invitation of the newly appointed bishop, John Brady of Perth, who had gone to Dublin seeking a community of Sisters for Australia, who would open schools 'for the rich, the poor and the natives'. After their arrival in Australia the first school was built, a simple timbered cabin, and others followed. The Sisters were also occupied in visiting the poor and needy and especially helping the Irish deportees in New South Wales and Victoria. Within the next fifty years the Sisters had made many foundations throughout Australia and Papua New Guinea. Today there are more than two thousand members continuing the work. The Sisters are much taken with justice and peace issues, especially among the Aborigines and Torres Strait Islanders, with refugee problems and with teaching and health care. They have members working in Pakistan, Malaysia, Thailand, Kampuchea, Ethiopia, Uganda, Kenya, South Africa, Chile and Vietnam.

✠ Institute of the Sisters of Mercy

MERCY, SISTERS OF – Ireland

The Irish Congregation was formed in 1994, when a union was effected between twenty-six Mercy Congregations in Ireland, which had been founded directly or indirectly by Mother Catherine herself from 1835 onwards, and the Sisters of Mercy of South Africa. The Congregation is divided into several provinces, a vice-province and several regions and mission areas. The Sisters are to be found working in Ireland, South Africa, the USA, Canada, Kenya, Nigeria, Rwanda, Zambia, Peru and Brazil.

✠ Congregation of the Sisters of Mercy

SISTERS OF MERCY – New Zealand

The New Zealand Federation was formed through an amalgamation of Congregations in 1968. The presence of the Congregation in New Zealand began through the efforts of Sister Cecilia Maher from Carlow, who arrived in Auckland together with eight companions in 1850, to serve the Maori people and the new immigrants in Auckland, Christchurch, Dunedin and Wellington. Today, the Sisters work throughout New Zealand and in Ireland, Western Samoa, Fiji, Tonga, Australia, Vietnam, South Africa, Chile, Peru and Jamaica.

✠ Institute of the Sisters of Mercy

MERCY, SISTERS OF – Newfoundland

The Newfoundland Congregation was founded in 1842, several months after Mother Catherine's death, by two Sisters from Dublin who accompanied the newly professed Mary Frances Creedon back to Canada at the invitation of Bishop Anthony Fleming. It had been his idea that she should go to Ireland for her novitiate and return with other Sisters to found a convent at St John's, Newfoundland, together with a day school for paying pupils. An outbreak of typhus involved the Sisters in nursing and caring for the sick and dying, and this led to the building of a modern hospital, which the Congregation ran. Today, the members work not only in Newfoundland, but elsewhere in Canada, as well as in Labrador and Peru.

✠ Institute of the Sisters of Mercy

MERCY, SISTERS OF – The Americas

By 1843 the first settlement of Mercy nuns had been made in Pittsburgh, Pennsylvania, by Mother Frances from the Irish foundation at Carlow. Thirty-nine foundations followed across the USA, the Sisters enduring much hardship and persecution as they nursed the sick and wounded from the Civil War and helped the sick miners during the Californian Gold Rush. By 1928, some 140 convents had been established in the USA, many of which united in 1929 to form the Sisters of Mercy of the Union. In 1991, members of the nine provinces of the Union and of some other Mercy Congregations founded the Sisters of Mercy of the Americas, which eased communication and common goal-setting. The six thousand and more members work across the USA, in Argentina, Belize, Chile, Guan, Guatemala, Guyana, Honduras, Jamaica, Panama, Peru, the Philippines, Haiti, Puerto Rico, the Bahamas, Romania, Saipan and Rota (a small island in the southern Marianas group).

✚ Institute of the Sisters of Mercy

MERCY, SISTERS OF – the Philippines

This group of Mercy Sisters was granted autonomy by Rome in 1981 and had its origins in 1954 when six Irish Sisters of Mercy responded to an invitation by Bishop Lino Gonzago to establish a foundation, which took the form of a high school, at Tacloban City in the south-east Philippines.

✚ Religious Sisters of Mercy

MERCY, SISTERS OF – United Kingdom Institute

The Institute was formed in 1983 by the union of sixteen Mercy Congregations originating from the 1839 foundation made in Bermondsey, London. The members of this group work in education, and in the care of the sick, elderly, unemployed and destitute, and those in need. Houses are to be found throughout England and in Wales. Other Sisters work overseas, in Italy, Peru and Kenya.

✚ Institute of Our Lady of Mercy

MERCY, SISTERS OF – United Kingdom Federation

A Federation of many autonomous Mercy Congregations in Great Britain, whose members share the same ministries as the other Mercy Congregations.

✚ Federation of the Sisters of Mercy

MERCY, SISTERS OF – United Kingdom Union

The Union was founded in 1976 from some thirty houses, with a dependent mission in South America. The communities can be found throughout England, Scotland and Wales as well as on the Falkland Islands, and the Sisters are engaged in teaching and health care programmes, youth and hospital chaplaincies, prison visiting and the usual parish ministries.

✚ Sisters of Mercy of the Union – United Kingdom

MERCY OF ALMA, RELIGIOUS SISTERS OF

Location: USA (Alma, Michigan)
RC (female) founded in the USA in 1973
Abbr: RSM
Original habit: a black habit and veil and a leather belt, into which is tucked a large crucifix, with a rosary.

The Congregation was granted diocesan status in Michigan, USA, in 1974 and given full pontifical approval in 1982. Apart from their work in the USA, the Sisters maintain foreign missions in Canada, Germany and Italy.

MERCY OF OUR LADY OF PERPETUAL HELP, BROTHERS OF

Location: Germany (Trier)
RC (male) founded in Germany in 1850 by Blessed Peter Friedhofen (beatified 1985)
Abbr: FMMA

The founder of this Brotherhood was born on a farm in Weitersburg, near Koblenz, Germany, in 1819, and from childhood was familiar with poverty and sickness. As one of eleven children when his mother was left widowed, he worked as a chimney sweep in order to support them as best he could. With the care of the poor and the sick much in his mind, he later formed the Fraternity of St Aloysius, which operated in many parishes, bringing help where it was needed. Inspired to found a Congregation of Brothers of Mercy, but lacking the necessary experience, he and a companion, Karl Marchand, went to live and work with the Alexian Brothers at Aachen. They returned to Weitersburg in 1850, where the foundation of the Congregation was started. Weitersburg, a tiny village, proved too small for such a venture, and they moved to Koblenz, where Peter and his companions were clothed in the habit in the Church of Our Lady. The following year saw the final profession of Peter, and the clothing of two novices who had joined the Congregation. But Peter's time with his foundation was limited. He died from TB in 1860. The Order continues today with its ministry to the poor and the sick, with houses in Germany, France, Switzerland, Italy, Luxemburg, Brazil and parts of Asia.

✚ Brothers of Charity of Mary Help of
   Christians

MERCY OF ST CHARLES BORROMEO, SISTERS OF

Location: Poland (Katowice)
RC (female) founded in France in 1626

A Congregation which had its beginnings in 1626 in Nancy, France, as an Association of pious women who cared for the sick in the hospital of St Charles in that city. By 1652 it had evolved into a religious community, having accepted a Rule and Constitutions that had been compiled for them by a Premonstratensian abbot, Fr Louys. With the passage of time the work expanded beyond nursing and came to include teaching. The Sisters were dispersed at the time of the French Revolution with the break-up of religious houses, but were reconstituted by Napoleon. These French Sisters adopted a change of Rule, to that of St Augustine, and received papal approval in 1892, by which time their work covered most fields, from vocational training in trades, catechesis, care for young people at risk and in need of reform, to care of the elderly and the sick. Some independent foundations were made, including one in Prague in 1838, with many daughter houses throughout Middle Europe. A house was opened at Neissa (present-day Nysa) in Poland at the invitation of the prince-bishop of Breslaw (Wroclaw). By 1857 this had become a separate Congregation. From this Polish foundation other, affiliated, foundations were made in the Near East.

MERCY OF SEES, SISTERS OF

Location: France (Sees)
RC (female) founded in France in 1823 by Canon J. J. Bazin
Original habit: a black habit and veil with a white cap and a cincture from which a large-beaded rosary was suspended; a crucifix was worn around the neck.

Concerned with the care of the sick and the poor in the diocese, a canon of Sees Cathedral, J. J. Bazin (later vicar-general of the diocese) formed a group of five members, who made use of a single room which they used as a chapel, dormitory, refectory, kitchen and workroom. Although their beginnings were very humble, it was not long before the canon, with the assistance of the duke of Montmorency, could give the Sisters sufficient funds with which to buy some houses, allowing their work to spread. There was great growth in France, with other foundations made in England and Scotland, as well as in other parts of Europe. Overseas expansion took the Sisters into North Africa and Mauritius.

MERCY OF THE BLESSED SACRAMENT, SISTERS OF

Location: Mexico (Coyoacan)
RC (female) founded in Mexico in 1910
Abbr: HMSS

A Pontifical Congregation founded in Mexico in 1910 and devoted to working in schools and performing the usual parish ministries. They maintain a presence in Texas and California as well as in Spain, Italy, Chile, Venezuela, Colombia, El Salvador and Guatemala. The American foundation dates from 1926.

MERCY OF THE CHRISTIAN SCHOOLS, SISTERS OF

Location: France (Saint-Sauveur-le-Vicomte)
RC (female) founded in France in 1807 by Julie Françoise Catherine Postel (St Marie-Madeleine – canonized 1925)
Abbr: SSC
Original habit: a black tunic with a square white wimple and black veil; a cross was worn over the wimple.

An Order originally established in Cherbourg, but in 1823 the Sisters moved to an old Benedictine abbey at Saint-Sauveur-le-Vicomte, which is now the mother house. The coming of the Association Laws in France at the start of the 20th century drove the Sisters to establish other houses, in Germany, Italy, The Netherlands and Eng-

land. The Rule is based on that of the De la Salle Brothers. The work of the Order is in education and nursing.

✠ Sisters of St Marie-Madeleine Postel

MERCY OF THE HOLY CROSS, SISTERS OF

Location: Switzerland (Ingenbohl)
RC (female) founded in Switzerland in 1856
Abbr: SCSC
Original habit: a brown tunic and cape with a white linen headdress, a small wimple and black veil; a metal crucifix on a cord was worn around the neck.

The congregation was founded in 1856 as an outgrowth from the Teaching Sisters of the Holy Cross, when Blessed Mother Maria Scherer (beatified in 1995) became the first superior of the house at Ingenbohl in Switzerland. The Sisters worked initially in nursing, but later included teaching in their apostolate. Boarding schools and schools for the poor were opened, together with training centres for teachers. The Sisters follow the Franciscan Third Order Rule and are now to be found in many European countries, the Far East, Africa and the USA.

✠ Ingenbohl Sisters

MICHAEL IN FRANCE, KNIGHTS OF ST

Defunct
RC (male Equestrian Order) founded in France in 1469
Original habit: a scarlet tunic with a white damask cloak over which was worn a gold collar from which hung a small representation in gold of St Michael forcibly removing a horned demon, complete with tail, by means of a long lance and with the words 'Immensi Tremor Oceani' (The Swell of a Mighty Ocean) inscribed upon it.

The Order was first founded by King Louis XI of France in 1469 and underwent a brief revival in 1816, after the French Revolution, but failed to survive the 1830 revolution.

MICHAEL'S WING, KNIGHTS OF ST

Defunct
RC (male Equestrian Order) founded in Portugal in the 12th century
Original habit: (insignia) a medallion, worn on the left shoulder of a white cloak, shaped like a large sun-burst in the centre of which is a wing. From the neck is suspended another medallion with a red cross in the centre of two small fleur-de-lis motifs, the whole surmounted by a scroll bearing the words 'Quis Ut Deus' (Who is Like Unto God?).

The Order of the Knights of St Michael's Wing was founded in the Cistercian monastery of Alcobazar in Portugal, around the year 1171, by King Alfonso I, in commemoration of a victory over the Moors in which he believed that he had been assisted by St Michael himself. The knights were under the jurisdiction of the abbey of Alcobazar.

✚ Knights of St Michael in Portugal

MILITIA JESU CHRISTI

Defunct
RC (male) founded in Italy in the 13th century

The origins of the Order are uncertain, but it was probably founded by Blessed Bartholomew of Vicenza (1200–71), a Dominican who had received the habit from St Dominic himself while he was in Bologna in 1233. There was an earlier foundation of the same name made in Languedoc, France. The main purpose of the Order was to maintain peace and order and defend the Church against the Albigensian heresy, which was flourishing at this time. The members would appear to have worked in parallel with the Dominicans, who acted as administrators. The merger of the Militia Jesu Christi with the Order of Penance of St Dominic occurred towards the close of the 13th century and so formed the Brothers and Sisters of the Penance of St

Dominic, which was known as the Third Order of St Dominic, with its distinctive habit and Rule.

✚ Fratres Gaudentes

MILL HILL FATHERS

Location: England (Mill Hill, London)
RC (male) founded in London in 1866 by (Cardinal) Herbert Vaughan
Abbr: MHM
Original habit: as for secular clergy

A Society founded at Mill Hill in North London by Fr (later Cardinal) Vaughan as a Missionary Society of secular priests and lay Brothers who would dedicate their lives to working in foreign missions. There are various novitiates and houses of formation in Europe and the USA, and missions are conducted in Asia, Australasia, Africa, South America, the Philippines and the Falkland Islands.

✚ Mill Hill Missionaries
   St Joseph's Missionary Society of Mill Hill
   Society of St Joseph of the Sacred Heart

MINIM DAUGHTERS OF MARY IMMACULATE

Location: Mexico (Leon)
RC (female) founded in Mexico in 1886
Abbr: CFMM

A Pontifical Congregation founded in Leon, Mexico. Because of anti-clerical and anti-Catholic persecution which broke out in 1926 and which continued into the 1930s, the Sisters fled Mexico and made a foundation in the USA, at Tucson, Arizona. They undertake academic and religious education in Our Lady of Lourdes High School in Nogales, Arizona, as well as health care in the Holy Cross Hospital and work also with the care of orphans and in parish ministries. The Congregation maintains a presence in Mexico.

MINIM FATHERS

Location: Italy (Rome)
RC (male) founded in Italy in 1436 by St Francis of
Paola (canonized 1519)
Abbr: OM
Original habit: a dark brown, or black, woollen
tunic with a round hood and a shortened scapular
retained by a rope, the free end of which is
knotted five times (three for a novice); a cloak
which reached below the knee was worn during
winter; the friars were originally discalced, but this
has been dispensed with.

St Francis (1416–1507) was born in the city
of Paola in Calabria, Italy, and at the age of
fifteen became a hermit, having been in a
Franciscan friary from the age of twelve to
honour a vow made by his parents if they
had a son after many years of childlessness.
During his time in the friary he gained a
reputation for sanctity, and as a hermit
practised great austerities. By the age of
twenty he had attracted a group of followers
who styled themselves the Hermits of
Brother Francis of Assisi. The year 1436
marked the foundation of the future Order
of Minims, which grew from this band of
hermits. A church and monastery were
built, and diocesan approval was granted to
the Order in 1471, with papal approval
from Pope Sixtus IV following in 1474.
Other foundations were made, one in Sicily,
when some of the hermits settled near
Paterno on the south side of Mount Etna,
and another at Milazzo, on the north of the
island. The Order had no written Rule until
1493, when the Rule of the Friars Minor
was adopted and later revised. The overall
emphasis was on humility and penance not
only for their own sins but for those of the
rest of mankind. The penitential and contemplative life of the Minims did not
exclude them from preaching. The major
austerities were concerned with fasting and
abstinence. Meat, milk and eggs were forbidden, and the diet was mainly restricted
to bread and water with occasional fish and
vegetables. Any infringement of the Rule
and Constitutions was punished by a penance determined by the superior, known as
the corrector, who was elected for six years.
In determining the penance he made use of
a 'Correctorium', a book of ten chapters
drawn up by St Francis of Paola which
listed appropriate penances. The Minims
were granted the privileges of being a mendicant Order in 1567 by Pope St Pius V.
The austerity attracted many vocations and
the Minims had earlier spread throughout
France. St Francis of Paola spent the rest of
his life there, following a summons by King
Louis XI, who was impressed by the saintliness of the man. He was detained there,
exercising an influence for good, until his
death in 1507 by which time the Order had
expanded through Italy, France, Spain and
Germany. The 16th century marked the
period of greatest expansion for the Order,
but during the French Revolution it disappeared from France, persisting only in Italy
and Spain. Since 1970 there has been a
Minim representation in the USA, in Los
Angeles, as well as a strong tertiary group
operating in South America.

✛ Friars Minims
   Friars of the Order of St Francis
   Hermits of St Francis of Asissi
   Minimi

MINIM SISTERS OF SORROWS

Location: Italy (Bologna)
RC (female) founded in Italy in the 16th century
Original habit: a brown or black woollen habit
with a shortened, round-ended scapular secured by
a rope cincture with five knots, a full-length cape,
small coif and a white veil with a black outer veil;
the Sisters were originally discalced, but this has
been dispensed with.

A very small Congregation, founded in
1506, at the end of St Francis of Paola's life

and approved by Pope Julius II in 1507. The Rule for the Sisters was almost identical with that of the Minim Fathers (see previous entry), with its emphasis on humility and a life of austerity and penance. The houses, which were not as widely spread as those of the Minim Fathers, are presently found mainly in Spain, with others in France and Italy. The life of the Sisters is heavily contemplative.

MISERICORDIA SISTERS

Location: Canada (Montreal, Quebec)
RC (female) founded in Canada in 1848 by
Madame Rosalie Jette (Mother Mary of the
Nativity)
Abbr: SM

An Institute founded in Montreal, Canada, for the care and protection of girls at risk. The founder, Mother Mary, did not become the first superior, but gave way to Sr Jane de Chantal. Papal approval was granted in 1867 and the Rule and Constitutions were given approbation in 1905. Young women who wished to remain in the convent after a period of rehabilitation were called The Daughters of St Margaret. If they persevered in their intention to join the religious life, they could become Magdalens. The Sisters made a foundation in the USA in 1887 where they still work in the archdiocese of New York, operating a large hospital with a maternity home for unmarried mothers. Other foundations were made, usually of hospitals or orphanages, in Illinois and Milwaukee.

✠ Congregation of Sisters of the Misericorde

MONS, CANONESSES OF

Defunct
RC (female) founded in Belgium in the 7th century
by St Valdetrudis
Original habit: a black dress with white sleeves, a
black veil reaching half-way down the back, and a

long black mantle lined in white. In choir the dress was a full-length white linen surplice, or cassock, braided with cord in ornamental knots and scrolls, and a peaked headdress with a long streamer was worn, together with a black silk mantle lined with mouse fur (black with white spots).

St Vaudru, or Valdetrudis, was a saintly widow and patroness of Mons, Belgium, who died c.688. When her saintly husband, St Vincent Madelgarus, became a monk she devoted herself to looking after the poor and sick, building a convent for canonesses on a site in the present-day town of Mons. The canonesses, who observed some form of Benedictine Rule, were really secular women, usually of noble birth, who were free to leave and marry as they were not under a vow of chastity. The Order underwent some reforms under St Bruno, archbishop of Cologne (c.925–65), sometimes called 'The Great'.

MONTE LUCO, HERMITS OF

Defunct
RC (male) founded in Italy in the 5th century by
John of Antioch
Original habit: a tawny-coloured tunic girded with
a knotted cord, short scapular, mantle and hood
and an optional hat, or cap. Some of the hermits
were discalced.

A group of hermits probably founded in the 5th century on the slopes of Monte Luco, which abounded in holly bushes, where some hermitages had been built. These were used by successive groups of solitaries well into the 17th century. The hermits would meet daily to pray in common and would support themselves with some useful work. The superior was elected annually and the hermits could leave at any time as they were not under any type of vow.

MONTE SENARIO, HERMITS OF

Defunct
RC (male) founded in Italy in 1593 by Fr Bernardino di Ricioni
Original habit: a black tunic and scapular with a hooded cloak extending below the knees.

A group of hermits who gathered together on Mt Senario, outside of Florence, at the birthplace of the Order of the Servants of Mary, or Servites, which had been founded in 1234. The hermits lived a most austere life, with long periods of fasting when they existed on bread and water alone, with total abstinence from meat. Much of this was mitigated in 1612 by Pope Paul V. The enthusiasm of the hermits waned in time and the foundation was abolished.

MONTESA, KNIGHTS OF

Defunct
RC (male Equestrian Order) founded in Spain in the 14th century
Original habit: a white mantle with a black cross on the left shoulder.

An Aragonese Order, founded c.1321 by several Mercedarian knights when their Order ceased to be military, together with some knights of Calatreve. The new Order took its name from its headquarters at Montesa. The members were nobly-born, but poor, with new postulants forced to pay for their own maintenance. There was a certain waiving of the very strict requirements to prove noble blood before admittance was granted; this could require no more than two such proofs, which would not have been sufficient for admittance to other Equestrian Orders. In 1400 the knights united with the Order of St George of Alfama, and the new foundation became known as the Order of Our Lady of Montesa and St George of Alfama, at which time the insignia of a red cross for the cloak was adopted.

MOST BLESSED TRINITY, MISSIONARY SERVANTS OF THE

Location: USA (Philadelphia, Pennsylvania)
RC (female) founded in the USA in 1912 by Fr Thomas Judge
Abbr: MSBT
Original habit: a plain dark dress with a simple white collar, dark stockings and shoes and a dark, unadorned, brimmed hat.

Founded in Baltimore, Maryland, by a Vincentian priest, Fr Thomas Judge, the Congregation was founded with the intention of combining the contemplative and active lives. The Sisters are found throughout the USA and are involved in developing the Missionary Cenacle Lay Apostolate. For this purpose the Congregation maintains several Missionary Cenacles at Philadelphia and in Stirling, New Jersey, a Retreat Cenacle at Holy Trinity, Alabama, and the Ecumenical Retreat Centre at New Hartford, Connecticut. The Sisters are also involved in home visiting the needy and poor, providing youth centres, nursing, teaching and various parish and campus ministries. Their apostolate has been extended to include missions to Cuba, Mexico and Puerto Rico.

✠ Trinitarians

MOST HOLY AND IMMACULATE HEART OF MARY, CALIFORNIA INSTITUTE OF THE SISTERS OF THE

Location:
RC (female) founded in Spain in 1848 by Fr Joaquin Masmitja y Puig
Abbr: IHM

An Institute founded in Spain and introduced to California, to Pico Heights, Los Angeles, and Monterey, where the Sisters have been involved in education from elementary to graduate-college level, with specialization in Braille instruction for the blind. They also work in hospitals and run a retreat house for married couples.

✠ Sisters of the Immaculate Heart of Mary

MOST HOLY REDEEMER, OBLATES OF THE

Location: Spain (Madrid)
RC (female) founded in Spain in 1864 by Antonia Maria de la Misericordia and Bishop Jose Maria Benito Serra
Abbr: OSSR

A Spanish Congregation founded in Ciempozuelos, near Madrid. The work of the Sisters is mainly concerned with helping women in need, especially those who have been drawn into prostitution. The Oblates of the Most Holy Redeemer are now found in Spain, Italy, Portugal, parts of South America, the USA, Angola and the Philippines.

MOST HOLY SACRAMENT, SISTERS OF THE – Lafayette

Location: USA (Lafayette, Louisiana)
RC (female) founded in France in 1851 by Fr Joseph A. Faller
Abbr: MHS

A Congregation founded in France, with the first American foundation made in 1872 and approved by the Holy See in 1935. There are houses in Lafayette, San Antonio, Baton Rouge, Biloxi and Gallup. The Sisters work in education, the social services, health care, parish ministries, pastoral work and the conducting of retreats.

MOST HOLY TRINITY, HANDMAIDS OF THE

Location: USA (South Bend, Indiana)
RC (female) founded in the USA in 1968
Abbr: HT

This small Public Association has a purely contemplative apostolate. The members live in community under the usual vows of religion, of poverty, chastity and obedience.

MOST HOLY TRINITY, MISSIONARY SERVANTS OF THE

Location: USA (Arlington, Virginia)
RC (male) founded in the USA in 1928 by Fr Thomas Judge
Abbr: MSSST (or ST)

An American Congregation founded in Maryland by the Vincentian priest Thomas Augustine Judge, for priests and Brothers who are willing to undertake parish ministries and work in specialised fields such as drug rehabilitation and prison chaplaincies. The members also work as military chaplains and in rest homes, hospitals and asylums and have a special ministry among the Appalachian and other rural communities and with Native and Afro-Americans. Houses are to be found throughout the USA, Mexico, Puerto Rico, Costa Rica and Colombia.

✠ Trinity Missions

MOST HOLY TRINITY, ORDER OF THE – FRIARS, CALCED AND DISCALCED

Location: Italy (Rome)
RC (male) founded in France in 1198 by St John of Matha
Abbr: OSST
Original habit: (calced friars) a white tunic, scapular and cape with a blue and red cross embroidered on the scapular and on the left-hand side of the cape; (discalced friars) as for calced friars with the addition of a white hood (France), or with a brown cape and a round black hood, embroidered as before with a cross on the scapular and cape (Spain).

The Order owes its origin to St John of Matha, of Provence, France (1160–1213), who founded it in 1198 during the times of the crusades. He was inspired to found an Order of clerics and lay Brothers dedicated to the ransoming of Christian slaves from the Muslims, who were reputed to have many thousands in captivity. The first Trinitarian House was established at Cerfroid, north-east of Paris. Lay assistants, given the privilege of wearing the Trinitarian scapular and gaining for themselves the spiritual benefits of membership of the Order, were authorized to collect the money necessary to fund the operation. The present Third Order Secular of Trinitarians may have evolved from this lay group. Further ministries were also undertaken by the Order, including hospitality, care of the sick and poor, education and evangelization. Houses in Spain, Luxemburg, Portugal, England, Scotland and Ireland were est blished, and by the close of the 15th century there were about a hundred and fifty houses in existence. Financial troubles and expenses, however, began to dog the Trinitarians, and reform movements began to take effect. In 1596 the Discalced, or barefoot, Trinitarians were introduced. This movement also became known as the Spanish discalced reform, and its influence spread. Discalced houses opened in various countries. Those in France were suppressed in 1771, and further suppressions, in Austria, England, Scotland and Wales, followed. The European revolutions did not spare the Trinitarians and many houses were closed, their members scattered. Restorations followed and new foundations were made. The first American house was opened in 1911 in New Jersey with others following in Pennsylvania and Maryland. The work of the Trinitarian Order continues today in many parts of the world, its members caring for the homeless and hospitalized, those in prison and people who are persecuted.

✠ Mathurins

MOST HOLY TRINITY, ORDER OF THE – INSTITUTES OF TRINITARIAN SISTERS

There are Institutes of Trinitarian Sisters as follows:

1 Institute of Trinitarian Sisters of Rome (founded 1762)
2 Institute of Trinitarian Sisters of Valence, France (founded 1685)
3 Institute of Trinitarian Sisters of Valencia, Spain (founded 1885)
4 Institute of Trinitarian Sisters of Madrid, Spain (founded 1885)
5 Institute of Trinitarian Sisters of Majorca, Spain (founded 1810)
6 Institute of Trinitarian Sisters of Seville, Spain (founded early 17th century)

The members are mainly concerned with education and the care of those in need.

MOST HOLY TRINITY, ORDER OF THE – NUNS, CALCED

Location: Italy (Rome)
RC (female) founded in Aragon in 1236
Abbr: OSST
Original habit: a white tunic and scapular and cape with the Trinitarian cross in red and blue embroidered on the scapular and on the left-hand side of the cape; a black veil over a white cap and small wimple.

The founders of this branch of the Trinitarian Order were Constanza and Sancha, the daughters of King Pedro II of Aragon (1196–1213). Constanza was moved to found a religious Order upon the death of her husband, and the first convent was established at Aitona, in Catalonia (northeast Spain) in 1236. Other women were attracted to the austere and rigorous life. The nuns were strictly enclosed, their work the spiritual help, through prayer and penance, of the Trinitarian Fathers and Brothers. Constanza remained prioress of this first foundation until her death. Other houses were opened in Spain, and from these, new foundations were made in Portugal and Italy. The work later expanded, and the nuns were able to undertake a more active life, involving themselves in teaching and nursing. They established houses in France where, despite their hospital work which protected many religious communities at the time of the French Revolution, they suffered many difficulties. Approbation was granted in 1891, by which time the Sisters had established convents in North Africa, and later in England and the USA. The members now support foreign missions in Madagascar, Colombia and South Korea. As well as teaching and being responsible for hospital ministries, the Sisters manage the National Shrine of Our Lady of Lourdes, at Euclid, Ohio.

✠ Trinitarian Sisters

MOST HOLY TRINITY, ORDER OF THE – NUNS DISCALCED

Location: Spain (Valencia)
RC (female) founded in Spain in 1612 by Francesca Romero
Abbr: OSST
Original habit: a white tunic and scapular, embroidered with the red and blue Trinitarian cross, with a brown cape and black sandals.

This Order of Discalced Trinitarians had its beginnings when a Spanish noblewoman, Francesca Romero, was widowed. Inspired by the reforms introduced into the Trinitarian Order of friars by Juan Bautista, she wanted a foundation with similar austerity for women. The first convent was opened in Madrid in 1613, the foundation approved by Pope Urban VIII in 1624. The Order is still functioning in Spain and elsewhere and has many houses, its members working largely for the needy and those in hospitals and other institutions.

✠ Trinitarian Sisters

MOST PRECIOUS BLOOD OF OUR LORD JESUS CHRIST, SISTERS OF THE

Location: Canada (St Hyacinthe, Quebec)
RC (female) founded in Canada in 1861 by Catherine Caouette (Mother Catherine-Aurélie du Précieux Sang)
Original habit: a white tunic and a black veil with a white turn-back; a red cincture and scapular on which are painted the instruments of the Passion; a white mantle is worn in chapel; external Sisters wore a black habit.

A contemplative Congregation founded in St Hyacinthe, Quebec. Mother Catherine saw her work as being both contemplative and reparational. The Congregation received papal approval in 1896. The life of the community is still completely contemplative and dedicated to devotion to the Precious Blood. The Sisters make religious articles, print prayer cards and pro-life literature, provide spiritual direction and make altar breads. The branch houses of this foundation are all independent and are to be found throughout Canada.

✠ Daughters of Mary Immaculate
  Sisters-Adorers of the Precious Blood

MOST SACRED HEART OF JESUS, MISSIONARY SISTERS OF THE – Hiltrup

Location: Italy (Sutri, diocese of Viterbo)
RC (female) founded in Germany in 1899 by Fr Hubert Linckens
Abbr: MSC
Original habit: a black habit with a black veil and white under-veil, a white wimple and coif; professed Sisters wear a small cross around the neck.

The Congregation was founded by the provincial of the Missionaries of the Sacred Heart, in Hiltrup, near Münster, Germany, and received diocesan approval in 1900. An American foundation, at Reading, Pennsylvania, followed in 1908. This is now a

Pontifical Congregation whose members provide ministries to the poor and needy, the sick and the elderly through their hospitals in Georgia and Pennsylvania, catechesis and education, especially in homecraft, and parish ministries and counselling. The Sisters are to be found throughout the USA and in New Guinea and the Marshall Islands.

MOST SACRED HEART OF JESUS, SERVANTS OF THE

Location: Poland (Krakow)
RC (female) founded in Poland in 1894
Abbr: SSCJ
Original habit: a black habit with a small collar and a leather belt, a black veil and white stiffened headband; a medallion of the Sacred Heart and a crucifix were worn around the neck.

The Congregation was founded in Poland, and an American foundation followed at Cresson, Pennsylvania, in 1959. The Sisters combine both contemplative and active apostolates, which are concerned with fostering reparation to the Sacred Heart in a spirit of Franciscan asceticsim.

MOTHER OF GOD, CLERKS REGULAR OF THE – Lucca

Location: Italy (Rome)
RC (male) founded in Italy in 1574 by St John Leonardi (canonized 1938)
Abbr: OMD
Original habit: as for secular clergy.

Following his ordination to the priesthood in 1572, John Leonardi (1542–1609) became increasingly concerned about the welfare and Christian education of those who were confined to hospitals and prisons in Lucca, west of Florence. With the help of many companions he began work to remedy the situation, and gradually the idea of founding a Congregation given to education and hospital and prison chaplaincy

work took shape. Its beginnings were not without local discord, particularly from the leading families of Lucca, but diocesan approval was granted and the Association of Clerks Regular of the Mother of God, with simple vows of chastity, perseverance and obedience, came into being, recognized as a religious Congregation by Clement VIII in 1595. In his work to make this foundation, St John Leonardi was helped by St Philip Neri and also by St Joseph Calasanctius, who had founded the Piarists. For a short time St John Leonardi's Association was united with the Piarists. In 1619 the Congregation was recognized as a religious Order and its members received the right to take solemn vows, an event which St John failed to see, as he had died from the plague in 1609. The Congregation continues its work in hospital and prison chaplaincy work and has houses in Rome, Naples and Monte Carlo.

MOTHER OF GOD, MISSIONARY SISTERS OF THE

Location: USA (Philadelphia, Pennsylvania)
RC – Byzantine Catholic Rite (female) founded in the USA
Abbr: MSMG

An American Congregation of women of the Byzantine Catholic Rite who are prepared to work largely in education from primary to secondary school level. The Sisters are to be found in the Ukrainian Catholic parishes of the archdiocese of Philadelphia and in the Ukrainian diocese of Stamford, Connecticut.

MOTHER OF GOD, POOR SERVANTS OF THE

Location: England (Roehampton, London)
RC (female) founded in England in 1869 by Frances Mary Taylor (Mother Magdalen of the Sacred Heart)
Abbr: SMG

Original habit: a black habit and veil with a dark blue scapular and black apron, a small, angular white wimple and a white coif, a cincture with rosary and a small crucifix suspended around the neck.

Frances (Fanny)Taylor (1832–1900), whose cause for canonization is now being researched, was a convert from Anglicanism. She is well known to history as one of the helpers of Florence Nightingale at the Crimean War, when she was stationed with the other nurses at Koulali Barrack Hospital in 1854. Her earlier interest and concern for the poor continued on her return to England after the war and brought her into contact with Lady Georgina Fullerton, with whose co-operation and help the foundations for the Institute of the Poor Servants of the Mother of God were laid. Frances visited Poland, to stay with the Congregation of Servants of the Mother of God, Mary Immaculate, at Posen, to see at first hand the type of Congregation she had in mind. With the help of the Oblates of Mary Immaculate at Tower Hill, London, and with three companions, Frances started a postulancy in premises off Grosvenor Square, London. She made her profession in 1872. By now the numbers attracted to join this Congregation had increased enough to cause the opening of another house in London, at Roehampton, which became the mother house. Approved by Rome in 1879, the work continued with the opening of the Providence Free Hospital in St Helens, Lancashire, as well as refuges in Liverpool and London and St Joseph's Asylum for single and elderly women in Dublin. More foundations followed. An American house was opened in 1947. The American Sisters work in North Carolina with an apostolate of care for the sick as well as teaching in schools and running a retreat centre. Houses of the Congregation are also to be found in France, South America, Italy and Africa.

MOTHERS OF THE HELPLESS

Location: Spain (Valencia)
RC (female) founded in Spain in 1881
Abbr: MD

A Diocesan Congregation founded in Malaga, Spain, and with an American foundation in New York dating from 1916. The Sisters in New York maintain the San Jose de la Montana Day Nursery and the Sacred Heart Residence for young women as well as caring for orphans and the elderly. Other houses have been opened in Guatemala, Colombia, Puerto Rico, Spain, Mexico, Chile, Argentina and Italy.

MOUNT CALVARY, DAUGHTERS OF

Defunct
RC (female) founded in the 17th century by Virginia Centurione
Original habit: Franciscan in style.

This Congregation was founded by the daughter of a doge of Venice, Virginia Centurione, who had been married to Gasparo Grimaldi Bracelli. When her husband died, in 1625, she gathered together some children who had been abandoned during a time of famine and established for them a refuge dedicated to the Blessed Virgin Mary. She and her companions led a communal Franciscan way of life and undertook to care for the sick and poor. No vows were made, only solemn promises to persevere in the Congregation. After her death, in 1651, the Congregation spread throughout Italy, and a house was established in Rome. The Congregation prospered under both Pope Pius VII and Pope Gregory XVI.

MOUNT CALVARY, MISSIONARY SOCIETY OF

Defunct

RC (male) founded in France in 1633 by Fr Hubert Charpentier

A Congregation of secular priests who were concerned with countering the work of the Huguenots, defending the Roman Catholic faith and honouring the Sacred Passion. They banded together in 1633 at Betharram (Bayonne) under the leadership of Hubert Charpentier, with another house opened near Toulouse. The Congregation did not survive the French Revolution.

MOUNT CALVARY, NUNS OF THE ORDER OF

Defunct

RC (female) founded in France in 1601 by Antoinette, Princess of Orléans

Original habit: a white habit, cloak, scapular and girdle with a black veil.

An Order founded by Antoinette of Orléans, the daughter of the duke of Longueville and widow of the marquis of Belleisle, dedicated to the Blessed Virgin Mary of Mount Calvary. The Order observed a strict Benedictine Rule and was approved by Rome. The founder died in 1618.

N

NAME OF JESUS, COMMUNITY OF THE

Defunct

Anglican (female) founded in England in 1881

An Anglican community founded at Great Maplestead, Essex, which became defunct in the 1940s. In addition to the usual parish and social ministries, the Sisters started a female rehabilitation centre and an orphanage in Stratford, East London. In 1891 the community moved to Glamorgan, in Wales, where they undertook parish work in several dioceses. The Rule followed by the Sisters was a compilation from several sources.

NATIVITY OF OUR LORD, INSTITUTE OF THE SISTERS OF THE

Location: France (Paris)

RC (female) founded in France in 1813 by the Abbé Enfantin and Madame de Franzu

Abbr: SC

Original habit: a black dress and cape with a corded girdle; a black veil beneath which was worn a frilled white cap, a white linen collar and a silver crucifix around the neck.

An Institute founded in Crest, south-east France, to provide education for the young, which was in a sad state in the years following the French Revolution. Madame de Franzu was appointed as the first superior-general and a further house was opened at Valence, south of Lyons. The Congregation received its approbation in 1888. Prior to its union with six other Congregations, to form the Union Mysterium Christi in 1976, there were houses in France, Italy, Madagascar and Cameroon. As well as teaching, the Sisters now run homes for girls, orphanages and various clubs and hostels.

NATIVITY OF THE BLESSED VIRGIN, SISTERS OF THE

Defunct

RC (female) founded in France in 1818 by Abbé Pierre Pourchon

Original habit: a black habit with a white headcap, and a deep white linen wimple, beneath which a cross was worn.

The Congregation was founded in Paris, at St Germain-en-Laye, by the Abbé Pourchon, assisted by Annette Perrier, who became its first superior as Mother St Francis de Sales, and Clare Veronique Gibot (Mother St Chantal), the first superior-general. The work of the Congregation was concerned with education, and many schools and foundations were made in France. With the enactment of the Association Laws in France at the start of the 20th century, which led to the closure of many religious houses, a school was opened at Genape, in Belgium, and a boarding and day school with a novitiate in Leicester, England, in 1904.

NAZARETH, POOR SISTERS OF

Location: England (Hammersmith, London)
RC (female) founded in England in 1851 by Victoire Larmenier (Mother St Basil)
Abbr: PSN
Original habit: a black or white habit and scapular, according to the climate, with blue trimming on the scapular and sleeves; the emblem of the Congregation was worn on a blue cord around the neck. A blue cloak was worn in choir on special occasions.

The founder, Victoire Larmenier (1827–78), who came from Brittany, was invited by Cardinal Wiseman to found this Congregation in London in 1851. Approval was granted in 1864. It took as its main theme the life of the Holy Family in Nazareth, for which reason every foundation of the Congregation is called Nazareth House. The need for this Congregation arose on account of the appalling conditions that many of the old and poor had to endure, which the Sisters sought to improve, extending the apostolate into caring for homeless and abandoned children. Today, the work continues in nursing, teaching, the care of children and the aged, dietetics, maternity work and various social and welfare programmes. The Sisters are found throughout the UK as well as in South Africa, Zimbabwe, Eastern Samoa, Australia, New Zealand and the USA, where they maintain houses in California and Wisconsin.

NAZARETH, THE LADIES OF

Defunct
RC (female) founded in France in 1822 by Fr Roger, the Duchesse de la Rochefoucauld and Elise Rollat
Original habit: a black woollen dress with a long black veil, beneath which was worn a white frilled

cap with pleated muslin border; and a silver crucifix bearing the words 'O Crux Ave, O Spes Unica, Jesus, Marie, Joseph'. In choir a long black mantle was worn. Lay Sisters wore a brown woollen habit with a large black bibbed apron, a shorter veil, a cloak and a silver cross with the I.H.S. monogram.

A Congregation founded for the purpose of educating young women in the wake of the French Revolution, so that they could take their place in a country which emerged with a very different social structure. The Sisters, aiming for simplicity, named their Congregation 'Nazareth' and strove to restore to the young women something of the standards and mores of the time before the Revolution. Approbation was granted by Pope Leo XIII in 1896. Further houses and schools were opened in Palestine, with a large boarding school in Beirut to provide education for girls of wealthy European and local families, and a Free School to cater for those who could not pay. Other houses were established throughout France, and a single foundation was made in both England (Ealing, London) and Italy (Rome).

NORTH AMERICAN UNION OF SISTERS OF OUR LADY OF CHARITY

Location: USA (Wisconsin Dells, Wisconsin)
RC (female) founded in France in 1641 by St John Eudes (canonized 1925)
Abbr: NAU – OLC

The Congregation was founded in Caen, Normandy by St John Eudes, who was distressed by the condition of many young women and girls who had been abandoned to their fate and were open to sexual exploitation. He was joined by a group of ladies in a rescue bid, and they formed the nucleus of the Order of Our Lady of Charity, which received papal approbation in 1666. The Congregation is still concerned with the protection of women and young girls who are at risk and others who are exploited and seeking rehabilitation. To this end the Sisters have created day care centres and residences which can help those in need. They also operate parish and educational ministries. The first American foundation was made in 1855, followed by many others, and in 1944 a Federation of these autonomous houses was made which resulted in the North American Union of Our Lady of Charity, receiving papal approval in 1979. The Sisters in America have a special ministry for Spanish-speakers.

NOTRE DAME, CONGREGATION OF SISTERS OF – Namur

Location: Italy (Rome)
RC (female) founded in France in 1804 by St Julie Billiart (canonized 1969) and the Viscountess Blin de Bourdon (Mother St Joseph)
Abbr: SNDdeN (or SND)
Original habit: a black habit with a starched, white linen wimple and binder and a black veil; a black cloak was used for outdoor wear.

A French Congregation founded in Amiens by Julie Billiart (1751–1816), who was born in Cuvilly, Picardy. From a tender age she showed great enthusiasm for teaching her fellows, which, in time, led to the foundation of her Congregation, with a ministry to help in the education of the poor. In 1804 permission was given for the founding of a school which had as its first resident pupils eight orphan girls. By 1807 several other houses had been founded and a large school was opened at Namur, in Belgium, which became the mother house of the Congregation. Free Schools for the poor were supported by the fees charged at the boarding schools. Papal approbation was not received until 1844, well after the death of the founder. The first American foundation was made by eight pioneer Sisters who went to Cincinnati, Ohio, in 1840, invited there to establish education for the American Indians. Declining the offer of a fine country property, on the grounds that the poor would never come there, the Sisters went to the city and opened their first house, which expanded a year later into a school for three types of pupils, those who boarded, those who were day pupils and those attending the Free School. So successful was their work that by 1848 they had established nine schools in Cincinnati. More schools were opened in other parts of the USA. Today, the Congregation is divided into eight provinces, and the work in education now encompasses every type of school, college and university. Communities are also to be found in Europe, Asia, Africa and South America, where the Sisters care for refugees and street children, migrant workers, and AIDS orphans.

NOTRE DAME, SCHOOL-SISTERS OF

Location: Italy (Rome)
RC (female) founded in Germany in 1833 by Caroline Gerhardinger (Blessed Mother Mary Teresa of Jesus; beatified 1985)
Abbr: SSND
Original habit: a black habit with a wide black girdle, a white wimple and binder, a long black veil with a white under-veil and a long, pleated mantle.

The founder, who had been educated by the Canonesses of Our Lady (founded 1597), was encouraged by the bishop of Ratisbon to form a Congregation of teachers who could take charge of education for the poor in Bavaria. The Rule was based on that of the Canonesses of Our Lady and the Congregation was unenclosed, to allow the Sisters to go about the country as teachers and catechists. In 1847 Blessed Mother Mary Teresa went to the USA to found more houses. The Sisters maintain a presence in the USA in seven Provinces, working as teachers but with an extended apostolate in health and social ministries, prison chaplaincies, spiritual direction and parish and diocesan administration. There are other foundations in Europe, South and Central America, Africa, Asia and the Pacific Islands.

NOTRE DAME, SISTERS OF

Location: Italy (Rome)
RC (female) founded in Germany in 1850 by Aldegonda Wolbring (Sr Mary Aloysia) and Lisette Kuehling (Sr Mary Ignatia)
Abbr: SND
Original habit: a black habit, and cape with a white linen collar.

The Congregation, founded in Coesfeld, Germany, came into existence when the two founders, encouraged by their parish priest, Fr Elting, took abandoned and neglected children into their home to educate and care for them. In 1852 the two founders made their vows, having undergone a period of religious formation helped by Sisters from the Notre Dame Community of Amersfoort, in The Netherlands. An American foundation was made at Cleveland, Ohio, in 1874 and other foundations followed, leading to the establishment of four American provinces. The work in the USA is extensive and covers teaching at all levels, providing support for single parents, care for the elderly and for the sick in hospitals, youth and campus ministries, migrant advice, retreats, missions, counselling and spiritual direction. Foreign missions have also been undertaken, and members now work in Papua New Guinea, Africa, India, Indonesia, Korea and Brazil as well as Europe.

NOTRE DAME, SISTERS OF THE CONGREGATION OF

Location: Canada (Montreal, Quebec)
RC (female) founded in Canada in 1653 by St Marguerite Bourgeouys (canonized 1982)
Abbr: CND
Original habit: a simple black tunic with a large divided white collar and a tight-fitting cap; a crucifix was worn around the neck.

This Canadian Congregation was founded by a Frenchwoman, St Marguerite Bourgeoys (1620–1700), who came from Troyes, France. Attracted to the religious life, she had been unable to find acceptance with either the Carmelites or the Poor Clares, both enclosed Orders, which probably led her to found an unenclosed Order. A compatriot, Paul de Chomedey de Maisonneuve, from Canada, met Marguerite in France when he was visiting his sister at the Augustinian Convent in Troyes. He invited her to Canada, anxious to provide a teacher to work at the Villa Marie which he had founded at Montreal in 1642. She accepted the challenge and arrived in Canada to find only one child of school age and a group of prospective brides, some as young as twelve. The area was poor, and she began a ministry by washing clothes for the sick and sharing her food with them. As the local community grew she was able to open a school in 1658 to cater for twelve pupils, and it became necessary for Marguerite to return to France to recruit more volunteers. It is claimed that 1659 marks the date of the foundation, for that was when she returned to Canada with some companions and opened a kindergarten and a vocational training school. Another visit to France resulted in the recruitment of six more helpers, and the idea of a religious Congregation grew. The Congregation of Notre Dame was canonically erected by Bishop François de Laval, the first bishop of Quebec, in 1676, a man described by contemporaries as being saintly but 'tight lipped under a big nose'. He was determined that the new Congregation should live an enclosed life, and despite appeals to France for ecclesiastical approval for an unenclosed Congregation with simple vows so that their work could continue, Marguerite failed to get her way at first. Bishop Laval finally gave way, but his successor made more difficulties for the French group, and it was not until 1698 that the Sisters were able to make their formal religious profession. Twenty-four Sisters made their vows, accepting the Rule which Marguerite had drawn up for them. The Sisters' work prospered and expanded to include the running of mission schools for Indians, with two young Iroquois women joining the Congregation. Much work was done with young immigrant women, providing workshops where they could learn trades and skills which would allow them to earn a living. Today, the Sisters are to be found in Canada and the USA, where a foundation was made in 1860, as well as in France, Japan, Cameroon, El Salvador, Guatemala, Honduras and Paraguay.

NOTRE DAME SISTERS

Location: Czech Republic (Javornik)
RC (female) founded in Czechoslovakia in 1853 by Fr Gabriel Schnieder
Abbr: ND

A Congregation founded in Javornik, Czechoslovakia, in the mid-19th century to provide teachers and parish helpers, who were in very short supply at the time. An American foundation was made at Omaha, Nebraska, in 1910, from which many other foundations have been made throughout the USA. The Sisters are involved in education at elementary and secondary level and provide pastoral ministries, catechesis, counselling for those who are drug-dependent, hospital chaplaincies and campus ministries, as well as a special ministry to the Sioux Indians.

O

OAK TREE, KNIGHTS OF THE

Defunct
RC (male Equestrian Order) founded in Spain in the 8th century
Original habit: a white tunic decorated with a red cross, whose horizontal and terminal arms terminated in a fleur-de-lis, suspended above an oak tree.

The Order had its origins in a vision experienced by Garcia Ximenes, a nobleman and military leader, who renounced his military career in order to embrace a solitary life having first distinguished himself and inspired others in the fight against the Moors. He had seen a vision of a cross above an oak tree which became the emblem of this Equestrian Order, instituted by the first king of Navarre during the pontificate of Pope St Gregory II (715–31) to celebrate the defeat of the Moors.

OBREGONIANS

Defunct
RC (male) founded in Spain in 1567 by Bernardino Obregon
Original habit: the grey habit of the Franciscan Third Order Regular with the addition of a black cross worn on the left breast, a privilege granted by Pope Paul V in 1609.

A Congregation of Franciscan regular tertiaries founded in Madrid by Bernardino Obregon, a nobleman who spent his career in the Spanish army. On retirement, he decided to dedicate his life to the care of the sick in the hospitals of Madrid. He was joined in this work by others who, like him, were Franciscan tertiaries. They lived together in community, taking the usual vows of religion, poverty, chastity and obedience, with an additional fourth vow of free hospitality. The Congregation spread throughout Spain and Belgium and extended as far as India, but became defunct.

OPUS DEI

Location: Italy (Rome)
RC (male and female) founded in Spain in 1928 by Blessed José Maria Escriva de Balaguer (beatified 1992)

The Society of Opus Dei was founded in Madrid, Spain, by José Maria Escriva de Balaguer (1902–75) and intended for professional people who were anxious to attain personal sanctification and to spread the life of Christian perfection among people of all classes, especially those in positions of great influence because of their professional lives. At the end of the Spanish Civil War, which had largely destroyed the structure of Spanish society, members of Opus Dei were in a position to fill many of the vacancies with the approval of General Franco, who was anxious to restore Spain as a major Roman Catholic power in Europe. In 1943 the Society received the approval of Pope Pius XII for the training of priests, and the movement spread widely following the end of World War II. Fr José Maria was granted the use of the former Hungarian Embassy in Rome, and this became the headquarters of Opus Dei. With increasing worldwide support, branches were established. In 1962, the Society approached Pope John XXIII with a view to becoming a 'personal prelature', which would exempt the members from the jurisdiction of any local hierarchy. This was a move that prompted some alarm in some parts of the Church, but permission was granted after the founder's death in 1975. The members of the Society, who may be clerics or laypeople, are noted for their traditionalist attitude to the practice of the faith, and their perceived secrecy has courted considerable criticism.

✠ Sacerdotal Society of the Holy Cross and Opus Dei

OPUS SPIRITUS SANCTI

Location: USA (Pocahontas, Iowa)
RC (male and female) founded in Germany in 1950

A Secular Institute of diocesan right, which received approbation in 1970. The Institute provides an opportunity for single and married laity to live communally alongside priests and deacons and to exercise missionary zeal for the creation of a 'New Pentecost'.

ORATORIANS

Location: Italy (Rome)
RC (male) founded in Italy in 1575 by St Philip Neri (canonized 1622)
Abbr: CO
Original habit: a double-breasted black cassock with cincture and a linen collar open at the front.

After his ordination, St Philip Neri (1515–95) led a community life with four other priests, including his confessor. His discourses and devotions attracted the attention of others, who wished to join the group. An oratory was built over the aisle of the church of St Jerome in Rome to accommodate the growing numbers. In 1564, Philip took charge of the church of St John of the Florentines in Rome, where he and his priest-associates could say a daily Mass and preach four sermons a day, interspersed with hymn-singing and popular devotions. It soon became apparent that the group needed a church of their own, and the pope gave them Santa Maria in Vallicella, which was rebuilt and is now known as the Chiesa Nuova. It was here that Pope Gregory XIII formally erected the Congregation in 1575. Its Constitutions were approved by Pope Paul V in 1612. The Oratory movement spread widely, and during St Philip's lifetime some fifty houses were either established or united with the Oratory. A period of suppression was imposed under Napoleon at the start of the 19th century and again in 1869, but the Congregation survived. The purpose of the Oratory of St Philip Neri was threefold and composed of prayer, preaching and the sacraments, through which the Oratorians sought to lead men to God. No vows are taken, and the members remain as secular priests and lay Brothers, united in a community to which all contribute according to their means. Each house is independent, and there are some national differences in administration. The French Oratorians, founded in 1611 by Cardinal Pierre de Bérulle, opted for a centralized Congregation with a superior-general elected for life, an arrangement which suited the needs of the Church in France at the start of the 17th century. The English Oratorians were founded in 1848 by Cardinal Newman, following his conversion to Roman Catholicism.

♰ Congregation of the Oratory of St Philip Neri

ORATORY, DAUGHTERS OF THE

Location: Italy (Lodi)
RC (female) founded in Italy in c.1900 by Blessed Vincent Grossi (beatified 1975)

The Congregation was founded in Vicobellignano, in the diocese of Cremona, by Vincent Grossi (1845–1917), who realized that the moral and religious education of girls in his parish was meagre. In order to remedy this, he founded a community of women, known as the Daughters of the Oratory, which received diocesan approval in 1901 and papal approbation in 1915 and 1926. The Sisters still work in the field of religious education and counselling throughout Europe.

ORATORY OF JESUS AND OF MARY IMMACULATE OF FRANCE

Location: France (Paris)
RC (male) founded in France in 1611 by Fr (later Cardinal) Pierre de Bérulle

The Oratory of Jesus and Mary Immaculate was founded by Pierre de Bérulle (1575–1629), who was inspired by the Oratorians of St Philip Neri. His principal aim in so doing was to train priests in 'the pursuit of sacerdotal perfection'. While never intended as a teaching Order, the Oratory organized seminaries in France along the lines recommended by the Council of Trent.

♰ French Congregation of the Oratory

ORATORY OF THE GOOD SHEPHERD

Location: England (Horsham, Sussex)
Anglican (male) founded in England in 1913

Abbr: OGS
Original habit: as for secular clergy.

An Anglican Society of priests and laymen which was founded in Cambridge. Its members do not live a communal life but undertake to observe a common Rule which involves daily Eucharist, the reading of the divine office, meditation and study, with regular meetings of members in chapters and retreats. It must not be confused with an Order, or a religious community, but is rather better described as a society, with the members, who are grouped into colleges each with its own chapter, observing a vow of celibacy and required to give an account of their assets, liabilities and expenses. Vows are taken after a period of probation, or novitiate, which may last up to two years. Profession is initially binding for one year, renewed annually for five years and finally a profession for life may be made. Members of the Oratory of the Good Shepherd currently live and work in five provinces throughout the world, the UK, Canada, the USA, Australia and South Africa.

OUR LADY HELP OF THE CLERGY, CONGREGATION OF

Location: USA (Vale, North Carolina)
RC (female) founded in the USA in 1961
Abbr: CLHC

An American Congregation founded to provide Sisters who will be able to visit those in hospital or confined to their own homes, and to care for the elderly. The members also provide counselling and spiritual direction, conduct retreats and operate day care centres.

♰ Maryvale Sisters

OUR LADY MOTHER OF MERCY, BROTHERS OF (and SISTERS OF)

Location: The Netherlands (Tilburg)
RC (male) founded in The Netherlands in 1844 by Fr (later Archbishop) Joannes Zwijsen
Abbr: CFMM

Joannes Zwijsen (1794–1877), aware of the needs of the poor and their lack of education, founded first a Congregation of Sisters in 1832, followed in 1844 by that of the Brothers of Our Lady of Mercy, in Tilburg. In 1845 he opened an orphanage for boys and a printing press for religious and school books, soon followed by a primary school for boys and a teacher training programme for Brothers. The work continued away from Tilburg, with attention directed at the educational needs of deaf or blind boys. After the founder's death, in 1877, the work of the Brothers was further extended and foreign missions were made to Surinam, Indonesia, Zaire, Kenya, Namibia, Brazil and California. The work now includes an AIDS ministry, pastoral work, teacher training programmes and the provision of sheltered accommodation for refugees.

OUR LADY OF AFRICA, MISSIONARY SISTERS OF

Location: Italy (Rome)
RC (female) founded in Algeria in 1869 by Cardinal Charles Martial Lavigerie
Abbr: WS (also MSOLA)
Original habit: a white tunic, belt, scapular, wimple and veil with a silver crucifix suspended from the neck on a red cord; a rosary composed of black and white beads is also worn and professed Sisters wear a silver ring. In non-African countries the Sisters could add a long black cloak and veil.

A missionary Congregation which was founded by Archbishop (later Cardinal) Lavigerie in response to the plight of orphans in Africa in the aftermath of famines and droughts. The first members were eight Breton girls who commenced their novitiate in Algiers in 1869, one of whom, Mother Marie Salome, became the first mother-general. The work expanded as the numbers increased and the Sisters were soon working alongside the White Fathers in many African countries. There are foundations in Europe, America and Canada where the Sisters work in education, medical and social services, manage homes for the elderly, give pastoral care, run youth retreats, and are active in helping with the formation of local Sisterhoods. In 1992, the Sisters started a lay association based on the teachings and spirit of Charles Lavigerie, which is attached to the Sisters' mission in Bukavu, Eastern Congo. The members of this association have a one-year training, make a retreat and can then go on to make a solemn promise to live according to the rules of the association, when they receive a scarf with the emblem of a pelican, symbolising self-sacrificing love. This promise is renewed annually.

✠ Sisters of Africa
   White Sisters

OUR LADY OF ALLTAGRACIA, INSTITUTE OF

Location: Dominican Republic (Santo Domingo)
RC (female) founded in the Dominican Republic in 1956 by Fr José Maria Uranga, SJ

A Secular Institute of diocesan right, which was founded by a Jesuit priest and received approbation in 1964. The members of the Institute, which has houses in the Dominican Republic, Puerto Rico, Nicaragua, Mexico and the USA, continue to live with their families, providing catechesis in schools and parishes. They also help in poor and rural communities, where they try to focus on Our Lady and to integrate a contemplative life within an active lifestyle.

OUR LADY OF BETHANY, MISSION OF

Location: USA (Boston, Massachusetts)
RC (female) founded in France in 1948

This Secular Institute of diocesan right was founded in Plesis-Chenet, France, and received diocesan approbation in 1965. The members aim to bring happiness and care to the most neglected and marginalized of society, to those in prison and those who are being exploited through prostitution. The Sisters are also present in the USA.

OUR LADY OF CHARITY, SISTERS OF

Location: Italy (Rome)
RC (female) founded in France in 1641 by St John Eudes
Abbr: OLC
Original habit: a cream habit and scapular with a black veil; a silver heart was worn on the chest; a cream cloak was worn in choir.

The Congregation of Our Lady of Charity was founded in Caen, France by St John Eudes (1601–80) to reform fallen women, work which is still maintained today. St John Eudes, ordained as a priest in 1625, spent some of his early working years in rural Normandy, and during this time he helped women who were being exploited through prostitution by making safe accommodation available for them in Caen. In this work he was helped by Madelaine Lamy. When new premises were needed they obtained a larger house, with the blessings of the local bishop and civic authorities for the work they had undertaken. The foundation of the Congregation was made in 1641 in the house of Our Lady of Charity. Other houses were founded throughout France, providing shelter, support and spiritual counselling for women. Early disputes, which led to the departure of some of the members, were overcome and the Congregation, which observed the Rule of St Augustine and adopted the Constitution of the Visitation Order, flourished despite difficulties in a sensitive situation. But stagnation developed in the mid-18th century and in 1792 eight of the independent houses of the Congregation were dissolved. An attempt was made after the end of the French Revolution to reassemble the Congregation at Tours. The future St Mary Euphrasia Pelletier, the founder of the Good Shepherd Sisters, an independent branch of the Congregation of Our Lady of Charity, joined the Tours Congregation in 1814. Autonomous houses of this Congregation were federated in 1944, and in 1979 the North American Union of the Sisters of Our Lady of Charity was established and approved by Rome. The Sisters' work is still concerned with the needs of women and girls who are in moral danger and the provision for them of safe housing, day care centres and drug counselling. Teaching and pastoral ministries are also undertaken. Houses are maintained in six European countries, the USA, Canada, Mexico, and Kenya.

✠ Sisters of Our Lady of Charity and Refuge

OUR LADY OF CHARITY OF THE GOOD SHEPHERD, SISTERS OF

Location: Italy (Rome)
RC (female) founded in France in 1829 by Rose Virginie Pelletier (St Mary Euphrasia) (canonised 1940)
Abbr: RGS and CGS
Original habit: (choir Sisters) a white tunic and scapular with a blue girdle, a white linen wimple and a black veil; an engraved silver heart was worn around the neck, with the image of the Good Shepherd on one side and the Virgin Mary and Infant Jesus with roses and lilies on the other; (external Sisters) a black habit.

This Congregation forms a branch of the Institute of Our Lady of Charity and Refuge, founded by St John Eudes at Caen,

France, in the 17th century. Rose Virginie Pelletier, who was born into a bourgeois family in the west of France in 1796, entered the Community of Our Lady of Charity and Refuge, in Tours, in 1814 and some eleven years later was elected as its superior. A woman of vision, she set about expanding her community's work among women in need of moral and physical help. Aware that two communities of the Good Shepherd, which had been disbanded at the time of the French Revolution, were anxious to be reactivated, she established a community incorporating them in Angers in 1829 under the title of the Order of Our Lady of Charity and the Good Shepherd. The foundation was approved by Rome in 1835, with centralized organization. Later foundations followed and the Order spread into Italy, Ireland, England, the USA, Canada, Australia and Chile. It has been estimated that by the time of her death in 1868, Mother Mary Euphrasia had established over a hundred convents on six continents. The work has expanded into many fields, and the Sisters now run rescue and rehabilitation centres, probation homes and approved schools, homes for unmarried mothers and their babies and foreign missions. There is also a contemplative branch of this Order.

OUR LADY OF CHRISTIAN DOCTRINE, SISTERS OF

Location: USA (Suffern, New York)
RC (female) founded in the USA in 1910 by Marion Frances Guerney (Mother Marianne of Jesus)
Abbr: RCD

A Congregation founded in New York in 1910 by Marion Frances Guerney, with its main apostolate in religious education and social justice. These goals are fulfilled in spiritual direction, retreat work, counselling, nursing and various parish ministries and social work. There are houses in New Hampshire, Illinois and New York and also in the Dominican Republic.

OUR LADY OF COMPASSION, SISTERS OF

Location: France (Toulouse)
RC (female) founded in France in 1817 by Abbé Maurice Marie Mathieu Garrigou

A Congregation which was founded at Toulouse in 1817 and later united with the Congregation of the Daughters of Compassion, Handmaids of the Lord (founded 1842 by Mother Mary of the Compassion). The Sisters are involved in education.

OUR LADY OF COMPASSION, SISTERS OF

Defunct
RC (female) founded in France in 1824 by Madame Gaborit (Sr Marie de la Compassion)
Original habit: a black habit and veil.

The Congregation of Sisters of Our Lady of Compassion was founded at Argenteuil, near Paris, in an attempt to form a community which would undertake the education of young girls. The original name was Daughters of the Cross, but when the community moved from Argenteuil to Saint-Denis the name was changed to the present one. The Congregation observed the Rule of St Augustine. In 1834 the work expanded when the Sisters ran a hospital in Paris.

✦ Religious of the Compassion of the Holy Virgin
   Sisters of St Denis

OUR LADY OF CONSOLATION, ORDER OF

Defunct
RC (male) founded in Italy in 1631 by Fr Boniface d'Antoine
Original habit: Camaldolese style.

This Order was founded from within the Camaldolese Congregation of the Hermits of Monte Corona and was responsible for the founding of the first Camaldolese hermitage in France, near Botheon, Lyons, which was approved by King Louis XIII in 1631. Other foundations followed, and the French Camaldolese Congregation was established as a separate foundation in 1634. The Rule of the Monte Corona Congregation was most austere. The French Congregation followed it assiduously, which led to the hermits becoming tainted by Jansenism, which some refused to recognize as heretical. The Congregation was consequently suppressed in 1770.

OUR LADY OF CONSOLATION, SISTERS OF

Location: Italy (Rome)
RC (female) founded in Spain by St Mary Rose Molas y Vallve (canonized 1988)

The founder of the Congregation of Our Lady of Consolation had unwittingly joined an irregular religious Order, which was dedicated to the care of the elderly, the sick, children and infants at Reus, near Tarragona, Spain. The matter was regularized when St Mary (1815–76), together with ten members of the community, placed themselves under diocesan jurisdiction and a new Congregation was established which undertook responsibility for teaching and providing health care, especially for children. The Sisters now have houses in Europe, South America, Africa and Asia.

OUR LADY OF FIDELITY, SISTERS OF

Location: France (Douvres La Delivrande)
RC (female) founded in France in 1831 by Henriette Leforestier D'Osseville (Mother Saint Mary)
Abbr: OLF

A Congregation founded in Rouen, France, which devotes itself to the care of poor and abandoned children and their education. The founder was persuaded to form a Congregation which would demonstrate the faithfulness of the Mother of God to those who invoke her under the title of 'Our Lady of Fidelity'. The Rule followed is Ignatian in spirit.

OUR LADY OF GOOD AND PERPETUAL SUCCOUR, SISTERS OF

Location: Italy (Rome)
RC (female) founded on the island of Mauritius in 1850 by Caroline Lenferna de Laresles (Mother Marie-Augustine)
Abbr: BPS
Original habit: a black habit, apron and cincture with a white linen wimple and a black veil over a white cap; a silver heart was suspended around the neck, engraved on one side 'Our Lady of Perpetual Succour' and on the reverse, 'Our Lady Help of Christians'.

A Congregation founded on the island of Mauritius, off the east coast of Africa, whose founder had decided when she was very young that she wanted to be a Sister of Charity. Her father disinherited her, and with slender resources she began, with four companions, to care for the poor. She took the name of Mother Marie-Augustine and at the age of twenty-four set about opening a hospital, a leper settlement and an orphanage, as well as free schools and crèches. Queen Victoria of England recognized her work and that of her Sisters by awarding a gold medal for their efforts during the epidemics that occurred in the mid-19th century on Mauritius. Papal approbation was granted in 1882. The work expanded and other houses were opened, in Belgium, Italy and South America, and a mother house was established in Rome. More expansion followed the founder's death in 1900, which took the Congregation into France, Argentina and England. The Sisters still continue the same work for which they were founded and have also undertaken missions to India and the Philippines.

OUR LADY OF MERCY, BROTHERS OF

Location: Italy (Rome)
RC (male) founded in Belgium in 1830 by Canon
Cornelius Scheppers
Abbr: FDM
Original habit: a black tunic with an open white
collar, a black scapular upon which is embroidered
a brown cross, a cincture and rosary and a black
cape

The Institute began in Malines, Belgium
and by 1839 was sufficiently well organised
to undertake the education of the young as
well as the care and welfare of the sick and
of prisoners. The work of the Institute
attracted the attention of the papal nuncio
in Brussels, Gioacchino Pecci (later Pope
Leo XIII), and through his influence papal
approbation was granted in 1857. The
Brothers were invited to England in 1855
by Cardinal Wiseman, and houses were set
up in London and Derby. The foundation
expanded into many parts of Europe, Canada, Africa and South America.

✠ Brothers of the Blessed Virgin Mary of
  Mercy

OUR LADY OF MERCY, DAUGHTERS OF

Location: Italy (Savona)
RC (female) founded in Italy in 1837 by Benedetta
Rosello (St Mary Josepha Rosello)
Abbr: DM

An inauspicious start marked the beginning
of the Congregation of the Daughters of
Our Lady of Mercy. The founder, Benedetta
Rosello, had been refused admission to one
Order because she lacked a dowry, but she
was determined on a religious life and
begged the bishop of Savona to allow her to
house and educate poor girls of the district.
He accepted her offer, and with two of her
cousins and a friend, Benedetta moved into
very run-down accommodation in Savona.
With very little money between them they

started to work among the poor girls, catechizing at first and beginning to educate
them. Hospitals, schools and hostels were
to follow. Diocesan approbation came in
1840 and the Congregation continued to
expand in Italy. Houses of Divine Providence were opened, which were to provide
refuges and rescue homes for young women
at risk. A foundation in Argentina was
made at Buenos Aires in 1875, and in 1919
the first American house was opened.
Today, the Sisters are to be found also in
Africa, India, the West Indies and the
Dominican Republic and in many parts of
Europe.

OUR LADY OF MERCY, ORDER OF

Location: Italy (Rome)
RC (male) founded in Spain in 1218 by St Peter
Nolasco and St Raymond of Peñafort
Abbr: O de M.
Original habit: a white tunic and scapular with a
short hood and cape, with the insignia of a small
shield bearing a red cross, beneath which are three
silver bars subtended from a horizontal bar which
stretched across the shield. The white habit was
chosen because it was thought to make it easier to
gain access to Muslim territory.

The Order of Our Lady of Mercy, also
known as Mercedarian Friars, was founded
in Barcelona in 1218 when a lay confraternity for the ransoming of captives was reorganized into a religious Order, receiving
papal approbation from Gregory IX in
1235. The original confraternity had been
formed in 1192 by some noblemen to care
for the sick in hospitals and redeem captives
taken by the Moors during the time of the
crusades. These nobles were, in effect, the
first monks of the Order and had their
headquarters in Barcelona in the convent of
St Eulalia, for which reason they were
sometimes known as the knights of St
Eulalia. St Peter Nolasco was the first
superior and was given the office of 'ran-

somer', who was the monk delegated to go to the Moors in order to arrange for the freeing of captives. It is said that he went twice to Africa to redeem Christian slaves, using funds from his own inheritance and from contributions. Pope John XXII, however, declared that the office of grand master should be restricted to the clergy. At this point the knights left the community and entered the Order of Montesa. This action caused the Congregation to become a mendicant Order which spread through France, England, Germany, Portugal and Spain. Members went to the New World with Christopher Columbus, and many foundations were set up in Latin America and were important in the conversion of Indians. In today's world the redemption of captives makes few demands on the Mercedarian friars, but they still concern themselves with those in prison and those in need of education. They also maintain the usual parish ministries and try to alleviate social injustices. In the USA, Mercedarians are to be found in many States, with other foundations in Italy, South America and Rwanda.

♰ Mercedarian Friars
   Nolascans

OUR LADY OF MERCY, ORDER OF NUNS OF

Location: Italy (Rome)
RC (female) founded in Spain in 1265
Abbr: SOLM
Original habit: a white habit, scapular and cincture with a black veil; the badge of the Mercedarians, a shield bearing a small red cross beneath which is a horizontal bar in silver and three small silver bars subtended to it, is worn.

Following the foundation of the male Mercedarian Order by Sts Peter Nolasco (canonized 1628) and Raymond of Peñafort (canonized 1601), two pious widows who were tertiaries of the Order, Isabella Berti and Eulalie Pins, wanted to live according to the Mercedarian Rule of life, to fast and practise austerities and voluntary penances, to aid with their prayers the Mercedarians' work and to collect alms for the redemption of Christian captives. Permission was granted, after many difficulties, by Pope Clement IV in 1265 and more women joined the Congregation, including St Mary of Succour. She became the first elected superior of the community, which made its first foundation in Barcelona. An attempt to found a discalced branch of the Mercedarian Nuns was made, successfully, in 1568, its first superior being Blessed Anne of the Cross. This reformed branch made several foundations throughout Spain. The Order experienced many problems, not least being that of recruitment, but is now represented by some fifty-nine houses in Spain, the USA, India and South America.

♰ Mercedarian Nuns
   Sisters of Our Lady of Mercy

OUR LADY OF MERCY, ORDER OF THE DISCALCED FATHERS OF

Location: Spain (Madrid)
RC (male) founded in Spain in the 17th century by Fr Juan Baptista Gonzalez
Abbr: MD
Original habit: a white tunic and scapular with a short hood and cape, with the insignia of a small shield bearing a red cross, beneath which are three silver bars subtended from a horizontal bar which stretched across the shield. The white habit was chosen because it was thought to make it easier to gain access to Muslim territory.

The history of this Order is identical to that of the Order of Our Lady of Mercy, the Mercedarian Friars (see above) until the start of the 17th century, when Fr Gonzalez from Olmedo, Spain, a fully professed Mercedarian friar since 1573, considered that a reform of the Order was necessary. He suggested his ideas to Alfonso de Monroy, the superior-general, or commander-general as he was then known, of the Order. De Monroy's initial enthusiasm and support waned, and it was with the encouragement and help of the countess of Castellan that Fr Gonzalez obtained the necessary authority from Pope Clement VIII (1592–1605), who made three convents available to him for his reformed Order. Fr Gonzalez took the name in religion of John the Baptist of the Blessed Sacrament and lived to see Pope Paul V grant his approval for the reform in 1606. The Order's independence from its parent Congregation was granted in 1621 by Pope Gregory XV.

OUR LADY OF MERCY AND THE DIVINE MASTER, DAUGHTERS OF

Location: Argentina (Buenos Aires)
RC (female) founded in Argentina in 1903 by Mgr Anthony Rasore and Mother Sofia Bunge
Original habit: a white tunic and scapular with a dark cincture, a black veil with a white headcap and wimple; a small medallion, resembling that of the Mercedarian Order, was also worn.

A Congregation founded in Buenos Aires by Mgr Rasor (1851–1929) and Sofia Bunge (1842–1927) for the sole purpose of providing a teaching force for children and young people. The Congregation was approved in 1950.

OUR LADY OF MONTJOIE IN THE HOLY LAND, KNIGHTS OF

Defunct
RC (male Equestrian Order) founded in Spain in 1180 by Count Rodrigo
Original habit: a white tunic bearing a red and white cross, the arms of which had concave-shaped extremities.

An Order of knights founded in the 12th century by a former knight of Santiago who gave the new Order lands in Castile and Aragon in return for ransoming captives and fighting the Saracens. The Order, which was confirmed by Pope Alexander III as following the Cistercian Rule, took its name from a small hill on the outskirts of Jerusalem. This name, the Mount of Joy, gets its reputation from the shouts of joy which pilgrims allegedly made when Jerusalem came into view as they reached its summit. The knights took the usual three vows of religion, poverty, chastity and obedience, and added a fourth one which was to defend the Catholic faith. The Order failed to flourish and had trouble in attracting prospective new members who usually preferred to join either the national, or the larger Equestrian Orders. What was finally left of the Order retired to Aragon where it became known as the Order of Trufac.

OUR LADY OF MOUNT CARMEL, HERMITS OF

Location: USA (Chester, New Jersey)
RC (female) founded in the USA in 1976

An American diocesan community of hermits whose members observe a fully eremitical and contemplative form of life. They take the three vows of religion, poverty, chastity and obedience, and observe a full regime of prayer and meditation.

OUR LADY OF MOUNT CARMEL, KNIGHTS OF

Defunct
RC (male Equestrian Order) founded in France by Henry IV

A Military Order of Hospitallers which united with the Knights of St Lazarus in 1607. The latter is still extant.

OUR LADY OF MOUNT CARMEL, SISTERS OF

Location: USA (Lacombe, Louisiana)
RC (female) founded in France in 1825 by Charles Boutelou; later refounded in the USA in 1830 with the help of Mother Mary Theresa Chevrel
Original habit: Carmelite in style.

An active Pontifical Institute whose members, who make simple vows, work as teachers and nurses.

OUR LADY OF PERPETUAL HELP, SISTERS OF

Location: Canada (St Damien de Buckland, Quebec)
RC (female) founded in Canada in 1892 by Abbé J. O. Brousseau and Virginia Fournier (Mother St Bernard)

A Congregation founded in the parish of St Damien de Buckland for the provision of education for children in city and country parishes in Canada. The Abbé Brousseau had started orphanages for children from an agricultural background, where they could receive education and catechesis and be prepared for working on the land when they were old enough. From this there emerged a plan which provided care and education for the children up to the age of twelve years with the Sisters of Our Lady of Perpetual Help, with a transfer then into the care of the Brothers of Our Lady of the Field, a Congregation which the abbé had founded in 1902. There was much expansion in the 20th century, with many schools opened throughout Quebec, as well as a hospital and an orphanage.

OUR LADY OF PITY, SISTERS OF

Location: England (Kiln Green, Reading, Berkshire)
RC (female) founded in England in 1936 by Mother Margaret Mary Lawder
Abbr: CLP
Original habit: a black tunic and scapular with a leather belt, a white wimple and binder and a black veil; a rosary and crucifix were worn.

The Congregation began in 1936, founded by a small group of Servite tertiaries led by Mother Margaret Mary Lawder and aimed at combining active and contemplative apostolates. The Sisters were prepared to carry out parish and social work as the need arose, and diocesan approval was granted

in 1948. The work continues still, the Sisters offering assistance to priests in parishes and providing care for sick and old clergy in purpose-built housing.

OUR LADY OF PROVIDENCE, DAUGHTERS OF

Location: France (Saintes, La Rochelle)
RC (female) founded in France in 1817 by Fr De Rupt and Elisabeth Vassal (Mother St Irenée)
Abbr: SOLP

In the wake of the French Revolution the provision of education for young people, and young girls in particular, was meagre. Anxious to remedy this, Fr De Rupt of Saintes and Elisabeth Vassal set about providing help. With two volunteers, Jeanne Soulignac and Justine Salmon, who both wished to join a religious Order, Elisabeth formed the the Association of St Mary of Providence, which in 1819 became known as the Congregation of the Daughters of Our Lady of Providence, with Elisabeth as superior. In 1835, with the revision of the Constitutions, the Sisters were given their names in religion, Elisabeth becoming superior-general as Mother St Irenée. In 1890, after her death, an affiliation was made with the Congregation of Perpetual Adoration of Montmartre. The Sisters had an apostolate in nursing, as well as education. Despite setbacks at the time of the Association Laws in France at the start of the 20th century, the Congregation survived and flourished. Houses were opened in Spain and England, where a foundation was made at Alton, Hampshire, in 1938. At the same time a further union was made between the Congregation and that of Sisters of St Joseph of Providence, of La Rochelle. Final approval was granted by Rome in 1958. Missionary work was then undertaken, in Peru (1963), Chad (1968, since closed) and India, where the Sisters continue to care for the young, the sick and the poor, and operate a special ministry among the Indian Untouchable caste. They have also started a mission in Colombia.

OUR LADY OF SION, CONGREGATION OF

Location: Italy (Rome)
RC (female) founded in France in 1843 by Theodore and Alphonse Ratisbonne
Abbr: NDS
Original habit: a black habit, veil and cape with a white linen wimple and binder; an ebony crucifix was worn on a chain around the neck.

A Congregation for women founded by two Jewish brothers in Paris in 1843. Theodore Ratisbonne had converted to Roman Catholicism in 1827 and was ordained as a priest in 1830. Following a miraculous experience of Our Lady, his brother Alphonse also converted and was also ordained as a priest. Together, they sought and obtained permission from Pope Gregory XVI to work for the conversion of Jews, to make reparation and to intercede for them as well as to perform works of charity. Fr Theodore was chaplain of an orphanage in Paris, known as 'La Providence', where many poor Jewish convert families sent their children. He recruited some female volunteers and founded a small group under the patronage of Our Lady of Sion. Although not at first planned as a religious community, this later came about through the wishes of some of the members. A novitiate was established in 1849 and approbation received from Rome in 1863. The Sisters soon became totally concerned with education, and the original ministry to the Jews became one of prayer. A foundation offering a more contemplative way of life was later opened in Paris. Work with the Jewish community was carried on by the so-called 'Ancillae' Sisters, who wore no religious habit so that their work remained unobtrusive, as it continues still, with the Sisters carrying on with their professional work as teachers, adminis-

trators, nurses and pastoral workers in parishes. Foundations have been made in Jerusalem, largely following the groundwork made by Fr Alphonse, and other communities have been established in the Eastern Mediterranean area, in North Africa, South America, Australia and in several major European cities, as well as in the USA, where the first foundation was made in 1892.

OUR LADY OF SORROWS, SISTERS OF

Location: Italy (Rome)
RC (female) founded in Italy in 1830 by Elizabeth Renzi
Abbr: OLS
Original habit: a black habit, with a small white collar and a black veil with a white turn-back.

The founder, Elizabeth Renzi (born 1786), had been educated by the Poor Clares and wanted to join their Congregation, but Napoleon's policy of suppression of all monasteries precluded this and she returned to her home in Coriano. The strong anti-clerical feelings that prevailed in Italy at the time had a serious effect on the education of the young, much of which had been in the hands of the religious Orders. Elizabeth became involved in the teaching of young children in Coriano, and this led her to consider founding a community which would undertake this work. A Congregation was formed and approved in 1839, attracting many postulants and making the opening of schools, oratories and orphanages possible. The Sisters still continue in this work in Italy where they have also given assistance to members of other Congregations in the troubled country of Albania. In 1947 the first foundation in the USA was made, in Louisiana, and it is here that the Sisters now have a large programme of work in education, the day care of children, and special education and care for the mentally retarded. Houses have also been opened in Brazil, Mexico, Bangladesh and Zimbabwe.

OUR LADY OF THE APOSTLES, MISSIONARY SISTERS OF

Location: Italy (Rome)
RC (female) founded in France in 1876 by Fr Augustine Planque
Abbr: OLA
Original habit: a black dress and veil with a white wimple and under-veil

A missionary Congregation founded by a member of the African Missions of Lyons, France, for Sisters to work alongside missionary priests on the west coast of Africa. The Sisters are presently found throughout Africa, where they teach, run dispensaries, hospitals and clinics and carry out catechetical work in schools and homes in villages which are a long way from a parish centre.

✦ Missionary Sisters of Our Lady of the Apostles for African Missions

OUR LADY OF THE HOLY ROSARY, SISTERS OF

Location: Canada (Rimouski, Quebec)
RC (female) founded in Canada in 1874
Abbr: RSR

The Sisters of this Congregation work mainly in education and the conducting of retreats. They maintain a campus and parish ministry in the Canadian provinces of Quebec and New Brunswick. An American foundation was made at the beginning of the 20th century, in Maine, and foreign missions have also been established in Honduras, Guatemala and Peru.

OUR LADY OF THE IMMACULATE CONCEPTION, SISTERS OF

Location: France (Briouze)
RC (female) founded in France in 1849 by Charlotte Delaunay

Original habit: a black habit with a blue girdle and a silver cross on a blue cord around the neck.

A Congregation of teaching Sisters founded at Briouze, near Alençon, France. The work began with the teaching of poor children of the district but expanded into the care of the sick. Gradually, a religious community emerged whose Rule and Constitutions were approved by the bishop of Sees. The work spread throughout France, where the Sisters ran many hospitals, schools and homes for the sick. Their vital work in these areas helped them to survive in France when the Association Laws at the start of the 20th century closed many Congregations. The Sisters were allowed to continue with their hospital work, but their schools were closed. The Congregation is almost entirely to be found in France, but it also has a limited representation in England.

OUR LADY OF THE MISSIONS, SISTERS OF

Location: Italy (Rome)
RC (female) founded in France in 1861 by Euphrasie Barbier (Mother Mary of the Heart of Jesus)
Abbr: NDM (or RNDM)
Original habit: a black habit, veil, scapular and cincture with a rosary, and a white linen cap, wimple and collar; a black cloak was used for outdoor wear; the sleeves of the habit were bound in blue, and a crucifix was worn around the neck.

The founder began her religious life in 1848 when she became a member of the Sisters of the Divine Word at Cuves, which later changed its name to the Sisters of Calvary. Changes to that Congregation made Sister Maria aware that her missionary goals would not be achieved if she stayed there, and with one of the novices she removed herself and began the formation of a separate Institute. With the help of the Marist Fathers in Lyons the Institute of Our Lady of the Missions came into being. Other foundations were made in France as well as in other parts of Europe, in Australasia, Oceania, Indo-China and India, where the Sisters pursue their missionary ideals, teaching at all levels, nursing and caring for those in need. The Congregation gained pontifical status in 1869, and with it came autonomy from the Marists. The Constitutions were approved in 1890 and confirmed in 1906.

OUR LADY OF THE MOST HOLY TRINITY, SOCIETY OF

Location: USA (Robstown, Texas)
RC (male and female) founded in the USA in 1958 by Fr James Flanagan
Abbr: SOLT

This Society of Apostolic Life is made up of men and women, clerical, religious and lay, who work together in groups called ecclesial teams. They serve throughout the world in parishes and mission out-stations, running orphanages and schools and providing counselling and care in drug rehabilitation centres, working with immigrant families and their children and assisting native-American families and those marginalized through poverty.

OUR LADY OF THE RETREAT IN THE CENACLE, CONGREGATION OF

Location: Italy (Rome)
RC (female) founded in France in 1826 by Marie Victoire Couderc (St Thérèse Couderc; canonized 1970) and the Abbé Jean-Pierre Terme
Abbr: RC
Original habit: a black habit and veil with a frilled-edged coif and a purple cape for use in choir. Lay and coadjutor Sisters wore an identical habit except that the cape was black and just edged in purple.

A Congregation which had its origins in a group of women who ran a hostel for pilgrims at the shrine of the Jesuit priest St Jean François Regis, at La Louvesc, France.

They formed the Institute of Our Lady of the Retreat in the Cenacle, led by Marie Couderc and Fr Terme, who were advocates of the Spiritual Exercises of St Ignatius and careful catechesis as the principal ways to revive faith and further the kingdom of God. The Sisters still have an apostolate in providing opportunities for people to make retreats and deepen their spiritual lives, conducting retreats and promoting Eucharistic devotions. They also provide catechetical instruction and RCIA programmes for converts and first communicants. A foundation was made in the USA in 1892 which is now divided into two provinces. The Congregation also has houses in Canada, Ghana, Italy and England.

♰ Religious of Our Lady of the Retreat in the Cenacle

OUR LADY OF THE SACRED HEART, DAUGHTERS OF

Location: Italy (Rome)
RC (female) founded in France in 1874 by Marie Louise Hartzer and Fr Jules Chevalier
Abbr: FDNSC
Original habit: a black habit, veil and scapular with a blue woollen cincture, a heart-shaped coif and a white linen wimple over which was suspended a large medal of the Sacred Heart.

A French Congregation founded at Issoudun, in the Indre region of France. The nucleus of the Congregation was composed of Sisters from another community but without a clear leader and this made for some difficulties. Some of them returned to their original houses and others decamped, but a loyal few remained, supporting themselves by maintaining a hostel for those pilgrims who wanted to visit the famous Shrine of Our Lady of the Sacred Heart at Issoudun. In 1881 a request came for missionaries to go to Oceania, but the Congregation was by then reduced to only three members. The situation was shortly to alter when, in the same year, the widowed Marie Louise Hartzer joined the Congregation and became its leader, resulting in an increase in numbers. She argued the case that the Congregation needed to be autonomous, and Rome eventually agreed. This is now a very large Congregation with an apostolate in teaching at all levels, nursing care and the training of catechists for the foreign missions. There are now houses in most European countries, in North and South America (the US foundation was made in 1955), Australia, Papua New Guinea, Oceania, Indonesia and some African countries.

OUR LADY OF THE SEVEN DOLOURS, LITTLE RELIGIOUS OF

Location: France (Vendée)
RC (female) founded in France in 1849 by Canon de Larnay

This small Congregation was founded in Larnay, France, for the care and education of the handicapped and received its approbation from Pope St Pius X. The work of the Larnay Institute was renowned for its progressive methods of instruction for those who were blind and for deaf-mutes. In 1898 the Congregation became affiliated to the Daughters of Wisdom.

OUR LADY OF THE WAY, SOCIETY OF

Location: USA (Los Angeles, California)
RC (female) founded in Austria in 1936 by Maria Elizabeth von Strachotinsky

A Secular Institute for women which was founded in Vienna in 1936 but which had an earlier origin in the work started by Fr Karl Dinkhauser, SJ, in Austria and Czechoslovakia. The aim of the Institute was to meet the need felt by many pious women to play a more useful role in the Church than was on offer at the time. In 1947 Pope Pius XII recognized the group, which received approbation as a Secular Institute of pontifical right in 1953. The members of the Institute, which has now spread to the USA, profess the usual three vows of religion, poverty, chastity and obedience, after a two-year period of formation.

OUR LADY OF VICTORY, MISSIONARY SISTERS OF

Location: USA (Huntington, Indiana)
RC (female) founded in the USA in 1922 by Fr John J. Sigstein
Abbr: OLVM

A Pontifical Congregation founded at Huntington, Indiana, whose work is concerned with caring for the marginalized and for the poor, providing social service and health care support as well as undertaking a pastoral ministry and catechesis. Members are to be found in many parts of the USA and in Bolivia.

OUR LADY QUEEN OF THE CLERGY, SERVANTS OF

Location: Canada (Rimouski, Quebec)
RC (female) founded in Canada in 1929
Abbr: SRC

The members of the Congregation are employed in domestic work for the clergy in presbyteries and seminaries. An American foundation was made in 1934 and there are houses in Massachusetts, New Hampshire and Rhode Island.

OUR MOTHER OF PEACE, DAUGHTERS OF

Location: USA (High Ridge, Missouri)
RC (female) founded in the USA in 1967
Abbr: SMP
Original habit: as for Carmelite Third Order Seculars.

A Public Association founded for the evangelization of non-Catholics which helps people through spiritual direction. The Sisters undertake communal living and the three vows of religion, poverty, chastity and obedience, and they also co-operate with the laity who, married or single, can live with the community and experience their structured way of life.

OUR SAVIOUR, CANONS REGULAR OF – Lorraine

Defunct
RC (male) founded in 1629 by St Peter Fourier (canonized 1897)
Original habit: a black robe with a narrow linen strip which hung down from the neck and passed to the left-hand side. In summer a cotta was worn with a grey almuce. In winter a full, sleeveless rochet with an ankle-length cape of black linen was worn, the front edges of which were decorated with a wide band of red cloth. A fur hood was also worn, and possibly a biretta.

A Congregation founded by St Peter Fourier (1565–1640), a member of the Canons Regular of St Augustine at Chamousey, who was ordained as a priest there in 1589. With a concern for education he founded the Congregation of Notre Dame for the free schooling of girls. An appeal came from the bishop of Toul for him to reform the canons regular in Lorraine, which he accepted. The reform was fully operational by 1629 and the Congregation was renamed the Congregation of Canons of Our Saviour,

receiving papal approval. It was his hope that the canons would be able to provide the type of schooling for boys which had been achieved by the Sisters of the Congregation of Notre Dame. The Order flourished throughout the duchy of Lorraine and extended into France and Savoy, but became defunct at the time of the French Revolution.

OUR SAVIOUR, CLERKS REGULAR OF

Defunct
RC (male) founded in France in 1851

A Congregation founded at Benoîte-Vaux, Verdun, France by four diocesan priests from the Verdun diocese in an attempt to revitalize the Order of Canons Regular of Our Saviour (see previous entry), which had been destroyed at the time of the French Revolution. The priests had retired to Benoîte-Vaux, where there is a shrine of Our Lady, and began to observe the Rule which had been given to the original canons regular of Lorraine in 1629 by St Peter Fourier (1565–1640) when they were reformed into the Congregation of Our Saviour. Papal approbation was granted in 1854 by Pope Pius IX, at which time the name was changed from canons regular to clerks regular. Many houses were established throughout France, but the Congregation did not finally succeed.

P

PACHOMIUS, MONKS OF ST

Defunct
Universal Church (male) founded in Egypt in the
4th century by St Pachomius
Original habit: a white woollen tunic and cowl, the
latter embroidered with a violet cross.

St Pachomius (*c.*290–346) was an Egyptian who had served in the Roman army. After his demobilization, in 316, he became a Christian and decided to pursue a monastic life, much influenced by the example of the hermit Palaemon, who was considered to be one of the strictest followers of St Antony. He founded a cenobitic, or communal, monastery at Tabbennesi, north of Thebes and composed a Rule, which has not survived, said to have been given to him by an angel. The plan was to build houses for groups of forty monks who would have enough skills between them to make the community self-sufficient, and each group of forty monks would constitute a monastery in the charge of an abbot to ensure that the Rule was followed and that the administration was sound. The lifestyle was very frugal, with Wednesdays and Fridays named as fast days; on the other days the monks were given a midday meal and supper. Each day had a full range of liturgical services, including a daily celebration of the divine liturgy. The growth of these monasteries was considerable. It is recorded that at Oxyrhynchus, a city in the Nile Valley famous for the early papyri found there, including copies of the New Testament and the Gospel of Thomas, the total monastic population was about thirty thousand, more than two-thirds of whom were nuns (see next entry). There were monasteries also in Palestine, in Asia Minor and along the North African coast, in Gaul, Greece, Spain, Sicily and Italy.

PACHOMIUS, NUNS OF ST

Defunct
Universal Church (female) founded in Egypt in the
4th century by St Pachomius
Original habit: a black tunic with a grey scapular and veil; the edge of the habit was decorated with many small, white Greek crosses.

St Pachomius (see previous entry), founder of the first monastic communities in the upper Nile region of Egypt in the early 4th century, followed his first foundation for men with another, on the opposite bank of the Nile, for women who were placed under the direction of his sister, Mary. Their main occupation, apart from prayer both individual and communal, was the learning of the Scriptures by heart and handiwork, to provide what was needed for the communities.

PALLOTTINE FATHERS

Location: Italy (Rome); Poland (Poznan – see below)
RC (male) founded in Italy in 1835 by St Vincent Pallotti (1795–1850; canonized in 1963)
Abbr: SAC
Original habit: as for secular clergy.

This Society of Apostolic Life was founded in Rome. Following his ordination to the priesthood in 1818, Vincent Pallotti dedicated himself to the care of those in need. He was determined to bring people to the faith and to the practice of charitable works. He formed the Pious Union of the Catholic Apostolate, which was open to any faithful Roman Catholic who wished to renew the apostolic spirit of the Church. In order to provide a full-time Congregation for priests who were needed to promote the aims of the Pious Union, Vincent Pallotti founded the Congregation of the Catholic Apostolate, a name later changed to the Pious Society of Missions, until, in 1947, it resumed its original name. The members take no vows but make promises of poverty, chastity and obedience as well as perseverance in the communal life. They must also be prepared to refuse any ecclesiastical dignity offered to them, except in obedience to the pope. The work of the Pallottines expanded throughout Italy and into other parts of Europe, spreading to Africa, Western Australia and North and South America. Those Pallottine Fathers who belong to the Infant Jesus Delegature of Christ the King Province, New York, whose mother house is in Poznan, Poland, are responsible for a hospital chaplaincy as well as providing a pro-life ministry.

✠ Society of the Catholic Apostolate

PALLOTTINE MISSIONARY SISTERS

Location: Italy (Rome)
RC (female) founded in Italy in 1835 by St Vincent Pallotti (canonized 1963)

Abbr: SAC (previously CMP.)
Original habit: a black tunic, scapular, veil and cloth girdle with a white linen wimple and binder.

The Pallottine Missionary Sisters evolved from the male foundation made in Rome. While some of the Sisters remained in Rome, caring for orphans, others were recruited from Germany by St Vincent Pallotti to be trained as missionaries. This led to a mother house being established at Limburg, in Germany, several years after the founder's death. The Sisters, specifically trained for foreign missions, went on to make an American foundation in 1912, where they are now involved in education, child and health care, the running of retreats and parish and renewal ministries. Missions are maintained in Europe, Africa, India, and Central and South America.

✠ Missionary Sisters of the Catholic Apostolate

PALLOTTINE SISTERS

Location: Italy (Grottaferrata)
RC (female) founded in Italy in 1838 by St Vincent Pallotti (canonized 1963)
Abbr: CSAC
Original habit: a black habit, scapular and outer veil, with a black cloth girdle with a rosary; a small white collar, binder and under-veil; a crucifix was worn around the neck.

Another Congregation founded in Rome by St Vincent Pallotti (see previous entries), which arose from a group of women who had banded together in order to care for young girls who had been orphaned as a result of the cholera epidemic in the city in 1837. The Congregation persisted in Italy despite the need arising in 1890 for Sisters to help the Pallottine Fathers who had gone as missionaries to Cameroon. The Sisters went instead to the USA, where they made their first American foundation. They work now in education and catechesis, with missions in India, South America and Mozambique, and are also represented in many parts of Europe.

✠ Sisters of the Catholic Apostolate

PAMPLONA, CANONS REGULAR OF

Defunct
RC (male) founded in Spain in the 12th century
Original habit: a white serge cassock with a white, sleeveless rochet and a grey mozetta.

A Congregation of canons regular founded in the city of Pamplona, the capital of Navarre, by its bishop, Peter, in thanksgiving for the defeat of the Saracens. The canons were to observe the Rule of St Augustine and were under solemn vows. The regulations provided for no more than twelve canons at any one time.

PARACLETE, ORDER OF THE

Defunct
RC (female) founded in France in the 12th century
by Héloïse

A small Order, founded near Troyes by Héloïse (1100–63/4), who had entered a nunnery at Argenteuil near Paris following her affair with Peter Abélard (1079–1142) and the birth of their son, Astrolabe. In 1129, through malicious means, the Sisters were evicted from their convent, and she turned for advice to Abélard, who gave the community his old oratory, the Paraclete, near Troyes, and it was here that Héloïse established a monastery for women. Abélard wrote a Rule for the Congregation, which was later modified by Héloïse. The Order was independent and autonomous and was ruled by an abbess. Héloïse survived Abélard's death and her Order flourished, with daughter foundations made. It survived until the time of the French Revolution.

PARIS FOREIGN MISSION SOCIETY

Location: France (Paris)
RC (male) founded in France in 1663
Abbr: MEP
Original habit: as for secular clergy.

A Society of Apostolic Life made up of secular priests who do not take vows, which was founded to provide missionaries for China and the Far East. Pope Alexander VII (1655–67) appointed two bishops, Francis Pallu and Pierre de la Motte Lambert, giving them the authority to nominate a vicar apostolic, to inaugurate a native clergy and to take decisions without reference to Rome, so great was the task. A missionary training establishment was opened in Paris in 1663. The first missionaries to set out for China in 1665 were Pierre de la Motte Lambert and Jacques de Bourge. The enterprise grew, spreading throughout China and the Far East. A mission to India was made following the suppression of the Jesuits there in 1773. The work still continues.

PASSION, MISSIONARIES OF THE

Location: USA (Nanticoke, Pennsylvania)
RC (male and female) founded in the USA in 1980

A Secular Institute composed of celibate men and women who are inspired by the charism of the Passion, and who are prepared to live lives in the world under vows of poverty, chastity and obedience and to preach the message of the Passion.

PASSION, SECULAR MISSIONARIES OF THE

Location: Italy (Mascalucia)
RC (male and female) founded in Italy in 1957 by Fr Costante Brovetto

A lay Institute, founded in Ovada, Italy. A similar Institute was established at Mascalucia in 1968 by two founders, Fr Gemeroso Privatera and Sarina Consoli. The two groups merged their work in 1974 and today the members are to be found in Italy, the USA, Mexico and Brazil, where they work among the marginalized poor as the opportunity arises. The Institute was approved in Catania, Sicily, in 1980.

PASSION OF JESUS CHRIST, KNIGHTS OF THE

Defunct
RC (male Equestrian Order) founded in France and England in 1380
Original habit: a calf-length blue tunic enclosed by a silk cincture which is secured with a buckle, and a red-hooded cape. Over the tunic was a white cloth mantle, open at the sides, the front adorned with a large plain red cross.

An Equestrian Order said to have been founded by King Richard II of England and King Charles VI of France jointly, in memory of the Passion of Our Lord. In 1396, after the death of his wife, Anne of Bohemia, Richard II married Isabella, the seven-year-old daughter of Charles VI, securing a thirty-year-long truce which ensured that if Richard should face civil disturbance at home, Charles would come to his aid.

PASSION OF OUR LORD JESUS CHRIST AND THE SORROWS OF MARY, DAUGHTERS OF THE

Location: Mexico (Mexico City)
RC (female) founded in Mexico in 1877
Abbr: CP
Original habit: a black habit with a Passionist badge embroidered on the breast; a white cap and black veil with a crimped border; a long black cloak and veil for outdoor wear.

A few years after the Passionist Sisters had arrived in America, towards the end of 1852, they attempted to enter Mexico to make a foundation there, but they were driven out. Undaunted, they returned there in 1877 and established a house at Tacubaya which was approved by the archbishop of Mexico City. The community was formally affiliated to the Passionist Congregation in

1901. Today, the Sisters work in the USA, Mexico, El Salvador, San Domingo, Guatemala, Spain and Italy, where they teach, give assistance in seminaries and run retreat houses.

✠ Mexican Passionist Sisters

PASSIONIST FATHERS

Location: Italy (Rome)
RC (male) founded in Italy in 1720 by Paolo Francesco Danei (St Paul of the Cross; canonized 1867)
Abbr: CP
Original habit: a black habit, belt and cloak; a badge of the Passion (a heart surmounted by a cross and the inscription 'Jesu XPI Passio' worked in white) was worn on the left-hand side of the habit and cloak; sandals were worn.

The Congregation was founded in a hermitage on Mount Argentaro, near Orbitello, on the coast of Tuscany, which had been established by St Paul of the Cross and his brother. The inspiration for the foundation was the Passion of Christ, a vision of which St Paul had experienced some time before. In that vision he was shown the Rule, while Our Lady showed him the habit of the new Order which God wanted him to found. This vision took place at Castelazzo, in the diocese of Allesandria del Paglia. The pope subsequently gave permission for the two brothers to accept novices for their Congregation, which was initially very austere in nature, with fasting three times a week. Pope Benedict XIV made it a condition of his approbation that the austerity be eased. Members took the three vows of religion, poverty, chastity and obedience, to which was added a fourth, the undertaking to spread the memory of Christ's Passion to the faithful. In 1765, the year in which St Paul's brother died, the Congregation was given the use of the Basilica of Sts John and Paul in Rome. It was not until the middle of the 19th century that the Order began to spread outside of Italy, with houses opened in France, Belgium, England, Ireland, the USA, South America, Canada and Australia. More recently, further foundations have been made in Germany, Japan, Poland, India, the Philippines and the West Indies. The work of the Passionist Fathers and Brothers is concerned with giving retreats and conducting missions. A general synod of the Passionists in 1972 proposed the formation of an international organization to promote the study of, and to work with, the problem of suffering as a result of social injustice. As a result 'Stauros International' was started, with its base at Louvain, Belgium.

✠ Congregation of Discalced Clerks of the Passion of the Most Holy Cross and Passion of Our Lord Jesus Christ

PASSIONIST NUNS

Location: (each convent is autonomous)
RC (female) founded in Italy in 1771 by St Paul of the Cross and Faustina Gertrude Constantini (Mother Mary Crucified)
Abbr: CP
Original habit: a black habit with a Passionist badge (a heart surmounted by a cross and the inscription 'Jesu XPI Passio' worked in white) embroidered on the breast; a white cap and black veil with a crimped border and a long black cloak and veil for outdoor wear.

When St Paul of the Cross gave a retreat in 1739 to the Benedictine nuns at the convent of St Lucy in Corneto (now Tarquinia), Italy, he met there Faustina Gertrude Constantini, who received spiritual direction from him and came to realize that her vocation was to belong to a community devoted to the Passion of Christ. A vision that came to her in 1741 persuaded her of the rightness of this decision, and when approbation was given to St Paul in 1771 to

form a Congregation of Passionist Nuns, ten women, together with Faustina, who took the name in religion of Sr Mary Crucified, received the Passionist habit and entered the first convent of Passionist nuns, their Rule and Constitutions composed by St Paul himself. The life was contemplative, with prayer day and night and the penance of perpetual abstinence and fasting and of being shoeless. For over a century the nuns were restricted to Italy, with the exception of one convent in France, but in 1910 a group left for the USA, where they made a foundation in Pittsburgh, Pennsylvania, from which they founded a convent at Daventry in England in 1963. Other nuns from Italy went to Mexico, but had to leave in 1916, going to Spain, where at Lexama, near Bilbao, they established the first Spanish Passionist convent in 1918. Passionist nuns are now to be found in many parts of the world. They support themselves through bookbinding, farming their own cattle, vegetable production, and recently through worm-breeding.

✠ Religious of the Passion of Christ

PASSIONIST SISTERS

Location: England (Dewsbury, West Yorkshire)
RC (female) founded in England in 1852 by Elizabeth Prout (Mother Mary Joseph)
Abbr: CP
Original habit: a black habit with a Passionist badge (a heart surmounted by a cross and the inscription 'Jesu XPI Passio' worked in white) embroidered on the breast; a white cap and black veil with a crimped border and a long black cloak and veil for outdoor wear.

An active Passionist Congregation founded by a convert from Anglicanism, Elizabeth Prout, who had taught poor girls in industrial Lancashire. A Passionist priest, Fr Rossi, aware of the difficulties that some young women faced when they wanted to become religious Sisters but lacked the dowry, or were not called to an enclosed life, suggested to Elizabeth that she start a community at St Chad's, in Manchester, which she did. The Congregation was initially known as the Sisters of the Holy Family and Passion of Our Lord Jesus Christ, and approbation came from Rome in 1875 and 1887. Today, the Sisters work and live with the poor in many parts of the world, in Europe, North and South America, Botswana, Jamaica and Papua New Guinea, where they teach, give pastoral support and retreats and work in hospitals and clinics.

✛ Sisters of the Cross and Passion
  Sisters of the Most Holy Cross and
    Passion of Our Lord Jesus Christ

PASSIONIST SISTERS OF ST PAUL OF THE CROSS

Location: Italy (Rome)
RC (female) founded in Italy in 1872 by Fr Joseph Fiammetti
Abbr: CP
Original habit: a black habit with a Passionist badge (a heart surmounted by a cross and the inscription 'Jesu XPI Passio' worked in white) embroidered on the breast; a white cap and black veil with a crimped border and a long black cloak and veil for outdoor wear.

A group of Sisters formed this community at Signa, near Pisa, in 1872 under the direction of Fr Fiammetti, in an attempt to revive an earlier community of women, the Handmaids of Florence, which had been founded in 1811 with an apostolate of reform for prostitutes and also with the education of young girls. The community had been affiliated with the Passionist Congregation, but was dispersed following the death of its founder, the marchesa Mary Magdalen Frescobaldi (1771–1843), later known as Mother Mary Magdalen. Two

members from this original foundation went to Signa and joined the Passionist Congregation. The principal work is concerned with the care of the poor through various pastoral and social ministries.

PATRICK, BROTHERS OF ST

Location: Ireland (Tullow, County Carlow)
RC (male) founded in Ireland in 1808 by Bishop Daniel Delaney
Abbr: FSP (formerly PB)
Original habit: similar to that worn by the Christian Brothers

A small Congregation founded at Tullow, County Carlow, Ireland, and approved in 1893. The Brothers live a community life and are involved in teaching, counselling in drug and alcohol dependency units, and all kinds of youth work. An American foundation was made in California in 1948. Members are to be found in Ireland, the USA, Australia, Kenya, India and New Guinea.

✛ Patrician Brothers

PATRICK'S MISSIONARY SOCIETY, ST

Location: Ireland (Kiltegan, County Wicklow)
RC (male) founded in Ireland in 1932 by Bishop Whitney
Abbr: SPS
Original habit: as for secular priests

St Patrick's Missionary Society was founded in Kiltegan, County Wicklow, Ireland, by Bishop Whitney and some diocesan priests who had been working in Nigeria as missionaries. The purpose of the Society is to evangelize in non-Christian countries, to establish local church units and to sustain the converts until they are strong enough to stand on their own. In the early days the activity was restricted to Nigeria, but the Society has now expanded its field of operation and maintains a presence in the USA,

Italy, Spain, Albania, Rumania, Sierra Leone, Brazil, Colombia, Argentina, Chile, Ecuador, Guinea Bissau and Mexico.

✟ Kiltegan Fathers
   St Patrick Fathers

PAUL, ANGELICAL SISTERS OF ST

Location: Italy (Rome)
RC (female) founded in Italy in 1530 by the Countess Torelli of Guastalla
Original habit: a white tunic and scapular with a cross embroidered on it; a short dark veil over a white linen headcloth and a very long knotted cord around the neck.

Following her widowhood, Countess Torelli took the name of Paula and consecrated herself to God, founding the Order of the Angelical Sisters of St Paul. Her chaplain, St Anthony Mary Zaccaria, had founded a Congregation of priests, the Barnabites, who were placed under the patronage of St Paul. The purpose of the Angelicals was to help with the repentance of prostitutes and the care of these women and their children. For this purpose the Order sought vocations from well-born women to run homes for abandoned and orphaned children and to provide for their care and for the running of hospitals in Venice. However, the arrival in Venice of Paula Antonia Negri, from the Angelicals in Padua, who was much given to 'prophesying', discredited the Order and they were cloistered from 1557.

✟ Angelicals

PAUL, BROTHERHOOD OF ST

Defunct
Anglican (male) founded in the USA in 1928
Abbr: BSP
Original habit: a black habit with a divided white collar.

The Brotherhood was founded in Kingston, New York, as a society of laymen within the Episcopalian (Anglican) Church. It was designed to help working men get employment and also to provide a Christian environment for young men in need of work. The Brothers were usually employed, and supported the society by sharing their wages through a common fund. The Rule was simple and modern, but the Congregation did not succeed.

PAUL, DAUGHTERS OF ST

Location: Italy (Rome)
RC (female) founded in Italy in 1915 by Fr James Alberione and Mother Thecla Merlo
Abbr: FSP (formerly DSP)
Original habit: a black tunic and veil with a white under-veil and a small, divided white collar; a small cloth emblem is worn on the upper left-hand side of the tunic. In tropical countries a white habit is worn.

A Congregation which was founded to spread Christian doctrine through the media of the times and whose members are very much involved with the information technology (IT) of today. The Sisters work in thirty-five countries, publishing books, magazines and every type of printed matter, bookbinding and illustrating, running book centres and producing a great deal of audio-visual material. They are also involved in the distribution of this material.

PAUL, HERMITS OF ST

Location: Poland (Czestochowa)
RC (male) founded in Poland in 1215
Abbr: OSPPE
Original habit: originally brown, but in the mid-14th century this changed to a white tunic, scapular and hood; sandals were worn.

The Order was founded in Hungary through the union of two pre-existing Orders, one founded by the Blessed Euse-

bius of Pilis in 1250 and an earlier foundation made at Patach by Bishop
Bartholomew of Pecs, in 1215, which is
taken as the founding date of the Congregation. Eusebius, who is reputed to have
died at the age of 112, renounced a lucrative
position as a canon of the Church and went
with some companions to the mountains of
Pilis to live a penitential life in imitation of
St Paul the first hermit (c.233–c.345).
Through a vision which urged Eusebius to
unite with other hermits, the new Congregation was born, with Eusebius as its
superior. From 1308 the hermits were
allowed to observe the Rule of St Augustine.
The Order enjoyed many privileges and
spread throughout Hungary, Germany,
Poland and Sweden. In 1382 the shrine of
Our Lady of Czestochowa, in Poland, was
given into their care. In time the eremitical
life was abandoned, and today this is a
contemplative–active Order. In the USA
they are responsible for the national shrine
of Our Lady of Czestochowa in Doylestown,
Pennsylvania, from which their apostolic
work of fostering devotion to Our Lady is
directed.

✠ Order of St Paul the First Hermit
  Pauline Fathers

PAUL, HERMITS OF ST – Portugal

Defunct
RC (male) founded in Portugal in c.1420 by Mendo
Gomez di Simbria
Original habit: a white tunic and cord with a black
hooded scapular.

The Order was founded at Mendoliva, near
Sebutal, which is south-east of Lisbon, by a
military officer, Mendo Gomez, who was
probably a captain in the army of King John
of Portugal. On leaving the army he retired
to a hermitage and oratory he had built for
himself at Mendoliva, where he gave himself
up to a life of prayer and penance. Some

hermits from Sierra de Ossa, who were without a leader, appealed successfully to Mendo
Gomez to unite with them under the patronage of St Paul the Hermit. Mendo Gomez
died in 1481. The Order was approved by
Pope Gregory XIII in 1578. The eremitical
life was replaced by the cenobitic and the
Rule of St Augustine was observed. The
Order was later suppressed.

PAUL THE APOSTLE, SOCIETY OF MISSIONARY PRIESTS OF ST

Location: USA (Jamaica Estates, New York)
RC (male) founded in the USA in 1857 by Fr Isaac
Thomas Hecker and others
Abbr: CSP

This Society had an unusual beginning,
founded by five ex-Redemptorist priests
who had been expelled from their Order,
accused of disobedience and disloyalty. The
founder is understood to be Isaac Hacker,
who, together with Augustine Hewitt,
George Deshon, Francis Baker and Clarence
Walworth, was dispensed from his vows.
The Society they subsequently founded was
in New York, where they were welcomed by
the archbishop and given a parish to administer. Their appeal for funds was successful,
and they were able to build a house, which
remains the mother house, and a church, at
Scarsdale, New York. Approbation was
granted by Rome in 1940. The principal
work undertaken is the conversion of non-
believers by making use of the media, by way
of the Paulist Press, the Paulist Radio–TV
Communications Services and the Paulist
National Catholic Evangelization Association as well as running various information
centres and missions. Its members also
preach, work in ecumenical programmes
and maintain university missions, adult education courses and RCIA programmes.
There are now houses throughout the USA.

✠ Paulist Fathers

PAULINE FATHERS AND BROTHERS

Location: Italy (Rome)
RC (male) founded in Italy in 1914 by Fr James
Alberione
Abbr: SSP
Original habit: as for secular clergy.

A society of priests and Brothers founded
at Alba in Italy for the propagation of the
Roman Catholic message through whatever
forms of media communication are available. The members live in communities,
and the main apostolate today is the publication and sale of books and illustrated
material, including cassettes, CDs and
videos, in accord with the vows taken at
profession and the Constitutions which
require them 'to work for the glory of God
and the salvation of other souls through the
modern media of communication' (Article
II). The Society maintains a presence in
some twenty-six countries.

✠ Paulines
    Society of St Paul for the Apostolate of
        Communications
    Pious Society of St Paul

PENANCE, RELIGIOUS ORDER OF

Defunct
RC (male) founded in Spain in 1752 by Juan Varella
y Losada
Original habit: Franciscan in style.

An Order founded in Salamanca, Spain, by
Juan Varella, a retired soldier who had
become a Franciscan Observant. With eight
like-minded companions he left the Franciscans and founded this Order which was
based on penance and austerity. The Rule
was approved by Pope Benedict XIV
(1740–58) and the Constitutions, based on
those of the Franciscans, by Pope Pius VI
many years after Juan's death. Early foundations in Hungary failed to thrive, however, and the Spanish and Portuguese

foundations were later dispersed, with the
Italian foundations being the last to survive
until the Order became defunct.

✠ Nazareni
    Scalzetti

PENITENTIAL ORDER OF HOLY MARTYRS

Defunct
RC (male) founded in Poland in the 1st century
(more likely the 13th century)
Original habit: a white habit and scapular with an
embroidered red cross and a heart.

This Congregation has a legendary origin
during the 1st-century pontificate of Pope
Cletus, but more likely dates from the 13th
century. There is evidence of a monastery
dedicated to St Mark as a centre for these
penitents in Krakow, Poland. The Order
flourished in Poland and Bohemia in the
16th century, at which time the monks were
observing the Rule of St Augustine.

PENITENTS OF OUR LADY OF REFUGE

Defunct
RC (female) founded in France in 1631 by Marie-
Elizabeth Dubois (Mother Marie-Elizabeth de la
Croix de Jésus)
Original habit: a red-brown habit with a white
scapular.

An Order founded at Nancy, France, by the
widowed Marie-Elizabeth Dubois, to provide a refuge for women who were at risk,
or who had been prostitutes. In this work
she was helped by her three daughters. At
the start the foundation was very *ad hoc*
and Marie was persuaded by some clergy to
put her work on a firmer, and more canonical, basis. In 1631 this was done, with
Marie, two of her daughters and nine other
companions entering the religious community which she founded and which was
approved by Rome in 1634. The Rule followed was that of St Augustine, and the

Constitutions were modified from those of the Jesuits. The Congregation spread throughout France. In order to provide for the many women who wished to join the Congregation, membership was divided into three classes, or groups. The first class was for women who enjoyed a good reputation; these took a fourth vow in addition to the usual vows of poverty, chastity and obedience, that of being of service to the penitents. The second class was for women who had reformed themselves but were unable to provide a dowry in order to enter, and were therefore unable to hold any office within the Congregation. The third class was for those who were penitents; these women were without any special habit and were not under any obligation of vows.

✙ Nuns-Hospitallers of Our Lady of Mercy

PERPETUAL ADORATION, INSTITUTE OF

Location: Belgium (Watermael, Boitsfort)
RC (female) founded in Belgium in 1856 by Anna de Meeus
Abbr: RE
Original habit: a black dress, cape, bonnet and veil, which has a slight central depression; during times of adoration a longer veil was worn, a white coif and starched linen collar; around the neck was a silver cross, given at final profession, engraved on one side with the image of the Sacred Heart and on the reverse with a chalice and raised Host.

When she was still quite young Anna de Meeus had been shown the perilous state of the vestments and linen at her local church and felt herself inspired and moved to found an association of people who would make reparation to Our Lord in the Blessed Sacrament through spending an hour a month in adoration as well as paying for the repair of altar wares and providing some material support for the upkeep of poor churches. This gave rise to the Association of Perpetual Adoration and Work for Poor

Churches, which was directed by a Jesuit priest, Fr Jean-Baptiste Boone and soon led to the foundation of the Institute of Perpetual Adoration, which would be the support of the Association; it was approved by Rome in 1872. The Congregation now provides for retreats, prepares first communicants and makes and supplies poor churches with altar linens and vestments. An American foundation was made in 1900 in the archdiocese of Washington, where the Sisters are involved in education.

✙ Congregation of the Perpetual Adoration of the Blessed Sacrament
Religious of the Eucharist

PERPETUAL ADORATION, SISTERS OF

Location: Ireland (Wexford)
RC (female) founded in Ireland in 1874 by Mother Mary of St Joseph and Mother Mary of St Rose
Abbr: CPAW

An Institute founded in Ireland to make reparation to the Blessed Sacrament through perpetual adoration, day and night. The Sisters support themselves through the making of altar breads, vestments and altar linens and provide catechesis and retreats for women. In 1895, two members of the Sisters of Perpetual Adoration – a small community which had been founded in Brisbane, Queensland, but lacked diocesan approval – went to Ireland to get guidance from the Wexford Congregation. They used the Wexford Constitutions, modified for their own needs, and were then approved by the archbishop of Brisbane in 1920.

PERPETUAL ADORATION OF THE BLESSED SACRAMENT, ORDER OF THE

Location: Each community is autonomous
RC (female) founded in Italy in 1807 by Mother Mary Magdalen of the Incarnation
Abbr: AP

The Order was founded in Rome, Italy. It is fully contemplative, with the Sisters supporting themselves through the making of altar breads and vestments. Each foundation of the Order is autonomous, and houses can be found in Spain, the USA, Mexico, Chile and Africa.

PERPETUAL ADORATION OF THE MOST BLESSED SACRAMENT, SISTERS OF THE

Location: France (Guipavas, diocese of Quimper)
RC (female) founded in France in 1835 by the Abbé François-Marie Langrez

The idea of making a foundation devoted to the perpetual adoration of the Blessed Sacrament coupled with the education of children had occurred to the Abbé Langrez in 1821. He shared his ideas with Marguerite Le Maitre, who cared for many orphans in her own home. By 1829, Marguerite had been joined by two other women, and together they began a community life. They were joined in this by Marguerite's employer, Olympe de Moelien, in 1832, and she became superior in the following year. Together, they all took the habit in 1835 and adopted a Rule composed for them by Abbé Langrez which was approved in 1845. The Congregation currently has five houses but only a very small number of Sisters.

PETER, COMMUNITY OF ST

Location: England (Woking, Surrey)
Anglican (female) founded in England in 1861 by Benjamin and Rosamira Lancaster
Abbr: CSP
Original habit: a grey dress and a simple cap tied with a blue ribbon; a small silver cross was suspended from the neck on a blue ribbon.

The community began as a means of providing convalescent care for patients discharged from hospital. Benjamin Lancaster, who was a governor of St George's Hospital in London, was a wealthy man who could provide the means for the community to begin to function. Two young women, Susan Oldfield and Ella Jones, went to live at 27 Brompton Square, which subsequently became known as St Peter's Home, a site that had been revealed to Rosamira Lancaster in a dream. Other houses in London were bought as the work expanded, many of which were lost during the bombing raids of World War II. In 1883, through the generosity of their benefactors, the Sisters were able to build a house at Maybury Hill, Woking, set in the fine Surrey countryside, which provided an excellent environment for their convalescing patients. A further development came at the start of the 20th century, when a home was opened in the London suburb of Hendon, St Peter's Ouvroir, where partially disabled young women and girls were employed. A print shop, laundry and needlework facilities were introduced, which provided training for useful employment. A home for invalids, the Smiles Home for Invalid Ladies, was established at Woking in 1923, where residents can remain for the rest of their lives. The Sisters also responded to the need for foreign missions, going to Korea in 1892. Today the work continues with great emphasis on retreats which are conducted at a purpose-built retreat centre at Woking. 'Retreat and Reflect Days' are presented here, which are often based on reflections on works of art, and more recently on poetry.

PETER, COMMUNITY OF ST – Horbury

Location: England (Horbury, Wakefield, Yorkshire)
Anglican (female) founded in England in 1858 by Canon John Sharp
Abbr: CSPH

A community which arose from a need for a refuge for women and girls at risk in the Yorkshire mill town of Horbury. A so-called 'penitentiary' or house of mercy, was opened there in 1858. Two of the original members were sent to train with the Sisters of St John the Baptist at Clewer, near Windsor. The cottage in which the Congregation started soon proved to be too small, and a large house was bought, allowing the Sisters to expand their work to include the running of a night school, and also of a day school. More refuges and two homes for abused children were opened, staffed by the Sisters who also now included prison visiting in their apostolate. Retreats were organized, initially for women and girls but later for clergy and their wives. In 1930 the Community divided into two unequally sized independent groups.

1 The Community of St Peter the Apostle at Westminster, London, which in 1937 acquired additional property at Laleham-on-Thames, Staines, Middlesex. This group, which followed the Benedictine style of religious life, continued the work of schooling, working in parishes, running missions and providing opportunities for retreats. The Sisters also made altar breads, church linen and vestments. Retreat houses for men and women were opened in Scotland. This community no longer exists.

2 The Community of St Peter in Chains, which remained associated with Horbury and maintains schools for maladjusted children and provides retreat facilities and some mission work. This community still functions and provides spiritual direction as well as social work for individuals in need.

PETER, PRIESTLY FRATERNITY OF ST

Location: Germany (Opfenbach-Wigratzbad)
RC (male) founded in Germany in 1988
Abbr: FSSP

A Pontifical Institute which was founded for priests living in community who wished to celebrate the divine liturgy and administer the sacraments according to the provisions of the liturgical books of 1962. They were founded 'for the formation and sanctification of priests in the framework of the traditional liturgy of the Roman rite'.

PETER, SOLITARY NUNS OF ST

Defunct
RC (female) founded in Portugal in 1676
Original habit: a rough habit tied with a rope; a scapular, mantle and veil.

An Order of solitary nuns, or hermitesses, founded at Faro, Portugal, living under the Rule of the Third Order of St Francis and heavily influenced by the reforms introduced by St Peter of Alcántara (1499–1562). The nuns were separated from the world, given to contemplation and an austere life. The Constitutions were approved by Pope Blessed Innocent XI in 1678, but the Order is no longer in existence.

PETER AD VINCULA, CONGREGATION OF ST

Location: Spain (Barcelona)
RC (male) founded in Spain in 1839

A Congregation, approved in 1931, which is designed to provide opportunities for the rehabilitation of young men who have fallen foul of the law.

✠ Congregation of St Peter in Chains

PETER CLAVER, MISSIONARY SISTERS OF ST

Location: Italy (Rome)
RC (female) founded in Austria in 1894 by Blessed Mary Theresa Ledóchowska (beatified 1975)
Abbr: SSPC
Original habit: a black tunic and veil, trimmed in white, with a red cord with a silver medal of St Peter Claver worn around the neck.

A sodality founded in Salzburg, Austria, which received approbation in 1904. A meeting between Countess Mary Theresa Ledóchowska and Cardinal Lavigerie in 1889 convinced her of two things, the need for missionaries to work in Africa and that she should become a religious Sister and organize lay groups to support the missions and to promote anti-slavery movements. The sodality came into existence in 1894, and members supported the missions in Africa with alms, prayer, fundraising appeals and the production and sale of literature. This literature included catechisms, Bibles and periodicals which have been translated into many different African languages. Mary was tireless in her efforts and today members of her Congregation are found throughout the world. There is a strong emphasis on communal living, and the Rule which is followed is marked by its Ignatian spirituality. The founder was beatified in 1975.

✠ Sisters of St Peter Claver for the African Missions

PETER OF ALCÁNTARA, FRIARS OF THE OBSERVANCE OF ST

Defunct (as such, but now part of the Franciscans of the Regular Observance)
RC (male) founded in Spain, in the mid-15th century by Peter Garavita (St Peter of Alcántara – canonized 1669)
Original habit: a brown tunic, hood and capuce with a seven-decade rosary and a cord girdle; sandals were worn, and in cold weather a knee-length cloak could be added.

Peter Garavita was born in Alcántara, Spain, in 1499. He joined the Franciscan Friars of the Observance at Manxarretes, in the province of Extremadura, and was ordained there in 1524. Seeing the need for a return to a stricter observance of the Rule in his community, he tried to bring this about, without success. Leaving the community he became a hermit at Arabida, where another

friar, Martin of Santa María, was attempting reforms along similar lines. The desire to found his own Congregation of friars incorporating these reforms led Peter to undertake a barefoot walk to Rome to seek the necessary permission from Pope Julius III. Opposition to his plans, coming mainly from the minister general of the Observant branch of the Franciscan Order, forced Peter to place himself under the Conventual branch of the same Order. Returning to Spain he founded a house at Pedrosa which was the start of the Friars of the Observance of St Peter of Alcántara. Their way of life was that of barefoot austerity, with complete abstinence from meat. Until 1897 the friars continued this separate existence, but they were then united with other Observant traditions by Pope Leo XIII. St Peter of Alcántara was a strong influence on St Teresa of Avila, and his support encouraged her to found her first monastery in 1562.

✠ Alcantarines

PETER OF MONTE CORBULO, CANONS REGULAR OF ST

Defunct
RC (male) founded in Italy in the 16th century by (reputedly) Peter of Reggio
Original habit: a grey cassock and rochet with an almuce; after 1521 this changed to a black cassock with a white-sleeved rochet and a black cloak.

A Congregation founded at Monte Corbulo, twelve miles from Siena, Italy. Its reputed founder, Peter of Reggio, had been a Carthusian monk and a canon regular of St Saviour, at Bologna. With the approval of Francesco Soderini, bishop of Volterra (Pisa) and with papal permission, he was given the use of the church of St Michael the Archangel at Monte Corbulo, where he installed a Congregation of canons regular under the patronage of St Peter. The canons were to observe a life of severe austerity under the Rule of St Augustine, characterized by much fasting, great poverty, manual labour, works of great charity and a seeking after silence and solitude.

PHILIP NERI, NUNS OF ST

Defunct
RC (female) founded in Italy in the 17th century by Retilio Brandi
Original habit: a black woollen tunic with a girded white, sleeveless surplice which bore a black cross in the centre of the chest; a black veil was worn over a white under-veil.

A Congregation of nuns under the protection of St Philip Neri (canonized 1622), founded in Rome towards the middle of the 17th century. The nuns observed the Rule of the Third Order of St Francis, and their work was concerned with the education of poor girls.

✠ Philippine Nuns of Rome

PIARIST FATHERS

Location: Italy (Rome)
RC (male) founded in Italy in 1617 by St John Calasanz (canonized 1767)
Abbr: SP or Sch P
Original habit: a plain black tunic with three leather buttons and a short mantle

The Order was founded in Rome by John Calasanz who was born into an aristoctratic Spanish family. Following a successful academic education in Spain he was ordained as a priest in 1583. He would seem to have been heading for a successful career in the Spanish Church, but a vision made him go to Rome where he began a ministry of caring for and educating poor and abandoned children. As a member of the Confraternity of Christian Doctrine, which undertook the teaching of children and adults on Sundays and Holy Days, he became aware of the need for educating those who could not afford school fees. Unable to get assistance for this work from the main religious Orders, he and three other priests set up a free school in Rome in 1597. As the number of pupils increased, so did the need for larger premises and more teachers who could live together in a community. This was the beginning of the Piarist Order. Further expansion received the support of Popes Clement VIII and Paul V. But the path was not smooth. Malicious and unfounded accusations were laid against John Calasanz, who was at one point suspended from his work and came close to imprisonment by the Holy Office. He was vindicated and the Piarists began a slow process of rehabilitation, culminating in the foundation of the Order of Clerks Regular of the Christian Schools in 1621. During the lifetime of the founder the Order spread rapidly through Spain, Italy and South America. Today, the members teach at all levels in schools and colleges throughout the world, including the USA where they have a special care for the poor families in the Appalachian Mountains. As well as teaching, the members undertake counselling, run drug dependency clinics and provide pastoral care and outreach programmes.

✠ Escolapios
  Order of Clerks Regular of the Mother of
    God of the Pious Schools
  Pious Workers of St Calasanctius
  Scolopii

PICPUS FATHERS, THE

Location: Italy (Rome)
RC (male) founded in France in 1800 by Fr Marie-Joseph Coudrin
Abbr: SSCC
Original habit: a white tunic and scapular with a knotted cincture and a cape; the scapular

has a large badge of the Sacred Hearts on the breast.

A Congregation founded at Coursay-les-Bois in Poiton, France. After his ordination in 1792, a time of persecution of the clergy in France, Fr Coudrin became aware of the great need for reparation to be made for all the wickedness of the times. He decided, with the help of some others, to promote devotion to the Sacred Hearts of Jesus and Mary, taking his solemn vows on Christmas Eve, 1800. By 1805 he was able to buy some old houses in the rue Picpus, in Paris, from which the Congregation takes its name. Here they started a seminary and a college for the training of young men. The work spread to other parts of France, where further colleges were opened, as well as free schools for the poor. The Congregation was approved in 1817 and responded to the need for foreign missions, especially to Oceania, in 1826. Missions were established in the Sandwich Islands, the Gambier Islands, Tahiti, Hawaii and the Marquesa Islands. Fr Damien lost his life from leprosy on the island of Molokai, where he was caring for sufferers from the disease. Today, the members' work has increased and now includes the running of hospital and prison chaplaincies, care of the elderly, the conducting of Roman Catholic charismatic prayer groups and parish retreats, while still fostering devotion to the Sacred Hearts. Other foundations have been made in North and South America, the Philippines, the Bahamas, Japan, India, Belgium, The Netherlands and England.

✠ Congregation of the Sacred Hearts of
    Jesus and Mary
   Congregation of the Sacred Hearts of
    Jesus and Mary and of Perpetual
    Adoration of the Most Blessed
    Sacrament of the Altar
   Damien Fathers

PICPUS SISTERS

Location: Italy (Rome)
RC (female) founded in France in 1797 by Fr Marie-Joseph Coudrin and Henriette Aymer de la Chevalerie
Abbr: SSCC
Original habit: a white tunic with a white woollen girdle, scapular, veil and cape with a frilled bonnet tied under the chin. An image of the Sacred Hearts was embroidered on the scapular. In choir a white cloak was worn, and a red cloak during the time of adoration.

The founders of the Congregation first met in 1794, when Fr Coudrin was in hiding from the mobs during the French Revolution. He had travelled to Poitiers in disguise, dressed as a baker. Here he became the spiritual director of an association of women which had been formed in honour of the Sacred Heart. Although some of them were living communally, there was no intention at that time to form a religious Congregation. But as other women joined the association, so the idea grew and a Congregation was formed, with Henriette Aymer de la Chevalerie as the first superior. The first five Sisters made their vows in 1797 and a school was opened in 1800 for the education of poor girls. The work of the Sisters is still concerned with education and with adoration of the Blessed Sacrament and reparation for sin, with a great emphasis on spreading devotion to the Sacred Hearts of Jesus and Mary and practising a life of penance and mortification. They undertake a variety of parish missions, teach in the field of religious education, provide hospital chaplaincies and visit the housebound and those in prison. Provision is also made for the homeless and for those in need of care and protection. Houses are to be found in Europe, the USA, South America, Africa, Asia and Oceania.

✠ Congregation of Sisters of the Sacred
   Hearts of Jesus and Mary and of
   Perpetual Adoration of the Holy
   Sacrament of the Altar

PIOUS KNIGHTS, PONTIFICAL ORDER OF

Defunct
RC (male Equestrian Order) founded in Rome in
1559 by Pope Pius IV
Original habit: (insignia) a medallion, on one side
of which was an engraving of the image of St
Ambrose with the pontifical arms on the other.
This was suspended around the neck; no particular
tunic was worn.

The Pontifical Order of the Pious Knights
was founded as a Military Order, and was
limited to 375 members, each getting a
pension in recognition of their earlier mon-
etary contributions to the papal coffers.

PIOUS SCHOOLS, SISTERS OF THE

Location: Italy (Rome)
RC (female) founded in Spain in 1829
Abbr: SchP

A Pontifical Congregation founded in
Figueras, Spain, from which an American
foundation was made at Northridge, California, in 1954. The Sisters are mainly occupied with religious education in parish
schools, and they work in many parts of
America as well as in foreign missions
in France, Germany, Austria, Poland and
India.

✠ Escolapias

PIUS IX, ORDER OF

Location: Italy (Rome)
RC (Equestrian Order), a papal award; instituted in
1847 by Pope Pius IX; reformed in 1939 and 1957
Original habit: (insignia) this varies according to
which of the four classes of knighthood is being
received, but is mainly an eight-pointed blue
enamelled star between whose points radiate

golden flames. In the centre of the star is a white
enamelled medal on which the motto 'Virtuti et
Merito' (for virtue and merit) is inscribed, with the
date '1847' on the reverse. The badge is suspended
on a dark blue silk ribbon bordered in red.

The Order was instituted by Pope Pius IX
to recognize noble and conspicuous deeds
which benefited both Church and State and
which served as an example to others.

PIUS X, BROTHERS OF ST

Location: USA (La Crosse, Wisconsin)
RC (male) founded in the USA in 1952 by Bishop
John P. Treacy
Abbr: CSPX

A Congregation of Brothers founded at La
Crosse, Wisconsin, which has not yet
received approbation. The Brothers are
involved in parish administration and
assistance to parish priests. They also teach
and provide health care services.

POLAND, CANONS REGULAR OF

Defunct
RC (male) founded in Poland in 976 by Mieszko
(Mieccislaus)
Original habit: a white cassock, a long white
rochet, a fur tippet and a black cap edged with fur.

The founder of the Order was the ruler, or
duke, of Poland, who had accepted Christianity in the name of his people in 963 and
brought Christian missionaries to the
country. The first bishopric was established
at Posen, and there followed a vigorous
programme of baptism and of the establishment of monasteries and convents. Canons
from Verona were introduced in 976, and
in 1129 three daughter foundations of the
Canons Regular of St Victor were made. In
1402, King Ladislaus II set up a flourishing
college of Canons Regular of the Most Holy
Sacrament.

PONTIFICAL INSTITUTE FOR MISSIONARY EXTENSION

Location: Italy (Rome)
RC (male) founded in Italy in 1926 from two earlier foundations
Abbr: PIME
Original habit: as for secular clergy.

The Institute was formed as a result of the union in 1926 between two organizations, the Lombard Seminary for Foreign Missions, which had been founded in Milan at the request of Pope Pius IX in 1850, and the Seminary of Sts Peter and Paul, founded in 1874. It retains its secular status since the priests and Brothers are not bound by vows of religion but only by a solemn undertaking to spread the Gospel wherever they may be sent by the Holy See, and to lay the foundations for foreign dioceses to be taken over by indigenous clergy. The missionaries are now also concerned with education, justice and peace issues, and the care of the sick and elderly and of orphans. Members staff hospitals, clinics, leprosy missions and orphanages. Houses are to be found in Italy, the USA, England, the Far East, West Africa, Papua New Guinea, Brazil and the Philippines.

✠ PIME Fathers

POOR, LITTLE SISTERS OF THE

Location: France (Saint-Pern, Rennes)
RC (female) founded in France in 1839 by Blessed Jeanne Jugan (beatified 1982)
Abbr: LSP
Original habit: a black habit, woollen cord girdle and veil, with a small white wimple, a bonnet secured under the chin and a headband of white linen; a hooded black cloak for use outside.

The founder was born at Cancale, on the Brittany coast, in 1792, into a poor, devout family. After some experience in nursing Jeanne went into service as companion to a pious woman, and together they undertook works of charity and taught catechism to the children of the parish. Jeanne had by now become a tertiary in the Society of the Heart of the Admirable Mother (founded by St John Eudes) and following the death of her employer she joined with some others and together they developed a regular pattern of life, devoting themselves to prayer and works of charity. In 1840 three of the women formed a small association based on the Franciscan Third Order Rule. Moving to larger premises as the numbers increased, and calling themselves the Servants of the Poor, with Jeanne as their superior, the members now extended their work to the care of orphans and destitute old men. In 1843 the first vows of religion, of poverty, chastity and obedience, were taken and the members assumed their names in religion, Jeanne becoming Sr Mary of the Cross. The name of the society was also changed, to the Little Sisters of the Poor, and other foundations were made throughout France and, later, in Germany and Belgium. The Congregation received papal approval in 1879 and 1907. The work of the Congregation is still among the elderly and the poor, and there are houses in thirty countries on five continents. The American foundation was made in 1868.

POOR, SISTERS-SERVANTS OF THE

Location: Poland (Krakow)
RC (female) founded in Poland in 1891 by St Albert Chmielowski (1845–1916; canonized 1989) and Bernardina Maria Jablonska
Original habit: Franciscan style.

The saintly founder of the Albertine Sisters, as they are commonly called, had been a painter before becoming a Jesuit. Unable to stay with the Order because of his poor health, having lost a leg during the uprising in Poland against the Tsar of Russia in 1863, he became a member of the Third

Order Secular of St Francis in 1888. He founded the Brothers of the Third Order of St Francis Servants of the Poor, which worked among society's outcasts, the homeless and abandoned. With the assistance of Bernardina Jablonska the work was extended and the Sisters-Servants of the Poor was founded, with an apostolate among women who were in the same position. The Sisters not only cared for these women, but also undertook to teach them crafts and trades so that they could improve their lives and care for themselves and their families, thereby gaining some measure of self-reliance. The work of both the Brothers and Sisters extended throughout Poland, where twenty-one refuges and shelters had been opened at the time of the founder's death in 1916. Five Albertine Sisters went to the USA in 1989 where they set up a foundation in Hammond, Indiana and worked in St Margaret's Hospital in order to validate their Polish nursing diplomas. The Sisters established an Albertine Home for retired priests and the elderly in the diocese of Gary, Indiana. They also work in homes for single mothers and their children, as well as providing soup kitchens for the hungry and homeless.

✠ Albertine Sisters

POOR CHILD JESUS, SISTERS OF THE

Location: The Netherlands (Simpelveld)
RC (female) founded in Germany in 1844 by Mother Clara Fey
Abbr: PCJ
Original habit: a black habit and girdle with a white scapular and rosary and a medal of the Holy Family and the Blessed Sacrament with a monstrance on the breast.

A Congregation founded at Aachen, Germany. The founder, Clara Fey (born 1815) together with friends from her schooldays, began to care for the poor and to feed and teach the poor and the orphaned children in a rented house. As their need for more space grew, they were able to make use of an old Dominican convent. In 1844 diocesan approval was granted for the founding of a religious Congregation. The original purpose of the Congregation was modified to allow the members to support themselves, and other activities were taken up including teaching at secondary level, church embroidery and the training of girls for domestic service and for careers in business. The Congregation grew, with other foundations made in Germany, Luxemburg and Austria. During the Franco-Prussian War (1870–71) some members were involved in nursing, and this may have been influential in postponing for a time their expulsion during Bismarck's *Kulturkampf*, when many religious houses were closed. Their eventual expulsion opened up foundations in other countries. This Congregation observes the nineteenth day of each month in honour of St Joseph, who is considered to be their chief patron. The twenty-fifth day of each month is also celebrated, in honour of the birth of Christ. The Sisters are now to be found in Europe, the USA (the American foundation dates from 1924), South America, Indonesia, Uganda and Australia.

POOR CLARE MISSIONARY SISTERS

Location: Italy (Rome)
RC (female) founded in Mexico by Mother Maria Ines Teresa Arias
Abbr: MC
Original habit: a grey, or brown, tunic with a knotted Franciscan cord and rosary, a black veil and sandals.

The Poor Clare Missionary Sisters work in education, the giving of retreats, in nursing and the provision of pastoral care. They are to be found on the West Coast of the USA and in Mexico, Costa Rica, parts of Europe including Russia, Africa and the Far East.

POOR CLARES

Location: Italy (Assisi)
RC (female) founded in Italy in 1212 by St Clare and St Francis of Assisi
Abbr: OSC (or PCC)
Original habit: a grey, or brown, tunic with, since the 15th century, a knotted Franciscan cord and rosary, a black veil and sandals.

This Second Order of St Francis was founded in the convent of San Damiano in Assisi. The members were originally known as the Poor Ladies, and only later as the Poor Clares after their founder. St Clare appealed to Pope Innocent III to confirm their absolute right to poverty, but this was later rescinded by his successor, Honorius III, when Cardinal Hugolini (later Pope Gregory IX) was appointed as protector of the Franciscans. He imposed a Benedictine Rule on the Ladies, enforced a strict form of enclosure, and removed their Privilege of Poverty. After the death of St Francis in 1226, the Poor Ladies began to expand beyond Italy. St Clare continued to battle with the Church over the imposed Rule, and in 1247, under Pope Innocent IV, a second Rule was sanctioned which contained several concessions regarding poverty and authority over women's monasteries. Just before her death in 1253, St Clare's own Rule was approved, but it was not observed in every monastery. It is of importance that it confirmed that the Poor Ladies were to possess no property, either individually or corporately. By then there were nearly a hundred monasteries throughout Europe, most of them in Italy but with a few in Spain, France and Germany. In France, a new Community of Poor Sisters had been founded at Longchamp in 1259 by Blessed Isabel of France, the sister of King St Louis, which intro-

duced the Rule of Longchamp. This permitted the ownership of property by the community, moderated various austerities and imposed perpetual claustration. Those who observed this Rule became known as 'Urbanists' (after Pope Urban IV who approved the Rule), or 'Second Rule Clarisses'. There was a marked increase in the number of monasteries during the 13th and 14th centuries, but with the increase in numbers came a corresponding increase in benefactions and dispensations, permitting various forms of luxury. A reform of the Order was undertaken by St Colette, giving her name to a branch of the Poor Clares, the Colettines. She aimed to restore the spirit and practice of strict poverty. St Colette opened her first reformed convent at Besançon, France, and travelled extensively throughout France and The Netherlands. By the time of her death in 1447 she had reformed or re-founded twenty-two convents of the Rule of St Clare with her own Constitutions. Later centuries were to see several more reforms which brought into being the Recollect Poor Sisters, the Discalced Poor Sisters (Poor Clare Sisters of St Peter of Alcántara), the Poor Clares of the Strictest Observance and the Capuchin Poor Sisters. The French Revolution caused massive expulsions of nuns from their monasteries and convents and the establishment of new foundations in Belgium and England. The first attempts to make a foundation in the USA came to nought when some of the American bishops felt that the lifestyle was incompatible with the culture of their country, but a house was eventually established at Omaha, Nebraska, in 1882 which led on to three daughter foundations. Today, the monasteries are grouped into two American provinces, the Mother Bentivoglio Federation and the Holy Name Federation. Members of this Order are now to be found throughout the world, each house being self-supporting and independent.

✠ Order of St Clare
   Poor Clares of the Capuchin Branch
   Poor Clares of the Primitive Observance
   Poor Clares of the Reform of St Colette

POOR CLARES – Newry

Location: Ireland (Newry, County Down)
RC (female) founded in France in 1625
Abbr: OSC
Original habit: Franciscan style

A community of Irish Poor Clares of the First Rule which was founded at Dunkirk from Gravelines in 1625 and returned to Ireland in 1629, opening a monastery in Dublin. Following the destruction of this house in 1641, some of the nuns stayed in Ireland, opening a house in Wexford, while others went to France and Spain. In 1649 another Irish House was established at Galway, where the nuns supported themselves through teaching and working in the local community, for which they had to surrender their enclosure. A return to Dublin in 1712 saw the opening of an orphanage for girls at Harold's Cross. The work later expanded to the running of elementary and secondary schools at Newry, County Down, which became the mother house of the Congregation. Other houses were founded in Wales and Australia, where a school was opened in Waverley, West Sydney, in 1886. At the suggestion of Pope Pius XII in 1944 many of the convents, all of which owed their origins to the 1629 foundation, amalgamated under a mother-abbess-general. The Australian foundation joined the federation in 1973, following Vatican II.

✠ Poor Clares of the Immaculate
   Conception

POOR CLARES OF PERPETUAL ADORATION

Location: each convent is autonomous
RC (female) founded in France in 1854 and in the USA in 1921
Abbr: PCPA
Original habit: Poor Clare style with a small medallion of a monstrance suspended around the neck on a cord which extends below the white wimple.

A Congregation of autonomous contemplative communities which was founded in France and from which foundation another was made in the USA. The Sisters are occupied with perpetual adoration of the Blessed Sacrament, with the privilege of solemn exposition both day and night. The work of some of the Sisters has taken them into the world of television and radio, where they now have an apostolate; other foundations are fully enclosed and contemplative. Foreign missions are undertaken in France, Germany, Poland, Austria and India.

POOR CLARES OF REPARATION AND ADORATION

Defunct
Episcopalian (female) founded in the USA in 1922 by Mrs Lily Dorrit Gray (Mother Mary Christine)
Original habit: a grey habit with a black veil and scapular and a Franciscan knotted cord with four knots from which hung a seven-decade rosary; sandals were worn.

A community founded at Merrill, Wisconsin, by Mrs Lily Gray and some friends, who moved in 1928 to Long Island, where they were able to found a convent next door to the Order of the Poor Brethren of St Francis. Here they observed the First Rule of St Clare, together with some amended and adapted Constitutions which provided for the recitation of the divine office according to the Seraphic Breviary and a full rota of adoration of the Blessed

Sacrament during the day. The community did not survive.

POOR INFIRMARIANS

Defunct
RC (male) founded in Spain in 1567 by Bernardino Obregon
Original habit: a grey Franciscan tertiary habit decorated with a black cross on the left-hand side.

A group of Franciscan tertiaries founded near Burgos, Spain, whose members worked in hospitals and also in their foundation in Portugal, which opened in 1592, where they set up an orphanage for boys. In addition to the usual three vows of poverty, chastity and obedience was added a fourth – that of hospitality. The Congregation had limited success in Spain and Belgium and did not survive the upheavals of the late 18th and early 19th centuries in Europe.

POOR OF ST CATHERINE OF SIENA, SISTERS OF THE

Location: Italy (Rome)
RC (female) founded in Italy in 1873 by Blessed Savina Petrilli (beatified 1988)

As a Child of Mary, Savina Petrilli began to teach children the catechism in her own home. In 1868, with three friends, she took temporary vows of religion, which led to the founding of the Congregation in 1873, whose principal focus was on the poor and needy. The members cared for the sick and elderly in their own homes and in hospitals. Today there are over seven hundred members, with houses in Italy, North and South America, India and the Philippines.

POPE ST SYLVESTER, ORDER OF

Location: Rome (Italy)
RC (Equestrian Order), a papal award; date of foundation uncertain; restored in 1841 by Pope Gregory XVI and in 1905 by Pope St Pius X

Original habit: (insignia) an eight-pointed gold cross with the image of St Sylvester on a medal at its centre. Around the periphery of the medal there is a blue circlet inscribed in gold with the words 'Sanc. Sylvester PM'; on its reverse it bears the date 1841 in Roman numerals and the words 'Gregorius XVI restituit'. The more recent medal also bears the inscription 1905, again in Roman numerals. A gold spur is suspended from the lower foot of the cross. The ribbon, originally of red and black stranded silk, is now of red silk with a black border.

This very old and valued Order has had several historical phases. It appeared first as the Order of the Golden Militia, or Militia of the Golden Spur, was later restored under Pope Gregory XVI in 1841 and then again in 1905 by Pope St Pius X. More recently the order was opened to women, by Pope John Paul II in 1996. The Order is intended to reward lay men and women who are active in their Christian apostolate and in the exercise of their professional duties.

PRADO, SOCIETY OF PRIESTS OF THE

Location: France (Lyons)
RC (male) founded in France in 1856 by Blessed Anthony Chevrier (beatified 1986)
Original habit: as for secular priests.

A Society of secular priests living in community, founded at Lyons, France, and receiving a decree of praise in 1959. After his ordination as a priest Anthony Chevrier was appointed to a working-class district of Lyons, where he saw at first hand the problems of the poor and homeless and realized the need of education for the children and care for the homeless. He acquired the use of a disused ballroom, the Prado, where he set up a residence for those in need and, with some other priests, formed the Providence of the Prado, which evolved into the Society of Priests of the Prado. In this work,

Anthony Chevrier was encouraged by St John Vianney, the Curé of Ars. The members adopted the Third Order Rule of St Francis, while still remaining as secular priests. In order to cater for the needs of the female poor and homeless, and to help with the catechizing and health care of young women, the Society of Sisters of the Prado was also formed. Today, the work of the Society continues in France, Africa, Japan and Chile.

PRECIOUS BLOOD, DAUGHTERS OF THE

Location: The Netherlands (Münstergeller, Roermond)
RC (female) founded in The Netherlands in 1862 by Maria Seraphina Spiehermans
Abbr: FPS

A Congregation, approved by Pope Leo XIII in 1890, founded at Sittard, south of Roermond. The work of the Sisters is concentrated in the care and education of young girls and the nursing of the elderly.

✥ Sisters of Christian Charity of the Most Precious Blood

PRECIOUS BLOOD, HANDMAIDS OF THE

Location: USA (Jemez Springs, New Mexico)
RC (female) founded in New Mexico in 1947 by Fr Gerald Fitzgerald
Abbr: HPB
Original habit: a wine-red full-length habit, scapular and cincture with a rosary attached and a white veil; professed Sisters wear a finger ring.

A fully contemplative, but not strictly enclosed, Congregation founded by a member of the Servants of the Paraclete. The foundation was made at Jemez Springs on Pentecost Sunday, 1947. The members are concerned with providing perpetual Eucharistic adoration with a view to praying for the sanctification of priests. Each Sister undertakes one hour of adoration before the exposed Blessed Sacrament each day and together they chant the divine office. Personal prayer and spiritual reading are also important parts of the Sisters' day. Houses can be found in the archdioceses of Sante Fa and Chicago, as well as in Rome, Italy.

PRECIOUS BLOOD, KNIGHTS OF THE

Defunct
RC (male Equestrian Order) founded in Italy in 1608 by the duke of Mantua
Original habit: a wide-sleeved, embroidered tunic of purple silk, lined with white and with the edge decorated with gold discs. (Insignia) a gold ribbon with a medallion, engraved on one side with two angels holding a vase containing three drops of the Precious Blood of Christ and the words 'Nihil Isto Triste Recepto' (Nothing is Sad After Receiving This). This is suspended from a collar composed of linked, ornate discs, alternately inscribed with the letters 'D.P.' to represent the opening words from Psalm 60 – Domine Probasti (O God, Thou Hast Tried Me).

An Order founded by Vincente del Gonzago, duke of Mantua, in 1608, on the occasion of the marriage of his son, Frederick II Gonzago, to Margaret of Savoy. The Order received the approval of Pope Paul V. The fourteen noble members were dedicated to the protection of a relic of the precious blood and to the defence of religion, the Holy See and their sovereign. The relic disappeared in 1848. With the declaration by the Emperor Joseph I (1705–11) that the dukedom of Mantua was abolished, the Order became defunct.

✥ Knights of the Redeemer

PRECIOUS BLOOD, MISSIONARY SISTERS OF THE

Location: Italy (Rome)
RC (female) founded in South Africa in 1885 by Abbot Francis Pfanner
Abbr: CPS

This Congregation was founded at Mariannhill, near Pinetown, not far from Durban in Kwazulu-Natal, South Africa. The founder had come from the Maria Stern Cistercian Monastery in Bosnia to South Africa with a view to founding a male branch of the Order there. His undertaking was successful, and from the abbey of Mariannhill numerous mission stations were established throughout South Africa. The Congregation of Missionary Sisters was founded to help the monks with their care of the native people by way of education, pastoral ministries and health care. The Sisters are to be found in many parts of the world, throughout Europe and the USA, with other houses in New Guinea and South Korea. The American foundation was made at Princeton, New Jersey, in 1925, with other houses in Pennsylvania and New Mexico. The Sisters have undertaken the care of the aged, catechesis, education at all levels, care of Hispanic communities, care of the physically and mentally handicapped and an AIDS ministry, as well as youth counselling and some parish ministries.

✠ Mariannhill Sisters
  Sisters of the Precious Blood

PRECIOUS BLOOD, SISTER ADORERS OF THE

Location: Italy (Rome)
RC (female) founded in Italy in 1834 by St Gaspar del Bufalo (canonized 1954) and Blessed Mother Mary de Mattias (beatified 1950)
Abbr: ASC (formerly AdPPS)
Original habit: unknown except that the Sisters wore a locket in the shape of a heart, engraved with three drops, representing Christ's blood.

Founded in Acuto, which is in the mountains south-east of Rome, by St Gaspar del Bufalo (1786–1837) and Blessed Mother Mary de Mattias (1805–55), the Sisters have a very varied apostolate. Their work began with catechesis and the spiritual direction of local women, but it quickly enlarged to include every type of care. An American foundation was made in 1870, and foreign missions were undertaken to South America, Africa and many parts of Europe. The Sisters teach at all levels, care for the aged, maintain retirement villages, provide retreats and campus ministries and care for abused children. They also provide a ministry to those who are alcohol and drug dependent. At present this Congregation is composed of three provinces in the USA, all with the same Constitutions. As part of a process of rationalization, the three provinces undertook a process of convergence in 1999.

✠ Adorers of the Blood of Christ

PRECIOUS BLOOD, SISTERS OF THE

Location: USA (Dayton, Ohio)
RC (female) founded in Switzerland in 1834 by Maria Anna Brunner
Abbr: CPPS
Original habit: a grey habit with a small white collar, a black veil with a white headband and a simple shoulder cape; a crucifix was worn around the neck.

The Congregation of the Sisters of the Precious Blood was founded in Grisons, Switzerland, by a widow, Maria Brunner, with the encouragement and help of her son, Fr Francis de Sales Brunner. They had undertaken a trip to Rome, where they were impressed by the devotion to the Precious Blood that St Gaspar del Bufalo had developed. The foundation of the Sisters of the Precious Blood followed, with the approval of the bishop of Chur, the Sisters adopting the Rule of St Benedict. They began to teach the young and care for orphans and destitute girls. Fr Brunner, a member of the Missionaries of the Most Precious Blood, was sent to the USA to make a foundation there in 1844, and this enabled the Sisters to follow. Their first American foundation was made in the same year near Norwalk, Ohio. The Sisters later adapted the Benedictine Rule to enhance the opportunities for adoration, and became an independent Congregation under the control of the archbishop of Cincinnati. Their work concerns education at all levels, as well as missions in hospitals, prisons and nursing homes and the conducting of retreats. They also operate soup kitchens and homeless shelters and have special ministries for minority groups and those marginalized by drug and alcohol abuse. Houses are to be found throughout the USA, and in Chile, Guatemala and Poland.

PRECIOUS BLOOD, SOCIETY OF THE

Location: Italy (Rome)
RC (male) founded in Italy in 1815 by St Gaspar del Bufalo
Abbr: CPPS
Original habit: a black tunic and veil and a large ebony crucifix, with a brass corpus.

This Congregation was founded in Giano, diocese of Spoleto, Italy, as a community of secular priests. St Gaspar was invited by Pope Pius VII to preach missions with the aim of restoring the spiritual life in Italy after the fall of Napoleon in 1814. With several priests he took up residence at the convent of San Felice at Giano, north of Rome. Other houses were opened and six missions set up throughout Naples with a view to combating the brigands of the area and converting many anti-clericals, including some Masonic lodges. One of the priests of the Society, Fr Francis de Sales Brunner, left for the USA in 1844, at the invitation of Bishop Purcell of Cincinnatti, to lay the foundation of the Society in Ohio. Today, there are four provinces of the Society in the USA, whose members work in parishes, schools, hospitals and clinics, and who also undertake preaching missions and retreats for those in need, both in the USA and abroad.

✠ Missionaries of the Most Precious Blood

PRECIOUS BLOOD, SOCIETY OF THE

Location: England (Burnham Abbey, Taplow, Maidenhead, Berkshire)
Anglican (female) founded in England in 1905 by Millicent Taylor and the Revd Arnold Pinchard
Abbr: SPB
Original habit: a black habit, scapular and veil, with a red girdle and collar; a crucifix was worn.

The origins of the Society of the Precious Blood, which was founded in Birmingham, England, lay in work undertaken by Millicent Taylor when she was asked to help with a factory girls' club in the evenings. Feeling that she needed a more organized religious life, Millicent made her profession and, joined by some other women, continued the active apostolate of the Society. After the purchase of Burnham Abbey, which had been founded in 1266 for a community of Augustinian canonesses, suppressed at the time of the Reformation, the Congregation moved there to start their contemplative life, which Sr Millicent had been inspired to consider after a visit she made to Malling Abbey, Kent, in 1910. The members observe the enclosure and the Rule of St Augustine, singing the divine office and observing perpetual adoration before the Blessed Sacrament. The Society is fully self-supporting and the Sisters provide opportunities for quiet days and private retreats for a small number of guests.

PRÉMONTRÉ, ORDER OF

Location: Italy (Rome)
RC (male) founded in France in 1120 by St Norbert (canonized 1582)
Abbr: OPraem
Original habit: a white tunic, scapular, sash, cappa, hood and biretta.

St Norbert, born in Xanten in Germany in
*c.*1080 into a noble family, turned away
from his life of comfort and ease following
a narrow escape from death during a thun-
derstorm. He sold his estates and turned to
a life of poverty in order that he might
minister to the poor, becoming at first a
wandering preacher. With thirteen companions he settled at Prémontré, in northern France, where he established the Order
of Prémontré, which was marked by strict
and rigorous asceticism based on that lived
by the Cistercians, whose founder, St Bernard of Clairvaux, was an influential friend.
It is said that the Blessed Virgin Mary had
requested St Norbert to adopt a white habit.
The history of the Order is chequered. It
spread rapidly to England and Ireland in
the mid-12th century, and there were many
foundations. The houses, often built in
places remote from towns, were generally
dedicated to Our Lady. The earliest English
abbey was founded in 1143 at Newhouse,
in Lincolnshire, manned by canons from
France, and eleven other abbeys sprang
from this foundation. But the Order saw a
decline in vigour and a general laxity of the
Rules, probably through affluence. Movements to reform the Order were made,
especially in France, which brought about
some new foundations during the 16th century. The French Revolution suppressed
most religious houses at the end of the 18th
century, in both France and Belgium, and
by the start of the 19th century the Order
was all but defunct. It has since enjoyed a
resurgence. The Order is made up of three
classes:

1 Priests and clerics under an abbot or
provost;
2 Nuns, who have taken the Rule of St
Norbert;
3 Tertiaries, who follow a modified Rule
and live in the world.

Five characteristics govern the life of the
canons, the singing of the divine office in
choir, zeal for the salvation of souls, a spirit
of habitual penance, a special devotion to
the Holy Eucharist, and another to the
Blessed Virgin Mary in her Immaculate
Conception.

✠ Canons Regular of Prémontré
Norbertines
Premonstratensians

PRESENTATION BROTHERS

Location: Ireland (Cork)
RC (male) founded in Ireland in 1802 by Blessed
Edmund Ignatius Rice (beatified 1996)
Abbr: FPM
Original habit: a black cassock, capuce and scapular
with a leather belt and a rosary.

When the founder of the Order, the Blessed
Edmund Ignatius Rice, became a widower,
he involved himself in many charitable
projects, caring for the poor and visiting
those in prison. He was instrumental in
introducing the Presentation Sisters to
Waterford, where they cared for the girls
of the city, and the idea was born in his
mind that there was a similar need for boys
and young men. He opened a school in
1803 and with two companions started a
literacy programme, which included religious instruction. The work of the school
increased, and the programme expanded to
include vocational subjects, including book-
keeping, navigation and architectural drawing, all aimed at giving the young men a
future career. Many schools were opened in
Ireland. Edmund and his companions took
vows according to the Presentation Rule
and assumed a religious habit, with
Edmund taking the name of Ignatius, as
superior. The Congregation was not without its birth pangs. Matters involving its
organization led to some divisions, but a
reorganization received papal approval in

1820 and 1889. Expansion of the work followed, with schools opening in most towns in Ireland. Foundations were made in England and in many other parts of the world. The Brothers are now to be found engaged in every sort of youth ministry and education in Canada, the USA, the West Indies, Peru and Ghana.

PRESENTATION OF MARY, SISTERS OF THE

Location: Italy (Castelgandolfo)
RC (female) founded in France in 1796 by Blessed Mary Rivier (beatified 1982)
Abbr: PM
Original habit: a black habit with a small black cape and a short black silk veil over a white muslin cap; a silver cross was worn around the neck.

The Institute was founded at Theuyts in France by Mary Rivier, who had taught the children from poor families and cared for the sick during the years of the French Revolution. Others joined her in this work and a Congregation was soon formed, with the decree of praise granted from Rome in 1836. Foundations abroad were subsequently made, in Canada in 1853 and at Glen Falls, New York, in 1873. When the French houses were closed because of the Association Laws at the beginning of the 20th century, the Sisters were dispersed, many leaving France to join their overseas foundations. The Institute now maintains a presence in France and other parts of Europe, the USA, Canada, Peru, Japan and the Philippines. The Sisters' work is largely educational, but also includes nursing and a ministry to the disabled, as well as the provision of spiritual retreats.

✝ Sisters of the Presentation of Our Lady

PRESENTATION OF MARY, SISTERS OF THE

Location: France (Broons, Saint-Brieuc)
RC (female) founded in France in 1826 by Louise Le Marchand

Abbr: PS
Original habit: a black habit and veil.

A Congregation founded at Broons in Brittany for the purpose of providing education for young people, especially in religion, and to care for the poor and the sick. There are foundations in France, Belgium, The Netherlands, England, including the Channel Islands, and the USA.

PRESENTATION OF THE BLESSED VIRGIN MARY, SISTERS OF THE

Location: Ireland (Monasterevan, Kildare)
RC (female) founded in Ireland in 1775 by Honoria (Nano) Nagle
Abbr: PBVM
Original habit: a black habit and veil with a white linen wimple and coif, and a leather belt.

This large Congregation has its origin in County Cork, Ireland. The founder, Nano Nagle, educated in her home country of Ireland and also in France, became a postulant in a French convent, but was convinced that her destiny lay in Ireland. She returned there and began to teach and to prepare children for their First Communion, opening her first school in a mud cabin at Cove Lane, Cork City. Her interest extended to the poor and to sick women, and with what resources she could muster she founded the Ursuline Convent in that city in 1771, but felt compelled to found another community whose members would be able to work among the needy. She built another convent, close to the Ursulines, and in 1775, with three companions, began her religious life, and in 1777 entered the new Congregation, which was known as the Sisters of the Sacred Heart until changing to its present name in 1791. The Rule followed was based on that of St Augustine, and papal approbation was received. The Congregation made many foundations throughout Ireland, and their first overseas community was established in Newfoundland in 1829. The first English foundation was made in Manchester in 1833, and others followed. There is now a presence in India, Australia and the USA, where the first foundation was made in San Francisco, California, in 1854. The work of the Sisters continues to include most aspects of education, from caring for children with special needs to university level. They also provide social and health ministries, retreat work and care for the elderly and sick. The members lived in autonomous, or diocesan, groups until 1976, when many joined together under a central administration which was subdivided into provinces, or regions. In 1989 the province of the Union of Sisters of the Presentation of the Blessed Virgin Mary was formed in the USA.

✠ Presentation Order

PROVIDENCE, DAUGHTERS OF

Location: France (Le Kremlin-Bicetre)
RC (female) founded in France in 1818 by the Venerable Jean-Marie de Lammenais and Marie-Anne Cartel
Abbr: DP
Original habit: a black habit, cape and veil with a square white coif.

A Congregation founded in Saint-Brieuc, Brittany, where there was much need for good catechesis and general education for the young at the time, as much damage had been done during the years of the French Revolution. Marie Cartel started a school, called 'Providence', which provided the poor children with clothing as well as the fundamentals of education. By 1821 there were enough pupils to move to a purpose-built convent which had been vacated by the Ursulines in Saint-Brieuc, and the community was formed and given a Rule which had been written for them by Fr Lammenais. By the end of the 19th century other foundations had been made, in Canada in 1897 and England in 1903 after the French Association Laws had driven the Sisters out of France. Today, the Sisters are to be found in many parts of Brittany, in Canada and the USA and in the Ivory Coast in Africa. The original apostolate has been expanded and as well as working in education the Sisters also nurse and take care of the elderly and the handicapped.

PROVIDENCE, OBLATE SISTERS OF

Location: USA (Baltimore, Maryland)
RC (female) founded in the USA in 1829
Abbr: OSP

An American Congregation, founded in Baltimore, Maryland, by an aristocratic French Sulpician priest, Jacques-Hector-Nicolas Joubert de la Muraille, who had gone into exile in the USA at the time of the French Revolution, when religious houses were closed and their communities scattered. The aim of the Congregation was to educate coloured children, and with this in mind he opened a house in Baltimore which was to be staffed by coloured nuns. He was encouraged to undertake this work by two other French priests and four coloured women who had maintained a private school in San Domingo, with a view to becoming a religious community in time. Fr Joubert's posting to a coloured parish in Baltimore provided the opportunity for introducing these four women from San Domingo. Permission to form a novitiate and ultimately make their profession as religious Sisters was given and papal approbation followed in 1831. The Sisters now work in education and conduct literacy programmes, especially in the Hispanic migrant community. They also have an outreach ministry and provide day care. There are houses in many parts of the USA, with missions to Costa Rica and the Dominican Republic.

PROVIDENCE, SISTERS OF

Location: Canada (Montreal, Quebec)
RC (female) founded in Canada in 1843 by Emilie
Gamelin and Bishop Ignace Bourget
Abbr: SP

A Congregation founded in Montreal, Canada, by Bishop Ignace Bourget, who had been very impressed by the works of charity which were being undertaken by Emilie Gamelin. Anxious to establish a community of Sisters in Montreal, he invited the Daughters of Charity in France to go to Montreal. When, at the last minute, they were unable to go to Canada, he established, with Emilie Gamelin, his own Congregation using the same Rule. An American foundation followed, in Seattle, Washington, in 1856 which now forms the headquarters of the Province of the Sacred Heart. Other American provinces were established, covering the whole of the USA. The Sisters have undertaken many ministries. They work in education and health care, low income and sheltered housing provision, prison visiting, and the care of the elderly and the handicapped, AIDS programmes, and the care and protection of victims of domestic violence.

PROVIDENCE, SISTERS OF – Rosminian

Location: Italy (Rome)
RC (female) founded in Italy in 1833 by Antonio
Rosmini
Abbr: SPR
Original habit: a black habit with a white collar,
and a black veil, cape and cincture.

The Congregation of the Sisters of Providence was founded at Domodossola, Italy, in a former Ursuline convent where the Sisters set up a novitiate and facilities for educating future teaching Sisters. This came about when some Sisters, who had trained in the novitiate of the Sisters of Charity at Portieux, France, found that they were unqualified to teach in a state-recognized school on their return to Locarno, which was then in Italy but has been part of Switzerland since 1925, where they were to make a foundation. The Congregation, which has houses in Italy and England, runs boarding and day schools and cares for orphans and the elderly as well as conducting prayer groups and retreats and providing opportunities for conferences and meetings. The Sisters also help the Rosminian Fathers in whatever work they have undertaken.

✚ Institute of Charity
  Rosminian Sisters

PROVIDENCE, SISTERS OF

Location: France (Rouen)
RC (female) founded in France in 1666 by Fr Nicolas
Barré
Abbr: SOP (formerly P. de R.)
Original habit: a black habit and veil with a large
white coif and a silver crucifix.

The Congregation was founded in Rouen by Fr Barré, a Minim friar, in order to educate the poor children of the town. The work continues today and the Sisters are still involved in education and the care of children, with houses in France and England, Madagascar and Central Africa.

PROVIDENCE, SISTERS OF

Location: France (Le Mans)
RC (female) founded in France in 1806 by Abbé
Jacques-François Dujarie
Abbr: SP
Original habit: a black tunic and veil with a linen
shawl worn over the shoulder; an ivory cross was
suspended from the neck.

The Sisters of Providence was founded at Ruille-sur-Loire, France, by the Abbé Dujarie with the assistance of the first superior-general, Josephine Zoe de Roscoat. The

Congregation is concerned with many works of charity and was for a time involved in education. In 1839 some Sisters, under the leadership of Mother Theodore Guérin, founded a branch Congregation at St Mary-of-the-Woods in Indiana, USA, which eventually became independent (see below).

PROVIDENCE AND OF THE IMMACULATE CONCEPTION, SISTERS OF

Location: Belgium (Champion, Namur)
RC (female) founded in Belgium in 1833 by Canon Jean-Baptist-Victor Kinet
Abbr: SPIC
Original habit: a black habit with a short veil and a black hooded cape for outdoor wear; a small wooden cross was worn around the neck.

The Congregation was founded at Jodoigne, near Namur, Belgium, and canonically recognized in 1836. The purpose of the foundation was to provide Sisters who would undertake the education and care of orphans, care for the sick and visit those in prisons and other institutions. At present the Sisters are represented in Belgium, Italy, England and South America.

PROVIDENCE OF ST ANDREW, SISTERS OF

Location: France (Peltre, Marly)
RC (female) founded in France in 1806 by Fr Anton Gapp

Founded at Hambourg-la-Forteresse, the Sisters of Providence of St Andrew was designed to provide teaching Sisters who would be able to catechize and teach children at primary and secondary schools. The first mother house was at Lorraine, but moved to Peltre in 1839, where it suffered damage during the Franco-Prussian War of 1870/71. It was fully restored and the Sisters carry on their work in education in Belgium and France.

PROVIDENCE OF ST MARY-OF-THE-WOODS, SISTERS OF

Location: USA (St Mary of the Woods, Indiana)
RC (female) founded in the USA in 1840 by Blessed Mother Theodore Guérin
Abbr: SP
Original habit: a black tunic and veil with a linen shawl worn over the shoulder; an ivory cross was worn around the neck.

At the invitation of Bishop Hailandiere of Vincennes, Indiana, Mother Guérin and five Sisters from the Congregation of the Sisters of Providence at Ruille-sur-Loire, France, went to the USA to establish a house and educate the children of pioneer families. The Sisters settled in a densely wooded area of Indiana, where at first they found accommodation in a farmhouse. A boarding school was soon built, and several more were opened in the next few years. But the progress was not smooth. Mother Guérin, in trying to maintain ties with the French community, so angered the local bishop, who tried to depose her, that she was denounced at the seventh Council of Baltimore as being rebellious, and a call was made for her expulsion and excommunication. Bishop Hollandiere resigned in 1847, and his replacement was to last for only a matter of months before he died. The maelstrom abated and papal approval was granted in 1887. The American foundation eventually became independent of the French Congregation. In 1920 the first Sisters left the USA for China, where they created a native Chinese Sisterhood, the Providence Sister-Catechists, who later became the Missionary Sisters of Providence. When they were forced to leave mainland China in 1948, the Sisters took up residence in Taiwan, where they remain. Other foundations were made, in England and the West Indies. The Sisters work in education at all levels, address social justice issues, and provide care for children with physical and mental disabilities, as well as running adult day-care centres and literacy programmes.

PROVIDENCE OF ST VINCENT DE PAUL, SISTERS OF

Location: Canada (Kingston, Lake Ontario)
RC (female) founded in Canada in 1861 by Catherine McKinley (Mother Mary Edward)
Abbr: SP
Original habit: a black habit, veil and cincture, with a rosary, and a silver cross worn around the neck; a white, gathered headdress secured under the chin with a large bow.

Bishop Horan of Kingston, Ontario, in 1861 turned his attention to the Congregation of the Sisters of Providence of Montreal, which had been founded by Emilie Gamelin and Bishop Bourget in 1843, when he was looking for Sisters to serve the sick, the aged, the poor and those in need within his diocese. Four Sisters were sent to Kingston in 1861, and this diocesan community was founded under the leadership of Mother Mary Edward. The necessary buildings were erected and the community began its work. The Congregation observes the Rule of St Vincent de Paul and undertakes works of charity as the diocesan bishop sees fit. An American foundation was made from the Kingston House in 1873 at Holyoke, Massachusetts, which has been independent since 1892. There are other American communities, in Boston, Springfield and Worcester, Massachusetts, and in Raleigh, North Carolina. The Sisters are to be found helping the marginalized and disadvantaged and they continue to teach and engage in hospital work, especially in the field of holistic medicine, and to provide spiritual direction.

REDEEMER, SISTERS OF THE

Location: Germany (Wurzburg)
RC (female) founded in Germany in 1854

A Congregation founded as a branch of the Sisters of the Divine Redeemer. The new Congregation achieved its independence in 1866, and several daughter foundations have been made in Germany, the USA and Tanzania.

REDEMPTORISTINES, THE

Location: Each monastery is independent, under the jurisdiction of the diocesan bishop
RC (female) founded in Italy in 1731 by Sr Mary Celeste Crostarosa and Fr Tommaso Falcoia
Abbr: OSSR
Original habit: a red habit, with a blue scapular, a white pleated wimple and a black outer veil over a white under-veil, the veil worn in such a way that part of it could be lowered to cover the face; a fifteen-decade rosary and a large medal engraved with the instruments of the Passion were worn, and a blue cape for use in chapel; white leather sandals were worn instead of shoes; a fully professed nun wears a gold ring representing two clasped hands.

The Redemptoristines were founded at Scala, near Amalfi, Italy, as a contemplative Order observing the Visitandine Rule, which was later revised in line with a revelation in which Mary Celeste was given instructions by Christ the Redeemer about the Rule they should be following. The Rule then adopted was based on that of St Augustine and later approved and confirmed by Pope Benedict XIV in 1750. The Order spread throughout Europe and now has a presence in the USA, Canada, Australia, Brazil and the Philippines. In 1995 a new foundation was made at Bielsko, in Poland. The Sisters observe the contemplative life centred around the divine liturgy, spiritual reading, meditation and the observance of silence. They support themselves by making vestments and altar breads as well as through various forms of artwork.

✠ Order of the Most Holy Redeemer

REDEMPTORISTS, THE

Location: Italy (Rome)
RC (male) founded in Italy in 1732 by St Alphonsus Liguori (canonized 1839)
Abbr: OSSR
Original habit: a black cassock with a white linen collar, a black cincture, cloak, and biretta; a crucifix and rosary are worn.

The Redemptorists were founded at Scala, near Amalfi, Italy. Alphonsus, a lawyer by training, was very concerned about the poor people in his native country. He became a priest in 1726 and set about organizing the many unemployed men in the city into groups for catechesis. On becoming chaplain to a missionary training college he met Tomasso Falcoia, later bishop of Castellamare, who became his friend and confessor. At Falcoia's insistence Alphonsus founded the Congregation of the Most Holy Redeemer, known as the Redemptorists, whose members would work among the rural communities, taking catechesis and education to them. Other foundations were made as the Congregation spread in Europe. A community established in Warsaw in 1787 attracted many postulants, but was suppressed by Napoleon in 1808 and only returned there some eighty years later. There are houses in many parts of the world, in North and South America, Australia, Africa and Asia, and the Congregation is divided into thirty-nine provinces, with an Eastern Catholic monastery in Winnipeg, Canada, where the priests celebrate the Byzantine Rite liturgy. The work of the Redemptorists continues in the missionary vein with the conducting of retreats and missions in parishes and schools. The members also undertake an AIDS ministry, work with the deaf and run renewal courses for clergy and laity. A group calling themselves the Transalpine Redemptorists, now living on the Scottish island of Papa Stronsay in the Orkneys, which they purchased in 1998, have nothing to do with the Redemptorist Order.

♰ Congregation of the Most Holy Redeemer

REMIGIUS, KNIGHTS OF ST

Defunct
Universal (male Equestrian Order) founded in the 5th century by King Clovis I
Original habit: (insignia) a cross, with fleur-de-lis finials, bearing a hand holding a small ampulla into which a dove, representing the Holy Spirit, places his beak.

The Order was instituted in the wake of the reception of the Merovingian king, Clovis I, into the Christian faith following his victory over the Germanic tribes at the battle of Tolbiac (Zulpich). His baptism, and that of his infant son and some three thousand of his soldiers, took place in Reims on Christmas Day, 496. According to a 9th-century legend, Hincmar, archbishop of Reims, alleged that the chrism for the baptismal ceremony was missing and more was brought down from heaven in a vase borne by a dove. This was known as the 'Sainte Ampoule' of Reims. It was this miraculous event that inspired Clovis to institute the Order of St Remigius in *c.*499.

REPARATION, SISTERS OF THE

Location: Italy (Milan)
RC (female) founded in Italy in 1859 by Fr Carlo Salerio and Maria Carolina Orsenigo (Mother Maria Carolina)

The Congregation of the Sisters of Reparation was founded in Milan, Italy, by Carlo Salerio (1827–70), a priest of the Pontifical Institute of Foreign Missions, who had returned from Oceania inspired to found a Congregation dedicated to those in need of help in his native Italy. He collaborated with Maria Orsenigo (1822–81), who also shared his vision, and the foundation was made in 1859. Originally called the Pious Ladies, the first Sisters vowed to make their work of reparation to the Eucharistic Heart of Jesus the purpose of their Congregation, which received its decree of praise from Rome in 1895 and was approved in 1923 and 1933. The Sisters work in Italy, Myanmar (Burma), and in Brazil, where they are concerned with the rehabilitation and care of girls with social difficulties, in the education of young people in institutions and boarding schools, and with various charitable works among the poor and those marginalized by society.

✠ Pious Ladies

REPARATION OF THE CONGREGATION OF MARY, SISTERS OF

Location: USA (Monsey, New York)
RC (female) founded in the USA in 1890 by Ellen O'Keefe (Mother Mary Zita)
Abbr: SRCM

Ellen O'Keefe was an Irish woman from County Limerick who emigrated to the USA and trained there as a nurse. Her experiences in New York showed her the need for a home, or shelter, for women in need of a refuge and protection, with nothing asked in return. With the help of two friends, Mary Finnegan and Katherine Dunne, such a home was started. The diocesan authorities, under Cardinal Farley, were fully supportive of the work, and approval was granted in 1903, with Ellen taking the name in religion of Mother Mary Zita. The work still continues today in St Zita's Villa, and none needing help are turned away. The Sisters also visit the sick in hospitals and run a home for adult women, another for business women and a residential home for the elderly.

REPARATION OF THE SACRED HEART OF JESUS, HANDMAIDS OF

Location: Italy (Messina)
RC (female) founded in Italy in 1918 by Mgr Antonino Celano and Sr Serafina Palermo
Abbr: AR
Original habit: a white tunic and belt with a short black veil over a white headcap; a small badge of the Sacred Heart was worn on the left-hand side of the tunic.

A Pontifical Congregation, founded by Antonino Celona (1863–1952) at Messina, Italy. After his ordination as a priest and further studies in Rome he returned to his native Messina, where he turned his attention to the spiritual reconstruction of the city following its destruction in the earthquake of December 1908. In 1915 he founded the lay Association of the Daughters of Mary, as well as an Association of young women called the Little Handmaids, from which grew the Congregation of the Handmaids of Reparation of the Sacred Heart, founded in 1918. Sr Serafina Palermo was chosen as the first mother-general and is regarded as the co-founder. The Congregation received diocesan approval in 1935 and approbation from Rome in 1951. The charism of the Congregation is reparation and the practice of perpetual adoration of the Blessed Sacrament. The Sisters are heavily involved in education at all levels, in various diocesan and parish ministries and the staffing of rehabilitation centres for those who are drug dependent. Foreign missions have been undertaken, to Brazil and Africa, and a presence is also maintained in Poland and the USA, where a foundation was made at Steubenville, Ohio, in 1958. In 1990 another house was opened in Burke, Virginia, from where a religious education programme is carried out.

REPARATION OF THE SACRED WOUNDS OF JESUS, SISTERS OF

Location: USA (Portland, Oregon)
RC (female) founded in the USA
Abbr: SR

A very small Congregation which relies heavily on lay helpers. The Sisters provide a variety of ministries in nursing and teaching and also undertake home and hospital visiting.

REPARATION TO JESUS IN THE BLESSED SACRAMENT, COMMUNITY OF

Location: England (c/o St John the Baptist Community, Clewer, Windsor, Berkshire)

Anglican (female) founded in England in 1869 by
Fr A. B. Goulden

Abbr: CRJBS

The decision to found a community of reparation was taken at a meeting of like-minded priests which was held at All Saints, Margaret Street, in London. They began initially as a group of tertiaries, but quickly felt that they wished to dedicate their lives more fully to the apostolate of reparation. Two of the community were sent to live with the Community of St John the Baptist, at Clewer in Berkshire, in order to complete a novitiate, to emerge in due time as Sr Catherine (later to be mother superior for twenty-seven years) and Sr Agnes, who died soon after her profession was made. When their founder, Fr Goulden, was appointed in 1871 to be in charge of the Mission District of St Alphege, in Southwark, London, the Sisters moved into the same district a year later. It was then that they started their missionary work in the parish and took over the running of an orphanage and home for girls. New houses were later founded in the south of England. The last remaining members of the community now live with the Community of St John the Baptist, at Clewer, Windsor, Berkshire.

✠ Mission Sisters of St Alphege

RESURRECTION, COMMUNITY OF THE

Location: England (Mirfield, West Yorkshire)
Anglican (male) founded in England in 1892 by
Charles Gore and others

Abbr: CR

Original habit: a black cassock with a light-coloured scapular.

The Community of the Resurrection began life as an Association of priests, many of them members of staff of the theological college at Pusey House, Oxford, together with its principal, Dr Charles Gore. The community was founded on St James' Day

(25 July) 1892, when the first six Brothers made their profession at Pusey House. A year later the community moved to Radley, five miles south of Oxford, where Charles Gore had been offered the living. In 1898 they made their first foundation at Mirfield in Yorkshire, where the College of the Resurrection still provides a theological education for prospective ordinands. Members of the community went to South Africa in 1903 to establish the Cathedral School of St John, at Pretoria, and to work to ease the plight of native African children and create a native clergy. For this purpose they built St Peter's Theological College, where most of the native priests received their theological training. Mission work was started in 1919 in Southern Rhodesia (Zimbabwe), where the Community members were helped by the Sisters of the Community of the Resurrection of Our Lord, at Grahamstown.

✠ Mirfield Fathers

RESURRECTION, SISTERS OF THE

Location: Italy (Rome)
RC (female) founded in Italy in 1891 by Celine and
Hedwig Borzeka

Abbr: CR

Original habit: a black tunic with a white collar and a black veil over a white turn-back; a cross, engraved with the symbols of alpha and omega, the Lamb of God and Chi Rho, is worn around the neck on a cord.

A Pontifical Congregation, founded in Rome by a mother and daughter, the Ven. Mother Celine Borzeka (1833–1913) and the Ven. Mother Hedwig Borzeka (1863–1906). An American foundation was made in 1900. Today, this large Congregation is involved in teaching at elementary and secondary school level as well as in catechetics, nursing and health care and a has a special ministry for geriatric patients.

The Sisters also maintain day care centres and soup kitchens.

RESURRECTION OF OUR LORD, COMMUNITY OF THE

Location: South Africa (Grahamstown)
Anglican (female) founded in South Africa in 1884 by Cecile Isherwood (Mother Cecile) and Bishop Webb of Grahamstown
Abbr: CR
Original habit: a black tunic and cincture with a black veil over a white under-veil and a white crimped headcap, a square linen wimple and a cross suspended from the neck.

Recruited in England by Bishop Webb to go to South Africa to teach children, Cecile Isherwood, Miss Pickthall and ten other women, nicknamed the 'Bishop's Widows' on account of their funereal bonnets and veils, travelled to Grahamstown. In a short time a community was founded, and in 1884 Cecile was clothed as a novice of the new community. Miss Pickthall later joined her in the Congregation, while the other women who had travelled with them returned to England. A school was started. The considerable poverty the new community endured made its progress perilous, but it survived and is now a missionary and educational presence with an emphasis on nursing, with schools, orphanages, child care centres and a training college for teachers established. Missions and retreats are still given by the Sisters, both in South Africa and in England.

RESURRECTION OF OUR LORD JESUS CHRIST, CONGREGATION OF THE

Location: Italy (Rome)
RC (male) founded in France in 1836 by Bohdan Janski, Peter Semenenko and Jerome Kajksiewicz
Abbr: CR
Original habit: a black soutane with a black woollen girdle.

A community founded in Paris by three men who had at one time given up their faith but later regained it. They moved their very poor community to Rome, where Semenenko and Kajksiewicz were studying for the priesthood. Janski, who was in poor health, died there in 1840. The others were ordained, and in 1842, with Semenenko chosen as superior, he and five other men took their vows and adopted the title of the Congregation of the Resurrection of Our Lord Jesus Christ. The Constitutions were approved in 1902, many years after Semenenko and Kajksiewicz had both died. The Congregation continues and the work is largely educational at all levels. The Brothers also maintain parish ministries and campus chaplaincies and are to be found in the USA, Canada, Mexico, the West Indies and Bolivia.

✚ Resurrectionists

RETREAT, CONGREGATION OF THE

Location: France (Le Russey, Besançon)
RC (female) founded in France in 1789 by the Venerable Antony Sylvester Receveur
Abbr: CR
Original habit: a white habit, cape, scapular and cap, but no veil; a crucifix was worn around the neck and a rosary suspended from a cincture; a black habit and long, black cloak were worn out of doors.

Antony Receveur, a man noted for his preaching, founded the Order at Fontenelles, Doubs, France. The first Sisters, threatened with execution during the French Revolution if they would not desert their founder, refused to bow to the revolutionary mob, which allowed them, instead, to go into exile in Switzerland. When the Sisters were allowed to return to France after the years of the Revolution, Fr Receveur found them a house at Aix-en-Provence, where they could lodge until, in 1804, the

Congregation moved to a foundation made at Autun, a little east of Nevers. Many other foundations were made, and the Sisters followed an apostolate in teaching. With the Association Laws enacted in France at the start of the 20th century, they were once more driven into exile, returning to Switzerland and making other foundations in Belgium, Italy, Ireland and England. In the early days of this Congregation the Sisters would rise at midnight to give thanks to God for the grace of their vocations and would go each afternoon to the chapel to make an exercise known as 'the adoration of the cross', during which prayers for the conversion of sinners and the 'Memorare' were said with their arms extended. This was in keeping with their founder's devotion to the cross and in part explains the Congregation's motto, 'Omnia per Crucem' (Everything through the Cross). The work of the Congregation is still in teaching but also in youth work, nursing, parish ministries and in the promotion of retreats.

RETREAT OF THE SACRED HEART, SISTERS OF THE

Location: France (Saint-Germain-en-Laye, Versailles)
RC (female) founded in France in 1675 by Catherine de Francheville and Fr Huby, SJ
Abbr: RLR
Original habit: a black habit and veil with a white coif; a silver heart was worn at the breast.

The Congregation of La Retraite is the result of a union in 1966 of three communities devoted to the provision of retreats. The oldest of the three communities began with an idea by Catherine de Francheville of creating a home for women. She purchased a large house in Vannes, where she formed a community in 1675. Women seeking advice and spiritual direction could go there and also attend the retreats conducted by Fr Huby in the town. Similar foundations were made, including one at Quimper in Brittany, which was started in 1678 by Mother Claude-Thérèse de Kermenom, and another in Rennes, which was founded by Madame Budes de Guebriand. The French Revolution took its toll and the communities were dispersed, to reassemble at the start of the 19th century. Three new foundations were made, at Redon (1820), Angers (1826) and Bruges, in Belgium (1875). Redon and Angers united with the Quimper community, and another union was made in 1966 of the Congregations of Vannes, Quimper and Bruges to form the single Congregation of La Retraite. The Sisters' work, which is based on the Ignatian Spiritual Exercises, is carried out in Europe, South America and Africa, where they provide spiritual direction, counselling, retreats and prayer guidance.

✛ La Retraite Sisters

REUILLY, DEACONESS COMMUNITY OF

Location: France (Reuilly, Paris)
Protestant (female) founded in France in 1841 by Pastor Antoine Vermeil

A community founded in Paris by Pastor Vermeil, who recognized the need for a community of dedicated women who would be able to care for those in need. In this work he was helped by a schoolteacher from Rennes, Caroline Malvesin. The first house was opened in Paris to offer opportunities for the rehabilitation of female ex-prisoners, and by the end of the first year the role of the deaconesses had expanded to include social work, home visiting and the running of a dispensary. The members of the community made life promises, rather than vows, of chastity, obedience and the community of goods.

RIEHEN, DEACONESS COMMUNITY OF

Location: Switzerland (Riehen bei Basel)
Protestant (female) founded in Switzerland in 1852
by Christian Friedrich Spittler

A deaconess community, founded in Riehen, near Basel, by Christian Spittler, who worked for the European Evangelical Society in Basel and came to realize the need for deaconesses, living in community, who would care for the sick and for ex-prisoners.

RITA, SISTERS OF ST

Location: Germany (Wurzburg)
RC (female) founded in Germany
Abbr: OSA
Original habit: a black tunic and veil with a white wimple and a leather cincture.

This Diocesan Institute follows the Augustinian tradition with the Sisters caring for the elderly and those in need, working in education, various pastoral ministries and the provision of spiritual and social care for families at risk. There is an American foundation in Wisconsin as well as houses in Germany and Switzerland.

ROGATIONIST FATHERS

Location: Italy (Rome)
RC (male) founded in Italy in 1887 by Blessed Hannibal Mary di Francia (1851–1927; beatified 1992)
Abbr: RCJ

The Rogationist Congregation was founded to pray for vocations to the priesthood and the religious life and to foster a sense of vocation in the young. The priests and Brothers work in schools and provide social assistance for the underprivileged and for orphans, and maintain a centre in California for those in need of assistance and houses of formation for those considering the priesthood, or Brotherhood, as well as producing vocational publications. Members work in parishes in the USA and have mission stations in several South American countries as well as houses in Africa, Italy, Spain, Poland, the Philippines and India.

✠ Rogationists of the Sacred Heart of Jesus

ROSARY, DAUGHTERS OF THE

Location: Italy (Pompeii, Naples)
RC (female) founded in 1875 by Blessed Bartolo Longo (beatified 1980)
Original habit: Dominican style.

The founder of the Congregation, Bartolo Longo (1841–1926), had been very anticlerical during his days as a law student, but he later changed his views and became a Dominican tertiary. As a lawyer, he was called upon to administer the affairs of a countess who lived near Pompeii. Seeing the difficulties that the country people of the area had to endure, from bandit attacks to poor drainage and illiteracy, he began the Confraternity of the Rosary, to provide help, and later founded the Dominican Sisters of the Holy Rosary of Pompeii, whose members were prepared to care for the young daughters of criminals. He also set up a parallel Institute for the sons of prisoners, and together these communities cared for children in need who would otherwise be at risk. The work has now expanded to include orphanages, schools for the education of the children of criminals, a printing house and a seminary and pilgrimage centre from which the apostolate of the Rosary foundation is fostered.

ROUEN, CANONESSES REGULAR OF

Defunct
RC (female) founded in France in the 13th century by King St Louis of France and Blanche of Castile
Original habit: originally a white habit, but this later changed to black, with a black mantle edged with white fur and a black veil over a white underveil.

The Canonesses Regular of Rouen were instituted by St Louis of France (1214–70) and his mother, Blanche of Castile. The Congregation observed the Rule of St Augustine for many years before adopting the Rule of St Benedict, at which point their habit changed from white to black.

RUFUS, CANONS REGULAR OF ST

Defunct
RC (male) founded in France in c.1000 (possibly) by four canons (see below)
Original habit: a white cassock buttoned at the front with a white girdle or sash passing over the left shoulder and knotted loosely on the right-hand side; a black biretta was worn

The Order of St Rufus was possibly founded in the 11th century by four canons of the church of St Mary of Avignon, and dedicated to the legendary first bishop of the city, although there is no historical evidence for the start of the foundation. The Order received approbation from Blessed Pope Urban II (1088–99) in a Bull dated 1092. Little is known of this Order except that houses were established in France, Italy and Spain. Pope Hadrian (Adrian) IV (1154–59), the only English pope, was prior and then abbot of the foundation of St Rufus at Avignon, with a reputation for strictness. Born in England as Nicholas Breakspear, and coming from a farming background, he was thwarted in his efforts to join an English abbey, possibly through the action of his father, who had become a monk, and his frustration sent Nicholas abroad, where he became a wandering scholar known for his sound learning. After his time at the abbey of St Rufus he was made a cardinal and finally elected pope in 1154. The canons of St Rufus fled from France at the time of the Albigensian heresy in the 12th and 13th centuries and settled in Spain, in the region of Valencia, where they built a church dedicated to St Rufus.

The daily life of the canons, which had been very austere, was eased during this time, the long periods of silence reduced in length and limited to certain hours of the day and wine and meat allowed, although strict fasting applied during Lent. The Order enjoyed some prosperity for a time, but periods of averted crises and then of laxity led to suppression in 1775.

RUPERT, KNIGHTS OF ST

Defunct
RC (male Equestrian Order) founded in Austria in 1703 by the Prince-Archbishop Joseph Ernest Thun
Original habit: (insignia) a gold collar from which hung a violet enamelled cross in the middle of which was an image of St Rupert in a mitre and bearing a crozier.

An Equestrian Order, founded in the city of Salzburg, Austria, for those nobles who had distinguished themselves in the defence of the Roman Catholic faith and of the archbishop of the city. Some twelve young sons of those noble families, including two of the prince-archbishop's nephews, were encouraged for the space of twelve years to live communally to learn the art of warfare and become acquainted with the liberal arts.

RURAL CATECHISTS, CONGREGATION OF

Location: Italy (Rome)
RC (male) founded in Italy in 1943 (see below)
Abbr: POCR

The present-day Congregation of Rural Catechists was formed from a union between the earlier Congregation of Pious Workmen, founded in 1600, with that of the Rural Catechists, founded in 1928. The union between the two was effected in 1943, and its members have undertaken to help young country people socially, as well as with catechesis, especially in those districts where it is difficult to maintain a parish setting.

S

SABBAS, MONKS OF ST

Location: Israel
Universal Church (male) founded near Jericho in the 5th century
Original habit: a tawny tunic with a girdle, a black scapular and sandals.

St Sabbas (or Sabas, 439–532) was born at Mutalaska in Cappadocia and entered a monastery near his birthplace at an early age. Moving from there first to Jerusalem and then to a place near Jericho, he was asked by many people to found a lavra, or anchorite colony. St Sabbas was ordained priest and appointed by the patriarch of Jerusalem, Salustius, to be superior-general of all the anchorites within the patriarch's jurisdiction. St Theodosius, a friend of St Sabbas, was to be in charge of the cenobitic monks. On the death of his father, with whom he had been in serious disagreement, the mother of St Sabbas came to Palestine and under her son's spiritual direction she undertook the building of several hospitals, a pilgrims' rest and a new monastery at the lavra. The lavra, called Mar Saba, is still functioning in the gorge of the Cedron, in the desert just a little south-east of Jerusalem. It is now occupied by Eastern Orthodox monks.

SACK, FRIARS OF THE

Defunct
RC (male) founded probably in France in the 13th century (see below)
Original habit: a tunic, hood and scapular of rough material resembling sackcloth; wooden sandals were worn on bare feet.

The origins of this Order are obscure. They may have been disciples of a follower of Hugh of Digne, an austere friar minor, with their earliest establishment in the south of France, but this is uncertain. A convent of this Order was known to have existed in Segovia, Spain, before 1216, with others established in France and Germany. The Order came to England during the 13th century with the first house opened, in London, with the help of Henry III, to which another fifteen were added as the Order grew. The members were variously known as Sack-bearers, Brethren of Penitence (or Penance) of Jesus Christ and Bonhommes, although this last name was given to other groups at various times. In England they were always known as the Brothers (or Brethren) of the Sack. The Order was suppressed in England in 1307, although some houses seem to have existed beyond this date. There is a suggestion that the suppression was because of growing laxity, which even allowed married couples to join the Order, the wives known as Sackettes. Peterhouse College, in Cambridge, England, is known to have bought some of their land on Trumpington Road, presumably following the suppression of the monastery in that city. The site now houses the Fitzwilliam Museum.

✣ Brothers of Penitence
Brothers of Penance of Jesus Christ

SACRED ADVENT, SOCIETY OF THE

Location: Australia (Albion, Brisbane, Queensland)
Anglican (female) founded in Australia in 1892 by
Bishop Stone-Wigg
Abbr: SSA

A community founded in Brisbane, whose
members maintain various schools as well
as the War Memorial Hospital in Brisbane
and some children's homes in different
parts of Queensland. Because of the vast
size of the state, the Sisters can only meet
when they come to Brisbane for an annual
chapter and take their retreat there together.

SACRED CROSS, SOCIETY OF THE

Location: Wales (Lydart, Monmouth, Gwent)
Anglican (female) founded in England in 1914 by
the Revd E. A. Glover
Abbr: SSC
Original habit: a dark tunic with a small white
collar and a black veil with a white turn-up.

The Society had its beginnings in Chichester, Sussex, when two young women wanted
to form a confraternity of a contemplative
nature. The confraternity evolved into the
Society of the Sacred Cross, and in 1923 the
Sisters left Chichester to take up residence
in a house, in much need of repair, in
Monmouth, Wales. The Sisters carried out
much of the repair themselves. They were
self-supporting and lived a Cistercian style
of life, with an emphasis on prayer, study,
manual work and silence. Today, the Sisters
still maintain themselves through the running of a small farm, making and selling
items of craftwork and offering opportunities for retreats, quiet days and
pilgrimages.

SACRED HEART, BROTHERS OF THE

Location: Italy (Rome)
RC (male) founded in France in 1821 by Fr André
Coindre
Abbr: SC

The Society of the Sacred Heart was
founded in Lyons, France, the members
following the Rule of St Augustine and the
Constitutions of St Ignatius, having made
simple vows at their profession. The development of the Congregation was slow,
mainly because of political unrest in France
but also through poor administration.
Upon the death of the founder in 1821, his
brother, Vincent, also a priest, took over,
but at the general chapter, held in 1840, a
unanimous decision was made that one of
the Congregation, which contained no
priests, should always be superior-general.
This was agreed and a period of remarkable
development followed. In 1847 a foundation was made in the USA at Mobile, Alabama, with others following in Canada,
which soon became a province of its own.
The French Laws of Association in 1901
caused the Brothers to move to Spain and
Belgium. There are now 1,700 Brothers
working in thirty-two countries throughout
the world, engaged in teaching, counselling,
school administration, religious education
and Christian doctrine and catechetical
work. The community recently developed
the Volunteer Service Community, through
which a small group of young men in their
twenties can share the life of the Brothers
for one year. They spend this time in voluntary work, to discern their future
vocations.

SACRED HEART, HOSPITALLER SISTERS OF THE

Location: Italy (Rome)
RC (female) founded in Spain in 1881 by Blessed
Benedict Menni (beatified 1985) and Maria Josepha

Recio (Mother Maria Josefa of the Blessed
Sacrament)
Abbr: HSC
Original habit: a black habit and scapular with a
leather belt, a white starched cap and a long black
veil.

The Congregation was founded in Ciempozuelos, about 20 miles from Madrid. Fr
Menni (1841–1914), who came from Milan,
Italy, was a member of the Brothers of St
John of God. The Order had been asked to
re-establish itself in Spain after the anti-
clerical disturbances there in the 1830s. The
work he began in Spain was halted during
the Second Carlist War (1872–76), but
when it was again possible, Fr Menni
returned to Spain and set up a psychiatric
hospital at Ciempozuelos, with other foundations and hospital refuges later established throughout Spain, Portugal and
Mexico. These foundations did not cater for
women. In 1881, with the help of Maria
Recio and Maria Jimenez, he was able to
found the Congregation of the Hospitaller
Sisters of the Sacred Heart. A novitiate was
started in the same year, and the work of
the Sisters began to spread. Today, the
members maintain psychiatric hospitals,
clinics and sanatoria as well as facilities for
caring for the elderly and chronically sick.
They also run orphanages and schools for
retarded children and hospitals for specialized treatments. There are houses in many
countries throughout Europe, Africa, Asia
and South America.

SACRED HEART, LITTLE SERVANTS OF THE

Location: Italy (Rome)
RC (female) founded in Italy in 1874 by Blessed
Anne Michelotti (beatified 1888)

Anne Michelotti (1843–88) was a member
of the Congregation of the Daughters of
Mary Help of Christians (Salesian Sisters),
but she was concerned that more could be

done to ease the plight of the poor and
neglected. The Congregation of the Little
Servants of the Sacred Heart was established
and remains dedicated to this work.

SACRED HEART, MISSION HELPERS OF THE

Location: USA (Baltimore, Maryland)
RC (female) founded in the USA in 1890 by Mrs
Hartwell
Abbr: MHSH
Original habit: a black habit, cincture and scapular,
upon which was embroidered a cross, and a black
veil with white under-veil with a white wimple.

A prominent non-Catholic charity worker,
Mrs Hartwell, on becoming a Roman Catholic in 1888 was asked to help with the
catechizing of some black children in Baltimore, Maryland, by the parish priest, Fr
Slattery. He was a member of St Joseph's
Society which was concerned with missions
to the coloured population. Together with
some volunteers she undertook the work,
and in 1890 they formed a community
under the name of the Mission Helpers,
Daughters of the Holy Ghost. The members
took the usual vows of religion, of poverty,
chastity and obedience, with an added
fourth vow which was to work exclusively
with and for coloured people. In 1895 the
name of the Congregation was changed to
the Mission Helpers of the Sacred Heart
and the fourth vow was dispensed with,
allowing for greater future expansion of the
work. The Sisters then began to care for all
neglected and poor people, especially for
the deaf, for whom they opened St Francis
Xavier's School in Baltimore. The Congregation underwent several changes from
1906, when Mother Mary Demetrias was
elected mother-general. Until then the Sisters had been required to maintain a programme of perpetual adoration of the
Blessed Sacrament, which was proving
impossible as their workload grew. Today,
the Congregation can be found throughout

much of the USA, and in Venezuela and Puerto Rico, where the Sisters continue to care for the poor, the neglected and those with handicaps. They also offer counselling to the bereaved, to those suffering from AIDS and to the homeless. Much work is undertaken with the Hispanic community.

SACRED HEART, MISSIONARIES OF THE

Location: Italy (Rome)
RC (male) founded in France in 1854 by the Abbé Jules Chevalier
Abbr: MSC
Original habit: a black cassock with a badge of the Sacred Heart on the left-hand side of the chest.

This Congregation was founded at Issoudun, south-west of Bourges, France, and approbation followed in 1877, the community having received the decree of praise in 1869. The priests and Brothers are committed to spreading devotion and reparation to the Sacred Heart of Jesus, according to the revelations received by St Margaret Mary Alocoque in the 17th century. The Society also has a close connection with the definition of the Immaculate Conception, and a shrine to Our Lady of the Sacred Heart was built by the founder in 1855. The members of this Congregation have spread from France to form sixteen provinces worldwide, and they maintain a presence in Europe, Australia, Papua New Guinea, the USA and Brazil as well as missions in many other countries. The priests and Brothers work in education, parish and retreat work.

SACRED HEART, SERVANTS OF THE

Location: France (Versailles)
RC (female) founded in France in 1866 by the Abbé Victor Braun
Original habit: a black habit with large sleeves and a violet cincture with a rosary, a black veil, white linen binder and wimple and a black scapular; a

crucifix is worn around the neck suspended on a violet cord.

The Sisters of this Congregation, which was founded in Paris, observe the Rule of St Augustine and are concerned with works of charity and the care of the sick in their own homes. They also have a ministry to those in hospitals, infirmaries and prisons as well as providing orphanages for children and safe housing for girls and women at risk. An English branch of the Congregation, the Sisters of the Sacred Hearts of Jesus and Mary, at Chigwell, Essex, became independent in 1901.

SACRED HEART, SISTERS OF THE

Location: Italy (Rome)
RC (female) founded in Italy in the mid-19th century by Blessed Mary Schinina (beatified 1990)

A Congregation founded by the Sicilian-born Mary Schinina, who came from Ragusa, in the south-east of the island. Born in 1844, at a time when Italy was experiencing the upheavals of unification, she saw the effects of suffering resulting from the troubles which accompany war and famine. Together with five companions she founded the Sisters of the Sacred Heart of Jesus with the blessing and support of the archbishop of Syracuse. The object of their work was to help those who become victims of war as prisoners, and to help rural communities and those who suffer through natural disasters, such as earthquakes.

SACRED HEART, SISTERS OF THE SOCIETY DEVOTED TO THE

Location: USA (Northridge, California)
RC (female) founded in Hungary in 1940
Abbr: SDSH

A Diocesan Congregation with its origins in Hungary, where it was founded in 1940, moving to the USA by 1956. The Sisters are involved in many types of work, mostly centred around the need for good catechesis among the Hispanic, Chinese and Korean immigrant communities. The members teach in schools and provide opportunities for family summer retreats and day retreats for children and adults, for which they maintain special retreat centres in California. Foreign missions are undertaken in Hungary and Taiwan.

SACRED HEART, SOCIETY OF THE

Location: Italy (Rome)
RC (female) founded in France in 1800 by St Madeleine Sophie Barat (canonized 1925)
Abbr: RSCJ
Original habit: a black habit with a white cape and frilled white cap, over which was worn a black gauze veil.

This Institute had its origins among a group of young seminarians at Saint Sulpice, Paris, which included Leonor de Tournely and Joseph Varin de Solmon, who formed themselves into the Association of the Sacred Heart, which was designed to help them to prepare for their apostolic futures. De Tournely had ideas of forming a parallel group for women who would be concerned with the education of girls. Sadly, he died from smallpox at the age of thirty. Fr Varin was introduced to the future St Madeleine Sophie Barat (1779–1865; canonized 1925) by her brother, and it was clear that she and some like-minded women would be the nucleus of such a society as he had in mind. Sophie Barat and her friends formed a religious community under the spiritual direction of Fr Varin and based on the Jesuit model. This became known as the *Dilette di Gesù*, or the Ladies of Faith, and the small group moved to Amiens to take over a school. In a short time their school had begun to enjoy a good academic reputation and was attracting the daughters of émigrés who had returned to France after the French Revolution. A board-

ing school was established for the children of wealthy parents as well as a school for poor children, and the Sisters expanded their work to include the spiritual direction of women and the giving of retreats. A visit to Grenoble in 1804 by Sophie Barat resulted in the introduction into the society of a group of women who had been Visitation Sisters, including St Rose-Philippine Duchesne (1769–1852; canonized 1988). In 1815 the title Society of the Sacred Heart of Jesus was adopted. St Rose-Philippine Duchesne established the Order in the USA in 1818, at St Charles on the Missouri River, and in 1821 a second house was opened at Grand Coteau, Louisiana. Many other foundations were made. Today the Sisters are to be found worldwide. Their ministries include teaching, concern and care for the poor, health care, counselling, pastoral work in hospitals, parishes and prisons, spiritual direction and the giving of retreats.

SACRED HEART OF JESUS, APOSTLES OF THE

Location: Italy (Rome)
RC (female) founded in Italy in 1894
Abbr: ASCJ

The Congregation was founded in Italy and by 1902 had opened its first American House. The Sisters work in education and provide special help for children who are mentally handicapped or who have learning difficulties. They also have a ministry to the poor, maintain a special legal ministry and run adult day care centres. Foreign missions have been undertaken in Mexico, South America, Taiwan and some European countries, including Albania and Italy.

SACRED HEART OF JESUS, CONGREGATION OF PRIESTS OF THE

Location: Italy (Rome)
RC (male) founded in France in 1878 by Canon Leo John Dehon

Abbr: SCJ
Original habit: a secular black soutane with a black
woollen cord with three knots

A Congregation of priests and Brothers
founded in Saint Quentin, north-east of
Paris, France, from where they spread
throughout the world into thirty-five
countries. The priests and Brothers are dedicated to helping the poor and unemployed.
The Congregation, which received papal
approval in 1906, is dedicated to the apostolate of reparation to the Sacred Heart and
care for those marginalized in society.

✙ Dehonian Priests

SACRED HEART OF JESUS, DAUGHTERS OF THE

Location: Italy (Rome)
RC (female) founded in Italy in 1841 by Blessed
Teresa Verzeri (beatified 1946)

A Congregation founded in Bergamo, Italy,
by Teresa Verzeri, whose first members
included her widowed mother and four
sisters. Diocesan approval was granted in
1842, and papal approbation was received
in 1841 and 1847. The work of the community was mainly concerned with teaching
and visiting the sick, which is still the apostolate of the Sisters, who now work in Italy,
Argentina, Brazil, India and Africa.

SACRED HEART OF JESUS, HANDMAIDS OF THE

Location: Italy (Rome)
RC (female) founded in Spain in 1877 by St
Raphaela Mary Poras (Mother Mary of the Sacred
Heart; canonized 1977)
Abbr: ACJ
Original habit: a black tunic and veil with a white,
angular wimple and a white mantle for use in
choir; a medal of the Sacred Heart was worn
around the neck. Lay Sisters wore a white veil.

The Congregation was founded in Madrid,
Spain, under the original title of the Sisters
of Reparation of the Sacred Heart. The
founder, along with her sister, Dolores,
entered the novitiate of the Society of Mary
Reparatrix in Cordoba upon the death of
their mother. This Congregation was
unpopular with the bishop of Cordoba,
who requested that the Sisters should leave
the city. Some of the novices went to Andu-
jar, where they were taken in and housed
by nuns who were running a hospital in the
town. Permission later came for them to
settle in Madrid, where Raphaela and her
sister were solemnly professed. The Congregation was approved in 1886 and the name
was later changed to the present one, but
not before Raphaela and Dolores had a
disagreement which resulted in Raphaela
resigning as superior-general in 1893. The
Congregation flourished and foundations
have been made in many parts of the world.
The work of the Sisters is concerned with
education at all levels, the running of
orphanages and the rehabilitation of those
who suffer from drug and alcohol addic-
tions. Special Vietnamese and Hispanic
ministries have been set up in the USA.
The Congregation has spread throughout
Europe, and there are now houses in the
USA, South America, South Africa, India,
Asia, Cuba and the Philippines.

SACRED HEART OF JESUS, MISSIONARY SISTERS OF THE

Location: Italy (Rome)
RC (female) founded in Italy in 1880 by Francesca
Cabrini (St Frances Xavier Cabrini – canonized in
1946).
Abbr: MSC
Original habit: a black habit with a short, elbow-
length cape and a black silk veil worn over a black
bonnet and tied with a large bow under the chin;
a black cloak was worn out of doors; a silver cross

was worn around the neck, and professed Sisters wore a gold ring.

The founder of the Order was born in Italy at Sant'Angelo, Lodigiano, near Pavia, in 1850. After a difficult early life she qualified as a primary school teacher and hoped to join a religious Order, but was rejected every time on account of her frailty and poor health. On the advice of her parish priest she began to work with orphans and gathered together some fellow workers, but the enterprise failed. Inspired to found a Congregation dedicated to foreign missions, especially in China, she was given permission to found the Missionary Sisters of the Sacred Heart in 1880, at Codogno near Piacenza, where, with seven companions, she took over an old, empty Franciscan friary. Persuaded to go to the USA to look after Italian immigrants, she arrived in New York in 1889 with members of her Congregation and won over her many critics. Houses were soon established throughout America, providing orphanages, workshops, schools and hospitals. Her work, and that of her Sisters, was not confined to the USA but extended to Central America, Argentina and Brazil. Other houses were opened in Europe, Australia and the Philippines. The longed-for missionary work in China was established in 1927, ten years after the founder's death. She died in the Columbus Hospital she had founded in Chicago, and since she had by then become a naturalized American citizen, she became known as the 'First Citizen Saint' of the USA.

✠ Cabrini Sisters

SACRED HEART OF JESUS, OBLATE SISTERS OF THE

Location: Italy (Rome)
RC (female) founded in Italy in 1894 by Mother Maria Teresa Casini
Abbr: OSHJ

A Congregation founded with the aim of supplying education at an elementary and primary school level. An American foundation was made in 1949 in Hubbard, Ohio. Today, the Sisters work with the secular clergy in the dioceses of Pittsburgh, Pennsylvania and Youngstown, Ohio, in the field of religious education. They also provide care for elderly clergy and run pastoral ministries as the needs arise.

SACRED HEART OF JESUS, PRIESTS OF THE

Location: Italy (Rome)
RC (male) founded in France in 1832 by St Michael Garicoits (1797–1863; canonized 1947)
Abbr: SCJ
Original habit: a black soutane with a broad black cincture and a small black shoulder cape.

The Congregation of Priests of the Sacred Heart of Jesus was founded in Betharram, near Lourdes, France. On account of the poverty of the founder's family, he had to support himself through his seminary training, which he did by teaching in a preparatory school, It was this early work that helped him to decide to train priests, through a community framework, for work in education in mission fields. When, after some years, his post as superior was lost when the seminary in which he was working united with another, he was encouraged by St Elizabeth Bichier des Ages, founder of the Community of the Daughters of the Cross for which Michael Garicoits was spiritual director, to found his Congregation. It received papal approval in 1877. The work of the priests and Brothers is largely mission-orientated, and they are engaged in teaching in seminaries and schools as well as undertaking parochial work when it is called for. Houses of the Congregation are to be found in Europe, including England, in Israel, where work was undertaken in philosophical and theological seminaries, South America, Africa and the Far East.

SACRED HEART OF JESUS, SISTERS OF THE

Location: Paris
RC (female) founded in France in 1817 by
Genevieve Freret (Mother St Joseph)
Abbr: SSHJ
Original habit: a black pleated habit with a white
bonnet and binder and a black cape; an ebony
crucifix with a silver corpus was worn around the
neck.

The Congregation was founded at St Aubin,
south of Rouen, France, in some outbuild-
ings of property owned by the founder's
parents, with the aim of caring for the poor.
With the encouragement of their parish
priest, the Abbé Lefebvre, the founding Sisters made their first vows in 1824 in the
Dominican convent at Rouen. Genevieve
had been concerned about the education
and health care of the rural poor in France
in the wake of the French Revolution, and
the Sisters began their work in these fields.
In time the apostolate was widened to
include social welfare and the education
and care of the handicapped. Driven from
France at the start of the 20th century
because of the Association Laws, the Sisters
made a foundation in England, but later
returned to France, where their work still
continues.

SACRED HEART OF JESUS, SISTERS OF THE

Location: France (Paris)
RC (female) founded in France in 1816 by
Angelique le Sourd
Abbr: SSCJ
Original habit: a black habit with a white collar,
black girdle and triangular black cape; a silver
crucifix is suspended from a black cord at the neck.

Angelique le Sourd was born into a peasant
family in Brittany on the eve of the French
Revolution and was later involved in hiding
priests from the revolutionary mobs at great
risk to her own life. She survived, and
became aware of the poor moral and relig-

ious standards that lingered in the wake of
the Revolution, and with the help of three
friends she formed a small and informal
association dedicated to teaching children
in various local parishes. With the encouragement of the parish priest of Saint-Jacut,
south of Rennes, and the permission of the
local bishop, the members were able to
form a Congregation in 1816, which has
flourished. The Association Laws in France
at the start of the 20th century drove the
Sisters into exile, and they made a foundation in the USA in 1903. Other houses have
been established in England, Ireland, Canada, Peru, Africa, Papua New Guinea and
Mexico. The Sisters still work in education
and provide social and pastoral care, health
care and missions in Mexico.

SACRED HEART OF JESUS AND OF THE POOR, SERVANTS OF THE

Location: Mexico (Puebla, Pue)
RC (female) founded in Mexico in 1885 by St Jose
Maria de Yermo y Parres (canonized 2000)
Abbr: SSHJP

A Congregation founded in Leon, Mexico
by Jose Maria de Yermo y Parres
(1851–1904). The work of the Sisters, which
extended into the USA in 1907, is concerned with education, from kindergarten
to high school, and the running of children's homes. They also work in dispensaries, clinics, nursing homes and mobile
clinics. Overseas activities have taken Congregation members to Guatemala, Nicaragua, Colombia, Italy and Kenya.

SACRED HEART OF MARY, RELIGIOUS OF THE

Location: Italy (Rome)
RC (female) founded in France in 1848 by Fr Pierre-
Jean Antoine Gailhac and Mother St Jean Pellissier
Cure
Abbr: RSHM
Original habit: a dark blue dress and a long black

veil, with a silver cross and a heart suspended from the neck; lay Sisters wore a black habit, the edges of which were bound in dark blue, and a black veil.

The Congregation of the Religious of the Sacred Heart of Mary was founded by the Abbé Gailhac in Beziers, in the diocese of Montpellier, France, with the help of a wealthy widow, Apollonie Pelissier Cure, who was able to use her money to fund the first establishment. The Rule observed is that of St Augustine, and the Congregation was approved by Pope Leo XIII in 1880. The Sisters have always been involved in education, especially of those who are deprived or disadvantaged. They also conduct retreats, undertake catechesis and provide a ministry for the homeless and those in prison. Houses of this Congregation can be found in many parts of Europe, the USA (from 1877) and some African countries.

SACRED HEARTS, LITTLE WORKERS OF THE

Location: Italy (Rome)
RC (female) founded in Italy in 1892
Abbr: POSC

A Pontifical Congregation, with a later American foundation made in 1948. The Sisters now have a mother house and novitiate at Stamford, Connecticut, and also conduct foreign missions in India, Argentina and Albania. The apostolate centres around those in need, with active care for drug and alcohol abusers, care for orphans, the elderly, the sick and convalescent. Some work is also undertaken in catechetics, with members working in seminaries.

SACRED HEARTS OF JESUS AND MARY, MISSIONARIES OF THE

Location: Italy (Rome)
RC (male) founded in Italy in 1833
Abbr: MSSCC

A Congregation founded in Naples, Italy, in 1833 and approved in 1846. The members are concerned with spreading devotion to the Sacred Hearts of Jesus and Mary and are involved in inner-city parish work. There are houses in the USA, in New Jersey and Pennsylvania. The members also provide retreats and chaplaincy work and support missions to Slovakia, India and Argentina.

SACRED HEARTS OF JESUS AND MARY, MISSIONARY CATECHISTS OF THE

Location: Mexico (Mexico City)
RC (female) founded in Mexico in 1918
Abbr: MCSH (or MCSSCCJM)

A missionary Congregation which was founded in Mexico City and went to the USA in 1943, establishing residence at the Our Lady of Sorrows Convent in Victoria, Texas. The Sisters are also responsible for missions in Africa, Bolivia, Mexico and Spain. They work in various parish pastoral and liturgical ministries, with drug and alcohol dependency and in catechesis.

SACRED HEARTS OF JESUS AND MARY, SISTERS OF THE

Location: Lebanon (Beirut)
RC (female) founded in Lebanon in 1860
Original habit: a Maronite religious habit.

This Congregation is composed of local women who have become Sisters within the jurisdiction of the Eastern Catholic Maronite Church. The Sisters teach in a variety of schools, at all levels, throughout Syria and Lebanon, often in partnership with European Sisters.

✠ Mariamettes
  Maronites

SACRED HEARTS OF JESUS AND MARY, SISTERS OF THE

Location: England (Chigwell, Woodford Bridge, Essex)
RC (female) founded in England in 1901
Abbr: SSHJM
Original habit: a black tunic with a leather belt, a black scapular and veil and a white linen wimple; a crucifix was worn around the neck.

A Congregation which was formed as an independent branch of the Society of the Servants of the Sacred Heart, which had been founded in France in 1866. The Rule of St Augustine is observed and the work of the Congregation is concerned with elementary education and the care of the underprivileged and those marginalized in the community, especially the elderly and handicapped, for whom the Sisters provide pastoral care and nursing. Houses are to be found throughout the UK, the USA (from 1953) and Zambia, while missions are maintained in El Salvador and Colombia.

SACRED HEARTS OF JESUS, MARY AND JOSEPH, HANDMAIDS OF THE

Location: USA (Ventura, California)
RC (female) founded in the USA in 1989 by Archbishop (later Cardinal) Roger Mahoney
Original habit: a blue tunic with a white blouse and a dark veil.

A Public Association founded in California which began as a Catholic lay women's community in 1978 when seven women responded to the call to an apostolate of Christian renewal which had been preached by a Picpus Father, Luke Zimmer. The work of the community is catechesis and evangelization in Ventura, California, at the San Buenaventura Mission, the last mission founded by Blessed Junipero Serra in 1782. The community was raised to the status of Public Association by Archbishop Mahoney.

SACRED MISSION, SOCIETY OF THE

Location: England (Milton Keynes, Buckinghamshire)
Anglican (male) founded in England in 1893 by Herbert Kelly
Abbr: SSM
Original habit: a dark grey tunic with a blue linen scapular.

The Society was arguably founded by Bishop Corfe of Korea in 1890, when he wanted to recruit missionaries to work in Korea. In response to this request the co-founder, Fr Herbert Kelly, who was a curate at St Paul's Church in Wimbledon Park, Surrey, offered himself for this work. Several men with various useful trades to offer also came forward, and a missionary college was established where the recruits could be trained for the mission field. The first members, some eight students and two priests, took up residence there in 1891. With a daily recitation of the divine office and a daily Eucharist, this was the beginnings of the religious community, which was granted formal recognition in 1896. The original name of the community, the Korean Ministry Brotherhood, was changed to its present name in 1897 and its scope enlarged to encompass more than Korea as a mission field. The accommodation was proving inadequate for the growing numbers who were offering themselves for this work, and a move was made to Mildenhall in Suffolk, where the society was recognised as a theological and missionary college by the diocesan Boards. In 1903 a further move was made, to Kelham Hall, near Newark, Nottinghamshire. By now the first members of the society had set out for South Africa to start their missionary work. The Society is very democratic in its organization and the priests and lay Brothers enjoy the same status. There are two provinces, that of Europe and a Southern Province. The European Province is responsible for the work in England and in the Anglican Centre in Rome, Italy, while the Southern Province is responsible for the work in South Africa, Lesotho, Australia, New Zealand and Papua New Guinea.

SACRED NAME, DEACONESS COMMUNITY OF THE

Anglican (female) founded in New Zealand in 1894 by Sr Edith

This community had its origin in Christchurch, New Zealand, when a member from the St Andrew Deaconess Community in London, Sr Edith, went out to found the Institution at the request of Archbishop Julius of Christchurch. The work of the community was to give assistance in the parishes to which they were licensed, to prepare altar breads, make altar linen, undertake parish visiting, organize retreats and care for children.

SACRED PASSION, COMMUNITY OF THE

Location: England (Effingham, Leatherhead, Surrey)
Anglican (female) founded in Zanzibar in 1911 by Bishop Frank Weston
Abbr: CSP

When the bishop of Zanzibar, Frank Weston, wanted to found a community of Sisters to work in East Africa, he arranged for the initial training of novices to take place in England, with the Community of the Holy Name. In 1910 the first six women were on their way to Zanzibar, where they were professed. Soon after their arrival a dispensary and boarding school were established. The charism of the community was to offer some reparation for all the wrongs inflicted upon Africa by white people. Very soon other houses were established in the dioceses of Zanzibar and Masasi, and the Sisters undertook missionary and parish work as well as the care of lepers. The

Community of the Sacred Passion withdrew from Africa in 1991, and is now in England with houses in London, Walsall, Norwich and Effingham, which is the mother house. Retreats are organized, and the Sisters work with the housebound and those in prison as well as providing various other ministries. When the community left Africa it left behind the Tanzanian Community of St Mary of Nazareth and of Calvary, which now has nine houses in Tanzania and one in Zambia.

SAINT-LOUP, DEACONESS COMMUNITY OF

Location: Switzerland (Saint-Loup, Pompales)
Protestant (female) founded in Switzerland in 1842 by Pastor Louis Germond

A community founded at Saint-Loup, which was the fulfilment of an idea that Pastor Louis Germond had when he was a theological student at the University of Lausanne, to revive the order of deaconess and to care for the sick and poor. The first foundation was made at Echallens, but trouble and disturbance forced its closure in 1848. The community moved to Saint-Loup, to resume its community life on an estate generously donated to the Congregation.

SALESIANS OF DON BOSCO

Location: Italy (Rome)
RC (male) founded in Italy in 1859 by St John (Don) Bosco (1815–88; canonized 1934);
Abbr: SDB
Original habit: as for secular clergy.

The founder of this large family of priests, Brothers and Sisters styled his companions 'Salesians' in honour of St Francis de Sales. The foundation was made following many long discussions between Don Bosco and Pope Pius IX. Gathering some fellow priests and helpers he began the work of educating and feeding young abandoned people in the

Oratory, in Turin. Night classes were started and, with the help of his mother, John Bosco was able to move to a larger house in a very poor part of the town, where he and his helpers could house many more young and vulnerable people. So successful was their work that the municipal authorities placed no obstacles in his path when workshops and technical schools were planned. A church was also built, dedicated to Our Lady Help of Christians. The Congregation was approved by Pope Pius IX in 1869 and 1874. There are now many thousand members of this Society spread among 120 countries with mission areas maintained in Africa, Asia and parts of South America. The work is largely educational and parochial, but the priests and Brothers also provide retreats, missions, youth and summer camps and centres for young people.

✟ Society of St Don Bosco
  Society of St Francis de Sales

SALVATORIAN FATHERS AND BROTHERS

Location: Italy (Rome)
RC (male) founded in Italy in 1881 by Fr Johann Baptist Jordan
Abbr: SDS
Original habit: a black tunic or cassock, a black cincture with four knots to represent the four vows taken at profession, and a rosary. A white cassock with a red cincture was sometimes worn on mission stations, and a black cloak was used for outdoor wear.

A society founded in Rome by a young German priest who took the name in religion of Francis Mary of the Cross. He had a poor start in life in terms of education, and his decision to become a priest rather than a painter and decorator meant some large adjustments in his life. Once his studies were under way, however, it was discovered that he had a great gift for languages. He founded the Society of the Divine Saviour, which was originally known as the Society of Christian Instruction, to propagate the faith, especially through missions both at home and overseas, and to teach, provide retreats and work in parishes as needed. The members, who now include counselling and various campus and youth ministries in their apostolate, take the usual three vows of religion, poverty, chastity and obedience, to which has been added a fourth, that of a vow of apostolic mission work. Houses of the Order are found throughout Europe, with an American foundation made in Corvallis, Oregon, in the early 1890s, which was followed by a foundation in Brazil in 1896. Others followed from 1893 to 1915, in Ecuador, Colombia, Switzerland, Czechoslovakia, Romania, Belgium, Poland, Yugoslavia, England and Germany, and most recently in India (1986), following the ordination of the first Indian Salvatorian priest. Further mission stations have been established in Tanzania, East Africa (1955).

✟ Society of the Divine Saviour

SASH, KNIGHTS OF THE

Defunct
RC (male Equestrian Order) founded in Spain in 1320 by King Alphonso XI of Castile and Leon ('the Avenger', 1312–50)
Original habit: a red band, or sash, of silk four fingers wide was worn over the left shoulder and secured beneath the right arm by means of a rosette.

The award of the insignia of a Knight of the Sash was intended for the firstborn sons of noble families, in return for which they were obliged to defend the faith, with arms if necessary, to uphold the king and to serve in court for at least ten years. The award was later extended by King John I of Castile and Leon (1379–90) to include more than just the firstborn son.

✠ Knights of the Band

SASH, LADIES OF THE

Defunct
RC (female) founded in Spain in the 14th century
Original habit: a gold band, or sash, worn over a mantle from the right-hand side and secured under the left arm by means of a rosette.

The award was granted to noblewomen as a recognition of their fortitude and courage during the siege of Palencia by the English. Palencia lies midway between modern Burgos and Valladolid in north-west Spain.

✠ Ladies of the Band

SAVIGNY, CONGREGATION OF

Defunct
RC (male) founded in France in the 12th century by Blessed Vital (Vitalis)
Original habit: a grey Benedictine habit.

Blessed Vital (c.1060–1122) was chaplain to William the Conqueror's half-brother, Robert de Mortain, and was made canon of the collegiate church of St Evroult. In 1095, Vital gave up his office and sought to become a hermit in the forest of Savigny in Normandy, where he built a hut for himself. He soon attracted followers, and this led him to establish the abbey of Savigny, where the Benedictine Rule was followed. Many were attracted to the way of life, both in France and in England; by 1145 fourteen houses in England and a further nineteen in France had been established. The entire Congregation of Savigny, by now including nuns, was invited to affiliate with that of Cîteaux at the general chapter of 1147. Some English monasteries resisted this move, but were obliged to affiliate under instructions from Pope Blessed Eugene III in 1148. For their part, the Cistercians were

not overwhelmed at the prospect of this affiliation and were determined not to let their own standards fall to those enjoyed by the Savigniacs. The English Abbot St Aelred of Rievaulx was said to have remarked, on the sending of Cistercians to the Savigniac community at Swineshead, that it would 'illuminate it with the Cistercian way of life'.

✠ Grey Brothers

SAVIOUR, COMPANY OF THE

Location: Spain (Madrid)
RC (female) founded in Spain in 1952
Abbr: CS

A Diocesan Congregation founded in Madrid. Ten years after its foundation, another was made in the USA at Bridgeport, Connecticut, where the Sisters now undertake various parish support ministries.

SAVIOUR AND THE BLESSED VIRGIN, SISTERS OF THE

Location: France (Villeneuve-d'Ascq, Lille)
RC (female) founded in France in 1834 by Josephine du Bourg (Mother Marie de Jésus)
Abbr: CSBV
Original habit: a blue habit with a black veil, a white wimple and a corded cincture with tassels; a small crucifix was worn around the neck.

The Congregation was founded at La Souteraine in the diocese of Limoges. Josephine du Bourg had intended to enter the Order of the Incarnate Word (later known as the Sisters of Charity of the Incarnate Word), but she realized that teaching and nursing were a priority in the diocese at that time and founded her Congregation with this in mind, receiving approbation in 1904. The Congregation soon spread to other countries, including Belgium, Switzerland, Italy, Morocco and England. The Sisters undertake parish work, teaching, catechesis, the nursing of the sick in their own homes and the care of the elderly.

SAVIOUR IN THE WOOD, CANONS REGULAR OF ST

Defunct
RC (male) founded in Italy in 1408 by Stephan Ciogni and Jacob Andrew
Original habit: a white woollen cassock and rochet with lace edging, over which was worn a scapular; a black cape could also be worn and a black biretta was customary.

The Canons Regular of St Saviour in the Wood was founded under the Rule of St Augustine, the founders being the Augustinian Hermits of Siena. The Congregation was approved by Pope Gregory XII in 1408.

SCARBORO FOREIGN MISSION SOCIETY, THE

Location: Canada (Scarborough, Ontario)
RC (male) founded in Canada in 1918
Abbr: SFM
Original habit: secular

A Foreign Missionary Society, founded at Scarborough and approved in 1940. The work of the members of this Society is totally dedicated to foreign missions.

SCHONSTATT SECULAR INSTITUTE

Location: Germany (Vallendar)
RC (male and female) founded in Germany in 1914 by Fr Joseph Kentenick

An all-embracing Secular Institute which includes different types of community and accepts male and female, married, single, clerical and lay members. It was founded by a Pallottine priest, Fr Kentenick, who erected a shrine to the Virgin Mary at Schonstatt, in Germany, with the help of his students at the seminary where he was spiritual director. The shrine later became a place of pilgrimage. This marked the start of the Schonstatt Movement, which is broken up into Institutes, Fraternities, Apostolic Leagues and the Pilgrim Movement. The Institutes are communities of consecrated lives and include the Congregations of the Sisters of Mary, of Our Lady of Schonstatt, of Families, of the Brothers of Mary, of the Schonstatt Fathers and of the Schonstatt Diocesan Priests. The Fraternities are communities that aspire to the highest degree of holiness and are committed to maintaining a permanent outreach programme; this group includes the Federations of Married People, of Women, of Mothers of the Diseased, of Men, of Youth, and of Diocesan Priests. The Apostolic League includes those groups of men and women who aspire to holiness and who try to live out the apostolic life in their professional and daily lives. The Popular and Pilgrim Movement was started in 1934 and involves pilgrims who have established an attachment to the shrine at Schonstatt and who try to enrich their lives through prayer. The Schonstatt Movement is worldwide and is divided into five provinces, Africa, America (North and South America and Canada), Asia (including India and Israel), Europe and Oceania.

✟ Schonstatt Movement

SERAPHIM, KNIGHTS OF THE

Defunct
RC (male Equestrian Order) founded in Scandinavia in 1334
Original habit: (insignia) a collar bearing the images of three seraphim separated by a small patriarchal two-barred cross with a central image of a seraph from which a larger patriarchal cross was suspended.

The Order of Knights of the Seraphim was founded by the royal families of Norway and Sweden to defend their respective families against invading hordes. It was also known as the Order of the Knights of the Name of Jesus.

SERVANTS OF THE CROSS, COMMUNITY OF THE

Location: England (Chichester, West Sussex)
Anglican (female) founded in England in 1877 by Dean Butler and Mother Lucy, CSMV
Abbr: CSC

The Community of the Servants of the Cross was a daughter foundation of the Community of St Mary the Virgin, Wantage, and became independent in 1893. When Bishop Jackson of London needed help with the rescue and rehabilitation of young women, some Sisters from Wantage settled in Fulham, London, and began their work. This foundation later became the headquarters of the Servants of the Cross. From Fulham, the Congregation moved to Worthing, West Sussex, in 1893, and it was here that they dedicated their convent to the Holy Rood. The community was later to move again, to settle in Lindfield, near Haywards Heath, Sussex. The Sisters observe the Augustinian Rule and undertake the care of elderly and infirm ladies. In 1997 the community divided, with some of the Sisters going to a retirement home in Chichester, West Sussex, and others now living with the Community of St Peter at Woking, Surrey.

✠ Community of Mother Angela and the Holy Rood Sisters

SERVANTS OF THE WILL OF GOD, COMMUNITY OF THE

Location: England (Crawley, Sussex)
Anglican (male and female) founded in England in 1953 by the Revd R. C. Gofton-Salmond
Abbr: CSWG

This contemplative Congregation was founded in Crawley, Sussex, as an attempt to create a purely contemplative community, originally for men only, both clerical and lay. This has since changed, and the community is now able to accommodate female religious as well, the Sisters living under the same monastic Rule as the men. The founder, Fr Gofton-Salmond, had been a vicar in London until 1938. He was then able to purchase an extensively forested piece of land on Crawley Downs, Sussex, where he began to create a 'hidden' community of silence, work and prayer, the members observing a Benedictine Rule with many Eastern Orthodox modifications and supporting themselves from the produce of their farm as well as through providing hospitality and retreat facilities and selling various items of craftwork and literature. Since the foundation at Crawley was made, another has been established at Hove, in Sussex.

SERVITIUM CHRISTI

Location: USA (Pueblo, Colorado)
RC (female) founded in The Netherlands in 1952

A Secular Institute for women, founded in The Netherlands and receiving diocesan approbation in 1963. It has since spread to the USA. The origin and spirituality of the Institute is based on the cult of the Blessed Sacrament and the work of St Peter-Julian Eymard.

SEVEN DOLOURS OF THE BLESSED VIRGIN MARY, DAUGHTERS OF THE

Defunct
RC (female) founded in Italy in 1652

The Congregation was founded indirectly by St Philip Benizi when, in 1652, some women who had belonged to a confraternity of the same name which had been founded by him decided to form a religious community in Rome. The new Congregation was prepared to accept women who were unable to enter more conventional religious Orders, often because of their ill-health or deformities. The Sisters followed the Rule of St Augustine and took promises of stability, the conversion of manners (*conversio morum*) and obedience at their profession.

SEVEN SORROWS OF THE BLESSED VIRGIN MARY, NUNS OF THE

Defunct
RC (female) founded in Italy in the 17th century by the Duchess Camilla Virginia Sabella Farnesi
Original habit: a black woollen tunic and girdle with a white linen head-covering and wimple; a long black head veil was worn out of doors.

A community of nuns which was formed by a pious noblewoman, the Duchess Farnesi, in imitation of the foundation of Servites made by St Philip Benizi. The members undertook to live a communal monastic life under vows of poverty, chastity and obedience and to observe the Rule of St Augustine together with the Constitutions drawn up for them by their founder. Approbation was received from Pope Alexander VII and his successor, Clement IX, and confirmed by Pope Clement X in 1671.

SHIP, ORDER OF THE KNIGHTS OF THE

Defunct
RC (male Equestrian Order) founded in France in 1269 by King St Louis of France (1214-70; canonized 1297)
Original habit: (insignia) a linked gold collar made up of five scallop shells (a symbol of Christian pilgrimage) which are separated by two intertwined half moons (a symbol of Islam); from the third, and central, shell is suspended a medallion with an engraving of a ship.

The Order of Knights of the Ship was allegedly founded in France just before St Louis set off on his second crusade against the Muslims. He died from dysentery while at the crusade, most probably a result of contracting typhus at Tunis, where he had landed in 1270.

SILENCE, KNIGHTS OF THE

Defunct
RC (male Equestrian Order) founded in Cyprus in 1195 by the de Lusignan family
Original habit: (insignia) a collar made up of a series of golden 'S's which were joined top to end; from a central 'S' a silver-edged sword was suspended, intertwined by a large letter 'S' on which was written the words 'Pro Fide Servanda' (For the Safeguarding of the Faith).

The de Lusignan family, founders of the Knights of Silence, had been appointed as rulers of Cyprus following the conquest of the island by Richard I, the Lionheart, in 1191. Guy de Lusignan, who was the deposed king of Jerusalem, founded a feudal monarchy on the island which lasted throughout the Middle Ages. The Order, which observed the Rule of St Basil, flourished until it was finally expelled from Cyprus by the Turks.

SOCIAL SERVICE, SISTERS OF

Location: USA (Buffalo, New York)
RC (female) founded in Hungary in 1923 by Sr Margaret Slachta
Abbr: SSS

A Pontifical Society of Apostolic Life founded in Budapest, Hungary. The Sisters of Social Service, now in the USA, are organized as a Diocesan Congregation and undertake responsibility for health care, retreats, parish ministries, religious education and a special ministry for Hispanics. The Sisters maintain foreign missions in Cuba, Hungary, Romania and Slovakia.

SOCIAL SERVICE, SISTERS OF

Location: USA (Los Angeles, California)
RC (female) foundedin Hungary in 1923 by Sr
Margaret Slachta
Abbr: SSS

A pontifical Society of Apostolic Life, founded in Budapest, Hungary in 1923 and with an American foundation made in 1926. The Sisters are heavily committed to all kinds of social work, dealing with poverty on the streets, homelessness of the young, counselling, education in parenting, and the management of summer camps for young people. The Californian Sisters have taken responsibility for foreign missions in the Far East, Taipei, Taiwan and parts of South America. They also maintain a presence in Buffalo, New York (see previous entry).

SOMASCA, CLERKS REGULAR OF

Location: Italy (Rome)
RC (male) founded in Italy in 1534 by St Jerome
Emiliani (canonized 1767)
abbr: CRS
Original habit: secular style.

The Order was founded at Somasca, between Milan and Bergamo, and is sometimes known as the Order of St Maieul because St Charles Borromeo gave them the Church of St Maieul at Pavia as a base for their apostolate among the poor and abandoned orphans. St Jerome Emiliani (1481–1537) had been a soldier in the republican army when he was captured and miraculously released after he prayed to Our Lady. He became a priest in Venice, where he was much concerned at the plight of the orphans in the city. He set up a house where they could be catechized, fed and accommodated. Similar foundations were made in other Italian cities, including Somasca, and it was here that he was joined by two other priests and the foundation of

his new Congregation was made. In his work he was helped by St Cajetan, the founder of the Theatines, with whom the Somaschi were temporaily united between 1547 and 1555, following the death of St Jerome when the Somaschi Congregation nearly disappeared. The Congregation was approved by Pope Paul III in 1540 and is still in existence, the members continuing to work for underprivileged youth through pastoral ministries. They are to be found in the USA, Mexico, South America, India and Sri Lanka as well as in Europe, where they have houses in Spain, Poland, Italy and Romania.

✠ Order of St Jerome Emiliani
Somaschan Fathers
Somaschi

SPIRITUAL LIFE INSTITUTE

Location: USA (Crestone, Colorado)
RC (male and female) founded in the USA in 1960
by Fr William McNamara and Mother Tessa Bielcki
Original habit: (men) a white tunic, cincture and
hood and a brown scapular and sandals; (women)
a similar habit but with a brown headscarf; as
novices the women would wear a white scapular
and cap with the tunic and cincture.

A Diocesan Institute based on Carmelite spirituality whose members live in community under vows of poverty, chastity and obedience and undertake manual labour, outdoor living, silence, solitude and communal worship. The community has created hermitages in Crestone, Colorado, and in Skreen, County Sligo, Ireland, where spirituality and the arts are being developed. Another hermitage, in Nova Scotia, Canada, was built but had to be sold because of ecological issues that were raised. The purpose of the hermitages is to provide an opportunity for people to live in the wilderness so that they can meditate at leisure. The principal apostolate of the community is contemplative, but they also publish books and a quarterly magazine, offer homilies, organize conferences and make and sell various items of handicraft.

STAR, KNIGHTS OF THE

Defunct
RC (male Equestrian Order) founded in France in 1352 by John of Valois
Original habit: a hooded tunic bearing an embroidered emblem with the initials 'M.R.A.V.' (Monstrans Regibus Astra Viam – The Stars Light Up the Way for the Kings) surrounding a seven-pointed tailed star on the left-hand side. (Insignia) a three-stranded linked gold collar with five rosettes placed along its length; from the third rosette a five-pointed star is suspended over the chest.

The Order of the Star was founded in Paris, where a church dedicated to St Audoenus (c.600–84) was its centre. It has been said that the Order venerated the memory of the three Magi who brought gifts to the Christ child. The Order must not be confused with the spurious 'Order of the Star of Our Lady', which was introduced into France during the reign of King Louis XIV (1643–1715) by a bogus 'prince' from the Gold Coast of Africa.

STEPHEN, KNIGHTS OF THE ORDER OF ST

Defunct
RC (male Equestrian Order) founded in Italy in 1560 by Cosimo de' Medici (1519–74)
Original habit: a full-length white linen tunic secured at the neck with two red silk cords which terminated in tassels and were decorated with a red Maltese cross outlined in gold cord; a white cloak lined with rose-coloured material; chaplains wore a white soutane and cape with the Maltese cross edged in yellow cord.

The Order of St Stephen was instituted in Tuscany, Italy, the function of the knights being to suppress the corsairs, those pirates

who were authorized by the Turks to harry the coasts of Christian countries. The Order had four classes of Brethren: knights, who had to be able to prove noble birth, and chaplains, serving Brethren and nuns. The ships operated by the Order were able to co-operate with the Knights of Malta in patrolling the Mediterranean, and they distinguished themselves at the Battle of Lepanto in 1571. The Order was confirmed by Pope Pius IV in 1562. Although himself a Medici, he was not from the same Florentine family as the founder, Cosimo de' Medici. The pope endowed the Order with many privileges. Members of the Order, with the grand master's residence in Pisa, observed the Rule of St Benedict. Married members were allowed, but they had to observe conjugal chastity.

STEPHEN, NUNS OF THE EQUESTRIAN ORDER OF ST

Defunct
RC (female) founded in Italy in 1562 by Eleanor da Toledo, wife of Cosimo de' Medici
Original habit: a white linen tunic and scapular decorated with a red cross after the fashion of the eight-pointed Maltese cross, and a black outer veil over a white under-veil. In choir an amply cut white silk over-garment, or cowl would be worn, lined in red with the sleeves turned back to display the lining.

After the Knights of St Stephen had been founded by Cosimo de' Medici (see previous entry), some nuns of this Equestrian Order were established in a Florentine monastery by Cosimo's first wife, Eleanor da Toledo, just prior to her death in 1561. The nuns observed the Rule of St Benedict under the jurisdiction of the monks of Vallombrosa. A second foundation was made in Florence under the title of the Order of the Immaculate Conception, which was approved by Pope Clement VIII in 1592.

SULPICE, SOCIETY OF THE PRIESTS OF ST

Location: France (Paris)
RC (male) founded in France in 1642 by Fr Jean-Jacques Olier
Abbr: SS
Original habit: secular style.

A Society of Apostolic Life which is an Association of diocesan priests who work to prepare candidates for the priesthood. It was founded in Paris by Fr Olier (1608–57), who realized that if the Church was going to be renewed, it would only do so through the renewal of its parish priests. An early attempt to found a seminary at Chartres had failed, and an attempt was made in the Vaugirard suburb of Paris to start a community for priests and seminarians. The effect it had on the local parish was immense, and Fr Olier was invited to take over the parish of Saint Sulpice, where he achieved the same results and also established a seminary which soon began to enjoy the reputation of forming fine, well-educated and capable priests. It was not long before he was asked to send priests to staff seminaries throughout France and abroad. The Sulpicians made their first American foundation at the end of the 18th century, going on to establish St Mary's College and Seminary at Baltimore, Maryland. Today, Sulpicians can be found throughout the world, and their Congregation is divided into three provinces, France, Africa and the USA.

✠ Sulpician Fathers

SWAN, KNIGHTS OF THE

Defunct
RC (male Equestrian Order) founded in Brabant
Original habit: (insignia) a collar made of linked gold chain, from the centre of which was suspended a golden swan.

A very early Order of Knights, the membership of which was restricted to some selected nobles from Flanders and Brabant, instituted by Duke Salucio of Brabant. The date of institution is not known.

SWORD, KNIGHTS OF THE

Defunct
RC (male Equestrian Order) founded in Latvia/Estonia in c.1204 by Bishop Albrecht von Buxhoeveden of Riga
Original habit: (insignia) a single cross and sword in red (later two crossed swords) worn as decoration on a white mantle.

The Order of the Sword was founded possibly as early as 1204, during the conquest and evangelization of Livonia (present day Estonia and Latvia). The bishop of Riga was anxious to defend the lands against the pagan Baltic people, described at the time as the northern Saracens. Members of the Order were noblemen who observed the three vows of religion, of poverty, chastity and obedience, and were to persuade the local pagans, perhaps forcibly, to accept Christianity. The Order was approved by Pope Innocent III (1198–1216). The knights suffered setbacks in their wars against the pagan fighters, and many, including the grand master, were killed at the Battle of Saule in 1236. After this serious blow the Order was required by the Holy Roman Emperor and the pope to become a branch of the Teutonic Knights of Germany, but they still retained much of their separate identity, largely because of the geographical isolation of the Livonian Province. There was a brief period in the 16th century when the knights continued to control Livonia, but with the break-up of the region the Order was finally suppressed in 1561.

T

TABORITE NUNS OF MARY IMMACULATE

Location: Ireland (Drummin, Westport, County Mayo)
RC (female) founded in the late 20th century

A Congregation of hermitesses who have dedicated themselves to a life of prayer, penance and mortification in silence for the salvation of all, especially priests. It has been said of these hermitesses that their lifestyle is inspired by the example of the Desert Fathers and the 12th-century Carthusians of St Bruno.

TAIZÉ, COMMUNITY OF

Location: France (Saône-et-Loire)
Protestant (male) founded in France in 1939 by Roger Schutz
Abbr: none
Original habit: none

An ecumenical monastic community founded by a student of theology at the University of Lausanne, Roger Schutz, who gathered together some friends for work and prayer in common which became known as the 'Grande Communauté', for which study groups and retreats were organized. Convinced that there was a need for regular monasticism within the Protestant tradition, Schutz acquired a property at Taizé, in south-east France, where he was in a good position to care for Jewish and other refugees until 1942, which marked the German occupation of France. He went to Geneva and began to live a communal life there with others, including the theologian Max Thurian. At the end of the war he returned to Taizé and opened a children's home, 'Le Manvin', and arranged retreats. In 1948 his sister, Geneviève, became the adopted mother of the home. At the same time Roger Schutz was busy making ecumenical contact with Roman Catholic clergy and representatives from other denominations. The first seven Brothers declared their vows at Taizé in 1949 'for life, to the service of God and of their neighbours, living in celibacy under authority and holding all things in common'. The Rule, which was drawn up by Roger Schutz, is similar to that of other monastic Orders, but the members of the Congregation wear no religious habit and the offices of the day are restricted to three. A Third Order later came into being, whereby groups were formed for prayer and study, in Switzerland, France and America. The community has produced a large amount of printed material, videos, and discs of the distinctive Taizé music and chant. While it is largely occupied with promoting ecumenism, other practical projects have been undertaken by the Congregation as well, including 'Operation Hope', which sets up agricultural co-operatives in the poorest rural communities in South American countries.

TEACHERS OF THE CHILDREN OF GOD, ORDER OF THE

Location: USA (Tucson, Arizona)
Episcopalian – Anglican (female) founded in the USA in 1935 by Dr Abbie Loveland Tuller
Abbr: TCG
Original habit: a white habit for life-professed Sisters with a blue and white habit for those under annual vows.

The Order was founded at Providence, Rhode Island, by Abbie Tuller, who had studied education at Harvard University and became well known in the USA in the 1920s for 'The Tuller Method of Education'. The Sisters combine the religious life with the vocation of teaching and to this end have established boarding, day and parish schools and teacher training colleges. They also maintain a publishing enterprise which produces business and educational material. The Congregation is represented in Tucson, Arizona, and in Fairfield, Connecticut, and Sag Harbour, New York.

TEMPLAR, KNIGHTS

Defunct
RC (male Equestrian Order) founded in Jerusalem in 1118/19 by Hugues de Payens and Godfrey de Saint Omer
Original habit: as for a Cistercian, with a white cloak emblazoned with a red cross on the back.

Originally called the Knights of the Temple of Jerusalem, from the quarters they occupied in the royal palace of Baldwin II, which was believed to have been above the ruins of the temple of Solomon, this was both a military and a religious Order. It developed from a military band formed in Jerusalem in 1119 by two French knights, Hugues de Payens and Godfrey de St Omer, expressly

to protect the recently captured kingdom of Jerusalem and to afford safe passage to Christian pilgrims visiting the Holy Land. The Rule of the Order was written by St Bernard of Clairvaux, who may have been a relative of Hugues de Payens, and was therefore Cistercian in outline with the conventual life spent against a background of simplicity, austerity and silence. On military duty, knights would dispense with their normal Cistercian habit and wear instead a white cloak decorated with a large red cross over their military dress. The recitation of the little office was also adjusted to meet the demands of the battlefield, with the Lord's Prayer recited in place of the daily Hours. The Order was composed of four ranks:

1 Knights – who alone were allowed to wear the white mantle
2 Chaplains
3 Sergeants
4 Craftsmen

– all led by a grand master. A contemporary description calls them 'lions of war and lambs of the hearth; rough knights on the battlefield and pious monks in chapel'. The services of the knights were gradually used to ensure the safe passage not only, as at first, of pilgrims but also of money and valuables between Europe and the Holy Land, and the banking system which developed brought great wealth to the Order and in time led to its downfall. With the fall of Jerusalem to the Muslims in 1187 and Acre in 1291 much of the Order's security work was at an end. In 1307 the grand master, Jacques de Molay, was seized together with some other senior members of the Order, betrayed by a renegade knight. Under torture they confessed to charges of sacrilege, sodomy, blasphemy and Satanism and went to the stake. It is almost certainly true that they were innocent of these charges, victims of the envy and greed of unscrupulous men. The assets were seized, ostensibly to be handed over to other Orders, but in reality used for their own ends by impecunious and ruthless monarchs. The Order was suppressed in 1312 and banned from England by Edward II.

☩ Knights of the Temple of Solomon
Poor Knights of Christ
Poor Knights of the Temple

TERESA, INSTITUTE OF ST

Location: Italy (Rome)
RC (female) founded in Spain in 1911 by Blessed Peter Poveda Castroverde (beatified 1993)

A Secular Institute founded in Linares, Spain. After his ordination in 1897, Peter Poveda taught briefly at the seminary, but he was anxious to work among the very poor who were living in caves in Guadix, in the archdiocese of Granada. He established some schools for the children and workshops for the adults who could learn skills, which would give them employment. Peter later became a canon of the basilica in Covadonga in north-west Spain and began the St Teresa of Avila Academy in Oviedo, which marked the start of the Teresian Association. By 1913 his educational methods were beginning to be noted, and diocesan and civil approvals were followed by approbation from Rome. The work of the Association spread from Spain to Chile and Italy, and in 1951 it was granted Secular Institute status. Peter Poveda's work in education made him a target for the militia of the revolutionary Left during the Spanish Civil War, and he lost his life in 1936. The members, who are now to be found throughout the world, promote a Roman Catholic solution to educational problems and work for the maintaining of Christian values in education and culture.

☩ Teresian Association

TERESA OF JESUS, SISTERS OF ST

Location: Italy (Rome)
RC (female) founded in Spain in 1876 by Enrique de Osso
Abbr: STJ

A Congregation, founded in Spain, which spread to the USA in 1910. The Sisters are involved in education, catechesis and youth work. They also provide a specialized Hispanic ministry in the USA and have a strong commitment to foreign missions. They maintain houses in Spain, Portugal, France, Italy, South America, Bolivia, Angola, the Ivory Coast and the Philippines.

☩ Teresian Sisters

THEATINE FATHERS

Location: Italy (Rome)
RC (male) founded in Italy in 1524 by St Cajetan and Peter Caraffa (later Pope Paul IV)
abbr: CR
Original habit: a black tunic with a cord cincture, perhaps with a rosary suspended, a black cloak and a clerical hat.

The name of the Order derives from 'Theate' (Chieti) in the Abruzzi, Italy, which was the See of Peter Caraffa, the co-founder with St Cajetan. After his ordination in 1516, Cajetan returned to his birthplace of Vicenza and entered the Oratory of St Jerome, which was noted for its care of outcasts and the sick. The scandalous lives of many of the clergy prompted Cajetan to found this Order of clerks regular, known as the Theatine Fathers, adopting the Rule of St Augustine. Pope Clement VII (1523–34) gave his approval in 1524, and Cajetan, with two companions, was professed in Rome before the pope. The aim of the Order was to restore the good name and practice of the clergy, to help the sick and to preach. On Cajetan's death in 1547 the Order continued to flourish in

Italy, and by the end of the 17th century it had spread to several European countries. Overseas missions had also been opened in Peru, Borneo, Sumatra, the Near East and Iran. An American foundation made at Denver, Colorado, is now a seminary from which priests undertake parish work, offer retreats and provide a special ministry to the Hispanic community. Missions have been conducted in South America, Mexico and Africa.

THEATINE HERMITESSES

Defunct
RC (female) founded in Italy in 1616 by the Venerable Ursula Benincasa (1550–1618)
Original habit: a white habit with a leather girdle and a blue scapular (in honour of the Immaculate Conception of the Blessed Virgin Mary), a black veil, white wimple and mantle.

An Order founded in Castel Sant'Elmo, Naples, where the founder and some thirty-three companions observed a most severe and austere life of perpetual abstinence from flesh meat, except during times of illness, with frequent fasts in addition to the usual church fasts on the vigils of Marian feasts, the Ascension, Corpus Christi and every Saturday. Adoration of the Blessed Sacrament, which was exposed on all Fridays, was accomplished in rotas of five Sisters at a time. At her solemn profession a hermitess was permitted to talk, for the last time ever, to her parents. The overall tenor was austere and contemplative. The Rule of the hermitesses was approved by Pope Gregory XV in 1623. Although the Congregation is now defunct, the devotion of the Blue Scapular of the Immaculate Conception is still practised today (see next entry).

✠ Hermitesses of the Immaculate
    Conception

THEATINE NUNS

Location: Italy (Rome)
RC (female) founded in Italy in c.1583 by the Venerable Ursula Benincasa
Original habit: a white tunic with a black outer garment with wide sleeves; a woollen girdle and white veil, but no wimple and only a small collar.

The founder, Ursula Benincasa (1550–1618) was precocious and had attempted to enter the monastery of St Mary of Jerusalem in Naples at the age of ten years. With her sister, Christina, who was elected as the first superior, and several nieces as part of her Congregation, Ursula Benincasa made her foundation of Theatine Nuns. The site of this first foundation was discerned with the aid and encouragement of the abbot of Francaville, Sicily, to whom Ursula had revealed details of visions she had been experiencing. These mystical experiences continued for two years preceding the foundation and attracted unpleasant attention and the accusation that she may have been possessed. The foundation was made, authorized and placed under the protection of the Blessed Virgin Mary, St Joseph, St Michael the Archangel and St Peter. A little like the more austere Theatine Hermitesses (see previous entry) which Ursula Benincasa later founded, the nuns were to observe simple vows, practise fasting, participate in manual labour and wear a hair shirt on Fridays. They recited both the little office and the divine office daily, with the addition of the *Veni Creator* and the *De Profundis*, recited after the office of None.

✠ Sisters of the Immaculate Conception of
    the Blessed Virgin Mary

THÉRÈSE, LITTLE WAY SISTERS OF ST

Location: Burma (Myanmar, diocese of Hahka)
RC (female) founded in Burma in the 1990s

This very young Congregation was co-founded by Bishop Nicholas Mang Thang and Sr Mary Doohan with a view to the evangelization of Burma. The first group of Sisters were due to make their final profession in 2000.

THOMAS OF VILLANOVA, SISTERS OF ST

Location: France (Neuilly-sur-Seine)
RC (female) founded in France in 1661 by Ange Le Proust
Abbr: SSTV

A Congregation founded by the prior of the Hermits of St Augustine, at Lamballe, south-east of St Brieuc, France. At the close of the 17th century, the Sisters were trying to cope with the demands of the poor and the sickness that came with poverty by maintaining poorhouses. The Congregation survived the French Revolution because of the value of the Sisters' nursing service to the community, and the work spread throughout France. The members still continue to care for the sick. A foundation was made in the USA in 1948, where the Sisters maintain a convalescent home, the Notre Dame Home, in Norwalk, Connecticut.

THOMAS THE MARTYR, COMMUNITY OF ST

Defunct
Anglican (female) founded in England in 1851 by the Revd Thomas Chamberlain

An Anglican Sisterhood which was founded in Oxford because of the concern of the founder for his parish of St Thomas the Martyr, which enjoyed a rather lugubrious reputation. He gathered together a group of women who were given to works of mercy and charity in the district, two of whom, Felicia Skene and Marian Hughes, were willing to live a community life, which Thomas Chamberlain organized in 1849. In 1851 this became the Sisterhood of St Thomas the Martyr. The first profession was made in 1852, and a school established at Rewley, Oxford, in 1859 for the girls of

wealthy parents. A boarding school for the middle classes was followed by the establishment of a vocational, or industrial, school for those girls destined for domestic service. These schools financed the charitable work of the Sisters and made possible the opening of an orphanage and nursery school near the mother house. The Sisters also baked altar breads and worked at church embroidery and the making of vestments, undertook the care of a penitentiary in the Winchester diocese and supported a mission in Barry Docks, South Wales. After Thomas Chamberlain's death in 1892, the Sisterhood declined and was forced to affiliate with the Community of St Mary the Virgin at Wantage, Oxfordshire, although remaining independent as far as the Rule and Constitutions were concerned.

TIRON, ORDER OF

Defunct
RC (male) founded in France in 1109 by St Bernard of Tiron

The Order of Tiron, was originally founded by St Bernard of Tiron (c.1046–1117), who was also known as Bernard of Abbeville. He had been a monk of the abbey of Saint-Cyprien but left there because of the growing laxity of the community and spent a time as a hermit. A brief return to the abbey soon sent him away again because of the internal wrangling he witnessed there. Living for a time on one of the islands off the Normandy coast, sheltering among the rocks and living on a diet of herbs and roots, he soon attracted many followers. In 1109 he went to Tiron where he founded the monastery, which observed a strict Benedictine Rule. Other houses were established, including a small settlement at Caldey Island, off the Welsh coast. In the 17th century the Order of Tiron merged with the Congregation of St Maur, a Benedictine Congregation founded under Cardinal Richelieu in 1618, but the Maurists failed to survive the French Revolution.

TRAPPISTINES / TRAPPISTS

A popular name for the female / male members of the Order of Cistercians of the Strict Observance.

TUSINUS, KNIGHTS OF

Defunct
RC (male Equestrian Order) founded in Austria in c.1562

Original habit: a red mantle decorated with a simple, unadorned green Greek cross.

The Order had its origins in Austria and present-day Czechoslovakia. The knights observed the Rule of St Basil and undertook vows of conjugal chastity, obedience to the Roman Catholic Church and a readiness to take up arms against its enemies. The grand master was said to be the Holy Roman Emperor, but details of the Order's history and decline are not readily available.

U

UNION MYSTERIUM CHRISTI

Location: France (Paris)
RC (female) founded in France in 1976
Abbr: SC

The Congregation, now called the Union Mysterium Christi, was formed when seven foundations, each dedicated to one of the mysteries of Christ's life, passion, death and resurrection, formed a union, which for the most part took over existing community property. The Sisters continue their work as before, but in a united Congregation. They teach, nurse, undertake parish ministries and missions and care for the aged and those who are handicapped. Foreign missions are conducted in Belgium, England, Italy, Chile, Madagascar and Cameroon.

✛ Sisters of Christ

URSULA, SOCIETY OF ST

Location: France (St Cyr, Loire)
RC (female) founded in France in 1606 by the Ven. Anne de Xainctonge
Abbr: SU
Original habit: a black habit with a deep white collar, a small black cape and a black cap, pointed at the forehead, over which was a black veil; a small crucifix was worn below the collar and a rosary was suspended from the girdle. Lay Sisters wore a similar habit except that beneath the veil a white starched bonnet was worn.

The Venerable Anne de Xainctonge (1587–1621), the founder, even as a small girl used to gather people together to catechize them and, as she grew, came to see that what she wanted to do with her life was to devote it to the care and education of girls, in a similar way to that devised by the Jesuits for boys. She had a vision in which the Virgin Mary urged her to found a new Order in Dole, which was then a part of Spain. Her father preferred that she found her Order in Dijon, and her refusal to comply with his wishes led to her banishment from the family home. With a servant for company she settled in Dole. It took some ten years before a community could be assembled. Anne, with the help of a Jesuit priest, began to draw up the Constitutions for her Order, which were very Ignatian in spirit, but she died before the task was completed. After some difficulties, the Constitutions were approved by Pope Innocent X. In 1606 she opened the first free school classes for girls and young women, a pioneer action in female education. Further foundations were made, in France, Switzerland and Germany, and approbation from Rome was received in 1648 and 1678. The French Revolution caused the dispersal of the Sisters, but they reassembled in the peace that followed, only to be dispersed again in 1901 on account of the French Association Laws. As a result, further foundations were made overseas, in the USA, Italy, The Netherlands and England. The Sisters still work in education but have increased their apostolate to include the care of the elderly and the giving of retreats. They also maintain a mission in Africa.

✝ Sisters of St Ursula of the Holy Virgin

URSULINE NUNS

Location: varies according to the Congregation; see under individual entries
RC (female) founded in Italy in 1535 by St Angela Merici (canonized 1807)
Abbr: OSU
Original habit: a black tunic and veil, but there are many differences in habit between the different Congregations.

St Angela Merici (1470/4–1540) was born in Desenzano, near Lake Garda in Lombardy, Italy, and became a Franciscan tertiary, wearing that habit for the rest of her life despite making her own foundation. With some companions she formed a self-help and support group for unmarried girls in the area, who could be taught various useful skills. The enterprise was successful, and St Angela was invited to found a similar institution in Brescia. In time this became the Company of St Ursula, made up of virgin women who could live at home with their families and wore no distinctive habit; the term 'Company' was used at this time to refer to lay Associations. The Ursuline Sisters date their foundation from the time when St Angela moved into a house which served as a centre for this group. In 1536, twelve members were allowed to form a new Institute with diocesan approval, and they undertook catechesis and the edu-

cation of young women and girls. St Angela died in 1540, four years before papal approbation was granted by Paul III. The Order grew and spread, and by 1582, observing a Rule written for them by St Charles Borromeo, had begun its transformation into a religious Order. Development and expansion was swift throughout Europe. Today, there are several thousand Ursulines in the world, both religious Sisters and secular members, the latter belonging to the Secular Institute of St Angela Merici. The separate Congregations are dealt with below.

1 THE PARIS CONGREGATION OF URSULINE NUNS AND SISTERS – The Irish Union

Location: Ireland (Booterstown, Dublin)
RC (female) founded in Cork in 1771
Abbr: OSU (Irish Union IUU)
Original habit: black habit with a square white linen wimple, a black veil and leather belt.

The Paris foundation was largely the work of Madame de Sainte Beuve, who endowed a monastery in the rue St Jacques in 1610 under the guidance of Françoise de Bermond, an Ursuline from the Avignon foundation, which had been made in 1596. From this Congregation, which observed a Rule known as the Primitive Rule of St Angela Merici, other French communities were developed. Four young Irishwomen came to Paris to complete their novitiate, returning to Ireland in 1771, where a school was opened in Cork City the following year. Other Irish foundations followed, at Tipperary (1787), Waterford (1816) and Sligo (1850). A more recent foundation has been made in Brecon, Wales (1948). These houses in turn all founded others. The four major houses amalgamated as the Irish Ursuline Union in 1978. Sisters of the IUU work in Great Britain, Kenya and the USA, where the first foundation was made from the Paris mother house to New Orleans in

1727. The members are mostly involved in teaching, some hospital chaplaincies, social and pastoral ministries, spiritual direction and retreats.

2 THE ROMAN UNION

Location: Italy (Rome)
RC (female) union founded in 1900 from earlier foundations
Abbr: OSU
Original habit: a black habit with wide sleeves, a round white wimple with an angular headdress and a leather belt.

A Union of some sixty Ursuline Congregations from a wide range of countries, arranged into provinces. The Sisters of the Roman Union are involved in education at all levels, parish religious education programmes, counselling, hospital chaplaincy work and care for the marginalized and disadvantaged in society. They are present throughout the world.

3 THE CONGREGATION OF BRENTWOOD

Location: England (Brentwood, Essex)
RC (female) founded in England in 1900 by Mother Clare Arthur
Abbr: OSU
Original habit: a black habit with a black cord girdle, a square-cut wimple and a round headcap with a black veil.

The Brentwood Congregation was founded, initially, by Ursulines from the Congregation at Tildonk, Belgium (see below). Following the arrival in England of Sisters from the Congregation at Tildonk in 1851, several foundations were made including the one at Brentwood. When other Ursuline houses in England joined the Roman Union in 1900, this house declared that it wished to remain autonomous. The Congregation today is mainly concerned with education

in England, although in the past it maintained a foreign mission in Kenya.

4 CONGREGATION OF TILDONK

Location: Belgium (Brussels)
RC (female) founded in Belgium in 1815 by Fr Lambertz
Abbr: OSU
Original habit: a black tunic, cord girdle and veil with a white wimple and headband.

The Congregation at Tildonk was founded when Fr Lambertz reconstituted some Ursulines who had fled to Belgium from France during the French Revolution. He adopted the Constitutions of the Ursulines of Bordeaux with some modifications, and these were approved by Rome in 1831. The Tildonk Congregation spread through Belgium, The Netherlands, Canada, the USA and England. The work of these Sisters is largely educational, ranging from elementary to college level, and they also provide pastoral and retreat facilities. Foreign missions are maintained in Asia and Africa, as well as throughout Central and South America.

5 THE CONGREGATION OF URSULINES OF BELLEVILLE (Ursuline Sisters of Mt Calvary)

Location: USA (Belleville, Illinois)
RC (female) founded in the USA in 1983
Abbr: OSU

The Ursuline Sisters of Belleville have been an autonomous Diocesan Congregation since 1983 and were formerly a mission of the Ursulines of Kalvarienberg, near Ahrweiler, Germany, which came to the USA in 1910. The Mt Calvary Ursulines originated from the 1535 foundation made by St Angela Merici and from the house at Bordeaux which had been founded in 1606, whose Constitutions were approved in 1618 by Pope Paul V. The Sisters of the present community at Belleville undertake retreat work, teach in elementary schools, nurse the sick and visit those who are housebound.

6 THE CANADIAN UNION

Location: Canada (Quebec)
RC (female) founded in Canada in 1953
Abbr: OSU

The Union was formed from all the Ursuline convents which sprang from the Quebec foundation of 1641. The founders of the Ursulines in Canada were Marie Guyard Marti (The Ven. Marie de l'Incarnation) and Madame de la Petrie, two widows from France who arrived in Quebec in 1639, with several Sisters from Dieppe and Paris, and immediately set about caring for and educating the Indians. They faced great difficulties, both with the local Iroquois and in their attempt to agree on a common habit and devotional regime for themselves, as the Sisters had come from different houses. The first Ursuline monastery was built in 1641, but was destroyed by fire nine years later. Another was built in 1651 and the Sisters faced the problems of teaching the Indian children. From Quebec, a convent of five Ursuline Sisters was founded at Trois Rivières in 1697 for the service of education and nursing. A hospital was opened, later transferred to the Sisters of Providence, and missionaries were sent to New Orleans (1822), Charleston (1824), Galveston (1849) and Montana (1893). The Canadian Union is divided into five provinces, Quebec, Trois Rivières, Rimouski, Japan and Peru.

URSULINES OF JESUS, THE

Location: France (Paris)
RC (female) founded in France in 1802 by Fr Louis Marie Baujdouin and Charlotte Gabrille Raufray de la Rochette (Mother St Benedict)

Abbr: UJ (previously U de J)
Original habit: a black habit with a violet girdle and a white frilled cap worn beneath a black veil; an ebony cross was worn around the neck.

The Congregation was founded at Chavagnes as a teaching Order. The Sisters soon became concerned with the care of orphans and the sick, and this remains the focus of their work today. This has now been extended into providing catechesis for children and potential converts, visiting the lonely, and sharing problems with those who live in deprived areas. The Congregation has many foundations in Great Britain, Spain, France, Italy, The Netherlands, Canada and Ireland. Missionary work has been undertaken in Cameroon, Chile, Nigeria and Bolivia.

URSULINES OF PARMA AND OF PIACENZA, THE

Defunct
RC (female) founded in Italy in 1575 by Ranuccio, duke of Parma
Original habit: (Parma) a black tunic with a very long dark blue cape, the hem of which was caught up into the girdle, and a long veil which in part obscured the eyes; (Piacenza) as for the Parma Congregation but with a dark violet cape.

A Congregation of nuns founded in Parma in the 16th century for virginal members of the most illustrious and noble families of the district. The Rule and Constitutions that were to be observed were the same as those for the Company of St Ursula, which had been founded by St Angela Merici. The members of the community were restricted in number to forty at any one time. In Piacenza, just a little north-west of Parma, was another Ursuline Congregation, founded from Parma by two selected noblewomen, Laura Masi and Isabella Lampugnana.

URSULINES OF THE HEART OF JESUS AGONIZING

Location: Italy (Rome)
RC (female) founded in Poland in 1920 by Blessed Mother Ursula Ledochowska (beatified 1983)
Original habit: a grey habit

Blessed Ursula Ledochowska had become an Ursuline nun at Krakow, Poland, and was sent as a missionary to Russia in 1907. She left there at the time of the Russian Revolution in 1917, and went to Scandinavia. At the end of the First World War Ursula returned to Poland, and with the help of her brother Vladimir, who was general of the Jesuits in Poland, she founded the Grey Ursulines, as they were commonly called from the colour of the habit, and a mother house was established at Pniewy, near Poznan. The foundation flourished, and today the Sisters, who work mainly in education and works of charity, can be found in Poland, France, Italy, Argentina, Canada, South Finland and Germany.

✟ Grey Ursulines

USETZ, CANONS REGULAR OF THE CITY OF

Defunct
RC (male) founded in France, date uncertain
Original habit: a white, buttoned tunic with a large enveloping surplice.

This Congregation of canons regular was founded in the cathedral city of Usetz (present day Uzes), which was an episcopal seat from the 5th to the 18th century. The canons observed the Rule of St Augustine and were housed in the present Church of St Theodorat. The effects of war and the inroads of heresies tarnished the splendour of the canons and their reputation and they were replaced in 1640 by the canons of St Genevieve.

V

VALLEY OF JEHOSOPHAT, CANONS REGULAR OF THE

Defunct
RC (male)
Original habit: a dark red cloak, or cowl, with a hood. The canons were bearded.

Jehosophat is a valley between the Temple Mount and Mount Olivet in Jerusalem. A church was built here and a chapter of canons regular was installed. It was destroyed at the time of the crusades.

✠ Canons Regular of the Valley of Josaphat

VALLEY OF RONCEAU, CANONS REGULAR OF THE

Defunct
RC (male) founded in Spain, possibly in the mid-9th century
Original habit: a black habit with a very small white scapular and cincture; a black cape was worn in choir.

The Canons Regular of Ronceau inhabited a monastery at Roncevalle, south of Santiago, Spain, and were installed there to offer hospitality to pilgrims who were *en route* to Compostela to venerate the relic of St James the Greater whose remains are reputedly enshrined there. The monastery was dedicated to the Blessed Virgin Mary.

VALLEY OF SCHOLARS, ORDER OF THE

Defunct
RC (male) founded in France in 1219 by four doctors of theology at the Paris University
Original habit: a white woollen tunic and scapular, a black cape lined with lambs' wool and a biretta.

An Order of canons regular, approved by Pope Honorius III (1216–27), which was founded at Luzy, near Chaumont, in the diocese of Langres as an Augustinian friary. The founders were all professors of theology, and they chose the location on account of its solitude, which ensured that they would to enjoy some silence. In 1646 the Order of the 'Val des Escoliers' was united with that of St Genevieve by Pope Innocent X.

✠ Scholari

VALLISCAULIAN ORDER

Defunct
RC (male) founded in France in the 12th century by Viard (or Guido)

The Order was started by a Carthusian lay Brother named Viard, or Guido, in Burgundy towards the end of the 12th century. He had intended to erect a hermitage for himself, but the duke of Burgundy, in fulfilment of a promise he had made, built a monastery on the site. Viard became prior of the foundation, which attracted many novices who were willing to take on a way of life which represented an amalgam of both Cistercian and Carthusian customs. The Order received approbation from Rome in 1205, and successive dukes of Burgundy endowed the monastery with land and wealth which allowed the original foundation to flourish and to develop independent foundations in France, Germany and Scotland, which are said to have numbered at least twenty. The monastery at Val-des-Choux survived for many years, but by the middle of the 18th century it had declined to such a point that the remaining members of the Order were easily persuaded to affiliate in 1764 with the Cistercians at Sept Fons, a daughter foundation of the Fontenoy monastery which had been founded in 1132.

✠ Brothers of Cabbage Valley

VANNES, CONGREGATION OF ST

Defunct
RC (male) founded in France in the 10th century
Original habit: Benedictine style.

A Benedictine Congregation which occupied a collection of buildings that had been founded as a college for clergy near Verdun, France, by St Vitonius, or Vannes, who died *c.*525. The buildings were handed over to the Benedictines in 952, who named the foundation the Congregation of the Abbey of St Vannes of Verdun. An important monastic reform, aimed at stopping the practice of giving benefits to some ecclesiastics and seculars *in commendam* started here in 1600 under the priorship of Dom Didier. In time this led to a collection of reformed houses in Lorraine, Champagne and Bourgogne, and eventually a new Congregation was formed, known as the Congregation of St Vannes and St Hydulphe, which is said to have numbered some forty

houses. It was approved by Pope Clement VIII in 1604. At a general chapter held at St Mansuet de Toul in 1618, the Congregation was divided along national lines. The French houses formed the Congregation of St Maur, and those of Lorraine, which was then a separate country, remained loyal to St Vannes. The French Revolution dealt badly with both Congregations, which were consequently suppressed. With the formation of the Benedictine Congregation of Solesmes in 1837, the privileges of St Vannes were handed over to the new Congregation, even though the continuity was simply artificial.

VERONA MISSIONARY SISTERS

Location: Italy (Rome)
RC (female) founded in Italy in 1872 by Bishop Daniel Comboni and Mother Maria Bollezoli
Abbr: CMS
Original habit: a black habit and cape, with five red buttons, and a black outer veil over a white linen under-veil; a small silver cross on a red cord was worn around the neck.

This international missionary Congregation was founded at Verona, Italy, following Bishop Comboni's appointment as pro-vicar-apostolic of Central Africa. Its aim was to provide help in the mission fields, especially in Africa, for the Comboni Missionary Fathers. The scope of the apostolate has now expanded to include work in Europe, the Middle East, Asia and the USA, where more than two thousand Sisters are to be found working in schools, pastoral centres, hospitals, leprosy centres and dispensaries. They also provide catechesis, marriage direction, counselling and help with promoting the cause of women in various parts of the world.

✠ Comboni Missionary Sisters

VERONICAN SISTERS OF THE HOLY FACE

Location: Italy (Calabria)
RC (female) founded in Italy in 1934 by Blessed
Gaetano Catanoso (beatified 1998)

The Congregation grew from the Pious
Union of the Holy Face, which had been
founded at Pentedattilo in 1919. In making
his foundation, Blessed Gaetano was
inspired by Blessed Aloysius Orione and his
'Little Work of Divine Providence'. The
Sisters of the Institute are concerned with
the welfare of refugees and also provide
catechesis in remote and rural districts.

VIATOR, CONGREGATION OF THE CLERICS OF ST

Location: Italy (Rome)
RC (male) founded in France in 1831 by Fr Louis
Querbes
Abbr: CSV
Original habit: secular,

A Congregation founded in Vourles,
France, and given approbation by Pope
Gregory XVI in 1838 and 1839. Fr Querbes
had been deeply concerned about the lack
of catechesis among the young people in his
parish, and he founded an Association, the
Catechists, or Parochial Clerics, of St Viator, which would teach Christian doctrine
and the service of the altar. St Viator was
chosen as patron because of his faithfulness
to the gospel and to the service of the altar
in 4th-century Lyons. The Association
formed itself into a community of priests
and Brothers, and the work expanded
through France and into Canada, where,
from 1848 to 1968 the members were
involved in the education of the deaf and
mute in Montreal. This work is now no
longer undertaken. The Congregation has
four provinces, France, Canada, the USA
and Spain, as well as missions in Peru,
Belize, Taiwan, the Ivory Coast, Haiti,
Japan, Colombia and Chile.

✚ Viatorians

VINCENTIAN SISTERS OF CHARITY

Location: USA (Bedford, Ohio)
RC (female) founded in the USA in 1928
Abbr: VSC

An American foundation whose members
work in education and in the care of the
elderly and those who are in need of assistance. The Sisters also provide pastoral and
counselling services. As well as maintaining
a presence in Ohio, Kentucky and New
York, the Sisters also run a mission in El
Salvador.

VINCENTIAN SISTERS OF CHARITY

Location: USA (Pittsburgh, Pennsylvania)
RC (female) founded in Austria in 1835 by the
Empress Caroline Augusta and in the USA in 1902
Abbr: VSC
Original habit: a black tunic with a large, starched
oval wimple and a white headband with a black
veil.

The Congregation, which was founded in
Austria, went to the USA in 1902 when five
Sisters left Szatmar, in Austria-Hungary,
and travelled to Braddock, Pennsylvania.
These five Sisters of Charity of St Vincent
de Paul, later known as the Vincentian
Sisters of Charity, were dedicated to teaching, to ministering to the sick and to providing a ministry to Slovak refugees. Today,
the work of the Sisters is largely educational
at every level, and they also maintain specialized ministries in hospitals, health care
clinics and nursing homes, day care centres,
a youth ministry and general parish work.
They are represented throughout the USA
and maintain missions in Canada, Peru and
Slovakia.

VINCENTIANS, THE

Location: Italy (Rome)
RC (male) founded in France in 1625 by St Vincent de Paul (canonized 1737)
Abbr: CM
Original habit: secular.

The early life of St Vincent de Paul, or Depaul (1581–1660) is obscure, but it is known that following his ordination he became alarmed at the state of the clergy and the lack of catechesis in the country, as well the general care of the poor. Much of his awareness was heightened by his early encounters with Pierre de Bérulle, who had organized the French Oratorians. In 1617, while he was serving as a parish priest at Chatillon-les-Dombes, he started the first 'Charité', whose female members were called the Servants of the Poor, in an effort to provide continued help for the poor that would always be available to them. Other groups were started as they were needed, and with the increase in membership came a change in name, to the Ladies of Charity. The first Association for men was the Congregation of the Mission, founded by St Vincent in 1625 with the financial help of the Gondi family, whose sons he had tutored. The members followed a Rule composed by St Vincent, to which he added continually until the end of his life. The first house was opened in Paris, in the rue St Victor. At the outset, the priests and Brothers took no vows, but this was changed following the general chapter in 1651 and simple vows of poverty, chastity and obedience were adopted. The community moved to the Priory of St Lazare, which had previously belonged to the Canons of St Victor, and this added the name 'Lazarists' to the Congregation. To their original apostolate of catechesis, care for the sick and the poor and the training of clergy was now added foreign mission work. Members were sent to Tunisia, Algeria, Scotland and Ireland, and later to Madagascar and Poland. It was Pope Innocent XII (1691–1700) who sent some of the Fathers as missionaries to China, Spain, Portugal and Austria as well as into present-day Iran and Ethiopia. In the 19th century further missions were established throughout South America, England and Australia. The Vincentians arrived in the USA, reaching Baltimore, Maryland, in 1816 and opening a seminary at Perryville, Missouri, in 1818 which is now the mother house of the Congregation in the USA. The work in North America so expanded from 1900 until 1967 that today Vincentian houses are to be found throughout the country, divided between five provinces.

✠ Congregation of the Mission
  Lazarists

VIRGINS OF THE INFANT JESUS, CONGREGATION OF THE

Defunct
RC (female) founded in Italy in 1661 by Anna Moroni
Original habit: a tawny woollen tunic sometimes worn with a very long black veil which nearly reached the feet.

A Congregation founded in Rome and very similar to an Ursuline Congregation. The members taught poor girls what were then termed 'the proper' feminine arts, good manners and the Christian faith.

✠ Sisters of the Infant Jesus

VISITATION NUNS

Location: each monastery is autonomous
RC (female) founded in France in 1610 by St Jane de Chantal (canonized 1767)
Abbr: VHM
Original habit: a black habit, girdle and binder with a white linen wimple; a silver cross, engraved with the letters 'I.H.S.' on one side and 'M.A.' with

a heart between the letters on the other, was worn around the neck, and a large ebony rosary with a plain black cross hung from the girdle.

The Order was founded at Annecy in Savoy, the result of a meeting of St Jane de Chantal (1572–1641) and St Francis de Sales (1567–1622), when the latter realized that a vision he had of founding an Order could be realized through Jane de Chantal. Jane had been married, but was widowed in 1601 through a hunting accident which left her to care for four young children. She took a vow of chastity after her husband's death and undertook many works of charity as she visited the sick and poor in the district. St Francis became her confessor and spiritual director, and she made an undertaking of total obedience to him. He suggested to Jane that a religious community for women could be founded which would serve as a refuge for girls with disabilities and for older women and widows with grown-up children who were often precluded from joining such communities. The first house was established at Gallery House on the edge of the lake at Annecy in 1610, with Jane as superior and twelve other nuns clothed in the habit with her. At this point they were known as Oblates. Initially, a modified cloister was instituted, allowing members to leave the convent for their work in visiting the sick and for widows to return to their homes if family matters needed their attention. The Visitation Institute was canonically erected in 1618 as a religious Order under the Rule of St Augustine, to which were added the Constitutions drawn up by St Francis, accepting enclosure and solemn vows. Each house was to be autonomous and subject to its diocesan bishop. By 1626, when the Order received the approbation of Pope Urban VIII, there were sixty-five houses in existence. Further houses were opened in Italy, Spain, Poland, The Netherlands, England and North America. The North American foundation was made in Georgetown, Washington DC, in 1799. Today, the Order is divided into two federations, the first being purely contemplative and the second engaged additionally in active work, such as teaching. In England the nuns provide opportunities for women to make their retreats within the enclosure. The Rule of the Visitation Order is characterized by its mildness, to suit the temperament of those who would not be able to bear a more austere regime.

✠ Order of the Visitation of Holy Mary
  Visitandines

VISITATION OF THE CONGREGATION OF THE IMMACULATE HEART OF MARY, SISTERS OF THE

Location: USA (Dubuque, Iowa)
RC (female) founded in the USA in 1952 by Bishop Leo Binz
Abbr: SVM

This Diocesan Congregation owes its origins to the formation of the Visitation Nuns at Annecy, France, in 1610 by St Jane de Chantal (see previous entry), from which a foundation was made in Georgetown, Washington, DC in 1799. It was from this foundation that Bishop Leo Binz established a house at Dubuque, Iowa, in 1952 in order to fill a need for sound catechetics. The Sisters at Dubuque undertake teaching and catechetical work, college counselling and some adult education. They are also represented in Indiana and California.

VISITATION SISTERS

Location: Belgium (Ghent)
RC (female) founded in Belgium in 1669 by Isabella Stoop
Abbr: VBVM
Original habit: a black habit, apron and girdle with a black rosary with copper links, a square white linen wimple, and a black binder and veil; a silver

cross, engraved with the letters 'I.H.S.' and inlaid with one of ebony, was worn around the neck; professed choir Sisters wore a gold ring on the third finger of the right hand. Lay Sisters wore a cap instead of the wimple and veil, and a silver ring.

This Congregation was formally founded in Ghent when Isabella Stoop and three hospital nurses decided to form themselves into a religious community, to visit the sick and catechize children. They adopted St Francis de Sales as their patron and came to be known as the Sales School Sisters. The community was broken up at the French Revolution, but was reorganized in 1826 along the lines of the Visitation Nuns, adopting the name of 'Sisters of the Visitation'. Their work was to be dedicated entirely to the training of poor children and the education of girls from all backgrounds. With the passage of time the work of the Sisters has expanded and now includes care for the aged and other ministries as needed. Houses are to be found in Belgium, Africa and England.

✛ Congregation of the Visitation of the
    Blessed Virgin Mary

VOCATION SISTERS

Location: England (Angmering, West Sussex)
RC (female) founded in England in 1945
Abbr: VS

A Congregation founded in London whose members organize retreats and promote religious vocation promotional material through parish missions and through exhibitions in schools. The Sisters help young men and women to obtain material about their possible future careers in the Church.

✛ Daughters of Our Lady of Good Counsel
    and St Paul of the Cross

VOCATIONIST FATHERS

Location: Italy (Rome)
RC (male) founded in Italy in 1920 by Fr Justin Russolillo
abbr: SDV
Original habit: secular.

The Society was founded at Pianure, Italy, by its parish priest, and received diocesan approval in 1927 and papal approbation in 1947. The priests and Brothers live in community under vows of poverty, chastity and obedience, and they work to help young people investigate and discern whether they may have a vocation either to the religious life or to the diocesan priesthood. This process of guidance is helped by means of vocation camps, parish missions and exhibitions, which may be carried out in special houses called vocationaries. Help and guidance can also be given to those men who have left the priesthood, or are in the process of so doing. The first vocationary was established in the USA at Florham Park, New Jersey, in 1989. Missionary work took the Society to Brazil in 1950 and then to the USA in 1962, where a house was established in 1989. There are also houses in Argentina, Nigeria, the Philippines and India.

✛ Society of the Divine Vocations

VOCATIONIST SISTERS

Location: Italy (Rome)
RC (female) founded in Italy in 1921 by Fr Justin Russolillo
Abbr: SDV
Original habit: a simple dark skirt and tunic with a white blouse and a dark veil with a white outer brim.

The Society was founded in Pianure, Italy, shortly after the foundation of the Vocationist Fathers (see previous entry). The aim of the Society is to help young men and women investigate whether they may have a vocation to the religious life or to the priesthood, through parish missions. The Vocationist Sisters work side by side with their male counterparts. They also work among the poor and those who have been marginalized by society.

✛ Sisters of the Divine Vocations

VOLUNTAS DEI

Location: Canada (Trois Rivières, Quebec)
RC (priests, laymen and married couples) founded in Canada in 1958 by Fr Louis-Marie Parent, OMI

This Secular Institute was founded at Trois Rivières in Canada with the approval of Bishop Henri Routhier, OMI, of Grouard, Alberta. Celibate men are allowed to make the usual three vows of religion, of poverty, chastity and obedience, but married couples, who have been admitted since 1970, have associate member status only and take no vows. All members make themselves available to serve the Church wherever a need arises. The first missionary work was undertaken in 1959, and by 1987 the Congregation had received its approval as a Secular Institute of pontifical right.

WAY OF THE CROSS, COMMUNITY OF THE

Defunct
Episcopal Church (female) founded in the USA in 1939 by Pattie Ellis and Gwendolyn Morgan
Abbr: CWC
Original habit: (worn in community) a dark green tunic and veil with a black girdle and a brown wooden cross; secular dress was worn at other times.

An American Community, under the patronage of St Catherine of Siena, founded at Buffalo, New York, for women who wanted to live the religious life but still retain their work in the world. Members, who underwent a two-year novitiate, undertook to recite daily the Benedictine day hours, speak at churches and youth fellowships and provide retreats and quiet weekends. The first professions were made in 1943, but the community was not successful.

WHITE FATHERS

Location: Italy (Rome)
RC (male) founded in France in 1868 by Cardinal Charles Martial Lavigerie
Abbr: WF (also M.Afr.)
Original habit: a white tunic and cloak; a rosary was worn around the neck.

An Institute of secular priests and missionary Brothers founded in response to the plight of children orphaned by famine and drought in Africa. Three seminarians were the first to answer the call for help by Archbishop (later Cardinal) Lavigerie, who was transferred from Nancy, France, to Algiers in 1867, at a time of great suffering. The volunteers undertook a novitiate with the Jesuits and by 1870 were ready to make a solemn oath of obedience, which substituted for vows, marking the start of the Society of the White Fathers. The work continues today, the priests and Brothers united by a missionary oath which obliges them to work among the people of Africa. Their work covers many facets of missionary activities, including education and medical work, but also extends to agricultural, social and pastoral activities.

✠ Missionaries of Africa

WILFRID, COMMUNITY OF ST

Defunct
Anglican (female) founded in England in 1866 by Fr John Gilberd Pearse
Abbr: CSW
Original habit: Benedictine style.

The Community of St Wilfrid was founded in Exeter, Devon, to provide for the care of the elderly and orphaned and to teach the young. The history of the community is not one of success. The first mother-superior was installed in 1873, but few were attracted to join, and the community was in a depressing state by the start of the 20th century. The appointment of a new chaplain produced a brief respite in their fortunes, but this lasted only until his death in 1927. Retreats were held for associates and friends, and at one time the Sisters ran an orphanage for girls in Torquay, Devon, which later transferred to Exeter. The community later became defunct.

WILLIAM, HERMITS OF ST

Defunct
RC (male) founded in Italy in the 12th century
Original habit: a white tunic with a sleeveless, girded over-garment and a scapular; after the union with the Augustinians, the habit changed to black.

An Order of hermits which was founded by a Frenchman, St William of Malavalla, near Siena. In 1155 he went to live in a cave at Malavalla (Stabulum Rhodis), where a local nobleman had built a cell for him and where he was joined by some followers, one of whom, Albert, later wrote an account of William's eremitical life. On St William's death in 1157, a chapel was built over his grave and a hermitage was later added. The community of hermits grew and the Order spread throughout Italy and into France, Flanders and Germany. The original austere Rule was moderated in the 13th century, with most Williamite houses adopting the Rule of St Benedict but a few accepting the Augustinian Rule. The last house to survive of this Order was in Germany, but this was closed in 1785.

✠ Gulielmites

WILLIAMITES

Defunct
RC (male and female) founded in Italy in 1119 by St William of Vercelli

Original habit: (monks) white tunic, scapular and cowl; (nuns) the same habit with the addition of a black veil.

St William of Vercelli (1085–1142) had been on a pilgrimage at the age of fifteen, to the Shrine of St James of Compostela, and upon his return to Italy he lived for a while as a hermit on Monte Solicoli. A planned pilgrimage to Jerusalem was abandoned after an encounter with robbers, and he went instead as a hermit to the slopes of Monte Vergiliano, near Naples. Others joined him there, and in 1119 he founded a community, and a church dedicated to Our Lady. The name of the mountain was then changed to Montevergine. The Rule was based on that of St Benedict and was most austere, with no meat, wine or dairy produce allowed, and on three days every week only vegetables and dried bread permitted. The Congregation was confirmed by Pope Celestine III in 1197. Other monasteries were built in the mountains of southern Italy, some for men alone and others for men and women together in a double monastery. It was at one of these double monasteries, at Guglietto, near Nusco, that St William died in 1142. In 1879 the abbey of Montevergine was affiliated with the Cassinese Congregation of the Primitive Observance, now known as the Benedictine Subiaco Congregation.

✠ Hermits of Monte Vergine
   Whitemantles

WINDESHEIM, CANONS REGULAR OF THE CONGREGATION OF

Location: Italy (Rome)
RC (male) founded in The Netherlands in 1386 by Florence Radewyns
Original habit: a white tunic and rochet, with a biretta and a fur almuce in winter.

When Geert de Groote (1340–84) was dying, he advised the Brethren of the Common Life, which he had founded, to adopt the Rule of an approved Congregation. His successor, Florence Radewyns, and six of the Brethren went to the monastery at Eymsteyn to familiarize themselves with the Augustinian usage there. In 1386 they returned to Windesheim and established a monastery and church. Further foundations were made and began to flourish, receiving approbation from Pope Boniface IX (1389–1404). The Constitutions, with their Augustinian additions, were approved by Pope Martin V (1417–31) at the Council of Constance. At the height of their success, the Congregation had eighty-six houses of canons and sixteen of nuns, mostly in The Netherlands and in Cologne, Germany. The Windesheim foundation itself was destroyed in 1572 during the Reformation and was suppressed in 1581, with other communities which survived the Reformation ultimately suppressed at the end of the 18th century. The Congregation was reconstituted in 1961, and at present there are three foundations with a membership of twenty-six canons, only a little over half of whom are priests.

WISDOM, DAUGHTERS OF

Location: Italy (Rome)
RC (female) founded in France in 1715 by St Louis Marie Grignion de Montfort (canonized 1947) and Blessed Marie-Louise of Jesus (beatified 1993)
Abbr: DW (also FDLS)
Original habit: a grey habit with a white cap forming a kind of veil, a white linen cape crossed at the neck and a large crucifix; a long black cloak and hood were used out of doors.

From the earliest years of his life it is said that St Louis had a great concern for the poor, and this increased following his ordination to the priesthood in 1700. With it came the desire to found a Congregation whose members would be able to help with the problems of the needy. His first attempt at founding such a group, in a hospital for the poor in Poitiers, was not very successful, but ten years later he founded the Daughters of Wisdom with greater success. Some women from the Poitiers foundation, including Marie-Louise Trichet, later Mother Marie-Louise of Jesus, later followed St Louis to Brittany, where he was living and where he had opened some schools for the poor boys of the town of La Rochelle. They began working there at the hospital and this marked the start of the Community of the Daughters of Wisdom which was founded a year before the death of St Louis. Blessed Marie-Louise, who had become superior of the Congregation, continued the charitable work, opening a small school, nursing the sick, providing food for beggars and visiting the poor. At the time of her death, in 1759, the small Congregation, which was approved by Pope Benedict XIV in 1748, had grown to number 174 Sisters distributed among thirty-six communities. The Congregation suffered badly during the French Revolution and many of the Sisters were killed. There are now houses in Europe, North, Central and South America, Asia and Oceania. The Sisters' work with deaf, mute and blind people, which was started in 1812, continues, and they are still running orphanages, hospitals and health clinics as well as working in schools and catechetical centres. The American foundation was made in 1904.

WOMEN MINISTERS TO THE SICK, ORDER OF

Defunct
Universal Church (female) founded in Italy in c.400 by St Fabiola
Original habit: a black dress with a white scapular and veil.

This Order of nuns was allegedly founded in the early 5th century by the Roman noblewoman St Fabiola, and while it is certain that she created a hospital for the sick in Rome, it is less certain that her work was continued in other parts of the Roman empire by women known as the Black Sisters, on account of their habit, as has sometimes been claimed. The link has not been established, but it is known that there were early communities of so-called Black Sisters living under the Rule of St Augustine in the Low Countries, where they cared for the sick.

WORKING SISTERS

Location: Italy (Botticino Sera, Brescia)
RC (female) founded in Italy in 1885 by Fr Arcangelo Tadini
Original habit: a black tunic with a small white collar and a simple black veil over a white cap; a cross was worn around the neck.

When he was appointed curate, later priest, of the town of Botticino, Fr Tadini found that there were no youth activities or charitable and welfare institutions in the area, and he set about righting this, creating new activities for every age group and catechizing the young. He established monthly retreats and was noted for his advice and skill at counselling. In order to discourage young women from leaving the town in search of employment he set up a spinning mill, which was opened in 1898. Gradually, the idea of worker-nuns came to his mind. The first group of ten nuns was organized under Mother Nazarena Maffeis in 1900, not without local opposition, and the foundation flourished. Today, the Working Sisters are to be found in Italy and England, organizing retreats, arranging youth activities and summer camps and working in factories, schools, surgeries and holiday houses. They also maintain a presence in Africa, where the Sisters are working in dispensaries and schools and helping women to develop their lives.

✠ Worker Nuns of the Holy House of Nazareth

XAVERIAN BROTHERS

Location: Italy (Rome) and England (Twickenham, Middlesex)
RC (male) founded in Belgium in 1839 by Theodore James Ryken
Abbr: CFX
Original habit: a black habit with a black cloth belt to which was attached a rosary on the left-hand side; a crucifix was worn.

Theodore Ryken, who was born in Elshout, North Brabant, trained originally as a shoe-maker and later became a catechist, helping to run an orphanage and caring for cholera patients in Groeningen. In 1831 he went to the USA with a view to becoming a cate-chist to the Native Americans, but he was instead drawn to the idea of founding a Congregation of Brothers who would work alongside the missionary priests. He returned to Europe and underwent a novi-tiate with the Redemptorists. Having com-pleted this, Ryken founded his Congregation in Bruges in 1839. Twelve men made their profession with him in 1846. The success of the foundation was threatened through lack of money, but an anonymous donation made expansion possible, and schools in Bruges and England were opened. In 1854 five of the Brothers took over some parochial schools in the USA, in Baltimore, Maryland. Today there are schools in Belgium, England, the USA, Bolivia, Haiti, Kenya, the Republic of Congo and Sudan. The Brothers undertake teaching at all levels and also work as cate-chists and counsellors, maintain prison and hospital ministries, care for the elderly and dying and run homes and hostels for the homeless and for immigrants.

XAVERIAN MISSIONARY FATHERS

Location: Italy (Rome)
RC (male) founded in Italy in 1895 by Blessed Guido Conforti
Abbr: SX

The Society was founded in Parma, Italy. Guido Conforti had been ordained as a priest in 1888, and in 1893 he approached Cardinal Ledochowski, who endorsed his plans to found a missionary Congregation. He bought a building near the diocesan seminary in Parma, and the Society was founded there. By 1898 the first members had made their vows of profession together with a promise to dedicate their lives exclu-sively to the missions. At the time of his profession, each man received a crucifix as a symbol of the forthcoming mission to China. Sufficient interest was aroused to warrant the opening of a minor seminary at Vicenza in 1919 and another at Ancona in 1920. The following year the Society received papal approbation. Further missions were opened in Great Britain and

Spain, throughout Asia, South America and in several African countries, and the latest mission was established in Mozambique in 1998. The Fathers conduct missions, especially in non-Christian and cross-cultural situations, and undertake social work, education and pastoral and community ministries.

✠ St Francis Xavier Foreign Mission Society

XAVERIAN MISSIONARY SOCIETY OF MARY, INC.

Location: Italy (Parma)
RC (female) founded in Italy in 1945 by Mother Celestina Healy Bottego and Fr Giacomo Spagnolo, SX
Abbr: XMM

A Pontifical Congregation, founded in Italy and with an apostolate in the USA, where a foundation was made in Massachusetts in 1954. Mother Celestina was born in Glendale, Ohio, in 1895 and went to live in Parma, Italy, with her parents in 1910. She taught English in the Parma state school, but she was always concerned about the needs of the poor and the young. In 1944 she was asked by Fr Spagnolo to co-found

a Congregation of religious women who would be prepared to work in foreign missions and among those with the greatest needs. The new Congregation was founded in 1945 and today the Sisters work in foreign missions in the Congo, Brazil, Mexico, Chad, Cameroon and Sierra Leone, undertaking catechism and the care of the elderly. They also have a special ministry to Hispanic families in the USA, where they are represented in New York and Massachusetts.

XAVIER SISTERS

Location: USA (Clinton Township, Michigan)
RC (female) founded in the USA in 1946 by Cardinal Edward Mooney
Abbr: XS

An American Diocesan Congregation, whose few members take private vows. When it was founded, the apostolate was intended to be concerned with retreats. If the numbers allowed, the Sisters were prepared to undertake foreign mission work, but there are very few remaining members.

✠ Society of Catholic Mission Sisters of St Francis Xavier

YOUTH APOSTLES INSTITUTE, THE

Location: USA (McLean, Virginia)
RC (male) founded in the USA

A Public Association, whose membership is open to all young men, single or married, consecrated laymen and clerics. The single members may take public vows of poverty, chastity, obedience and a life of service to youth. The work of the Institute is to encourage and inspire young people to live fuller Roman Catholic lives. This is done by means of college outreach ministries, human sexuality education, social action, teaching and other parish-based programmes.

Z

ZELATRICES OF THE SACRED HEART, MISSIONARY

Location: Italy (Rome)
RC (female) founded in Italy in 1894 by Mother Clelia Merloni
Abbr: ASCJ

The Congregation of Zelatrices was founded in Viarreggio, Italy. Clelia Merloni had made several attempts to enter the religious life, all of which had failed, until it became clear to her that she was intended to found an Institute of her own. With some companions, known as the Apostles of the Sacred Heart, she began to teach children and later opened a sheltered workshop and a home for eleven elderly people. Within the space of two years the number of Sisters had increased to twenty, and their work had expanded to include nurseries, shelters, elementary schools, orphanages and parish work. New foundations were made in Broni and Montebello, in Piedmont, in 1895. But financial mismanagement by an advisor caused the collapse of the Viarregio foundation, and only twelve Sisters remained loyal to Mother Clelia. The intervention of Bishop Scalabrini of Piacenza saved the day and allowed the Congregation not only to recover but to become officially established in 1900. Within three years there were two hundred Sisters in thirty houses. Foreign missions were undertaken to Brazil, in 1900, and then to Boston, USA, in 1902. The Sisters still work in education, including that of the mentally handicapped and of those with learning difficulties. They also run day nurseries, and provide health care and legal services for the poor. The foreign mission work has now expanded to include missions in Africa, Chile, Uruguay, Mexico and Taiwan, and the Congregation still maintains a presence in Italy and Albania.

✠ Apostles of the Sacred Heart of Jesus

ZITA, SOCIETY OF ST

Location: Italy (Rome)
RC (female) founded in Italy in c.1860 by Blessed Francis Faa di Bruno (beatified 1988)

The Society of St Zita was founded in Turin by Francis di Bruno, who had been ordained as a priest late in life. The purpose of the foundation was to provide charity for those employed in domestic service, an apostolate which developed to include the administration of hostels for students and single mothers and homes for the elderly, the poor, sick women and the clergy. The Sisters are still working in the same fields, and in addition now have a ministry of care for prostitutes who are trying to become rehabilitated.

GLOSSARY

abstinence: a refusal to take certain food or drink, in accordance with some ecclesiastical ruling. It should be distinguished from fasting, which is concerned with the quantities of food and drink consumed.

active life: a mode of religious life dedicated to various works of mercy, for example nursing, education and missions.

Albigenses (Albigensian heresy): 12th- and 13th-century heretics, also known as the Cathars, found in southern France and northern Italy. They preached that Christ was not a human but an angel, was not the Son of God, or the Redeemer, and would not rise again. A crusade was organized against them by Pope Innocent III in 1208 and they were completely routed by the end of the 14th century.

almuce: a scarf of linen or fur worn over choir dress in church, as a protection against the cold. It could also be carried over the left arm as a sign of office.

anchorite: a person who has withdrawn from the world for religious reasons; also a hermit.

anti-pope: a false claimant to the Holy See, in opposition to the canonically elected pope.

apostolate: the work to which the members of a religious Congregation are committed.

apostolic life, societies of: societies of men and women who live a common life without taking vows and who pursue an apostolic purpose. The societies may be clerical or lay, male or female.

approbation (papal): the last stage in the establishment of a religious Institute in the Roman Catholic Church, which is marked by the release of a decree of approval from the Holy See. The Institute is then free from diocesan control and is described as being of pontifical right.

Augustinian Rule (Rule of St Augustine): St Augustine wrote no Rule as such, but his teaching on many matters is found in several of his letters, which were written in the early 5th century. The Rule is the basis of the Constitutions of various canons regular, the Dominicans, the Trinitarians, the Mercedarians and many modern religious Orders.

beatification: an official papal declaration in the Roman Catholic Church that a candidate for canonization, the process which declares a person to be a saint, has upon investigation satisfied the various standards of sanctity and can be called Blessed; this attests that the person may be venerated and is believed to be in heaven.

Benedictine Rule: the Rule followed by Benedictines proper, Cistercians, Camaldolese and, in the past, Cluniacs; many modern Congregations observe the Rule with certain modifications. It was composed in Italy in the first half of the 6th century by St Benedict for his own monastery at Monte Cassino.

binder: a white linen cloth passing over a nun's head to cover the hair, and then folded under the chin.

biretta: a hard, four-cornered clerical hat with three raised divisions, sometimes supporting a pompon.

blue scapular: two pieces of blue cloth, similar to the brown scapular (below) which are worn under their ordinary clothes by members of the Confraternity of the Blessed Virgin Mary.

brother: a lay member of a male religious community.

brown scapular: two pieces of brown cloth, about three inches by two inches, joined by strings and worn back and front under the clothes by members of the Confraternity of Our Lady of Mt Carmel. Carmelite secular tertiaries may wear a larger scapular, about ten inches by nine inches, joined by a narrow band and also worn under secular clothes.

canonization: a papal decision in the Roman Catholic Church that a person may be called a saint. The candidate, who has already been beatified and declared Blessed, may become a saint after two miracles have been credited to their intercession. The miracles are investigated thoroughly by the Holy See before the declaration of sainthood is made.

canons: (i) secular canons are diocesan priests who are attached to a religious foundation, such as a cathedral, and may form a chapter, or college, with responsibility for its maintenance; (ii) regular canons, or can-ons regular, are priests who are not monks or friars, but who live in a religious community observing a Rule.

capuce: a hood.

cassock: an ankle-length, sleeved tunic which may be held in at the waist by a belt, or may be buttoned from neck to foot as in the Roman Catholic soutane; it may be of any colour.

catechesis: religious instruction, either as part of a programme of religious education in or out of school, or in a programme of instruction preparing adults for reception into the Roman Catholic faith.

Cathars: a heretical sect which arose in Germany in the Middle Ages and spread to Italy and southern France, where they were more commonly known as Albigenses (see above).

Cenacle: the upper room in which the Last Supper was celebrated and where Christ revealed himself after the Resurrection; also the place where the descent of the Holy Spirit took place.

cenobite: a person living in a religious community, as against an eremite, or hermit, who lives in solitude.

Child of Mary: a member of a Roman Catholic association founded in Rome in 1864 to encourage devotion to Our Lady among young women and to prepare them for adult life. Members attend regular parish meetings and may wear a medal of Our Lady.

Church Army: an Anglican organization of voluntary lay and ordained men and women, founded by Wilson Carlile in 1882 along the lines of the Salvation Army; its members work among the poor and needy and those in institutions.

cincture: a cord, or sash of cloth, worn around the waist.

clothing: the formal giving of a religious habit to a person who is being admitted to an Order or Congregation.

coif: a close-fitting cap worn under her veil by a nun.

confraternity: an association of the faithful which has been canonically established by an ecclesiastical authority, usually for some work of piety or charity.

Congregation: a religious community in which simple vows are taken.

Constitution: the statutes, or enactments, by which a religious community is administered, which explain how the Rule is applied.

cowl: an enveloping, wide-sleeved monastic garment, sometimes hooded.

Day Hours: parts of the divine office taken from the breviary, but not including matins. They can therefore include those taken from the other canonical Hours of lauds, prime, terce, sext, none, vespers and compline.

decree of praise: after a diocesan religious Institute in the Roman Catholic Church has approached the Holy See to get papal approval, it can be issued with a decree of praise, which releases the Institute from diocesan control and places it under pontifical control.

diaconate: a Holy Order, received by a candidate when he or she is ordained as a deacon, through the laying on of hands by a bishop together with a consecratory prayer. The work of a deacon is to assist the priest in preaching, baptizing, performing marriages and helping with parish ministries, especially the visiting of the sick.

discalced: barefoot, but most discalced

Orders now allow the use of sandals, made from leather or wood.

divine office: a collection of prayers, psalms, hymns and readings which were collected together and were meant to be recited or sung at specific moments, or Hours, of the day.

enclosure: that part of a religious community building or land which is strictly private and reserved for the members of the community alone, with very few exceptions.

Episcopalian Church: in the USA, the Anglican Church, which was declared the Protestant Episcopal Church in 1783.

fasting: a reduced intake of food at certain times, or during certain seasons of the church year.

First Order: some religious Orders are divided into first, second and third Orders. The first Order consists of men only.

flagellation: a method of punishment at one time practised in monasteries and convents; or a method of self-mortification, for which a scourge, or whip (sometimes known as a discipline) was used, but often more symbolically than actually.

fleury: a heraldic cross, the arms each terminating in the three leaves of the fleur-de-lis.

friar: a member of a male mendicant Order dedicated to mission preaching.

girdle: a broad belt, or rope, worn around the waist; also known as a cincture.

great silence: a period of time which extends from the end of the canonical hour of compline until the end of prime the next morning. It is observed in those religious communities which follow the Rule of St Benedict, and in some other Orders.

gremial: a white cloth secured over the head

and around the throat and breast of some nuns, worn under the veil.

habit: the distinctive religious dress of an Order or Congregation; receiving the habit usually marks the start of the novitiate, or period spent as a novice, and indicates the wearer's entrance into the religious life.

hôtel-dieu: a hospital run by a religious Order or Congregation.

Huguenots: French Calvinists of the 16th and 17th centuries who were forced to flee from France in 1685; it was only from 1802 that their status was recognized. In 1938 most French Calvinists united in the Reformed Church of France.

in commendam: when the revenues of an abbey or religious house were granted either to a cleric who was not a member of that Order, or to a layman for his own use, the abbey was then said to be recommended to his care; this practice understandably led to abuses which were at their worst during the 13th and 14th centuries.

kamilavkion: a black, cylindrical hat worn by Eastern Catholic and Orthodox clergy; it is sometimes worn under a veil and gives it a characteristic shape.

Kulturkampf: an attempt by Otto von Bismarck, the Prussian Chancellor, to subject the Roman Catholic Church in his country to state control and remove the running of schools from its hands in order to make Prussia a foremost Protestant power; this was prompted by the decree of papal infallibility which was made by Rome in 1870. Many Roman Catholic religious Congregations left Germany at this time, most of them making foundations in other countries so that they could continue with their work in education.

lavra (or laura): a colony of solitaries, or hermits, who live in individual cells around a church.

laus perennis: the custom of singing the divine office using relays of monks so that there is never a time when God is not being praised within the monastery.

laws of association: French legislation which was enacted at the start of the 20th century and was designed to restrict the growth of new religious Congregations and to prevent existing Congregations from carrying out any educational work. It had much the same effect as the *Kulturkampf* in Germany in the 1870s.

lectio divina: spiritual reading.

Manichaean heresy: a 3rd-century, dualistic heresy started by Mani, or Manichaeus, a Persian. It held that there were two ultimate sources of creation – one good, the other evil.

monk: a member of a religious Order for men, specially devoted to the contemplative life in a monastery and the recitation, or singing, of the divine office in choir. Monks should not be confused with friars, who are members of preaching Orders.

monstrance: a sacred vessel which has a clear glass panel set into it, behind which a consecrated Host, or wafer, may be placed, enabling it to be venerated, exposed, carried in processions and used in the service of Benediction of the Blessed Sacrament.

Nestorian heresy: a heresy believed by followers of Nestorius, Patriarch of Constantinople (428–31), who taught that Christ had two distinct natures, one human and the other divine, and that the Blessed Virgin Mary was the mother of his human nature only. The heresy was condemned in 430 by Pope Celestine I.

novice: a person preparing to take vows in

a religious Order or Congregation; this period of training is called the novitiate.

nun: a member of a religious Order for women, usually enclosed and contemplative.

Order: a religious community in which solemn vows are taken. Some communities require their members to take only simple vows.

perpetual vows: those vows taken with the intention of lifelong obligation.

personal prelatures: juridical structures in the Roman Catholic Church composed of secular clergy governed by a cleric who is authorized by the Holy See, in order that specific work may be carried out. Laity in sympathy with the apostolic work of the prelature may join it.

postulant: a person preparing to become a novice; the period of postulancy varies.

Public Associations: associations of the faithful established by a competent ecclesiastical authority.

RCIA: The Rite of Christian Initiation of Adults – the steps and process of Christian initiation adopted by the Roman Catholic Church following Vatican II.

regular: a person who lives under an authorized Rule of life.

religious: a term used to describe a person who has been formally admitted to the religious state, having first been a postulant and then a novice.

religious Institute: a society whose members pronounce public vows and live a community life. Some Institutes are called Orders, in which solemn vows are made by at least some of its members, while others are called Congregations, whose members are called religious of simple vows; some

Institutes are called clerical, if they are governed by clerics.

rochet: an overgarment with either narrow sleeves, or none at all, made of fine linen or lace; it usually falls to just below the knees.

Rule: a Rule sets out the spiritual, disciplinary and moral principles which govern the lives of members of a religious community.

Salian Franks: tribes of Franks, called the Salii, who had settled on both sides of the Lower Rhine near the Zuyder Zee in the 4th century.

scapular: a length of cloth with a hole in its centre for the head to pass through so that the cloth can hang down evenly at the back and front; the colour and shape of the scapular can vary, and it is sometimes decorated.

Second Order: some religious Orders are divided into first, second and third Orders. The second Order consists of women only.

secular Institute: an Institute of consecrated life whose members live in the world but may make the three vows of religion – poverty, chastity and obedience – after a period of probation; they may be clerical or lay, male or female.

secular priest: a priest who is not a member of a religious community but is under obedience to a bishop.

Seraphic breviary: the breviary used by members of the Franciscan Order. The term 'Seraphic' is used as an epithet commonly associated with St Francis of Assisi, the Seraphic Father, and his Order.

seven-decade Rosary: a Servite devotion in which the Seven Sorrows of Mary are meditated upon during the recitation of the Rosary.

simple vows: vows that are made publicly but are not recognized by the Church as being solemn. Acts that are contrary to a simple vow are illicit, but not invalid, which is not the case with solemn vows.

Sister: a member of a religious community, Congregation, Institute or society for women, with an active apostolate. The term 'nun' and 'Sister' are often confused; nuns are enclosed contemplatives while Sisters work in fields such as education and nursing.

society of apostolic life: a society of men or women who live in community but without making vows; they may be clerical or lay, male or female.

solemn vows: vows which are recognized by the Church as binding.

superior: the head of a Congregation with the authority to administer religious obedience to those under his or her control.

Statutes: the Constitutions of an Order are applied to a particular locality through the use of national, regional and provincial Statutes.

surplice: a short, white, wide-sleeved garment worn over a cassock by all grades of clergy.

temporary vows: those vows which are taken with a specific time limit in mind.

Third Order: some religious Orders are divided into first, second and third Orders. The third Order consists of secular tertiaries, living in the world, and regular tertiaries, who live in community and follow the Rule of the relevant third Order. Tertiaries may be male or female.

tunic: a garment, usually extending from the neck to the feet, which is worn beneath the cowl and scapular and is secured with a belt, cord, girdle or sash. The colour may vary according to the Order or Congregation.

veil: a cloth covering placed over the head of a female at the time of her religious profession, or her acceptance into the novitiate; the colour may vary.

vows of religion: the three vows of poverty, chastity and obedience; a fourth vow can sometimes be made.

wimple: a cloth covering worn over the head and around the neck and chin by some nuns.

ABBREVIATIONS

AA	Assumptionists	BA	Allepine Basilian Order of Melkites
AASC	Handmaids of the Blessed Sacrament and Charity	BBSF	Byzantine Brothers of St Francis
ACJ	Handmaids of the Sacred Heart of Jesus	BC	Basilian Order of St John the Baptist of the Melkites
AD	Sisters of the Lamb of God	BE	Oxford Mission Brotherhood of the Epiphany
ADC	Handmaids of the Divine Heart	Bethl	Bethlemita Daughters of the Sacred Heart of Jesus
AdPPS	Sister Adorers of the Precious Blood	BGS	Little Brothers of the Good Shepherd
AP	Order of the Perpetual Adoration of the Blessed Sacrament	BPS	Sisters of Our Lady of Good and Perpetual Succour
APB	Sisters-Adorers of the Precious Blood	BS	Daughters of the Good Saviour
APG	Sisters of Perpetual Adoration of Guadalupe	BSC	Bon Secours Sisters
AR	Handmaids of Reparation of the Sacred Heart of Jesus	BSO	Basilian Order of the Most Holy Saviour of the Melkites
ASC	Sisters-Adorers of the Most Precious Blood Sister Adorers of the Precious Blood	BSP	Brotherhood of St Paul
		BVM	Sisters of Charity of the Blessed Virgin Mary
ASCJ	Apostles of the Sacred Heart of Jesus Missionary Zelatrices of the Sacred Heart	CAH	Community of All Hallows
		CBE	Bernardine Cistercians
ASSP	Angelicals of St Paul Society of All Saints Sisters of the Poor	CBS	Congregation of Bon Secours Sisters of the Blessed Sacrament
		CCRRMM	Caracciolo Fathers

CCV	Carmelite Sisters of Charity	CIJ	Congregation of the Infant Jesus
CCVI	Sisters of Charity of the Incarnate Word	CJ	Josephite Fathers
CCW	Carmelite Community of the Word	CJC	Poor Sisters of Jesus Christ Crucified and the Sorrowful Mother
CDP	Sisters of Divine Providence		
CFA	Brothers of St Alexius; Cellites	CJGS	Community of the Companions of Jesus the Good Shepherd
CFC	Christian Brothers		
CFIC	Sons of the Immaculate Conception	CJM	Congregation of Jesus and Mary
CFMM	Sisters of Our Lady of Mercy Brothers of Our Lady of Mercy Minim Daughters of Mary Immaculate	CK	School Sisters of Christ the King
		CLHC	Congregation of Our Lady Help of the Clergy
		CLP	Sisters of Our Lady of Pity
CFP	Poor Brothers of St Francis Seraphicus	CM	Carmelite Missionary Sisters Vincentians
CFR	Franciscan Friars of the Renewal	CMF	Claretian Fathers
CFX	Xaverian Brothers	CMI	Carmelites of Mary Immaculate
CGA	Community of the Glorious Ascension	CMM	Brothers of the Blessed Virgin Mary Mother of Mercy Community of St Mary of Nazareth and Calvary Mariannhill Missionaries
CGS	Sisters of our Lady of Charity of the Good Shepherd		
CHC	Holy Cross Community		
CHF	Community of the Holy Family Congregation of the Sisters of the Holy Faith	CMP	Pallottine Missionary Sisters
		CMS	Verona Missionary Sisters
CHM	Congregation of the Humility of Mary	CMST	Carmelite Missionary Sisters of St Teresa Missionary Carmelites of St Teresa
CHN	Community of the Holy Name		
CHS	Community of the Holy Spirit	CMV	Order of Mechitarists
CIC	Sisters of the Immaculate Conception	CND	Canonesses Regular of the Order of St Augustine of the Congregation of Our Lady Congregation of Notre Dame
CICM	Congregation of the Immaculate Heart of Mary		
		CO	Oratorians

COp	Congregation of the Christian Workers of St Joseph Calasanzio	CRL	Canonesses Regular of St Augustine Canons Regular of St John Lateran Canons Regular of the Lateran
CP	Daughters of the Passion of Our Lord Jesus Christ and the Sorrows of Mary Passionists Congregation of the Passion	CRM	Caracciolo Fathers
		CROSA	Canonesses Regular Hospitallers of the Merciful Heart of Jesus
CPAW	Sisters of Perpetual Adoration		
CPM	Priests of Mercy Congregation of the Fathers of Mercy	CRS	Clerks Regular of Somasca
		CRSP	Clerks Regular of St Paul (Barnabite Fathers)
CPS	Congregation of the Holy Stigmata Missionary Sisters of the Precious Blood	CRSS	Canonesses Regular of the Holy Sepulchre
		CS	Company of the Saviour Missionaries of St Charles Borromeo (Scalabrini Fathers) Sisters of Charity of Sts Bartolomea Capitanio and Vincenza Gerosa
CPPS	Sisters of the Adoration of the Most Precious Blood Sisters of the Precious Blood Society of the Precious Blood		
CR	Clerks Regular Community of the Resurrection (Mirfield Fathers) Community of the Resurrection of Our Lord Congregation of the Resurrection of Our Lord Jesus Christ Congregation of the Retreat Sisters of Christian Retreat Sisters of the Resurrection Theatine Fathers	CSA	Augustinian Sisters of Charity Brothers of St Aloysius Gonzaga Canonesses Regular of Charity Canonesses Regular of St Augustine Community of St Andrew Sisters of Charity of St Augustine Sisters of St Agnes
		CSAC	Pallottine Sisters
CRIC	Canons Regular of the Immaculate Conception	CSB	Priests of the Community of St Basil Sisters of St Brigid
CRJBS	Community of Reparation to Jesus in the Blessed Sacrament		
CRL	Canons Regular of St John Lateran	CSBV	Sisters of the Saviour and the Blessed Virgin

CSC	Community of the Holy Rood	CSS	Congregation of the Holy Stigmata
	Congregation of the Holy Cross		Holy Stigmatics of Our Lord Jesus Christ
	Servants of the Cross	CSSF	Sisters of St Felix (Felician Sisters)
	Sisters of the Church		
	Sisters of the Holy Cross	CSSp	Sisters of the Holy Ghost
CSCL	Community of St Clare		Sisters of the Holy Spirit
CSD	Community of St Denys	CSSp	Congregation of the Holy Ghost and of the Immaculate Heart of Mary
CSF	Community of St Francis		
CSFN	Sisters of the Holy Family of Nazareth	CST	Carmelite Sisters of St Thérèse of the Infant Jesus
CSJ	Congregation of St Joseph of Murialdo	CSV	Congregation of the Clerics of St Viator
	Sisters of St Joseph	CSW	Community of St Wilfrid
CSJB	Community of St John the Baptist	CSWG	Community of the Servants of the Will of God
	Sisters of St John the Baptist	CTC	Community of Teresian Carmelites
CSJD	Nursing Sisters of St John the Divine	CVD	Sisters of Bethany
CSJE	Sisters of St John the Evangelist	CVI	Religious of the Incarnate Word
CSJP	Sisters of St Joseph of Peace		Sisters of the Incarnate Word and the Blessed Sacrament
CSK	Community of St Katharine of Egypt	CWC	Community of the Way of the Cross
CSL	Community of St Laurence	CZR	Community of the Holy Name – Zimbabwe
CSMV	Community of St Mary the Virgin		
CSP	Community of St Peter	DC	Daughters of Charity of St Vincent de Paul
	Community of the Sacred Passion		Daughters of the Cross
	Missionary Priests of St Paul the Apostle (Paulist Fathers)		Fathers of Christian Doctrine
		DCJ	Carmelite Sisters of the Divine Heart of Jesus
CSPH	Community of St Peter – Horbury	DCPB	Daughters of Charity of the Precious Blood
CSPX	Brothers of St Pius X	DDR	Daughters of the Divine Redeemer
CSrR	Congregation of the Most Holy Redeemer		
CSR	Sisters of the Holy Redeemer	DHM	Daughters of the Heart of Mary

DHS	Daughters of the Holy Spirit	FDLC	Daughters of the Cross
DJ	Daughters of Jesus	FDLS	Daughters of Wisdom
DLJC	Disciples of the Lord Jesus Christ	FDM	Brothers of Our Lady of Mercy
DM	Daughters of Mary of the Immaculate Conception Daughters of Our Lady of Mercy	FDNSC	Daughters of Our Lady of the Sacred Heart
		FDP	Sons of Divine Providence (Don Orione)
DMJ	Daughters of Mary and Joseph Sisters of Mary-Joseph and of Mercy Ladies of Mary	FFSC	Franciscan Brothers of the Holy Cross
		FHM	Franciscan Handmaids of the Most Pure Heart of Mary
DMMC	Daughters of Mary Mother of the Church	FI	Daughters of Jesus
		FICP	Brothers of Christian Instruction of Ploermel
DP	Daughters of Providence	FJ	Daughters of Jesus
DSF	Daughters of St Francis of Assisi	FMA	Daughters of Mary Help of Christians Sisters of Mary Help of Christians
DSMP	Daughters of St Mary of Providence		
DSP	Daughters of St Paul	FMDC	Franciscan Missionary Sisters of the Divine Child
DW	Daughters of Wisdom		
		FMDM	Franciscan Missionaries of the Divine Motherhood
ECMC	Camaldolese Hermits of Mount Corona	FMI	Daughters of Mary Immaculate Marianist Sisters Sons of the Blessed Virgin Mary Immaculate
EFMS	Eucharistic Franciscan Missionaries Eucharistic Franciscan Missionary Sisters		
		FMIJ	Franciscan Missionary Sisters of the Infant Jesus
FBP	Franciscan Brothers of Peace	FMJC	Franciscan Missionaries of Jesus Crucified
FC	Brothers of Charity Daughters of the Cross	FMM	Brothers of Mercy Franciscan Missionaries of Mary Missionary Fraternity of Mary
FCJ	Faithful Companions of Jesus		
FCSCJ	Daughters of Charity of the Sacred Heart of Jesus		
FCSP	Sisters of Charity of Providence		
FDC	Daughters of Divine Charity	FMMA	Brothers of Mercy of Our Lady of Perpetual Help
FDCC	Canossian Daughters of Charity of Verona	FMS	Marist Brothers

FMSC	Franciscan Missionary Sisters of the Sacred Heart
FMSI	Daughters of Mary Health of the Sick Missionary Society of Mary
FMSJ	Franciscan Missionaries of St Joseph
FMSL	Franciscan Missionary Sisters – Littlehampton
FPM	Presentation Brothers Congregation of the Presentation
FPO	Franciscans of the Primitive Observance
FPS	Daughters of the Precious Blood
FSA	Franciscan Sisters – Allegany
FSC	Brothers of the Christian Schools
FSE	Brothers of the Holy Eucharist Daughters of the Holy Spirit Franciscan Sisters of the Eucharist
FSF	Brothers of the Holy Family – Belley
FSG	Brothers of St Gabriel
FSJ	Religious Daughters of St Joseph
FSJM	Franciscan Servants of Jesus and Mary
FSM	Franciscan Sisters of St Mary Franciscan Minoresses
FSMA	Franciscans of St Mary of the Angels
FSP	Brothers of St Patrick Daughters of St Paul Franciscan Sisters of Peace Franciscan Sisters of the Poor

FSPA	Franciscan Sisters of Perpetual Adoration – La Crosse
FSR	Brothers of Our Lady of the Holy Rosary
FSSE	Franciscan Sisters of St Elizabeth
FSSJ	Franciscan Sisters of St Joseph
FSSP	Priestly Fraternity of St Peter
GHMS	Home Mission Sisters of America
GNSH	Grey Nuns of the Sacred Heart
HB	Handmaids of the Precious Blood
HFB	Association of the Holy Family
HHS	Helpers of the Holy Souls Helpers of the Souls in Purgatory
HIHM	Hermits of the Immaculate Heart of Mary
HJEP	Hermits of Jesus the Eternal Priest
HM	Sisters of the Holy Humility of the Blessed Virgin Mary
HMSS	Mercedarian Sisters of the Blessed Sacrament Sisters of Mercy of the Blessed Sacrament
HPB	Handmaids of the Precious Blood
HSC	Hospitaller Sisters of the Sacred Heart
HT	Handmaids of the Most Holy Trinity
HVM	Home Visitors of Mary Sisters-Home Visitors of Mary

IBVM	Institute of the Blessed Virgin Mary	LSG	Little Sisters of the Gospel of Charles de Foucauld
IC	Institute of Charity	LSIC	Little Servant-Sisters of the Immaculate Conception
ICM	Missionary Sisters of the Immaculate Heart of Mary	LSJ	Little Sisters of Jesus
IHM	Brothers of the Immaculate Heart of Mary	LSJM	Little Sisters of Jesus and Mary
	Sisters of the Most Holy and Immaculate Heart of Mary	LSP	Little Sisters of the Poor
	Sisters of the Immaculate Heart of Mary	MA	Society of Sisters of Marie-Auxiliatrice
	Sisters-Servants of the Immaculate Heart of Mary	MAfr	White Fathers
IJ	Sisters of the Infant Jesus	MC	Consolata Missionary Sisters
IMC	Consolata Fathers		Missionaries of Charity
	Sisters of the Immaculate Conception – St Meen		Missionary Brothers of Charity
			Missionary Sisters of Charity
IUU	Irish Ursuline Union		Poor Clare Missionary Sisters
IWBS	Sisters of the Incarnate Word and the Blessed Sacrament	MCCJ	Missionaries of the Heart of Jesus (Comboni Fathers)
		MCDP	Missionary Catechists of Christ the King
JT	Sisters of Jesus in the Temple (Blue Sisters)		Missionary Catechists of Divine Providence
	Sisters of the Finding of Jesus in the Temple	MCSH	Missionary Catechists of the Sacred Hearts of Jesus and Mary
KG	Knight of the Garter		
KHS	Knight of the Holy Sepulchre	MCSSCCJM	Missionary Catechists of the Sacred Hearts of Jesus and Mary
LBSF	Little Brothers of St Francis		
LC	Legionaries of Christ	MD	Discalced Fathers of Our Lady of Mercy
LCM	Little Company of Mary		Mothers of the Helpless
LCSJE	Sisters of St John the Evangelist	MEP	Paris Foreign Mission Society
			Society of Foreign Missions of Paris
LHC	Lovers of the Holy Cross Sisters	MG	Missionaries of Guadalupe
LMSC	Little Missionary Sisters of Charity	MGSpS	Guadalupan Missionaries of the Holy Spirit
LS	Little Sisters of Jesus	MHM	Mill Hill Fathers
LSA	Little Sisters of the Assumption	MHS	Sisters of the Most Holy Sacrament

MHSH	Mission Helpers of the Sacred Heart
MI	Clerks Regular Ministers of the Infirm
MIC	Clerks Regular of the Mother of God (Marian Fathers) Marian Fathers of the Immaculate Conception of the Blessed Virgin Mary Marianists of the Immaculate Conception Missionary Sisters of the Immaculate Conception Sisters of the Immaculate Conception of the Blessed Virgin Mary
MId	Idente Missionaries of Christ Crucified
MJMJ	Missionaries of Jesus, Mary and Joseph Missionary Sisters of Jesus, Mary and Joseph
MM	Catholic Foreign Mission Society of America
MMM	Medical Missionaries of Mary
MMS	Medical Missionary Sisters
MOM	Missionary Sisters of Our Lady of Mercy
MPF	Filippini Religious Teachers
MPV	Maestre Pie Venerini Sisters
MS	International Institute of Sisters of St Marcellina La Salette Fathers Marian Sisters Marist Sisters
MSBT	Missionary Servants of the Most Blessed Trinity (Trinitarians)

MSC	Marianites of the Holy Cross Missionaries of the Sacred Heart Missionary Servants of Christ Missionary Sisters of the Most Sacred Heart of Jesus Missionary Sisters of the Sacred Heart of Jesus (Cabrini Sisters)
MSCGpe	Sisters of the Sacred Heart of Jesus and of Our Lady of Guadalupe
MSCK	Missionary Sisters of Christ the King for Polish Emigrants
MSCS	Missionary Sisters of St Charles Borromeo (Scalabrini Sisters)
MSF	Missionaries of the Holy Family
MSFS	Missionaries of St Francis de Sales
MSHR	Missionary Sisters of the Holy Rosary
MSJ	Medical Sisters of St Joseph
MSMG	Missionary Sisters of the Mother of God
MSOLA	Missionary Sisters of Our Lady of Africa
MSpS	Missionaries of the Holy Spirit
MSS	Missionaries of the Blessed Sacrament
MSSA	Missionary Servants of St Anthony Missionary Sisters of St Anthony
MSSCB	Missionary Sisters of St Charles Borromeo
MSSCC	Missionaries of the Sacred Hearts of Jesus and Mary

MSSp	Mission Sisters of the Holy Spirit	OCSO	Cistercians of the Strict Observance
	Missionaries of the Holy Spirit	O de M	Order of Our Lady of Mercy
	Sisters of the Holy Ghost	ODN	Sisters of the Company of Mary Our Lady
MSSS	Missionary Sisters of the Most Blessed Sacrament	OFM	Franciscan Friars Minor
MSSST	Missionary Servants of the Most Holy Trinity	OFMCap	Franciscan Friars Minor Capuchin
MVP	Religious Venerini Sisters	OFMConv	Franciscan Friars Minor Conventual
MXY	Institute for Foreign Missions – Yarumal	OFMI	Franciscan Friars of Mary Immaculate
NAU-OLC	North American Union of the Sisters of Our Lady of Charity	OGS	Oratory of the Good Shepherd
		OH	Friars of the Order of Charity – Hospitallers
ND	Notre Dame Sisters		Order of Hospitallers
NDM	Sisters of Our Lady of the Missions		Brothers of Hospitallers of St John of God
NDS	Congregation of Our Lady of Sion	OHP	Order of the Holy Paraclete
		OIC	Order of the Imitation of Christ (Bethany Fathers and Sisters)
OA	Oblate Missionary Sisters of the Assumption	OLA	Missionary Sisters of Our Lady of the Apostles
OAM	Order of the Maronite Antonians	OLC	Sisters of Our Lady of Charity
OAR	Order of the Recollects of St Augustine	OLF	Daughters of the Faithful Virgins
OBT	Sisters Oblates to the Blessed Trinity		Sisters of Our Lady of Fidelity
OBVM	Annunciades	OLM	Order of Maronites of Lebanon
OC	Order of Carmelites		Sisters of Charity of Our Lady of Mercy
	Order of Cistercians		
OCarm	Order of Carmelites	OLS	Sisters of Our Lady of Sorrows
OCart	Order of Carthusians		
OCD	Order of Discalced Carmelites	OLVM	Missionary Sisters of Our Lady of Victory
OCDH	Carmelite Sisters of Mercy		
OCDT	Carmelite Sisters of St Teresa	OM	Minim Fathers
OCist	Order of Cistercians		

OMar	Congregation of Maronite Monks	OSH	Order of St Helena Order of St Jerome
OMD	Clerks Regular of the Mother of God	OSHJ	Oblate Sisters of the Sacred Heart of Jesus
OMI	Oblates of Mary Immaculate	OSJ	Oblates of St Joseph
OMM	Maronite Order of the Blessed Virgin Mary	OSJD	Brothers Hospitallers of St John of God
OMO	Oblates of the Mother of Orphans	OSM	Mantellate Sisters-Servants of Mary Order of St Mary Servants of Mary
OMV	Oblates of the Blessed Virgin Mary		
OP	Order of Preachers (Dominicans)	OSP	Oblate Sisters of Providence
		OSPPE	Hermits of St Paul
OPraem	Order of Prémontré	OSS	Religious of the Order of the Blessed Sacrament and of Our Lady
OSA	Order of St Anne Order of St Augustine (Augustinians; Austin Friars)		
		OSSR	Redemptoristines Redemptorists Oblates of the Most Holy Redeemer
OSB	Order of St Benedict (Benedictines)		
OSBI	Basilian Order of Grottaferrata	OSSS	Bridgettine Nuns and Monks Bridgettine Sisters Brigittine Monks
OSBM	Order of St Basil the Great (Basilian Order of St Josaphat) Catechists of the Heart of Jesus Sisters of the Order of St Basil the Great	OSST	Order of the Most Holy Trinity
		OSU	Ursuline Nuns
		PB	Brothers of St Patrick
OSBS	Oblate Sisters of the Blessed Sacrament	PBVM	Sisters of the Presentation of the Blessed Virgin Mary
OSC	Order of St Clare Order of the Holy Cross Poor Clares	PCC	Poor Clares
		PCJ	Sisters of the Poor Child Jesus
OSCam	Order of St Camillus (Camillans)	PCPA	Poor Clares of Perpetual Adoration
OSCCap	Capuchin Poor Clare Sisters	PDDM	Pious Disciples of the Divine Master
OSF	Order of St Francis (Franciscans)		
		PdeR	Sisters of Providence
OSFS	Oblate Sisters of St Francis de Sales Oblates of St Francis de Sales	PFM	Little Franciscans of Mary
		PHJ	Institute of the Heart of Jesus

PHJC	Poor Handmaids of Jesus Christ	RDC	Compassionists Sisters of Divine Compassion
PIME	Pontifical Institute for Foreign Missions Pontifical Institute for Missionary Extension	RE	Religious of the Eucharist Institute of Perpetual Adoration
PM	Sisters of the Presentation of Mary	RGS	Sisters of Our Lady of Charity of the Good Shepherd
PME	Foreign Mission Society of Quebec	RHF	Sisters of the Holy Family
POCR	Congregation of Rural Catechists	RHSJ	Religious Hospitallers of St Joseph
POSC	Little Sisters Workers of the Sacred Hearts	RJM	Religious of Jesus and Mary
		RLR	Sisters of the Retreat of the Sacred Heart
PS	Sisters of the Presentation of Mary	RMI	Daughters of Mary Immaculate Religious of Mary Immaculate
PSDP	Poor Servants of Divine Providence		
PSN	Poor Sisters of Nazareth	RNDM	Sisters of Our Lady of the Missions
PSSC	Missionaries of St Charles Borromeo	ROLC	Religious of Our Lady of Charity
PSSF	Little Sisters of the Holy Family	RSA	Religious of St Andrew
PSSJ	Poor Sisters of St Joseph	RSCJ	Society of the Sacred Heart
PVMI	Parish Visitors of Mary Immaculate	RSHM	Religious of the Sacred Heart of Mary
RA	Religious of the Apostolate of the Sacred Heart of Jesus Sisters of the Assumption	RSJ	Congregation of St Joseph of the Sacred Heart
		RSM	Religious Sisters of Mercy of Alma Sisters of Mercy Sisters of St Martha
RC	Religious of Our Lady of the Retreat in the Cenacle		
RCD	Sisters of Our Lady of Christian Doctrine	RSR	Sisters of Our Lady of the Holy Rosary
RCE	Religious of Christian Education	SA	Franciscan Sisters of the Atonement Society of the Atonement Sons of the Atonement
RCI	Sisters of Christian Instruction – Flone-lez-Amay		
RCJ	Rogationist Fathers		
RCM	Sisters of the Immaculate Conception	SAA	Sisters Auxiliaries of the Apostolate

SAC	Pallottine Fathers Pallottine Missionary Sisters Sisters of the Guardian Angel
SASV	Sisters of the Assumption of the Blessed Virgin Mary
SBB	Brotherhood of St Barnabas
SBS	Sisters of the Blessed Sacrament for Indians and Coloured People
SBST	Bon Secours Sisters
SC	Brothers of the Sacred Heart Guanellians Servants of Charity Sisters of Charity Sisters of Charity of St Elizabeth Sisters of Christ Sisters of St Clothilde Sisters of the Nativity of Our Lord Union Mysterium Christi
SCC	Sisters of Christian Charity of the Blessed Virgin Mary
SCE	Sisters of Charity of Our Lady of Evron
SCh	Society of Christ
SChP	Sisters of the Pious School
SChr	Society of Christ for Polish Immigrants
SCI	Sisters of Christian Instruction
SCIM	Sisters-Servants of the Immaculate Heart of Mary and of the Good Shepherd
SCJ	Congregation of Priests of the Sacred Heart of Jesus Priests of the Sacred Heart of Jesus
SCJM	Sisters of Charity of Jesus and Mary
SCL	Sisters of Charity – Leavenworth

SCMM	Sisters of Charity of Our Lady Mother of Mercy
SCN	Sisters of Charity – Nazareth Sisters of Charity and Christian Instruction – Nevers
SCO	Grey Nuns of the Cross
SCQ	Sisters of Charity of Quebec
SCS	Sisters of St Marie-Magdalen Postel
SCSC	Sisters of Mercy of the Holy Cross
SCSH	Sisters of Charity of St Hyacinthe
SCSJA	Sisters of Charity of St Joan Antide
SCSL	Sisters of Charity of St Louis
SCSP	Sisters of Charity of St Paul the Apostle – Selly Park
SDB	Salesians of Don Bosco
SDC	Society of Divine Compassion
SDE	Society of the Daughters of the Eucharist
SdeC	Sisters of Charity of St Joan Antide
SdeJ	Sisters-Servants of Jesus of Charity
SDM	Institute of the Servants of Divine Mercy
SDR	Sisters of the Divine Redeemer
SDS	Salvatorian Fathers and Brothers Sisters of the Divine Saviour
SDSH	Sisters of the Society Devoted to the Sacred Heart
SDV	Vocationist Fathers Vocationist Sisters
SdeM	Handmaids of Mary

SF	Holy Family Fathers Sons of the Holy Family	SJT	Sisters of St Joseph – Tarbes
SFM	Scarboro Foreign Mission Society	SJW	Sisters of St Joseph the Worker
SFMA	Franciscan Missionary Sisters of Assisi	SL	Sisters of Loretto at the Foot of the Cross
SG	Brothers of Christian Instruction – St Gabriel	SLG	Sisters of the Love of God
		SLO	Sisters of the Little Ones
SGM	Sisters of Charity – Montreal Sisters of Charity of the General Hospital of Montreal Grey Sisters – Montreal	SLW	Sisters of the Living Word
		SM	Handmaids of Mary Sisters of Mercy Misericordia Sisters Society of Mary (Marianists) Society of Mary (Marist Fathers and Sisters)
SHC	Society of the Holy Cross		
SHCJ	Society of the Holy Child Jesus		
SHF	Sisters of the Holy Family	SMA	Society of African Missions
SHJM	Sisters of the Sacred Hearts of Jesus and Mary	SMB	Bethlehem Fathers
SHN	Sisterhood of the Holy Nativity	SMDC	Daughters of Mercy of St Vincent de Paul
SHS	Sisters of the Holy Spirit	SMG	Poor Servants of the Mother of God
SHSp	Sisters-Servants of the Holy Spirit and Mary Immaculate	SMI	Sisters of Mary Immaculate
SHT	Society of the Holy Trinity	SMIC	Missionary Sisters of the Immaculate Conception of the Mother of God
SIJ	Sisters of the Infant Jesus		
SIM	Missionaries of the Kingship of Christ	SMM	Missionaries of the Company of Mary (Montfort Fathers)
SIW	Sisters of the Incarnate Word and the Blessed Sacrament	SMMG	Sisters of Mary Mother of God
SJ	Servants of Jesus Society of Jesus (Jesuits)	SMP	Daughters of Our Mother of Peace Sisters of Mary of the Presentation
SJA	Sisters of St Joan of Arc Sisters of St Joseph of the Apparition		
SJC	Sisters of St Joseph Cluny Sisters	SMR	Sisters of Mary Immaculate Institute of Marie Reparatrice Society of St Mary Reparatrix
SJG	Sisters of St John of God		
SJS	Sisters-Servants of the Blessed Sacrament	SMSM	Missionary Sisters of the Society of Mary (Marists)
SJSM	Sisters of St Joseph of St Mark	SND	Sisters of Notre Dame

SND deN	Sisters of Notre Dame – Namur	SSA	Society of the Sacred Advent Sisters of St Anne
SNJM	Sisters of the Holy Names of Jesus and Mary	SSB	Bethany Sisters
		SSC	Missionary Sisters of St Columban
SOL	Sisters of Our Lady		Missionary Society of St Columban
SOLM	Order of Nuns of Our Lady of Mercy		Sisters of Charity Sisters of Mercy of the Christian Schools
SOLP	Daughters of Our Lady of Providence		Sisters of St Casimir
SOLT	Society of Our Lady of the Most Holy Trinity		Society of the Sacred Cross
SOP	Sisters of Providence	SSCC	Congregation of the Sacred Hearts of Perpetual Adoration
SP	Piarists Servants of the Holy Paraclete Sisters of Providence		Picpus Fathers Picpus Sisters
SPB	Society of the Precious Blood	SSCh	Sisters of St Chrétienne
SPC	Sisters of Charity of St Paul the Apostle – Chartres	SSCH	Institute of the Holy Childhood of Jesus
SPF	Franciscan Sisters of the Poor	SSCJ	Servants of the Most Sacred Heart of Jesus Sisters of the Sacred Heart of Jesus
SPIC	Sisters of Providence and of the Immaculate Conception	SSCK	Sister Servants of Christ the King
SPM	Priests of Mercy		
SPR	Sisters of Providence (Rosminians) Sisters of Providence of the Institute of Charity	SSCM	Sisters-Servants of the Holy Heart of Mary Society of Sts Cyril and Methodius
SPS	St Patrick's Missionary Society	SSCME	Missionary Society of St Columban
SPSF	Franciscan Sisters of the Poor	SSD	Institute of the Sisters of St Dorothy
SR	Sisters of Reparation of the Sacred Wounds of Jesus	SSE	Sisters of St Elizabeth Society of St Edmund
SRC	Servants of Our Lady Queen of the Clergy	SSF	Sisters of the Holy Family Society of St Francis
SRCM	Sisters of Reparation of the Congregation of Mary	SSHJ	Sisters of the Sacred Heart of Jesus
SS	Society of the Priests of St Sulpice	SSHJM	Sisters of the Sacred Hearts of Jesus and Mary

SSHJP	Poor Servants of the Sacred Heart of Jesus and of the Poor	SSSF	School Sisters of St Francis
SSJ	Franciscan Sisters of St Joseph	SSTV	Sisters of St Thomas of Villanova
	Order of St Joseph	ST	Missionary Servants of the Most Holy Trinity
	Servants of St Joseph		
	Sisters of St Joseph	STJ	Sisters of St Teresa of Jesus
	Society of St Joseph of the Sacred Heart	SU	Society of St Ursula
SSJA	Sisters of St Joseph – Annecy	SUSC	Sisters of the Holy Union of the Sacred Hearts of Jesus and Mary
SSJB	Sisters of St Joseph – Bordeaux	SV	Sisters of Life
SSJD	Sisterhood of St John the Divine	SVD	Society of the Divine Word
	Society of St John the Divine	SVM	Sisters of the Visitation of the Congregation of the Immaculate Heart of Mary
SSJE	Society of St John the Evangelist (Cowley Fathers)	SX	Foreign Mission Society of St Francis Xavier
SSL	Sisters of St Louis		The Xaverian Missionary Fathers
SSM	Franciscan Sisters of the Third Order Regular of the Sorrowful Mother		
	Society of St Margaret	TCG	Order of Teachers of the Children of God
	Society of the Sacred Mission	TChr	Society of Christ for Polish Emigrants
SSMI	Sisters-Servants of Mary Immaculate	TOSF	Sisters of the Third Order of St Francis
SSMN	Sisters of St Mary – Namur		
SSMO	Sisters of St Mary of Oregon		
SSND	School-Sisters of Notre Dame	UJ	Ursulines of Jesus
SSP	Society of St Paul		
	Pauline Fathers and Brothers	VBVM	Visitation Sisters
SSPC	Missionary Sisters of St Peter Claver	VHM	Visitation Nuns
		VS	Vocation Sisters
SSpS	Missionary Sisters of the Holy Spirit	VSC	Vincentian Sisters of Charity
SSpSdeAP	Sisters-Servants of the Holy Spirit of Perpetual Adoration	WF	White Fathers
		WS	Missionary Sisters of Our Lady of Africa
SSS	Sisters of Social Service		
	Fathers of the Blessed Sacrament	XMM	Xaverian Missionary Sisters of Mary
	Servants of the Blessed Sacrament	XS	Xavier Sisters

ALTERNATIVE NAMES

Alternative Name	See entry
Adorers of the Blood of Christ	Precious Blood, Sister Adorers of the
Adorno Fathers	Caracciolo Fathers
Adrian Dominicans	Dominican Sisters of the Congregation of the Most Holy Rosary
Agonizants	Camillus, Order of St
Albertine Sisters	Poor, Sisters-Servants of the
Alcantarines	Peter of Alcantara, Friars of the Observance of St
Alexian Brothers	Alexius, Brothers of St
Alexian Nuns	Alexius, Sisters of St
Amadeans	Amadists
Ambrosian Sisters	Ambrose, Sisters of St
Ambrosians	Ambrose, Oblates of St
Ancilla Domini Sisters	Jesus Christ, Poor Handmaids of
Angelical Sisters of St Paul	Angelicals of St Paul
Angelicals	Paul, Angelical Sisters of St
Angelics of St George	Constantinian Order of St George
Annunciates of Lombardy	Marcellina, Sisters of St
Antonines	Anthony of Egypt, Order of St
Apostles of the Sacred Heart of Jesus	Zelatrices of the Sacred Heart, Missionary
Apostolic Clerics of St Jerome	Jesuats, Congregation of
Apostolini	Apostles, Order of the
Armenian Religious of Genoa	Bartholomites
Assumptionists	Austria, Canons Regular of
Augustinians of the Assumption	Assumptionists
Austin Friars	Augustine, Order of St
Baccanarists	Faith of Jesus, Clerks Regular of the
Baladites	Basil the Great, Order of St
Barettini	Humiliati
Basilian Salvatorian Fathers	Basil the Great, Order of St

Alternative Name	See entry
Bearers of the Star	Bethlehem, Brothers of
Bedlam Beggars	Abraham-Men
Beghines	Beguines
Belemites	Bethlehemites
Bernardine Cistercians	Bernardine Cistercians of Esquermes
Bethany Fathers	Imitation of Christ
Bethany Sisters	Imitation of Christ
Bethlehem Missionaries of Switzerland	Bethlehem Fathers
Bianchi	Albati, Order of
Black Canons	John Lateran, Canons Regular of St
Black Friars	Dominicans
Black Monks	Benedictines
Black Sisters	Alexius, Sisters of St
Blessed Sacrament Sisters	Blessed Sacrament for Indians & Coloured People, Sisters of the
Blessed Virgin Mary Sisters	Charity of the Blessed Virgin Mary, Sisters of
Blue Annunciades	Annunciation, Sisters of the Blessed
Blue Nuns	Mary, Little Company of
Bonites	Boni Homines
Boniti	Boni Homines
Bonnes Capotes	Christian Schools, Sisters of the
Bridgettine Knights	Bridget, Knights of St
Bridgettines	Bridget, Order of the Most Holy Saviour & St
Brignole Sisters	Mount Calvary, Daughters of
Brotherhood of St Barnabas	Bush Brotherhood
Brothers Crossbearers	Crutched Friars
Brothers of Bethlehem	Bethlehemites
Brothers of Cabbage Valley	Valliscaulian Order
Brothers of Charity of Mary Help of Christians	Mercy of Our Lady of Perpetual Help, Brothers of
Brothers of Charity of St Hippolytus	Hippolites
Brothers of Mary	Mary, Society of
Brothers of Penance of Jesus Christ	Sack, Friars of the
Brothers of Penitence	Sack, Friars of the
Brothers of Santa Maria of Evora	Aviz of Portugal, Knights of
Brothers of St Barnabas	Apostles, Order of the
Brothers of St Hippolytus	Charity of St Hippolytus, Friars of
Brothers of St John the Baptist of Penitence	Baptistines
Brothers of St Joseph	Joseph, The Working Brothers of St
Brothers of the Blessed Virgin Mary of Mercy	Our Lady of Mercy, Brothers of

Alternative Name	*See entry*
Brothers of the Christian Schools In Ireland	Christian Brothers
Brown Joeys	Joseph of the Sacred Heart of Jesus, Sisters of St
Bush Sisters	Joseph of the Sacred Heart of Jesus, Sisters of St
B.V.M.	Charity of the Blessed Virgin Mary, Sisters of
Cabrini Sisters	Sacred Heart of Jesus, Missionary Sisters of the
Caelestes	Annunciation, Sisters of the Blessed
Calvarians	Calvary, Order of Our Lady of Calvarists
Calvary Benedictines	Calvary, Order of Our Lady of
Camillans	Camillus, Order of St
Canonesses Regular Hospitallers of the Merciful Heart of Jesus of the Order of St Augustine	Augustinian Sisters of the Mercy of Jesus
Canons of St Laudo	Laudus, Canons Regular of St
Canons of St Lo	Laudus, Canons Regular of St
Canons Regular of Prémontré	Prémontré, Congregation of
Canons Regular of St Anthony	Anthony of Egypt, Order of St
Canons Regular of St Autbert	Aubert, Canons Regular of St
Canons Regular of St Saviour	John Lateran, Canons Regular of St
Canons Regular of the Austrian Lateran Congregation	Austria, Canons Regular of
Canons Regular of the Mother of God & of the Pious Schools	Piarist Fathers
Canons Regular of the Priory of the Two Lovers	Amanti, Canons Regular of the Priory of
Canons Regular of the Valley of Josaphat	Valley of Jehosophat, Canons Regular of the
Canossian Sisters	Canossian Daughters of Charity of Verona
Capitanio Sisters	Charity of St Bartholomea Capitanio and St Vincent Gerosa, Sisters of
Caritas Christi Union	Caritas Christi
Carriers of the Star	Bethlehem, Brothers of
Cassinese of the Primitive Observance	Benedict, Order of St (Subiaco Congregation)
Catechist Sisters of Mary Immaculate Help of Christians	Mary Immaculate, Sisters of
Celestial Annunciades	Annunciation, Sisters of the Blessed
Celestine Hermits	Celestines
Cellites	Alexius, Brothers of St

Alternative Name	See entry
Cellitine Sisters	Alexius, Sisters of St
Chama Cha Maria Mtakatifu	Mary of Nazareth & Calvary, Community of St
Charitable Mistresses of the Holy Infant Jesus	Infant Jesus, Sisters of the
Clerks Regular Ministers of the Infirm	Camillus, Order of St
Clerks Regular Minor	Caracciolo Fathers
Clerks Regular of St Paul	Barnabite Fathers
Clerks Regular of the Order of the Holy Ghost	Holy Ghost, Order of the – Clerks Regular
Cluniac Monks	Cluny, Order of
Cluniac Nuns	Cluny Sisters
Colettans	Colettines
Columban Fathers	Columban, Missionary Society of St
Columban Sisters	Columban, Missionary Sisters of St
Comboni Fathers	Heart of Jesus, Missionaries of the
Comboni Missionary Sisters	Verona Missionary Sisters
Community of Mother Angela & The Holy Rood Sisters	Servants of the Cross, Community of the
Community of St Katharine	Katharine of Egypt, Community of St
Community of St Katharine of Alexandria	Katharine of Egypt, Community of St
Community of St Katharine of Fulham	Katharine of Egypt, Community of St
Company of Jesus	Jesus, Society of
Company of Mary	Company of Mary Our Lady, Sisters of the
Company of Our Lady of the Blessed Sacrament	Grey Sisters – Melbourne
Company of the Daughters of Mary Our Lady (Notre Dame)	Company of Mary Our Lady, Sisters of the
Congregation of Discalced Clerks of the Passion of the Most Holy Cross and Passion of Our Lord Jesus Christ	Passionist Fathers
Congregation of Our Lady of Fidelity	Faithful Virgins, Daughters of the
Congregation of Scheutveld	Immaculate Heart of Mary, Congregation of the
Congregation of Sisters of the Misericorde	Misericordia Sisters
Congregation of the Sacred Hearts of Jesus and Mary	Picpus Fathers, The
Congregation of Sts Ambrose and Barnabas	Ambrose, Order of St
Congregation of St Ambrose at Nemus	Apostle Brothers of the Poor Life, The
Congregation of St Felix of Catalice of the Third Order of St Francis	Felix, Sisters of St
Congregation of St Peter in Chains	Peter ad Vincula, Congregation of St
Congregation of St Rose of Lima	Dominican Sisters of the Relief of Incurable Cancer

Alternative Name	*See entry*
Congregation of the Apostle Brothers of the Poor Life	Ambrose, Order of St
Congregation of the Blessed Sacrament	Blessed Sacrament, Fathers of the
Congregation of the Dove	Andrew, Hermits of St
Congregation of the Holy Union of the Sacred Hearts of Jesus and Mary	Holy Union of the Sacred Hearts of Jesus and Mary, Sisters of the
Congregation of the Mission	Vincentians, The
Congregation of the Most Holy Redeemer	Redemptorists, The
Congregation of the Oratory of St Philip Neri	Oratorians
Congregation of the Perpetual Adoration of the Blessed Sacrament	Perpetual Adoration, Institute of
Congregation of the Sacred Hearts of Jesus and Mary	Picpus Fathers, The
Congregation of the Sacred Hearts of Jesus and Mary and of Perpetual Adoration of the Most Blessed Sacrament of the Altar	Picpus Fathers, The
Congregation of the Sisters of Mercy	Mercy, Sisters of
Congregation of the Visitation of the Blessed Virgin Mary	Visitation Sisters
Consolata Society for Foreign Missions	Consolata Fathers
Cowley Fathers	John the Evangelist, Society of St
Crosier Fathers	Holy Cross, Order of the
Crosiers	Holy Cross, Order of the
Crossed Friars	Crutched Friars
Dames de St Maur	Infant Jesus, Sisters of the
Damianissines	Damianites
Damianistes	Damianites
Damien Fathers	Picpus Fathers, The
Daughters of Mary	Guastella, Virgins of
Daughters of Mary	Marianist Sisters
Daughters of Mary and Joseph	Mary, The Ladies of
Daughters of Mary Immaculate	Most Precious Blood of Our Lord Jesus Christ, Sisters of the
Daughters of Mary Immaculate for the Protection of Working Girls	Mary Immaculate, Daughters of
Daughters of Mary of Bannabikira	Bannabikira Sisters
Daughters of Our Lady of Good Counsel and St Paul of the Cross	Vocation Sisters
Daughters of the Blessed Virgin Mary of the Immaculate Conception	Christian Charity of the Blessed Virgin Mary, Sisters of
Daughters of the Cross	Andrew, Sisters of St

Alternative Name	*See entry*
Daughters of the Holy Family	Genevieve, Daughters of St
Daughters of the Most Holy Redeemer	Holy Redeemer, Sisters of the
De La Mennais Brothers	Christian Instruction of Ploermel, Brothers of
De La Salle Brothers	Christian Schools, Brothers of the
Deaconess Community of St Andrew	Andrew, Community of St
Dehonian Priests	Sacred Heart of Jesus, Congregation of Priests of the
Disciples of St Anthony	Antonian Order
Divine Word Missionaries	Divine Word, Society of the
Doctrinarians	Christian Doctrine, Fathers of
Dominican Sisters of Charity of the Presentation of Our Lady	Dominican Sisters of the Presentation of Tours
Dominican Sisters of Marywood	Dominican Congregation of Our Lady of the Sacred Heart
Dominican Sisters of the Presentation	Dominican Sisters of the Presentation of Tours
Don Orione Congregation	Divine Providence, Sons of
Edmundite Fathers	Edmund, Society of St
Edmundites	Edmund, Society of St
English Ladies	Blessed Virgin Mary, Institute of the
Escolapias	Pious Schools, Sisters of the
Escolapios	Piarist Fathers
Eudist Fathers	Jesus and Mary, Congregation of
Evangelical Sisters of Jesus of Nazareth	Jesus of Nazareth, Community of
Evangelical Sisters of Mary	Mary, Evangelical Society of – Darmstadt
Fate Bene Fratelli	John of God, Brothers Hospitallers of St
Fathers of a Good Death	Camillus, Order of St
Fathers of Charity	Charity, Institute of
Fathers of the Shirt	John Lateran, Canons Regular of St
Federation of the Sisters of Mercy	Mercy, Sisters of
Felician Sisters	Felix, Sisters of St
Felicians	Felix, Sisters of St
Finthen Sisters	Divine Providence of Ribeauville, Sisters of
Foreign Mission Society of Bethlehem	Bethlehem Fathers
Franciscan Sisters of Jesus and Mary	Franciscan Sisters, Daughters of the Sacred Hearts of Jesus and Mary
Franciscan Sisters of St Bernard of Siena	Bernardine Sisters of the Third Order of St Francis
Fransalians	Francis de Sales, Missionaries of St
Fratres Cruciferi	Crutched Friars

Alternative Name	*See entry*
Fratres Gaudentes	Militia Jesu Christi
French Congregation of the Oratory	Oratory of Jesus & of Mary Immaculate of France
Friars Minims	Minim Fathers
Friars of the Order of St Francis	Minim Fathers
Friends of God	Amadists
Friends of God	Amedians
Gilbertines	Gilbert of Sempringham, Canons Regular of St
Gilbertines	Gilbert of Sempringham, Nuns of St
Glenmary Home Missioners	Home Missioners of America, The
Glenmary Sisters	Home Mission Sisters of America
Good Shepherd Sisters	Immaculate Heart of Mary and of the Good Shepherd, Sisters-Servants of the
Grey Brothers	Savigny, Congregation of
Grey Friars	Franciscans – Roman Catholic
Grey Ursulines	Ursulines of the Heart of Jesus Agonizing
Guanellians	Charity, Servants of
Guanellians	Mary of Providence, Daughters of St
Guastallines	Guastella, Virgins of
Gulielmites	William, Hermits of St
Hermit Sisters of St John the Baptist	Baptistines
Hermitesses of the Immaculate Conception	Theatine Hermitesses
Hermits of Fonte-Avellana	Andrew, Hermits of St
Hermits of Monte Bello	Jerome of Blessed Peter of Pisa, Hermits of St
Hermits of Monte Vergine	Williamites
Hermits of Murrone	Celestines
Hermits of Our Lady of Gonzaga	Gonzaga, Hermits of
Hermits of St Augustine	Augustine, Order of St
Hermits of St Damian	Celestines
Hermits of St Francis of Assisi	Minim Fathers
Hermits of St Jerome	Jerome, Monks of the Order of St
Hermits of St John of Penance	John the Baptist of Penitence, Hermits of St
Hermits of St John the Baptist	Baptistines
Hermits of St John the Baptist in France	Baptistines
Hieronymite Nuns	Jerome, Nuns of the Order of St
Hieronymites	Jerome, Monks of the Order of St
Holy Cross Fathers	Holy Cross, Congregation of
Holy Family Fathers	Holy Family, Sons of the

Alternative Name	*See entry*
Holy Ghost Fathers	Holy Ghost and of the Immaculate Heart of Mary, Congregation of the
Holy Ghost Missionaries	Holy Ghost and of the Immaculate Heart of Mary, Congregation of the
Holy Ghost Missionary Sisters	Holy Spirit, Missionary Sisters of the
Holy Spirit Adoration Sisters	Holy Spirit of Perpetual Adoration, Sisters-Servants of the
Holy Union Sisters	Holy Union of the Sacred Hearts of Jesus and Mary, Sisters of the
Hospital Sisters of the Mercy of Jesus	Augustinian Sisters of the Mercy of Jesus
Hospitaller Brothers of St Anthony	Anthony of Egypt, Order of St
Hospitallers of Bethlehem	Bethlehemites
Hospitallers of Ernemont	Christian Schools, Sisters of the
Hospitallers of St Lazarus	Lazarus of Jerusalem, Order of St
Hospitallers of the Holy Ghost	Holy Ghost, Order of the
Hospitallers of the Observance	Humiliati
Humble Ladies	Humiliati
Idente Association of Christ the Redeemer	Idente Missionaries of Christ Crucified
Illuminati	Alumbrados
Immaculata Sisters	Immaculate Conception of the Mother of God, Missionary Sisters of the
Ingenbohl Sisters	Mercy of the Holy Cross, Sisters of
Institute of Charity	Providence, Sisters of – Rosminians
Institute of Mary	Blessed Virgin Mary, Institute of the
Institute of Our Lady of Mercy	Mercy, Sisters of
Institute of the Sisters of Mercy	Mercy, Sisters of
Jeronimite Hermits	Jerome, Monks of the Order of St
Jesuatesses	Jesuats
Jesuati	Jesuats, Congregation of
Jesuits	Jesus, Society of
Josephites	Joseph of the Sacred Heart of Jesus, Sisters of St
Josephites	Joseph of the Sacred Heart of Jesus, Society of St
Kaiserswerth Deaconess Community	Kaiserswerth Alliance
Karmilitha Nishpatkuka Munnam Sabha	Carmelites of Mary Immaculate
Kiltegan Fathers	Patrick's Missionary Society, St
Knights of Avis	Aviz of Portugal, Knights of
Knights of Evora	Aviz of Portugal, Knights of
Knights of St Benedict of Aviz	Aviz of Portugal, Knights of
Knights of St Lazarus	Lazarus of Jerusalem, Order of St

Alternative Name	*See entry*
Knights of St Michael in Portugal	Michael's Wing, Knights of St
Knights of the Band	Sash, Knights of the
Knights of the Lily of the Valley	Lily, Knights of the
Knights of the Order of Calatrava	Calatreve, Knights of – Toledo
Knights of the Redeemer	Precious Blood, Knights of the
Knights of the Temple of Solomon	Templar, Knights
Knights of the Whip and the White Eagle	Discipline & the White Eagle, Knights of the
La Retraite Sisters	Retreat of the Sacred Heart, Sisters of the
La Sainte Union	Holy Union of the Sacred Hearts of Jesus & Mary, Sisters of the
Ladies of the Band	Sash, Ladies of the
Lazarists	Vincentians, The
Little Brothers of Mary	Marist Brothers
Little Franciscan Sisters of Mary	Mary, Little Franciscans of
Loreto Sisters	Blessed Virgin Mary, Institute of the
Loretto Community	Loretto at the Foot of the Cross, Sisters of
Loretto Sisters	Blessed Virgin Mary, Institute of the
Lyons Missionaries	African Missions, Society of
Madelonnettes	Mary Magdalen, The Order of St
Magdalens	Magdalen, Nuns of St
Mantellate Sisters	Mary, Servants of
Mariamettes	Sacred Hearts of Jesus and Mary, Sisters of the – Lebanon
Marian Fathers	Marian Fathers of the Immaculate Conception of the Blessed Virgin Mary, Congregation of the
Marianists	Mary, Society of
Mariannhill Brothers	Mariannhill, Congregation of Missionaries of
Mariannhill Fathers	Mariannhill, Congregation of Missionaries of
Mariannhill Sisters	Precious Blood, Missionary Sisters of the
Marist Brothers of the Schools	Marist Brothers
Maronite Antonians	Antonian Order
Maronite Order of St Anthony of Aleppo	Antonian Order
Maronites	Sacred Hearts of Jesus and Mary, Sisters of the
Maryknoll Fathers	Catholic Foreign Mission Society of America, Inc.
Maryknoll Sisters	Catholic Foreign Mission Society of America

Alternative Name	*See entry*
Maryknoll Society for Foreign Missions	Catholic Foreign Mission Society of America, Inc.
Maryvale Sisters	Our Lady Help of the Clergy, Congregation of
Mathurins	Most Holy Trinity, Order of the – Friars, Calced and Discalced
Maurists	Maur, Congregation of St
Mercedarian Friars	Our Lady of Mercy, Order of
Mercedarian Nuns	Our Lady of Mercy, Order of Nuns of
Mexican Passionist Sisters	Passion of Our Lord Jesus Christ and the Sorrows of Mary, Daughters of the
Mill Hill Missionaries	Mill Hill Fathers
Minimi	Minim Fathers
Ministers of the Sick	Mary, Handmaids of
Mirfield Fathers	Resurrection, Community of the
Mission Sisters of St Alphege	Reparation to Jesus in the Blessed Sacrament, Community of
Mission Sisters of the Holy Name of Jesus	Holy Name, Community of the
Missionaries of Africa	White Fathers
Missionaries of Guadalupe	Mary of Guadalupe for Foreign Missions, Institute of St
Missionaries of Our Lady of La Salette	La Salette Fathers
Missionaries of Rennes	Immaculate Conception, Mission Priests of the
Missionaries of St Charles	Charles Borromeo, Missionaries of St
Missionaries of the Most Precious Blood	Precious Blood, Society of the
Missionary Carmelites of St Teresa	Carmelites
Missionary Community of St Denys	Denys, Community of St
Missionary Oblates of Mary Immaculate	Mary Immaculate, Oblates of
Missionary Priests of St John the Baptist	Baptistines
Missionary Sisters of Our Lady of the Apostles for African Missions	Our Lady of the Apostles, Missionary Sisters of
Missionary Sisters of Our Lady of the Holy Rosary	Holy Rosary, Missionary Sisters of the
Missionary Society of Provence	Mary Immaculate, Oblates of
Missionary Sisters of St Dominic	Catholic Foreign Mission Society of America
Missionary Sisters of the Catholic Apostolate	Pallottine Missionary Sisters
Missionary Sisters of the Society of Mary	Marist Missionary Sisters, The
Missionary Sisters-Servants of the Holy Ghost	Holy Spirit, Missionary Sisters of the
Missionary Society of Mount Calvary	Calvarists
Missionary Society of Provence	Mary Immaculate, Oblates of

Alternative Name	*See entry*
Missionary Sons of the Immaculate Heart of Mary	Claretian Fathers
Missionhurst Congregation of the Immaculate Heart of Mary	Immaculate Heart of Mary, Congregation of the
Monk-Hermits of St Jerome	Jerome, Hermits of St – Lupo Olmedo Reform
Monks of Fonte Avellana	Andrew, Hermits of St
Monks of St Andrew	Andrew, Hermits of St
Montfort Fathers	Mary, Missionaries of the Company of
Montfortian Society of Mary	Mary, Missionaries of the Company of
Montfortians	Mary, Missionaries of the Company of
Nazareni	Penance, Religious Order of
Nolascans	Our Lady of Mercy, Order of
Norbertines	Prémontré, Order of
Notre Dame Nuns	Company of Mary Our Lady, Sisters of the
Nuns of St Ambrose	Marcellina, Sisters of St
Nuns of St Cesarius	Caesarius, Nuns of St
Nuns-Hospitallers of Our Lady of Mercy	Penitents of Our Lady of Refuge
Nursing Sisters of the Sick Poor	Infant Jesus, Congregation of the
Oblates of St Charles	Ambrose, Oblates of St
Oblates of St Frances of Rome in Tor de'Specci	Frances of Rome, Oblates of St
Oblates of St Hilary	Blessed Virgin Mary Immaculate, Sons of the
Oblates Regular of St Benedict	Frances of Rome, Oblates of St
Oratory of St Philip Neri	Oratorians
Order of Clerks Regular of the Mother of God of the Pious Schools	Piarist Fathers
Order of Discalced Augustinians	Augustine, Order of the Recollects of St
Order of Humility	Humiliati
Order of Santiago	James of the Sword, Knights of St
Order of Servites	Mary, Servants of
Order of St Clare	Poor Clares
Order of St Hubert of Lorraine	Fidelity, Order of
Order of St James of Compostella	James of the Sword, Knights of St
Order of St Jerome Emiliani	Somasca, Clerks Regular of
Order of St Paul the First Hermit	Brothers of Death – France
	Hermits of St Paul – Portugal
Order of the Most Holy Redeemer	Redemptoristines, The
Order of the Most Holy Saviour	Bridget, Order of the Most Holy Saviour and St
Order of the Resurrection	Holy Sepulchre, Canonesses Regular of the

Alternative Name	*See entry*
Order of the Servants of the Sick	Camillus, Order of St
Order of the Tau	James of Altopascio, Order of St
Order of the Visitation of Holy Mary	Visitation Nuns
Paccanarists	Faith of Jesus, Clerks Regular of the
Paraclete Fathers	Holy Paraclete, Servants of the
Patrician Brothers	Patrick, Brothers of St
Pauline Fathers	Paul, Hermits of St
Paulines	Pauline Fathers and Brothers
Paulist Fathers	Paul the Apostle, Society of Missionary Priests of St
Penitents of St John the Baptist	Baptistines
Philippine Nuns of Rome	Philip Neri, Nuns of St
P.I.M.E. Fathers	Pontifical Institute for Missionary Extension
Pink Sisters	Holy Spirit of Perpetual Adoration, Sisters-Servants of the
Pious Ladies	Reparation, Sisters of the
Pious Society of St Paul	Pauline Fathers and Brothers
Pious Society of the Missionaries of St Charles	Charles Borromeo, Missionaries of St
Pious Workers of St Calasanctius	Piarist Fathers
Pontifical Institute of Religious Teachers Filippini	Filippini Religious Teachers
Poor Clares	Damianites
Poor Clares of the Primitive Observance	Poor Clares
Poor Clares of the Reform of St Colette	Poor Clares
Poor Hermits of the Lord Celestine	Celestines
Poor Knights of Christ	Templar, Knights
Poor Knights of the Temple	Templar, Knights
Precious Blood Sisters	Adoration of the Most Precious Blood, Sisters of the
Premontratensians	Prémontré, Order of
Presentation Order	Presentation of the Blessed Virgin Mary, Sisters of the
Priests of Christian Doctrine	Christian Doctrine, Fathers of
Racine Dominican Sisters	Dominican Sisters of St Catherine of Siena of Racine
Religious of Christian Instruction of Ghent	Christian Instruction, Sisters of
Religious of Mary Immaculate	Mary Immaculate, Daughters of
Religious of Our Lady of the Retreat in the Cenacle	Our Lady of the Retreat in the Cenacle, Congregation of
Religious of Provins	Celestines – Provins

Alternative Name	*See entry*
Religious of the Assumption	Assumption, Sisters of the
Relgious of the Compassion of the Holy Virgin	Our Lady of Compassion, Sisters of
Religious of the Eucharist	Perpetual Adoration of the Most Holy Sacrament, Religious of
	Perpetual Adoration, Institute of
Religious of the Passion of Christ	Passionist Nuns
Religious Sisters of Mercy	Mercy, Sisters of
Resurrectionists	Resurrection of Our Lord Jesus Christ, Congregation of the
Rogationists of the Sacred Heart of Jesus	Rogationist Fathers
Rosminian Sisters	Providence, Sisters of – Rosminian
Rosminians	Charity, Institute of
Sacerdotal Society of the Holy Cross and Opus Dei	Opus Dei
Sacramentine Nuns	Blessed Sacrament and of Our Lady, Religious of the
Sacramentines	Blessed Sacrament, Fathers of the
Salesian Sisters of St John Bosco	Mary Help of Christians, Daughters of
Salvatorian Sisters	Divine Saviour, Sisters of the
Savannah Franciscans	Franciscan School Sisters
Scalabrini Fathers	Charles Borromeo, Missionaries of St
Scalabrini Sisters	Charles Borromeo, Missionary Sisters of St
Scalabrinians	Charles Borromeo, Missionaries of St
Scalzetti	Penance, Religious Order of
Schervier Sisters	Franciscan Sisters of the Poor
Scheut Fathers	Immaculate Heart of Mary, Congregation of the
Scholari	Valley of Scholars, Order of the
Schonstatt Movement	Schonstatt Secular Institute
Scolopii	Piarist Fathers
Servants of the Cross	Holy Rood, Community of the
Servants of the Poor	James, Sisterhood of St
Servites	Mary, Servants of
Shuwairite Basilians	Basil the Great, Order of St
Sinsinawa Dominicans	Dominican Congregation of the Sinsinawa Congregation of the Most Holy Rosary
Sisterhood of St John the Evangelist	John the Evangelist, Sisters of the Community of St
Sisterhood of the Epiphany	Epiphany, Oxford Mission Sisterhood of the
Sisters of Africa	Our Lady of Africa, Missionary Sisters of

Alternative Name	*See entry*
Sisters of Charity of Quebec	Grey Nuns – Beauport
Sisters of Charity of St Hyacinthe	Grey Nuns – St Hyacinthe
Sisters of Charity of St Vincent de Paul	Charity, Sisters of – New York
Sisters of Charity of the General Hospital of Montreal	Grey Sisters – Montreal
Sisters of Christ	Union Mysterium Christi
Sisters of Christian Charity	Christian Charity of the Blessed Virgin Mary, Sisters of
Sisters of Christian Charity of the Most Precious Blood	Precious Blood, Daughters of the
Sisters of Divine Compassion	Compassionists
Sisters of Divine Vocations	Vocationist Sisters
Sisters of Jesus in the Temple	Finding of Jesus in the Temple, Sisters of the
Sisters of Mary and Joseph	Mary, Joseph and of Mercy, Sisters of
Sisters of Mercy of the Blessed Sacrament	Mercedarian Sisters of the Blessed Sacrament
Sisters of Our Lady of Charity and Refuge	Our Lady of Charity, Sisters of
Sisters of Our Lady of Mercy	Our Lady of Mercy, Order of Nuns of
Sisters of St Chretienne	Holy Childhood of Jesus, Institute of the
Sisters of St Columban	Columban, Missionary Sisters of St
Sisters of St Columban for Missions among the Chinese	Columban, Missionary Sisters of St
Sisters of St Denis	Our Lady of Compassion, Sisters of
Sisters of St Dominic	Catholic Foreign Mission Society of America
Sisters of St Gildas	Christian Instruction, Sisters of
Sisters of St John the Baptist	Baptistines
Sisters of St Juilly	Louis, Sisters of St
Sisters of St Louis – Monaghan	Louis, Sisters of St
Sisters of St Lucy	Filippini Religious Teachers
Sisters of St Marie-Madeleine Postel	Mercy of the Christian Schools, Sisters of
Sisters of St Peter Claver for the African Missions	Peter Claver, Missionary Sisters of St
Sisters of St Ursula of the Holy Virgin	Ursula, Society of St
Sisters of the Catholic Apostolate	Pallottine Sisters
Sisters of the Cross	Cross, Religious of the
Sisters of the Cross and Passion	Passionist Sisters
Sisters of the Divine Vocations	Vocationist Sisters
Sisters of the Holy Child Jesus	Infant Jesus, Sisters of the
Sisters of the Holy Cross	Holy Cross, Teaching Sisters of the – Menzingen
Sisters of the Holy Ghost	Holy Spirit and Mary Immaculate, Sisters-Servants of the

Alternative Name	*See entry*
Sisters of the Holy Name of Mary	Marist Sisters, The
Sisters of the Humility of Mary	Holy Humility of the Blessed Virgin Mary, Sisters of the
Sisters of the Immaculate Conception of the Blessed Virgin Mary	Theatine Nuns
Sisters of the Immaculate Heart of Mary	Most Holy and Immaculate Heart of Mary, California Institute of the Sisters of the
Sisters of the Infant Jesus	Virgins of the Infant Jesus, Congregation of
Sisters of the Infant Mary	Charity of St Bartolomea Capitanio and St Vincenza Gerosa, Sisters of
Sisters of the Junior Schools	Little Schools, Sisters of the
Sisters of the Love of Jesus	John the Evanglist, Sisters of St
Sisters of the Most Holy Cross and Passion of Our Lord Jesus Christ	Passionist Sisters
Sisters of the Oaks	Little Schools, Sisters of the
Sisters of the Precious Blood	Precious Blood, Missionary Sisters of the
Sisters of the Presentation of Our Lady	Presentation of Mary, Sisters of the
Sisters of the Sacred Hearts of Jesus and Mary	Little Schools, Sisters of the
Sisters of the Temple	Finding of Jesus in the Temple, Sisters of the
Sisters of the Visitation of Mary	Jesuats
Sisters-Adorers of the Most Precious Blood of Our Lord Jesus Christ of the Union of St Hyacinthe	Blood of Christ, Sisters-Adorers of the
Sisters-Adorers of the Precious Blood	Most Precious Blood of Our Lord Jesus Christ, Sisters of the
Sisters-Disciples of the Divine Master	Divine Master, Pious Disciples of the
Sisters-Servants of Mary	Mary, Handmaids of
Sleeping Fathers	Genevieve, Canons Regular of St
Society of Catholic Medical Missionaries	Medical Missionary Sisters, Society of
Society of Catholic Mission Sisters of St Francis Xavier	Xavier Sisters
Society of Mary the Helper	Marie-Auxiliatrice, Society of Sisters of
Society of Mary	Marist Fathers
Society of Mary of Montfort	Mary, Missionaries of the Company of
Society of Mary Reparatrice	Institute of Marie Reparatrice
Society of Oblate Fathers of St Edmund and of the Sacred Heart of Jesus and the Immaculate Heart of Mary	Edmund, Society of St
Society of Our Lady of Charity of the Orphans	Faithful Virgins, Daughters of the

Alternative Name	*See entry*
Society of St Don Bosco	Salesians of Don Bosco
Society of St Francis de Sales	Salesians of Don Bosco
Society of St Joseph of the Sacred Heart	Mill Hill Fathers
Society of St Paul for the Apostolate of Communications	Pauline Fathers & Brothers
Society of the Catholic Apostolate	Pallottine Fathers
Society of the Divine Saviour	Salvatorian Fathers and Brothers
Society of the Divine Vocations	Vocationist Fathers
Society of the Faithful Virgins	Faithful Virgins, Daughters of the
Society of the Most Holy Trinity	Holy Trinity, Society of the
Society of the Sisters of Bethany	Bethany Sisters
Somaschan Fathers	Somasca, Clerks Regular of
Somaschi	Somasca, Clerks Regular of
Sons of Mary, Health of the Sick	Mary, Missionary Society of
Sons of St Joseph	Josephite Fathers
Spanish Nursing Sisters	Mary, Handmaids of
Sparkhill Dominicans	Dominican Sisters of the Congregation of Our Lady of the Rosary
Spinola Sisters	Divine Heart, Handmaids of the
Spiritans	Holy Ghost and of the Immaculate Heart of Mary, Congregation of the
Spiritual Franciscans of the Marches	Celestines
St Columban's Missionary Society	Columban, Missionary Society of St
St Francis Xavier Foreign Missionary Society	Xaverian Missionary Fathers
St Joseph of Cluny Sisters	Cluny Sisters
St Joseph's Missionary Society of Mill Hill	Mill Hill Fathers
St Joseph's Society for Coloured Missions	Joseph of the Sacred Heart, Society of St
St Patrick Fathers	Patrick's Missionary Society, St
Steyl Missionaries	Divine Word, Society of the
Stigmatines	Holy Stigmata, Congregation of the
Studites	Acoemetae
Sulpician Fathers	Sulpice, Society of Priests of St
Swedish Bridgettines	Bridget, Order of the Most Holy Saviour and St
Teresian Association	Teresa, Institute of St
Teresian Sisters	Teresa of Jesus, Sisters of St
Tom o'Bedlam's Men	Abraham-Men
Trappists	Cistercians of the Strict Observance
Trappistines	Cistercians of the Strict Observance
Trinitarian Sisters	Most Holy Trinity, Order of the

Alternative Name	*See entry*
Trinitarians	Most Blessed Trinity, Missionary Servants of the
Trinity Missions	Most Holy Trinity, Missionary Servants of the
United Brethren	Bartholomites
Vatellotes	Christian Doctrine, Sisters of
Verona Fathers	Heart of Jesus, Missionaries of the
Viatorians	Viator, Congregation of the Clerics of St
Visitandines	Visitation Nuns
Votaries of the Cross	Lovers of the Holy Cross Sisters
Watchers, The	Acoemetae
White Friars	Carmelites
White Ladies	Magdalen, Nuns of St
White Sisters	Holy Spirit, Congregation of Daughters of the
White Sisters	Our Lady of Africa, Missionary Sisters of
Whitemantles	Williamites
Worker Nuns of the Holy House of Nazareth	Working Sisters

SUMMARY LIST OF ORDERS

ABANDONED AGED, SISTERS OF THE

ABRAHAM-MEN

ACOEMETAE

ADORATION OF THE MOST PRECIOUS BLOOD, SISTERS OF THE

ADORATION REPARATRICE, SISTERS OF THE INSTITUTE OF

AFRICAN MISSIONS, SOCIETY OF

AGNES, SISTERS OF ST – Dordrecht

AGNES, SISTERS OF ST – Fond du Lac

ALBATI, ORDER OF

ALCÁNTARA, KNIGHTS OF

ALEXIUS, BROTHERS OF ST

ALEXIUS, SISTERS OF ST

ALL HALLOWS, COMMUNITY OF

ALL SAINTS SISTERS OF THE POOR

ALL SAINTS SISTERS OF THE POOR, SOCIETY OF

ALOYSIUS GONZAGO, BROTHERS OF ST

ALUMBRADOS

AMADISTS

AMANTI, CANONS REGULAR OF THE PRIORY OF

AMARANTA, KNIGHTS OF

AMBROSE, OBLATES OF ST

AMBROSE, ORDER OF ST

AMBROSE, SISTERS OF ST

AMEDIANS

ANAWIM

ANDREW, COMMUNITY OF ST

ANDREW, HERMITS OF ST

ANDREW, RELIGIOUS OF ST

ANDREW, SISTERS OF ST

ANGELICALS OF ST PAUL

ANGELO OF CORSICA, BROTHERS OF ST

ANNE, ORDER OF ST

ANNE, SISTERS OF ST

ANNE, SISTERS OF ST – Lachine

ANNE OF PROVIDENCE, SISTERS OF ST

ANNUNCIADES

ANNUNCIATION, SISTERS OF THE BLESSED

ANNUNCIATION OF SAVOY, KNIGHTS OF THE

ANTHONY, MISSIONARY SISTERS OF ST

ANTHONY OF EGYPT, ORDER OF ST

ANTHONY OF ETHIOPIA, KNIGHTS OF ST

ANTHONY OF SYRIA, NUNS OF ST

ANTONIAN ORDER

APOSTLE BROTHERS OF THE POOR LIFE, THE

APOSTLES, ORDER OF THE

APOSTOLATE, SISTERS AUXILIARIES OF THE

APOSTOLIC OBLATES

APOSTOLIC SODALES

APOSTOLINES, FRIARS OF THE ORDER OF THE

ARROUAISIANS

ASSUMPTION, LITTLE SISTERS OF THE

ASSUMPTION, MISSIONARY SISTERS OF THE

ASSUMPTION, OBLATE MISSIONARY SISTERS OF THE

ASSUMPTION, SISTERS OF THE

ASSUMPTION OF THE BLESSED VIRGIN MARY, SISTERS OF THE

ASSUMPTIONISTS

AUBERT, CANONS REGULAR OF ST

AUGUSTINE, CANONESSES REGULAR OF ST – Neuilly-sur-Seine

AUGUSTINE, CANONESSES REGULAR OF ST – WINDESHEIM-LATERAN CONGREGATION

AUGUSTINE, MISSIONARY SISTERS OF ST

AUGUSTINE, ORDER OF ST
AUGUSTINE, ORDER OF THE RECOLLECTS OF ST
AUGUSTINE, PENITENTS OF ST
AUGUSTINIAN (DISCALCED) NUNS IN PORTUGAL
AUGUSTINIAN (DISCALCED) NUNS IN SPAIN
AUGUSTINIAN RECOLLECTS OF THE HEART OF
    JESUS
AUGUSTINIAN RELIGIOUS OF THE MONASTERY
    OF THE VIRGINS – Venice
AUGUSTINIAN SISTERS – Meaux
AUGUSTINIAN SISTERS – Pont de Beauvoisin
AUGUSTINIAN SISTERS OF CHARITY
AUGUSTINIAN SISTERS OF OUR LADY OF
    CONSOLATION
AUGUSTINIAN SISTERS OF THE HOLY HEART OF
    MARY
AUGUSTINIAN SISTERS OF THE HÔTEL-DIEU –
    Carpenteras
AUGUSTINIAN SISTERS OF THE MERCY OF JESUS
AUGUSTINIAN SISTERS OF THE MERCY OF JESUS
AUGUSTINIAN SISTERS OF THE PRECIOUS
    BLOOD
AUGUSTINIAN SISTERS SERVANTS OF JESUS AND
    MARY
AUSTRIA, CANONS REGULAR OF
AUSTRIAN CONGREGATION
AVIZ OF PORTUGAL, KNIGHTS OF
BANNABIKIRA SISTERS
BAPTISTINES
BAPTISTINES
BAPTISTINES
BAPTISTINES
BAPTISTINES
BARNABAS, BROTHERHOOD OF ST – Pennsylvania
BARNABITE FATHERS
BARRATI
BARTHOLOMITES
BARTHOLOMITES
BASIL THE GREAT, ORDER OF ST
BASIL, PRIESTS OF THE COMMUNITY OF ST
BASIL THE GREAT, SISTERS OF THE ORDER OF ST
BEAR, KNIGHTS OF THE
BEC, MONKS OF
BEGHARDS
BEGUINES
BENEDICT, ORDER OF ST – ANGLICAN
BENEDICT, ORDER OF ST – ROMAN CATHOLIC

BENEDICTINE NUNS AND SISTERS – ROMAN
    CATHOLIC
BENEDICTINE SISTERS, MISSIONARY
BENEDICTINE SISTERS OF OUR LADY OF GRACE
    AND COMPASSION
BENEDICTINE SISTERS OF PERPETUAL
    ADORATION
BERNARDINE CISTERCIANS OF ESQUERMES
BERNARDINE SISTERS OF THE THIRD ORDER OF
    ST FRANCIS
BERNARDINES
BETHANY SISTERS
BETHLEHEM, BROTHERS OF
BETHLEHEM FATHERS
BETHLEHEM SISTERS
BETHLEMITA DAUGHTERS OF THE SACRED
    HEART
BETHLEHEMITE FRIARS
BETHLEHEMITES
BLAISE AND ST MARY, KNIGHTS OF ST
BLESSED SACRAMENT, FATHERS OF THE
BLESSED SACRAMENT, MISSIONARIES OF THE
BLESSED SACRAMENT, OBLATE SISTERS OF THE
BLESSED SACRAMENT, POOR VIRGINS OF THE
BLESSED SACRAMENT, SERVANTS OF THE
BLESSED SACRAMENT, SISTERS OF THE
BLESSED SACRAMENT AND OF OUR LADY,
    RELIGIOUS OF THE
BLESSED SACRAMENT FOR INDIANS AND
    COLOURED PEOPLE, SISTERS OF THE
BLESSED TRINITY MISSIONARY INSTITUTE
BLESSED VIRGIN MARY, INSTITUTE OF THE
BLESSED VIRGIN MARY, INSTITUTE OF THE
BLESSED VIRGIN MARY, INSTITUTE OF THE
BLESSED VIRGIN MARY, OBLATES OF THE
BLESSED VIRGIN MARY IMMACULATE, SONS OF
    THE
BLESSED VIRGIN MARY MOTHER OF MERCY,
    BROTHERS OF THE – Tilburg
BLIND SISTERS OF ST PAUL
BLOOD OF CHRIST, SISTERS-ADORERS OF THE
BON SECOURS SISTERS – Paris
BON SECOURS SISTERS – Troyes
BONI HOMINES
BONIFACE, BROTHERHOOD OF ST
BONS HOMMES
BRIDGE-BUILDING BROTHERHOOD

BRIDGET, KNIGHTS OF ST
BRIDGET, ORDER OF THE MOST HOLY SAVIOUR
    AND ST
BRIGID, CONGREGATION OF ST
BRIGITTINE MONKS
BRIGITTINES OF THE RECOLLECTION
BRITTINIANS
BROOM, KNIGHTS OF THE
BUSH BROTHERHOOD
CAESARIUS, NUNS OF ST
CALATREVE, KNIGHTS OF – Toledo
CALATREVE, NUNS OF
CALVARISTS
CALVARY, DAUGHTERS OF MOUNT
CALVARY, ORDER OF OUR LADY OF
CAMALDOLESE NUNS
CAMALDOLESE ORDER
CAMILLUS, ORDER OF ST
CANONESSES REGULAR
CANONESSES SECULAR
CANOSSIAN DAUGHTERS OF CHARITY OF
    VERONA
CAPUCHIN POOR CLARE SISTERS
CARACCIOLO FATHERS
CARITAS CHRISTI
CARITON, MONKS OF THE ORDER OF
CARMELITES
CARMELITES OF MARY IMMACULATE
CARMELITES OF OUR LADY OF PEACE
CARTHUSIANS, ORDER OF
CASIMIR, SISTERS OF ST
CASSIAN MONKS
CASSIAN NUNS
CATECHISTS OF CHRIST THE KING, MISSIONARY
CATECHISTS OF THE HEART OF JESUS
CATHERINE, KNIGHTS OF ST – Mount Sinai
CATHOLIC FOREIGN MISSION SOCIETY OF
    AMERICA
CATHOLIC FOREIGN MISSION SOCIETY OF
    AMERICA, INC.
CELESTINES
CELESTINES
CELESTINES – Provins
CESARIUS, MONKS OF ST
CESARIUS, SISTERS OF ST
CHAPEL, ORDER OF THE
CHARITY, BROTHERS OF – Ghent

CHARITY, BROTHERS AND SISTERS OF
CHARITY, HANDMAIDS OF
CHARITY, INSTITUTE OF
CHARITY, MISSIONARIES OF
CHARITY, MISSIONARY BROTHERS OF
CHARITY, SERVANTS OF
CHARITY, SISTERS OF
CHARITY, SISTERS OF – THE FEDERATION
CHARITY, SISTERS OF – Australia
CHARITY, SISTERS OF – Cincinnati
CHARITY, SISTERS OF – Halifax, Nova Scotia
CHARITY, SISTERS OF – Ireland
CHARITY, SISTERS OF – Leavenworth
CHARITY, SISTERS OF – Nazareth
CHARITY, SISTERS OF – New York
CHARITY, SISTERS OF – Seton Hill
CHARITY AND CHRISTIAN INSTRUCTION,
    SISTERS OF – Nevers
CHARITY OF JESUS AND MARY, SISTERS OF
CHARITY OF OUR LADY MOTHER OF MERCY,
    SISTERS OF
CHARITY OF OUR LADY OF EVRON, SISTERS OF
CHARITY OF OUR LADY OF MERCY, SISTERS OF
CHARITY OF PROVIDENCE, SISTERS OF
CHARITY OF ST AUGUSTINE, SISTERS OF
CHARITY OF ST BARTOLOMEA CAPITANIO AND
    ST VINCENZA GEROSA, SISTERS OF
CHARITY OF ST ELIZABETH, SISTERS OF
CHARITY OF ST HIPPOLYTUS, FRIARS OF
CHARITY OF ST JOAN ANTIDE, SISTERS OF
CHARITY OF ST LOUIS, SISTERS OF – Vannes
CHARITY OF ST PAUL THE APOSTLE, SISTERS OF
    – Chartres
CHARITY OF ST PAUL THE APOSTLE, SISTERS OF
    – Selly Park
CHARITY OF ST VINCENT DE PAUL, DAUGHTERS
    OF
CHARITY OF THE BLESSED VIRGIN MARY, ORDER
    OF
CHARITY OF THE BLESSED VIRGIN MARY,
    SISTERS OF
CHARITY OF THE IMMACULATE CONCEPTION,
    SISTERS OF
CHARITY OF THE INCARNATE WORD, SISTERS OF
    – Houston
CHARITY OF THE INCARNATE WORD, SISTERS OF
    – San Antonio

CHARITY OF THE MOST PRECIOUS BLOOD, DAUGHTERS OF
CHARITY OF THE SACRED HEART OF JESUS, DAUGHTERS OF
CHARLES BORROMEO, MISSIONARIES OF ST
CHARLES BORROMEO, MISSIONARY SISTERS OF ST
CHRIST FOR POLISH EMIGRANTS, SOCIETY OF
CHRIST, MISSIONARY SERVANTS OF
CHRIST, ORDER OF
CHRIST JESUS, MISSIONARIES OF
CHRIST THE KING, KNIGHTS OF
CHRIST THE KING, MISSIONARY SISTERS OF
CHRIST THE KING, MISSIONARY SISTERS OF
CHRIST THE KING, SCHOOL SISTERS OF
CHRIST THE KING, SERVANTS OF
CHRIST THE KING, SISTER-SERVANTS OF
CHRISTA SEVA SANGHA
CHRISTIAN BROTHERS
CHRISTIAN CHARITY OF THE BLESSED VIRGIN MARY, SISTERS OF
CHRISTIAN DOCTRINE, FATHERS OF
CHRISTIAN DOCTRINE, SISTERS OF
CHRISTIAN EDUCATION, RELIGIOUS OF
CHRISTIAN INSTRUCTION, BROTHERS OF – St Gabriel
CHRISTIAN INSTRUCTION, SISTERS OF
CHRISTIAN INSTRUCTION, SISTERS OF – Flone-lez-Amay
CHRISTIAN INSTRUCTION OF PLOERMEL, BROTHERS OF
CHRISTIAN RETREAT, SISTERS OF
CHRISTIAN SCHOOLS, BROTHERS OF THE
CHRISTIAN SCHOOLS, SISTERS OF THE
CHRISTIAN VIRGINS, INSTITUTE OF
CHURCH, SISTERS OF THE
CISTERCIANS (ANGLICAN)
CISTERCIANS (ROMAN CATHOLIC)
CISTERCIANS, ORDER OF (MONKS)
CISTERCIANS, ORDER OF (NUNS)
CISTERCIANS OF THE STRICT OBSERVANCE
CLARETIAN FATHERS
CLERKS REGULAR
CLOTHILDE, SISTERS OF ST
CLUNY, ORDER OF (MONKS)
CLUNY, ORDER OF (NUNS)
CLUNY SISTERS

COLETTINES
COLLEGE OF FOOLS, KNIGHTS OF THE
COLORITO, HERMITS OF
COLUMBAN, MISSIONARY SISTERS OF ST
COLUMBAN, MISSIONARY SOCIETY OF ST
COLUMBANUS, ORDER OF ST
COMMON LIFE, BRETHREN OF THE
COMMON LIFE, ORATORY OF THE
COMPANIONS OF JESUS THE GOOD SHEPHERD, COMMUNITY OF THE
COMPANY OF MARY OUR LADY, SISTERS OF THE
COMPANY OF ST PAUL
COMPASSION OF JESUS, COMMUNITY OF THE
COMPASSIONISTS
CONSOLATA FATHERS
CONSOLATA MISSIONARY SISTERS
CONSTANTINIAN ORDER OF ST GEORGE
CRESCENT MOON, KNIGHTS OF THE
CROSS, DAUGHTERS OF THE – Liège
CROSS, DAUGHTERS OF THE – Torquay
CROSS, DAUGHTERS OF THE HOLY
CROSS, KNIGHTS OF THE
CROSS, RELIGIOUS OF THE
CROSS OF JESUS, BROTHERS OF THE
CROSS OF SAINT ANDREW, DAUGHTERS OF THE
CRUSADERS OF ST MARY
CRUTCHED FRIARS
CULDEES
CYRIL AND METHODIUS, SOCIETY OF STS
DAMIANITES
DEATH, BROTHERS OF
DENIS, CANONS REGULAR OF ST
DENMARK, KNIGHTS OF
DENYS, COMMUNITY OF ST
DIJON AND LANGRES, HOSPITALLERS OF
DIOCESAN LABORER PRIESTS
DISCIPLINE AND THE WHITE EAGLE, KNIGHTS OF THE
DIVINE CHARITY, DAUGHTERS OF
DIVINE COMPASSION, SOCIETY OF
DIVINE HEART, HANDMAIDS OF THE
DIVINE MASTER, PIOUS DISCIPLES OF THE
DIVINE MERCY, INSTITUTE OF
DIVINE MERCY, INSTITUTE OF THE SERVANTS OF
DIVINE MERCY, SOCIETY OF
DIVINE PROVIDENCE, SISTERS OF – San Antonio

DIVINE PROVIDENCE, MISSIONARY CATECHISTS OF

DIVINE PROVIDENCE, POOR SERVANTS OF

DIVINE PROVIDENCE, SISTERS OF

DIVINE PROVIDENCE, SISTERS OF

DIVINE PROVIDENCE, SONS OF

DIVINE PROVIDENCE OF RIBEAUVILLE, SISTERS OF

DIVINE PROVIDENCE OF ST ANDREW OF PELTRE, SISTERS OF

DIVINE PROVIDENCE OF ST MAURITZ, SISTERS OF

DIVINE REDEEMER, SISTERS OF THE

DIVINE SAVIOUR, DAUGHTERS OF THE

DIVINE SAVIOUR, SISTERS OF THE

DIVINE SHEPHERD OF DIVINE PROVIDENCE, SISTERS OF THE

DIVINE WORD, SOCIETY OF THE

DOMINIC, MISSIONARIES OF ST

DOMINIC, ORDER OF ST – Anglican

DOMINIC, ORDER OF ST – Roman Catholic

DOMINICAN CONGREGATION OF OUR LADY OF THE ROSARY OF FATIMA

DOMINICAN CONGREGATION OF OUR LADY OF THE SACRED HEART

DOMINICAN CONGREGATION OF THE SINSINAWA CONGREGATION OF THE MOST HOLY ROSARY

DOMINICAN MISSIONARY SISTERS OF THE MOST SACRED HEART OF JESUS

DOMINICAN NUNS – Farmington Hills

DOMINICAN NUNS – Menlo Park

DOMINICAN NUNS – Oslo

DOMINICAN NUNS – The Bronx

DOMINICAN SISTERS – Amityville

DOMINICAN SISTERS – Bethany

DOMINICAN SISTERS – Caldwell

DOMINICAN SISTERS – Malta

DOMINICAN SISTERS – Maryknoll

DOMINICAN SISTERS OF HOPE

DOMINICAN SISTERS OF ST CATHARINE OF SIENA

DOMINICAN SISTERS OF ST CATHERINE DE RICCI

DOMINICAN SISTERS OF ST CATHERINE OF SIENA – King William's Town

DOMINICAN SISTERS OF ST CATHERINE OF SIENA – Newcastle

DOMINICAN SISTERS OF ST CATHERINE OF SIENA – Oakford

DOMINICAN SISTERS OF ST CATHERINE OF SIENA OF RACINE

DOMINICAN SISTERS OF ST CECILIA

DOMINICAN SISTERS OF ST DOMINIC – Akron

DOMINICAN SISTERS OF ST MARY OF THE SPRINGS

DOMINICAN SISTERS OF THE CONGREGATION OF BROOKLINE

DOMINICAN SISTERS OF THE CONGREGATION OF OUR LADY OF THE ROSARY

DOMINICAN SISTERS OF THE CONGREGATION OF ST CATHERINE OF SIENA – Kenosha

DOMINICAN SISTERS OF THE CONGREGATION OF THE HOLY CROSS

DOMINICAN SISTERS OF THE CONGREGATION OF THE MOST HOLY ROSARY

DOMINICAN SISTERS OF THE ENGLISH CONGREGATION OF ST CATHERINE OF SIENA

DOMINICAN SISTERS OF THE MOST HOLY NAME OF JESUS – San Rafael

DOMINICAN SISTERS OF THE PRESENTATION OF TOURS

DOMINICAN SISTERS OF THE QUEEN OF THE MOST HOLY ROSARY

DOMINICAN SISTERS OF THE RELIEF OF INCURABLE CANCER

DOMINICAN SISTERS OF THE ROMAN CONGREGATION

DOMINICAN SISTERS OF THE SACRED HEART

DOMINICAN SISTERS OF THE THIRD ORDER – Great Bend

DOMINICAN SISTERS OF THE THIRD ORDER – Springfield

DOMINICAN SISTERS – Western Australia

DON BOSCO INSTITUTE

DON BOSCO VOLUNTEERS

DOROTHY, ORDER OF ST

DOROTHY OF CEMMO, SISTERS OF ST

DRAGON, KNIGHTS OF THE

EAR OF CORN, KNIGHTS OF THE

EDITH STEIN COMMUNITY, THE ST

EDMUND, SOCIETY OF ST

ELEPHANT, KNIGHTS OF THE

ELIGIUS IN FRANCE, THE NUNS OF ST

ELIZABETH, SISTERS OF ST

EPIPHANY, COMMUNITY OF THE
EPIPHANY, OXFORD MISSION BROTHERHOOD OF THE
EPIPHANY, OXFORD MISSION SISTERHOOD OF THE
EPIPHANY, SOCIETY OF THE
EUCHARIST, RELIGIOUS OF THE
EUCHARIST, SOCIETY OF THE DAUGHTERS OF THE
EUCHARISTIC FRANCISCAN MISSIONARIES
EVORA AND AVIZ, KNIGHTS OF
FAITH OF JESUS, CLERKS REGULAR OF THE
FAITHFUL COMPANIONS OF JESUS
FAITHFUL VIRGINS, DAUGHTERS OF THE
FATHER KOLBE MISSIONARIES OF THE IMMACULATA
FELIX, SISTERS OF ST
FEUILLANTS, ORDER OF
FIDELITY, ORDER OF
FILIPPINI RELIGIOUS TEACHERS
FINDING OF JESUS IN THE TEMPLE, SISTERS OF THE
FLEURY, ABBEY OF
FONTEVRAULT, ORDER OF
FOREIGN MISSION SOCIETY OF QUEBEC
FOREIGN MISSIONS, INSTITUTE FOR – Yarumal
FOREIGN MISSIONS OF PARIS, SOCIETY OF
FRANCES OF ROME, OBLATES OF ST
FRANCIS DE SALES, MISSIONARIES OF ST
FRANCIS DE SALES, OBLATE SISTERS OF ST
FRANCIS DE SALES, OBLATES OF ST
FRANCISCANS – ANGLICAN
FRANCISCAN SERVANTS OF JESUS AND MARY
FRANCISCANS – ROMAN CATHOLIC
FRANCISCAN CONGREGATIONS
FRISIA, KNIGHTS OF
FRUCTUOSUS, ORDER OF ST
GABRIEL, BROTHERS OF ST
GENEVIEVE, CANONS REGULAR OF ST
GENEVIEVE, DAUGHTERS OF ST
GEORGE IN ALGA, CANONS REGULAR OF ST
GEORGE, ORDERS OF KNIGHTS OF ST
GEORGE OF ALFAMA, KNIGHTS OF ST
GEREON IN THE EAST, KNIGHTS OF ST
GILBERT OF SEMPRINGHAM, CANONS REGULAR AND NUNS OF ST
GIRDLE, LADIES OF THE

GLORIOUS ASCENSION, COMMUNITY OF THE
GOLDEN FLEECE, KNIGHTS OF THE
GOLDEN SPUR, ORDER OF THE
GONZAGA, HERMITS OF
GOOD SAMARITAN, SISTERS OF THE
GOOD SAVIOUR, DAUGHTERS OF THE
GOOD SHEPHERD, LITTLE BROTHERS OF THE
GOOD SONS, CONGREGATION OF THE
GOSPEL OF CHARLES DE FOUCAULD, LITTLE SISTERS OF THE
GRANDMONT, HERMITS AND THE ORDER OF
GREEN SHIELD, KNIGHTS OF THE
GREGORY THE GREAT, ORDER OF ST
GREY NUNS – Beauport
GREY NUNS – St Hyacinthe
GREY NUNS OF THE CROSS
GREY NUNS OF THE SACRED HEART
GREY SISTERS – Melbourne
GREY SISTERS – Montreal
GREY SISTERS OF THE IMMACULATE CONCEPTION
GUARDIAN ANGEL, SISTERS OF THE
GUASTALLA, VIRGINS OF
HATCHET, ORDER OF THE
HEART OF JESUS, INSTITUTE OF PRIESTS OF THE
HEART OF JESUS, MISSIONARIES OF THE
HEART OF MARY, DAUGHTERS OF THE
HEDWIG, SOCIETY OF ST
HELENA, ORDER OF ST
HIPPOLITES
HOLY AND UNDIVIDED TRINITY, SOCIETY OF THE
HOLY CHILD JESUS, SOCIETY OF THE
HOLY CHILD JESUS OF THE THIRD ORDER REGULAR OF ST FRANCIS, SERVANTS OF THE
HOLY CHILDHOOD OF JESUS, INSTITUTE OF THE
HOLY CROSS, BROTHERHOOD OF THE
HOLY CROSS, CONGREGATION OF
HOLY CROSS, MARIANITES OF
HOLY CROSS, ORDER OF THE
HOLY CROSS, SERVANTS OF THE
HOLY CROSS, SISTERS OF THE – USA
HOLY CROSS, SOCIETY OF THE
HOLY CROSS, TEACHING SISTERS OF THE – Menzingen
HOLY FAITH, SISTERS OF THE
HOLY FAMILY, ASSOCIATION OF THE – Bordeaux

HOLY FAMILY, BROTHERS OF THE – Belley
HOLY FAMILY, COMMUNITY OF THE
HOLY FAMILY, INSTITUTE OF THE SISTERS OF
  THE
HOLY FAMILY, LITTLE SISTERS OF THE
HOLY FAMILY, LITTLE SISTERS OF THE –
  Sherbrooke
HOLY FAMILY, MISSIONARIES OF THE
HOLY FAMILY, MISSIONARY SISTERS OF THE
HOLY FAMILY, SISTERS OF THE – New Orleans
HOLY FAMILY, SISTERS OF THE – San Jose
HOLY FAMILY, SISTERS OF THE – Villefranche-de-
  Rouergue
HOLY FAMILY, SONS OF THE
HOLY FAMILY OF NAZARETH, SISTERS OF THE
HOLY GHOST, HOSPITALLERS OF THE
HOLY GHOST, ORDER OF THE – CLERKS
  REGULAR
HOLY GHOST, ORDER OF THE – NUNS
HOLY GHOST, SISTERS OF THE – Ohio
HOLY GHOST, SISTERS OF THE – Pittsburgh
HOLY GHOST AND OF THE IMMACULATE HEART
  OF MARY, CONGREGATION OF THE
HOLY HEART OF MARY, DAUGHTERS OF THE
HOLY HEART OF MARY, SISTERS-SERVANTS OF
  THE
HOLY HUMILITY OF THE BLESSED VIRGIN MARY,
  SISTERS OF THE
HOLY INFANCY, BROTHERS OF THE
HOLY MARTYRS IN PALESTINE, KNIGHTS OF THE
HOLY NAME, COMMUNITY OF THE
HOLY NAME, COMMUNITY OF THE
HOLY NAME, COMMUNITY OF THE – Lesotho
HOLY NAME, COMMUNITY OF THE – Zululand
HOLY NAME COMMUNITY
HOLY NAME OF JESUS, CONGREGATION OF THE
HOLY NAME OF JESUS, SISTERHOOD OF THE
HOLY NAMES OF JESUS AND MARY, SISTERS OF
  THE
HOLY NATIVITY, SISTERHOOD OF THE
HOLY PARACLETE, ORDER OF THE
HOLY PARACLETE, SERVANTS OF THE
HOLY REDEEMER, CONGREGATION OF THE –
  Bologna
HOLY REDEEMER, SISTERS OF THE
HOLY ROOD, COMMUNITY OF THE
HOLY ROSARY, MISSIONARY SISTERS OF THE

HOLY SAVIOUR, KNIGHTS OF THE ORDER OF
  THE – Aragon
HOLY SEPULCHRE, CANONESSES REGULAR OF
  THE
HOLY SEPULCHRE, CANONS REGULAR OF THE
HOLY SEPULCHRE OF JERUSALEM, KNIGHTS/
  DAMES OF THE
HOLY SOULS, HELPERS OF THE
HOLY SPIRIT, COMMUNITY OF THE
HOLY SPIRIT, CONGREGATION OF DAUGHTERS
  OF THE
HOLY SPIRIT, MISSION SISTERS OF THE
HOLY SPIRIT, MISSIONARIES OF THE
HOLY SPIRIT, MISSIONARY SISTERS OF THE
HOLY SPIRIT, ORDER OF THE
HOLY SPIRIT AND MARY IMMACULATE, SISTERS-
  SERVANTS OF THE
HOLY SPIRIT OF PERPETUAL ADORATION,
  SISTERS-SERVANTS OF THE
HOLY STIGMATA, CONGREGATION OF THE
HOLY TRINITY, SOCIETY OF THE
HOLY UNION OF THE SACRED HEARTS OF JESUS
  AND MARY, SISTERS OF THE
HOME MISSION SISTERS OF AMERICA
HOME MISSIONERS OF AMERICA, THE
HOPE, SISTERS OF
HUBERT, KNIGHTS OF ST
HUMILIATI
HUMILIATI
IDENTE MISSIONARIES OF CHRIST CRUCIFIED
IMITATION OF CHRIST
IMMACULATE CONCEPTION, CANONS REGULAR
  OF THE
IMMACULATE CONCEPTION, KNIGHTS OF THE
  ORDER OF THE
IMMACULATE CONCEPTION, LITTLE SERVANT-
  SISTERS OF THE
IMMACULATE CONCEPTION, LITTLE SISTERS OF
  THE
IMMACULATE CONCEPTION, MISSION PRIESTS
  OF THE
IMMACULATE CONCEPTION, MISSIONARIES OF
  THE – Lourdes
IMMACULATE CONCEPTION, MISSIONARY
  SISTERS OF THE
IMMACULATE CONCEPTION, SISTERS OF THE
IMMACULATE CONCEPTION, SISTERS OF THE

IMMACULATE CONCEPTION, SISTERS OF THE

IMMACULATE CONCEPTION, SISTERS OF THE

IMMACULATE CONCEPTION, SISTERS OF THE – Armenian

IMMACULATE CONCEPTION, SISTERS OF THE – St Meen

IMMACULATE CONCEPTION OF OUR LADY OF LOURDES, SISTERS OF THE

IMMACULATE CONCEPTION OF THE BLESSED VIRGIN MARY, CONGREGATION OF THE

IMMACULATE CONCEPTION OF THE BLESSED VIRGIN MARY, SISTERS OF THE – Lithuania

IMMACULATE CONCEPTION OF THE MOTHER OF GOD, MISSIONARY SISTERS OF THE

IMMACULATE HEART OF MARY, BROTHERS OF THE

IMMACULATE HEART OF MARY, CONGREGATION OF THE

IMMACULATE HEART OF MARY, DAUGHTERS OF THE – Rennes

IMMACULATE HEART OF MARY, HERMITS OF THE

IMMACULATE HEART OF MARY, MISSIONARY SISTERS OF THE

IMMACULATE HEART OF MARY, SISTERS OF THE – Arizona

IMMACULATE HEART OF MARY, SISTERS OF THE – Blon

IMMACULATE HEART OF MARY, SISTERS OF THE – Porto Alegre

IMMACULATE HEART OF MARY, SISTERS OF THE – Wichita

IMMACULATE HEART OF MARY, SISTERS-SERVANTS OF THE – Immaculata

IMMACULATE HEART OF MARY, SISTERS-SERVANTS OF THE – Michigan

IMMACULATE HEART OF MARY, SISTERS-SERVANTS OF THE – Scranton

IMMACULATE HEART OF MARY AND OF THE GOOD SHEPHERD, SISTERS-SERVANTS OF THE

INCARNATE WORD, INSTITUTE OF THE

INCARNATE WORD AND THE BLESSED SACRAMENT, SISTERS OF THE

INCARNATE WORD AND THE BLESSED SACRAMENT, SISTERS OF THE

INCARNATE WORD AND THE BLESSED SACRAMENT, SISTERS OF THE

INCARNATE WORD AND THE BLESSED SACRAMENT, SISTERS OF THE – Corpus Christi

INCARNATION OF THE ETERNAL SON, SOCIETY OF THE

INFANT JESUS, CONGREGATION OF THE

INFANT JESUS, SISTERS OF THE

INFIRMARIANS OF ST FRANCIS, SISTERS

INSTRUCTION OF THE INFANT JESUS, SISTERS OF THE

ISIDORE, NUNS OF ST

JAMES, BROTHERHOOD OF ST

JAMES, SISTERHOOD OF ST

JAMES OF ALTOPASCIO, ORDER OF ST

JAMES OF HAUT-PAS, ORDER OF ST

JAMES OF THE SWORD, CANONS REGULAR OF ST

JAMES OF THE SWORD, KNIGHTS OF ST

JAMES OF THE SWORD, NUNS OF ST

JAMES THE APOSTLE, MISSIONARY SOCIETY OF ST

JEROME, HERMITS OF ST – LUPO OLMEDO REFORM

JEROME, MONKS OF THE ORDER OF ST

JEROME, NUNS OF THE ORDER OF ST

JEROME OF BLESSED PETER OF PISA, HERMITS OF ST

JEROME OF FIESOLE, HERMITS OF ST

JESUATS

JESUATS, CONGREGATION OF

JESUS, CONGREGATION OF THE DAUGHTERS OF

JESUS, DAUGHTERS OF

JESUS, FRATERNITY OF THE LITTLE BROTHERS OF

JESUS, MISSIONARIES OF

JESUS, FRATERNITY OF THE LITTLE SISTERS OF

JESUS, SOCIETY OF

JESUS AND MARY, CONGREGATION OF

JESUS AND MARY, LITTLE SISTERS OF

JESUS AND MARY, RELIGIOUS OF

JESUS CARITAS FRATERNITY

JESUS CHRIST, POOR HANDMAIDS OF

JESUS CHRIST CRUCIFIED AND THE SORROWFUL MOTHER, POOR SISTERS OF

JESUS CRUCIFIED, CONGREGATION OF

JESUS ETERNAL PRIEST, MISSIONARY SISTERS OF

JESUS, MARY AND JOSEPH, MISSIONARY SISTERS OF

JESUS OF CHARITY, SISTERS-SERVANTS OF

JESUS OF NAZARETH, COMMUNITY OF

JESUS THE ETERNAL PRIEST, HERMITS OF

JESUS THE GOOD SHEPHERD, COMMUNITY OF
THE COMPANIONS OF

JOAN OF ARC, CONGREGATION OF SISTERS OF
ST

JOHN, CONTEMPLATIVE SISTERS OF ST

JOHN, SOCIETY OF ST

JOHN AND THOMAS, KNIGHTS OF THE ORDER
OF STS

JOHN LATERAN, CANONS REGULAR OF ST

JOHN OF CHARTRES, CANONS REGULAR OF ST

JOHN OF GOD, BROTHERS HOSPITALLERS OF ST

JOHN OF GOD, SISTERS OF ST

JOHN OF JERUSALEM, CANONESSES OF THE
ORDER OF ST

JOHN THE BAPTIST, CANONS REGULAR OF ST

JOHN THE BAPTIST, COMMUNITY OF ST

JOHN THE BAPTIST, COMMUNITY OF ST

JOHN THE BAPTIST, HERMITS OF ST

JOHN THE BAPTIST, SISTERS OF ST

JOHN THE BAPTIST OF PENITENCE, HERMITS OF
ST

JOHN THE BELOVED, ORDER OF ST

JOHN THE DIVINE, NURSING SISTERS OF

JOHN THE DIVINE, SISTERHOOD OF ST

JOHN THE DIVINE, SOCIETY OF ST

JOHN THE EVANGELIST, SISTERS OF ST

JOHN THE EVANGELIST, SISTERS OF THE
COMMUNITY OF ST

JOHN THE EVANGELIST, SOCIETY OF ST

JOSEPH, CONGREGATION OF SISTERS OF ST –
Annecy

JOSEPH, CONGREGATION OF SISTERS OF ST –
Baden

JOSEPH, CONGREGATION OF SISTERS OF ST –
Bordeaux

JOSEPH, CONGREGATION OF SISTERS OF ST –
Boston

JOSEPH, CONGREGATION OF SISTERS OF ST –
Brentwood

JOSEPH, CONGREGATION OF SISTERS OF ST –
Buffalo

JOSEPH, CONGREGATION OF SISTERS OF ST –
Burlington

JOSEPH, CONGREGATION OF SISTERS OF ST –
Canada

JOSEPH, CONGREGATION OF SISTERS OF ST –
Carondelet

JOSEPH, CONGREGATION OF SISTERS OF ST –
Chambéry

JOSEPH, CONGREGATION OF SISTERS OF ST –
Chestnut Hill

JOSEPH, CONGREGATION OF SISTERS OF ST –
Cleveland

JOSEPH, CONGREGATION OF SISTERS OF ST –
Cluny

JOSEPH, CONGREGATION OF SISTERS OF ST –
Concordia

JOSEPH, CONGREGATION OF SISTERS OF ST – Erie

JOSEPH, CONGREGATION OF SISTERS OF ST –
Lafayette/Tipton

JOSEPH, CONGREGATION OF SISTERS OF ST – La
Grange

JOSEPH, CONGREGATION OF SISTERS OF ST – Le
Puy

JOSEPH, CONGREGATION OF SISTERS OF ST –
Lyons

JOSEPH, CONGREGATION OF SISTERS OF ST –
Medaille

JOSEPH, CONGREGATION OF SISTERS OF ST –
Nazareth

JOSEPH, CONGREGATION OF SISTERS OF ST –
Orange

JOSEPH, CONGREGATION OF SISTERS OF ST –
Rochester

JOSEPH, CONGREGATION OF SISTERS OF ST – St
Augustine

JOSEPH, CONGREGATION OF SISTERS OF ST – St
Vallier

JOSEPH, CONGREGATION OF SISTERS OF ST –
Springfield

JOSEPH, CONGREGATION OF SISTERS OF ST –
Watertown

JOSEPH, CONGREGATION OF SISTERS OF ST –
Wheeling

JOSEPH, CONGREGATION OF SISTERS OF ST –
Wichita

JOSEPH, HOSPITALLERS OF ST

JOSEPH, LITTLE DAUGHTERS OF ST – Canada

JOSEPH, LITTLE DAUGHTERS OF ST – Italy

JOSEPH, MEDICAL SISTERS OF ST

JOSEPH, OBLATES OF ST – Asti

JOSEPH, ORDER OF ST

JOSEPH, POOR SISTERS OF ST
JOSEPH, RELIGIOUS DAUGHTERS OF ST
JOSEPH, SERVANTS OF ST
JOSEPH, SISTERS OF ST – St Hyacinthe
JOSEPH, SISTERS OF ST – Tarbes
JOSEPH, THE WORKING BROTHERS OF ST
JOSEPH CALASANZIO, CONGREGATION OF THE
   CHRISTIAN WORKERS OF ST
JOSEPH OF MURIALDO, CONGREGATION OF ST
JOSEPH OF NAZARETH, SISTERHOOD OF ST
JOSEPH OF PEACE, SISTERS OF ST
JOSEPH OF ST MARK, SISTERS OF ST
JOSEPH OF THE APPARITION, SISTERS OF ST
JOSEPH OF THE SACRED HEART, SOCIETY OF ST
JOSEPH OF THE SACRED HEART OF JESUS,
   SISTERS OF ST
JOSEPH OF THE THIRD ORDER OF ST FRANCIS,
   SISTERS OF ST
JOSEPH THE WORKER, SISTERS OF ST
JOSEPHITE FATHERS
JULIAN OF NORWICH, ORDER OF
KAISERSWERTH ALLIANCE
KATHARINE OF EGYPT, COMMUNITY OF ST
KINGSHIP OF CHRIST, MISSIONARIES OF THE
KNOT, KNIGHTS OF THE
LA SALETTE FATHERS
LAMB OF GOD, KNIGHTS OF THE
LAMB OF GOD, SISTERS OF THE
LAUDUS, CANONS REGULAR OF ST
LAURENCE, BROTHERHOOD OF ST
LAURENCE, COMMUNITY OF ST
LAZARUS AND OUR LADY OF MOUNT CARMEL,
   KNIGHTS OF ST
LAZARUS OF JERUSALEM, ORDER OF ST
LEGIONARIES OF CHRIST
LÉRINS, THE ABBEY OF
LIFE, SISTERS OF
LILY, KNIGHTS OF THE
LITTLE ONES, SISTERS OF THE
LITTLE SCHOOLS, SISTERS OF THE
LIVING WORD, SISTERS OF THE
LOCHES, HOSPITALLERS OF
LORD JESUS CHRIST, DISCIPLES OF THE
LORETTO AT THE FOOT OF THE CROSS, SISTERS
   OF
LOUIS, SISTERS OF ST
LOVE OF CHRIST, THE BROTHERHOOD OF THE

LOVE OF GOD, COMMUNITY OF SISTERS OF THE
LOVE OF GOD, SISTERS OF THE
LOVERS OF THE HOLY CROSS SISTERS
MACARIUS, HERMITS OF ST
MACARIUS IN EGYPT, NUNS OF ST
MADONNA HOUSE
MAESTRE PIE VENERINI SISTERS
MAGDALEN, NUNS OF ST
MALTA, KNIGHTS (and DAMES) OF THE
   SOVEREIGN MILITARY ORDER OF
MARCELLINA, SISTERS OF ST
MARCELLINA, INTERNATIONAL INSTITUTE OF
   SISTERS OF ST
MARGARET, SOCIETY OF ST
MARIAN FATHERS OF THE IMMACULATE
   CONCEPTION OF THE BLESSED VIRGIN
   MARY, CONGREGATION OF THE
MARIAN INSTITUTE OF ST FRANCIS DE SALES
MARIAN SISTERS OF THE DIOCESE OF LINCOLN
MARIAN SOCIETY OF DOMINICAN CATECHISTS
MARIANIST SISTERS
MARIANNHILL, CONGREGATION OF
   MISSIONARIES OF
MARIE, CONGREGATION OF SAINTE
MARIE-AUXILIATRICE, SOCIETY OF SISTERS OF
MARIE-MAGDALEN POSTEL, SISTERS OF ST
MARIE REPARATRICE, INSTITUTE OF
MARIST BROTHERS
MARIST FATHERS, THE
MARIST MISSIONARY SISTERS, THE
MARIST SISTERS, THE
MARK, CANONS REGULAR OF ST
MARK OF VENICE, KNIGHTS OF ST
MARTHA, SISTERS OF ST – Périgueux
MARTHE, SISTERS HOSPITALLERS OF ST
MARTIN, CANONS REGULAR OF ST
MARTIN OF TOURS, CONGREGATION OF SISTERS
   OF ST
MARY, EVANGELICAL SOCIETY OF – Darmstadt
MARY, HANDMAIDS OF
MARY, LITTLE COMPANY OF
MARY, LITTLE FRANCISCANS OF
MARY, MEDICAL MISSIONARIES OF
MARY, MISSIONARIES OF THE COMPANY OF
MARY, MISSIONARY SOCIETY OF
MARY, SERVANTS OF
MARY, SERVANTS OF

MARY, SISTERS OF ST – Namur
MARY, SISTERS-HOME VISITORS OF
MARY, SOCIETY OF
MARY, THE LADIES OF
MARY, XAVERIAN MISSIONARY SISTERS OF
MARY HEALTH OF THE SICK, DAUGHTERS OF
MARY HELP OF CHRISTIANS, DAUGHTERS OF
MARY IMMACULATE, DAUGHTERS OF
MARY IMMACULATE, OBLATE MISSIONARIES OF
MARY IMMACULATE, OBLATES OF
MARY IMMACULATE, PARISH VISITORS OF
MARY IMMACULATE, SISTERS OF
MARY IMMACULATE, SISTERS-SERVANTS OF
MARY IMMACULATE AND THE SACRED HEART,
   THE HANDMAIDS OF
MARY-JOSEPH AND OF MERCY, SISTERS OF
MARY MAGDALEN, THE ORDER OF ST
MARY MOTHER OF GOD, SISTERS OF
MARY MOTHER OF THE CHURCH, DAUGHTERS
   OF
MARY MOTHER OF THE CHURCH, SISTERS OF
MARY MOTHER OF THE EUCHARIST, SISTERS OF
MARY OF GUADALUPE FOR FOREIGN MISSIONS,
   INSTITUTE OF ST
MARY OF JERUSALEM, ORDER OF TEUTONIC
   KNIGHTS OF ST (Teutonic Order)
MARY OF NAZARETH AND CALVARY,
   COMMUNITY OF ST
MARY OF OREGON, SISTERS OF ST
MARY OF PROVIDENCE, DAUGHTERS OF ST
MARY OF THE IMMACULATE CONCEPTION,
   DAUGHTERS OF
MARY REPARATRIX, SOCIETY OF ST
MARY THE VIRGIN, COMMUNITY OF ST
MAUR, CONGREGATION OF ST
MAURICE, CANONS REGULAR OF THE ABBEY OF
   ST
MAURICE AND LAZARUS, KNIGHTS OF ST
MECHITARISTS, ORDER OF
MEDICAL MISSIONARY SISTERS, SOCIETY OF
MERCEDARIAN SISTERS OF THE BLESSED
   SACRAMENT
MERCY, BROTHERS OF
MERCY, PRIESTS OF
MERCY, SISTERS OF
MERCY OF ALMA, RELIGIOUS SISTERS OF

MERCY OF OUR LADY OF PERPETUAL HELP,
   BROTHERS OF
MERCY OF ST CHARLES BORROMEO, SISTERS OF
MERCY OF SEES, SISTERS OF
MERCY OF THE BLESSED SACRAMENT, SISTERS
   OF
MERCY OF THE CHRISTIAN SCHOOLS, SISTERS
   OF
MERCY OF THE HOLY CROSS, SISTERS OF
MICHAEL IN FRANCE, KNIGHTS OF ST
MICHAEL'S WING, KNIGHTS OF ST
MILITIA JESU CHRISTI
MILL HILL FATHERS
MINIM DAUGHTERS OF MARY IMMACULATE
MINIM FATHERS
MINIM SISTERS OF SORROWS
MISERICORDIA SISTERS
MONS, CANONESSES OF
MONTE LUCO, HERMITS OF
MONTE SENARIO, HERMITS OF
MONTESA, KNIGHTS OF
MOST BLESSED TRINITY, MISSIONARY SERVANTS
   OF THE
MOST HOLY AND IMMACULATE HEART OF
   MARY, CALIFORNIA INSTITUTE OF THE
   SISTERS OF THE
MOST HOLY REDEEMER, OBLATES OF THE
MOST HOLY SACRAMENT, SISTERS OF THE –
   Lafayette
MOST HOLY TRINITY, HANDMAIDS OF THE
MOST HOLY TRINITY, MISSIONARY SERVANTS OF
   THE
MOST HOLY TRINITY, ORDER OF THE – FRIARS,
   CALCED AND DISCALCED
MOST HOLY TRINITY, ORDER OF THE –
   INSTITUTES OF TRINITARIAN SISTERS
MOST HOLY TRINITY, ORDER OF THE – NUNS,
   CALCED
MOST HOLY TRINITY, ORDER OF THE – NUNS
   DISCALCED
MOST PRECIOUS BLOOD OF OUR LORD JESUS
   CHRIST, SISTERS OF THE
MOST SACRED HEART OF JESUS, MISSIONARY
   SISTERS OF THE – Hiltrup
MOST SACRED HEART OF JESUS, SERVANTS OF
   THE

MOTHER OF GOD, CLERKS REGULAR OF THE – Lucca

MOTHER OF GOD, MISSIONARY SISTERS OF THE

MOTHER OF GOD, POOR SERVANTS OF THE

MOTHERS OF THE HELPLESS

MOUNT CALVARY, DAUGHTERS OF

MOUNT CALVARY, MISSIONARY SOCIETY OF

MOUNT CALVARY, NUNS OF THE ORDER OF

NAME OF JESUS, COMMUNITY OF THE

NATIVITY OF OUR LORD, INSTITUTE OF THE SISTERS OF THE

NATIVITY OF THE BLESSED VIRGIN, SISTERS OF THE

NAZARETH, POOR SISTERS OF

NAZARETH, THE LADIES OF

NORTH AMERICAN UNION OF SISTERS OF OUR LADY OF CHARITY

NOTRE DAME, CONGREGATION OF SISTERS OF – Namur

NOTRE DAME, SCHOOL-SISTERS OF

NOTRE DAME, SISTERS OF

NOTRE DAME, SISTERS OF THE CONGREGATION OF

NOTRE DAME SISTERS

OAK TREE, KNIGHTS OF THE

OBREGONIANS

OPUS DEI

OPUS SPIRITUS SANCTI

ORATORIANS

ORATORY, DAUGHTERS OF THE

ORATORY OF JESUS AND OF MARY IMMACULATE OF FRANCE

ORATORY OF THE GOOD SHEPHERD

OUR LADY HELP OF THE CLERGY, CONGREGATION OF

OUR LADY MOTHER OF MERCY, BROTHERS OF (and SISTERS OF)

OUR LADY OF AFRICA, MISSIONARY SISTERS OF

OUR LADY OF ALLTAGRACIA, INSTITUTE OF

OUR LADY OF BETHANY, MISSION OF

OUR LADY OF CHARITY, SISTERS OF

OUR LADY OF CHARITY OF THE GOOD SHEPHERD, SISTERS OF

OUR LADY OF CHRISTIAN DOCTRINE, SISTERS OF

OUR LADY OF COMPASSION, SISTERS OF

OUR LADY OF COMPASSION, SISTERS OF

OUR LADY OF CONSOLATION, ORDER OF

OUR LADY OF CONSOLATION, SISTERS OF

OUR LADY OF FIDELITY, SISTERS OF

OUR LADY OF GOOD AND PERPETUAL SUCCOUR, SISTERS OF

OUR LADY OF MERCY, BROTHERS OF

OUR LADY OF MERCY, DAUGHTERS OF

OUR LADY OF MERCY, ORDER OF

OUR LADY OF MERCY, ORDER OF NUNS OF

OUR LADY OF MERCY, ORDER OF THE DISCALCED FATHERS OF

OUR LADY OF MERCY AND THE DIVINE MASTER, DAUGHTERS OF

OUR LADY OF MONTJOIE IN THE HOLY LAND, KNIGHTS OF

OUR LADY OF MOUNT CARMEL, HERMITS OF

OUR LADY OF MOUNT CARMEL, KNIGHTS OF

OUR LADY OF MOUNT CARMEL, SISTERS OF

OUR LADY OF PERPETUAL HELP, SISTERS OF

OUR LADY OF PITY, SISTERS OF

OUR LADY OF PROVIDENCE, DAUGHTERS OF

OUR LADY OF SION, CONGREGATION OF

OUR LADY OF SORROWS, SISTERS OF

OUR LADY OF THE APOSTLES, MISSIONARY SISTERS OF

OUR LADY OF THE HOLY ROSARY, SISTERS OF

OUR LADY OF THE IMMACULATE CONCEPTION, SISTERS OF

OUR LADY OF THE MISSIONS, SISTERS OF

OUR LADY OF THE MOST HOLY TRINITY, SOCIETY OF

OUR LADY OF THE RETREAT IN THE CENACLE, CONGREGATION OF

OUR LADY OF THE SACRED HEART, DAUGHTERS OF

OUR LADY OF THE SEVEN DOLOURS, LITTLE RELIGIOUS OF

OUR LADY OF THE WAY, SOCIETY OF

OUR LADY OF VICTORY, MISSIONARY SISTERS OF

OUR LADY QUEEN OF THE CLERGY, SERVANTS OF

OUR MOTHER OF PEACE, DAUGHTERS OF

OUR SAVIOUR, CANONS REGULAR OF – Lorraine

OUR SAVIOUR, CLERKS REGULAR OF

PACHOMIUS, MONKS OF ST

PACHOMIUS, NUNS OF ST

PALLOTTINE FATHERS

PALLOTTINE MISSIONARY SISTERS
PALLOTTINE SISTERS
PAMPLONA, CANONS REGULAR OF
PARACLETE, ORDER OF THE
PARIS FOREIGN MISSION SOCIETY
PASSION, MISSIONARIES OF THE
PASSION, SECULAR MISSIONARIES OF THE
PASSION OF JESUS CHRIST, KNIGHTS OF THE
PASSION OF OUR LORD JESUS CHRIST AND THE
   SORROWS OF MARY, DAUGHTERS OF THE
PASSIONIST FATHERS
PASSIONIST NUNS
PASSIONIST SISTERS
PASSIONIST SISTERS OF ST PAUL OF THE CROSS
PATRICK, BROTHERS OF ST
PATRICK'S MISSIONARY SOCIETY, ST
PAUL, ANGELICAL SISTERS OF ST
PAUL, BROTHERHOOD OF ST
PAUL, DAUGHTERS OF ST
PAUL, HERMITS OF ST
PAUL, HERMITS OF ST – Portugal
PAUL THE APOSTLE, SOCIETY OF MISSIONARY
   PRIESTS OF ST
PAULINE FATHERS AND BROTHERS
PENANCE, RELIGIOUS ORDER OF
PENITENTIAL ORDER OF HOLY MARTYRS
PENITENTS OF OUR LADY OF REFUGE
PERPETUAL ADORATION, INSTITUTE OF
PERPETUAL ADORATION, SISTERS OF
PERPETUAL ADORATION OF THE BLESSED
   SACRAMENT, ORDER OF THE
PERPETUAL ADORATION OF THE MOST BLESSED
   SACRAMENT, SISTERS OF THE
PETER, COMMUNITY OF ST
PETER, COMMUNITY OF ST – Horbury
PETER, PRIESTLY FRATERNITY OF ST
PETER, SOLITARY NUNS OF ST
PETER AD VINCULA, CONGREGATION OF ST
PETER CLAVER, MISSIONARY SISTERS OF ST
PETER OF ALCÁNTARA, FRIARS OF THE
   OBSERVANCE OF ST
PETER OF MONTE CORBULO, CANONS REGULAR
   OF ST
PHILIP NERI, NUNS OF ST
PIARIST FATHERS
PICPUS FATHERS, THE
PICPUS SISTERS

PIOUS KNIGHTS, PONTIFICAL ORDER OF
PIOUS SCHOOLS, SISTERS OF THE
PIUS IX, ORDER OF
PIUS X, BROTHERS OF ST
POLAND, CANONS REGULAR OF
PONTIFICAL INSTITUTE FOR MISSIONARY
   EXTENSION
POOR, LITTLE SISTERS OF THE
POOR, SISTERS-SERVANTS OF THE
POOR CHILD JESUS, SISTERS OF THE
POOR CLARE MISSIONARY SISTERS
POOR CLARES
POOR CLARES – Newry
POOR CLARES OF PERPETUAL ADORATION
POOR CLARES OF REPARATION AND ADORATION
POOR INFIRMARIANS
POOR OF ST CATHERINE OF SIENA, SISTERS OF
   THE
POPE ST SYLVESTER, ORDER OF
PRADO, SOCIETY OF PRIESTS OF THE
PRECIOUS BLOOD, DAUGHTERS OF THE
PRECIOUS BLOOD, HANDMAIDS OF THE
PRECIOUS BLOOD, KNIGHTS OF THE
PRECIOUS BLOOD, MISSIONARY SISTERS OF THE
PRECIOUS BLOOD, SISTER ADORERS OF THE
PRECIOUS BLOOD, SISTERS OF THE
PRECIOUS BLOOD, SOCIETY OF THE
PRECIOUS BLOOD, SOCIETY OF THE
PRÉMONTRÉ, ORDER OF
PRESENTATION BROTHERS
PRESENTATION OF MARY, SISTERS OF THE
PRESENTATION OF MARY, SISTERS OF THE
PRESENTATION OF THE BLESSED VIRGIN MARY,
   SISTERS OF THE
PROVIDENCE, DAUGHTERS OF
PROVIDENCE, OBLATE SISTERS OF
PROVIDENCE, SISTERS OF
PROVIDENCE, SISTERS OF – Rosminian
PROVIDENCE, SISTERS OF
PROVIDENCE, SISTERS OF
PROVIDENCE AND OF THE IMMACULATE
   CONCEPTION, SISTERS OF
PROVIDENCE OF ST ANDREW, SISTERS OF
PROVIDENCE OF ST MARY-OF-THE-WOODS,
   SISTERS OF
PROVIDENCE OF ST VINCENT DE PAUL, SISTERS
   OF

REDEEMER, SISTERS OF THE

REDEMPTORISTINES, THE

REDEMPTORISTS, THE

REMIGIUS, KNIGHTS OF ST

REPARATION, SISTERS OF THE

REPARATION OF THE CONGREGATION OF MARY, SISTERS OF

REPARATION OF THE SACRED HEART OF JESUS, HANDMAIDS OF

REPARATION OF THE SACRED WOUNDS OF JESUS, SISTERS OF

REPARATION TO JESUS IN THE BLESSED SACRAMENT, COMMUNITY OF

RESURRECTION, COMMUNITY OF THE

RESURRECTION, SISTERS OF THE

RESURRECTION OF OUR LORD, COMMUNITY OF THE

RESURRECTION OF OUR LORD JESUS CHRIST, CONGREGATION OF THE

RETREAT, CONGREGATION OF THE

RETREAT OF THE SACRED HEART, SISTERS OF THE

REUILLY, DEACONESS COMMUNITY OF

RIEHEN, DEACONESS COMMUNITY OF

RITA, SISTERS OF ST

ROGATIONIST FATHERS

ROSARY, DAUGHTERS OF THE

ROUEN, CANONESSES REGULAR OF

RUFUS, CANONS REGULAR OF ST

RUPERT, KNIGHTS OF ST

RURAL CATECHISTS, CONGREGATION OF

SABBAS, MONKS OF ST

SACK, FRIARS OF THE

SACRED ADVENT, SOCIETY OF THE

SACRED CROSS, SOCIETY OF THE

SACRED HEART, BROTHERS OF THE

SACRED HEART, HOSPITALLER SISTERS OF THE

SACRED HEART, LITTLE SERVANTS OF THE

SACRED HEART, MISSION HELPERS OF THE

SACRED HEART, MISSIONARIES OF THE

SACRED HEART, SERVANTS OF THE

SACRED HEART, SISTERS OF THE

SACRED HEART, SISTERS OF THE SOCIETY DEVOTED TO THE

SACRED HEART, SOCIETY OF THE

SACRED HEART OF JESUS, APOSTLES OF THE

SACRED HEART OF JESUS, CONGREGATION OF PRIESTS OF THE

SACRED HEART OF JESUS, DAUGHTERS OF THE

SACRED HEART OF JESUS, HANDMAIDS OF THE

SACRED HEART OF JESUS, MISSIONARY SISTERS OF THE

SACRED HEART OF JESUS, OBLATE SISTERS OF THE

SACRED HEART OF JESUS, PRIESTS OF THE

SACRED HEART OF JESUS, SISTERS OF THE

SACRED HEART OF JESUS, SISTERS OF THE

SACRED HEART OF JESUS AND OF THE POOR, SERVANTS OF THE

SACRED HEART OF MARY, RELIGIOUS OF THE

SACRED HEARTS, LITTLE WORKERS OF THE

SACRED HEARTS OF JESUS AND MARY, MISSIONARIES OF THE

SACRED HEARTS OF JESUS AND MARY, MISSIONARY CATECHISTS OF THE

SACRED HEARTS OF JESUS AND MARY, SISTERS OF THE

SACRED HEARTS OF JESUS AND MARY, SISTERS OF THE

SACRED HEARTS OF JESUS, MARY AND JOSEPH, HANDMAIDS OF THE

SACRED MISSION, SOCIETY OF THE

SACRED NAME, DEACONESS COMMUNITY OF THE

SACRED PASSION, COMMUNITY OF THE

SAINT-LOUP, DEACONESS COMMUNITY OF

SALESIANS OF DON BOSCO

SALVATORIAN FATHERS AND BROTHERS

SASH, KNIGHTS OF THE

SASH, LADIES OF THE

SAVIGNY, CONGREGATION OF

SAVIOUR, COMPANY OF THE

SAVIOUR AND THE BLESSED VIRGIN, SISTERS OF THE

SAVIOUR IN THE WOOD, CANONS REGULAR OF ST

SCARBORO FOREIGN MISSION SOCIETY, THE

SCHONSTATT SECULAR INSTITUTE

SERAPHIM, KNIGHTS OF THE

SERVANTS OF THE CROSS, COMMUNITY OF THE

SERVANTS OF THE WILL OF GOD, COMMUNITY OF THE

SERVITIUM CHRISTI
SEVEN DOLOURS OF THE BLESSED VIRGIN
    MARY, DAUGHTERS OF THE
SEVEN SORROWS OF THE BLESSED VIRGIN
    MARY, NUNS OF THE
SHIP, ORDER OF THE KNIGHTS OF THE
SILENCE, KNIGHTS OF THE
SOCIAL SERVICE, SISTERS OF
SOCIAL SERVICE, SISTERS OF
SOMASCA, CLERKS REGULAR OF
SPIRITUAL LIFE INSTITUTE
STAR, KNIGHTS OF THE
STEPHEN, KNIGHTS OF THE ORDER OF ST
STEPHEN, NUNS OF THE EQUESTRIAN ORDER OF
    ST
SULPICE, SOCIETY OF THE PRIESTS OF ST
SWAN, KNIGHTS OF THE
SWORD, KNIGHTS OF THE
TABORITE NUNS OF MARY IMMACULATE
TAIZÉ, COMMUNITY OF
TEACHERS OF THE CHILDREN OF GOD, ORDER
    OF THE
TEMPLAR, KNIGHTS
TERESA, INSTITUTE OF ST
TERESA OF JESUS, SISTERS OF ST
THEATINE FATHERS
THEATINE HERMITESSES
THEATINE NUNS
THÉRÈSE, LITTLE WAY SISTERS OF ST
THOMAS OF VILLANOVA, SISTERS OF ST
THOMAS THE MARTYR, COMMUNITY OF ST
TIRON, ORDER OF
TRAPPISTINES / TRAPPISTS
TUSINUS, KNIGHTS OF
UNION MYSTERIUM CHRISTI
URSULA, SOCIETY OF ST
URSULINE NUNS
URSULINES OF JESUS, THE
URSULINES OF PARMA AND OF PIACENZA, THE
URSULINES OF THE HEART OF JESUS AGONIZING
USETZ, CANONS REGULAR OF THE CITY OF

VALLEY OF JEHOSOPHAT, CANONS REGULAR OF
    THE
VALLEY OF RONCEAU, CANONS REGULAR OF
    THE
VALLEY OF SCHOLARS, ORDER OF THE
VALLISCAULIAN ORDER
VANNES, CONGREGATION OF ST
VERONA MISSIONARY SISTERS
VERONICAN SISTERS OF THE HOLY FACE
VIATOR, CONGREGATION OF THE CLERICS OF ST
VINCENTIAN SISTERS OF CHARITY
VINCENTIAN SISTERS OF CHARITY
VINCENTIANS, THE
VIRGINS OF THE INFANT JESUS, CONGREGATION
    OF THE
VISITATION NUNS
VISITATION OF THE CONGREGATION OF THE
    IMMACULATE HEART OF MARY, SISTERS OF
    THE
VISITATION SISTERS
VOCATION SISTERS
VOCATIONIST FATHERS
VOCATIONIST SISTERS
VOLUNTAS DEI
WAY OF THE CROSS, COMMUNITY OF THE
WHITE FATHERS
WILFRID, COMMUNITY OF ST
WILLIAM, HERMITS OF ST
WILLIAMITES
WINDESHEIM, CANONS REGULAR OF THE
    CONGREGATION OF
WISDOM, DAUGHTERS OF
WOMEN MINISTERS TO THE SICK, ORDER OF
WORKING SISTERS
XAVERIAN BROTHERS
XAVERIAN MISSIONARY FATHERS
XAVERIAN MISSIONARY SOCIETY OF MARY, INC.
XAVIER SISTERS
YOUTH APOSTLES INSTITUTE, THE
ZELATRICES OF THE SACRED HEART,
    MISSIONARY
ZITA, SOCIETY OF ST